FIFTH EDITION

Language

INTRODUCTORY READINGS

FIFTH EDITION

Language

INTRODUCTORY READINGS

EDITED BY

Virginia P. Clark
Paul A. Eschholz
Alfred F. Rosa

University of Vermont

ST. MARTIN'S PRESS

NEW YORK

Senior editor: Karen J. Allanson
Managing editor: Patricia Mansfield-Phelan
Associate project editor: Nicholas Webb
Production supervisor: Alan Fischer
Art director: Sheree Goodman
Cover and text design: Anna George

Library of Congress Catalog Card Number: 92-50044

87654
fedcb

For information, write:
St. Martin's Press, Inc.
175 Fifth Avenue
New York, NY 10010

ISBN:0-312-00508-3

Published and distributed outside North America by
THE MACMILLAN PRESS LTD
Houndmills, Basingstoke, Hampshire RG21 2XS and London Companies
and representatives throughout the world.

ISBN 0-333-60894-1

A catalogue record for this book is available from the British Library.

Preface

The limits of my language mean the limits of my world.
— LUDWIG WITTGENSTEIN

Our language is central to everything we do. Language, more than any other human attribute, distinguishes us from all other forms of life on earth. Because we cannot function without our language, and because the language we use and how we use it set strict boundaries to what we can do, new discoveries and changes in linguistics can profoundly affect what we think of ourselves and our place in society. In appreciating the complexities of the medium through which we all communicate, we can understand more fully our humanity.

This fifth edition of *Language: Introductory Readings* maintains, with one notable exception, the organizational structure of the fourth edition. On the recommendation of reviewers and teachers, we have combined the old section "Syntax and Language Processing" with "Semantics and Pragmatics" to form the new Part Five, "Syntax, Semantics, and Discourse." In conflating these two sections we are now able to give more extensive coverage to the other seven subject areas.

In addition to providing more focused and in-depth coverage, the selections have been updated. Fourteen of the forty-four readings are new and two—Julia Falk's essay "To Be Human: A History of the Study of Language" and Jeannine Heny's "Learning and Using a Second Language"—were written especially for this edition. Four articles originally written for the fourth edition have been revised and updated: Jeannine Heny's "Brain and Language," William Kemp and Roy Smith's "From Speaking Act to Natural Word: Animals, Communication, and Language," Edward Callary's "Phonetics," and Frank Heny's "Syntax: The Structure of Sentences."

The professional literature of linguistics and related fields ranges greatly in its demands on the reader's knowledge. We have therefore tried to choose selections that are consistent in level of difficulty and that are accessible to undergraduates who have no previous formal study of linguistics but have a serious interest in the subject. The sequence of the eight parts represents one possible syllabus for a course in language.

However, instructors with other preferences will find that the order can easily be rearranged and that all sections may not be needed for some courses. Even so, we do recommend that Part One, "Language and Its Study," be assigned first, and that students read Edward Callary's "Phonetics" in Part Four before tackling any of the selections that make use of the phonetic alphabet (i.e., those by Morris Halle, H. A. Gleason, and Roger W. Shuy).

The new edition retains the teaching aids familiar from its predecessors: an introduction and discussion-and-review questions for each selection, an annotated bibliography and a variety of projects at the end of each part, and a general introduction for each part that describes the topics it covers and relates the readings to one another. In addition, a glossary of frequently used terms and a complex topical index are provided.

We received valuable criticism of the fourth edition and advice toward the fifth from teachers around the country, who, in a real sense, were collaborators in setting the new proportions and coverage of this book: Barbara Abbott, Michigan State University; Helen Aristar-Dry, University of Texas–San Antonio; Linda Armspaugh, University of Cincinnati; Mark Aronoff, SUNY Stonybrook; Janet G. Auten, Bowling Green State University; Guy Bailey, Texas A&M University; Beatrice Bartlett, Stephens College; Byron W. Bender, University of Hawaii; Janet Bing, Old Dominion University; James Blodgett, Indiana University–South Bend; Theodora Bofman, Northeastern Illinois University; Thomas R. Brooks, Wheaton College; Irene Brosnahan, Illinois State University; Thomas J. Buchholz, University of Wisconsin–Stevens Point; Kevin G. Burne, California State University–San Bernardino; Arthur F. Butler, Fort Valley State University; Alexander Butrym, Seton Hall University; Patrice Caldwell, Eastern New Mexico State University; Larry Carucci, Montana State University; Richard Chartier, Framingham State College; Mary Morris Clark, University of New Hampshire; Roger W. Cole, University of South Florida; Ann Charlotte Conway, Holy Names College; Stanley J. Cook, California State Polytechnic University–Pomona; Lucretia Crawford, Lakeland College; Bernard Crook, University of Texas–San Antonio; Helga H. Delisle, New Mexico State University; Robert B. Dewell, Loyola University; Angeline Dufner, College of Saint Benedict; Christopher Dunne, Ohio University; R. Durst, University of Hawaii; Esteban Egea, University of Texas–Dallas; Peter K. Fei, Marshall University; Donald N. Flemming, Keene State College; Antonia Folarin, University of Kansas; Lawrence M. Foley, James Madison University; Susan R. Ford, Northeastern Illinois State University; Virginia Gassner, Moorhead State University; Walker Gibson, University of Massachusetts; Francis G. Greco, Clarion University; Thomas A. Green, Texas A&M University; Dorothy G. Grimes, University of Montevallo; Allan W. Grundstrom, Bucknell University; Christopher Hall, University of Wyoming; Richard Hankins, Baldwin Wallace College; Marta P. Harley, Florida State University; Winifred C. Harris, Delaware State College; Gerald W. Haslam, Sonoma State University; C. W. Hayes, University of Texas–San Antonio; Jeannine Heny, Middlebury College; Vera M. Henzl, Foothill College; William Hofelt, Juniata College; Yuphaphaan Hoonchamlong, University of Wisconsin–Madison; David Hoover, New York University–Washington Square; Mary Howe, University of Kansas; Nina Hyams, University of California–Los Angeles; Kenneth Roy Johnson, Chicago State University; Joseph Keller, Indiana University–Purdue University; Susan Ann Kendall, University of Illinois; Thomas C. Kennedy, Washburn University of Topeka; Joan M. Kerns, Shoreline Community College; Carolyn Kessler, University of Texas–San Antonio; Daniel Kies, Governors State University; Elizabeth Kimball, University of New Hampshire; Kenneth Kirkpatrick, University of Tulsa; John V. Klapp, Northern Illinois University; Turner Kobler, Texas Woman's University; Barbara Law, California State University–Chico; David Lawton, Central Michigan University; Catherine Lewicke, Worchester State College; Rochelle Lieber, University of New Hampshire; Joseph E. Littlejohn, Southeastern Oklahoma State University; Kathy Lyday-Lee, Elon College; Mary Anne Loewe, Western Michigan University; Peggy M. Maki, Beaver College; Sonia Manuel-Dupont, Utah State University; Richard Maxwell, Valparaiso University; Mary Meiser, University of Wisconsin; Mildred C. Melendez, Sinclair Community College; Kenneth L. Miner, University of Kansas; Nancy H. Mitchell, Mary Washington College; Toni J. Morris, University of Indianapolis; Rae Moses, Northwestern University; Salikoko S. Mufwene, University of Georgia; Denise Murray, San Jose State University; Thomas E. Murray, Ohio State University; Doris T. Myers, University of Northern Colorado; Robert E. Nichols, Purdue University–Calumet Campus; Neal R. Norrick, Northern Illinois University; John F. O'Donnell II, Millersville University; Robert O'Hara, University of South Florida; Alexander Hennessey Olsen, University of Denver; Patrick O'Neill, University of North Carolina–Chapel Hill; Andrea G. Osburne, Central Connecticut State University; Robert A. Palmatier, Western Michigan University; William Park, University of North Carolina–Charlotte; Elinore H. Partridge, California State University–San Bernardino; Marian Paul, College of Saint Mary; Jennifer Peterson, University of Wisconsin; James R. Pickett, Western Connecticut State University; Willis L. Pitkin, Jr., Utah State University; Richard Pollnac, University of Rhode Island; Ronna Randall, Bellevue Community College; Linda S. Rashidi, Central Michigan University; Lawrence A. Reid, University of Hawaii; Robert W. Reising, Pembroke State University; Joan Retallack, University of Maryland–College Park; Kenneth A. Robb, Bowling Green State University; Sharon Robinson, Russell Sage College; M. Augustine Roth, Mount Mercy College; C. Rudin, Miami University; Deborah Schaffer, Eastern Montana College; Mary A. Seeger, Grand Valley State College; Norma Shanebrook, University of Wisconsin; Kenneth Shields, Millersville University; Ronald C. Shumaker, Clarion University; Riley B. Smith, Bloomsburg University; William L. Smith, University of Pittsburgh; William Snyder, Northwestern University; Bruce Southard, Oklahoma State University; Timothy S. Studlack, Pennsylvania State University; Joseph L. Subbiondo, University of Santa Clara; Richard Suter, California State Polytechnic University–Pomona; William Tanner, Texas Woman's University; Josephine Tarvers, Rutgers University; Talbot J. Taylor, College of William and Mary; Christian Todenhagen, California State University–Chico; James Tollefson, University of Washington; Donald M. Topping, University of Hawaii; Hector A. Torres, University of Texas at Austin; Susana B. Tuero, Michigan State University; Joseph F. Tuso, University of Science and Arts; Bruce Urquhart, Nassau Community College; Rebecca Vallette, Boston College; Robert S. Wachal, University of Iowa; Peter B. Waldeck, Susquehanna University; Eugene Washington, Utah State University; Charlotte Webb, San Diego State University; William F. Williams, Slippery Rock University; Michael M. Williamson, Indiana University of Pennsylvania; Douglas Woken, Saginaw State University; Ina Jane Wundram, Georgia State University; Chris Zahn, Cleveland State University; and James A. Zeller, San Joaquin Delta College.

As with the previous editions of *Language: Introductory Readings*, St. Martin's Press provided us with an excellent editorial team—Cathy Pusateri, Karen Allanson, and Nicholas Webb. Their individual efforts made our work on this new edition a pleasure. Special thanks go to Julie Young, our graduate research assistant, for her work on this new edition. Finally, we'd like to acknowledge our students at the University of Vermont, whose continued enthusiasm for language study and responses to and evaluations of materials included in this edition, as well as in the first four, have been most helpful.

VIRGINIA CLARK
PAUL ESCHHOLZ
ALFRED ROSA

Contents

PART THREE
LANGUAGE AND THE BRAIN
197

PART FOUR
PHONETICS, PHONOLOGY, AND MORPHOLOGY
297

PART FIVE
SYNTAX, SEMANTICS, AND DISCOURSE
383

PART SIX
LANGUAGE VARIATION: REGIONAL AND SOCIAL
507

PART SEVEN
HISTORICAL LINGUISTICS AND LANGUAGE CHANGE
597

PART EIGHT
BROADER PERSPECTIVES
645

FIFTH EDITION

Language

INTRODUCTORY READINGS

LANGUAGE AND ITS STUDY

Language is not only the principal medium that human beings use to communicate with each other but also the bond that links people together and binds them to their culture. To understand our humanity, we must understand the language that makes us human. The study of language, then, is a very practical, as well as a very challenging, pursuit. In beginning this study, we must consider some fundamental questions: What is language? What are its unique characteristics? Are there some commonly held misconceptions that impede our understanding of language—and if so, what are they? What effect does language have on people and on their culture? The selections in Part One raise these basic questions and suggest some answers.

Most people take their language ability for granted; speaking and understanding speech seem as natural as breathing or sleeping. But human language is extremely complex and has unique characteristics. In the first selection in this section, W. F. Bolton discusses the properties of human language that make it species-specific and explains the intricate physiological adaptations that make speech and hearing possible. He also points out that all languages are systematic and that no language is "simple" or "primitive," and he alerts us to the harm of ethnocentric attitudes.

Following this definition of human language and introduction to the physiology of speech and hearing, Harvey A. Daniels discusses nine "facts" about human language that most contemporary linguists believe to be demonstrably true. These ideas are important in their own right; in addition, understanding them will make the selections in other parts of this book more enjoyable and meaningful.

In the tnird essay, Lewis Thomas, noted physician and essayist, speculates on the origins of language and the ways in which humans acquire it. Of particular interest is his emphasis on the importance of childhood and adolescence as the period in which our brains are

1

receptive to the creative and humanizing power of language. In the concluding essay, Julia Falk provides a comprehensive historical overview of the study of language today, all of which increases, as she writes, "the depth of our understanding of what it is to be human."

The selections in Part One provide an introduction to the study of language: its physiology and unique properties, and facts that refute nine commonly held misconceptions about language. Reading these four articles should help us begin to understand the complexity of both human language and the problems involved in studying it. Moreover, doing so should make it impossible to take for granted the unique and complicated phenomenon that is human language.

1

Language: An Introduction

W. F. Bolton

The ability to use language is the most distinctive human characteristic, and yet most people take this ability for granted, never considering its richness and complexity. In the following selection, W. F. Bolton, professor of English at Douglass College, analyzes the intricate physiological mechanisms involved in speech production and in speech reception, or hearing. Especially interesting is his discussion of the differences between "speech breathing" and "quiet breathing." Professor Bolton also explains the "design features" that characterize human language; this explanation is important for understanding many of the later selections in this book. His concluding warning against ethnocentricity is particularly important today.

Language is so built into the way people live that it has become an axiom of being human. It is the attribute that most clearly distinguishes our species from all others; it is what makes possible much of what we do, and perhaps even what we think. Without language we could not specify our wishes, our needs, the practical instructions that make possible cooperative endeavor ("You hold it while I hit it"). Without language we would have to grunt and gesture and touch rather than tell. And through writing systems or word of mouth we are in touch with distant places we will never visit, people we will never meet, a past and a future of which we can have no direct experience. Without language we would live in isolation from our ancestors and our descendants, condemned to learn only from our own experiences and to take our knowledge to the grave.

Of course other species communicate too, sometimes in ways that seem almost human. A pet dog or cat can make its needs and wishes known quite effectively, not only to others of its own species but to its human owner. But is this language? Porpoises make extremely complex sequences of sounds that may suggest equally complex messages, but so far no way has been found to verify the suggestion. Chimpanzees have been taught several humanly understandable languages, notably AME-SLAN (American Sign Language) and a computer language, but there has been heated debate whether their uses of these languages are like ours or merely learned performances of rather greater subtlety than those of trained circus animals. If the accomplishments of dolphins and chimpanzees remain open questions, however, there is no question but that human uses of language, both everyday and in the building of human cultures, are of a scope and power unequaled on our planet.

It seems likely that language arose in humans about a hundred thousand years ago. How this happened is at least as unknowable as how the universe began, and for the same reason: there was nobody there capable of writing us a report of the great event. Language, like the universe, has its creation myths; indeed, in St. John's Gospel both come together in the grand formulation, "In the beginning was the Word, and the Word was with God, and the Word was God." Modern linguists, like modern cosmologists, have adopted an evolutionary hypothesis. Somehow, over the millennia, both the human brain and those parts of the human body now loosely classed as the organs of speech have evolved so that speech is now a part of human nature. Babies start to talk at a certain stage of their development, whether or not their parents consciously try to teach them; only prolonged isolation from the sounds of speech can keep them from learning.

Writing is another matter. When the topic of language comes up, our first thoughts are likely to be of written words. But the majority of the world's languages have never been reduced to writing (though they all could be), and illiteracy is a natural state: we learn to write only laboriously and with much instruction. This is hardly surprising, since compared with speech writing is a very recent invention—within the past 5,000 years. Still more recently there have been invented complex languages of gesture for use by and with people unable to hear or speak; these too must be painstakingly learned. What do the spoken, written, and sign languages have in common that distinguishes them from other ways to communicate?

PROPERTIES OF LANGUAGE

Perhaps the most distinctive property of language is that its users can create sentences never before known, and yet perfectly understandable to their hearers and readers. We don't have to be able to say "I've heard that one before!" in order to be able to say, "I see what you mean." And so language can meet our expressive needs virtually without limit, no matter how little we have read or heard before, or what our new experiences call on us to express. Another way of describing this property is to say that language is *productive*. We take this productivity for granted in our uses of language, but in fact it is one of the things that make human communication unique.

Less obvious is the fact that language is *arbitrary:* the word for something seldom has any necessary connection with the thing itself. We say *one, two, three*—but the Chinese say *yi, er, san.* Neither language has the "right" word for the numerals, because there is no such thing. (It might seem that a dog's barking, or a blackbird's call, were equally arbitrary, as both might be translated into various languages as "Go away!" or "Allez-vous-en!"—but within the species the sound is universally understandable. A chow and a German shepherd understand each other without translation—unlike speakers of Chinese and German.)

Even the sounds of a language are arbitrary. English can be spoken using only 36 significantly different sounds, and these are not all the same as the sounds needed to speak other languages. These 36 sounds are in turn arbitrarily represented by 26 letters, some standing for two or more sounds, others overlapping. (Consider *c*, *s*, and *k*.) And the patterns into which these sounds, and indeed words, may be arranged are also arbitrary. We all know to well what *tax* means but, in English at least, there is no such word as *xat*. In English we usually put an adjective before its noun—*fat man*; in French it's the other way around, *homme gros*. This patterning is the key to the productivity of language. If we use intelligible words in proper patterns, we can be sure of being understood by others who speak our language. Indeed, we seem to understand nonsense, provided it is fitted into proper patterns—the silly nonsense of double-talk, the impressive nonsense of much bureaucratese.

This ability to attach meaning to arbitrary clusters of sounds or words is like the use and understanding of symbolism in literature and art. The word *one* does not somehow represent the numeral, somehow embody its essence the way a three-sided plane figure represents the essence of triangularity. Rather, *one* merely stands for the prime numeral 1, giving a physical form to the concept, just as the word *rosebuds* gives a physical form to the concept "the pleasures of youth" in the poetic line, "Gather ye rosebuds while ye may." Thus the sound /wʌn/, spelled *one*, has a dual quality as a sound and as a concept. This can be seen from the fact that /wʌn/, spelled *won*, matches the identical sound to a wholly different concept. This feature of *duality* is both characteristic of and apparently unique in human communication, and so linguists use it as a test to distinguish language from other kinds of communication in which a sound can have only a single meaning. (Such sounds are called signs, to distinguish them from the symbols that are human words.)

Sounds can be made into meaningful combinations, such as language, only if they are first perceived as meaningfully distinct, or *discrete*. We can find an analogy in music. Musical pitch rises continuously without steps from the lowest frequency we can hear to the highest, sliding upward like the sound of a siren. But most of music is not continuous; it consists of notes that move upwards in discrete steps, as in a scale (from *scalae*, the Latin for "stairs"). This is why we can talk about notes being the same or different, as we could not easily do if all possible tones from low to high were distributed along a continuous line. Similarly, in speech we can slide through all the vowels from "ee" in the front of the mouth to "aw" in the throat—but then how could we tell *key* from *Kay* from *coo* from *caw?* Likewise we distinguish between *v* and *f*, so that *view* is different from *few*. But these distinctions are arbitrary. They are not even common to all languages. For example, in German the letters *v* and *f* both represent the sound /f/, the letter *w* represents the sound /v/ — and there is no sound /w/. What all languages do have in common, however, is the property of discreteness.

These four properties, or "design features," of language were first set down by Charles Hockett in 1958 as part of an attempt to see how human language differs from animal communication systems. There are of course other design features — their number has varied from seven to sixteen — but these four (discreteness, arbitrariness, duality, and productivity) appear to be the most important. Among the others:

Human language uses the *channel of sound,* generated by the vocal organs and perceived by the ear, as its primary mode. As a consequence, speech is *nondirectional:* anyone within hearing can pick it up, and we can hear from sources which we cannot see. Our hearing, being stereophonic, can also tell from what direction the sound is coming. Also, our language acts *fade rapidly* (unless recorded on tape or in writing). We do not, as a rule, repeat these acts the way animals often do their signals.

In human language, *any speaker can be a listener and any listener can be a speaker,* at least normally. Some kinds of animal communication, such as courtship behavior, are one-way. And we get *feedback* of our own utterances through our ears and through bone conduction. Nonsound animal communication, like the dances of bees, can often only be invisible to the originator of the message.

Our language acts are *specialized.* That is to say, they have to do only with communication; they do not serve any other function. For example, speech is not necessary for breathing, nor is it the same as other sounds we make, such as a laugh or a cry of pain or fear. Of course, such sounds can communicate, but only by accident to those within earshot. Their main purpose is a reflexive one: they happen more or less involuntarily, like the jerk of a tapped knee.

Italian children grow up speaking Italian; Chinese children learn Chinese. *Human language is transmitted by the cultures we live in,* not by our parentage: if the Chinese infant is adopted by an Italian couple living in Italy, he or she will grow up speaking perfect Italian. But a kitten growing up among human beings speaks neither Italian nor Chinese; it says *meow.* Its communication is determined by its genetic makeup, not by its cultural context.

NONLANGUAGES

Other kinds of human communication are sometimes called language: body language, or *kinesics,* is one example. The way we use our bodies in sitting, standing, walking, is said to be expressive of things we do not say. It probably is, but that does not make it language. Body language lacks duality, in that it is not symbolic but rather a direct representation of a feeling; discreteness, in that there is no "alphabet" of distinctive movements or postures; and productivity, in that "original" expressions are likely not to be understood. Moreover, it appears to be only partly arbitrary, for the movement or posture is often selected by its "meaning" as representational, not arbitrary; "barrier signs" such as crossing one's arms or legs need no dictionary. Try testing body language against the other design features.

THE PHYSIOLOGY OF SPEECH

Speech is a kind of specialized exhalation, so it follows that we breathe while we speak. But the two sorts of breathing are not at all the same. "Quiet" breathing is more rapid and shallow than breathing during speech. Quiet breathing is also more even and restful than speech breathing, for during speech the air is taken in quickly and then expelled slowly against the resistance of the speech organs. Quiet breathing is mostly through the nose, speech breathing through the mouth. These differences, and others, would normally affect the accumulation of carbon dioxide (CO_2) in the blood, and the level of CO_2 is the main regulator of breathing—the rate or volume of breathing responds to the level of CO_2 so as to keep us from getting too uncomfortable. If we consciously use "speech" breathing but remain silent, we resist this response and our discomfort grows rapidly. That discomfort does not take place during actual speech, however; some other mechanism comes into play.

> Thus, it is quite clear that breathing undergoes peculiar changes during speech. What is astonishing is that man can tolerate these modifications for an apparently unlimited period of time without experiencing respiratory distress, as is well demonstrated by the interminable speech with which many a statesman embellishes his political existence. Cloture is dictated by motor fatigue and limited receptivity in the audience — never by respiratory demands.[1]

Our neural and biochemical makeup is in fact specially adapted so that we can sustain the speech act. Other animal species are equally adapted to their systems of communication, but none of them can be taught ours because ours is species-specific, a set of abilities that have evolved in humankind over a very long time. The evolution has included the most intricate adaptations of the body and its workings, particularly the neural system (including, above all, the brain); the motor system

---

[1] Eric H. Lenneberg, *Biological Foundations of Language* (New York: John Wiley & Sons, Inc., 1967), p. 80.

(especially the muscles that the neural system controls); and the sensory system (especially hearing, of course, but also touch).

The speech act involves an input of meaning and an output of sound on the part of the speaker, the reverse on the part of the listener. But a great deal takes place between the input and the output, and it takes place in the brain. That means that the organ for thinking, the brain, is by definition the seat of language. And the brain is also the control center for the intricate virtuoso muscular performance we call speech, commanding the vocal activities and — most important — ensuring their coordination and sequencing.

The brain is not just an undifferentiated mass in which the whole organ does all of its tasks. The different tasks that the brain does are localized, and in a more general way, the whole brain is lateralized. In most people, the right half (or hemisphere) controls the left half of the body and vice versa, and many brain functions are also lateralized. Language is one of them; it is localized in several areas of the left hemisphere. The language centers are not motor control centers for the production of speech. Instead, they are "boardrooms" in which decisions are made, decisions that motor control centers in both hemispheres of the brain implement by issuing the orders to the body. The orders are carried by electric impulses from the central nervous system (brain and spinal cord) into the peripheral nervous system (activating the muscles).

Wernicke's area lies in the left hemisphere of the brain, just above the ear. It takes its name from the German Carl Wernicke (1848–1905), who in 1874 showed that damage to that part of the brain leads to a disrupted flow of meaning in speech. A decade earlier the Frenchman Paul Broca (1824–1880) had shown that damage to another area of the left hemisphere, several inches further downward, led instead to disrupted pronunciation and grammar. There are also differences in the areas when it comes to receptive ability: damage to Broca's area does not much affect comprehension, but damage to Wernicke's area disrupts it seriously.

These differences suggest that the two chief language areas of the brain have functions that are distinct but complementary. It seems that the utterance gets its basic structure in Wernicke's area, which sends it on to Broca's area through a bundle of nerve fibers called the *arcuate fasciculus*. In Broca's area the basic structure is translated into the orders of the speech act itself, which go on to the appropriate motor control area for implementation. In reverse order, a signal from the hearing or the visual system (speech or writing) is relayed to Wernicke's area for decoding from language to linguistic meaning. Broca's area, which seems to write the program for the speech act, is not so important to listening or reading as Wernicke's area is.

All of this, naturally, is inferential: the evidence as we know it points to these conclusions, but no one has ever actually seen these brain activities taking place. The conclusions are also incredible. It is difficult to imagine all that activity for a simple "Hi!" But those conclusions are the simplest ones that will account adequately for the evidence.

All sound, whether a cat's meow, a runner's "Hi!," or a sonar beep, is a disturbance of the air or other medium (water, for example) in which it is produced. When the sound is speech it can be studied in terms of its production (articulatory phonetics), its physical properties in the air (acoustic phonetics), or its reception by the ear and other organs of hearing (auditory phonetics). The first of these is the easiest to study without special instruments, and it is the only one of the three that directly involves the motor system.

The vocal organs are those that produce speech. They form an irregular tube from the lungs, the windpipe, the larynx (and the vocal cords it contains), and the throat, to the mouth (including the tongue and lips) and nose (Fig. 1.1). All the organs except the larynx have other functions, so not all their activities are speech activities. The lungs are central to breathing, for example, to provide oxygen to the blood, and so many animals that cannot speak have lungs. In that sense speech is a secondary function of the lungs and of all the vocal organs; it has been said that they are "vocal organs" only in the sense that the knees are prayer organs. The action of forming the sound we write with the letter *p* is very similar

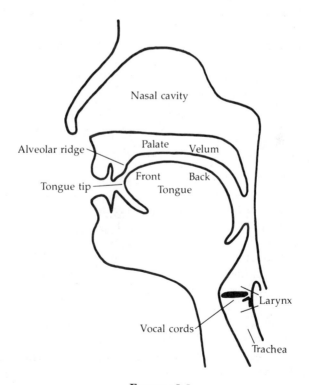

FIGURE 1.1

to that of spitting, but *p* is a part of a language system while spitting is not.

Nonetheless, to regard the speech function of these organs as secondary is to overlook the profound language adaptation of the whole human anatomy. The language functions of the motor system are not simply "overlaid" on their other functions, for the language functions in many ways conflict with the others: the tongue is far more agile than is needed for eating, the ear more sensitive than is needed for nonspeech sounds, and the esophagus much too close to the pharynx for safety (hence the need for the Heimlich maneuver). In human beings, there is nothing really secondary about the speech activities of the vocal organs.

The lungs produce a steady stream of exhaled air which the other speech organs specialize into speech. For vowels and for many consonants, the air is set into rapid vibration by the vocal cords in the larynx or "Adam's apple." The more rapid the vibration, the higher the pitch of the speech. The air can also be set in motion by a partial constriction farther up the vocal tract in the mouth, or by a complete stoppage followed by an abrupt release. The vocal cords produce a buzzlike vibration, constriction produces a hissing sound, stoppage and release produce a small explosion. A buzz alone gives us one or another of the vowels, such as the *u* in *buzz*. A stop without buzz will be like the *p* in *stoppage*, with buzz like the *b* in *buzz*.

Whether buzzing or not, the column of air driven by the lungs next passes through the pharynx, a tube that extends from the larynx through the back of the mouth as far as the rear opening of the nasal cavity. The nasal cavity itself is a chamber about four inches long, opening in front at the nostrils and at the rear into the pharynx. The nasal cavity is divided in two by the septum. The nostrils cannot open and close, but the entrance into the pharynx is controlled by the soft palate or velum. The velum is open for *n* and *m* (and often for sounds adjacent to them), closed for other sounds. You can probably feel, or with a mirror even see, the velum open at the end of a word like *hang*.

Within the mouth, the air column is molded by the tongue and the lips. The lips can cause constriction or stoppage; they constrict the air when the upper teeth touch the lower lip to make an *f* or *v* sound, and they stop the air when they close to make a *p* or *b* sound. They also close for the *m* sound, which is emitted through the nose, not the mouth. The lips can further mold the air by rounding, as they do when making the vowel sound in *do* or the consonant sound in *we*, among others.

The tongue — which has a surprising shape for those familiar only with the tip and the upper surface of it — can cause constriction or stoppage of the airflow at any point from the back of the teeth to the roof of the mouth near the velum. Like the lips, the tongue is involved in making both vowel sounds and consonant sounds. It makes both with the tip in a word like *eat*. Or the rear of the tongue can arch up toward the roof of the mouth to make a "back" consonant or vowel. It makes both in a word like *goo*. The tongue can approach the roof of the mouth in other positions farther forward as well, and it can change the shape of the oral cavity in other ways without actually approaching or touching the roof of the mouth.

So the speech sounds are formed in the larynx, in the mouth, and in the nasal cavity. They are formed by the action of the larynx, the velum, the tongue, and the lips. The lips may touch the teeth, and the tongue may touch the teeth or the roof of the mouth. That sounds a trifle complicated, but it is only a small part of what goes on in the motor system. To begin with, all the vocal organs are controlled by muscles, from those that cause the lungs to inhale and exhale air to those that shape the lips in speech. These muscles are not single — a lung muscle, a lip muscle, and so forth — but arranged in intricate groups. In reality, the vocal organs are not only those that articulate but those that activate the articulators.

Other parts of the anatomy too are involved in articulation although we do not usually think of them as vocal organs. The pharynx changes shape as we talk, and so do the cheeks. Some of the vocal organs move in ways that coordinate with articulation but do not seem to be part of it: the larynx moves up and down, for example, in speaking as it does more obviously in swallowing.

Finally, all the vocal organs are in constant motion during speech. The vowels in *house* and in *white* are formed by a change of position in the mouth, not by a single position. And as the mouth moves from the first consonants in these words, through the complex vowel sound, to the final consonants, it is always in motion. What is more, these actions must be coordinated. To take a simple example, the buzz of the larynx must be "on" for the first sounds of *mat* but "off" for the *t*; meanwhile, the mouth closes and the velum opens for the *m*, but they reverse roles for the *a* and *t*. The whole performance adds up to a virtuoso display that far exceeds in complexity . . . the minute adjustments required for even the finest violinist's playing. To observe that "The cat is on the mat" is, from the standpoint of the motor skills required, so demanding that we would think it impossible if we paused to analyze it. We usually do not.

THE SENSORY SYSTEM

In a way, the main sensory system of language, hearing, is the reverse of speech. Speech turns meaning into sound, while hearing turns sound into meaning. Speech encodes meaning as language in the brain, and the brain sends neural messages to the motor system for action; the motor system produces speech. Hearing turns the speech sounds back into neural messages which go to the brain where they are decoded into language and interpreted for meaning.

Sound, as we have seen, is a disturbance of the air — a kind of applied energy. The ear is designed to pick up and process that energy, often in incredibly small amounts. The ear is good not only at amplifying small sounds but at damping loud ones, within limits: a very sudden, very loud noise, or even sound that is not sudden (if it is loud enough), can cause damage to the sensitive sound-gathering mechanisms of the ear, damage which if severe or prolonged can be permanent.

What we usually mean by *ear* is the appendage earrings hang from, but that is only the ear's most visible part. In fact it has three divisions: the outer ear, which extends into the eardrum; the middle ear; and the inner ear. The outer ear collects the sound, passes it through the ear canal, and focuses it on the eardrum. The eardrum is a tightly stretched membrane which is set into motion by the vibrations of sound energy; it is really a "drum" in reverse, for while the bass drum in a marching band converts the energy of motion (a blow from a drumstick) into sound waves, the eardrum converts sound waves into motion energy which is picked up in the middle ear. That motion is carried through the middle ear by three tiny bones; here weak sounds are amplified and very strong sounds are damped. The last of the three bones delivers the sound motion to a membrane called the oval window, which is smaller than the eardrum; the difference in size helps to concentrate the sound energy.

The oval window divides the middle ear from the inner ear. The inner ear is composed of several cavities in the bones of the skull; in one of these, the cochlea, the energy that arrived at the outer ear as sound, and is now motion, will be converted by a set of intricate organs into electrical impulses and fed into the central nervous system for delivery to the auditory center of the brain. The remaining steps in the process are then neural, not sensory.

The process here described, and our idea of hearing in general, relates to sound that reaches us from outside by conduction through the air, water, or other medium. But there is another way in which we can receive sound. A vibrating tuning fork held against the skull will be "heard" by conduction through the bone itself, even if the ear-hole is effectively plugged. Bone-conduction helps us monitor our own speech by providing continuous feedback; thus we can pick out our own words even when surrounded by loud conversation or noise. Bone-conduction has a different sound quality from air-conduction, which is why your voice sounds to you one way when you are speaking and another when you hear it played back from a tape. And bone-conduction can sometimes substitute for air-conduction — for example, when a hearing aid "plays" sound waves directly into the bones of the skull.

LANGUAGE AND CULTURE

Language is species-specific to humankind. By *humankind* we mean the genus *Homo*, species *sapiens* — no other species of this genus survives. Any smaller subdivisions, such as sex or race, may differ among themselves in other very visible ways, but the neural, motor, and sensory equipment necessary to language is common to all. Not that the equipment is identical; otherwise everyone would speak at about the same pitch. But racial, sexual, or individual differences in the shape and size of the nose and lips, or of the internal speech organs, do not override the structural similarity of the vocal organs among all human groups, and they definitely do not result in any functional differences. The members of any group, that is, have the vocal organs to articulate any human language with complete mastery. The same is true of other genetic factors: the intellectual ability to use language is the same in all the varieties of humankind and in all normal individuals.

That is not the same as saying that adult individuals can learn a foreign language as easily as they learned their own in childhood. The physiological habits of the speech organs are complex, and they are learned early. We observe that a native speaker of Chinese has difficulty with the sound of *r* in *very*, a native speaker of Japanese with the sound of *l* in *hello*. That is because their native languages have given them no opportunity to practice those sounds. On the contrary, the languages have reinforced other sounds that tend to crop up when the Chinese speaker attempts English *r* or the Japanese speaker English *l*. The problem, however, is one of habit and not heredity. An American of Chinese ancestry has no trouble with the sounds of English, including *r*, while a person of European ancestry raised to speak Chinese would.

Our virtuosity in our own language carries with it other commitments, some easily understandable and some less so. Speakers of English easily handle a system of pronouns that distinguishes among masculine *(he)*, feminine *(she)*, and neuter *(it)* forms. They may have trouble with a language like German, however, where the nouns, adjectives, and articles (equivalents of *the* and *a*) make a similar three-way distinction, often in apparent disregard of the sex of the noun—a *maiden (das Mädchen)* is neuter, [but changes to feminine] when she becomes a *wife (die Frau)*—or with a language like French which makes only a two-way distinction between masculine and feminine, so that *table* is feminine *(la table)* but *floor* is masculine *(le plancher)*.

We should not rush to conclude, however, that the Germans and the French see sexual characteristics in inanimate objects or concepts, or do not see them in people. Rather, their languages have grammatical features that English lacks. True, words like *he, she,* and *it* do reflect the sex of their antecedent (except for a few oddities, like referring to a ship as "she"). But their equivalents in French and German refer not to sex but to *gender,* which is an entirely linguistic, and therefore arbitrary, matter. No French speaker regards a table as having any feminine properties other than grammatical ones.

In more remote languages the differences are still greater. When a Chinese speaker counts items, he or she puts a "measure word" between the number and the item: "one [measure word] book," and so forth. There is nothing quite like this in English, although when we arrange numbers in order we signify that we are ordering rather than counting by inserting expressions like *number, No.,* or #: "We're number 1," "Love Potion No. Nine," and the like. But our practice is invariable, while the Chinese measure word is not; it varies according to the thing being counted. The most common one is *ga,* "one *ga* book." But for flat objects it is *zhang,* "one *zhang* table"; and for other kinds of objects there are many other measure words. Sometimes it is far from obvious what the objects have in common that makes them take a common measure word: the measure word *ba* is used for both chairs and umbrellas!

This all sounds formidably difficult, but only to us — not to the Chinese. The Mandarin variety of Chinese is the native language of over half a billion people in the world today, and they all master their language at the same rate and by the same age as English speakers do. No language, no matter how strange and difficult it may seem to outsiders, is too hard for its native speakers to master. All languages are systematic, which makes their complexities intelligible to their native speakers, but each system is arbitrary in its own way, which makes it something of a closed book to others.

Equally, no language is especially "simple," if by that word we mean lacking complexity in its phonological and grammatical systems. More likely, people who speak of simplicity in language have a restricted vocabulary in mind. But even this judgment needs to be well-informed if it is to be at all valid. Of course, some languages have larger vocabularies than others; English may comprise half a million words, depending on your manner of counting, while a small tribal group out of touch with the complexities of industrial and urban civilization would probably have a markedly smaller vocabulary. But that vocabulary might be more subtle than English in those areas of thought and experience vital to its users. For example, Eskimos have many different words for different kinds of snow. Moreover, the tribal vocabulary could rapidly expand to deal with new needs as they come along, by borrowing or creating new words. Borrowing, indeed, is one of the most important ways that the English vocabulary has grown to such size. (And, of course, no individual speaker of English has all its half-million words at his or her disposal.)

So the equation of language with culture, one we tend to make, has two possibilities of misleading us. First, we are likely to judge another culture as "simple" because we do not understand it or even know much about it; cultural anthropologists would quickly remedy that error for us. Second, we are likely to think that a "primitive" culture has a primitive language. Yet such remote languages, we now know, seem forbiddingly complex to outsiders who try to learn them.

These attitudes are forms of *ethnocentricity* — a point of view in which one culture is at the center of things and all others are more or less "off the target," either because they never got on target (they are too primitive) or they have wandered away from it (they are decadent).

Language is very fertile ground for ethnocentricity. We are quick to judge even small differences from our own variety of English as "wrong," either laughably or disgustingly. When another people's language is different in more than just small ways, we are inclined to doubt the native intelligence of those who use it, its adequacy for serious purposes, or both.

A more enlightened and indeed more realistic view is the opposite of ethnocentricity. It often goes by the name of "cultural relativism," but learning the name is not the same thing as adopting the view. Only an objective eye on the facts, and a careful eye on our own attitudes, will raise us above ethnocentricity.

To compare linguistics with the study of other forms of human behavior is instructive, but a still grander comparison comes to mind: In many ways the study of language is like the study of life itself. Languages, like species, come into being, grow, change, are sometimes grafted to each other, and occasionally become extinct; they have their histories and, in the written record, their fossils. The origins of both life and language, and their processes, are mysteries that can be penetrated (if at all) by reasoning from incomplete and perhaps ultimately inadequate evidence. And linguists, the scientists of language, study language and its environment with a biologist's care and intensity in order to approach an understanding of the nature of language itself—the most characteristic attribute of all humanity.

In the following pages you can read about the tools and methods of that study, and about the current state of linguistic knowledge. The nature of language and its internal laws, how we learn it, how languages and dialects differ and why, how to reconstruct the linguistic past, how people and animals communicate without words: these are some of the topics discussed in the rest of this book. Its essays offer a compact résumé of the science of linguistics.

FOR DISCUSSION AND REVIEW

1. Why is the fact that human language is *productive* one of its most distinctive properties? In answering this question, consider both your ability to create sentences you have never seen or heard before and also your ability to understand such sentences.

2. Another important property of human language is that it is *arbitrary*. Discuss the several aspects of language characterized by this property.

3. Two other significant "design features" of human language are *duality* and *discreteness*. One way to be sure that you understand these concepts is to try to explain them in your own words to someone else. Write brief explanations of these two concepts, and ask a friend to evaluate the clarity of your explanations.

4. Review the seven additional "design features" discussed by Bolton. Do they seem to you to be of equal importance? Why or why not?

5. According to Bolton, body language *(kinesics)* lacks the distinctive properties of human language. Discuss this statement in terms of the design features he describes.

6. In what ways does human physiology support the conclusion that speech is not simply an "overlaid function"?

7. Summarize the differences between "quiet" breathing and "speech" breathing. *Without speaking,* use "speech" breathing for at least a minute. Write a brief description of your physical sensations.

8. Explain the functions in the hearing process of (a) the outer ear, (b) the middle ear, and (c) the inner ear.

9. For what reasons does Bolton insist that "all languages are systematic" and that "no language is especially 'simple' "? In what way is an understanding of these principles important to our understanding of different cultures and their peoples? What is *ethnocentricity?*

10. In the preface to this book, we quote the philosopher Ludwig Wittgenstein: "The limits of my language mean the limits of my world." Discuss the implications of this statement, considering the points Bolton makes and paying particular attention to the concepts of *ethnocentricity* and *cultural relativism*.

11. Bolton asserts that "we seem to understand nonsense, provided it is fitted into proper patterns." Consider the following "nonsense," the opening stanza of "Jabberwocky" by Lewis Carroll (Charles Lutwidge Dodgson [1832–1898]):

> 'Twas brillig, and the slithy toves
>   Did gyre and gimble in the wabe;
> All mimsy were the borogroves,
>   And the mome raths outgrabe.

What do you "know" about the meaning of this stanza? For example, can you identify any nouns? Any verbs? Do you know that something will or did happen? If so, what is that something? Try to describe *how* you "understand" these and other aspects of the stanza.

2

Nine Ideas about Language

Harvey A. Daniels

In the following chapter adapted from his book Famous Last Words: The American Language Crisis Reconsidered, *Harvey A. Daniels, a director of the Illinois Writing Project and a professor at the National College of Education, presents nine fundamental ideas about language that are widely accepted by contemporary linguists. In doing so, he dispels a number of myths about language that are all too prevalent among Americans. The ideas introduced here provide a foundation for readings in later parts of this book, where they are discussed in more detail.*

Assuming we agree that the English language has in fact survived all of the predictions of doom which have been prevalent since at least the early eighteenth century, we also have reason to believe that current reports of the death of our language are similarly exaggerated. The managers of the present crisis of course disagree, and their efforts may even result in the reinstatement of the linguistic loyalty oath of the 1920s or of some updated equivalent ("I promise to use good American unsplit infinitives") in our schools. But it won't make much difference. The English language, if history is any guide at all, will remain useful and vibrant as long as it is spoken, whether we eagerly try to tend and nurture and prune its growth or if we just leave it alone.

Contemporary language critics recognize that language is changing, that people use a lot of jargon, that few people consistently speak the standard dialect, that much writing done in our society is ineffective, and so forth — but they have no other way of viewing these phenomena except with alarm. But most of the uses of and apparent changes in language which worry the critics *can* be explained and understood in unalarming ways. Such explanations have been provided by linguists during the past seventy-five years.

I have said that in order to understand the errors and misrepresentations of the language critics, we need to examine not only history but also "the facts." Of course, facts about language are a somewhat elusive commodity, and we may never be able to answer all of our questions about this wonderfully complex activity. But linguists have made a good start during this century toward describing some of the basic features, structures, and operations of human speech. This section presents a series of nine fundamental ideas about language that form, if not exactly a list of facts, at least a fair summary of the consensus of most linguistic scholars.

1. Children learn their native language swiftly, efficiently, and largely without instruction. Language is a species-specific trait of human beings. All children, unless they are severely retarded or completely deprived of exposure to speech, will acquire their oral language as naturally as they learn to walk. Many linguists even assert that the human brain is prewired for language, and some have also postulated that the underlying linguistic features which are common to all languages are present in the brain at birth. This latter theory comes from the discovery that all languages have certain procedures in common: ways of making statements, questions, and commands; ways of referring to past time; the ability to negate, and so on.[1] In spite of the underlying similarities of all languages, though, it is important to remember that children will acquire the language which they hear around them—whether that is Ukrainian, Swahili, Cantonese, or Appalachian American English.

In spite of the commonsense notions of parents, they do not "teach" their children to talk. Children *learn* to talk, using the language of their parents, siblings, friends, and others as sources and examples—and by using other speakers as testing devices for their own emerging ideas about language. When we acknowledge the complexity of adult speech, with its ability to generate an unlimited number of new, meaningful utterances, it is clear that this skill cannot be the end result of simple instruction. Parents do not explain to their children, for example, that adjectives generally precede the noun in English, nor do they lecture them on the rules governing formation of the past participle. While parents do correct some kinds of mistakes on a piecemeal basis, discovering the underlying rules which make up the language is the child's job.

From what we know, children appear to learn language partly by imitation but even more by hypothesis-testing. Consider a child who is just beginning to form past tenses. In the earliest efforts, the child is likely to produce such incorrect and unheard forms as *I goed to the store* or *I seed a dog*, along with other conventional uses of the past tense: *I walked to Grandma's.* This process reveals that the child has learned the basic, general rule about the formation of the past tense—you add *-ed* to the verb—but has not yet mastered the other rules, the exceptions and irregularities. The production of forms that the child has never heard suggests that imitation is not central in language learning and that the child's main strategy is hypothesizing—deducing from the language she hears an idea about the underlying rule, and then trying it out.

---

[1] Victoria Fromkin and Robert Rodman, *An Introduction to Language* (New York: Holt, Rinehart and Winston, 1978), pp. 329–342.

My own son, who is now two-and-a-half, has just been working on the *-ed* problem. Until recently, he used present tense verb forms for all situations: *Daddy go work!* (for: *Did Daddy go to work?*) and *We take a bath today!* (for: *Will we take a bath today?*). Once he discovered that wonderful past tag, he attached it with gusto to any verb he could think up and produced, predictably enough, *goed, eated, flied,* and many other overgeneralizations of his initial hypothetical rule for the formation of past tenses. He was so excited about his new discovery, in fact, that he would often give extra emphasis to the marker: *Dad, I swallow-ed the cookie.* Nicky will soon learn to deemphasize the sound of *-ed* (as well as to master all those irregular past forms) by listening to more language and by revising and expanding his own internal set of language rules.

Linguists and educators sometimes debate about what percentage of adult forms is learned by a given age. A common estimate is that 90 percent of adult structures are acquired by the time a child is seven. Obviously, it is quite difficult to attach proportions to such a complex process, but the central point is clear: schoolchildren of primary age have already learned the great majority of the rules governing their native language, and can produce virtually all the kinds of sentences that it permits. With the passing years, all children will add some additional capabilities, but the main growth from this point forward will not so much be in acquiring new rules as in using new combinations of them to express increasingly sophisticated ideas, and in learning how to use language effectively in a widening variety of social settings.

It is important to reiterate that we are talking here about the child's acquisition of her native language. It may be that the child has been born into a community of standard English or French or Urdu speakers, or into a community of nonstandard English, French, or Urdu speakers. But the language of the child's home and community *is* the native language, and it would be impossible for her to somehow grow up speaking a language to which she was never, or rarely, exposed.

2. Language operates by rules. As the *-ed* saga suggests, when a child begins learning his native language, what he is doing is acquiring a vast system of mostly subconscious rules which allow him to make meaningful and increasingly complex utterances. These rules concern sounds, words, the arrangement of strings of words, and aspects of the social act of speaking. Obviously, children who grow up speaking different languages will acquire generally different sets of rules. This fact reminds us that human language is, in an important sense, arbitrary.

Except for a few onomatopoetic words *(bang, hiss, grunt),* the assignment of meanings to certain combinations of sounds is arbitrary. We English speakers might just as well call a chair a *glotz* or a *blurg,* as long as we all agreed that these combinations of sounds meant *chair.* In fact, not just the words but the individual sounds used in English have been arbitrarily selected from a much larger inventory of sounds which the human vocal organs are capable of producing. The existence of African languages employing musical tones or clicks reminds us that the forty phonemes used in English represent an arbitrary selection from hundreds of available sounds. Grammar, too, is arbitrary. We have a rule in English which requires most adjectives to appear before the noun which they modify *(the blue chair)*. In French, the syntax is reversed *(la chaise bleue)*, and in some languages, like Latin, either order is allowed.

Given that any language requires a complex set of arbitrary choices regarding sounds, words, and syntax, it is clear that the foundation of a language lies not in any "natural" meaning or appropriateness of its features, but in its system of rules — the implicit agreement among speakers that they will use certain sounds consistently, that certain combinations of sounds will mean the same thing over and over, and that they will observe certain grammatical patterns in order to convey messages. It takes thousands of such rules to make up a language. Many linguists believe that when each of us learned these countless rules, as very young children, we accomplished the most complex cognitive task of our lives.

Our agreement about the rules of language, of course, is only a general one. Every speaker of a language is unique; no one sounds exactly like anyone else. The language differs from region to region, between social, occupational and ethnic groups, and even from one speech situation to the next. These variations are not mistakes or deviations from some basic tongue, but are simply the rule-governed alternatives which make up any language. Still, in America our assorted variations of English are mostly mutually intelligible, reflecting the fact that most of our language rules do overlap, whatever group we belong to, or whatever situation we are in.

3. All languages have three major components: a sound system, a vocabulary, and a system of grammar. This statement underscores what has already been suggested: that any human speaker makes meaning by manipulating sounds, words, and their order according to an internalized system of rules which other speakers of that language largely share.

The sound system of a language — its phonology — is the inventory of vocal noises, and combinations of noises, that it employs. Children learn the selected sounds of their own language in the same way they learn the other elements: by listening, hypothesizing, testing, and listening again. They do not, though it may seem logical, learn the sounds first (after all, English has only forty) and then go on to words and then to grammar. My son, for example, can say nearly anything he needs to say, in sentences of eight or ten or fourteen words, but he couldn't utter the sound of *th* to save his life.

The vocabulary, or lexicon, of a language is the individual's storehouse of words. Obviously, one of the young child's most conspicuous efforts is aimed at expanding his lexical inventory. Two- and three-year-olds are notorious for asking "What's that?" a good deal more often than even the most doting parents can tolerate. And not only do children constantly and spontaneously try to enlarge their vocabularies, but they are always working to build categories, to establish classes of words, to add connotative meanings, to hone and refine their sense of the semantic properties—the meanings—of the words they are learning. My awareness of these latter processes was heightened a few months ago as we were driving home from a trip in the country during which Nicky had delighted in learning the names of various features of the rural landscape. As we drove past the Chicago skyline, Nicky looked up at the tall buildings and announced "Look at those silos, Dad!" I asked him what he thought they kept in the Sears Tower, and he replied confidently, "Animal food." His parents' laughter presumably helped him to begin reevaluating his lexical hypothesis that any tall narrow structure was a silo.

Linguists, who look at language descriptively rather than prescriptively, use two different definitions of *grammar.* The first, which I am using, says that grammar is the system of rules we use to arrange words into meaningful English sentences. For example, my lexicon and my phonology may provide me with the appropriate strings of sounds to say the words: *eat four yesterday cat crocodile the.* It is my knowledge of grammar which allows me to arrange these elements into a sentence: *Yesterday the crocodile ate four cats.* Not only does my grammar arrange these elements in a meaningful order, it also provides me with the necessary markers of plurality, tense, and agreement. Explaining the series of rules by which I subconsciously constructed this sentence describes some of my "grammar" in this sense.

The second definition of *grammar* often used by linguists refers to the whole system of rules which makes up a language—not just the rules for the arrangement and appropriate marking of elements in a sentence, but all of the lexical, phonological, and syntactic patterns which a language uses. In this sense, *everything* I know about my language, all the conscious and unconscious operations I can perform when speaking or listening, constitutes my grammar. It is this second definition of grammar to which linguists sometimes refer when they speak of describing a language in terms of its grammar.

4. Everyone speaks a dialect. Among linguists the term *dialect* simply designates a variety of a particular language which has a certain set of lexical, phonological, and grammatical rules that distinguish it from other dialects. The most familiar definition of dialects in America is geographical: we recognize, for example, that some features of New England language—the dropping r's *(pahk the cah in Hahvahd yahd)* and the use of *bubbler* for *drinking fountain*—distinguish the speech of this region. The native speaker of Bostonian English is not making mistakes, of course; he or she simply observes systematic rules which happen to differ from those observed in other regions.

Where do these different varieties of a language come from and how are they maintained? The underlying factors are isolation and language change. Imagine a group of people which lives, works, and talks together constantly. Among them, there is a good deal of natural pressure to keep the language relatively uniform. But if one part of the group moves away to a remote location, and has no further contact with the other, the language of the two groups will gradually diverge. This will happen not just because of the differing needs of the two different environments, but also because of the inexorable and sometimes arbitrary process of language change itself. In other words, there is no likelihood that the language of these two groups, though identical at the beginning, will now change in the same ways. Ultimately, if the isolation is lengthy and complete, the two hypothetical groups will probably develop separate, mutually unintelligible languages. If the isolation is only partial, if interchange occurs between the two groups, and if they have some need to continue communicating (as with the American and British peoples) less divergence will occur.

This same principle of isolation also applies, in a less dramatic way, to contemporary American dialects. New England speakers are partially isolated from southern speakers, and so some of the differences between these two dialects are maintained. Other factors, such as travel and the mass media, bring them into contact with each other and tend to prevent drastic divergences. But the isolation that produces or maintains language differences may not be only geographical. In many American cities we find people living within miles, or even blocks of each other who speak markedly different and quite enduring dialects. Black English and midwestern English are examples of such pairs. Here, the isolation is partially spatial, but more importantly it is social, economic, occupational, educational, and political. And as long as this effective separation of speech communities persists, so will the differences in their dialects.

Many of the world's languages have a "standard" dialect. In some countries, the term *standard* refers more to a *lingua franca* than to an indigenous dialect. In Nigeria, for example, where there are more than 150 mostly mutually unintelligible languages and dialects, English was selected as the official standard. In America, we enjoy this kind of national standardization because the vast majority of us speak some mutually intelligible dialect of English. But we also have ideas about a standard English which is not just a *lingua franca* but a prestige or preferred dialect. Similarly, the British have Received Pronunciation, the Germans have High German, and the French, backed by the authority of the Académie Française, have "Le Vrai Français." These languages are typically defined as the speech of the upper, or at least educated, classes of the society, are the predominant dialect of written communication, and are commonly taught to schoolchildren. In the past, these prestige dialects have sometimes been markers which conveniently set the ruling classes apart from the rabble — as once was the case with Mandarin Chinese or in medieval times when the English aristocracy adopted Norman French. But in most modern societies the standard dialect is a mutually intelligible version of the country's common tongue which is accorded a special status.

A standard dialect is not *inherently* superior to any other dialect of the same language. It may, however, confer considerable social, political, and economic power on its users, because of prevailing attitudes about the dialect's worthiness.

Recently, American linguists have been working to describe some of the nonstandard dialects of English, and we now seem to have a better description of some of these dialects than of our shadowy standard. Black English is a case in point. The most important finding of all this research has been that Black English is just as "logical" and "ordered" as any other English dialect, in spite of the fact that it is commonly viewed by white speakers as being somehow inferior, deformed, or limited.

5. Speakers of all languages employ a range of styles and a set of subdialects or jargons. Just as soon as we accept the notion that we all speak a dialect, it is necessary to complicate things further. We may realize that we do belong to a speech community, although we may not like to call it a dialect, but we often forget that our speech patterns vary greatly during the course of our everyday routine. In the morning, at home, communication with our spouses may consist of grumbled fragments of a private code:

Uhhh.

Yeah.

More?

Um-hmm.

You gonna . . . ?

Yeah, if . . .

'Kay.

Yet half an hour later, we may be standing in a meeting and talking quite differently: "The cost-effectiveness curve of the Peoria facility has declined to the point at which management is compelled to consider terminating production." These two samples of speech suggest that we constantly range between formal and informal styles of speech — and this is an adjustment which speakers of all languages constantly make. Learning the sociolinguistic rules which tell us what sort of speech is appropriate in differing social situations is as much a part of language acquisition as learning how to produce the sound of /b/ or /t/. We talk differently to our acquaintances than to strangers, differently to our bosses than to our subordinates, differently to children than to adults. We speak in one way on the racquetball court and in another way in the courtroom; we perhaps talk differently to stewardesses than to stewards.

The ability to adjust our language forms to the social context is something which we acquire as children, along with sounds, words, and syntax. We learn, in other words, not just to say things, but also how and when and to whom. Children discover, for example, that while the purpose of most language is to communicate meaning (if it weren't they could never learn it in the first place) we sometimes use words as mere acknowledgments. (Hi. How are you doing? Fine. Bye.) Youngsters also learn that to get what you want, you have to address people as your social relation with them dictates (Miss Jones, may I please feed the hamster today?). And, of course, children learn that in some situations one doesn't use certain words at all — though such learning may sometimes seem cruelly delayed to parents whose offspring loudly announce in restaurants: "I hafta go toilet!"

Interestingly, these sociolinguistic rules are learned quite late in the game. While a child of seven or eight does command a remarkably sophisticated array of sentence types, for example, he has a great deal left to learn about the social regulations governing language use. This seems logical, given that children *do* learn language mostly by listening and experimenting. Only as a child grows old enough to encounter a widening range of social relationships and roles will he have the experience necessary to help him discover the sociolinguistic dimensions of them.

While there are many ways of describing the different styles, or registers, of language which all speakers learn, it is helpful to consider them in terms of levels of formality. One well-known example of such a scheme was developed by Martin Joos, who posited five basic styles, which he called *intimate, casual, consultative, formal,* and *frozen.*[2] While Joos's model is only one of many attempts to find a scale for the range of human speech styles, and is certainly not the final word on the subject, it does illuminate some of the ways in which day-to-day language varies. At the bottom of Joos's model is the *intimate* style, a kind of language which "fuses two separate personalities" and can only occur between individuals with a close personal relationship. A husband and wife, for example, may sometimes speak to each other in what sounds like a very fragmentary and clipped code that they alone understand. Such utterances are characterized by their "extraction" — the use of extracts of potentially complete sentences, made possible by an intricate, personal, shared system of private symbols. The *intimate* style, in sum, is personal, fragmentary, and implicit.

The *casual* style also depends on social groupings. When people share understandings and meanings which are not complete enough to be called intimate, they tend to employ the *casual* style. The earmarks of this pattern are ellipsis and slang. Ellipsis is the shorthand of shared meaning; slang often expresses these meanings in a way that defines the group and excludes others. The *casual* style is reserved for friends and insiders, or those whom we choose to make friends and insiders. The *consultative* style "produces cooperation without the integration, profiting from the lack of it."[3] In this style, the speaker provides more explicit background

---

[2] Martin Joos, *The Five Clocks* (New York: Harcourt, Brace and World, 1962).
[3] Ibid., p. 40.

information because the listener may not understand without it. This is the style used by strangers or near-strangers in routine transactions: co-workers dealing with a problem, a buyer making a purchase from a clerk, and so forth. An important feature of this style is the participation of the listener, who uses frequent interjections such as *Yeah, Uh-huh* or *I see* to signal understanding.

This element of listener participation disappears in the *formal* style. Speech in this mode is defined by the listener's lack of participation, as well as by the speaker's opportunity to plan his utterances ahead of time and in detail. The *formal* style is most often found in speeches, lectures, sermons, television newscasts, and the like. The *frozen* style is reserved for print, and particularly for literature. This style can be densely packed and repacked with meanings by its "speaker," and it can be read and reread by its "listener." The immediacy of interaction between the participants is sacrificed in the interests of permanence, elegance, and precision.

Whether or not we accept Joos's scheme to classify the different gradations of formality, we can probably sense the truth of the basic proposition: we do make such adjustments in our speech constantly, mostly unconsciously, and in response to the social situation in which we are speaking. What we sometimes forget is that no one style can accurately be called better or worse than another, apart from the context in which it is used. Though we have much reverence for the formal and frozen styles, they can be utterly dysfunctional in certain circumstances. If I said to my wife: "Let us consider the possibility of driving our automobile into the central business district of Chicago in order to contemplate the possible purchase of denim trousers," she would certainly find my way of speaking strange, if not positively disturbing. All of us need to shift between the intimate, casual, and consultative styles in everyday life, not because one or another of these is a better way of talking, but because each is required in certain contexts. Many of us also need to master the formal style for the talking and writing demanded by our jobs. But as Joos has pointed out, few of us actually need to control the frozen style, which is reserved primarily for literature.[4]

Besides having a range of speech styles, each speaker also uses a number of jargons based upon his or her affiliation with certain groups. The most familiar of these jargons are occupational: doctors, lawyers, accountants, farmers, electricians, plumbers, truckers, and social workers each have a job-related jargon into which they can shift when the situation demands it. Sometimes these special languages are a source of amusement or consternation to outsiders, but usually the outsiders also speak jargons of their own, though they may not recognize them. Jargons may also be based on other kinds of affiliations. Teenagers, it is often remarked by bemused parents, have a language of their own. So they do, and so do

---

[4] Ibid., pp. 39–67.

other age groups. Some of the games and chants of youngsters reflect a kind of childhood dialect, and much older persons may have a jargon of their own as well, reflecting concerns with aging, illness, and finances. Sports fans obviously use and understand various abstruse athletic terms, while people interested in needlecrafts use words that are equally impenetrable to the uninitiated. For every human enterprise we can think of, there will probably be a jargon attached to it.

But simply noting that all speakers control a range of styles and a set of jargons does not tell the whole story. For every time we speak, we do so not just in a social context, but for certain purposes of our own. When talking with a dialectologist, for example, I may use linguistic jargon simply to facilitate our sharing of information, or instead to convince him that I know enough technical linguistics to be taken seriously — or both. In other words, my purposes — the functions of my language — affect the way I talk. The British linguist M. A. K. Halliday has studied children in an attempt to determine how people's varying purposes affect their speech.[5] Halliday *had* to consider children, in fact, because the purposes of any given adult utterance are usually so complex and overlapping that it is extremely difficult to isolate the individual purposes. By examining the relatively simpler language of children, he was able to discover seven main uses, functions, or purposes for talking: *instrumental, regulatory, interactional, personal, heuristic, imaginative,* and *representational.*

The *instrumental* function, Halliday explains, is for getting things done; it is the *I want* function. Close to it is the *regulatory* function, which seeks to control the actions of others around the speaker. The *interactional* function is used to define groups and relationships, to get along with others. The *personal* function allows people to express what they are and how they feel; Halliday calls this the *here I come* function. The *heuristic* function is in operation when the speaker is using language to learn, by asking questions and testing hypotheses. In the *imaginative* function, a speaker may use language to create a world just as he or she wants it, or may simply use it as a toy, making amusing combinations of sounds and words. In the *representational* function, the speaker uses language to express propositions, give information, or communicate subject matter.

Absent from Halliday's list of functions, interestingly, is one of the most common and enduring purposes of human language: lying. Perhaps lying could be included in the representational or interactional functions, in the sense that a person may deceive in order to be a more congenial companion. Or perhaps each of Halliday's seven functions could be assigned a reverse, false version. In any case, common sense, human history, and our own experience all tell us that lying — or misleading or covering

---

[5] M. A. K. Halliday, *Explorations in the Functions of Language* (London: Edward Arnold, 1973).

up or shading the truth—is one of the main ends to which language is put.

As we look back over these three forms of language variation—styles, jargons, and functions—we may well marvel at the astounding complexity of language. For not only do all speakers master the intricate sound, lexical, and grammatical patterns of their native tongue, but they also learn countless, systematic alternative ways of applying their linguistic knowledge to varying situations and needs. We are reminded, in short, that language is as beautifully varied and fascinating as the creatures who use it.

6. Language change is normal. This fact, while often acknowledged by critics of contemporary English, has rarely been fully understood or accepted by them. It is easy enough to welcome into the language such innocent neologisms as *astronaut, transistor*, or *jet lag*. These terms serve obvious needs, responding to certain changes in society which virtually require them. But language also changes in many ways that don't seem so logical or necessary. The dreaded dangling *hopefully*, which now attaches itself to the beginning of sentences with the meaning *I hope*, appears to be driving out the connotation *full of hope*. As Jean Stafford has angrily pointed out, the word *relevant* has broadened to denote almost any kind of "with-it-ness." But these kinds of lexical changes are not new, and simply demonstrate an age-old process at work in the present. The word *dog* (actually, *dogge*), for example, used to refer to one specific breed, but now serves as a general term for a quite varied family of animals. Perhaps similarly, *dialogue* has now broadened to include exchanges of views between (or among) any number of speakers. But word meanings can also narrow over time, as the word *deer* shrank from indicating any game animal to just one specific type.

The sounds of language also change, though usually in slower and less noticeable ways than vocabulary. Perhaps fifty years ago, the majority of American speakers produced distinctly different consonant sounds in the middle of *latter* and *ladder*. Today, most younger people and many adults pronounce the two words is if they were the same. Another sound change in progress is the weakening distinction between the vowel sounds in *dawn* and *Don*, or *hawk* and *hock*. Taking the longer view, of course, we realize that modern pronunciation is the product of centuries of gradual sound changes.

Shifts in grammar are more comparable to the slow process of sound change than the sometimes sudden one of lexical change. Today we find that the *shall/will* distinction, which is still maintained among some upper-class Britishers, has effectively disappeared from spoken American English. A similar fate seems to await the *who/whom* contrast, which is upheld by fewer and fewer speakers. Our pronouns, as a matter of fact, seem to be a quite volatile corner of our grammar. In spite of the efforts of teachers, textbooks, style manuals, and the SAT tests, most American speakers now find nothing wrong with *Everyone should bring their books to class* or even *John and me went to the Cubs game*. And even the hoary old double negative (which is an obligatory feature of degraded tongues like French) seems to be making steady, if slow progress. We may be only a generation or two from the day when we will again say, with Shakespeare, "I will not budge for no man's pleasure."

While we may recognize that language does inexorably change, we cannot always explain the causes or the sequences of each individual change. Sometimes changes move toward simplification, as with the shedding of vowel distinctions. Other changes tend to regularize the language, as when we de-Latinize words like *medium/media* (The newspapers are one media of communication), or when we abandon *dreamt* and *burnt* in favor of the regular forms *dreamed* and *burned*. And some coinages will always reflect the need to represent new inventions, ideas, or events: *quark, simulcast, pulsar, stagflation*. Yet there is plenty of language change which seems to happen spontaneously, sporadically, and without apparent purpose. Why should *irregardless* substitute for *regardless*, meaning the same thing? Why should handy distinctions like that between *imply* and *infer* be lost? But even if we can never explain the reasons for such mysterious changes — or perhaps *because* we can't — we must accept the fact that language does change. Today, we would certainly be thought odd to call cattle *kine*, to pronounce *saw* as *saux*, or to ask about "thy health," however ordinary such language might have been centuries ago. Of course, the more recent changes, and especially the changes in progress, make us most uncomfortable.

But then our sense of the pace of language change is often exaggerated. When we cringe (as do so many of the language critics) at the sudden reassignment of the word *gay* to a new referent, we tend to forget that we can still read Shakespeare. In other words, even if many conspicuous (and almost invariably lexical) changes are in progress, this doesn't necessarily mean that the language as a whole is undergoing a rapid or wholesale transformation.

However, once we start looking for language change, it seems to be everywhere, and we are sorely tempted to overestimate its importance. Sometimes we even discover changes which aren't changes at all. Various language critics have propounded the notion that we are being inundated by a host of very new and particularly insidious coinages. Here are some of the most notorious ones, along with the date of their earliest citation in the *Oxford English Dictionary* for the meaning presently viewed as modern and dangerous: *you know* (1350); *anxious* for *eager* (1742); *between you and I* (1640); *super* for *good* (1850); *decimate* for *diminish* by other than one-tenth (1663); *inoperative* for nonmechanical phenomena (1631); *near-perfect* for *nearly perfect* (1635); *host* as in *to host a gathering* (1485); *gifted*, as in *He gifted his associates* (1660); *aggravate* for *annoy* (1611).[6]

---

[6] With many thanks to Jim Quinn and his *American Tongue and Cheek* (New York: Pantheon, 1981).

If we find ourselves being aggravated (or annoyed) by any of these crotchety old neologisms, we can always look to the Mobil Oil Corporation for a comforting discussion of the problem. In one of its self-serving public service magazine ads, Mobil intoned: "Change upsets people. Always has. Disrupts routine and habit patterns. Demands constant adaptation. But change is inevitable. And essential. Inability to change can be fatal."[7] And Mobil inadvertently gives us one last example of a language change currently in progress: the increasing use of sentence fragments in formal written English.

    7. Languages are intimately related to the societies and individuals who use them. Every human language has been shaped by, and changes to meet, the needs of its speakers. In this limited sense, all human languages can be said to be both equal and perfect. Some Eskimo languages, for example, have many words for different types of snow: wet snow, powdery snow, blowing snow, and so forth. This extensive vocabulary obviously results from the importance of snow in the Eskimo environment and the need to be able to talk about it in detailed ways. In Chicago, where snow is just an occasional annoyance, we get along quite nicely with a few basic terms — snow, slush, and sleet — and a number of adjectival modifiers. Richard Mitchell has described a hypothetical primitive society where the main preoccupation is banging on tree-bark to harvest edible insects, and this particular people has developed a large, specialized vocabulary for talking about the different kinds of rocks and trees involved in this process. In each of these cases, the language in question is well adapted to the needs of its speakers. Each language allows its speakers to easily talk about whatever it is important to discuss in that society.

    This does not mean, however, that any given language will work "perfectly" or be "equal" to any other in a cross-cultural setting. If I take my Chicago dialect to the tundra, I may have trouble conversing with people who distinguish, in Eskimo, ten more kinds of snow than I do. Or if one of Mitchell's tree-bangers came to Chicago, his elaborate rock-and-bark vocabulary would be of little use. Still, neither of these languages is inherently inferior or superior; inside its normal sphere of use, each is just what it needs to be.

    There is a related question concerning the differences between languages. Many linguists have tried to determine the extent to which our native language conditions our thought processes. For all the talk of similarities between languages, there are also some quite remarkable differences from one language to another. The famous studies of American Indian languages by Benjamin Lee Whorf and Edward Sapir have suggested, for example, that Hopi speakers do not conceptualize time in the

---

    [7] "Business Is Bound to Change," Mobil Oil advertisement, *Chicago Tribune*, January 5, 1977.

same way as speakers of English.[8] To the Hopi, time is a continuing process, an unfolding that cannot be segmented into chunks to be used or "wasted." The words and constructions of the Hopi language reflect this perception. Similarly, some languages do not describe the same color spectrum which we speakers of English normally regard as a given physical phenomenon. Some of these name only two, others three, and so on. Are we, then, hopelessly caught in the grasp of the language which we happen to grow up speaking? Are all our ideas about the world controlled by our language, so that our reality is what we *say* rather than what objectively, verifiably exists?

The best judgment of linguists on this subject comes down to this: we are conditioned to some degree by the language we speak, and our language does teach us habitual ways of looking at the world. But on the other hand, human adaptability enables us to transcend the limitations of a language—to learn to see the world in new ways and voice new concepts—when we must. While it is probably true that some ideas are easier to communicate in one language than another, both languages and speakers can change to meet new needs. The grip which language has on us is firm, but it does not strangle; we make language more than language makes us.

It is also important to realize that a language is not just an asset of a culture or group, but of individual human beings. Our native language is the speech of our parents, siblings, friends, and community. It is the code we use to communicate in the most powerful and intimate experiences of our lives. It is a central part of our personality, an expression and a mirror of what we are and wish to be. Our language is as personal and as integral to each of us as our bodies and our brains, and in our own unique ways, we all treasure it. And all of us, when we are honest, have to admit that criticism of the way we talk is hard not to take personally. This reaction is nothing to be ashamed of: it is simply a reflection of the natural and profound importance of language to every individual human being.

To summarize: all human languages and the concept systems which they embody are efficient in their native speech communities. The languages of the world also vary in some important ways, so that people sometimes falsely assume that certain tongues are inherently superior to others. Yet it is marvelous that these differences exist. It is good that the Eskimo language facilitates talk about snow, that the Hopi language supports that culture's view of time, and, I suppose, that Chicago speech has ample resources for discussing drizzle, wind, and inept baseball teams.

8. Value judgments about different languages or dialects are matters

---

[8] See Edward Sapir, *Culture, Language, and Personality* (Berkeley: University of California Press, 1949).

of taste. One of the things we seem to acquire right along with our native tongue is a set of attitudes about the value of other people's language. If we think for a moment about any of the world's major languages, we will find that we usually have some idea — usually a prejudice or stereotype — about it. French is the sweet music of love. German is harsh, martial, overbearing. The language of Spain is exotic, romantic. The Spanish of Latin Americans is alien, uneducated. Scandinavian tongues have a kind of silly rhythm, as the Muppet Show's Swedish chef demonstrates weekly. British English is refined and intelligent. New York dialect (especially on Toity-Toid Street) is crude and loud. Almost all southern American speakers (especially rural sheriffs) are either cruelly crafty or just plain dumb. Oriental languages have a funny, high-pitched, singsong sound. And Black English, well, it just goes to show. None of these notions about different languages and dialects says anything about the way these tongues function in their native speech communities. By definition — by the biological and social order of things — they function efficiently. Each is a fully formed, logical, rule-governed variant of human speech.

It is easy enough to assert that all languages are equal and efficient in their own sphere of use. But most of us do not really believe in this idea, and certainly do not act as if we did. We constantly make judgments about other people and other nations on the basis of the language they use. Especially when we consider the question of mutually intelligible American dialects, we are able to see that most ideas about language differences are purely matters of taste. It isn't that we cannot understand each other — Southerners, Northerners, Californians, New Yorkers, blacks, whites, Appalachian folk — with only the slightest effort we can communicate just fine. But because of our history of experiences with each other, or perhaps just out of perversity, we have developed prejudices toward other people's language which sometimes affect our behavior. Such prejudices, however irrational, generate much pressure for speakers of disfavored dialects to abandon their native speech for some approved pattern. But as the linguist Einar Haugen has warned:

> And yet, who are we to call for linguistic genocide in the name of efficiency? Let us recall that although a language is a tool and an instrument of communication, that is not all it is. A language is also a part of one's personality, a form of behavior that has its roots in our earliest experience. Whether it is a so-called rural or ghetto dialect, or a peasant language, or a "primitive" idiom, it fulfills exactly the same needs and performs the same services in the daily lives of its speakers as does the most advanced language of culture. Every language, dialect, patois, or lingo is a structurally complete framework into which can be poured any subtlety of emotion or thought that its users are capable of experiencing. Whatever it lacks at any given time or place in the way of vocabulary and syntax can be supplied in very short order by borrowing and imitation from other languages. *Any scorn for the language of others is scorn for*

those who use it, and as such is a form of social discrimination. [Emphasis mine.]⁹

It is not Haugen's purpose—nor is it mine—to deny that social acceptability and economic success in America may be linked in certain ways to the mastery of approved patterns of speech. Yet all of us must realize that the need for such mastery arises *only* out of the prejudices of the dominant speech community and not from any intrinsic shortcomings of nonstandard American dialects.

9. Writing is derivative of speech. Writing systems are always based upon systems of oral language which of necessity develop first. People have been talking for at least a half million years, but the earliest known writing system appeared fewer than 5,000 years ago. Of all the world's languages, only about 5 percent have developed indigenous writing systems. In other words, wherever there are human beings, we will always find language, but not necessarily writing. If language is indeed a biologically programmed trait of the species, writing does not seem to be part of the standard equipment.

Although the English writing system is essentially phonemic—an attempt to represent the sounds of language in graphic form—it is notoriously irregular and confusing. Some other languages, like Czech, Finnish, and Spanish, come close to having perfect sound-symbol correspondence: each letter in the writing system stands for one, and only one, sound. English, unfortunately, uses some 2,000 letters and combinations of letters to represent its forty or so separate sounds. This causes problems. For example, in the sentence: *Did he believe that Caesar could see the people seize the seas?* there are seven different spellings for the vowel sound /ē/. The sentence: *The silly amoeba stole the key to the machine* yields four more spellings of the same vowel sound. George Bernard Shaw once noted that a reasonable spelling of the word *fish* might be *ghoti: gh* as in *enough, o* as in *women,* and *ti* as in *nation.* In spite of all its irregularities, however, the English spelling system is nevertheless phonemic at heart, as our ability to easily read and pronounce nonsense words like *mimsy* or *proat* demonstrates.

Writing, like speech, may be put to a whole range of often overlapping uses. And shifts in the level of formality occur in writing just as they do in talk. An author, like a speaker, must adjust the style of her message to the audience and the occasion. A woman composing a scholarly article, for example, makes some systematically different linguistic choices than those she makes when leaving a note for her husband on the refrigerator. Both writers and speakers (even good ones) employ various jargons or specialized vocabularies that seem comfortable and convenient to the people they are addressing. Rules change with time in both writing and

---

⁹ Einar Haugen, "The Curse of Babel," in Einar Haugen and Morton Bloomfield, *Language as a Human Problem* (New York: W. W. Norton, 1974), p. 41.

speech. Most obviously, changes in speech habits are reflected in writing: today we readily pen words which weren't even invented ten or a hundred years ago. And even some of the rules which are enforced in writing after they have been abandoned in speech do eventually break down. Today, for example, split infinitives and sentence fragments are increasingly accepted in writing. Our personal tastes and social prejudices, which often guide our reactions to other people's speech, can also dictate our response to other people's writing.

Our beliefs about writing are also bound up with our literary tradition. We have come to revere certain works of literature and exposition which have "stood the test of time," which speak across the centuries to successive generations of readers. These masterpieces, like most enduring published writing, tend to employ what Joos would call formal and frozen styles of language. They were written in such language, of course, because their authors had to accommodate the subject, audience, and purpose at hand — and the making of sonnets and declarations of independence generally calls for considerable linguistic formality. Given our affection for these classics, we quite naturally admire not only their content but their form. We find ourselves feeling that only in the nineteenth or sixteenth century could writers "really use the language" correctly and beautifully. Frequently, we teach this notion in our schools, encouraging students to see the language of written literature as the only true and correct style of English. We require students not only to mimic the formal literary style in their writing, but even to transplant certain of its features into their speech — in both cases without reference to the *students'* subject, audience, or purpose. All of this is not meant to demean literature or the cultivation of its appreciation among teenagers. It simply reminds us of how the mere existence of a system of writing and a literature can be a conservative influence on the language. The study, occasionally the official worship, of language forms that are both old and formal may retard linguistic changes currently in progress, as well as reinforce our mistaken belief that one style of language is always and truly the best.

The preceding nine ideas about language are not entirely new. Many of them have been proclaimed by loud, if lonely, voices in centuries long past. It has only been in the last seventy or eighty years, however, that these ideas have begun to form a coherent picture of how language works, thanks to the work of the descriptive and historical linguists. It is their research which has been, I hope, accurately if broadly summarized here.

A look at the history of past crises offered a general kind of reassurance about the present language panic. It suggested that such spasms of insecurity and intolerance are a regular, cyclical feature of the human chronicle, and result more from social and political tensions than from actual changes in the language. The review of research presented in this section broadens that perspective and deflates the urgency of the 1983-model literary crisis in some other ways. It shows us that our language cannot "die" as long as people speak it; that language change is a healthy and inevitable process; that all human languages are rule governed, ordered, and logical; that variations between different groups of speakers are normal and predictable; that all speakers employ a variety of speech forms and styles in response to changing social settings; and that most of our attitudes about language are based upon social rather than linguistic judgments.

And so, if we are to believe the evidence of historical and linguistic research, our current language crisis seems rather curious. This is a crisis which is not critical, which does not actually pose the dangers widely attributed to it. If anything, the crisis is merely a description of linguistic business as usual, drawn by the critics in rather bizarre and hysterical strokes. It seems fair to ask at this point: What's the problem?

=

FOR DISCUSSION AND REVIEW

1. In presenting his "nine ideas about language," Daniels attempts to dispel some commonly held but inaccurate beliefs about language. List as many of these myths as you can. How successful is Daniels in dispelling them?

2. As Daniels notes, children learn relatively late the "rules" about the kinds of speech that are appropriate in various circumstances. From your own experience, give some examples of children's use of language that, given the social context, was inappropriate.

3. You probably would describe a particular event—for example, a party, a camping trip, an evening with a friend—differently to different people. Jot down the way you would tell a good friend about some event. Then write down the way you would describe the same occurrence to your parents. When you compare the two accounts, what differences do you find? Are they the differences that Daniels leads you to expect?

4. Daniels believes that most people have "some idea—usually a prejudice or stereotype"—about different languages and dialects. Define the terms *prejudice* and *stereotype*. Then test Daniels's theory by asking five people what they think of (a) the languages and dialects, or (b) the speakers of the languages and dialects, that Daniels mentions under point 8 on pp. 30–32. Study the responses and describe any prejudices or stereotypes that you find.

3

Song of the Canary

Lewis Thomas

Physician, administrator, teacher, and writer, Lewis Thomas was born in 1913 in New York and attended Princeton and Harvard Medical School. He is currently a scholar-in-residence at Cornell University. Beginning in 1971, Lewis wrote a series of articles for the New England Journal of Medicine, *the best of which were collected in* The Lives of a Cell: Notes of a Biology Watcher, *which won a National Book Award in 1974. He has since published several other books. In this selection, Thomas examines the hypothesis that humans are "compulsively, biologically, obsessively social . . . because of language." Thomas explores different theories about the origins of language and the probability of the existence of a common ancestral language, Indo-European. He also discusses the purposes for language, as well as a possible universal scheme underlying all languages. Thomas speculates about whether we became human as a result of acquiring language or if language was gained as a result of acquiring human brains. His aim is to clarify, if possible, the wonderful mystery of human language.*

Other creatures, most conspicuously from our point of view the social insects, live together in dense communities in such interdependence that it is hard to imagine the existence of anything like an individual. They are arranged in swarms by various genetic manipulations, they emerge in foreordained castles, some serving as soldiers for defending the anthill or beehive, some as workers, bringing in twigs of exactly the right size needed for whatever the stage of construction of the nest, some as the food-gatherers tugging along the dead moth toward the hill, some solely as reproductive units for the replication of the community, even some specialized for ventilating and cleaning the nest and disposing of the dead. Automatons, we call them, tiny genetic machines with no options for behavior, doing precisely what their genes instruct them to do, generation after mindless generation. They communicate with each other by chemical signals, unambiguous molecules left behind on the trail to signify all sorts of news items of interest to insects: the dead moth is on the other side of the hill behind this rock, the intruders are approaching from that direction, the queen is upstairs and asking after you, that sort of news. Bees, the earliest and greatest of all geometricians, dance in darkness to tell where the sun is and where it will be in exactly twenty minutes.

We, of course, are different. We make up our minds about the world as individuals, we look around at the world and plan our next move, we remember what happened last week when we made a mistake and got in trouble, and we keep records for longer memories, even several generations back. Also we possess what we call consciousness, awareness which most of us regard as a uniquely human gift: we can even think ahead to dying, and we cannot imagine an insect, much less a wolf or a dolphin or even a whale, doing *that*. So, we are different. And marvelously higher.

Nonetheless, we are a social species. We gather in communities far denser and more complex than any termite nest or beehive, and we depend much more on each other for individual survival than any troop of army ants. We are compulsively, biologically, obsessively social. And we are the way we are because of language.

Of all the acts of cooperative behavior to be observed anywhere in nature, I can think of nothing to match — for the free exchange of assets and the achievement of equity and balance in the trade — human language. When we speak to each other, it is not like the social insects laying out chemical trails, it contains the two most characteristic and accommodating of all human traits, ambiguity and amiability. Almost every message in human communication can be taken in two or more ways. There are choices to be made all over the place, in the sending of messages and in their reception. We are, in this respect, unlike the ants and bees. We are obliged to listen more carefully, to edit whatever we hear, and to recognize uncertainty when we hear it, or read it.

Another difference is that the communication systems of animals much older than our species are fixed in place and unchangeable. Our system, language, is just at its beginning, only a few thousand years old, still experimental and flexible. We can change it whenever we feel like, and have been doing so right along. How many of us can speak Chaucerian English or Anglo-Saxon, or Indo-European, or Hittite? Or read them?

But it is still a genetically determined gift, no doubt about it. We speak, and write, and listen, because we have genes for language. Without such genes, we might still be the smartest creatures on the block, able to make tools and outthink any other animal in combat, even able to think and plan ahead, but we would not be human.

It is not clear whether the gift of language turned up because of a mutation, suddenly transforming us from one kind of species into a distinctly different creature by the installation of brand-new centers for language, or whether you get language automatically, with a big enough brain. It could be either way. We could be human because of specialized centers designed for grammar, as songbirds evolved identifiable neurone clusters on one side of their brains for generating birdsong, or we could be generating grammar, and transforming it, simply because we acquired brains huge enough to do this sort of thing.

It is not a trivial question, and sooner or later we can hope to settle it since it is a question open not only to speculation but also to scientific inquiry. Did we become human because of acquiring the property of language, or did we gain language as the result of acquiring human brains?

It is not a question for the birds, although the birds have hypotheses for us if we like them. A song sparrow sings his elaborate song, stereotyped in its general message but ornamented by himself alone, because he possesses a large, sharply-delineated cluster of neurones in the left fronto-temporal cortex. If he hears the typical song of his species early in his life, as a nestling, he will remember it ten months later and sing it accurately, with a few modulations of his own. If he is kept from hearing it in his childhood, he will never learn it. If he is exposed to the song of another species, a swamp sparrow, say, he will sing a strange medley of song — sparrow and swamp-sparrow sounds on maturity. If deafened as a nestling, he will sing nothing beyond a kind of buzz. The calls responsible for the song of a canary are typical, conventional-looking neurones, easily recognized in strained sections of the brain, but between mating seasons they die away and vanish; then, with the next spring, they reappear as full-fledged brain cells, synaptic connections and all, and the song center is back in place. This is a nice piece of news: brain cells can die off and then can regenerate themselves. Until Nottebohm and his associates at Rockefeller University learned this from their studies of birdsong, a year or so ago, we had taken it for granted that brain cells could not regenerate; once dead they were gone for good. We knew that the olfactory receptor cells out in the open nose can regenerate all the time, every three weeks or so, but that seemed an extraordinary exception. Now, with the canary to contemplate, we can begin to guess that maybe any part of the brain might be given the same capacity for regeneration, if only we knew more about the regulatory mechanisms involved. I never used to like canaries much, nor their song, but now, as a once-neurologist, I hear them differently.

As I said a moment ago, human language is probably at its earliest stage, just beginning to emerge and evolve as a useful trait for our species. When we first acquired it is not known, but we do possess something resembling a fossil record. Around 20,000 years ago, our human ancestors scratched marks on rocks which Marshak and other scholars have interpreted as primordial arithmetic and accountancy. The proto-Sumerian tablets from the fourth millennium B.C. contain clear records of calculation, mostly concerned with barley measures, based on sequences of sixty rather than the tens used in our system. We can make good guesses about the origins, even the dates of origin, of many of the words in our language today, thanks to the scholarship of comparative philologists over the past two centuries. We can even see now, from this distance, how we made most of our metaphors from their words: *true,* for instance, from their *deru* for "tree," *world,* for instance, from their *wiros* for "man." Someone remarked, just a few years back, that we are much more knowledgeable than any preceding generation, we know much more than they knew. T. S. Eliot, when told this, remarked yes, but they are what we know.

Human culture has evolved in a manner somewhat similar to biological evolution. If, in studying the development and variation of several different languages, you can find consistent similarities between certain words of those languages, you are permitted to deduce that another word, parental to all the rest, existed at some time in the past in an earlier language. It is the same technique as is now used by today's molecular biologists for tracking back to the origin of today's genes. The ordinary bacteria, for instance, have sequences in their DNA which are significantly different from those in the DNA of modern, nucleated cells, and also just as different from those in the so-called archaebacteria — the ancient, anaerobic methane-producing bacteria of very long ago. The molecular geneticists viewed this problem in the same way that the early nineteenth-century philologists viewed the similarities of Greek to Latin and all the Celtic, Germanic and Slavic languages, and of these to Sanskrit and before, and deduced the existence of an original language, Indo-European, antedating all the rest. For the molecular geneticists, a theoretical species called the "U-bacteria," speaking in ancient but still recognizable biochemical words, serves the same function as in Indo-European philology.

I have invented my own taxonomy of language, not for the purpose of classifying different national or ethnic modes of speech but simply to divide up language into the several different purposes for which it is used. My classification reduces language to four principal categories.

1. Small-talk. This is human speech without any underlying meaning beyond the simple message that there is a human being present, breathing, and at hand. We use this communication mainly at social gatherings. The modern cocktail party is the best place to listen for it, but I have no doubt that an equivalent mode of speech has existed as long as society. The words do not matter, nor is grammar or syntax involved. The only messages conveyed are indications of presence: I am here. For this purpose, ritual phrases describing the weather, the route just taken by automobile, the flowers on the piano, the piano itself, suffice.

This usage of language is also employed by humans for the declaration of territory, for the competitive acquisition of space within a room filled with other humans, and, on occasion, for the beginning of courtship.

2. Proper, meaningful language is where real cooperation begins. This is the marketplace of humanity. Thoughts are thought up, packaged, unwrapped and packaged again, worried over, then finally put out for whomever, but never for sale, only given away. It is the strangest market in the world. Nothing is sold, no payment ever asked or received, everything is given away in expectation of something to be given in return, but without any assurance.

Speech is, at its best, the free exchange of thought. When it is working well, one human being can tell another everything that has just happened as the result of the explosive firing of one hundred billion nerve cells in his brain, wired together by a trillion or more synaptic connections. No amount of probing with electrodes inserted into the substance of the brain, no array of electroencephalographic tracings, can come close to telling you what the brain is up to, while a simple declarative sentence can sometimes tell you everything. Sometimes a phrase will do to describe what human beings in general are like, and even how they look at themselves. There is an ancient Chinese phrase, dating back millennia, which is still used to say that someone is in a great hurry, in too much of a hurry. It is *zou-ma guan-hua;* the *zou* means traveling, the *ma* means horse, the *guan* is looking at, the *hua* is flowers; the whole phrase means riding on horseback while looking, or trying to look, at the flowers. Precipitously, as we might say, meaning to look about while going over a cliff.

Language is more than a system of signals and directions, it is a mechanism for describing what is going on within a mind; most often it is used for pointing out the connections between one thing and another, seemingly different thing. It relies heavily on metaphor, using words and images fitted together in such a way that something quite new and different is revealed. The fourteenth-century nun Julian of Norwich, wanting to describe how the world seemed to her, wrote this: "And He showed me a little thing the size of a hazelnut in the palm of my hand, and it was round as a ball. I looked thereupon with the eye of my understanding and thought: Why may this be? And it was answered generally thus: It is all that is made." The language is itself very simple and the sentences seem and sound crystal clear, but this short section of Julian's Revelations has reverberated in all its ambiguity down through six centuries, serving even the purposes of today's advanced cosmological physicists.

Nobody knows when human language first began, or how. It is anyone's guess. One sort of guess is that the brain centers for generating speech turned up as a mutation, and was then selected for because of its obvious Darwinian advantage and thereafter spread through the species. This strikes me as highly improbable. The earliest human beings whose brains resemble those of *Homo sapiens* did not live together in one interbreeding community capable of passing special genes along. They were continents apart, with no possible way for that first mutant to get around from one community to another like Johnny Appleseed, spreading the new kind of seed. Mutations come at random, affecting individual members of a species long before they can affect the whole species, and language is so complex and intricate a mechanism that to suppose a mutation in the brain for just that one function would presuppose an extremely rare event. It could not possibly have occurred repeatedly and independently in one human population after another, always the same mutation.

More likely, the gift of speech came along with the gradual evolution of the human brain itself, needing nothing more than the great size and intricate connections between cells to become a possibility, along with the lucky accident of having the right kind of oral cavity, tongue, palate and larynx to permit vocalization. Sooner or later, given a big enough brain, any creature would begin communicating in this way. Even the tongue and larynx are not essential, not even the ears for listening to speech. Children who are born deaf and mute can learn sign language just as quickly as normal children, and they go through developmental stages of language acquisition that are remarkably similar to those among speaking children. The first sign language in young deaf-mute children exhibits the same kind of baby-talk, with the same mistakes in syntax and the same early difficulty in distinguishing between the terms for "you" and "me," that are the normal experience of speaking children. Mature sign language is very much like mature speech; there are a great many ways of signing the same meaning, ambiguity can be expressed easily, and the signs for ordinary language can even be transformed to something like poetry.

If language is a universal gift of human beings — part of what comes along from possessing an ordinary human brain — and if we therefore do not have to puzzle over the near-impossibility of a solitary mutant starting up the business somewhere on earth, we are still left with the problem of how language itself started. Did everyone just begin talking, all at once, as soon as our brains reached a certain size? Did grammar and syntax, flexible sentence structure and a real vocabulary, simply pop into our heads all at once? Or did it come gradually, in stages? As we look around at the several thousand different languages now in use around the world, there is little to help us here at hand. Noam Chomsky, who was the first to propose a coherent theory for the biological origin of language, has not yet succeeded in identifying the necessary underlying structures required for a complete theory of universal language, and perhaps the various languages now in existence are fundamentally too different from each other. Many linguists maintain that there is no such thing as a primitive tongue; all languages are adapted to the environments in which the speakers live, but all are equally complex and subtle. Indeed, some of the languages spoken by people in remote, primitive communities are more complicated and certainly much more highly inflected than English, and the oldest of all existing languages, Chinese, is the least inflected and in some ways the simplest and clearest. Benjamin Lee Whorf pointed out that not only do different environments result in the emergence of totally different languages, the languages themselves impose totally different ways of looking at the world. The Hopi language has no words or idiomatic constructions for what we call time; the world simply *is*, it does not change over time in any causal way; Whorf says the language is better than English for mapping the terrain of twentieth-century physics. The Algonkian languages are incredibly subtle in the terms available for intricate social relations. Whorf wrote, "A fair realization of the incredible degree of the diversity of linguistic system that ranges over the globe leaves one with an inescapable feeling that the human spirit is inconceivably old; that the few thousand years of history covered by our written records are no more than the thickness of a pencil mark on the scale that measures our past experience on this planet . . . , that the race has only played a little with a few of the linguistic formulations and views of nature bequeathed from an inexpressibly longer past." This, wrote Whorf, need not be "discouraging to science but should, rather, foster that humility which accompanies the true scientific spirit and thus forbid that arrogance of the mind which hinders real scientific curiosity and detachment."

There simply *must* be a universal scheme for making language, even though the languages that are put together by that scheme are wildly different in detail from each other, even though very few if any details of real importance can be identified as universal to all languages. Whether Chomsky is right, that the same deep structures in the mind are the source of generative transformational grammar in whatever language, cannot yet be established, but the failure thus far is the fault of the still primitive state of neurobiology. Perhaps indeed we all have centers for grammar in our brains, analogous to but far more complex than the known centers for speech itself, perhaps broadly analogous to the centers for birdsong in Marler and Nottebohm's birds.

But even when we reach this level of understanding, and have some neuroscience to account for the existence of physiology of language, we will still be stuck with the other question: How did it start, and who started it? Did committees get themselves appointed in the earliest tribes of hunters and gatherers, chosen from the wisest and most experienced elders, to figure out better ways of communication beyond simply pointing at things and howling or growling? Did the committees then make up lists of words and then lay out rules for stringing them together to make sense? Or was something more spontaneous at work?

Ma, mama, pa and *papa* are as close to linguistic universals as you can get. These words, or words sounding like them, exist in many of the world's languages, and they were probably first spoken by very young children. That is, of course, a guess.

The word *pupil*, with the two meanings of the pupil of the eye and a small child, may have acquired both meanings in the same way from children. The Indo-European root was *pap*, the word for the nipple or the breast, which with some kind of logic turned into terms for very small children: *pupus* and *pupa* in Latin, then *pupillae*, then *pupil*. Every language derived from Indo-European has the same connection, and for the same reason: when someone looks very closely into someone else's eye, he sees the reflection of himself, or part of himself. But why call that part of the eye a pupil? The same duplication, using identical terms for the pupil of the eye and a child, occurs in totally unrelated languages, including Swahili, Lapp, Chinese, and Samoan. Who would most likely have made such a connection, and decided then to use the same word for a child and the center of the eye? Most likely, I should think, a child. Who else but a child would go around peering into someone else's eye and seeing there the reflection of a child, and then naming that part of the eye a pupil? Surely not, I should think, any of the members of a committee of tribal elders charged with piecing together a language; it would never cross their minds. The pupil-eye connection must have turned up first in children's talk.

Which brings me to Derek Bickerton and his theory to explain the origin of Creole languages. Bickerton, a professor of linguistics at the University of Hawaii, has spent much of his career on the study of Hawaiian Creole, a language that developed sometime after 1880, when the Hawaiian Islands were opened up for sugar plantations and needed lots of imported labor quickly. The new arrivals, joining the existing communities of English-speakers and native Hawaiians, came from China, Korea, Japan, the Philippines, Puerto Rico, and the United States, each group, with its own language, unable to communicate with any of the rest. As always happens in such a circumstance, a common pidgin speech quickly emerged, not really a language, lacking most of the essential elements of grammar, more a crude system for pointing and naming items and giving simple directions. Most of the words were hybrids made by combining words from the collected languages, or imitations of English words. Pidgin is itself such a word, a mispronunciation of "business English."

At some period between 1880 and 1910, Hawaiian Creole emerged as the universal speech of the islands, enabling all the younger workers to speak together. The Creole was qualitatively different from Pidgin, a genuine formed language with its own tight rules for sentence structure, grammar, and word order, its own variants of articles and prepositions, its own inflections and indicators of tense and gender — in short a brand-new human speech.

According to Bickerton, who had the opportunity to interview some of the first settlers, when Hawaiian Creole first appeared it could neither be spoken nor understood by the original adult workers. It was the language of the first generation of children, and must have been constructed, in almost its entirety, by those children.

Bickerton asserts that Hawaiian Creole is a unique language, fundamentally different from the tongues spoken by the parents of the language makers. He claims, in addition, that this Creole resembles, in important linguistic details, other Creoles that have appeared at other times after similar language catastrophes in other parts of the world, in the Seychelles for example. Other scholars, especially the linguistic specialists known professionally as Creolists, have disagreed with him on these claims, and argue that Hawaiian Creole contains linguistic features similar enough to the parent languages to allow for the possibility of borrowing some grammar. But they do not argue, so far as I know, with his central point: that Hawaiian Creole could not possibly have become the common speech of the plantations as the result of any participation by the adults. It was neither taught nor learned by the adults, and it must therefore have been invented by children.

Bickerton has another point to make. Hawaiian Creole has certain features which make it technically similar to the word arrangements and syntax of young children being raised everywhere in the world. Thus, in his view, it recapitulates a stage partway along in the acquisition of language by children. From this, he argues that it can be taken as hard evidence for the existence of what he calls a universal "bioprogram" for language acquisition and language itself, which I take to mean a center or centers within the human brain responsible for both the generation and learning of grammar.

If Bickerton is right, or even partly right, his observations place children in a new role as indispensable participants — prime movers indeed — in the evolution of human culture. Everyone knows that young children are spectacularly skilled at acquiring new languages, the younger the better. They are positively brilliant when compared to adolescents, and most adults are out of the game altogether. All that a young child needs to pick up a new language is to be placed at close quarters with other children speaking that language. It is, literally, child's play.

I can imagine a time, long ago, I can't guess how many thousands of years ago, when there were only a few human beings of our sort, with our kinds of brains, scattered in small clusters around the earth: the early tool makers, cave dwellers, hunters and gatherers, some living in isolated family households, others beginning to form groups, bands, tribes. No language yet, lots of hoots, whistles, warning cries, grunts. Then some words, the names of animals, trees, fish, birds, water, death maybe. A good many of these must have been imitative, like the Indo-European root *ul*, which originally meant simply to howl, later becoming *uurvalon* in Germanic, then *ule* in Old English, and finally, in English, owl the bird. Along the way, it drifted into Latin as *ululare*, meaning to howl, into Middle Dutch as *hulen*, finally into English as the words with precisely the same meaning as in the original Indo-European, from *ul* to howl and ululation in heaven knows how many generations.

Let us assume, then, the spontaneous development of some sort of lexicon, antedating any sort of language, within every early human community. Things in the environment would have agreed-upon names. Very likely people would have names as well. Human speech, at that stage, would be limited to signals and markers, rather like a modern pidgin speech, but it would still be a poor way to transmit human thought from one mind to another. At the same time, every human brain would be capable of language, although language did not yet exist. How then did it begin?

I suggest that it began in the children, and it probably began when the earliest settlements, or the earliest nomadic tribes, reached a sufficient density of population so that there were plenty of very young children in close contact with each other, a critical mass of children, playing together all day long. They would already have learned the names of things and people from their elders, and all that remained for them to do was to string the words together so that they made sense. For this, they used the language centers in their brains, assembling grammar and constructing syntax, maybe at the outset, in much the same fashion that birds compose birdsong. To set off the explosion, and get it right, you would need a dense mass of children, a critical mass, at each other all day long for a long time.

When it first happened, it must have come as an overwhelming surprise to the adults. I can imagine the scene, the tribe gathered together in a communal compound of some sort, ready to make plans for the next hunt or the next move, or just trying to discuss the day's food supply as best they can in grunts and monosyllables, mildly irritated by the rising voices from the children playing together in a nearby clearing. The children have been noisier than ever in recent weeks, especially the three- and four-year-olds. Now they begin to make a clamor never heard before, a tumult of sounds, words tumbling over words, the newest and wildest of all the human sounds ever made, rising in volume and intensity, exultant, and all of it totally incomprehensible to the adults holding their meeting. In that moment, human culture was away and running.

A while back I ventured on a classification of human language but got only as far as small-talk and ordinary language and then tripped over the children. I have two more to add to the taxonomy.

The third is an entirely new form of communication, assembled from bits and pieces of logic over the past several centuries and now beginning to turn into the first and thus far the only genuinely universal human language. Parts of it can be spoken, all of it is written, and it bears no relation whatever to the parent languages of those who use it. It is the language of mathematics.

If you want to explain to someone else how the universe operates at its deepest known levels, all the way from occurrences in the distant cosmos to events within the nucleus of an atom, you cannot do so with any clarity or even any real meaning using any language but mathematics. The twentieth-century world of quantum mechanics is the strangest of all worlds, incomprehensible to most of us and getting stranger all the time. Yet it is indisputably the real world. It seems to change everything we have always taken as reality into unreality, threatening our fixed ideas about time, space, and causality, leaving us in a new kind of uncertainty and bewilderment perhaps never before experienced by our species. A wave is a wave, but it is also a particle, depending on how we choose to observe it.

None of this can be expressed or understood or explored in any language other than mathematics, nor can the real substance of it be translated into English. Written rapidly in chalk on a blackboard, the ideas can be taken in and then debated by an audience whose members need share no other common language, English, French, Germans, Italians, Russians, the lot. You can't buy a cup of coffee in mathematics, but you can explain, by all accounts, nearly everything. There are some theoretical physicists here and abroad who are so confident of the recent progress in their field that they believe all of the essential non-trivial questions about the material universe can be satisfactorily answered by a grand unifying theory, perhaps before the end of this century. This may indeed happen, but if it does, all the answers will only be expressible in the language of mathematics. For most of us, lacking mastery of that tongue, the world will then be an even stranger place than ever. The philosophers, carrying their traditional responsibility for explaining matters like this to the rest of us, will be out of business unless they are schooled in the highest mathematics beforehand; perhaps one of them will learn to translate, or at least to interpret, the real substance. Parenthetically, this might turn out to be the most pressing of all reasons to begin transforming our educational system at the secondary and university level. We will need a much larger population of young mathematics-speakers (or writers), not just for the future of technology and engineering or science in general, but for catching at least a glimpse of how the world works in its new reality.

I have a fourth category of language in mind, but only to mention in closing. It is poetry, which I take to be an extension of communication beyond all the normal usages of language itself. It is not as indecipherable to the untutored mind, but in some ways it is just as different from ordinary language as is higher mathematics. At its best, it is as hard to explain as music, and I have no intention of coming close to either of those formidable problems.

Only to say this much: children have had a hand in it, and childhood may be the single period in a human life when poetry begins to take hold. Without that long, puzzling period of immaturity which characterizes our species, poetry might never have entered human culture and would surely never have swept along the evolution of culture as it has since as far back as anyone can remember.

Where the children come in is at the beginning, setting in place this ungovernable and wonderful aspect of the human mind. They do so with their nursery rhymes, as close to music as speech can come. Nobody claims that nursery rhymes were written by children, but they were surely ornamented and converted into a dance of language by children, and very young children at that. They have been passed along from generation to generation by the children themselves, no doubt with the help of mothers but mostly child to child. They exist in all languages, always with the same beat, rhythm and rhyme. Iona and Peter Opie, in their introduction to *The Oxford Dictionary of Nursery Rhymes,* say that they are "the best known of verses in the world, not at all the doggerel they are popularly believed to be." Robert Graves wrote, "the best of the older ones are nearer to poetry than the greater part of *The Oxford Book of English Verse.*" G. K. Chesterton asserted that "Over the hills and far away" is one of the most beautiful lines in all English poetry, and Swift, Burns, Tennyson, Stevenson, and Henley each swiped the line for their own purposes.

Some of the rhymes seem to have been passed around among the world's children as though they were a separate tribe from the rest of us, speaking a common language none of the rest of us know anything about. The counting rhymes used for choosing the players in a children's game are just one example among many:

Eeny, meeny, miny, mo

Barcelona, bona, stry

is the Opie's recording of the song of Wisconsin children.

In Germany it goes:

Ene, tene, mone, mei

Pastor, lone, bone, strei

In Cornwall, England:

Ena, mena, mina, mite,

Basca, lora, hora, bite.

In New York, dating back to 1820:

Hana, aman, mona, mike,

Barcilona, bona, strike.

There are other older variants, in which some of the seemingly nonsense words are different, and the differences may be important.

In Edinburgh:

Inty, tinty, tethere, methera

In America, an old counting rhyme known as "Indian counting":

Een, teen, tether, fether, fip.

These are nearly the same words as those used for counting sheep by Celtic shepherds before and after the Roman occupation of Britain, and passed along by oral tradition for centuries. They may have been picked up by Welsh children two thousand or more years ago.

Compare, for instance, the nineteenth-century American rhyme:

Een, teen, tether, fether, fip,

And one from Scotland:

Eetern, feetern, peeny, pump,

And the shepherd's numbers in ancient Northumberland:

Eeen, tean, tether, mether, pimp: 1,2,3,4,5.

The Opies conclude that the Celtic language was best preserved during the Roman occupation by people who lived in isolation, especially those needed most by the Roman garrisons, the shepherds and stockbreeders. They believe that it may have been from these adults that Welsh children picked up their numbers, and preserved them, with some modifications ever since, spreading them by their own oral tradition across Europe and then over the Atlantic.

It is another good reason for respecting children, even standing in awe of them. The long period of childhood is not just a time of fragile immaturity and vulnerability, not just a phase of development to be got through before the real show of humanity emerges on stage. It is the time when the human brain can set to work on language, on taste, on poetry and music, with centers at its disposal that may not be available later on in life. If we did not have childhood, and were able somehow to jump catlike from infancy to adulthood, I doubt very much that we would turn out human.

FOR DISCUSSION AND REVIEW

1. When Thomas discusses differences between animal communication and language, he asserts: "We are compulsively, biologically, obsessively social. And we are the way we are because of language." How does Thomas support this statement?

2. In what ways does the "song sparrow" in the process of acquiring its song parallel human language acquisition theories?

3. Thomas asks the question: "Did we become human because of acquiring the property of language, or did we gain language as the result of acquiring human brains?" Continuing this line of study, he says, "human language is probably at its earliest stage, just beginning to emerge and evolve as a useful trait for our species." What explanations does Thomas offer to explain his assertions? Do you agree?

4. How have scientists deduced that English has evolved from an "original" Indo-European language?

5. Discuss the four main purposes of language Thomas describes. Add to your discussion any instances in your own speech in which you use language as Thomas describes.

6. In his study of when human language first began, Thomas presents an argument for the "genetic mutation" theory. What are Thomas's reasons for disputing this theory of language development? Do you agree? What arguments would you propose to support this theory?

7. What does Thomas propose as the "more likely" theory for language development?

8. Thomas says, "There simply must be a universal scheme for making language, even though the languages that are put together by that scheme are wildly different in detail from each other, even though very few if any details of real importance can be identified as universal

to all languages." If this is the case, then what problems face scientists even after we reach this level of understanding?

9. The terms "ma, mama, pa, and papa" are described as the closest to linguistic universals that we can get. Thomas proposes that the words were probably first spoken by children. How does Thomas account for his "educated guess"?

10. From what you know of the Hawaiian Creole language, what arguments support the assumption that children were the ones responsible for its development?

4

To Be Human: A History of the Study of Language

Julia S. Falk

Julia Falk is professor of linguistics at Michigan State University where she has been on the faculty since 1966. The author of many articles on various aspects of language study, Falk is the author of Linguistics and Language: A Survey of Basic Concepts and Implications. *In the following essay, written especially for this book, Falk presents an overview of the history of language study. She investigates the use of language as the quality that separates us from all other creatures and makes us essentially human. She examines the contributing roles played by the Greeks, the Stoics, and the Christian church, as well as the influences of individuals such as Dionysus Thrax and "speculative grammarians" in the growth and development of our language. She also explores complicated areas of language study in the United States in fields such as dialect study, transformational grammar, psycholinguistics, and sociolinguistics. At every point, Falk acknowledges the controversial and continually changing world of knowledge about human language and its study.*

To be human is to be capable of reason, to exercise free will, to have the ability to solve mathematical problems, to possess a visual system that perceives depth, color, and movement in particular ways, but, above all, to be human is to have language.

More than two millennia have passed since the Athenian Isocrates (436–338 B.C.) identified language as the characteristic that distinguishes human beings from other animals: "In most of our abilities we differ not at all from the animals; we are in fact behind many in swiftness and strength and other resources. But because there is born in us the power to persuade each other and to show ourselves whatever we wish, we not only have escaped from living as brutes, but also by coming together have founded cities and set up laws and invented arts, and speech has helped us attain practically all the things we have devised" (quotation from Harris and Taylor, p. xi). The same theme appears in the seventh-century writings of Isidore of Seville (c. 560–636): "No one is so idle as to be ignorant of their own language when they live among their own people. For what else could be thought of such a man or woman, than that he or she is worse than the brute animals" (adapted from a quotation given in Dinneen, p. 149). A thousand years later, René Descartes (1596–1650) made the point: "It is a very remarkable fact that there are none so depraved and stupid . . . that they cannot arrange different words together, forming of them a statement by which they make known their thoughts; while, on the other hand, there is no other animal, however perfect and fortunately circumstanced it may be, which can do the same" (quotation from Chomsky 1966, p. 4).

It is virtually impossible for us to even imagine a human culture, a human society, that is entirely indifferent to language. We preserve our heritage through language, maintaining libraries and archives for written documents, retelling stories and legends as part of oral history. In all aspects of our lives, from infancy until death, we interact with other human beings through language. If "intelligent life" exists elsewhere in the universe, we expect to find language there, perhaps not exactly like the languages of Earth, but similar enough so that, with some effort, we might be able to communicate. When we say that language is universal, we presume that it is literally so.

Language is an integral part of human nature, and, as such, it has been a subject of human study in every part of the world and in every period of recorded history. When we seek knowledge about human language, we seek knowledge about ourselves, as individuals and as members of the human species. What is it that we want to know? Throughout the centuries, recurring themes have included connections between language and the natural world, including questions on the origin of language; the relationship between languages and the cultures in which they are spoken; the uses of language in literature and in speech; the place of language in philosophy; the role of language in science; how to describe a language; how to learn one. Most of all, we want to know what language is. What is the nature of language? What are its properties? How does it work? What is common to all languages? By how much and in what ways do languages differ from one another? Why and how do languages change over time and from one place to another?

To some of these questions, modern linguists believe there are satisfactory answers. With others, we continue the search for understanding, at this point in our own lives and at this point in human history.

LANGUAGE AND NATURE

The formal intellectual history of Europe and the Americas is rooted in ancient Greece with traditions of recorded scholarship beginning there some 2,500 years ago and continuing without pause until our own time. Other cultures and traditions have also influenced the evolution of our understanding of language. The study of language in ancient India, for example, significantly affected European scholarship at the beginning of the nineteenth century, and we will discuss it when we reach that point. But to find the sources of many of our contemporary views and beliefs about language, we must begin with the extensive inquiries conducted by the Greeks. Readers who would like more detailed information on other traditions may wish to consult the book by Itkonen listed in the bibliography.

Most consequential of all Greek activity involving language was the development of the alphabet that, in modified form, is now used for the great majority of written languages throughout the world. At a time before most of recorded history—obviously so, since written records require writing—the Greeks adopted from the Phoenicians a way of representing language through written symbols that correspond to sounds. Expanding upon earlier writing that recorded only consonants, the Greeks introduced signs for vowels as well, thus creating the kind of alphabet familiar to us today.

As with many other aspects of Greek culture, their alphabet was later adopted, and adapted, by the Romans, who extended this writing system across their domain. The dissemination of the Roman alphabet continues in our own age and, just as in the early days of Christianity, in many regions the work is done by missionaries who modify the alphabet for languages without writing, usually with the goal of translating, printing, and distributing the Bible.

For the Greeks, writing was a fundamental aspect of language. Indeed, our modern word *grammar* comes from Greek *gramma* "letter". But the Greeks did not restrict their consideration of language to writing. The Sophists, in the fifth century B.C., were greatly concerned with rhetoric, the art of convincing oral argument, and they taught public speaking with as much emphasis on the forms of speech as on the content. This concern for form led to studies of syllable structure and the types of sentences used in successful speeches. It set a foundation for the study of language based on eloquent and effective spoken use.

The Sophists left no written records of their work on language. We learn of them through Plato (c. 427–347 B.C.), writing a century later, and he was not sympathetic. He compares them to his teacher Socrates (469–399 B.C.), recording that the Sophists "profess knowledge of all sorts, [Socrates] professes ignorance; they parade skill in public speaking, he can only ask questions, and rejects the elegant prepared answer; they offer to teach, to make men better, he merely offers to confirm man's ignorance; they charge high fees, his teaching is free" (*The Oxford History of the Classical World*, p. 229). (The use of *men* and *man* in this quotation, by the way, is historically accurate. Although women sometimes learned to write and to read in classical Greece, they were not encouraged to do so; schools were for boys only and, more specifically, for boys whose families could pay for the education.)

It is from Plato, too, that we learn first of a philosophical issue concerning not only language, but all human institutions. The question is: Do human institutions reflect nature *(physis)* or are they matters of convention *(nomos)?* For the Greeks, the choice was between natural rights and permitted behavior, between what is fundamentally just and what is societally legal, between nature as immutable and unchanging as opposed to conventions that are agreed to and therefore subject to change.

Language is a human faculty with which all people are familiar, and therefore it was an area in which the *physis-nomos* issue could be thoroughly discussed. Beginning in the fourth century B.C., some Greek philosophers supported the *physis* position, maintaining that words had a natural connection to reality, that the sounds of a word directly reflected the concept it conveyed. So, in Plato's dialogue *Cratylus*, Socrates discusses the Greek letter *lambda*, representing the sound *l*, and finds it "natural" in a Greek word like *leios*, meaning "slippery," because in making the *l* sound, "the tongue has a gliding movement" (see the chapter "Socrates on Names" in Harris and Taylor, pp. 1–19). It was easy enough for the Greeks of this time to find "evidence" for the *physis* position on language in their own language; all human languages have instances of onomatopoeia and sound symbolism. If you know only English, for example, the *physis* position might seem confirmed by the recurrence of word-initial *sn* in *sneeze-snivel-sniff-snore.* But if you also speak French, you know that the corresponding verbs are *éternuer, pleurnicher, renifler,* and *ronfler.* The key point here is that the specific sounds that seem related to particular concepts differ from one language to another. When we look beyond our own language and survey even a small sample of the 4,000 to 6,000 languages spoken in the world today, we find little evidence of a natural connection between sound and meaning.

The *nomos* position held that the words of language are arbitrary, unrelated to the nature of things, agreed upon by users of the language, and subject to change over time. Human beings, in the normal course of events, create words and these new words are understood and accepted by society. Thus, from the word *photogenic,* "appearing attractive when photographed," English speakers recently created the word *telegenic* to describe those who look good on television. There is nothing remarkable about this new word. Every language contains devices for such creation, and since words are arbitrary, whatever words are created will serve their purpose, so long as the speakers of that language accept and use them. In this sense the *nomos* position is the one that survived the debate. Aristotle (384–322 B.C.) repeatedly affirmed that words exist by convention, and by the time of the major Roman grammarians after the birth of Christ, the issue was so well settled that it no longer required discussion.

While the question raised by the *physis-nomos* controversy about the basic nature of words in human languages was answered long ago, another aspect of the debate persists into our own time. What was the origin of human language?

In the *nomos* view, humans created language; Socrates and Aristotle mention "those who first assigned the name" when discussing the origin of words. Later scholars, strongly affected by religious beliefs, viewed language as a gift from a higher power, a legendary Great Spirit, God, while others believed that mythical heroes or biblical figures were the source of language. There were also proposals based more directly on nature. Perhaps words somehow evolved from the animal noises made by primal humans. Or maybe the early humans imitated the noises they heard in nature and these imitations became more and more complex, eventually resulting in languages through which everything imaginable could be expressed. The origin of words remained a topic of discussion and debate among Western philosophers for 2,000 years.

Toward the end of the nineteenth century, serious students of language and of history concluded that it was impossible to answer the question about the origin of language. All of our records, no matter how old, reveal human language just as it is today. We have no evidence of "primitive" languages now or in the recorded past. There are no languages with vocabularies limited to a few hundred words, no languages that have verbs and nouns but no modifiers, no languages that use only a half dozen sounds, no languages where people cannot construct long and complex sentences. All languages that we know of are remarkably complex systems of sounds (or, in sign languages, gestures), words, and grammatical structures. In fact, it is the grammatical systems of human languages that are unique. Noam Chomsky (1928–), the most important linguist of the twentieth century, has written: "There is a long history of study of origin of language, asking how it arose from calls of apes and so forth. That investigation in my view is a complete waste of time, because language is based on an entirely different principle than any animal communication system. It's quite possible that human gestures . . . have evolved from animal communication systems, but not human language. It has a totally different principle" (*Language and Problems of Knowledge*, p. 183). The origin of human language is one of the questions to which we do not have an answer, and to which we may never have an answer, but it continues to intrigue us. Contemporary research in the cognitive sciences on evolution and the human brain may yet provide insights.

We have had more success in answering another fundamental question raised by the Greeks, a question about nature itself. Does nature operate according to laws and principles (the *analogy* position) or is it chaotic and free (the *anomaly* position)? Language, as part of nature, served as a testing ground for both sides of this issue.

Aristotle, as we have seen, held the *nomos* view on the nature of words, and it is not surprising that he also maintained an analogist position. Language, established by human convention, was regular and orderly; as such, it was a suitable vehicle for reasoning and for logic, central concerns in Aristotle's philosophical writings. The Alexandrians also followed this view. The Alexandrians were librarians, literary critics, and teachers of classical literature, centered in Egypt, in the city of Alexandria, founded by Alexander the Great after his conquest there in 331 B.C. The principles of analogy in language were entirely consistent with their work. If language lacked regularity and order, how could the older forms of Greek be taught to the young students who, by this time, spoke a language that differed substantially from that of Homer and the other great literature? The language data used by the Alexandrians in their teachings, unlike those of the earlier Sophists, were drawn from classical literature, and thus we find the beginning of a tradition that was to become very strongly established—the use of literary texts for examples in the study of language.

In order to demonstrate the regularities in language, the Alexandrians prepared summaries of the recurring patterns found in Greek literature for words, their roots, and their prefixes and suffixes. (The patterns, or paradigms, of nouns are known as declensions; for verbs, we refer to conjugations.) This study of words and the patterns by which they are formed is today known as morphology. The summation of work on Greek morphology came in the first century B.C. with a grammar usually attributed to Dionysius Thrax, an Alexandrian scholar about whom almost nothing is known. Translated into Latin in the first century A.D., the *Art of Grammar* was widely used in the schools of Greece and Rome; it became a model for language description for many centuries, surviving even today in the use of paradigms such as those we sometimes encounter when we study another language: Latin *amo, amas, amat* ("I, you, he/she loves"), Spanish *canto, cantas, canta* ("I, you, he/she sings").

But the principles of analogy were not undisputed. The Stoics were philosophers in Greece, rivals of the Alexandrians in Egypt, and they challenged the paradigms of the Alexandrians by citing irregularities in Greek. Since the Stoics dealt with contemporary life and language, it was no problem for them to find anomalies. Actual speech is not as obviously well-ordered as are paradigms. And the Stoics, too, assembled lists by "dividing their data into as many distinguishable parts as they could and assigning a technical term to each division" (Dinneen, p. 89). It is partly to the Stoics that we owe the classification of words into the parts of speech still widely used in language descriptions today.

Plato had divided the sentence *(logos)* into two parts—the subject or noun *(onoma)* and the predicate or verb *(rhema)*. Aristotle added a third category *(syndesmos)* which included such words as prepositions, conjunctions, and pronouns. The Stoics and the Alexandrians made further subdivisions, and by the time of Dionysius Thrax, eight parts of speech had been identified: nouns, verbs, adverbs, participles, prepositions, conjunctions, pronouns, and articles. You may notice that one part of speech is absent. Adjectives were considered part of the class of nouns by the Greeks, as well as by the Romans who adopted this system.

And now we may ask for the answer to the *analogy-anomaly* question. Is language regular or irregular? The answer is that it is both, but the regularities far exceed the irregularities. It is regularity that holds central position in any modern description of a language, and it is the existence of regularity that allows humans to learn languages. Were languages not regular, their complexity would make them extremely difficult, maybe even impossible, to learn, a point forcefully expressed 2,000 years ago by the Roman scholar Marcus Terentius Varro (116–27 B.C.).

Varro was one of the few Roman scholars of language who produced original studies, though his work had no detectable influence at the time. Others are important primarily because they adopted and adapted Greek studies, translating Greek works into Latin and transforming descriptions of Greek into descriptions of Latin. In these ways Greek scholarship was preserved and presented to the following generations, along with descriptive data about the Greek and Latin languages and the framework within which these two languages were described. Two grammars of Latin were exceptionally well known to later students of language. These were the works of Aelius Donatus in the fourth century A.D. and of Priscian in the sixth. We know little about these men, not even their dates of birth and death, but their linguistic studies were influential for many centuries. Donatus used as his model a Latin translation of Thrax's grammar, and his study became the teaching grammar of the schools well into the Middle Ages. Priscian, writing in Constantinople after the invasion of the western Roman empire by the Goths, also wrote a teaching grammar based on the Greek model. His work survived in "hundreds of manuscripts, and formed the basis of mediaeval Latin grammar and the foundation of mediaeval linguistic philosophy" (Robins, p. 70). To survive in so many copies was a sure sign of major influence, for Priscian's work extended to twenty volumes, each of which had to be copied by hand.

FAITH AND REASON

Already in Roman times, the study of language had moved away from the philosophical concerns of the Greeks to descriptivism, and what was described was primarily the language of classical Latin literature, modeled on Alexandrian descriptions of classical Greek literature. As Christianity assumed prominence the Scriptures became more important as written texts, and much of the study of language in the first part of the Middle Ages, from the sixth through the twelfth centuries, consisted of commentaries on the grammars of Priscian and Donatus — commentaries that "corrected" the classical Latin examples by replacing them with forms drawn from religious writing.

Faith overshadowed philosophy for several centuries, and accounts of language became part of encyclopedic works in which medieval scholars attempted to set down in one manuscript all that was known, or believed, about the world. In the seventh century, for example, Isidore of Seville prepared an encyclopedia entitled *Twenty Books of Etymologies or*

Origins. Etymology is the study of the historical development of words, tracing their forms and meanings back in time using old texts and citations as evidence. Even today, it is widely practiced, and you will find etymological information in every major dictionary. For Isidore, however, etymology was based, not on evidence drawn from historical documents, but on a combination of faith and fancy. For example, he proposed that the Latin word for "human being," *homo,* had originated with *humo* "the slime of the earth" (see Dinneen, pp. 148–50, for other examples). Not only had philosophy been displaced for a time by faith, but so had empirical observation, evidence, and the use of data.

It is not surprising that today we find in this period of history little that contributes to our understanding of the nature of language. What we do find, however, is a wealth of examples of language change in progress. There were commentaries on Priscian and Donatus that documented changes that had taken place in the Latin language from the classical period of Cicero, Virgil, and Horace in the first century B.C. to the Vulgate version of the Bible prepared in the fourth century A.D. by Saint Jerome. By the eighth century, Latin had changed even more, in different ways in different places, and we find evidence of what were eventually to be the separate Romance languages — French, Italian, Portuguese, Romanian, and Spanish, as well as Catalan, Provençal, and Sardinian. In 813 a council of bishops was held at Tours and it was agreed that sermons should be given no longer in Latin but in *rustica Romana lingua,* language spoken and understood by the people.

In England, as well, a new language was emerging. Late in the fifth century, members of three Germanic tribes — Angles, Saxons, and Jutes — settled in England and by the end of the seventh century, there are written records of "Englisc" — a language which, from that time until about 1100, shortly after the Norman Conquest, is referred to as Old English by modern scholars.

Throughout Europe, Latin remained the language of the liturgy in the churches, the language of scholarship carried out in large part by members of religious orders, and the language of the educated, but all who used Latin now had to study it as a foreign language. Teaching materials continued to include the grammars of Priscian and Donatus, but new materials were also prepared.

Aelfric (c. 955–1020), an English abbot, composed teaching materials on Latin for English children, including a grammar, a conversation book, and a dictionary. R. H. Robins, a modern historian of the study of language, says of Aelfric: "he told his readers that his book would be equally suitable as an introduction to (Old) English grammar. Though he was aware of differences between the two languages, . . . he did not question or discuss the applicability of the Priscianic system to Old English, and as his was one of the first known grammars specifically directed at English-speaking learners, it may be taken as setting the seal on several centuries of Latin-inspired English grammar" (*A Short History of Linguistics,*

p. 80). Today we still encounter descriptions of English, or foreign language teaching material for another language, with terms originally used for the various forms and functions of Latin nouns (and prior to that, for Greek), such as nominative, genitive, dative, and accusative. We may credit Aelfric for extending this tradition of grammatical description to English and to foreign language teaching.

Classical Greek philosophy regained prominence beginning in the eleventh century. The Crusades brought western Europe into renewed contact with the East; Greek documents, particularly on Aristotelian thought, became widely available, not only through Latin translations begun in Roman times, but also directly in Greek manuscripts transported back to Europe following the entry of the crusaders into Constantinople in 1096. Arab domination of Spain, begun in the eighth century, had continued without interruption until the Christians seized Toledo in 1085; Toledo had been a center of Arab scholarship and Aristotle's work was greatly admired there. And so, from Constantinople in the east and from Toledo in the west, reason and logic once again significantly influenced the study of language. Descriptive work alone was no longer satisfactory; explanation was required.

The most famous of the medieval scientists in this revitalized period was Roger Bacon (c. 1214–94), an English friar, philosopher, and writer. Responding to a request by Pope Clement IV, Bacon prepared several encyclopedic volumes summarizing his views on all areas of human study. His position on grammar established a major theme that continues without significant interruption to our own time. Bacon maintained that grammar is substantially the same in all languages and that whatever differences might occur among languages were "accidental" and superficial. He suggested that there are universal properties which are present in all human languages. This is not the same as the earlier unquestioned use of the Greek system of grammatical description for Latin, nor is it the same as Aelfric's belief that Latin grammar could be used for English. Rather, it assumes a set of principles and properties common to all human languages. It now became the task of the scholar of language to determine these universal principles and properties and, if possible, to explain why they exist. This was the focus of the scholastic philosophers of the thirteenth and fourteenth centuries.

The university system of higher education was formalized in Europe in the thirteenth century, as were opportunities for secondary school education. Teachers at these schools were called *scholastici*, and the scholastic philosophers came from this group. Many such schools were under the control of religious orders, and issues of faith and morality remained important, but the Scholastics, influenced by Aristotelian philosophy, supplemented understanding gained through faith with understanding gained through reason. Although scholars searched for natural laws to explain natural phenomena, science was still a part of philosophy and was considered "speculative." Science was the product of reason, of thinking, of logic. Its results could not be certain because they were not provided by faith. In this sense, the search for universal properties of human language was a science, and the grammars produced were called speculative grammars.

The writers of these speculative grammars attempted to unite their understanding of the world and the properties of the human mind with the principles of language. Such unity of knowledge had its foundation in the encyclopedia works of earlier church scholars, but now it was to be based on thought and reason. The speculative grammarians created a complex system to provide this unified theory, and they often disagreed among themselves. But basic to all of their work was the following line of argument: the nature of the world determines the nature of thought and the nature of thought determines the nature of language; since the world is constant, thought is constant and thereby universal in all humans; since thought is universal, so must be the essential properties of human language. Today we are less certain of such a direct connection between thought and language, but the scholastic philosophers believed that the structure of thought was revealed by the structure of sentences. Petrus Hispanus (?–1277), later Pope John XXI, argued that sentences should be investigated through their systematic relationship to other sentences. In order to explain the thought behind, and the meaning of, "No animal except man is rational," Hispanus argued that we must consider such related sentences as "No animal other than man is rational," "Man is an animal," and "Man is rational." This approach goes well beyond the study of morphology carried out so extensively by Greek and Roman scholars; it introduces in some detail the study of syntax, the structure of sentences.

The speculative grammarians broadened the scope of the study of language in important ways. They based argument and analysis on reason; they explored meaning; they considered the relationship between language and the mind; they included extended discussions of syntax; and they sought, although often unsuccessfully, explanations for the properties of language. But their work remained limited to Latin, the language of their faith and of all European scholarship at that time. Theoretically and descriptively, many discoveries about human language remained for the following centuries.

NEW HORIZONS

The greatest advances in the study of language from the fifteenth through the seventeenth centuries occurred as scholars prepared descriptions of an enormous variety of languages. The Reformation and the humanism of the Renaissance, nationalism and the development of modern nation-states, and the Age of Exploration all focused attention on the great diversity of languages used by the peoples of Europe and the many parts of the world that they finally came to know. European scholars no longer limited their linguistic studies to classical languages and the language of religion.

The shift in focus toward the vernacular languages occurred gradually during these centuries. Latin was no longer anyone's first language, but it remained the language of higher education and scholarship in many parts of Europe into the eighteenth century and continued as a compulsory subject even in American high schools well into the twentieth century. On the other hand, people used their native languages for ordinary conversation, for business and commerce, in routine legal matters, in secular songs, and in poetry. The fourteenth century had already produced two of the greatest early vernacular poets, Dante Alighieri (1265–1321) in Italy and Geoffrey Chaucer (c. 1340–1400) in England. Europeans began to write grammars describing modern languages: among the first was an account of Castillian Spanish in the fifteenth century; then Arabic, French, and Hungarian in the sixteenth; Finnish, Turkish, Persian, Russian, Armenian, Chinese, Tamil in the seventeenth. Some of the languages of the Americas were described for interested readers in Europe: from 1555 to 1560 two volumes were published on Mexican languages, and a study of the Quechua language of Peru appeared at the same time.

Many of these early grammars were textbooks intended for foreign language teaching. For trade and commerce, exploration, colonization, and for proselytizing, knowledge of foreign languages became increasingly important not only to members of the ruling elite, but also to an emerging middle class. At the same time, heightened nationalism on the one hand and, on the other, the invention of movable type and the resulting spread of literacy to a growing segment of the population drew attention to the native languages of Europe. Across the continent, language academies were founded by scholars, intellectuals, and even politicians with the goal of "regulating" and "purifying" their national languages. Members of these academies mistakenly believed that the languages of the time were chaotic; they were comparing spoken languages of recent written record to the neatly organized traditional descriptions that had existed for centuries for Greek and Latin. In 1582, the Italian *Accademia della Crusca* was founded; the *Académie française* was established in 1635. No official academy was created in Germany, but in various cities those concerned with "protecting" the German language from "invasion" by foreign words organized language societies; the first was in Weimar in 1617. All of the academies, and even some of the regional societies, proclaimed themselves the final authority on the national language. Dictionaries and grammars were prepared to present a single "correct" spelling for words, to define "hard" words for a new and expanding literate population, to provide words of native origin to replace borrowings from other languages, and to prescribe rules for "proper" grammatical usage. The latter were almost invariably based on formal written style.

England was not immune from this movement to reform the language of its people, although no official academy was ever created. By the beginning of the eighteenth century, however, many British writers had called for one. Jonathan Swift (1667–1745), author of *Gulliver's Travels*, in 1712 wrote *A Proposal for Correcting, Improving and Ascertaining the English Tongue*, arguing that royal officials had a responsibility to establish an academy to oversee the principles of English grammar and to keep the language from changing. Actually, there was no hope of preventing language change since all human languages—indeed all human institutions—change over time, but attempts to codify English in grammars and dictionaries became a major industry of eighteenth-century England. In 1755 Samuel Johnson (1709–84) published his famous *Dictionary of the English Language*. Americans, opponents of the British not only in the Revolution but also in the War of 1812, saw language as a political instrument in the early years of the republic. Noah Webster (1758–1843) attempted to record uniquely American usage, to propose distinctive American spellings, and to provide an authoritative source on American vocabulary in *The American Dictionary of the English Language*, published in 1828. No corresponding grammar was printed for American English at the time, probably because there were really no significant grammatical differences between British and American speakers.

In England, many grammars were published. Even Joseph Priestley (1733–1804), the British scientist who first produced oxygen in a laboratory, wrote a grammar in 1761, *Rudiments of English Grammar*. Following his scientific training, Priestley observed and described the language of his contemporaries. This objective description of the language, however, was not what his contemporaries wanted. They were looking for a prescriptive grammar, one that would set down rules to be followed for usage that others would consider "correct." The need was met the next year with the appearance in 1762 of *Short Introduction to English Grammar* by Robert Lowth (1710–87). Lowth did not hesitate to criticize current usage and to suggest "rules," many of which he simply made up, sometimes using his knowledge of Latin. It is from this prescriptive tradition that we encounter the rules still taught in some school grammars: "don't end a sentence with a preposition," "don't split infinitives," "don't say *taller than me*, say *taller than I*." Not until the twentieth century did English grammars return to describing what people actually say and write, rather than what some self-appointed authority thinks they "should" produce.

At the same time that academies, societies, and individuals were engaged in the practical work of writing dictionaries and grammars of the European languages, human language once again became an important topic of philosophical interest. For the most part, the philosophers of the seventeenth and eighteenth centuries belonged to the movement known as the Enlightenment, in which reason replaced faith in the study of natural phenomena and human institutions. When we last considered philosophy, with the speculative grammarians of the thirteenth and fourteenth centuries, reason was used as a supplement to faith. Now there was a major effort to establish science and human reason as the sole bases of all political, social, and educational matters.

In the study of language, the *Port-Royal Grammar* of 1660 marked an important turning point. The original French title of this work begins *Grammaire générale et raisonnée*—"general and rational grammar"—and reveals something of its approach. Here language was viewed as a human invention, rational because it developed from the human mind and general because the basic principles of all languages were assumed to be the same. The authors, Antoine Arnauld (1612–94) and Claude Lancelot (c. 1615–95), used examples from French, but since the grammar was general, they also drew on other modern European languages, as well as Greek, Latin, and Hebrew, to illustrate what they believed were universal properties common to all languages. Following the *Port-Royal Grammar*, other French scholars produced works that distinguished between *grammaire générale* (general, universal grammar) and *grammaire particulière* (particular grammar). Grammaire générale was the rational investigation of the unchanging and universal principles common to all languages and to the use of language in all human societies. Grammaire particulière, on the other hand, dealt with the properties of individual languages. It was grammaire générale that these rationalist scholars of the eighteenth century considered important for understanding the human mind.

Language was considered the creation of the human intellect, and like all human institutions, its development could serve as an appropriate object of study. In eighteenth-century France, this prompted a new search for the origin of human language. The search was not based on data or on observation, but on the application of principles of reason. Various points of view were expressed, but there was no evidence to sustain them, and one view was as good (or as bad) as another. Jean-Jacques Rousseau (1712–78), for example, offered several different opinions: language originated in the interaction of mother and child; language resulted from the expression of human passions; language arose when human beings came together in social groups. Although such views on the origin of human language were not based on scientific investigation, the interest in language origin in the eighteenth century set the stage for the development of a science of language in the nineteenth.

LANGUAGE CHANGE

By the end of the eighteenth century, a number of factors had come together in the study of language, and the result was the establishment during the nineteenth century of a specific field of study called *linguistics* in English, *Sprachwissenschaft* in German. The German name clearly specifies the new approach; it translates as "language science." Today linguistics is defined as the scientific study of language, a discipline of very broad scope dealing with a wide range of topics related to language. In the nineteenth century, however, attention was concentrated on language change.

A strong foundation for the scientific study of language change had been laid in the previous centuries. Some scholars had devoted their lives to the preservation and transmission of classical and religious texts in Greek and Latin. Others, in the spirit of nationalism, sought and published old texts from their own languages. The interest in older texts was supported by a more widespread interest in historical study, and the history of words, texts, and languages was pursued with some vigor. At the same time, explorers and missionaries, emissaries and ambassadors, ordinary travelers and learned teachers had all participated in preparing and collecting descriptions of languages from around the world. By the start of the nineteenth century, the libraries of Europe contained books and manuscripts on every language that Western scholars considered important in human history.

Toward the end of the eighteenth century, some students of language combined information on separate languages into comparative texts, often with parallel lists of words with similar forms and meanings from several different languages. For example, in 1786 Peter Simon Pallas (1741–1811), a German scholar serving in the court of Catherine the Great of Russia, edited and published lists of words from more than two hundred languages of Europe and Asia. The data had been collected by members of Catherine's diplomatic corps, and the title of Pallas's work reflected a somewhat naive view of their domain: *A Comparative Vocabulary of the Languages of the Entire World.* From works like this it became possible, and popular, to compare languages to one another, noting similarities and attempting to explain how these similarities had come about.

Earlier scholars had concluded that such similarities among different languages were due to development from a single source language (frequently said to be Hebrew), or to the borrowing of words by one language from another, or to universal properties common to all languages. Such conclusions were often reached without the benefit of observable data or objective analysis; they were based on national pride, or religious affiliation, or place of birth, or the supposed use of logic. But with the growing nineteenth-century belief in the importance of scientific inquiry and the extensive data available from many different languages, it became widely acknowledged that these early accounts had been inadequate.

Historical and comparative linguistic studies combined in the nineteenth century to provide compelling explanations of how languages change over time and why some languages have many systematic similarities in sounds, words, and grammar while others do not. A major impetus was the "discovery" of Sanskrit by European scholars. An ancient language of India, the oldest form of Sanskrit is found in the Vedic texts, religious rituals composed sometime around 1500 B.C. Sanskrit came to the attention of Europeans as one consequence of the extension of the British empire into India late in the eighteenth century. In 1786 Sir William Jones (1746–94), serving as chief justice at a British outpost in India, gave a talk in Calcutta that was printed and widely circulated back in England. In his talk he compared Sanskrit to Greek and Latin and claimed that its similarities to these well-known European languages were so great that they could not "possibly have been produced by accident." Jones stated that no student of language could examine Sanskrit, Greek, and Latin "without believing them to have sprung from some common source, which, perhaps, no longer exists."

As scholars learned more about the Sanskrit language, they were able to compare it to Greek and Latin, as well as to other European languages. The similarities noted by Sir William were immediately obvious: "mother" is *matar* in Sanskrit, *mater* in Greek, *mater* in Latin; "foot" is *padas* in Sanskrit, *podos* in Greek, *pedis* in Latin; "he/she is" is *asti* in Sanskrit, *esti* in Greek, *est* in Latin. Many such correspondences of basic vocabulary items could be listed. Clearly, this was not an accident. The reasonable explanation was a historical one: at some time in remote history, these different languages had been the same language. Their similarities were due to a common source. Whatever differences could be observed in more recent times were due to changes that had occurred over the centuries in different places.

The linguists of the nineteenth century set about systematically comparing the languages of India and of Europe, attempting to determine what the source language had been like and what changes had occurred over time in each of the modern languages. Rather than taking a great philosophical leap back to prehistory, as scholars of the Enlightenment had done, nineteenth-century linguists attempted to actually trace the development of language back through time, using data from existing languages and records of older languages. As their work progressed, they determined that the source language for much of India and Europe was not the same as any one of the languages for which they had records, and they called it Indo-European. From this hypothesized Indo-European, spoken long before historical records begin, changes occurred in different regions, resulting in different languages — still before written records. These languages — including Germanic, Greek, Latin, Slavic, Indo-Aryan, and Iranian — were in turn the ancestral sources of various modern languages. Other source languages, similarly reconstructed by comparing modern languages, were proposed for different language groups in other regions of the world.

The success of the nineteenth-century historical-comparative approach to the study of language was so great that linguistics was widely accepted as a science throughout the European and American scholarly communities. Language change was systematic and could be stated by formulas, or rules. Earlier stages of languages could be determined, even in the absence of written records, by comparing more modern stages.

Speculation was undesirable; recourse to logic, reason, or philosophy was unnecessary. Empirical data and scientific analysis were sufficient.

In all of this work, much of it conducted in Germany, the focus was on language change, and studies were diachronic (meaning "throughout time"). In 1880 the German scholar Hermann Paul (1846–1921), justifying the title of his book *Principles of the History of Language,* said: "It has been objected that there is another view of language possible besides the historical. I must contradict this." For Paul, only diachronic study of language could be scientific. Although many agreed with him at the time, the times were already changing.

The Sanskrit materials that had attracted Western scholars at the beginning of the century included descriptions of the Sanskrit language written by Indian scholars long before the earliest written descriptions of the Greek language. These accounts were extremely detailed, and included among them were extensive descriptions of Sanskrit pronunciation. Unlike the European history of language study in which letters were considered the smallest units of human language, the Indian scholars had focused on sounds. The seventeenth- and eighteenth-century efforts at spelling reform in England had also called attention to pronunciation, and there were a number of attempts to describe how speech sounds are produced. But a scientific understanding of the nature of speech sounds did not develop fully until advances in physiology were made by nineteenth-century scientists. As more became known about the human vocal tract, the accuracy of the Indian descriptions of Sanskrit pronunciation was more and more appreciated. By the last quarter of the nineteenth century, the field of phonetics (the study of speech sounds) was well established, particularly in England and France. Included in the work on phonetics was the creation of the International Phonetic Alphabet (IPA), a system of letters and marks that can be used to represent the speech sounds of all languages.

These developments in phonetics provided important tools for two major areas of investigation at the end of the nineteenth century and the beginning of the twentieth — the detailed recording of regional variations in pronunciation and the systematic, consistent description of all languages, including those without writing systems.

LINGUISTIC DIVERSITY

Much of the data collected and analyzed by the historical and comparative linguists of the nineteenth century had been drawn from those varieties of languages accepted as "standard" by speakers and scholars alike. These standard varieties typically reflected the language of people from major cultural, educational, and political centers and were often the varieties most widely represented in written documents. Concentrated attention on standard, written varieties of language had simply ignored the large majority of human beings whose language use was different. Virtually no one uses formal literary style in their ordinary daily speech. People from different regions speak differently from one another and those in rural areas speak differently from those in cultural centers. These oral and regional varieties of language soon became objects of linguistic study.

Until the end of the nineteenth century, it was not uncommon for the regional forms of a language to be called "dialects" while the standard variety was sometimes assumed to be "the language." Soon, however, the results of dialect study demonstrated conclusively that the regional varieties are linguistically equal to the standard varieties of languages — just as complete, just as complex, just as regular, and just as effective for communication. Today we know that a dialect is simply a variety of a language, standard or not.

Initial scholarly interest in local, regional dialects in Europe first arose at the start of the nineteenth century along with Romanticism and its emphasis on nature "uncorrupted" by the complexities of modern societies and civilizations. Just as the Grimm brothers at this time collected folktales as reflections of the lives and beliefs of ordinary people, so others began to record aspects of their speech. Dictionaries included regional words, and the first major description of a regional dialect appeared in 1821, *The Dialects of Bavaria* by Johann Schmeller (1785–1852). By the end of the nineteenth century, regional dialectology was thriving in all parts of Europe. Diversity across languages over time had been a center of attention for the historical and comparative linguists; now diversity within languages in the present also became a focus.

Two major projects established approaches to the investigation of regional dialect variation and the presentation of results. During the last quarter of the nineteenth century, Georg Wenker (1852–1911) distributed a questionnaire containing some forty sentences to German school teachers. He asked them to rewrite the sentences to reflect the pronunciation of the people living in their school region, and after he had received the responses, he recorded the different dialect features on maps. The maps formed the basis of a dialect atlas of Germany, a format for presenting the results of regional dialect studies that has been used since that time. But Wenker's use of teachers to collect information, though convenient, was flawed. The teachers varied enormously in how they chose to record their local dialects, and their reports were inconsistent and unreliable, especially in regard to pronunciation. But it was precisely pronunciation that Wenker had set out to investigate, and much of his massive study was later revised by other scholars.

Jules Gilliéron (1854–1926), a Swiss who had long been interested in the French language, was appointed in 1883 to the faculty of l'École des Hautes Études in Paris with a specific assignment to teach about the dialects of French. As part of his work he designed a dialect study of the language, not only in France, but in all of the neighboring areas where French is spoken — Belgium, Switzerland, and Italy. Gilliéron avoided

Wenker's problem by sending an investigator trained in phonetics into the field to collect the data directly from speakers of the dialects. Starting in 1897 Edmond Edmont (1849–1926) visited over 600 sites, often using his bicycle for transportation, and beginning in 1902 Gilliéron and Edmont started to publish the results as the *Atlas linguistique de la France.* It took a decade to complete publication.

These two major methods of regional dialect study, the use of a field investigator trained in phonetics and the presentation of results by means of maps, were adopted in the United States. In 1930 the American Council of Learned Societies and the Linguistic Society of America announced sponsorship of research on American English dialects. European dialectologists came to the United States the next year to train the investigators who were to collect data for a linguistic atlas of the United States and Canada. At its peak in the 1930s this project resulted in the publication of a linguistic atlas for New England (Kurath, 1939–43) and, later, for the Upper Midwest (Allen, 1973–76); books on pronunciation and word variation for several regions have also been published.

Some dialects of the United States and Canada still have not been investigated, and much of the dialect material that has been gathered remains unpublished. It is available to scholars in archives, though not accessible to more casual readers. The reasons are both logistical and economic. Compared to the dialect situations in Europe described in the German study by Wenker or the French study by Gilliéron and Edmont, for example, the United States and Canada cover enormous expanses of territory. Hundreds of investigators might be required and thousands of people should be interviewed for a thorough study; then the results must be plotted on detailed maps, each map covering an area no larger than a small town. To comprehend the magnitude of the task, recall that it took Gilliéron and Edmont ten years to publish the results obtained from the work of just one field worker covering an area about the size of the state of Texas.

Since a regional dialect is simply the variety of a language spoken in a particular region, we all have a dialect. Do you say *firefly* or *lightning bug? Soda* or *pop? Quarter to two, quarter of two,* or *quarter till two?* Are *merry, marry,* and *Mary* homonyms in your speech, or do they have different vowels? These are just a few features of various regional dialects of American English. Awareness of our own dialect and other dialects as well enables us to see ourselves as participants in the universal, human experience of linguistic diversity. This is particularly important for those many monolingual Americans who, unlike much of the world's population, are unaccustomed to and uninformed about other languages.

At the same time that regional dialects were engaging the attention of European linguists, a new direction was emerging in the United States, one that revealed yet another type of linguistic diversity. Franz Boas (1859–1942), a German educated in physics and geography, came to North America in 1886 on a field trip intending to study the geography of the region and the cultures of the native peoples. Boas devoted the remaining fifty years of his life to the investigation of native American languages and cultures.

As an educated person, Boas knew about the historical approach to linguistic studies and he was also familiar with the traditional framework for describing languages based on the Greek and Latin models. He recognized that neither approach was suitable to the languages of native Americans. The written documents of such importance to historical work of the time did not exist for most native American languages, for many did not have writing systems. The labels, categories, and patterns of Greek and Latin, and even of the other Indo-European languages, were inappropriate for native American languages, which differed greatly from the familiar languages of Europe. Not bound to a particular framework for the study of language, Boas forged a new approach. In 1888 he wrote: "If we desire to understand the development of human culture we must try to free ourselves of [the] shackles" imposed by "not only our knowledge, but also our emotions" which "are the result of the form of our social life and of the history of the people to whom we belong" (cited in Jakobson, p. 190). Through the objective study of native American languages, seeking their own patterns and structures, Boas believed that we would learn more about language, culture, and ourselves than could ever be possible with the ethnocentric approach that had dominated European linguistic studies since the time of the Greek Sophists.

PROMINENCE OF DESCRIPTION

The description of native American languages became one of the major goals of twentieth-century American linguists. Two great contributors were Edward Sapir (1884–1939) and Leonard Bloomfield (1887–1949). Both had studied historical and comparative linguistics, and both did research within that framework, enlarging its principles and extending them to native American languages despite the absence of written historical documents. Sapir was primarily interested in the native languages of western America, including the Uto-Aztecan languages of the southwestern United States and Central America; Bloomfield focused on the Algonquian languages around the Great Lakes. Although they continued and expanded upon the diachronic approach developed in nineteenth-century Europe, they are best known today for their synchronic work.

Synchronic study of language involves description of a language at a particular point in time, a snapshot without recourse to historical information. Contrary to the conclusion of Hermann Paul, twentieth-century students of language determined that nonhistorical, synchronic study could be objective and rigorous, that is, scientific, so long as the analysis of a language was based on its structure. Such structural analysis required that all units of the language (sounds, words, sentences) be viewed in relation to one another, as a unified system, independent of other languages, independent of popular assumptions, and independent of other fields of study. Conducted in this way, linguistics is an autonomous science, with its own goals, theories, and methods.

Establishing the autonomy of the discipline can be seen as a major achievement of American linguists in the twentieth century. In the early years, the historical and comparative approach was identified primarily with the study of European languages, modern and classical, while the study of cultures and languages conducted by Boas was considered part of anthropology. Indeed, Sapir, a student of Boas, received his doctoral degree in anthropology; Bloomfield's doctoral dissertation was a historical study of Germanic, and for many years his appointments as a university professor were in German. But as Sapir and Bloomfield, their students, and others studied the native languages of America, they developed field procedures, analytic principles, and a substantial agenda for the autonomous, synchronic, structural description of languages. Many of the concepts and procedures dealt with phonology, the structure of human language sound systems.

Phonetics had developed in the nineteenth century, describing specific speech sounds and explaining how they are produced by the human vocal tract. But in the twentieth century linguists discovered a number of additional important aspects of language sounds. Through phonetics we can describe the particular sound made when someone produces a [p]. But what is the role of that sound within the structure of the language? What similar sounds are perceived by speakers as the same, even though they are physically different? (The [p] in *spin* is not the same as that in *pin*.) Which sounds, when substituted for [p] in a word, produce a different word with a different meaning? (English *gap* and *gab*.) Where does a sound occur in relation to other sounds? ([p] can occur after [s] at the beginning of an English word, but [b] cannot.) Such details differ from one language to another. Spanish uses only the [p] in *spin*, not that of *pin*; German speakers do not use the sound [b] at the ends of words; Italian allows words that begin with the spelling *sb* although the actual pronunciation is [zb], another initial sequence that does not occur in English. These facts are as important as the sounds themselves. They are part of the reason why other languages sound different from our own, why other people may speak our language with a foreign accent, and why we tend to do the same when we speak their language. They also explain certain judgments we make about our language, e.g., that *sben* is not a possible English word but *spen* could be one even if it does not happen to be at this time.

The primary descriptive concern of the 1930s in the United States was phonology. The principles that were developed through the description of the phonology of native American languages were used as well to describe the phonology of other languages, some not familiar to many Americans of the time (Chinese, Japanese, Korean), others better known (French,

German), and, most of all, English. Accuracy and completeness in phonetics and phonology enabled the linguist to overcome the ethnocentrism to which Boas had objected and it established a firm empirical base of observable data. The focus on spoken language began in America with Boas; obviously, this continued with the concentration on phonology.

Although Sapir and Bloomfield both played major roles in all these developments, it was Bloomfield who wrote and lectured most about the scientific nature of linguistics. His 1933 textbook *Language* fundamentally altered the way in which American linguists approached the study of human languages. As they became more and more concerned with careful methodology, precise procedures, and clearly defined terms, the focus of mainstream American linguistics began to narrow until it became predominantly descriptive, structural, and synchronic in the 1940s and the early 1950s.

This narrow focus was not what Boas and Sapir had envisaged. In his introductory remarks to the first issue of the *International Journal of American Linguistics*, which Boas founded in 1917 and which was to be, and still is, devoted to the study of native American languages, he wrote: "The variety of American languages is so great, that they will be of high value for the solution of many fundamental psychological problems. The unconsciously formed categories found in human speech have not been sufficiently exploited for the investigation of the categories into which the whole range of human experience is forced" (p. 5). And Boas went on to proclaim the importance not only of describing the sounds, words, and sentences of these languages, but also of recording and studying conversations, tales, literary forms, poetry, and songs. Similarly, Sapir described the broadly encompassing aim of his 1921 book *Language:* "Its main purpose is to show what I conceive language to be, what is its variability in place and time, and what are its relations to other fundamental human interests — the problem of thought, the nature of the historical process, race, culture, art. . . . Knowledge of the wider relations of their science is essential to professional students of language if they are to be saved from a sterile and purely technical attitude" (p. v).

Sapir died in 1939, Boas in 1942, and their generous views of the scope of linguistics were overshadowed for a time in America by the more narrow concerns of scientific synchronic descriptivism. But this restricted view was not shared by the European linguists of this period. The illustrious Danish linguist Otto Jespersen (1860–1943), for example, not only wrote unsurpassed descriptions of English vocabulary and syntax but also major works on such diverse topics as children's language development, international auxiliary languages, foreign language teaching, and language change. Linguistic principles set forth in the 1916 book *Course in General Linguistics*, based on the lectures of the Swiss linguist Ferdinand de Saussure (1857–1913), were extended to anthropology, literary criticism, semiotics (the study of signs), and even psychoanalysis under the general rubric of structuralism. In central Europe an exceptionally talented assembly of scholars known as the Prague School applied structural principles to the analysis of folklore, standard literary languages, poetry, and regional dialects as well as particular languages; they actively sought universals of human language and some were especially interested in the nature of the phonological systems of the languages of the world. Foremost among the latter was Roman Jakobson (1896–1982). Educated in Russia, an intellectual leader in Prague, he escaped the Second World War in Europe in 1941 by immigrating to the United States. Jakobson brought twentieth-century European views of language to America, but he most influenced linguistics in the United States through his development of distinctive features, the binary component features of sounds. Today our understanding of phonology is the joint legacy of American structuralism and Jakobsonian distinctive features.

SYNTAX, SEMANTICS, AND BEYOND

The principles of observation and description that worked so well in phonology seemed to resist extension to syntax (the study and analysis of sentences), and the American insistence on observable data for a time placed semantics (the study of meaning) beyond the domain of linguistic science. These were serious problems. The primary purpose of human language is to convey meaning from one person to another, and the failure of American structural linguistics to produce a significant account of semantics was a major factor in the development of new approaches to the study of language in the 1950s and beyond. The changes began slowly as a number of linguists sought ways of describing syntax, where a key issue is the infinite number of sentences possible in every human language. Unlike phonological systems in which limited numbers of sounds occur in restricted combinations and patterns, or morphological systems with large but still listable numbers of words and their component roots and affixes, syntactic systems operate according to different principles.

In 1957 Noam Chomsky published *Syntactic Structures*, a slim volume of just over 100 pages that has been called "revolutionary" for the development of modern linguistics. Chomsky proposed explicit rules as a way of describing the sentences of a language. Basic sentences (e.g., active, affirmative, simple statements) could be produced, or generated, by a set of phrase structure rules, and a different type of rule, the transformation, derived all other sentences (e.g., passives, negatives, questions, complex sentences) from the basic types. This approach became known as transformational generative grammar, and it placed syntax at the center of linguistic investigation in the United States.

Chomsky did not restrict his work to the description of language structures; he sought explanations for the properties of human language. As a philosophical basis, he returned to some of the ideas about human language expounded by the rationalist philosophers of the seventeenth and eighteenth centuries. Recalling the rationalist distinction between grammaire générale and grammaire particulière, Chomsky reemphasized the importance of seeking universal properties of human language as a means to understand human nature and the human mind.

Chomsky challenged the narrow characterization of science that had bound so much of American linguistics in the 1940s and early 1950s to the directly observable data of actual samples of speech. He began to raise questions about how language exists in the minds of human beings and about what it is that permits speakers of a language to use that language creatively, producing and understanding sentences that they have never before heard or seen. Chomsky maintained that a grammar must account for the creativity that all speakers of a human language possess. Writing such a grammar became a central goal of American linguistics in the second half of the twentieth century; the task has not been easy and the goal has not yet been achieved. As Chomsky said in *Aspects of the Theory of Syntax:* "Any interesting generative grammar will be dealing, for the most part, with mental processes that are far beyond the level of actual or even potential consciousness; furthermore, it is quite apparent that [speakers'] reports and viewpoints about [their] behavior and [their] competence may be in error. Thus a generative grammar attempts to specify what [speakers] actually [know], not what [they] may report about [their] knowledge" (p. 8).

With an interest in all of the linguistic knowledge speakers possess, the study of semantics soon joined syntax as a major focus for American linguistics. Both of these topics require an investigator who is willing to go beyond the observable data of speech; they also require native or nativelike knowledge of the language under investigation. Thus, much of the work in transformational generative grammar has been done on English.

What is it that speakers of a language know that enables them to use the language as they do? This fundamental question became the basis for linguistic research, and it continues to be important today. Efforts to answer it have given rise to other questions. How do human beings acquire their linguistic knowledge? How is this knowledge stored in the brain? How do different contexts and situations affect the use of this knowledge? In Chomsky's words, "What contribution can the study of language make to our understanding of human nature?" (*Language and Mind*, p. 1). One approach to these questions is through the interdisciplinary field of psycholinguistics where researchers from linguistics and psychology are exploring questions about language acquisition, cognition, language comprehension and processing, and language and the brain. From its beginnings in the 1950s, this field has expanded to the point where for 1990 the *MLA International Bibliography* of linguistics listed almost 2,000 books and articles published on such topics in that one year alone.

The most widespread area of interest within psycholinguistics has been children's acquisition of their native language. It is a remarkable characteristic of the human species that its young, without conscious effort or overt teaching, and sometimes despite serious physical or mental disorders, acquire a complete linguistic system. Every human language is so complex that none has ever been completely described, yet somehow all children master the language of their environment. How do they accomplish this amazing feat? Not by imitating those around them, although that is sometimes the common belief. All children, from their earliest words, produce utterances that they have never heard, e.g., *she hitted me*. It has become clear that there are properties of the human mind that direct the acquisition of language. What these properties are and how they are activated by the environment are central concerns in psycholinguistic study.

During the same time period in which psycholinguistics developed, a different interdisciplinary field called sociolinguistics evolved, where language is considered in conjunction with aspects of the society in which it is used. Sociolinguistic studies in the United States have often related directly to broader social concerns. The study of the dialect known as Black English, for example, received a major impetus from the American civil rights movement, while the women's movement created interest in issues of language and gender, and population shifts fostered studies of language contact, bilingualism, and language attitudes.

Related to developments in psycholinguistics and in sociolinguistics, but not actually within their domain, have been extensions of linguistic research into the practical arenas of language teaching and language learning. The grammar-translation method of foreign language teaching can be traced back to the Middle Ages, even to the Romans who studied the Greek language at the same time that they adopted the Greek form of grammatical description. In the 1940s American linguists had participated actively in the preparation of teaching materials for the languages that they were describing. Consistent with their focus on the structure of spoken language, they created a new method of foreign language teaching called the audio-lingual approach, a method widely used in the United States during the 1950s and 1960s. Students memorized samples of spoken language, usually in the form of dialogues, and practiced the structural patterns of sentences. As American linguistics changed its emphasis from form alone to meaning and use, the audio-lingual approach (never accepted in Europe) was replaced by a variety of teaching methods that focus on using the foreign language for communicative purposes. The study of foreign- or second-language learning is sometimes referred to as "applied linguistics," although there are certainly other areas to which linguistic research has been applied, including the study and treatment of language loss and speech disorders, the use of language in law and medicine, and the teaching and learning of reading and writing.

Unlike scholars of language in other centuries and in other countries, very few twentieth-century linguists in the United States have worked extensively with literary prose or poetry, although some, like Edward Sapir, have themselves been poets, and a few, like Roman Jakobson, made important contributions in this area. A number of factors may be responsible: the early focus on native American languages without written literatures, the concentration on phonology in the 1930s, the attention to developing objective scientific principles of analysis during the 1940s and early 1950s, and, finally, the success of linguistics in the United States in achieving autonomy. With the widespread creation of university linguistics programs and departments independent from the traditional departments of English and foreign languages, many linguists became academically separated from their literary colleagues. Will a renewed interest in interdisciplinary work foster greater connections between linguistics and the literary arts? Perhaps this will be the next area of expansion in the scope of modern American linguistics, but at this time we simply do not know what lies ahead in the study of language.

The developments of the past, the changes in emphasis, and the insights achieved in the study of language could not have been predicted in advance. Even with the hindsight of centuries, we have not been able to explain why the Greeks were intellectually so productive. Nothing that we know about earlier centuries could have foretold the extensive understanding of language change that resulted from nineteenth-century historical and comparative work. The study of the native languages of North and Central America in the twentieth century was not predestined; there are still languages of South America that remain uninvestigated. Nor could anyone have predicted that linguistics in the United States would become so narrowly focused on structural description and the methodology of science and then would expand its scope so broadly. Modern American linguistics is no longer isolated from other fields of human inquiry, nor is it internationally isolated. Linguists from the United States lecture and conduct research in many other countries, and international scholars come to the United States to teach and to do their research. Professional societies, scholarly journals, technical books, and collections of essays extend the study of language around the world. In this sense, language and the study of language unite us all.

Linguistics today encompasses almost every conceivable topic related to human language — description and explanation, universals and properties of particular languages, synchronic and diachronic perspectives, regional and social variation, native-language acquisition and foreign-language learning, language as knowledge and language in use, philosophical questions and practical applications — all increasing the depth of our understanding of what it is to be human.

BIBLIOGRAPHY

Allen, Harold B. *The Linguistic Atlas of the Upper Midwest.* 3 volumes. Minneapolis: University of Minnesota Press, 1973–1976.

Andresen, Julie Tetel. *Linguistics in America 1769–1924.* London and New York: Routledge, 1990.

Bacon, Roger. *Opus Majus.* Translated by Robert Belle Burke. 2 volumes. New York: Russell and Russell, 1928.

Bloomfield, Leonard. *Language.* New York: Holt, Rinehart and Winston, 1933.

Boas, Franz. "Introductory." *International Journal of American Linguistics* 1: 1.1–8 (1917).

Chomsky, Noam. *Syntactic Structures.* The Hague: Mouton, 1957.

———. *Aspects of the Theory of Syntax.* Cambridge: The MIT Press, 1965.

———. *Cartesian Linguistics: A Chapter in the History of Rationalist Thought.* New York: Harper & Row, 1966.

———. *Language and Mind.* Enlarged edition. New York: Harcourt Brace Jovanovich, 1972.

———. *Language and Problems of Knowledge: The Managua Lectures.* Cambridge: The MIT Press, 1988.

Culler, Jonathan. *Ferdinand de Saussure.* Revised edition. Ithaca: Cornell University Press, 1986.

Darnell, Regna. *Edward Sapir: Linguist, Anthropologist, Humanist.* Berkeley: University of California Press, 1990.

Dinneen, Francis P. *An Introduction to General Linguistics.* New York: Holt, Rinehart and Winston, 1967.

Finegan, Edward. *Attitudes toward English Usage: The History of a War of Words.* New York: Teachers College Press, 1980.

Hall, Robert A., Jr. *A Life for Language: A Biographical Memoir of Leonard Bloomfield.* Amsterdam and Philadelphia: John Benjamins, 1990.

———, ed. *Leonard Bloomfield: Essays on His Life and Work.* Amsterdam and Philadelphia: John Benjamins, 1987.

Harris, Roy, and Talbot J. Taylor. *Landmarks in Linguistic Thought: The Western Tradition from Socrates to Saussure.* London and New York: Routledge, 1989.

Hymes, Dell, and John Fought. *American Structuralism.* The Hague: Mouton, 1981.

Itkonen, Esa. *Universal History of Linguistics: India, China, Arabia, Europe.* Amsterdam and Philadelphia: John Benjamins, 1991.

Jakobson, Roman. "Franz Boas' Approach to Language." *International Journal of American Linguistics* 10:4, 188–195 (1944).

———and Krystyna Pomorska. *Dialogues.* Cambridge: The MIT Press, 1983.

Juliard, Pierre. *Philosophies of Language in Eighteenth-Century France.* The Hague: Mouton, 1970.

Juul, Arne, and Hans F. Nielsen, eds. *Otto Jespersen: Facets of His Life and Work.* Philadelphia: John Benjamins, 1989.

Kurath, Hans, Miles L. Hanley, Bernard Bloch, et al. *Linguistic Atlas of New England.* 3 volumes. Providence: Brown University Press, 1939–1943.

Newmeyer, Frederick J. *Linguistic Theory in America.* Second edition. Orlando, Fla.: Academic Press, 1986.

The Oxford History of the Classical World. Edited by John Boardman, Jasper Griffin, and Oswyn Murray. Oxford: Oxford University Press, 1986.

Paul, Hermann. *Principles of the History of Language.* Translated from the second edition of the original by H. A. Strong. London: Swan Sonnenschein, Lowrey, 1888.

Pedersen, Holger. *The Discovery of Language: Linguistic Science in the Nine-

teenth Century. Translated by John Webster Spargo. Bloomington: Indiana University Press, 1962.

Robins, R. H. *A Short History of Linguistics*. Third edition. London: Longman, 1990.

Rousseau, Jean-Jacques. "Essay on the Origin of Languages." Translated by John H. Moran in *On the Origin of Language*. New York: Frederick Unger, 1966.

Sampson, Geoffrey. *Schools of Linguistics*. Stanford: Stanford University Press, 1980.

Sapir, Edward. *Language: An Introduction to the Study of Speech*. New York: Harcourt, Brace, 1921.

Saussure, Ferdinand de. *Course in General Linguistics*. Translated by Wade Baskin. New York: Philosophical Library, 1959.

Sebeok, Thomas A., ed. *Portraits of Linguists: A Biographical Source Book for the History of Western Linguistics, 1746–1963*. 2 volumes. Bloomington: Indiana University Press, 1966.

FOR DISCUSSION AND REVIEW

1. What is the Greek contribution to language growth? How was this made possible?

2. Falk says: "When we seek knowledge about human language we seek knowledge about ourselves as individuals and as members of the human species." What does Falk mean? Do you agree? Why or why not?

3. Briefly describe the *physis-nomos* debate that Falk discusses. Which position has become more powerful? Why is this so?

4. Who was Dionysius Thrax? Who were the Stoics? What role did they play in fostering language growth?

5. What does Falk describe as the Christian church's role in language development? What effect did the Crusades have on language in Europe?

6. Who were the speculative grammarians? In what ways did they broaden the scope of language's study?

7. What does Falk credit as "the greatest advances in the study of language from the fifteenth through the seventeenth centuries"? What political events of this time affected language study?

8. Describe the origins of language science, or linguistics, as a field of study. In what ways did this foster our knowledge of languages? What discoveries during the historical-comparative approach to language study encouraged the acceptance of linguistics as a science?

9. What is the earliest recorded language of which we have evidence? How have scientists made connections between this language and our own?

10. Which languages were accepted as standard in the eighteenth-century

linguistic community? Can you make any connections between this and modern notions of standard language forms?

11. What problems existed and still exist in attempts to study dialects in great detail? What efforts have been made in the United States for dialect study? Have they been successful?

12. What did Edward Sapir and Leonard Bloomfield contribute to the study of native American languages? What is their synchronic approach to language study? Why is the study of native American language so important?

13. In what ways did linguistic study in the United States of the 1950s change its scope and focus? What is transformational generative grammar? Who was responsible for its origins?

14. What is the focus of psycholinguistic study? How has sociolinguistics played a significant role in this area, especially in the United States? Why is the study of sociolinguistics so important in our society?

Projects for "Language and Its Study"

1. In "Language: An Introduction," W. F. Bolton points out that "perhaps the most distinctive property of language is that its users can create sentences never before known, and yet perfectly understandable to their hearers and readers." He calls this property *productivity*. To illustrate Bolton's point, show a photograph or a cartoon to the members of your class, and ask each of them to describe in one sentence what they see. Write down the sentences, and have the class compare them. What conclusions can be drawn?

2. Discussing the origin of human language, Bolton writes: "How this happened is at least as unknowable as how the universe began." However, a number of theories (e.g., the ding-dong and bow-wow theories) about the origin of language that used to be taken seriously have now been discredited. Read about four of these early theories in your library, and prepare an oral or written report describing the theories and evaluating their adequacy. Good starting places for this research are such standard textbooks as *The Origins and Development of the English Language* (Thomas Pyles and John Algeo) and *A History of the English Language* (Albert C. Baugh and Thomas Cable).

3. In describing the vocal organs that produce speech, Bolton notes that all of them except the larynx have other functions. Although disease sometimes necessitates the removal of an individual's larynx, speech is not always impossible for such a person. Both the artificial larynx and a technique involving swallowing air and talking while the air is "exhaled" have made speech possible for many people who have had this surgery. Prepare a report on one of these techniques. A great deal of published material will be available in your library; you may also find it useful to interview a speech pathologist or a specialist in this kind of rehabilitative medicine.

4. In some cases of deafness, as Bolton indicates, "bone-conduction can sometimes substitute for air-conduction." Prepare a brief report describing how hearing aids work; you may want to pay particular attention to bone-conduction.

5. Harvey A. Daniels presents "nine fundamental ideas about language." List the nine one-sentence ideas, and show them to five people who are not in your class. Summarize their reactions. Are some of the ideas more controversial or less accepted than others?

6. On pp. 29–30, Daniels describes the Sapir-Whorf hypothesis that the structure and vocabulary of people's languages influence their cultural and social beliefs, as well as their view of the world. Prepare a written or oral report explaining and analyzing the Sapir-Whorf hypothesis. Be sure to include examples of the ways in which language allegedly conditions perceptions.

7. In "To Be Human: A History of the Study of Language," Julia Falk examines several historical events, individual people, and groups or organizations that have significantly contributed to the growth and development of our language.

Among them are:

Individuals	Groups	Events
Dionysus Thrax	The Sophists	Invasion of England
Donatus	Greek philosophers	The Crusades
Priscian	Alexandrians	Invention of movable
Roger Bacon	Angles, Saxons, Jutes	type
Jonathan Swift	Speculative	
Samuel Johnson	grammarians	

All of the above mentioned fostered the growth of the English language in some manner. Your task is to prepare a report on one of these individuals, groups, or events demonstrating the contributions made by your selection to the development of language. Feel free to select a topic not included in the lists. You may find helpful resources in the bibliography at the end of this section. You may also turn to encyclopedia research or history books for your information. Compare reports in class in order to get an idea of the complications historical linguists face in their study of our language's history.

8. An interesting group project is to debate the validity of the Sapir-Whorf hypothesis. An excellent summary of the pro and con arguments can be found in Danny D. Steinberg's *Psycholinguistics: Language, Mind and World* (London and New York: Longman, 1982), pp. 101–120.

9. In his book *The Word-A-Day Vocabulary Builder*, lexicographer Bergen Evans states:

> Words are the tools for the job of saying what you want to say. And what you want to say are your thoughts and feelings, your desires and your dislikes, your hopes and your fears, your business and your pleasure — almost everything, indeed, that makes up you. Except for our vegetable-like growth and our animal-like impulses, almost all that we are is related to our use of words. Man has been defined as a tool-using animal, but his most important tool, the one that distinguishes him from all other animals, is his speech.

Do you agree with Evans's statement? Is it possible to think without language? Are there some creative activities for which people do not need speech? Write a brief essay in which you defend your position.

10. In his book *Humankind*, Peter Farb writes:

> Social scientists have long known that the way people perceive the world is influenced by the culture in which they are brought up. It has been noted, for example, that cultures give varying emphasis to round objects as distinct from rectangular ones. In Western cultures, rectangular ob-

jects tend to predominate, as witness the shapes of houses, furniture, television and movie screens, books, doorways, and numerous things constructed with carpenter's tools. Circular objects are much more common in many other cultures; thus the Zulus of South Africa live in circular houses inside circular compounds, keep their cattle in circular pens, and use circles in the imagery of their religious ceremonies. The way these traditional shapes affect perception has been formulated into what is known as the carpentered-world hypothesis, and has been tested by means of the optical illusion known as the Sander Parallelogram, shown.

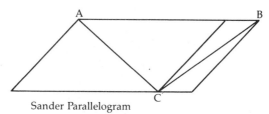

Sander Parallelogram

A person brought up in a Western culture who looks at this parallelogram tends to suppose that the diagonal line *AC* is longer than the diagonal *CB.* Measurement with a ruler, though, proves that *AC* is actually about fifteen percent shorter than *CB.* A moment's thought explains why a Westerner is likely to make this error. The carpentered world in which we live exposes us to rectangular surfaces, but these are rarely seen as right angles because objects are usually viewed from one side or another. We almost never see the rectangular top of a coffee table from directly overhead. Rather, we usually view it from one side and at an acute angle, which distorts it into the form of a parallelogram. Our everyday experience thus tells us that diagonal *AC* on a coffee table or any other three-dimensional rectangular object would be longer than diagonal *CB,* and so in a two-dimensional parallelogram we also automatically perceive *AC* as though it were longer. But people in rural Africa, who live in a circular world, are not hampered by any such preconception concerning rectangular forms. To them, that *CB* is longer is thus obvious. On the other hand, people in rural Africa are much more likely to be susceptible to various optical illusions involving circles.

Using "Language Shapes Reality" as the thesis and title of a short paper, describe incidents from your own experience that clearly exemplify the shaping power of language. For example, consider some of the recent purchases you have made. Have any of them been influenced by brand names, advertisements, or language used by salespersons? Did you ever find yourself taking or avoiding a course primarily because of its name?

11. As Daniels notes, "Although the English writing system is essentially phonemic—an attempt to represent the sounds of language in graphic form—it is notoriously irregular and confusing." (Consider, for example, the various ways the vowel sound in the word *keep* can be spelled: k*ee*p, k*ey*, tr*ea*t, p*eo*ple, qu*ay*, am*oe*ba, th*ie*f, rec*ei*ve.) It is no wonder that there have been many attempts to reform the spelling of English to make it more closely reflect its actual pronunciation. From

Benjamin Franklin to Noah Webster, from Theodore Roosevelt to George Bernard Shaw, many people have devised "improved" spelling systems for English. Prepare a report on (a) the proposals of one of the major would-be reformers, or (b) the history of the spelling-reform movement as a whole, summarizing both the arguments for and against spelling reform.

12. Daniels's book *Famous Last Words: The American Language Crisis Reconsidered*, from which "Nine Ideas about Language" is taken, disputes the idea that the English language is deteriorating and argues against what Daniels believes to be the trivializing attacks of such self-proclaimed experts as Edwin Newman, William Safire, John Simon, and the authors of usage handbooks. The subjects of just what is "correct usage" and of whether English is deteriorating are fascinating ones about which people have strong opinions.

Divide the class into three groups. Basing its arguments on facts, not opinions, each group should prepare a logical, well-documented position paper on one of the following: (a) the English language is deteriorating; (b) the English language is not deteriorating; and (c) there is an absolute standard for "correct" English and its basis is clear and defensible.

13. Consult at least four introductory linguistics texts (not dictionaries), and copy the definitions of *language* that each gives. After carefully comparing the definitions, write a paper discussing which points recur and explaining their significance. (If you decide to do this assignment as a class project, class members should collect as many different definitions of *language* as they can, being sure to identify the source of each. Copy and distribute the definitions; and discuss, as a group or in small groups, the significance of the similarities and differences among the definitions.)

Selected Bibliography

Akmajian, Adrian, Richard A. Demers, and Robert M. Harnish. *Linguistics: An Introduction to Language and Communication,* 2nd ed. Cambridge: The MIT Press, 1984. [An excellent introduction to the field of linguistics.]

Berko-Gleason, Jean. *The Development of Language,* 2nd ed. New York: Merrill Publishing Company, 1989. [An all-encompassing textbook for students of linguistics, with interesting sections on social language use and atypical language development.]

————. *The Development of Language,* 3rd ed. New York: Merrill Publishing Company, 1993. [Revised extensively with many new features of the 2nd ed. An introductory text that studies language development as a lifelong process.]

Bloomfield, Leonard. *Language.* New York: Holt, Rinehart and Winston, 1933. [Still a classic work for students of linguistics.]

Bolinger, Dwight. *Aspects of Language,* 2nd ed. New York: Harcourt Brace Jovanovich, 1975. [An extensive and readable treatment of a wide variety of topics.]

————. *Language: The Loaded Weapon.* New York: Longman Group, 1980. [A short but insightful introduction to language, with an emphasis on the importance of meaning.]

Burling, Robbins. *Patterns of Language: Structure, Variation, Change.* San Diego: Academic Press Inc., 1992. [Includes topics other introductory textbooks avoid with plenty of references from a variety of languages.]

Chase, Stuart. "How Language Shapes Our Thoughts," in *Harper's Magazine,* April 1954, pp. 76–82. [A discussion of language as a shaper of thought with examples drawn from many different cultures.]

Cook, V. J. *Chomsky's Universal Grammar: An Introduction.* New York: Basil Blackwell Inc., 1988. [Yet another invaluable collection of linguistic material from the field's master.]

Farb, Peter. *Humankind.* Boston: Houghton Mifflin, 1978. [Very readable discussion of all aspects of human behavior, including language.]

————. *Word Play: What Happens When People Talk.* New York: Alfred A. Knopf, 1973; rpt. New York: Bantam, 1975. [Entertaining, knowledgeable discussion.]

Fromkin, Victoria, and Robert Rodman. *An Introduction to Language,* 3rd ed. New York: Holt, Rinehart and Winston, 1983. [One of the most popular introductory books.]

Hattiangadi, J. N. *How is Language Possible? Philosophical Reflections on the Evolution of Language and Knowledge.* La Salle, IL: Open Court Publishing Company, 1987. [An interesting philosophical look at everything from acquisition through development of language. A very accessible reference work.]

Hulit, Lloyd M., M. R. Howard. *Born to Talk: An Introduction to Speech and Language Development.* New York: Macmillan Publishing Company, 1993. [An easily accessible detailed study of the "stages" of language development with inviting chapter titles and thorough exploration of the subject matter.]

Human Ancestors: Readings from "Scientific American." San Francisco: W. H. Freeman and Company, 1979. [A collection of eleven articles describing a number of aspects of the search for evidence regarding the origin and development of human beings.]

Kluckholm, Clyde. "The Gift of Tongues," in *Mirror for Man: The Relation of Anthropology to Modern Life.* New York: Whittlesey House, 1949. [An anthropologist's view of language, culture, and the Whorfian hypothesis.]

Langer, Suzanne K. *Philosophy in a New Key: A Study in the Symbolism of Reason, Rite, & Art,* 3rd ed. Cambridge: Harvard University Press, 1956. [A classic work on the human symbol-making process and its relationship to language.]

Lehmann, Winfred P. *Language: An Introduction.* New York: Random House, 1983. [A good, brief introduction to current areas of interest in linguistics.]

Lieberman, Philip. *On the Origins of Language.* New York: Macmillan, 1975. [A careful analysis of paleontological and archeological evidence.]

Michaels, Leonard, and Christopher Ricks, eds. *The State of the Language.* Berkeley: University of California Press, 1980. [A collection of sixty-three short, interesting essays on topics of widespread interest.]

Milner, Jean-Claude. *For the Love of Language.* New York: The Macmillan Press Ltd., 1990. [A translation of a 1978 publication with an extensive helpful introduction entitled "What do Linguists Want?"]

Nilsen, Don L. F., and Alleen Pace Nilsen. *Language Play: An Introduction to Linguistics.* Rowley, M. A.: Newbury House Publishers, 1978. [Interesting; includes topics often omitted. See Chapter 1, "What Is Language?"]

Pei, Mario. *The Story of Language,* rev. ed. Philadelphia: J. B. Lippincott Company, 1965. [A popular and readable introduction.]

Quinn, Jim. *American Tongue and Cheek: A Populist Guide to Our Language.* New York: Penguin Books, 1982. [Delightful and informative; traces changing attitudes toward usage, takes on the current "usage experts," and demonstrates that the English language is alive and well.]

Sagan, Carl. *The Dragons of Eden: Speculations on the Evolution of Human Intelligence.* New York: Random House, 1977. [Controversial but fascinating.]

Salus, P. H., ed. *On Language: Plato to Von Humboldt.* New York: Holt, Rinehart and Winston, 1969. [Includes several essays on the nature and origin of language.]

Sapir, Edward. *Language: An Introduction to the Study of Speech.* 1921; rpt. New York: Harcourt Brace & World, 1949. [A classic book that explores the relationship between speech and culture.]

Saussure, Ferdinand de. *Course in General Linguistics.* Trans. by Wade Baskin; Charles Bally and Albert Sechehaye, eds. 1915; rpt. New York: Philosophical Library, 1959. [A classic; based on lecture notes collected by former students.]

Stam, J. *Inquiries in the Origin of Language: The Fate of a Question.* New York: Harper & Row, 1976. [Traces the history of theories about the origin of language.]

Ullmann, Stephen. *Words and Their Use.* New York: Philosophical Library, 1951. [Contains an excellent chapter on the symbol-making process in language.]

Whorf, Benjamin Lee. *Language, Thought, and Reality.* John B. Carroll, ed. Cambridge: The MIT Press, 1956. [A classic work on the relationship between language and culture.]

Wilson, Edward O. *On Human Nature.* Cambridge: Harvard University Press, 1978. [Difficult but rewarding; attempt to join biological thought to the social sciences and the humanities.]

PART TWO

LANGUAGE ACQUISITION

A child is born, and grows, and learns to speak and to understand others when they speak. What could be more ordinary, more easily taken for granted? But that children — all children — master a large part of their native language(s) at as early an age as five is astonishing. We still do not fully understand how children learn language. However, once linguists and psychologists realized how extraordinary an accomplishment language acquisition is, they began to investigate and gain an understanding of the process. What they have discovered in recent years about language acquisition is the subject of the articles in this section.

In "The Acquisition of Language," Breyne Arlene Moskowitz provides an overview of the language acquisition process. She shows how children, in learning all the systems of grammar — phonology, syntax, lexicon, and pragmatics — use the same basic technique of developing a general rule and testing it, modifying the rule and narrowing its scope gradually, until near-mastery is achieved. Following this discussion, Eric H. Lenneberg juxtaposes, in chart format, a description of motor skills and language development for children aged twelve weeks to four years. Broadening the focus, Jean Aitchison, in "Predestinate Grooves," argues explicitly that language acquisition is a biologically triggered behavior which must occur during a specific critical period if it is to occur normally. She discusses the characteristics of biologically triggered behaviors — walking, for example — and explains in what ways speech shares these features.

According to George A. Miller and Patricia M. Gildea, "the average child learns at the rate of 5,000 words per year, or about thirteen per day." Surprisingly, linguists know very little about how children learn words, but Miller and Gildea believe, on the basis of their research, that computers can help children increase their vocabulary. In the next selection, Robert E. Owens, Jr., reports on his research on the importance of morphemes in preschool language development in

English-speaking children. With the increase of international trade and the rise of the global community, learning a second and even a third language is becoming imperative. In the final article in this section, Jeannine Heny reviews the process by which people learn a second language. By highlighting the differences between this process and that of learning a first language, she sheds light on some of the difficulties we experience while struggling to learn a new language.

Much has been learned in recent years about the language acquisition process, but there is still much that we do not fully understand. The selections in Part Two suggest that future research will significantly increase our understanding of the unique phenomenon that most people take for granted — language acquisition.

5

The Acquisition of Language

Breyne Arlene Moskowitz

*The image of proud parents leaning over their young baby's crib, urging
the infant to repeat such words as "mama" and "dada," is an American
stereotype. The acquisition of language, however, follows quite a different path than such a picture suggests. Language acquisition occurs in
all children in the same succession of stages, as linguistics professor
Breyne Arlene Moskowitz describes in the following selection. Professor
Moskowitz explores the prerequisites for language learning, the holophrastic stage (one-word utterances), the two-word stage, the telegraphic
stage, the acquisition of function words, the process of rule formation,
semantic processes, and the phonology and actual articulation of utterances. She shows that in all areas of language acquisition, children are
active learners and follow the same basic procedure: hypothesizing rules,
trying them out, and then modifying them. Children formulate the most
general rules first and apply them across the board; narrower rules are
added later, with exceptions and highly irregular forms. Although the
examples discussed in this selection concern children who are learning
English, the same process has been observed in children learning other
languages. While reading the selection, reflect on the language development of any young children you know to see if you can identify the stages
described by Moskowitz.*

An adult who finds herself in a group of people speaking an unfamiliar
foreign language may feel quite uncomfortable. The strange language
sounds like gibberish: mysterious strings of sound, rising and falling in
unpredictable patterns. Each person speaking the language knows when
to speak, how to construct the strings and how to interpret other people's
strings, but the individual who does not know anything about the language cannot pick out separate words or sounds, let alone discern meanings. She may feel overwhelmed, ignorant and even childlike. It is possible
that she is returning to a vague memory from her very early childhood,
because the experience of an adult listening to a foreign language comes
close to duplicating the experience of an infant listening to the "foreign"
language spoken by everyone around her. Like the adult, the child is
confronted with the task of learning a language about which she knows
nothing.

The task of acquiring language is one for which the adult has lost most of her aptitude but one the child will perform with remarkable skill. Within a short span of time and with almost no direct instruction the child will analyze the language completely. In fact, although many subtle refinements are added between the ages of five and ten, most children have completed the greater part of the basic language-acquisition process by the age of five. By that time a child will have dissected the language into its minimal separable units of sound and meaning; she will have discovered the rules for recombining sounds into words, the meanings of individual words and the rules for recombining words into meaningful sentences, and she will have internalized the intricate patterns of taking turns in dialogue. All in all she will have established herself linguistically as a full-fledged member of a social community, informed about the most subtle details of her native language as it is spoken in a wide variety of situations.

The speed with which children accomplish the complex process of language acquisition is particularly impressive. Ten linguists working full time for ten years to analyze the structure of the English language could not program a computer with the ability for language acquired by an average child in the first ten or even five years of life. In spite of the scale of the task and even in spite of adverse conditions — emotional instability, physical disability and so on — children learn to speak. How do they go about it? By what process does a child learn language?

WHAT IS LANGUAGE?

In order to understand how language is learned it is necessary to understand what language is. The issue is confused by two factors. First, language is learned in early childhood, and adults have few memories of the intense effort that went into the learning process, just as they do not remember the process of learning to walk. Second, adults do have conscious memories of being taught the few grammatical rules that are prescribed as "correct" usage, or the norms of "standard" language. It is difficult for adults to dissociate their memories of school lessons from those of true language learning, but the rules learned in school are only the conventions of an educated society. They are arbitrary finishing touches of embroidery on a thick fabric of language that each child weaves for herself before arriving in the English teacher's classroom. The fabric is grammar: the set of rules that describe how to structure language.

The grammar of language includes rules of phonology, which describe how to put sounds together to form words; rules of syntax, which describe how to put words together to form sentences; rules of semantics, which describe how to interpret the meaning of words and sentences; and rules of pragmatics, which describe how to participate in a conversation, how to sequence sentences and how to anticipate the information needed by an interlocutor. The internal grammar each adult has constructed is identical with that of every other adult in all but a few superficial details. Therefore each adult can create or understand an infinite number of sentences she has never heard before. She knows what is acceptable as a word or a sentence and what is not acceptable, and her judgments on these issues concur with those of other adults. For example, speakers of English generally agree that the sentence "Ideas green sleep colorless furiously" is ungrammatical and that the sentence "Colorless green ideas sleep furiously" is grammatical but makes no sense semantically. There is similar agreement on the grammatical relations represented by word order. For example, it is clear that the sentences "John hit Mary" and "Mary hit John" have different meanings although they consist of the same words, and that the sentence "Flying planes can be dangerous" has two possible meanings. At the level of individual words all adults speakers can agree that "brick" is an English word, that "blick" is not an English word but could be one (that is, there is an accidental gap in the adult lexicon, or internal vocabulary) and that "bnick" is not an English word and could not be one.

How children go about learning the grammar that makes communication possible has always fascinated adults, particularly parents, psychologists, and investigators of language. Until recently diary keeping was the primary method of study in this area. For example, in 1877 Charles Darwin published an account of his son's development that includes notes on language learning. Unfortunately most of the diarists used inconsistent or incomplete notations to record what they heard (or what they thought they heard), and most of the diaries were only partial listings of emerging types of sentences with inadequate information on developing word meanings. Although the very best of them, such as W. F. Leopold's classic *Speech Development of a Bilingual Child*, continue to be a rich resource of contemporary investigators, advances in audio and video recording equipment have made modern diaries generally much more valuable. In the 1960s, however, new discoveries inspired linguists and psychologists to approach the study of language acquisition in a new, systematic way, oriented less toward long-term diary keeping and more toward a search for the patterns in a child's speech at any given time.

An event that revolutionized linguistics was the publication in 1957 of Noam Chomsky's *Syntactic Structures*. Chomsky's investigation of the structure of grammars revealed that language systems were far deeper and more complex than had been suspected. And of course if linguistics was more complicated, then language learning had to be more complicated. In the . . . years since the publication of *Syntactic Structures* the disciplines of linguistics and child language have come of age. The study of the acquisition of language has benefited not only from the increasingly sophisticated understanding of linguistics but also from the improved understanding of cognitive development as it is related to language. The improvements in recording technology have made experimentation in this area more reliable and more detailed, so that investigators framing new and deeper questions are able to accurately capture both rare occurrences and developing structures.

The picture that is emerging from the more sophisticated investigations reveals the child as an active language learner, continually analyzing what she hears and proceeding in a methodical, predictable way to put together the jigsaw puzzle of language. Different children learn language in similar ways. It is not known how many processes are involved in language learning, but the few that have been observed appear repeatedly, from child to child and from language to language. All the examples I shall discuss here concern children who are learning English, but identical processes have been observed in children learning French, Russian, Finnish, Chinese, Zulu and many other languages.

Children learn the systems of grammar—phonology, syntax, semantics, lexicon and pragmatics—by breaking each system down into its smallest combinable parts and then developing rules for combining the parts. In the first two years of life a child spends much time working on one part of the task, disassembling the language to find the separate sounds that can be put together to form words and the separate words that can be put together to form sentences. After the age of two the basic process continues to be refined, and many more sounds and words are produced. The other part of language acquisition—developing rules for combining the basic elements of language—is carried out in a very methodical way: the most general rules are hypothesized first, and as time passes they are successively narrowed down by the addition of more precise rules applying to a more restricted set of sentences. The procedure is the same in any area of language learning, whether the child is acquiring syntax or phonology or semantics. For example, at the earliest stage of acquiring negatives a child does not have at her command the same range of negative structures that an adult does. She has constructed only a single very general rule: Attach "no" to the beginning of any sentence constructed by the other rules of grammar. At this stage all negative sentences will be formed according to that rule.

Throughout the acquisition process a child continually revises and refines the rules of her internal grammar, learning increasingly detailed subrules until she achieves a set of rules that enables her to create the full array of complex, adult sentences. The process of refinement continues at least until the age of ten and probably considerably longer for most children. By the time a child is six or seven, however, the changes in her grammar may be so subtle and sophisticated that they go unnoticed. In general children approach language learning economically, devoting their energy to broad issues before dealing with specific ones. They cope with clear-cut questions first and sort out the details later, and they may adopt any one of a variety of methods for circumventing details of a language system they have not yet dealt with.

(1)	(2)	(3)	(4)	(5)	(6)
boy		boys	boysəz	boys	boys
cat		cats	catsəz	cats	cats
			catəz		
man	men	mans	mansəz	mans	men
			menəz		
house		house	housəz	houses	houses
foot		foots	footsəz	feets	feet
feet		feets	feetsəz		

Sorting out of competing pronunciations that result in the correct plural forms of nouns takes place in the six stages shown in this illustration. Children usually learn the singular forms of nouns first (1), although in some cases an irregular plural form such as "feet" may be learned as a singular or as a free variant of a singular. Other irregular plurals may appear for a brief period (2), but soon they are replaced by plurals made according to the most general rule possible: To make a noun plural add the sound "s" or "z" to it (3). Words such as "house" or "rose," which already end in an "s"- or "z"-like sound, are usually left in their singular forms at this stage. When words of this type do not have irregular plural forms, adults make them plural by adding an "əz" sound. (The vowel "ə" is pronounced like the unstressed word "a.") Some children demonstrate their mastery of this usage by tacking "əz" endings indiscriminately onto nouns (4). That stage is brief and use of the ending is quickly narrowed down (5). At this point only irregular plurals remain to be learned, and since no new rule-making is needed, children may go on to harder problems and leave final stage (6) for later.

PREREQUISITES FOR LANGUAGE

Although some children verbalize much more than others and some increase the length of their utterances much faster than others, all children overgeneralize a single rule before learning to apply it more narrowly and before constructing other less widely applicable rules, and all children speak in one-word sentences before they speak in two-word sentences. The similarities in language learning for different children and different languages are so great that many linguists have believed at one time or another that the human brain is preprogrammed for language learning. Some linguists continue to believe language is innate and only the surface details of the particular language spoken in a child's environment need to be learned. The speed with which children learn language gives this view much appeal. As more parallels between language and other areas of cognition are revealed, however, there is greater reason to believe any language specialization that exists in the child is only one aspect of more general cognitive abilities of the brain.

Whatever the built-in properties the brain brings to the task of language learning may be, it is now known that a child who hears no language learns no language, and that a child learns only the language spoken in her environment. Most infants coo and babble during the first six months of life, but congenitally deaf children have been observed to cease babbling after six months, whereas normal infants continue to babble. A child does not learn language, however, simply by hearing it spoken. A boy with normal hearing but with deaf parents who communicated by the American Sign Language was exposed to television every day so that he would learn English. Because the child was asthmatic and was confined to his home he interacted only with people at home, where his family and all their visitors communicated in sign language. By the age of three he was fluent in sign language but neither understood nor spoke English. It appears that in order to learn a language a child must also be able to interact with real people in that language. A television set does not suffice as the sole medium for language learning because, even though it can ask questions, it cannot respond to a child's answers. A child, then, can develop language only if there is language in her environment and if she can employ that language to communicate with other people in her immediate environment.

CARETAKER SPEECH

In constructing a grammar children have only a limited amount of information available to them, namely the language they hear spoken around them. (Until about the age of three a child models her language on that of her parents; afterward the language of her peer group tends to become more important.) There is no question, however, that the language environments children inhabit are restructured, usually unintentionally, by the adults who take care of them. Recent studies show that there are several ways caretakers systematically modify the child's environment, making the task of language acquisition simpler.

Caretaker speech is a distinct speech register that differs from others in its simplified vocabulary, the systematic phonological simplification of some words, higher pitch, exaggerated intonation, short, simple sentences and a high proportion of questions (among mothers) or imperatives (among fathers). Speech with the first two characteristics is formally designated Baby Talk. Baby Talk is a subsystem of caretaker speech that has been studied over a wide range of languages and cultures. Its characteristics appear to be universal: in languages as diverse as English, Arabic, Comanche, and Gilyak (a Paleo-Siberian language) there are simplified vocabulary items for terms relating to food, toys, animals and body functions. Some words are phonologically simplified, frequently by the duplication of syllables, as in "wawa" for "water" and "choo-choo" for "train," or by the reduction of consonant clusters, as in "tummy" for "stomach" and "scambled eggs" for "scrambled eggs." (Many types of phonological simplification seem to mimic the phonological structure of an infant's own early vocabulary.)

Perhaps the most pervasive characteristic of caretaker speech is its syntactic simplification. While a child is still babbling, adults may address long, complex sentences to her, but as soon as she begins to utter meaningful, identifiable words they almost invariably speak to her in very simple sentences. Over the next few years of the child's language development the speech addressed to her by her caretakers may well be describable by a grammar only six months in advance of her own.

The functions of the various language modifications in caretaker speech are not equally apparent. It is possible that higher pitch and exaggerated intonation serve to alert a child to pay attention to what she is hearing. As for Baby Talk, there is no reason to believe the use of phonologically simplified words in any way affects a child's learning of pronunciation. Baby Talk may have only a psychological function, marking speech as being affectionate. On the other hand, syntactic simplification has a clear function. Consider the speech adults address to other adults; it is full of false starts and long, rambling, highly complex sentences. It is not surprising that elaborate theories of innate language ability arose during the years when linguists examined the speech adults addressed to adults and assumed that the speech addressed to children was similar. Indeed, it is hard to imagine how a child could derive the rules of language from such input. The wide study of caretaker speech conducted over the past eight years has shown that children do not face this problem. Rather it appears they construct their initial grammars on

(1)	(2)	(3)	(4)	(5)	(6)
walk		walked	walkedəd	walked	walked
play		played	playedəd	played	played
need		need	needəd	needed	needed
			camedəd		
come	came	comed	comedəd	comed	came
			goed		
go	went	goed	wentəd	goed	went

Development of past-tense forms of verbs also takes place in six stages. After the present-tense forms are learned (1) irregular past-tense forms may appear briefly (2). The first and most general rule that is postulated is: To put a verb into the past tense, add a "t" or "d" sound (3). In adult speech, verbs such as "want" or "need," which already end in a "t" or "d" sound, are put into the past tense by adding "əd" sound. Many children go through a brief stage in which they add "əd" endings to any existing verb forms (4). Once the use of "əd" ending has been narrowed down (5), only irregular past-tense forms remain to be learned (6).

the basis of the short, simple, grammatical sentences that are addressed to them in the first year or two they speak.

CORRECTING LANGUAGE

Caretakers simplify children's language-analysis task in other ways. For example, adults talk with other adults about complex ideas, but they talk with children about the here and now, minimizing discussion of feelings, displaced events and so on. Adults accept children's syntactic and phonological "errors," which are a normal part of the acquisition process. It is important to understand that when children make such errors, they are not producing flawed or incomplete replicas of adult sentences; they are producing sentences that are correct and grammatical with respect to their own current internalized grammar. Indeed, children's errors are essential data for students of child language because it is the consistent departures from the adult model that indicate the nature of a child's current hypotheses about the grammar of language. There are a number of memorized, unanalyzed sentences in any child's output of language. If a child says, "Nobody likes me," there is no way of knowing whether she has memorized the sentence intact or has figured out the rules for constructing the sentence. On the other hand, a sentence such as "Nobody don't like me" is clearly not a memorized form but one that reflects an intermediate stage of a developing grammar.

Since each child's utterances at a particular stage are from her own point of view grammatically correct, it is not surprising that children are fairly impervious to the correction of their language by adults, indeed to any attempts to teach them language. Consider the boy who lamented to his mother, "Nobody don't like me." His mother seized the opportunity to correct him, replying, "Nobody likes me." The child repeated his original version and the mother her modified one a total of eight times until in desperation the mother said, "Now listen carefully! Nobody likes me." Finally her son got the idea and dutifully replied, "Oh! Nobody don't likes me." As the example demonstrates, children do not always understand exactly what it is the adult is correcting. The information the adult is trying to impart may be at odds with the information in the child's head, namely the rules the child is postulating for producing language. The surface correction of a sentence does not give the child a clue about how to revise the rule that produced the sentence.

It seems to be virtually impossible to speed up the language-learning process. Experiments conducted by Russian investigators show that it is extremely difficult to teach children a detail of language more than a few days before they would learn it themselves. Adults sometimes do, of course, attempt to teach children rules of language, expecting them to learn by imitation, but Courtney B. Cazden of Harvard University found that children benefit less from frequent adult correction of their errors than from true conversational interaction. Indeed, correcting errors can interrupt that interaction, which is, after all, the function of language. (One way children may try to secure such interaction is by asking "Why?" Children go through a stage of asking a question repeatedly. It serves to keep the conversation going, which may be the child's real aim. For example, a two-and-a-half-year-old named Stanford asked "Why?" and was given the nonsense answer: "Because the moon is made of green cheese." Although the response was not at all germane to the conversation, Stanford was happy with it and again asked "Why?" Many silly answers later the adult had tired of the conversation but Stanford had not. He was clearly not seeking information. What he needed was to practice the form of social conversation before dealing with its function. Asking "Why?" served that purpose well.)

In point of fact adults rarely correct children's ungrammatical sentences. For example, one mother, on hearing "Tommy fall my truck down," turned to Tommy with "Did you fall Stevie's truck down?" Since imitation seems to have little role in the language-acquisition process, however, it is probably just as well that most adults are either too charmed by children's errors or too busy to correct them.

Practice does appear to have an important function in the child's language learning process. Many children have been observed purposefully practicing language when they are alone, for example in a crib or a playpen. Ruth H. Weir of Stanford University hid a tape recorder in her son's bedroom and recorded his talk after he was put to bed. She found that he played with words and phrases, stringing together sequences of similar sounds and of variations on a phrase or on the use of a word: "What color . . . what color blanket . . . what color mop . . . what color glass . . . what color TV . . . red ant . . . fire . . . like lipstick . . . blanket . . . now the blue blanket . . . what color TV . . . what color horse . . . then what color table . . . then what color fire . . . here yellow spoon." Children who do not have much opportunity to be alone may use dialogue in a similar fashion. When Weir tried to record the bedtime monologues of her second child, whose room adjoined that of the first, she obtained through-the-wall conversations instead.

THE ONE-WORD STAGE

The first stage of child language is one in which the maximum sentence length is one word; it is followed by a stage in which the maximum sentence length is two words. Early in the one-word stage there are only a few words in a child's vocabulary, but as months go by her lexicon expands with increasing rapidity. The early words are primarily concrete nouns and verbs; more abstract words such as adjectives are acquired later. By the time the child is uttering two-word sentences with some regularity, her lexicon may include hundreds of words.

When a child can say only one word at a time and knows only five words in all, choosing which one to say may not be a complex task. But how does she decide which word to say when she knows 100 words or more? Patricia M. Greenfield of the University of California at Los Angeles and Joshua H. Smith of Stanford have suggested that an important criterion is informativeness, that is, the child selects a word reflecting what is new in a particular situation. Greenfield and Smith also found that a newly acquired word is first used for naming and only later for asking for something.

Superficially the one-word stage seems easy to understand: a child says one word at a time, and so each word is a complete sentence with its own sentence intonation. Ten years ago a child in the one-word stage was thought to be learning word meanings but not syntax. Recently, however, students of child language have seen less of a distinction between the one-word stage as a period of word learning and the subsequent period, beginning with the two-word stage, as one of syntax acquisition. It now seems clear that the infant is engaged in an enormous amount of syntactic analysis in the one-word stage, and indeed that her syntactic abilities are reflected in her utterances and in her accurate perception of multiword sentences addressed to her.

Ronald Scollon of the University of Hawaii and Lois Bloom of Columbia University have pointed out independently that important patterns in word choice in the one-word stage can be found by examining larger segments of children's speech. Scollon observed that a nineteen-month-old named Brenda was able to use a vertical construction (a series of one-word sentences) to express what an adult might say with a horizontal construction (a multiword sentence). Brenda's pronunciation, which is represented phonetically below, was imperfect and Scollon did not understand her words at the time. Later, when he transcribed the tape of their conversation, he heard the sound of a passing car immediately preceding the conversation and was able to identify Brenda's words as follows:

BRENDA: "Car [pronounced 'ka']. Car. Car. Car."
SCOLLON: "What?"
BRENDA: "Go. Go."
SCOLLON: [Undecipherable.]
BRENDA: "Bus [pronounced 'baish']. Bus. Bus. Bus. Bus. Bus. Bus. Bus. Bus."
SCOLLON: "What? Oh, bicycle? Is that what you said?"
BRENDA: "Not ['na']."
SCOLLON: "No?"
BRENDA: "Not."
SCOLLON: "No. I got it wrong."

Brenda was not yet able to combine two words syntactically to express "Hearing that car reminds me that we went on the bus yesterday. No, not on a bicycle." She could express that concept, however, by combining words sequentially. Thus the one-word stage is not just a time for learning the meaning of words. In that period a child is developing hypotheses about putting words together in sentences, and she is already putting sentences together in meaningful groups. The next step will be to put two words together to form a single sentence.

THE TWO-WORD STAGE

The two-word stage is a time for experimenting with many binary semantic-syntactic relations such as possessor-possessed ("Mommy sock"), actor-action ("Cat sleeping") and action-object ("Drink soup"). When two-word sentences first began to appear in Brenda's speech, they were primarily of the following forms: subject noun and verb (as in "Monster go"), verb and object (as in "Read it") and verb or noun and location (as in "Bring home" and "Tree down"). She also continued to use vertical constructions in the two-word stage, providing herself with a means of expressing ideas that were still too advanced for her syntax. Therefore once again a description of Brenda's isolated sentences does not show her full abilities at this point in her linguistic development. Consider a later conversation Scollon had with Brenda:

BRENDA: "Tape corder. Use it. Use it."
SCOLLON: "Use it for what?"
BRENDA: "Talk. Corder talk. Brenda talk."

Brenda's use of vertical constructions to express concepts she is still unable to encode syntactically is just one example of a strategy employed by children in all areas of cognitive development. As Jean Piaget of the University of Geneva and Dan I. Slobin of the University of California at Berkeley put it, new forms are used for old functions and new functions are expressed by old forms. Long before Brenda acquired the complex syntactic form "Use the tape recorder to record me talking" she was able to use her old forms — two-word sentences and vertical construction — to express the new function. Later, when that function was old, she would develop new forms to express it. The controlled dovetailing of form and function can be observed in all areas of language acquisition. For example, before children acquire the past tense they may employ adverbs of time such as "yesterday" with present-tense verbs to express past time, saying "I do it yesterday" before "I dood it."

Bloom has provided a rare view of an intermediate stage between the one-word and the two-word stages in which the two-word construction — a new form — served only an old function. For several weeks Bloom's daughter Alison uttered two-word sentences all of which included the word "wida." Bloom tried hard to find the meaning of "wida" before realizing that it had no meaning. It was, she concluded, simply a placeholder. This case is the clearest ever reported of a new form preced-

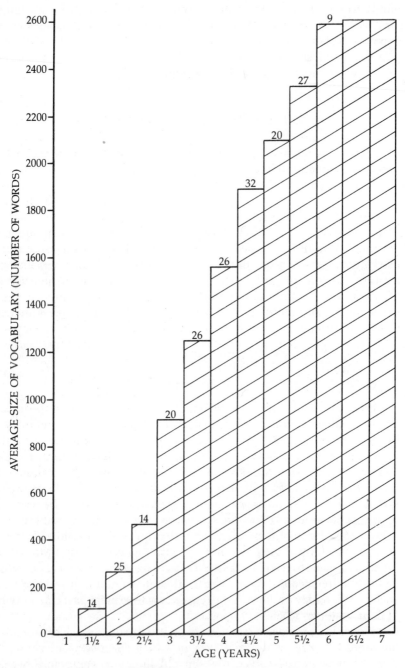

FIGURE 5.1   Children's average vocabulary size increases rapidly between the ages of one-and-a-half and six-and-a-half. The numbers over the first ten columns indicate the number of children tested in each sample age group. Data are based on work done by Madorah E. Smith of the University of Hawaii.

ing new functions. The two-word stage is an important time for practicing functions that will later have expanded forms and practicing forms that will later expand their functions.

TELEGRAPHIC SPEECH

There is no three-word stage in child language. For a few years after the end of the two-word stage children do produce rather short sentences, but the almost inviolable length constraints that characterized the first two stages have disappeared. The absence of a three-word stage has not been satisfactorily explained as yet; the answer may have to do with the fact that many basic semantic relations are binary and few are ternary. In any case a great deal is known about the sequential development in the language of the period following the two-word stage. Roger Brown of Harvard has named that language telegraphic speech. (It should be noted that there is no specific age at which a child enters any of these stages of language acquisition and further that there is no particular correlation between intelligence and speed of acquisition.)

Early telegraphic speech is characterized by short, simple sentences made up primarily of content words: words that are rich in semantic content, usually nouns and verbs. The speech is called telegraphic because the sentences lack function "words": tense endings on verbs and plural endings on nouns, prepositions, conjunctions, articles and so on. As the telegraphic-speech stage progresses, function words are gradually added to sentences. This process has possibly been studied more thoroughly than any other in language acquisition, and a fairly predictable order in the addition of function words has been observed. The same principles that govern the order of acquisition of function words in English have been shown to operate in many other languages, including some, such as Finnish and Russian, that express the same grammatical relations with particularly rich systems of noun and verb suffixes.

In English many grammatical relations are represented by a fixed word order. For example, in the sentence "The dog followed Jamie to school" it is clear it is the dog that did the following. Normal word order in English requires that the subject come before the verb, and so people who speak English recognize "the dog" as the subject of the sentence. In other languages a noun may be marked as a subject not by its position with respect to the other words in the sentence but by a noun suffix, so that in adult sentences word order may be quite flexible. Until children begin to acquire suffixes and other function words, however, they employ fixed word order to express grammatical relations no matter how flexible adult word order may be. In English the strong propensity to follow word order rigidly shows up in children's interpretations of passive sentences such as "Jamie was followed by the dog." At an early age children may interpret some passive sentences correctly, but by age three they begin to ignore the function words such as "was" and "by" in passive sentences and adopt the fixed word-order interpretation. In other words, since "Jamie" appears before the verb, Jamie is assumed to be the actor, or the noun doing the following.

FUNCTION WORDS

In spite of its grammatical dependence on word order, the English language makes use of enough function words to illustrate the basic principles that determine the order in which such words are acquired. The progressive tense ending "-ing," as in "He going," is acquired first, long before the present-tense third-person singular ending "-s," as in "He goes." The "-s" itself is acquired long before the past tense endings, as in "He goed." Once again the child proves to be a sensible linguist, learning first the tense that exhibits the least variation in form. The "-ing" ending is pronounced only one way, regardless of the pronunciation of the verb to which it is attached. The verb endings "-s" and "-ed," however, vary in their pronunciation: compare "cuts (s)," "cuddles (z)," "crushes (əz)," "walked (t)," "played (d)" and "halted (əd)." (The vowel "ə," called "schwa," is pronounced like the unstressed word "a.") Furthermore, present progressive ("-ing") forms are used with greater frequency than any other tense in the speech children hear. Finally, no verb has an irregular "-ing" form, but some verbs do have irregular third-person present-tense singular forms and many have irregular past-tense forms. (The same pattern of learning earliest those forms that exhibit the least variation shows

(1) Laura (2:2)	(4) Andrew (2:0)
Her want some more.	Put that on.
Her want some more candy.	Andrew put that on.
(2) Laura (2:2)	(5) Andrew (2:1)
Where my tiger?	All wet.
Where my tiger book?	This shoe all wet.
(3) Laura (2:2)	(6) Benjy (2:3)
Let's dooz this.	Broke it.
Let's do this.	Broke it.
Let's do this puzzle.	Broke it I did.

Children correct their speech in ways that reflect the improvements they are currently making on their internal grammar. For example, Laura (1–3) is increasing the length of her sentences, encoding more information by embellishing a noun phrase. Andrew (4, 5) and Benjy (6) appear to be adding subjects to familiar verb-phrase sentences.

---

(7) Jamie (6:0)

Jamie: Why are you doing that?
Mother: What?
Jamie: Why are you writing what I say down?
Mother: What?
Jamie: Why are you writing down what I say?

(8) Jamie (6:3)

Jamie: Who do you think is the importantest kid in the world except me?
Mother: What did you say, Jamie?
Jamie: Who do you think is the specialest kid in the world not counting me?

(9) Jamie (6:6)

Jamie: Who are you versing?
Mother: What?
Jamie: I wanted to know who he was playing against.

(10) Jamie (6:10)

Jamie: I figured something you might like out.
Mother: What did you say?
Jamie: I figured out something you might like.

Jamie (7–10) seems to be working on much more subtle refinements such as the placement of verb particles, for example the "down" of "writing down." (Each child's age at time of correction is given in years and months.) Corrections shown here were recorded by Judy S. Reilly of University of California at Los Angeles.

up much more dramatically in languages such as Finnish and Russian, where the paradigms of inflection are much richer.)

The past tense is acquired after the progressive and present tenses, because the relative time it represents is conceptually more difficult. The future tense ("will" and a verb) is formed regularly in English and is as predictable as the progressive tense, but it is a much more abstract concept than the past tense. Therefore it is acquired much later. In the same way the prepositions "in" and "on" appear earlier than any others, at about the same time as "-ing," but prepositions such as "behind" and "in front of," whose correct usage depends on the speaker's frame of reference, are acquired much later.

It is particularly interesting to note that there are three English morphemes that are pronounced identically but are acquired at different times. They are the plural "-s," the possessive "-s" and the third-person singular tense ending "-s," and they are acquired in the order of listing. Roman Jakobson of Harvard has suggested that the explanation of this phenomenon has to do with the complexity of the different relations the morphemes signal: the singular-plural distinction is at the word level, the possessive relates two nouns at the phrase level and the tense ending relates a noun and a verb at the clause level.

The forms of the verb "to be" — "is," "are" and so on — are among the last of the function words to be acquired, particularly in their present-tense forms. Past- and future-tense forms of "to be" carry tense information, of course, but present-tense forms are essentially meaningless, and omitting them is a very sensible strategy for a child who must maximize the information content of a sentence and place priorities on linguistic structures still to be tackled.

PLURALS

When there are competing pronunciations available, as in the case of the plural and past tenses, the process of sorting them out also follows a predictable pattern. Consider the acquisition of the English plural, in which six distinct stages can be observed. In English, as in many other (but not all) languages, nouns have both singular and plural forms. Children usually use the singular forms first, both in situations where the singular form would be appropriate and in situations where the plural form would be appropriate. In instances where the plural form is irregular in the adult model, however, a child may not recognize it as such and may use it in place of the singular or as a free variant of the singular. Thus in the first stage of acquisition, before either the concept of a plural or the linguistic devices for expressing a plural are acquired, a child may say "two cat" or point to "one feet."

When plurals begin to appear regularly, the child forms them according to the most general rule of English plural formation. At this point it is the child's overgeneralization of the rule, resulting in words such as "mans," "foots" or "feets," that shows she has hypothesized the rule: Add the sound /s/ or /z/ to the end of a word to make it plural. (The slashes indicate pronounced sounds, which are not to be confused with the letters used in spelling.)

For many children the overgeneralized forms of the irregular nouns are actually the earliest /s/ and /z/ plurals to appear, preceding "boys," "cats" and other regular forms by hours or days. The period of overgeneralization is considered to be the third stage in the acquisition of plurals because for many children there is an intermediate second stage in which irregular plurals such as "men" actually do appear. Concerned parents may regard the change from the second-stage "men" to the third-stage "mans" as a regression, but in reality it demonstrates progress from an individual memorized item to the application of a general rule.

In the third stage the small number of words that already end in a sound resembling /s/ or /z/, such as "house," "rose" and "bush," are used without any plural ending. Adults normally make such words plural by adding the suffix /əz/. Children usually relegate this detail to the remainder pile, to be dealt with at a later time. When they return to the problem, there is often a short fourth stage of perhaps a day, in which the child delightedly demonstrates her solution by tacking /əz/ endings indiscriminately onto nouns no matter what sound they end in and no matter how many other plural markings they may already have. A child may wake up one morning and throw herself into this stage with all the zeal of a kitten playing with its first ball of string.

Within a few days the novelty wears off and the child enters a less flamboyant fifth stage, in which only irregular plurals still deviate from the model forms. The rapid progression through the fourth stage does not mean that she suddenly focused her attention on the problem of /əz/ plurals. It is more likely that she had the problem at the back of her mind throughout the third stage. She was probably silently formulating hypotheses about the occurrence of /əz/ and testing them against the plurals she was hearing. Finding the right rule required discovering the phonological specification of the class of nouns that take /əz/ plurals.

Arriving at the sixth and final stage in the acquisition of plurals does not require the formulation of any new rules. All that is needed is the simple memorizing of irregular forms. Being rational, the child relegates such minor details to the lowest-priority remainder pile and turns her attention to more interesting linguistic questions. Hence a five-year-old may still not have entered the last stage. In fact, a child in the penultimate stage may not be at all receptive to being taught irregular plurals. For example, a child named Erica pointed to a picture of some "mouses," and her mother corrected her by saying "mice." Erica and her mother each repeated their own version two more times, and then Erica resolved the standoff by turning to a picture of "ducks." She avoided the picture of the mice for several days. Two years later, of course, Erica was perfectly able to say "mice."

NEGATIVE SENTENCES

One of the pioneering language-acquisition studies of the 1960s was undertaken at Harvard by a research group headed by Brown. The group studied the development in the language of three children over a period of several years. Two members of the group, Ursula Bellugi and Edward S. Klima, looked specifically at the changes in the children's negative sentences over the course of the project. They found that negative structures, like other subsystems of the syntactic component of grammar, are acquired in an orderly, rule-governed way.

When the project began, the forms of negative sentences the children employed were quite simple. It appeared that they had incorporated the following rule into their grammar: To make a sentence negative attach "no" or "not" to the beginning of it. On rare occasions, possibly when a child had forgotten to anticipate the negative, "no" could be attached to the end of a sentence, but negative words could not appear inside a sentence.

In the next stage the children continued to follow this rule, but they had also hypothesized and incorporated into their grammars more complex rules that allowed them to generate sentences in which the negatives "no," "not," "can't" and "don't" appeared after the subject and before the verb. These rules constituted quite an advance over attaching a negative word externally to a sentence. Furthermore, some of the primitive imperative sentences constructed at this stage began with "don't" rather than "no." On the other hand, "can't" never appeared at the beginning of a sentence, and neither "can" nor "do" appeared as an auxiliary, as they do in adult speech: "I can do it." These facts suggest that at this point "can't" and "don't" were unanalyzed negative forms rather than contractions of "cannot" and "do not," but that although "can't" and "don't" each seemed to be interchangeable with "no," they were no longer interchangeable with each other.

In the third stage of acquiring negatives many more details of the negative system had appeared in the children's speech. The main feature of the system that still remained to be worked out was the use of pronouns in negative sentences. At this stage the children said "I didn't see something" and "I don't want somebody to wake me up." The pronouns "somebody" and "something" were later replaced with "nobody" and "nothing" and ultimately with the properly concorded forms "anybody" and "anything."

Many features of telegraphic speech were still evident in the third stage. The form "is" of the verb "to be" was frequently omitted, as in "This no good." In adult speech the auxiliary "do" often functions as a dummy verb to carry tense and other markings; for example, in "I didn't see it," "do" carries the tense and the negative. In the children's speech at this stage "do" appeared occasionally, but the children had not yet figured out its entire function. Therefore in some sentences the auxiliary "do" was omitted and the negative "not" appeared alone, as in "I not hurt him." In other sentences, such as "I didn't did it," the negative auxiliary form of "do" appears to be correct but is actually an unanalyzed, memorized item; at this stage the tense is regularly marked on the main verb, which in this example happens also to be "do."

Many children acquire negatives in the same way that the children in the Harvard study did, but subsequent investigations have shown that there is more than one way to learn a language. Carol B. Lord of U.C.L.A. identified a quite different strategy employed by a two-year-old named Jennifer. From twenty-four to twenty-eight months Jennifer used "no" only as a single-word utterance. In order to produce a negative sentence she simply spoke an ordinary sentence with a higher pitch. For example, "I want put it on" spoken with a high pitch meant "I don't want to put it on." Lord noticed that many of the negative sentences adults addressed to Jennifer were spoken with an elevated pitch. Children tend to pay more attention to the beginning and ending of sentences, and in adult speech negative words usually appear in the middle of sentences. With good reason, then, Jennifer seemed to have hypothesized that one makes a

Stage 1	Stage 2	Stage 3
No . . . wipe finger.	I can't catch you.	We can't make another broom.
No a boy bed.	I can't see you.	I don't want cover on it.
No singing song.	We can't talk.	I gave him some so he won't cry.
No the sun shining.	You can't dance.	No, I don't have a book.
No money.	I don't want it.	I am not a doctor.
No sit there.	I don't like him.	It's not cold.
No play that.	I don't know his name.	Don't put the two wings on.
No fall!	No pinch me.	**A**
Not . . . fit.	Book say no.	I didn't did it.
Not a teddy bear.	Touch the snow no.	You didn't caught me.
More . . . no.	This a radiator no.	I not hurt him.
Wear mitten no.	No square . . . is clown.	Ask me if I not made mistake.
	Don't bite me yet.	**B**
	Don't leave me.	Because I don't want somebody to wake me up.
	Don't wake me up . . . again.	I didn't see something.
	He not little, he big.	**C**
	That no fish school.	I isn't . . . I not sad.
	That no Mommy.	This not ice cream.
	There no squirrels.	This no good.
	He no bite you.	I not crying.
	I no want envelope.	That not turning.
	I no taste them.	He not taking the walls down.

Three stages in the acquisition of negative sentences were studied by Ursula Bellugi of the Salk Institute for Biological Studies and Edward S. Klima of the University of California at San Diego. They observed that in the first stage almost all negative sentences appear to be formulated according to the rule: Attach "no" or "not" to the beginning of a sentence to make it negative. In the second stage additional rules are postulated that allow the formation of sentences in which "no," "not," "can't" and "don't" appear after the subject and before the verb. In the third stage several issues remain to be worked out, in particular the agreement of pronouns in negative sentences (B), the inclusion of the forms of the verb "to be" (C), and the correct use of the auxiliary "do" (A). In adult speech the auxiliary "do" often carries tense and other functional markings such as the negative; children in the third stage may replace it by "not" or use it redundantly to mark tense that is already marked on the main verb.

sentence negative by uttering it with a higher pitch. Other children have been found to follow the same strategy. There are clearly variations in the hypotheses children make in the process of constructing grammar.

SEMANTICS

Up to this point I have mainly discussed the acquisition of syntactic rules, in part because in the years following the publication of Chomsky's *Synctatic Structures* child-language research in this area flourished. Syntactic rules, which govern the ordering of words in a sentence, are not all a child needs to know about language, however, and after the first flush of excitement over Chomsky's work investigators began to ask questions about other areas of language acquisition. Consider the development of the rules of semantics, which govern the way words are interpreted. Eve V. Clark of Stanford reexamined old diary studies and noticed that the development in the meaning of words during the first several months of the one-word stage seemed to follow a basic pattern.

The first time children in the studies used a word, Clark noted, it seemed to be as a proper noun, as the name of a specific object. Almost immediately, however, the children generalized the word based on some feature of the original object and used it to refer to many other objects. For example, a child named Hildegard first used "tick-tock" as the name for her father's watch, but she quickly broadened the meaning of the word, first to include all clocks, then all watches, then a gas meter, then a firehose wound on a spool and then a bathroom scale with a round dial. Her generalizations appear to be based on her observation of common features of shape: roundness, dials and so on. In general the children in the diary studies overextended meanings based on similarities of movement, texture, size and, most frequently, shape.

As the children progressed, the meanings of words were narrowed down until eventually they more or less coincided with the meanings accepted by adult speakers of the language. The narrowing-down process has not been studied intensively, but it seems likely that the process has no fixed end point. Rather it appears that the meanings of words continue to expand and contract through adulthood, long after other types of language acquisition have ceased.

One of the problems encountered in trying to understand the acquisition of semantics is that it is often difficult to determine the precise meaning a child has constructed for a word. Some interesting observations have been made, however, concerning the development of the meanings of the pairs of words that function as opposites in adult language. Margaret Donaldson and George Balfour of the University of Edinburgh asked children from three to five years old which one of two cardboard trees had "more" apples on it. They asked other children of the same age which tree had "less" apples. (Each child was interviewed individually.) Almost

Child's Lexical Item	First Referents	Other Referents in Order of Occurrence	General Area of Semantic Extension
mooi	moon	cake round marks on windows writing on windows and in books round shapes in books tooling on leather book covers round postmarks letter "o"	shape
bow-wow	dog	fur piece with glass eyes father's cufflinks pearl buttons on dress bath thermometer	shape
kotibaiz	bars of cot	large toy abacus toast rack with parallel bars picture of building with columns	shape
bébé	reflection of child (self) in mirror	photograph of self all photographs all pictures all books with pictures all books	shape
vov-vov	dog	kittens hens all animals at a zoo picture of pigs dancing	shape
ass	goat with rough hide on wheels	things that move: animals, sister, wagon . . . all moving things all things with a rough surface	movement texture
tutu	train	engine moving train journey	movement
fly	fly	specks of dirt dust all small insects child's own toes crumbs of bread a toad	size
quack	ducks on water	all birds and insects all coins (after seeing an eagle on the face of a coin)	size
koko	cockerel's crowing	tunes played on a violin tunes played on a piano tunes played on an accordion tunes played on a phonograph all music merry-go-round	sound
dany	sounds of a bell	clock telephone doorbells	sound

Children overgeneralize word meanings, using words they acquire early in place of words they have not yet acquired. Eve V. Clark of Stanford University has observed that when a word first appears in a child's lexicon, it refers to a specific object but the child quickly extends semantic domain of word, using it to refer to many other things. Eventually meaning of the word is narrowed down until it coincides with adult usage. Clark found that children most frequently base the semantic extension of a word on shape of its first referent.

all the children in both groups responded by pointing to the tree with more apples on it. Moreover, the children who had been asked to point to the tree with "less" apples showed no hesitation in choosing the tree with more apples. They did not act as though they did not know the meaning of "less"; rather they acted as if they did know the meaning and "less" meant "more."

Subsequent studies have revealed similar systematic error making in the acquisition of other pairs of opposites such as "same" and "different," "big" and "little," "wide" and "narrow" and "tall" and "short." In every case the pattern of learning is the same: one word of the pair is learned first and its meaning is overextended to apply to the other word in the pair. The first word learned is always the unmarked word of the pair, that is, the word adults use when they do not want to indicate either one of the opposites. (For example, in the case of "wide" and "narrow," "wide" is the unmarked word: asking "How wide is the road?" does not suggest that the road is wide, but asking "How narrow is the road?" does suggest that the road is narrow.)

Clark observed a more intricate pattern of error production in the acquisition of the words "before" and "after." Consider the four different types of sentence represented by (1) "He jumped the gate before he patted the dog," (2) "Before he patted the dog he jumped the gate," (3) "He patted the dog after he jumped the gate" and (4) "After he jumped the gate he patted the dog." Clark found that the way the children she observed interpreted sentences such as these could be divided into four stages.

In the first stage the children disregarded the words "before" and "after" in all four of these sentence types and assumed that the event of the first clause took place before the event of the second clause. With this order-of-mention strategy the first and fourth sentence types were interpreted correctly but the second and third sentence types were not. In the second stage sentences using "before" were interpreted correctly but an order-of-mention strategy was still adopted for sentences that used "after." Hence sentences of the fourth type were interpreted correctly but sentences of the third type were not. In the next stage both the third and the fourth sentence types were interpreted incorrectly, suggesting that the children had adopted the strategy that "after" actually meant "before." Finally, in the fourth stage both "before" and "after" were interpreted appropriately.

It appears, then, that in learning the meaning of a pair of words such as "more" and "less" or "before" and "after" children acquire first the part of the meaning that is common to both words and only later the part of the meaning that distinguishes the two. Linguists have not yet developed satisfactory ways of separating the components of meaning that make up a single word, but it seems clear that when such components can be identified, it will be established that, for example, "more" and "less" have a large number of components in common and differ only in a single component specifying the pole of the dimension. Beyond the studies of opposites there has been little investigation of the period of semantic acquisition that follows the early period of rampant overgeneralization. How children past the early stage learn the meanings of other kinds of words is still not well understood.

PHONOLOGY

Just as children overgeneralize word meanings and sentence structures, so do they overgeneralize sounds, using sounds they have learned in place of sounds they have not yet acquired. Just as a child may use the word "not" correctly in one sentence but instead of another negative word in a second sentence, so may she correctly contrast /p/ and /b/ at the beginnings of words but employ /p/ at the ends of words, regardless of whether the adult models end with /p/ or /b/. Children also acquire the details of the phonological system in very regular ways. The ways in which they acquire individual sounds, however, are highly idiosyncratic, and so for many years the patterns eluded diarists, who tended to look only at the order in which sounds were acquired. Jakobson made a major advance in this area by suggesting that it was not individual sounds children acquire in an orderly way but the distinctive features of sound, that is, the minimal differences, or contrasts, between sounds. In other words, when a child begins to contrast /p/ and /b/, she also begins to contrast all the other pairs of sounds that, like /p/ and /b/, differ only in the absence or presence of vocal-cord vibration. In English these pairs include /t/ and /d/, and /k/ and the hard /g/. It is the acquisition of this contrast and not of the six individual sounds that is predictable. Jakobson's extensive examination of the diary data for a wide variety of languages supported this theory. Almost all current work in phonological theory rests on the theory of distinctive features that grew out of his work.

My own recent work suggests that phonological units even more basic than the distinctive features play an important part in the early acquisition process. At an early stage, when there are relatively few words in a child's repertory, unanalyzed syllables appear to be the basic unit of the sound system. By designating these syllables as unanalyzed I mean that the child is not able to separate them into their component consonants and vowels. Only later in the acquisition process does such division into smaller units become possible. The gradual discovery of successively smaller units that can form the basis of the phonological system is an important part of the process.

At an even earlier stage, before a child has uttered any words, she is accomplishing a great deal of linguistic learning, working with a unit of phonological organization even more primitive than the syllable. That unit can be defined in terms of pitch contours. By the late babbling period children already control the intonation, or pitch modulation, contours of the language they are learning. At that stage the child sounds as if she is uttering reasonably long sentences, and adult listeners may have the impression they are not quite catching the child's words. There are no words to catch, only random strings of babbled sounds with recognizable, correctly produced question or statement intonation contours. The sounds may accidentally be similar to some of those found in adult English. These sentence-length utterances are called sentence units, and in the phonological system of the child at this stage they are comparable to the consonant-and-vowel segments, syllables and distinctive features that appear in the phonological systems of later stages. The syllables and segments that appear when the period of word learning begins are in no way related to the vast repertory of babbling sounds. Only the intonation contours are carried over from the babbling stage into the later period.

No matter what language environment a child grows up in, the intonation contours characteristic of adult speech in that environment are the linguistic information learned earliest. Some recent studies suggest that it is possible to identify the language environment of a child from her babbling intonation during the second year of life. Other studies suggest that children can be distinguished at an even earlier age on the basis of whether or not their language environment is a tone language, that is, a language in which words spoken with different pitches are identifiable as different words, even though they may have the same sequence of consonants and vowels. To put it another way, "ma" spoken with a high pitch and "ma" spoken with a low pitch can be as different to someone speaking a tone language as "ma" and "pa" are to someone speaking English. (Many African and Asian languages are tone languages.) Tones are learned very early, and entire tone systems are mastered long before other areas of phonology. The extremely early acquisition of pitch patterns may help to explain the difficulty adults have in learning the intonation of a second language.

PHONETICS

There is one significant way in which the acquisition of phonology differs from the acquisition of other language systems. As a child is acquiring the phonological system she must also learn the phonetic realization of the system: the actual details of physiological and acoustic phonetics, which call for the coordination of a complex set of muscle movements. Some children complete the process of learning how to pronounce things earlier than others, but differences of this kind are usually not related to the learning of the phonological system. Brown had what has become a classic conversation with a child who referred to a "fis." Brown repeated "fis," and the child indignantly corrected him, saying "fis." After several such exchanges Brown tried "fish," and the child, finally satisfied, replied, "Yes, fis." It is clear that although the child was still not able to pronounce the distinction between the sounds "s" and "sh," he knew such a systematic phonological distinction existed. Such phonetic muddying of the phonological waters complicates the study of this area of acquisition. Since the child's knowledge of the phonological system may not show up in her speech, it is not easy to determine what a child knows about the system without engaging in complex experimentation and creative hypothesizing.

Children whose phonological system produces only simple words such as "mama" and "papa" actually have a greater phonetic repertory than their utterances suggest. Evidence of that repertory is found in the late babbling stage, when children are working with sentence units and are making a large array of sounds. They do not lose their phonetic ability overnight, but they must constrain it systematically. Going on to the next-higher stage of language learning, the phonological system, is more important to the child than the details of facile pronunciation. Much later, after the phonological system has been acquired, the details of pronunciation receive more attention.

In the period following the babbling period the persisting phonetic facility gets less and less exercise. The vast majority of a child's utterances fail to reflect her real ability to pronounce things accurately; they do, however, reflect her growing ability to pronounce things systematically. (For a child who grows up learning only one language the movements of the muscles of the vocal tract ultimately become so overpracticed that it is difficult to learn new pronunciations during adulthood. On the other hand, people who learn at least two languages in early childhood appear to retain a greater flexibility of the vocal musculature and are more likely to learn to speak an additional language in their adult years without the "accent" of their native language.)

In learning to pronounce, then, a child must acquire a sound system that includes the divergent systems of phonology and phonetics. The acquisition of phonology differs from that of phonetics in requiring the creation of a representation of language in the mind of the child. This representation is necessary because of the abstract nature of the units of phonological structure. From only the acoustic signal of adult language the child must derive successively more abstract phonological units: first intonations, then syllables, then distinctive features and finally consonant-and-vowel segments. There are, for example, few clear segment boundaries in the acoustic signal the child receives, and so the consonant-and-vowel units could hardly be derived if the child had no internal representation of language.

At the same time that a child is building a phonological representation of language she is learning to manipulate all the phonetic variations of language, learning to produce each one precisely and automatically.

The dual process of phonetics and phonology acquisition is one of the most difficult in all of language learning. Indeed, although a great deal of syntactic and semantic acquisition has yet to take place, it is usually at the completion of the process of learning to pronounce that adults consider a child to be a full-fledged language speaker and stop using any form of caretaker speech.

ABNORMAL LANGUAGE DEVELOPMENT

There seems to be little question that the human brain is best suited to language learning before puberty. Foreign languages are certainly learned most easily at that time. Furthermore, it has been observed that people who learn more than one language in childhood have an easier time learning additional languages in later years. It seems to be extremely important for a child to exercise the language-learning faculty. Children who are not exposed to any learnable language during the crucial years, for example children who are deaf before they can speak, generally grow up with the handicap of having little or no language. The handicap is unnecessary: deaf children of deaf parents who communicate by means of the American Sign Language do not grow up without language. They live in an environment where they can make full use of their language-learning abilities, and they are reasonably fluent in sign language by age three, right on the developmental schedule. Deaf children who grow up communicating by means of sign language have a much easier time learning English as a second language than deaf children in oral-speech programs learning English as a first language.

The study of child language acquisition has made important contributions to the study of abnormal speech development. Some investigators of child language have looked at children whose language development is abnormal in the hope of finding the conditions that are necessary and sufficient for normal development; others have looked at the development of language in normal children in the hope of helping children whose language development is abnormal. It now appears that many of the severe language abnormalities found in children can in some way be traced to interruptions of the normal acquisition process. The improved understanding of the normal process is being exploited to create treatment programs for children with such problems. In the past therapeutic methods for children with language problems have emphasized the memorizing of language routines, but methods now being developed would allow a child to work with her own language-learning abilities. For example, the American Sign Language has been taught successfully to several autistic children. Many of these nonverbal and antisocial children have learned in this way to communicate with therapists, in some cases becoming more socially responsive. (Why sign language should be so successful with some autistic children is unclear; it may have to do with the fact that a sign lasts longer than an auditory signal.)

There are still many questions to be answered in the various areas I have discussed, but in general a great deal of progress has been made in understanding child language over the past 20 years. The study of the acquisition of language has come of age. It is now a genuinely interdisciplinary field where psychologists, neurosurgeons and linguists work together to penetrate the mechanisms of perception and cognition as well as the mechanisms of language.

BIBLIOGRAPHY

Bloom, Lois. *One Word at a Time.* The Hague: Mouton, 1975.

Brown, Roger. *A First Language: The Early Stages.* Cambridge, Mass.: Harvard University Press, 1973.

Dil, Anwar S., ed. *Language Structure and Language Use: Essays by Charles A. Ferguson.* Stanford, Calif.: Stanford University Press, 1971.

McNeill, David. *The Acquisition of Language: The Study of Developmental Psycholinguistics.* New York: Harper & Row, 1970.

FOR DISCUSSION AND REVIEW

1. Explain how the tables showing the development of correct noun plural forms and of correct past tense forms of verbs illustrate and support the claim that "children approach language learning economically, devoting their energy to broad issues before dealing with specific ones."

2. What are the characteristics of "caretaker speech"? Why is its use important to children in their acquisition of language? How has the recognition of caretaker speech modified linguists' thinking about the process of language acquisition?

3. Explain how and why children in the one-word and two-word stages of language acquisition use vertical constructions. In what sense is this linguistic strategy an example of a technique that children use in all areas of cognitive development?

4. Children's acquisition of function words (including inflectional affixes such as noun plurals and the -*ing* and past-tense forms of verbs) in English and in other languages follows a very predictable order. Using examples from English, explain what principles govern the sequence of function-word acquisition.

5. Discuss how children expand their semantic understanding and use of a word. What features of the referent are most important? Although less is known about the narrowing-down process, consider what the

results of semantic overgeneralization and subsequent narrowing-down may be in the communication process—both among older children and adults, especially since "the meanings of words continue to expand and contract through adulthood."

6. With regard to the manner in which children learn the meanings of pairs of words with opposite meanings (e.g., *more* vs. *less*), explain the statement that "children acquire first the part of the meaning that is common to both words and only later the part that distinguishes the two."

7. What part of the language system do children learn first? What are some implications of this very early learning for adults who are trying to learn a new language?

8. Explain the statement that "learning to pronounce . . . , a child must acquire a sound system that includes the divergent systems of phonology and phonetics."

6

Developmental Milestones in Motor and Language Development

Eric H. Lenneberg

All normal children, whatever their native language, go through the same stages of language acquisition in nearly the same order, although not all progress at the same rate. All normal children also move through the same stages of motor development—though again at different rates. However, the relationship between language acquisition and sensorimotor development is not clear. Some researchers believe that some level of sensorimotor knowledge must be present in order for language acquisition to proceed; others argue that it is cortical maturation itself that is the essential prerequisite both for the development of language and for sensorimotor development. The issue is whether language is an autonomous cognitive system or whether it is only one way of many in which development of general cognitive ability is manifested. A further question is whether and to what extent children possess an innate capacity specifically for language acquisition. The following chart juxtaposes the stages of motor and language development typically reached by children from twelve weeks through four years of age.

AT THE COMPLETION OF:	MOTOR DEVELOPMENT	VOCALIZATION AND LANGUAGE
12 weeks	Supports head when in prone position; weight is on elbows; hands mostly open; no grasp reflex	Markedly less crying than at 8 weeks; when talked to and nodded at, smiles, followed by squealing-gurgling sounds usually called *cooing*, which is vowel-like in character and pitch-modulated; sustains cooing for 15–20 seconds
16 weeks	Plays with a rattle placed in his hands (by shaking it and staring at it), head self-supported; tonic neck reflex subsiding	Responds to human sounds more definitely; turns head; eyes seem to search for speaker; occasionally some chuckling sounds

(continued)

113

AT THE COMPLETION OF:	MOTOR DEVELOPMENT	VOCALIZATION AND LANGUAGE
20 weeks	Sits with props	The vowel-like cooing sounds begin to be interspersed with more consonantal sounds; labial fricatives, spirants, and nasals are common; acoustically, all vocalizations are very different from the sounds of the mature language of the environment
6 months	Sitting: bends forward and uses hands for support; can bear weight when put into standing position, but cannot yet stand with holding on; reaching: unilateral; grasp: no thumb apposition yet; releases cube when given another	Cooing changing into babbling resembling one-syllable utterances; neither vowels nor consonants have very fixed recurrences; most common utterances sound somewhat like *ma, mu, da,* or *di*
8 months	Stands holding on; grasps with thumb apposition; picks up pellet with thumb and finger tips	Reduplication (or more continuous repetitions) becomes frequent; intonation patterns become distinct; utterances can signal emphasis and emotions
10 months	Creeps efficiently; takes side-steps, holding on; pulls to standing position	Vocalizations are mixed with sound-play such as gurgling or bubble-blowing; appears to wish to imitate sounds, but the imitations are never quite successful; beginning to differentiate between words heard by making differential adjustment
12 months	Walks when held by one hand; walks on feet and hands—knees in air; mouthing of objects almost stopped; seats self on floor	Identical sound sequences are replicated with higher relative frequency of occurrence and words *(mamma* or *dadda)* are emerging; definite signs of understanding some words and simple commands (show me your eyes)
18 months	Grasp, prehension, and release fully developed; gait stiff, propulsive, and precipitated; sits on child's chair with only fair aim; creeps downstairs backward; has difficulty building tower of 3 cubes	Has a definite repertoire of words—more than three, but less than fifty; still much babbling but now of several syllables with intricate intonation pattern; no attempt at communicating information and no frustration for not being understood; words may include items such as *thank you* or *come here,* but there is little ability to join any of the lexical items into spontaneous two-item phrases; understanding is progressing rapidly

(continued)

AT THE COMPLETION OF:	MOTOR DEVELOPMENT	VOCALIZATION AND LANGUAGE
24 months	Runs, but falls in sudden turns; can quickly alternate between sitting and stance; walks stairs up or down, one foot forward only	Vocabulary of more than 50 items (some children seem to be able to name everything in environment); begins spontaneously to join vocabulary items into two-word phrases; all phrases appear to be own creations; definite increase in communicative behavior and interest in language
30 months	Jumps up into air with both feet; stands on one foot for about two seconds; takes few steps on tip-toe; jumps from chair; good hand and finger coordination; can move digits independently; manipulation of objects much improved; builds tower of six cubes	Fastest increase in vocabulary with many new additions every day; no babbling at all; utterances have communicative intent; frustrated if not understood by adults; utterances consist of at least two words, many have three or even five words; sentences and phrases have characteristic child grammar, that is, they are rarely verbatim repetitions of an adult utterance; intelligibility is not very good yet, though there is great variation among children; seems to understand everything that is said to him
3 years	Tiptoes three yards; runs smoothly with acceleration and deceleration; negotiates sharp and fast curves without difficulty; walks stairs by alternating feet; jumps 12 inches; can operate tricycle	Vocabulary of some 1000 words; about 80% of utterances are intelligible even to strangers; grammatical complexity of utterances is roughly that of colloquial adult language, although mistakes still occur
4 years	Jumps over rope; hops on right foot; catches ball in arms; walks line	Language is well-established; deviations from adult norm tend to be more in style than in grammar

FOR DISCUSSION AND REVIEW

1. Study Lenneberg's table showing typical stages of motor and language development for young children. Do motor development and language development seem to progress at similar rates—that is, do children develop more rapidly in one area than in the other?

2. Jean Piaget has argued that children acquire meanings as an extension of sensorimotor intelligence and that the development of vocabulary

categories, for example, depends upon motor development (things can be "graspable" or "suckable"). Thus, abilities in different areas (e.g., motor skills and language) that appear at the same age should be similar because they are based on the same cognitive knowledge. Can you support or refute this argument on the basis of Lenneberg's table, or do you need additional information? If you believe that you need additional information, describe the kind(s) of data that you would want to have.

7

Predestinate Grooves: Is There a Preordained Language "Program"?

Jean Aitchison

One possible and increasingly accepted explanation for why all children go through the same stages of language acquisition in the same order but at different rates is that language acquisition is biologically triggered. In the following chapter from her book The Articulate Mammal, *Jean Aitchison, a British linguist who teaches at the London School of Economics, describes the characteristics of biologically determined behaviors and considers whether and to what extent language acquisition fits this model. She also describes a "critical period" for language acquisition. In addition, using examples of specific children, Aitchison discusses certain aspects of language acquisition, such as crying, cooing, babbling, the acquisition order of various grammatical forms, and the significance of the mean length of utterance (MLU) measure.*

> There once was a man who said, "Damn!"
> It is born in upon me I am
> An engine that moves
> In predestinate grooves,
> I'm not even a bus, I'm a tram.
> —MAURICE EVAN HARE

Language emerges at about the same time in children all over the world. "Why do children normally begin to speak between their eighteenth and twenty-eighth month?" asks one researcher. "Surely it is not because all mothers on earth initiate language training at that time. There is, in fact, no evidence that any conscious and systematic teaching of language takes place, just as there is no special training for stance or gait" (Lenneberg 1967, p. 125).

This regularity of onset suggests that language may be set in motion by a biological time-clock, similar to the one which causes kittens to open their eyes when they are a few days old, chrysalises to change into butterflies after several weeks, and humans to become sexually mature at around 13 years of age. However, until relatively recently, few people had considered language within the framework of biological maturation. But in 1967 E. H. Lenneberg, then a biologist at the Harvard Medical School, published an important book, entitled *The Biological Foundations of Language.* Much of what is said in this chapter is based on his pioneering work.

THE CHARACTERISTICS OF BIOLOGICALLY TRIGGERED BEHAVIOR

Behavior which is triggered off biologically has a number of special characteristics. In the following pages we shall list these features, and see to what extent they are present in language. If it can be shown that speech, like sexual activities and the ability to walk, falls into the category of biologically scheduled behavior, then we shall be rather clearer about what is meant by the claim that language is "innate."

Exactly how many "hallmarks" of biologically controlled behavior we should itemize is not clear. Lenneberg lists four. The six listed below were obtained mainly by subdividing Lenneberg's four:

1. The behavior emerges before it is necessary.
2. Its appearance is not the result of a conscious decision.
3. Its emergence is not triggered by external events (though the surrounding environment must be sufficiently "rich" for it to develop adequately).
4. There is likely to be a "critical period" for the acquisition of the behavior.
5. Direct teaching and intensive practice have relatively little effect.
6. There is a regular sequence of "milestones" as the behavior develops, and these can usually be correlated with age and other aspects of development.

Let us discuss these features in turn. Some of them seem fairly obvious. We hardly need to set about testing the first one, that "the behavior emerges before it is necessary"—a phenomenon sometimes pompously labeled the "law of anticipatory maturation." Language develops long before children need to communicate in order to survive. Their parents still feed them, clothe them, and look after them. Without some type of inborn mechanism, language might develop only when parents left children to fend for themselves. It would emerge at different times in different cultures, and this would lead to vastly different levels of language skills. Although children differ enormously in their ability to knit or play the violin, their language proficiency varies to a much lesser extent.

Again, little explanation is needed for the second characteristic of biologically triggered behavior: "Its appearance is not the result of a conscious decision." Clearly, a child does not suddenly think to himself,

"Tomorrow I am going to start to learn to talk." Children acquire language without making any conscious decision about it. This is quite unlike a decision to learn to jump a four-foot height, or hit a tennis ball, when a child sets himself a target, then organizes strenuous practice sessions as he strives toward his goal.

The first part of feature 3 also seems straightforward: "The emergence of the behavior is not triggered by external events." Children start to talk even when their surroundings remain unchanged. Most of them live in the same house, eat the same food, have the same parents, and follow the same routine. No specific event or feature in the child's surroundings suddenly sets him off talking. However, we must here digress briefly in order to point out an aspect of biologically scheduled behavior that is sometimes misunderstood: although no external event *causes* the behavior, the surrounding environment must be sufficiently "rich" for it to develop adequately. Biologically programmed behavior does not develop properly in impoverished or unnatural surroundings. We have the apparent paradox that some types of "natural" behavior require careful "nurturing." Just as Chris and Susie, two gorillas reared away from other gorillas in Sacramento Zoo, are unable to mate satisfactorily (according to an item in the *Evening Standard*) — so an impoverished linguistic environment is likely to retard language acquisition. Children brought up in institutions, for example, tend to be backward in speech development. Lenneberg notes that a child raised in an orphanage will begin to talk at the same time as other noninstitutionalized children. But his speech will gradually lag behind the norm, being less intelligible, and showing less variety of construction. . . .

Rather more discussion is needed to justify the existence in language of a fourth characteristic of biologically controlled behavior: "There is likely to be a critical period for the acquisition of the behavior." It is clear that there is a biologically scheduled starting point for language acquisition, but far less clear that there is a biologically scheduled finishing point.

We know for certain that language cannot emerge before it is programmed to emerge. Nobody has ever taught a young baby to talk — though it seems that there is nothing much wrong with the vocal cords of a new-born infant, and from five or six months onwards it can "babble" a number of the sounds needed in speech. Yet children utter few words before the age of eighteen months. It is clear that they have to wait for some biological trigger. The "trigger" appears to be connected with brain growth. Two-word utterances, which are usually regarded as the beginning of "true language," begin just as a massive spurt in brain growth slows down. Children do not manufacture any new brain cells after birth. They are born with millions, perhaps billions. At first the cells are not all interconnected, and the brain is relatively light (about 300 g). From birth to around two years, many more cells interconnect, and brain weight increases rapidly. By the age of two, it weighs nearly 1000 g (Lenneberg 1967).

It is not nearly so easy to tell when a child has finished acquiring a language. Nevertheless, there are a number of indications that, after the onset of adolescence, humans can acquire a new language only after a considerable struggle.

First of all, almost everybody can remember how difficult it was to learn French at school. Even the best pupils had a slightly odd accent, and made numerous grammatical mistakes. The difficulty was not that one was learning a second language, since children who are brought up speaking French and English as equal "mother tongues" do not experience similar problems. Nor is there much difficulty for children who emigrate to France around the age of five or six, when they already speak fluent English. Moreover, the failure to learn perfect French cannot be due simply to lack of exposure to the language. There are numerous people who have emigrated to France as adults, and converse only in French — yet few, if any acquire a mastery of the new language equivalent to that of their native tongue. It seems that the brain loses its "plasticity" for language learning after a certain age.

However, evidence concerning difficulties with French at school is mainly anecdotal. Perhaps the most impressive evidence for the existence of a critical period comes from comparing the case histories of two socially isolated children, Isabelle and Genie. Both these children were cut off from language until long after the time they would have acquired it, had they been brought up in normal circumstances.

Isabelle was the illegitimate child of a deaf mute. She had no speech, and made only a croaking sound when she was found in Ohio in the 1930s at the age of six and a half. Mother and child had spent most of the time alone in a darkened room. But once found, Isabelle's progress was remarkable: "Isabelle passed through the usual stages of linguistic development at a greatly accelerated rate. She covered in two years the learning that ordinarily occupies six years. By the age of eight and one half Isabelle was not easily distinguishable from ordinary children of her age" (Brown 1958, p. 192).

Genie, however, was not so lucky. She was not found until she was nearly fourteen. Born in April 1957, she had lived most of her life in bizarre and inhuman conditions. "From the age of twenty months, Genie had been confined to a small room. . . . She was physically punished by her father if she made any sounds. Most of the time she was kept harnessed into an infant's potty chair; otherwise she was confined in a homemade sleeping bag in an infant's crib covered with wire mesh" (Curtiss et al. 1974, p. 529). When found, she was totally without language. She began acquiring speech well after the onset of adolescence — after the apparent "critical period."

Although she learnt to speak in a rudimentary fashion, she progressed more slowly than normal children (Curtiss 1977). For example, ordinary children go through a stage in which they utter two words at a time ("want milk," "Mummy play"), which normally lasts a matter of weeks. Genie's two-word stage lasted for more than five months. Again, ordinary children briefly pass through a phase in which they form negative sentences by putting the word *no* in front of the rest of the utterance, as in "no Mummy go," "no want apple." Genie used this primitive form of negation for over two years. Normal children start asking questions beginning with words such as *where, what,* at the two-word stage ("where Teddy?"). Genie finds this kind of question impossible to grasp, occasionally making inappropriate attempts such as "where is stop spitting?" The only aspect of speech in which Genie outstripped normal children was her ability to learn vocabulary. She knew many more words than ordinary children at a comparable stage of grammatical development. However, the ability to memorize lists of items is not evidence of language capacity — even the chimps Washoe and Sarah found this relatively easy. It is the rules of grammar which are the important part, and this is what Genie finds difficult. Her slow progress compared with that of Isabelle seems to provide evidence in favor of there being a "cut-off" point for language acquisition. We must be cautious however. Two individual cases cannot provide firm proof, especially as each is problematical. Isabelle was not studied by linguists, so her speech may have been more deficient than was reported. Genie, on the other hand, shows some evidence of brain damage. Tests suggest that her left hemisphere is atrophied, which means that she may be functioning with only one half of her brain, the half not usually associated with language (Curtiss 1977; Curtiss et al. 1974).

According to Lenneberg, further evidence in favor of a critical period is provided by mentally handicapped children, such as "mongols" (Down's syndrome cases) (Lenneberg 1967). These follow the same general path of development as normal children, but much more slowly. Lenneberg claims that they never catch up because their ability to learn language slows down dramatically at puberty. But some researchers have disputed this claim, arguing that the children's language ceases to develop through lack of stimulation, not lack of ability.

The recovery possibilities of brain-damaged patients give further support, and in addition, indicate that the critical period coincides with the period of lateralization — the gradual specialization of language to one side of the brain. Lenneberg suggests that this process occurs between the ages of 2 and 14, though others have suggested that its completion occurs around the age of 5 or 6. If a child under the age of 2 sustains severe damage to the left (language) hemisphere of the brain, his speech will develop normally, though it will be controlled by the right hemisphere. But as the child gets older, the likelihood of left hemisphere damage causing permanent impairment gets progressively greater. At the age of 7 or 8, the damage is usually long-lasting, whereas in an adolescent or adult it often results in lifelong speech disturbance. When lateralization is complete, the brain seems to have lost a natural "bent" for learning languages.

We have now considered several pieces of indirect evidence for the existence of a "critical period." They all suggest (though do not conclusively prove) that toddler time to adolescence is a time set aside by nature for the acquisition of language. Lenneberg notes:

> Between the ages of two and three years language emerges by an interaction of maturation and self-programmed learning. Between the ages of three and the early teens the possibility for primary language acquisition continues to be good; the individual appears to be most sensitive to stimuli at this time and to preserve some innate flexibility for the organization of brain functions to carry out the complete integration of subprocesses necessary for the smooth elaboration of speech and language. After puberty, the ability for self-organization and adjustment to the physiological demands of verbal behavior quickly declines. The brain behaves as if it had become set in its ways and primary, basic skills not acquired by that time usually remain deficient for life. [Lenneberg 1967, p. 158]

A similar critical period is found for the acquisition of their song by some species of birds. A chaffinch's song, for example, becomes fixed and unalterable when it is around fifteen months old. If the chaffinch has not been exposed to chaffinch song before that time, it never learns to sing normally (Thorpe 1972).

Let us now turn to the fifth characteristic of biologically triggered behavior, "Direct teaching and intensive practice have relatively little effect." In activities such as typing or playing tennis, a person's achievement is often directly related to the amount of teaching he receives and the hours of practice he puts in. Even people who are not "naturally" superb athletes can sometimes win tennis tournaments through sheer hard work and good coaching. But the same is not true of language, where direct teaching seems to be a failure. Let us consider the evidence for this.

When one says that "direct teaching is a failure," people smile and say, "Of course—whoever tries to *teach* a child to speak?" Yet many parents, often without realizing it, try to persuade their children to imitate them. They do this in two ways: firstly, by means of overt correction, secondly, by means of unconscious "expansions."

The pointlessness of overt correction has been noted by numerous researchers. One psychologist attempted over a period of several weeks to persuade his daughter to say *other* + noun instead of *other one* + noun. The interchanges went somewhat as follows:

CHILD: Want other one spoon, Daddy.
FATHER: You mean, you want the other spoon.

CHILD: Yes, I want other one spoon, please Daddy.
FATHER: Can you say "the other spoon"?
CHILD: Other . . . one . . . spoon.
FATHER: Say "other."
CHILD: Other.
FATHER: "Spoon."
CHILD: Spoon.
FATHER: "Other spoon."
CHILD: Other . . . spoon. Now give me other one spoon?

[Braine 1971, p. 161]

Another researcher tried vainly to coax a child into saying the past tense form *held:*

CHILD: My teacher holded the baby rabbits and we patted them.
ADULT: Did you say your teacher held the baby rabbits?
CHILD: Yes.
ADULT: What did you say she did?
CHILD: She holded the baby rabbits and we patted them.
ADULT: Did you say she held them tightly?
CHILD: No, she holded them loosely.

[Cazden 1972, p. 92]

In fact, repeated corrections are not merely pointless: they may even hinder a child's progress. The mother of seventeen-month-old Paul had high expectations, and repeatedly corrected his attempts at speech. He lacked confidence, and his progress was slow. But the mother of fourteen-month-old Jane was an accepting person who responded uncritically to everything Jane said. Jane made exceptionally fast progress, and knew eighty words by the age of fifteen months (Nelson 1973, p. 105).

So forcing children to imitate is a dismal failure. Children cannot be trained like parrots. Equally unsuccessful is the second type of coaching often unconsciously adopted by parents — the use of "expansions." When talking to a child an adult continuously "expands" the youngster's utterances. If the child says, "There go one," a mother is likely to expand this to "Yes, there goes one." "Mommy eggnog" becomes "Mommy had her eggnog," and "Throw Daddy" is expanded to "Throw it to Daddy." Children are exposed to an enormous number of these expansions. They account for perhaps a third of parental responses. Brown and Bellugi note:

> The mothers of Adam and Eve responded to the speech of their children with expansions about 30 percent of the time. We did it ourselves when we talked with the children. Indeed, we found it very difficult to withhold expansions. A reduced or incomplete English sentence seems to constrain the English-speaking adult to expand it into the nearest properly formed complete sentence. [Brown and Bellugi 1964, p. 144]

At first researchers were uncertain about the role of expansions. Then

Courtney Cazden carried out an ingenious experiment using two groups of children, all under three and a half (Cazden 1972). She exposed one group to intensive and deliberate expansions, and the other group to well-formed sentences which were *not* expansions. For example, if a child said, "Dog bark," an expanding adult would say, "Yes, the dog is barking." An adult who replied with a nonexpanded sentence might say "Yes, he's trying to frighten the cat" or "Yes, but he won't bite," or "Yes, tell him to be quiet." After three months the rate of progress of each group was measured. Amazingly, the expansion group were *less advanced* than the other group, both in average length of utterance and grammatical complexity.

Several explanations of this unexpected result have been put forward. Perhaps adults misinterpret the child's intended meaning when they expand. Erroneous expansions could hinder his learning. Several "wrong" expansions have been noted. For example:

CHILD: What time it is?
ADULT: Uh huh, it tells what time it is.

Alternatively, a certain degree of novelty may be needed in order to capture a child's attention, since he may not listen to apparent repetitions of his own utterances. Or it may be that expansions overrestrict the data the child hears. His speech may be impoverished because of an insufficiently rich verbal environment. As we noted earlier, the child *needs* copious and varied samples of speech.

The last two explanations seem to be supported by a Russian experiment (Slobin 1966, p. 144). One group of infants was shown a doll, and three phrases were repeatedly uttered, "Here is a doll . . . Take the doll . . . Give me the doll." Another group of infants was shown the doll, but instead, *thirty* different phrases were uttered, such as "Rock the doll . . . Look for the doll." The total number of words heard by both groups was the same, only the composition differed. Then the experimenters showed the children a selection of toys, and asked them to pick out the dolls. To their surprise, the children in the second group, the ones who had heard a richer variety of speech, were considerably better at this task.

We may conclude then that parents who consciously try to "coach" their children by simplifying and repeating may be actually *interfering* with their progress. It does not pay to talk to children as if one was telling a foreign tourist how to get to the zoo. Language that is impoverished is harder to learn, not simpler. Children appear to be naturally "set" to extract a grammar for themselves, provided they have sufficient data at their disposal. Direct teaching is irrelevant, and those who get on best are those who are exposed to a rich variety of language — in other words, those whose parents talk to them in a normal way.

But what does "talk in a normal way" mean? Before we go on to discuss the role of practice, this is perhaps the best place to clear up a misunderstanding which seems to have originated with Chomsky. He claims that what children hear "consists to a large extent of utterances that break rules, since a good deal of normal speech consists of false starts, disconnected phrases and other deviations" (Chomsky 1967, p. 441). Certainly, children are likely to hear *some* deviant sentences. But recent research indicates that the speech children are exposed to is not particularly substandard. Adults tend to speak in shorter sentences and make fewer mistakes when they address children. There is a considerable difference between the way a mother talks to another adult, and the way she talks to her child. One researcher recorded a mother talking to an adult friend. Her sentences were an average fourteen to fifteen words long, and she used several polysyllabic medical terms:

> I was on a inhalation series routine. We wen' aroun' from ward to ward. People, are, y'know, that get all this mucus in their chest, and it's very important to breathe properly an' to be able to cough this mucus up and out an' through your chest, y'know as soon as possible. And we couldn't sterilize the instruments 'cause they were plastic.

But when she spoke to her child the same mother used five- or six-word sentences. The words were shorter, and referred to things the child could see or do:

> Come look at Momma's colorin' book.
> You wanna see my coloring book?
> Look at my coloring book.
> Lookit, that's an Indian, huh?
> Is that an Indian?
> Can you say Indian?
> Talk to me.
>   [Drach, quoted in Ervin-Tripp 1971]

It seems that parents automatically simplify both the content and syntax when they talk to children. This is not particularly surprising — after all, we do not address bus conductors and boyfriends in the same way. The use of language appropriate to the circumstances is a normal part of a human's language ability. "Motherese," as it is sometimes called, consists of short, well-formed sentences spoken slowly and clearly. . . . Direct teaching, in the sense of correction and [expansion], does not accelerate the speed of learning and might even be a hindrance.

Let us now return to the question of practice. What is being claimed here is that practice alone cannot account for language acquisition. Children do not learn language simply by repetition and imitation. Two types of evidence support this view.

The first concerns the development of "inflections" or word endings. English has a number of very common verbs which have an "irregular" past tense (e.g., *came, saw, went*) as opposed to the "regular" forms such as *loved, worked, played*. It also has a number of irregular plurals such as *feet* and *mice*, as well as the far more numerous plurals ending in -*s* such as *cats, giraffes,* and *pythons*. Quite early on, children learn correct past tense and plural forms for common words such as *came, saw,* and *feet*. Later, they abandon these correct forms and replace them with over-generalized "regular" forms such as *comed, seed,* and *foots* (Ervin 1964). The significance of this apparent regression is immense. It means that language acquisition cannot possibly be a straightforward case of "prac-tice makes perfect" or of simple imitation. If it were, children would never replace common forms such as *came* and *saw*, which they hear and use all the time, with odd forms such as *comed, seed,* and *foots* which they are unlikely to have come across.

The second type of practice which turns out to be unimportant for language acquisition is spontaneous imitation. Just as adults subcon-sciously imitate and expand their children's utterances, so children ap-pear to imitate and "reduce" sentences uttered by their parents. If an adult says "I shall take an umbrella," a child is likely to say "Take rella." Or "Put the strap under her chin" is likely to be repeated and reduced to "Strap chin." At first sight, it looks as if this might be an important mechanism in the development of language. But Susan Ervin of the Uni-versity of California at Berkeley came to the opposite conclusion when she recorded the spontaneous utterances of a small group of toddlers (Ervin 1964). To her surprise she found that when a child spontaneously imitates an adult, her imitations are not any more advanced than her normal speech. She shortens the adult utterance to fit in with her current average length of sentence and includes the same number of endings and "little" words as in her nonimitated utterances. Not a single child pro-duced imitations which were more advanced. And one child, Holly, actu-ally produced imitations that were less complex than her spontaneous sentences! Susan Ervin notes: "There is not a shred of evidence supporting a view that progress toward adult norms of grammar arises merely from practice in overt imitation of adult sentences" [Ervin 1964, p. 172].

We may conclude, then, that mere practice — in the sense of direct repetition and imitation — does not affect the acquisition of language in a significant way. However, we must be careful that such a statement does not lead to misunderstandings. What is being said is that practice alone cannot account for language acquisition: children do not learn merely by constant repetition of items. In another sense, they do need to "practice" talking but even this requirement is not as extensive as might be expected. They can learn a surprising amount by just listening. It has been shown that the amount of talking a child needs to do in order to learn language varies considerably. Some children seem to speak very little. Others are constantly chattering, and playing with words. One re-searcher wrote a whole book on the presleep monologues of her first child, Anthony, who murmured paradigms to himself as he prepared for sleep:

Go for glasses
Go for them
Go to the top
Go throw
Go for blouse
Pants
Go for shoes
    [Weir 1962]

To her disappointment, her second child, David, was nowhere near as talkative although he eventually learned to speak just as well. These repetitious murmurs do not seem to be essential for all children.

So far, then, we have considered five of the six characteristics of biologically triggered behavior which we listed at the beginning of this chapter. All these features seem to be present in language. We now come to the sixth and final feature, "There is a regular sequence of 'milestones' as the behavior develops, and these can usually be correlated with age and other aspects of development." We shall deal with this in a section by itself.

THE PREORDAINED PROGRAM

All children seem to pass through a series of more or less fixed "stages" as they acquire language. The age at which different children reach each stage or "milestone" varies considerably, but the relative chronology remains the same. The milestones are normally reached in the same order, though they may be nearer together for some children and farther apart for others.

LANGUAGE STAGE	BEGINNING AGE
Crying	birth
Cooing	6 weeks
Babbling	6 months
Intonation patterns	8 months
1-word utterances	1 year
2-word utterances	18 months
Word inflections	2 years
Questions, negatives	2¼ years
Rare or complex constructions	5 years
Mature speech	10 years

Consequently, we can divide language development up into a number of approximate phases. The [accompanying table] is highly oversimplified.

The stages overlap, and the ages given are only a very rough guide—but it does give some idea of a child's likely progress.

In order to illustrate this progression we shall describe the successive phases which a typical (and nonexistent) English child is likely to go through as she learns to speak. Let us call this child *Barbara*—a name derived from the Greek word for "foreigner" and meaning literally "someone who says bar-bar, who talks gibberish."

Barbara's first recognizable vocal activity was *crying*. During the first four weeks of her life, she was truly:

> An infant crying in the night:
> An infant crying for the light:
> And with no language but a cry.
> —TENNYSON

A number of different types of cry could be detected. She cried with hunger when she wanted to be fed. She cried with pain when she had a tummy-ache, and she cried with pleasure when she was fed, comfortable, and lying in her mother's arms. However, strictly speaking, it is perhaps inaccurate to speak of crying as a "language phase," because crying seems to be instinctive communication and may be more like an animal call system than a true language. This seems to be confirmed by some research which suggests that the different "messages" contained in the crying of babies may be universal, since English parents could identify the "messages" of a foreign baby as easily as those of English babies (Ricks 1975). So although crying may help to strengthen the lungs and vocal cords (both of which are needed for speech), crying itself perhaps should not be regarded as part of true language development.

Barbara then passed through two reasonably distinct prelanguage phases, a *cooing* phase and a *babbling* phase. Early researchers confused these stages and sometimes likened them to bird song. . . .

The first of these two phases, *cooing,* began when Barbara was approximately six weeks old. To a casual observer, she sounded as if she was saying, "goo goo." But cooing is difficult to describe. Some textbooks call it "gurgling" or "mewing." The sound is superficially vowel-like, but the tracings produced on a sound spectogram show that it is quite unlike the vowels produced by adults. Cooing seems to be universal. It may be the vocal equivalent of arm and leg waving. That is, just as babies automatically strengthen their muscles by kicking their legs and moving their arms about, so cooing may help them to gain control over their vocal apparatus.

Gradually, consonant-type sounds become interspersed in the cooing. By around six months, Barbara had reached the *babbling* stage. She gave the impression of uttering consonants and vowels together, at first as single syllables—but later strung together. The consonants were often made with the lips, or the teeth, so that the sequences sounded like *mama, dididi,* or *papapa.* On hearing these sounds, Barbara's parents confidently but wrongly assumed that she was addressing them. Such wishful thinking accounts for the fact that *mama, papa,* and *dada* are found as nursery words for mother and father all over the world (Jakobson 1962). Barbara soon learned that a cry of *mama* meant immediate attention—though she often used it to mean, "I am hungry" rather than to refer to a parent. This phenomenon has been noted by numerous researchers.

Throughout the babbling period Barbara seemed to enjoy experimenting with her mouth and tongue. She not only babbled, she blew bubbles, gurgled and spluttered. Superficially, she appeared to be uttering an enormous variety of exotic sounds. At one time, researchers wrongly assumed that children are naturally capable of producing every possible speech sound. . . . More recent investigators have noted that the variety of sounds used in babbling is not particularly great. But because the child does not yet have complete control over his vocal organs, the noises are often unlike adult sounds, and seem exotic to an untrained observer. In general, babbling seems to be a period when a child experiments and gradually gains muscular control over his vocal organs. Many people claim that babbling is universal. But there are a few puzzling records of children who did not babble, which provide problems for this point of view. All we can say at the moment is that babbling is sufficiently widespread to be regarded as a normal stage of development.

Some investigators have tried to compare babbling babies who have been exposed to different languages. It has been reported that Chinese babbles are distinguishable from American, Russian, and Arabic ones (Weir 1966). Because Chinese is a language which distinguishes words by means of a change in "tone" or "pitch," Chinese babies tend to produce monosyllabic utterances with much tonal variation. American babies produce polysyllabic babbles with intonation spread over the whole sequence. The nontone babies sound superficially similar—though American mothers could often pick out the American baby, Russians the Russian baby, and Arabs the Arab baby. But the mothers could not distinguish between the babies babbling the other two languages. This research supports the notion of a "babbling drift," in which a child's babbling gradually moves in the direction of the sounds he hears around him. In this respect babbling is clearly distinct from crying, which has no discernible relationship with any one language.

A question which perhaps should be asked at this stage is the following: how much can children actually distinguish of their parents' speech? It is sometimes assumed that babies hear merely a general mish-mash of sound, and only gradually notice the difference between say *p* and *b*. However, recent research indicates that infants are capable of discriminating a lot more than we realize. Eimas and his colleagues (1971), for example, have shown that babies between one and four months old *can* distinguish between *p* and *b*. They started by playing a repeated *b* sound to selected infants. They then switched to *p*. A clear change in the babies' sucking behavior showed that they had noticed the alteration. So even though infants may not listen carefully to everything their parents say, they may well be capable of hearing a considerable amount from a very young age. Somewhat surprisingly, these results of Eimas have been replicated with rhesus and chinchilla monkeys (Morse 1976; Kuhl and Miller 1974, 1975), and so may be due to the hearing mechanisms in certain types of mammals, and not just humans alone. In brief, a child's perception may be much sharper than had previously been supposed, even though it may not be equivalent to an adult's for some time (Fourcin 1978).

Simultaneously with babbling, and from around eight or nine months, Barbara began to imitate *intonation patterns*. These made her output sound so like speech that her mother sometimes said, "I'm sure she's talking, I just can't catch what she's saying. . . ." English mothers have noted that their children often use a "question" intonation, with a rise in tone at the end of the sentence. This may be due to a normal parent's tendency to bend over the child, asking, "What are you trying to say then?" "Do you want some milk?" "Do you know who this is?" and so on.

Somewhere between one year and eighteen months Barbara began to utter *single words*. She continued to babble as well, though her babbling gradually diminished as true language developed. The number of single words acquired at around this time varies from child to child. Some have only four or five, others have around fifty. As an average child Barbara acquired about fifteen. Many of them were names of people and things, such as *uf* (woof) "dog," *daba* "grandma," *da* "doll." Then as she neared her second birthday, she reached the more impressive *two-word stage*.

From the time Barbara started to put words together she seemed to be in a state of "language readiness," and mopped up language like a sponge. The most noticeable feature of this process was a dramatic increase in her vocabulary. By the time she was 2½ years old, she knew several hundred words. Meanwhile, there was a gradual but steady increase in her average or mean length of utterance — usually abbreviated to MLU. MLU is calculated in terms of grammatical items or "morphemes": plural -s and past tense -d, for example, each count as one item and so do ordinary words such as *mummy* and *bath*. Compound words such as *birthday* and *quack-quack* also count as a single item (Brown 1973, p. 54). Many (but not all) researchers accept this as a useful gauge of progress — though the child with the longest utterances does not necessarily have the most grammatically advanced, or even the most grammatically correct utterances (Garman 1979).

The fact that a steady increase in MLU occurs from the age of around 2 onwards has been shown by Roger Brown of Harvard University, who carried out a detailed study of the speech development of three unacquainted children, Adam, Eve, and Sarah — though he found that the chronological age at which different children reached an MLU stage differed considerably (Brown, Cazden, and Bellugi 1968; Brown 1973). A

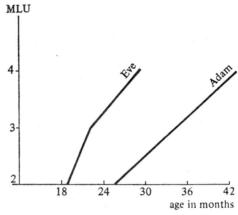

FIGURE 7.1

comparison of Adam and Eve showed that Eve outstripped Adam by far. Eve's MLU was two items at around twenty months, three at twenty-two months, and four at twenty-eight months. Adam was over twenty-six months old before he achieved an MLU of two items. He was nearly 3 years old before his MLU reached three items and 3½ before it reached four items—a whole year behind Eve. [See Figure 7.1.]

If we assume that Barbara is not as advanced as Eve, but ahead of Adam, she possibly had an MLU of two items a little before her second birthday, an MLU of three items at 2½, and four items around her third birthday.

In the early part of the two-word stage, when she was around 2 years old, Barbara's speech was "telegraphic." She sounded as if she was sending urgent telegrams to her mother: "Want milk," "Where duck?" As in a real telegram, she tended to preserve the nouns and verbs in the correct order, but omitted the "little" words such as *the, a, has, his,* and. She also left out word endings, such as the plural -*s* or past tense -*d*, as in *two shoe* and *milk spill.*

Then, gradually, the "little" words and *inflections* were added. "All these, like an intricate work of ivy, began to grow up between and upon the major construction blocks, the nouns and verbs" (Brown 1973, p. 249).

In this aspect of language, Barbara is following the same path of development as the Harvard child Adam, but at a slightly earlier age (Brown 1973, p. 271). Between the ages of 2 and 3½, Barbara acquired the following grammatical forms:

Age 2

Progressive -*ing*	I singing
Plural -*s*	Blue shoes
Copula *am, is, are*	He is asleep
Articles *a, the*	He is a doctor

Age 3

3rd person singular -*s*	He wants an apple
Past tense -*d*	I helped Mummy
Full progressive *am, is, are* + -*ing*	I am singing
Shortened copula	He's a doctor
Shortened progressive	I'm singing

Note that it is important to distinguish between the *emergence*, or first appearance of an ending, and its *acquisition*, its reliable use in the places where an adult would expect to find it. An ending can be considered acquired if it occurs in at least 90 percent of the contexts where it is needed (Brown 1973, p. 258).

The actual age at which Barbara acquired each form is not significant because it varies widely from child to child. What is important and interesting is the *order* of acquisition. The sequence seems surprisingly similar among English-speaking children. Roger Brown notes that in the unacquainted Harvard children, the developmental order of these grammatical forms was "amazingly consistent." There were one or two minor variations: Sarah, for example, acquired the progressive -*ing* after the plural, whereas Adam and Eve acquired it before. But in all the children, both the progressive -*ing* and the plural -*s* occurred before the past tense, the third person singular -*s*, and the copula *am, is, are*.

Perhaps even more surprising, is the fact that in all the Harvard children the copula *am, is, are* as in *I am a doctor* developed before *am, is, are* when it was part of the progressive construction, for example, *I am singing*. And the shortened copula as in *He's a bear* came before the shortened progressive, for example *He's walking*. This is really quite an astonishing discovery. Although we might expect children to go through similar general lines of development, there seems to be no obvious reason why a variety of English children should correspond so closely in their acquisition of specific items.

A similar consistency of order is found in the acquisition of more complicated constructions, such as *questions* and *negatives*. For example, in the acquisition of *wh-* questions (questions beginning with *what, why, where, who,* etc.), we can safely assume that Barbara, like Adam, Eve, and Sarah, went through three intermediate stages before she acquired them perfectly (Klima and Bellugi 1966). First of all, soon after her second birthday, she placed the *wh-* word in front of the rest of the sentence:

What	Mummy doing?
Why	you singing?
Where	Daddy go?

A second stage occurred three or four months later when she added an auxiliary verb such as *can* or *will* to the main verb:

Where	you	will go?
Why	kitty	can't see?
Why	you	don't know?

Finally, before she was 3, she realized that the subject noun must change places with the auxiliary and produced correct sentences such as:

Where	will you	go?
Why	can't kitty	see?
Why	don't you	know?

Once again [we have] the rather surprising finding that all English children tend to follow the same pattern. . . . As already noted, the actual *age* at which each stage is reached is irrelevant. It is the order which matters.

By the age of 3½, Barbara, like most children, was able to form most grammatical constructions—and her speech was reasonably intelligible to strangers. Her constructions were, however, less varied than those of an adult. For example, she tended not to use the "full" passive such as *The man was hit by a bus.* But she was able to converse quite adequately on most topics.

By 5, she gave the superficial impression of having acquired language more or less perfectly. But this was an illusion. Language acquisition was still continuing, though more slowly. The grammar of a child of 5 differs to a perhaps surprising degree from adult grammar. But the 5-year-old is not usually aware of his shortcomings. In comprehension tests, children readily assign interpretations to the structures presented to them—but they are often the wrong ones. "They do not, as they see it, fail to understand our sentences. They understand them, but they understand them wrongly" (Carol Chomsky 1969, p. 2). To demonstrate this point, the researcher (Chomsky's wife) showed a group of 5- to 8-year-olds a blindfolded doll, and said: "Is this doll hard to see or easy to see?" All the 5- and 6-year-olds said *hard to see,* and so did some of the 7- and 8-year-olds. The response of 6-year-old Lisa was typical:

> CHOMSKY: Is this doll easy to see or hard to see?
> LISA: Hard to see.

CHOMSKY: Will you make her easy to see?
LISA: If I can get this untied.
CHOMSKY: Will you explain why she was hard to see?
LISA: (to doll): Because you had a blindfold over your eyes.

Some psychologists have criticized this particular test. A child sometimes believes, ostrich-fashion, that if his own eyes are covered, others will not be able to see him. And he may be partly switching to the doll's viewpoint when he says a blindfolded doll is hard to see. But a rerun of this experiment using wolf and duck puppets, and sentences such as:

The wolf is hard to bite.
The duck is anxious to bite.

confirmed the original results (Cromer 1970). Children of 5 and 6 just do not realize that pairs of sentences such as *The rabbit is nice to eat* and *The rabbit is eager to eat* have completely different underlying meanings.

In fact, the gap between child and adult speech lasts longer than was once realized. More recently, detailed experiments on French children's understanding and use of the articles *le/la* "the" and *un/une* "a" have shown quite surprising differences between child and adult usage, which remained in some cases up till the age of 12 (Karmiloff-Smith 1979).

But the discrepancies between Barbara's speech and that of the adults around her gradually disappeared over the next few years. By the age of about 11, Barbara exhibited a command of the structure of her language comparable to that of an adult. At the age of puberty, her language development was essentially complete. She would continue to add individual vocabulary items all her life, but her grammatical rules were unlikely to change except in trivial respects. The "critical period" set by nature for the acquisition of language was over.

Note, incidentally, that language milestones tend to run parallel with physical development. Clearly, there is no essential correlation between language and motor development, since there are numerous examples of children who learn to talk, but never walk, and vice versa. However, researchers are agreed that in normal children the two often go together. Language milestones are often loosely linked to physical milestones. For example, the gradual change of cooing to babbling occurs around the time an infant begins to sit up. A child utters single words just before he starts to walk. Grammar becomes complex as hand and finger coordination develops.

Let us now summarize our conclusions. . . . [We] have shown that language seems to have all the characteristics of biologically programmed behavior. It emerges before it is necessary, and its emergence cannot be accounted for either by an external event, or by a sudden decision taken by the child. There seems to be a "critical period" set aside by nature for its acquisition, and direct teaching and intensive practice have relatively little effect. Language acquisition follows a regular sequence of milestones in its development, which can be loosely correlated with other aspects of the child's development. In other words, there is an internal mechanism both to trigger it off and to regulate it.

However, it would be wrong to think of language as something which is governed *only* by internal mechanisms. These mechanisms require external stimulation in order to work properly. The child needs a rich verbal environment during the critical acquisition period.

This suggests that the so-called nature-nurture controversy . . . may be misconceived. Both sides are right: nature triggers off the behavior, and lays down the framework, but careful nurture is needed for it to reach its full potential. The dividing line between "natural" and "nurtured" behavior is by no means as clear-cut as was once thought. In other words, language is "natural" behavior — but it still has to be carefully "nurtured" in order to reach its full potential. . . .

BIBLIOGRAPHY

Bernstein, B. (1972), "Social class, language, and socialization," in P. P. Giglioli (ed.), *Language and Social Context*, Harmondsworth: Penguin.

Braine, M. D. S. (1971), "The acquisition of language in infant and child," in C. E. Reed (ed.), *The Learning of Language*, New York: Appleton-Century-Crofts.

Brown, R. (1958), *Words and Things*, New York: The Free Press.

———. (1973), *A First Language*, London: Allen & Unwin.

Brown, R., and Bellugi, U. (1964), "Three processes in the child's acquisition of syntax," in E. H. Lenneberg (ed.) (1964), *New Directions in the Study of Language*, Cambridge, Mass.: MIT Press. Also in R. Brown (ed.), *Psycholinguistics: Selected Papers*, New York: The Free Press.

Brown, R., Cazden, C., and Bellugi, U. (1968). "The child's grammar from I to III," in J. P. Hill (ed.), *Minnesota Symposium on Child Psychology*, vol. II, Minneapolis: University of Minnesota Press.

Cazden, C. (1972), *Child Language and Education*, New York: Holt, Rinehart and Winston.

Chomsky, C. (1969), *The Acquisition of Syntax in Children from 5 to 10*, Cambridge, Mass.: MIT Press.

Chomsky, N. (1967), "The formal nature of language," in E. H. Lenneberg, *Biological Foundations of Language*, New York: Wiley.

Curtiss, S. (1977), *Genie: A Psycholinguistic Study of a Modern-Day "Wild Child,"* New York: Academic Press.

Curtiss, S., Fromkin, V., Krashen, S., Rigler, D., and Rigler, M. (1974), "The linguistic development of Genie," *Language* 50, pp. 528–554.

Eimas, P., Siqueland, E., Jusczyk, P., and Vigorito, J. (1971), "Speech perception in infants," *Science* 171, pp. 303–306.

Ervin, S. M. (1964), "Imitation and structural change in children's language," in

E. H. Lenneberg (ed.) (1964), *New Directions in the Study of Language*, Cambridge, Mass.: MIT Press.

Ervin-Tripp, S. (1971), "An overview of theories of grammatical development," in D. I. Slobin (ed.), *The Ontogenesis of Grammar*, New York: Academic Press.

Fourcin, A. J. (1978), "Acoustic patterns and speech acquisition," in N. Waterson and C. Snow (eds.), *The Development of Communication*, Chichester: John Wiley & Sons.

Garman, M. (1979), "Early grammatical development," in P. Fletcher and M. Garman (eds.), *Language Acquisition*, Cambridge: Cambridge University Press.

Jakobson, R. (1962), "Why 'Mama' and 'Papa'?" in A. Bar-Adon and W. F. Leopold (eds.) (1971), *Child Language: A Book of Readings*, Englewood Cliffs, N.J.: Prentice-Hall.

Karmiloff-Smith, A. (1979), *A Functional Approach to Child Language: A Study of Determiners and Reference*, Cambridge: Cambridge University Press.

Klima, E., and Bellugi, U. (1966), "Syntactic regularities in the speech of children," in J. Lyons and R. J. Wales (eds.), *Psycholinguistics Papers*, Edinburgh: Edinburgh University Press. Revised version in A. Bar-Adon and W. F. Leopold (eds.) (1971), *Child Language: A Book of Readings*, Englewood Cliffs, N.J.: Prentice-Hall.

Kuhl, P., and Miller, J. D. (1974), "Discrimination of speech sounds by the chinchilla: /t/ vs /d/ in CV syllables," *Journal of the Acoustical Society of America* 57, series 41 (abstract).

———. (1975). "Speech perception by the chinchilla: phonetic boundaries for synthetic VOT stimuli," *Journal of the Acoustical Society of America* 57, series 49 (abstract).

Lenneberg, E. H. (1967), *The Biological Foundations of Language*, New York: Wiley.

Morse, P. A. (1976), "Speech perception in the human infant and rhesus monkey," in S. Harnad, H. Steklis, and J. Lancaster (eds.), *Origins and Evolution of Language and Speech*, Annals of the New York Academy of Sciences, vol. 280.

Nelson, K. (1973), "Structure and strategy in learning to talk," *Monograph of the Society for Research in Child Development* 38, pp. 1–2.

Ricks, D. M. (1975), "Vocal communication in pre-verbal normal and autistic children," in N. O'Connor (ed.), *Language, Cognitive Deficits, and Retardation*, London: Butterworth.

Slobin, D. I. (1966), "The acquisition of Russian as a native language," in F. Smith and G. A. Miller (eds.), (1966), *The Genesis of Language*, Cambridge, Mass.: MIT Press.

Thorpe, W. H. (1972), "Vocal communication in birds," in R. A. Hinde (ed.), *Non-Verbal Communication*, Cambridge: Cambridge University Press.

Weir, R. H. (1962), *Language in the Crib*, The Hague: Mouton.

———. (1966), "Some questions on the child's learning of phonology," in F. Smith and G. A. Miller (1966), *The Genesis of Language*, Cambridge, Mass.: MIT Press.

=

FOR DISCUSSION AND REVIEW

1. What does Aitchison mean by "a biological time-clock"? Give four examples of its effects in animals that are not mentioned by Aitchison.

2. Aitchison discusses six features of biologically scheduled behavior in addition to its one predominant characteristic. Consider each of these seven in turn. To what extent is each actually a characteristic of human language? Are there any qualifications or caveats that need to be added? What are they?

3. Discuss the importance of the interaction of a child's environment and his or her biological predisposition for language acquisition. What conclusions, if any, can you draw concerning the function of day care centers, nursery schools, and kindergartens?

4. Explain the term "critical period." Summarize the arguments for both a biologically controlled starting point and a similarly controlled finishing point for language acquisition.

5. Reread the two examples of parent-child dialogue and the paragraph that follows them. How do the dialogues support the concept of language acquisition as biologically determined behavior? Consider outright correction, attempts to force imitation, and adult expansions of children's utterances.

6. Compare and contrast Aitchison's description of the way that parents talk to young children with Moskowitz's description of "caretaker speech." What similarities do you find? What differences?

7. What is the significance, in terms of theories of language acquisition, of the fact that children learn and use correct plural forms of some irregular nouns and correct past tense forms of some irregular verbs, but subsequently "regress"—i.e., cease using the correct irregular forms, replacing, for example, *went* with *goed* or *feet* with *foots?*

8. Explain the apparent paradox that practice is in one sense unimportant for language acquisition, but that in another sense children need to practice.

9. Moskowitz and Aitchison discuss the stages of normal language acquisition, although they do so in different ways. (For example, Moskowitz deals in generalizations, whereas Aitchison discusses specific children, both real and imaginary.) Compare and contrast the two discussions, looking especially for similarities and differences. Summarize your conclusions in a chart or table.

10. Review Lenneberg's "Developmental Milestones in Motor and Language Development" in light of Aitchison's discussion and examples of the fact that "Language milestones are often closely linked to physical milestones." Are her examples persuasive? What about the linkage between cognitive development and language milestones?

8

How Children Learn Words

George A. Miller
Patricia M. Gildea

Picture the traditional image of a mother leaning over her newborn's crib, coaxing the infant to make sounds and words. The only surprise that surfaces in detailed examinations of the word-learning process is that we may not in fact teach children as much about words and speech as we think we do. In this selection scientists George A. Miller of Purdue University and Patricia H. Gildea of Rutgers University examine the complicated word-learning process of children. The authors discuss the two stages of the word-learning process: how and in what manner words are learned, and the remarkable ability of children to learn much more than they are actually taught. Miller and Gildea demonstrate children's tendency toward "overextension" of meaning as new words are acquired. The authors discuss computers as new and helpful tools for teaching new words, along with the more traditional uses of definitions and sentence contexts. Miller and Gildea examine these teaching techniques with the hope that they will discover the most efficient method of facilitating the complicated process of word learning.

Listening to a child who is just learning to talk, one is most aware of the child's limited command of the language. What one tends to overlook is the sheer magnitude of the child's achievement. Simply learning the vocabulary is an enormous undertaking. The fact is that for many years after starting to talk a child learns new words at a rate of more than 10 per day! Yet little is known about how children do it. Certainly they do not do it by memorizing dictionary entries. Our findings and those of other workers suggest that formal efforts to build vocabulary by sending children to the dictionary are less effective than most parents and teachers believe. We are exploring the possibility that a computer program providing lexical information about new words encountered in the context of a story might be more effective.

When adults set out to learn a new language, they know what is in store. They realize they will have to learn a new pronunciation, a new grammar, a new vocabulary and a new style of using language. They know they will have to spend many hours every day for years before they can call themselves fluent in the new language. They also know, however, that they will be able to rely on teachers to explain, in their first language, everything they need to learn about the second language.

How different it is for infants. Having no language, they cannot be told what they need to learn. Yet by the age of three they will have mastered the basic structure of their native language and will be well on their way to communicative competence. Acquiring their first language is the most impressive intellectual feat many people will ever perform.

Students of how children learn language generally agree that the most remarkable aspect of this feat is the rapid acquisition of grammar. Nevertheless, the ability of children to conform to grammatical rules is only slightly more wonderful than their ability to learn new words.

How many words must one know in order to use English effectively? The answer depends on several variables, including the definition of "word." For the purpose of counting, a word can be defined as the kind of lexical unit a person has to learn; all the derivative and compound forms that are merely morphological variations on the conceptual theme would not be counted as separate words. For example, *write* is a word and its morphological variants (*writes, writ, wrote, written, writing, writer* and so on) are relatives in the same family. If such a family is counted as a single word and knowing a word is defined as being able to recognize which of four definitions is closest to the meaning, the reading vocabulary of the average high school graduate should consist of about 40,000 words. If all the proper names of people and places and all the idiomatic expressions are also counted as words, that estimate would have to be doubled.

This figure says something about the ability of children to learn words. If the average high school graduate is 17 years old, the 80,000 words must have been learned over a period of 16 years. Hence the average child learns at the rate of 5,000 words per year, or about 13 per day. Children with large vocabularies probably pick up new words at twice that rate. Clearly, a learning process of great complexity goes on at a rapid rate in every normal child.

No one teaches children 13 or more words a day. Children must have a special talent for this kind of learning. Some valuable hints as to how they do it were uncovered a decade ago by Susan Carey and Elsa J. Bartlett, who were then at Rockefeller University. They worked with the name of colors. First they established that a group of three-year-olds did not know the color olive. Most of the children called it green and some of them called it brown.

Carey and Bartlett taught the children a nonsense name for olive — a name they would not have heard anywhere else. They took two cafeteria trays and painted one tray olive and the other blue. Each child was then told casually, "Hand me the chromium tray. Not the blue one, the chromium one." The child would pause and perhaps point to the olive tray. "This one?" "Yes, that one. Thank you."

A week later, with no further guidance, the children were again asked to name the colors. When olive was presented, they paused. They did not remember *chromium*, but now they knew that this color was not called green or brown. A single exposure was enough to begin a reorganization of their color lexicon.

This simple experiment demonstrated some important points about how children learn words. First, in order to learn a word a child must be able to associate its sound with its meaning. Mastering the mechanics of uttering and recognizing a word and mastering the concept that it expresses are separate learning processes. After their experience with the trays the children knew that olive has a special name—that it is not called green or brown—but they did not remember the particular spoken sound associated with that perceived color. Many repetitions may be necessary before the sound of a new word becomes familiar.

Second, a child's appreciation of the meaning of a word seems to grow in two stages, one rapid and the other much slower. Children are quick to notice new words and to assign them to broad semantic categories. After hearing *chromium* just once the three-year-olds assigned it to the semantic field of color names. Children are able to keep such fields separate even before they know what the individual words mean. Asked the color of something, they may respond with almost any color term at random, but they never answer *round* or *five* or *lunch*.

The slow stage entails working out the distinctions among words within a semantic category. A child who has correctly assigned *red*, *green*, *yellow* and *blue* to the semantic field of color terms still has to learn the differences between and relations among those words. This stage ordinarily takes much longer than the first and may never be completely finished; some adults, for example, correctly assign *delphinium* and *calceolaria* to the semantic field of flowering-plant names but have not learned what plants the words denote and cannot identify the flowers on sight. At any given time many words will be in this intermediate state in which they are known and categorized but still not distinguished from one another.

A related aspect of word learning by preschoolers that has attracted wide attention is called overextension. For example, a small child learning the word *apple* may apply it to a tomato. *Apple* is thought to mean, say, round, red and of a certain size; without further qualification those attributes define ripe tomatoes as well as ripe apples. Overextension can occur when a child's conception of a word's meaning is incomplete.

The opposite error also occurs, but it is revealed only by special questioning. For example, a child who thinks that being round, red and of a certain size defines *apple* might fail to use *apple* to refer to green or yellow apples. The only way to identify such an underextension is to show the child green or yellow apples and ask what they are called.

The ability of preschoolers to soak up words has attracted increasing attention in recent years. Much more is known about it than was known when Carey and Bartlett did their pioneering study with color names.

The word-learning process becomes even more complex, however, during the school years.

In the early grades schoolchildren are expected to learn to read and write. At first they read and write familiar words they have already learned by means of conversation. In about the fourth grade they begin to see written words they have not heard in conversation. At this point it is generally assumed that something special must be done to teach children these unfamiliar words.

This educational assumption runs into serious problems. Although children can recognize that they have not seen a word before, learning it well enough to use it correctly and to recognize it automatically is a slow process. Indeed, learning a new word entails so much conceptual clarification and phonological drill that there simply is not enough classroom time to teach more than 100 or 200 words a year in this way. Since learning runs so far ahead of teaching—some 5,000 words learned in a year compared with 200 taught—it is hard to avoid the question: How do schoolchildren learn so much more than they are taught?

Many words are acquired through reading. Children learn words at school in the same way as they do at home: by observing how the words are used in intelligible contexts. The difference is that the academic environment depends more on written contexts. Both public opinion and scientific evidence are converging on the view that the best way to facilitate vocabulary growth in schoolchildren is to have them read as much as possible.

Learning words by reading them in context is effective but not efficient. Some contexts are uninformative, others misleading. If the word in question expresses an unfamiliar concept, a single context of use will seldom support more than one hypothesis about the word's meaning. In order for reading to have any substantial effect on vocabulary a great deal of reading must be done.

How much? A child who spent fifty minutes of every school day reading at, say, 200 words per minute would read one million words in a 100-day school year. A million running words of English prose would typically contain no more than 50,000 distinct word types, representing roughly 10,000 word families. Schoolbooks would probably contain fewer different words. Even among 10,000 different words, it is unlikely that more than 1,000 would be totally new lexical items. Since multiple encounters are required in order to learn a new word, it is clear that reading one million words per year is not enough. In order to account for a growth rate of 5,000 words in a year it seems necessary to think about continued learning from conversational interactions supplemented by reading several million words per year. Indeed, children who read little outside the classroom generally do poorly on vocabulary tests.

The fact that children learn many more words than anyone has time to teach them also carries implications for the role of teachers in this learning process. Learning new words from purely literary contexts of use—from the contexts provided on the printed page—is harder than learning them through interaction with a person. In conversation it is usually possible to ask the speaker what an unfamiliar word means. Moreover, in most conversations visual information supplements the linguistic information. Such help is missing from the printed page.

Given this additional difficulty, it seems reasonable to ask teachers to help children to be more efficient in learning new words from context. If they cannot teach all the words children need to know, perhaps teachers could help their students learn how to work out such things for themselves.

One way to figure out what an unfamiliar word means is to use a dictionary. In about the fourth grade, therefore, most schools begin to teach dictionary skills: spelling, alphabetizing, pronunciation, parts of speech and a little morphology and etymology. The idea, which is perfectly reasonable, is that children should learn how to find unfamiliar words in a dictionary and how to understand what they read there.

One trouble with this approach is that most healthy, right-minded children have a strong aversion to dictionaries. There may be good reason. We have looked at some of the tasks teachers assign in order to get students to use dictionaries. In our opinion these exercises do not merit the faith that teachers and parents have put in them.

Two tasks are often assigned when children are being taught how to use a dictionary. One task entails disambiguation: the child is given a sentence that contains an ambiguous word—a word with two or more senses—and told to find it in the dictionary and to decide which sense the author of the sentence had in mind. The other task calls for production: the child is given a word and told to look it up in the dictionary and to write a sentence incorporating it. On the face of it both tasks look as though they should be instructive. It is therefore surprising to discover how ineffectual they are.

Learning from a dictionary requires considerable sophistication. Interrupting your reading to find an unfamiliar word in an alphabetical list, all the while keeping the original context in mind so that you can compare it with the alternative senses given in the dictionary, then selecting the sense that is most appropriate in the original context—that is a high-level cognitive task. It should not be surprising that children are not good at it. Even when most of the complications are removed, children are still not good at it. On a simplified disambiguation task, in which fourth-grade students were given just two senses and asked to choose the one that was intended in a particular sentence, the students did little better than chance.

The second task, producing a sentence incorporating a new word, has the virtue of requiring the student to use the word and so, presumably, to think about its meaning. We have studied this production task extensively. After reading several thousand sentences that were written by children in the fifth and sixth grades we have concluded that it too is a waste of time.

Typical of the curious sentences we encountered was "Mrs. Morrow stimulated the soup." It illustrates the most frequent kind of error made by children in that age range. If they already know the word, their sentences are usually all right. If the word is unfamiliar, however, the results are often mystifying. In order to understand what the child did, you have to read carefully the same dictionary definitions the child read. The child who looked up *stimulate* found *stir up* among the definitions.

The example provides a key to what happens when children consult a dictionary. They find the unfamiliar word and then look for a familiar word or phrase among the definitions. Next they compose a sentence using the familiar word or phrase and substitute the new word for it. One of our favorite examples came from a fifth-grader who looked up the unfamiliar word *erode,* found the familiar phrases *eat out* and *eat away* in the definition and thought of the sentence "Our family eats out a lot." She then substituted *erode* for *eats out;* the resulting sentence was "Our family erodes a lot."

If children are so good at learning new words when they hear or see them used in context, why do they have trouble learning new words when they see them in a dictionary? We decided to look more closely at what goes on when an unfamiliar word is encountered in the context of a typical sentence. A preliminary study indicated that children can write better sentences when they are given a model sentence employing the word than when they are given a definition of the word. Since many of the sentences they wrote were patterned on the models, this result could not be interpreted to mean that the children learned more about the meaning of a word from illustrative sentences than they learned from definitions. Nevertheless, the observation was encouraging, and we pressed on.

The next step was simple: if one example is good, three should be better. When we made this comparison, however, we found that the number of examples made little difference. The acceptability ratings of sentences written after seeing one model sentence were the same as the ratings of sentences written on the basis of three examples.

That observation made us think again about what was going on. Apparently three unrelated sentences are hard for children to integrate, and so they simply focus on one of three examples and ignore the others. This behavior resembles what children do in reading dictionary definitions.

We were surprised by one result, although perhaps in retrospect we should have expected it. Mistakes resembling simple substitutions appeared even when model sentences were given instead of dictionary definitions. For example, given the model sentence "The king's brother tried to usurp the throne" to define the unfamiliar word *usurp*, the children wrote such sentences as "The blue chair was usurped from the room," "Don't try to usurp that tape from the store," "The thief tried to usurp the money from the safe" and so on. They had gathered from the model sentence that *usurp* means *take*, and so they composed sentences using *take* and then substituted *usurp* for it.

Children can appreciate at least part of the meaning of an unfamiliar word from its context, as in the case of *take* as one component of the meaning of *usurp*. Just as younger children may overextend *apple* because they know only part of its meaning, so this partial definition of *usurp* resulted in its being overextended. That is to say, if *usurp* is incompletely defined as *take*, it can be said of anything takable: chairs, tape, money or whatever. When it is seen from this perspective, the behavior of these children in the fifth and sixth grades is merely a later stage in the development of a word-learning process employed by preschool children.

The substitution strategy therefore seems to be quite general. In the context of a model sentence, however, something more than a simple substitution error appears. The children cannot search through an illustrative sentence for a familiar word as they could in a dictionary definition. First they must abstract a familiar concept from the context of the unfamiliar word. Only then can they apply the substitution rule.

Might there be a better way to foster the growth of vocabulary? What we and others have found out about the word-learning process will support some plausible suggestions. Put at the front of your mind the idea that a teacher's best friend in this endeavor is the student's motivation to discover meaning in linguistic messages. Then the problems with the traditional modes of instruction will begin to make sense. Drill on arbitrarily preselected lists of words seldom takes place at a time when the student feels a need to know those words; it fails to draw on the natural motivation for learning the associations between word and meaning. Learning through reading faces the opposite problem: not enough information about the word is available at the moment the student is motivated to learn its meaning.

What is needed is reading, which can make students curious about unfamiliar words, supplemented by immediate information about the meaning and use of those words. The important thing is to provide the information while the reader still wants it. Dictionaries are too slow. Recourse to a dictionary may help a mature and well-motivated student, but for the average child in the elementary grades it is likely to compound interruption with misunderstood information. A human tutor—someone immediately available to detect and resolve lexical misunderstandings—would be much better than a dictionary.

Given the shortage of attentive tutors to sit at every young reader's elbow, it is natural to wonder how much of the tutoring task might be carried out by a suitably programmed computer. For example, suppose reading material was presented to the student by a computer that had been programmed to answer questions about the meanings of all the words in the material. No alphabetical search would be needed: the student would simply point to a word and information about it would appear. No sophisticated disambiguation would be necessary: the computer would know in advance which particular sense of a word was appropriate in the context. Indeed, no definition would be necessary: the phrase or sentence containing the word could be rephrased to show what the word meant in the context.

As a case in point, imagine what such a computer might do with *erode* and *usurp*. It might present a text containing the sentence "The president's popularity was eroded by his bad relations with Congress." If the student asked for information about *erode,* the computer might state: "Things can erode; when soil is eroded by rain or wind, it breaks up and so is slowly destroyed and removed. Someone's power or authority can erode too, being slowly destroyed or removed by unfavorable developments. That kind of erosion is meant in the sentence about the president."

Suppose that for *usurp* the computer presented a text containing the sentence "The king's brother failed in his effort to usurp the throne." Asked for information, the computer might say: "When you usurp a title, job or position from someone else, you seize it or take it away even though you have no right to it. In the sentence about the king's brother, *throne* means not just the piece of furniture the king sits on; it also stands as a symbol of the king's authority."

Providing such explanations almost instantly is well within the range of currently available computer technology. It is even possible to add a voice that pronounces the target word and explains it, or to show pictures indicating what the word denotes in the context.

We are exploring some of these possibilities with a setup in which children in the fifth and sixth grades interact with a video display. They are asked to read a text that describes an episode from a motion picture they have just seen. Included in the text are certain marked words the reader is expected to learn. When one of them comes up, the child can ask for information about its meaning in any or all of three forms: definitions, sentences and pictures.

For some children illustrative sentences are more informative than definitions or pictures. When such children are given a definition, they read it and quickly return to the story. When they are given a sentence that is relevant to the story and uses the word in the same context, they interpret it as a puzzle to be solved. They spend more time thinking about the meaning of the word and remember it better a week later.

We found that providing information when it is wanted can significantly improve the children's grasp of unfamiliar words, as is demonstrated by their ability to recognize the meanings and to write acceptable sentences incorporating the words. The results reinforce our belief that much can be done with computers to make learning words easier.

FOR DISCUSSION AND REVIEW

1. The opening abstract suggests that readers compare how they learned or were taught new words as a child with how they learn new words now. Try to recall your earliest memories and make some comparisons. Compare your results with classmates.

2. How do Miller and Gildea describe the early processes children use in their acquisition of language?

3. As children learn new words, there are two stages through which they must pass. What are these two stages and what characterizes each? Do you pass through any similar stages today when you learn new words?

4. What is meant by the term "overextension"? Describe some instances in which you have heard a child "overextend" the meaning of a word.

5. Miller and Gildea propose the question: "How do children learn so much more than they are taught?" What explanations can be offered as a solution? How might an answer to this question support the work of Noam Chomsky?

6. Miller and Gildea suggest that children can learn new words in textual context, through interaction, as well as through the use of dictionaries. "If children are so good at learning new words when they hear or see them in context, why do they have trouble learning new words when they see them in a dictionary?" What difficulties are associated with the use of dictionaries?

7. We have observed how "overextension" is apparent in the speech of young children. Miller and Gildea demonstrate several instances in which older grade-school children employ this "overextension" technique as well. What are some suggestions for the continued use of such a technique?

8. What do the authors suggest as a means to foster the growth of vocabulary in children? Can you think of any other methods to aid in this complicated process?

9

Preschool Language Development: Brown's Stages of Development

Robert E. Owens, Jr.

A "morpheme" is the smallest unit in a language that carries meaning. Morphemes may be words or parts of words. This single unit of meaning is essential for the study of language acquisition. Morphemes are the units used to determine communicative competence in children and to measure and record progress. In this selection Robert E. Owens, Jr., professor of speech pathology and audiology at SUNY–Geneseo, examines the role that morphemes play in the process of language acquisition. Owens presents evidence that illustrates a regular pattern and order in the acquisition of language through morphemes and that these patterns coincide with certain nonlinguistic developments in children. That all children in normal linguistic environments seem to pass through Brown's stages of development suggests the existence of an underlying universal scheme for language acquisition.

STAGES OF SYNTACTIC AND MORPHOLOGICAL DEVELOPMENT

It may be helpful to our understanding if we divide the preschool period into stages of syntactic and morphological development. Several researchers have suggested just such a framework (R. Brown, 1973; Wells, 1985). After considering these frameworks, I have decided to organize this discussion on the model of Roger Brown because of its ease of understanding. Other significant studies, especially the exhaustive work of Wells (1985), will be highlighted throughout. Naturally, any discussion of language form requires the use of syntactic terms (parts of speech).

After completing a longitudinal study of child language, Brown noted that there are certain characteristic periods of language development that correspond to increases in the child's average utterance length, measured in morphemes. This value, the mean length of utterance (MLU), is a moderately reliable predictor of the complexity of the language of English-speaking young children. Some researchers have found that for English-speaking preschoolers, MLU relates well to age, is reliable, and is a good predictor of language development (Rondal, Ghiotto, Bredart & Bachelet, 1987). Up to an MLU of 4.0, increases in MLU correspond to increases in utterance complexity. Above an MLU of 4.0, complexity of utterances relates more to the context, and utterance length is not necessarily increased (D'Odorico & Franco, 1985).

At best, MLU is a crude measure that is sensitive to only those language developments that increase utterance length. For example, the movement of elements within the utterance may result in more mature utterances but will not increase the MLU. Although there is a positive correlation between MLU and age, MLU may vary widely for children with the same chronological age (J. Miller, 1981; J. Miller & Chapman, 1981; Wells, 1985). It is also important to note that although MLU is a rough estimate of language complexity for English-speaking preschoolers, it is not so for users of other languages such as modern Hebrew, in which complexity does not necessarily result in longer utterances (Dromi & Berman, 1982).

From age 1½ to 5 years, MLU may increase by approximately 1.2 morphemes per year, although there is some indication of a decreased rate after 42 months (Scarborough, Wyckoff, & Davidson, 1986). MLU is a simplistic predictor of language development, a gross developmental index that itself provides no information on specific structural complexity or grammatical competence, even among children with the same MLU (Cazden, 1968; Klee & Fitzgerald, 1985). We use it here because of its conceptual simplicity for discussion.

Computing MLU

In general, 50 or 100 utterances are considered a sufficient sample from which to generalize about a speaker's overall production. An utterance may be a sentence or a shorter unit of language that is separated from other utterances by a drop in the voice, a pause, and/or a breath that signals a new thought. Once transcribed, each utterance is analyzed by morphemes; the total sample is then averaged to determine the speaker's MLU.

When analyzing the language of young children, several assumptions about preschool language must be made. Let's use the past tense as an example. The regular past tense includes the verb stem plus -ed, as in *walked* or *opened.* Hence, the regular past equals two morphemes. In contrast, the irregular past is signaled by a different word, as in *eat/ate* and *sit/sat.* As adults, we realize that *eat* plus a past tense marker equals *ate.* It could thus be argued that *ate* should also be counted as two morphemes. It seems, however, that young children learn separate words for the present and the irregular past, and are not necessarily aware of the relationship between the two (R. Brown, 1973). Therefore, the irregular

TABLE 9.1   Brown's Rules for Counting Morphemes

RULE	EXAMPLE
Count as one morpheme:	
Reoccurrences of a word for emphasis	*No! No! No!* (3 morphemes)
Compound words (two or more free morphemes)	*Railroad, birthday*
Proper names	*Billy Sue*
Ritualized reduplications	*Night-night, choo-choo*
Irregular past tense verbs	*Went, ate, got, came*
Diminutives	*Daddie, doggie*
Auxiliary verbs and catenatives	*Is, have, do; gonna, hafta*
Irregular plurals	*Men, feet*
Count as two morphemes (inflected verbs and nouns):	
Possessive nouns	*Tom's, daddie's*
Plural nouns	*Doggies, kitties*
Third person singular present tense verbs	*Walks, eats*
Regular past tense verbs	*Walked, jumped*
Present progressive verbs	*Walking, eating*
Do not count:	
Dysfluencies, except for most complete form	*C-c-c-candy, bab-baby*
Fillers	*Um-m, ah-h, oh*

Source: Adapted from R. Brown, *A First Language: The Early Stages*, Cambridge: Harvard University Press, 1973.

---

past counts as one morpheme for young children. A similar logic exists for words such as *gonna* and *wanna*. As adults we can subdivide these words into their components: *going to* and *want to*. Young children, however, cannot perform such analyses. Therefore, *gonna* counts as one morpheme for the child, not as the three represented by *going to*.

Although we may not agree with this rationale, we must adopt it if we are to discuss language development within Brown's framework. Guidelines for counting morphemes are presented in Table 9.1. Applying these rules, we would reach the following values:

Daddy bring me choo-choo s. = 5 morphemes

Mommy eat-ed a-a-a- sandwich. = 5 morphemes

Doggie-'s bed broke baboom. = 5 morphemes

Smokie Bear go-ing night-night. = 4 morphemes

He hafta. = 2 morphemes

Once the morphemes for each utterance are counted, they are totaled and then divided by the total number of utterances. The formula is very simple:

$$\text{MLU} = \frac{\text{Total number of morphemes}}{\text{Total number of utterances}}$$

Thus, if the total number of morphemes for a 100-utterance sample is 221, the MLU will equal 2.21 morphemes per utterance. Remember that this is an average value and does not identify the length of the child's longest utterance. In other words, an MLU of 2.0 does *not* mean that the child uses only two-word utterances. The shortest and longest utterances are also important when considering the child's overall performance.

MLU and Stage of Development

The thrust of development changes with increased MLU. Major developments occur that can characterize certain MLU phases or stages. These stages are as follows (R. Brown, 1973):

Stage	*MLU*	*Approximate Age (months)*	*Characteristics*
I	1.0–2.0	12–26	Linear semantic rules
II	2.0–2.5	27–30	Morphological development
III	2.5–3.0	31–34	Sentence form development
IV	3.0–3.75	35–40	Embedding of sentence elements
V	3.75–4.5	41–46	Joining of clauses
V+	4.5+	47+	

Stage I is characterized by single-word utterances and by the word-order rules of early multiword combinations. . . . Stage II is characterized by the appearance of grammatical morphemes, which mark many of the relations expressed previously by the child with word order in stage I. By stage III the child exhibits simple sentence forms, and he begins to modify these forms to mirror more adultlike forms for different sentence modalities, such as yes/no questions, *wh-* questions, negatives, and imperatives. Stage IV is marked by the beginning of embedding of phrases and clauses within another sentence. For example, the clause *who laughed* can be embedded in the clause *the boy is funny* to produce "The boy *who laughed* is funny." Finally, stage V is characterized by conjoining or by compound sentences. For example, the clauses *Mary washed* and *John dried* can be combined to form "Mary washed and John dried." Although each stage has some characteristic linguistic modifications, it should be noted that other, less obvious changes are also occurring.

MORPHOLOGICAL DEVELOPMENT

Several morphological developments begin in stage II but continue well into the school-age years. "Overt grammar or morpheme-combining begins really as soon as the MLU rises above 1.00" (R. Brown, 1973,

p. 65), although the period of greatest acquisition is from 4 to 7 years. Since many morphemes are redundant or have alternative forms of expression, it is difficult to determine their age of acquisition. Even as adults, we are not aware of many morphological differences, such as the difference between *data* and *datum* or between *uninterested* and *disinterested*. (In court, however, we would clearly prefer a disinterested judge over an uninterested one.) Only the most commonly used morphemes will be discussed in the following section.

Stage II: Brown's 14 Morphemes

Stage II can be described by the appearance of morphemes that signify the semantic relations specified in stage I through word order. R. Brown (1973) isolated 14 morphemes for study. Selection was based on obligatory use. If use is obligatory rather than optional, then absence of the morpheme would indicate nonacquisition, not choice.

The 14 selected morphemes, presented in Table 9.2, have the following characteristics:

1. They are phonetically minimal forms. In general, they include simple phonemic additions or changes, such as the addition of an *s*.
2. They receive only light vocal emphasis.
3. They belong to a limited class of constructions, as opposed to the larger number of nouns and verbs.
4. They possess multiple phonological forms and can vary with the grammatical and phonetic properties of the words to which they are attached. For example, the *s* in *cats* is pronounced /s/, whereas the *s* in *dogs* is pronounced /z/.
5. Their development is slow.

Each morpheme emerges in stage II, but most morphemes are not fully mastered (used correctly 90% of the time) until later. The order presented in Table 9.2 reflects the order of mastery, not of appearance.

Present Progressive

The present progressive verb tense is used in English to indicate an activity that is currently in progress and is of temporary duration, such as *I am swimming*. The form consists of the auxiliary or helping verb *to be* (*am, is, are, was, were*), the main verb, and the -*ing* verb ending. Children initially express this verb with only the -*ing* ending. For example, a child might say "Swimming" or "Mommy eating." The present progressive verb tense without the auxiliary is the earliest verb inflection acquired in English and is mastered within stage II for most verbs used by young children (R. Brown, 1973; Kuczaj, 1978; J. Miller, 1981).

TABLE 9.2 Brown's 14 Morphemes

MORPHEME	EXAMPLE	AGE OF MASTERY* (IN MONTHS)
Present progressive -ing (no auxiliary verb)	Mommy *driving*.	19–28
In	Ball *in* cup.	27–30
On	Doggie *on* sofa.	27–30
Regular plural -s	Kitties eat my ice cream. Forms: /s/, /z/, and /ɪz/ *Cars* (/kæts/) *Dogs* (/dɔgz/) *Classes* (/klæsɪz/), *wishes* (/wɪʃɪz/)	24–33
Irregular past	*Came, fell, broke, sat, went*	25–46
Possessive *'s*	Mommy*'s* balloon broke. Forms: /s/, /z/, and /ɪz/ as in regular plural	26–40
Uncontractible copula (verb *to be* as main verb)	He *is*. (response to "Who's sick?")	27–39
Articles	I see *a* kitty. I throw *the* ball to daddy.	28–46
Regular past -ed	Mommy pull*ed* the wagon. Forms: /d/, /t/, /ɪd/ *Pulled* (/pʊld/) *Walked* (/wɔkt/) *Glided* (/g l aɪ d ɪ d/)	26–48
Regular third person -s	Kathy hit*s*. Forms: /s/, /z/, and /ɪz/ as in regular plural	26–46
Irregular third person	*Does, has*	28–50
Uncontractible auxiliary	He *is*. (response to "Who's wearing your hat?")	29–48
Contractible copula	Man*'s* big. Man *is* big.	29–49
Contractible auxiliary	Daddy*'s* drinking juice. Daddy *is* drinking juice.	30–50

* Used correctly 90% of the time in obligatory contexts. Adapted from Bellugi (1964), R. Brown (1973), and Miller (1981).

The present progressive can be used with action verbs in English but not with verbs of state, such as *need, know,* and *like.* Young children learn this distinction early; and few overgeneralization errors result (R. Brown et al., 1969). The child probably learns the rule one-verb-at-a-time by applying it to individual verbs to determine whether they are "*-inga-ble*" (R. Brown, 1973). Later the child abandons this strategy as being too cumbersome.

The child is capable of making a semantic distinction between action and state verbs and applying the rule for the present progressive appropriately. State verbs are not capable of expressing the present progressive meaning of temporary duration. When a child says "I eating," it is assumed that he'll stop soon. The action is temporary. On the other hand, adults don't say "I am knowing," because with *know* it is assumed that this state is of some duration. Thus a child learns some general rule of application that enables him to generalize the progressive form while not overgeneralizing to inappropriate verbs. Early learning may also reflect the difference between the progressive and many other morphological inflections (Kuczaj, 1978). There are no irregular progressive forms, resulting in less confusion for the child. Forms that are overgeneralized by children, such as the regular past tense *-ed*, have both regular and irregular forms. For example, *walked* and *ran* both express "past-ness," though only *walk* employs the regular past tense form *-ed*.

Prepositions

In and *on* are the only two prepositions to occur frequently enough for Brown to have declared that they are acquired within stage II (R. Brown, 1973; J. Miller, 1981). Often the child relates the preposition to the object itself. For example, you can put something *in* a cup but rarely *on* it. Other early prepositions include *away, out, over,* and *under* (W. Miller & Ervin-Tripp, 1964). Simple topographic or locational relations, such as *in, on,* and *under,* appear to be easier for the child to comprehend than dimensional spatial relations, such as *behind, beside, between,* and *in front of* (Washington & Naremore, 1978). Spatial relations describe a position relative to some object. In turn, these spatial relations are easier for the child if applied to an object with a recognizable side, such as the front of the television, rather than to an object such as a stool that does not have distinct sides. In the latter case, spatial directions relate to the perspective of the speaker and therefore require greater cognitive and pragmatic skill development.

Plural

In English there is no morpheme to indicate the singular form of a noun; thus a singular noun is called *uninflected* or *unmarked*. The regular form of the plural, marked in writing by *-s*, is acquired within stage II (R. Brown, 1973; J. Miller, 1981). Learning of irregular forms takes considerably longer and largely depends upon how frequently these forms are used in the preschooler's environment.

The regular plural appears in short phrases first, then in short sentences, and finally in longer sentences. In addition, there appear to be four phases of development (W. Miller & Ervin-Tripp, 1964). Initially there is no difference between the singular and plural, and a number or the word *more* may be used to mark the plural. In other words, the child might say "Puppy" for one or more than one, or he might say "Two puppy" or "More puppy" to indicate plural. Next, the plural marker will be used for selected instances, probably on plural words that are used frequently. In the third phase, the plural generalizes to many instances, some of which are inappropriate. Thus, we get such delightful forms as *foots* and *mouses*. Finally, the regular and irregular plural are differentiated.

Acquiring the English plural involves phonological learning as well. Three different speech sounds are used with the plural: /s/, /z/, and /Iz/. If a word ends in a voiced consonant, the voiced plural marker /z/ is used, as in *beds* (/bɛdz/). In contrast, voiceless consonants are followed by the voiceless /s/, as in *bets* (/bɛts/). These rules do not apply if the final consonant is similar to the /s/ and /z/. The /s/, /z/, /ʃ/, /ʒ/, /tʃ/, and /dʒ/ are called *sibilant sounds,* or *sibilants.* If a word ends in a sibilant, the plural marker is /Iz/ or /əz/, as in *bridges* (/brIdʒIz/). The /s/ and /z/ rules are learned first, followed by the rule for /Iz/. The child may be in stage V or beyond before these phonological rules are acquired. This distinction is especially difficult for deaf children because of the relatively high frequency or pitch and the complexity of sibilant sounds.

Irregular Past

Irregular past tense verbs, those that do not use the *-ed* ending, are a small but very frequently used class of words in English. A small subset of these verbs appears in single-word utterances and is acquired in stage II, probably learned individually by rote. These include *came, fell, broke, sat,* and *went.* Although the child acquires these forms early, he may later use the regular *-ed* marker to produce *goed/wented* or *falled/felled.* The irregular past of common verbs is once again produced correctly by stage V. Many irregular verbs are not learned until school age. Even some adults have difficulty with irregular verbs such as *drink, lie,* and *lay.* I avoid writing or saying the last two whenever possible. Like adults, children may generalize from a known form to one being learned. Thus, knowledge of *sing/sang* may yield *bring/brang.* Likewise, knowledge of *drink, drank, drunk* may result in *think, thank, thunk.*

Possessive

The possessive is originally marked with word order and stress; the use of the possessive marker *('s)* appears relatively late. Initially, the possessive is attached only to single animate nouns, such as *Mommy* or *doggie,* to form *Mommy's* or *doggie's.* The earliest entities capable of being "possessed" are alienable objects, such as clothing, rather than inalienable entities, such as body parts. The morphological form is mastered by stage III. Phonological mastery takes much longer, however, as in the case of the plurals /s/, /z/, and /Iz/.

Uncontractible Copula

The verb *to be (am, is, are, was, were)* may serve as a main verb or as an auxiliary, or helping, verb. As a main verb it is called the copula and is followed by a noun, an adjective, or some adverbs or prepositional phrases. For example, in the sentences "He *is* a teacher," "I *am* sick," and "They *are* late," the verb *to be* is the only verb, and hence the main verb. All of these sentences contain the copula. In one sentence the copula is followed by a noun, *teacher;* in the second, by an adjective, *sick;* and in the third, by an adverb, *late.*

The copula appears initially in an uncontractible or full form (R. Brown, 1973). The notion of uncontractibility is based on those adult uses of the copula in which it is not permissible to form a contraction. In the sentence "She *is* angry," we can contract the copula to form "She's angry." Thus, the copula is contractible. It is not permissible to contract the copula when the answer to a question omits known or redundant information, leaving only the verb *to be.* For example, in response to the question "Who is hungry?", it is acceptable only to say "I *am,*" not "I'm." In addition, the copula may not be contracted when it is the first or last word in a question ("*Is* he ill?" or "Do you know where she *is?*") or appears in negative sentences in which *not* is contracted *(n't),* as in "He *isn't* a lawyer." It would be incorrect to say "He'sn't a lawyer." The copula may be contracted, however, if the negative is in its full form, as in "He's not a lawyer." Finally, the copula may not be contracted in the past tense, as in "She *was* here." "She's here" is clearly present tense and would thus be incorrect because it changes the tense of the sentence.

In general, the copula, both uncontractible and contractible, is not fully mastered until stage V (J. Miller, 1981). It takes some time before the child sorts through all the copular variations for person and number *(am, is, are)* and tense *(was, were, will be, been).*

Articles

The articles *the* and *a* appear in stage II but take some time to be mastered. Initial use of *a* and *the* is probably undifferentiated, and it is sometimes difficult to ascertain from the child's pronunciation which article is being used. For adults, the indefinite article *a* is used for nonspecific reference and the definite *the* denotes specific reference. In addition, pragmatic considerations of informativeness influence article use. New information is generally marked with *a,* whereas old information is signaled by *the.* For example, you might introduce a new topic with "I need *a* new car." The subject of an automobile is new information, and the specific vehicle has not been identified. In your next sentence you might say, "*The* red one I saw last night was beautiful." Since *car* has already been mentioned, it is old information, and you have now identified a specific automobile. For both reasons, *the* is appropriate.

Distinctions in article use do not appear early. In general, articles are first acquired in a nominative, or naming, function. For example, the child might point to an object and say, "See the puppy." Initially the indefinite article tends to predominate, as in expressions such as "That's *a* kitty." As the child begins to use articles for reference, he uses the definite article predominantly, as in "*The* kitty go meow" when he's describing the behavior of cats in general. Use of the indefinite article in referencing expressions is acquired later (Emslie & Stevenson, 1981).

The age of article acquisition varies widely among children. Three-year-olds generally observe the indefinite-definite distinction, although they tend to overuse the definite article (Warden, 1976). This overuse, discussed under presuppositional skills, may reflect the child's egocentric assumption that more is known by his listener than adult speakers would assume. By age 4, the child is more capable of making complicated inferences about the listener's needs (Emslie & Stevenson, 1981; J. Miller, 1981). In addition, the 4-year-old knows that he must use *some* and *any* rather than *a* and *the* with mass nouns, such as *sand* and *salt* (Gordon, 1982). It has been noted that some children as old as 9 years, however, continue to overuse the definite article (Warden, 1976).

Regular Past

As we mentioned earlier, the regular past tense *-ed* marker is acquired after the child has demonstrated the use of a limited number of irregular past verbs. Few regular past inflected verbs appear at the single-word level (Trantham & Pedersen, 1976). Once the child acquires the regular past tense rule, he overgeneralizes it to irregular past tense verbs, producing forms such as *comed, eated,* and *falled.* Like other morphemes, the regular past has several phonological variations. The voiced /d/ follows voiced consonants, as in *begged* (/bɛgd/), and the unvoiced /t/ follows unvoiced consonants, as in *walked* (/wɔkt/). The third variation, /Id/ or /əd/, follows words ending in /t/ or /d/, such as *sighted* (/saItId/). The /Id/ form is acquired later than the voiced-voiceless /d-t/ distinction, which may explain why the regular past ending only occasionally overgeneralizes to irregular verbs ending in /t/ or /d/, such as *heard, told,* and *hurt* (Slobin, 1971).

Third Person Singular Marker: Regular and Irregular

The person marker on the verb is governed by the person (I, you, he/she) and number (he/she, they) of the subject of the sentence. In English the only present tense marker is an *s* on the third person singular verb, as in "That dog barks too much" or "She runs quickly." All other forms are uninflected, as in *I run, you dance, we sit,* and *they laugh.* The third person singular marker is redundant in most instances, since the subject generally expresses person and number. Only a few English verbs, such as *do* and *have*, are irregular. Although the regular and irregular forms appear in stage II, they are not mastered until stage V, and there is a long period of inconsistent use (Trantham & Pedersen, 1976).

Uncontractible Auxiliary

In general, the auxiliary or helping verb *to be* develops more slowly than the copula. Brown did not report on other helping verbs, such as *do* and *have*. Unlike the copula, the auxiliary is followed by a verb, as in "She *is* singing," which is a present progressive form. The uncontractible auxiliary is most frequent in the past tense, in which contraction of "He *was* eating" to "He's eating" would change the meaning. Like the copula, the uncontractible auxiliary *to be* is also used when it is the first or last word in a sentence, when the negative is contracted, or when redundant information is omitted, as in "He *is*" in response to the question "Who's painting?" The uncontractible auxiliary is mastered by stage V (J. Miller, 1981).

Contractible Copula

The contractible copula is mastered in late stage V or afterward (J. Miller, 1981). The copula is contractible if it can be contracted, whether or not it is actually contracted. Therefore, "Mommy *is* tall" and "Mommy's tall" are both examples of the contractible copula. The form does not alter the meaning of the sentence.

The copula may take many forms to reflect person and number. In general, the *is* and *are* forms develop before *am* (Trantham & Pedersen, 1976). The *is* form tends to be overused, contributing to singular-plural confusion, such as "He *is* fast" and "They *is* big" or "We *is* hungry." The overlearning of contractions, such as *'s* and *'re*, also seems to add to the confusion. Contracted forms are short, often unemphasized, and therefore easily undetected when used incorrectly.

There is considerable variation with *it's*. Initially, young children use *it's* and *it* interchangeably (Bellugi-Klima, 1969; R. Brown, 1973). In addition, the copula that appears on *it's* generalizes only very gradually.

Contractible Auxiliary

The development of the auxiliary is similar to that of the copula in the contractible form. The auxiliary *is* and *are* forms precede the *am* form, as in the copula. The contractible auxiliary is mastered after stage V.

≡

FOR DISCUSSION AND REVIEW

1. What is the importance of Roger Brown's "MLU" and how is it used in the study of language development of young children?

2. What is the formula used to calculate a child's MLU? What variables must be considered in its calculation? Is this unit sufficient to determine a child's language complexity? Are there any shortcomings? Why or why not?

3. Summarize Brown's rules for counting morphemes. Be sure to include examples.

4. Brown proposes several stages of development that change with increased MLU. Conduct some research of your own to determine whether or not these stages coincide with certain cognitive skills in young children.

5. In Brown's second stage of development, what criteria does he use to isolate specific morphemes that determine the requirements of this stage? What are the characteristics of these morphemes? Give examples of each.

6. Brown discovered that in the majority of cases, the prepositions "in" and "on" are the only two that occur frequently enough in the children's speech to declare that they are acquired in stage two of development. What reasons might there be to account for the presence of these prepositions in particular as opposed to such words as "beside" or "near"?

7. Summarize the process of verb acquisition that Brown describes. Which verbs are learned first? Which verbs last? How do we account for this?

10

Learning and Using a Second Language

Jeannine Heny

Remember trying to learn a second language and all of the frustrations of an endless list of conjugations, proper spellings, pronunciations, and intonations? The essays in this section have focused on the process of language acquisition, the developmental stages involved in acquiring language, and the possibility of universal characteristics in the acquisition process of children and adults alike. In this selection, Jeannine Heny, professor of English at Indiana University of Pennsylvania, offers a detailed look at the process of learning a second language and discusses the reasons for the frustrations we experience when we attempt to do so. She discusses the differences between the acquisition processes of first and second languages with regard to the "descriptivist" and "native language interference" theories. Heny also examines Chomsky's theory of "universal grammar" in the context of newer theories that investigate topics such as "competition models" and "creative construction" in the process of acquiring a second language. Heny's study presents a clear illustration of the important and somewhat controversial impact bilingualism is making on the world of modern linguistics and education.

INTRODUCTION

English is taking over the globe. A newsmagazine recently reported that nearly one of every seven people in the world claims some knowledge of English, a required subject in just over 100 countries.[1] Obviously, this leads to some comical situations: imagine the puzzled native speaker abroad who finds "half-fresh grapefruit," "raped carrots," or "frightened eggs" on her breakfast menu.[2] A small and popular pamphlet available in airports documents the problem of international English usage through simple pictures of signs. A Belgian tailor proudly proclaims "Come in and have a fit." An Athens hotel displays a carefully adorned sign at its

---

[1] McBee (1985).
[2] Cited from Nigel Rees, "Quote . . . Unquote" in Duff (1981), introduction.

main desk: "If you consider our help impolite, you should see the manager!" A baker's shop in Bombay insists, "We are number one loafers."[3]

If these anecdotes seem funny to speakers of English, they are nevertheless an uncomfortable reminder of how difficult it is to master the intricacies of a foreign language. Many a reader will recall the experience of trying to use a phrase she has carefully drilled for years in the classroom, only to see her hopes of communication crushed as her hearer's eyes fill with confusion or bemusement.

Why is it so easy to learn a first language, but so difficult to learn a second? Why can a mere infant achieve with ease a task that remains beyond the reach of many a mature, sophisticated, college-educated twenty-year-old, even after years of hard work? The widespread idea that children learn languages more readily than adults is not new: Quintillian argued for the teaching of Greek to young boys in ancient Rome. But only in the past two decades have the causes of this disparity been so intensely debated.

The three sections that follow each focus on one of three complex domains where answers to this elusive question have emerged:

1. Native language interference
2. The adult mind: biological and cognitive issues
3. Social factors

Each area raises special theoretical problems of interest to language learners and teachers alike, while offering some possible clues to adult-child learning differences, which we adopt as a guiding theme. Finally, the conclusion examines briefly some popular beliefs and recent scholarly opinions about the advantages and disadvantages of having a second language in childhood.

NATIVE LANGUAGE INTERFERENCE

In the forties and fifties, the *descriptivist* thinking that dominated linguistics viewed language acquisition in children as a matter of "habit formation," much like other kinds of learning. Heavily influenced by learning theories then current in psychology, linguists assumed that children learn language much as they learn, say, the names of the planets, or the "Star-Spangled Banner." Parents provide model sentences, children repeat them; children make mistakes, parents correct; children practice, parents repeat again. The end result, after a few years, is articulate human beings armed with all of the linguistic patterns needed to communicate.

Under this descriptivist view, there was no reason to distinguish first-

---

[3] Lo Bello (1986).

and second-language learning: both were thought to consist largely of memorization, repetition, and drill. Presumably, if older learners had more trouble doing the job, it was because they were less motivated, had less time, or because their first set of habits was so firmly entrenched that it "interfered" with their ability to properly master a second set.

In learning anything new, one draws on prior knowledge. Often, this helps: since I learned to type on a conventional typewriter, I was able to "transfer" my typing skills directly to the computer keyboard being used to write this article. But transfer can also hinder learning: had my computer's manufacturer decided to put all the letters in unfamiliar places, I would have been at a considerable disadvantage, as anyone with experience with two different keyboards knows: inevitably, knowledge of one system will get in the way when the typist is trying to master another.

Extending this commonsense reasoning to language, linguists and educators assumed that firmly established habits from people's native language would carry over to any new language they tried to learn. If your first language has verbs at the end of the sentence, it was thought that you would put them there in your second language (or L2). If this turned out to be undesirable, as in English, you would need to practice hard to "unlearn" the familiar native language (or L1) pattern and internalize the correct one. Many who accepted this view felt that the learner's most important task was to overcome transfer. They advocated extensive comparative study of language pairs, called *contrastive analysis*, to determine the points of difference between languages. The results were considered useful for teachers, who could identify learner errors beforehand, and thus prevent them. The examples below suggest how diverse the phenomena are that have been attributed to transfer in the few decades since contrastive analysis became popular.

Most obvious are patterns that never occur in English, but look like word-for-word translations from the native language — for instance, when a German or Dutch speaker says one of the following:

* Speak you English?
* Yesterday have I the letter not written.
* When learned you German?[4]

Equally easy to see are transfers of sound patterns. Many readers will recognize the stereotypical English speaker's rendition of French *parlay-voo Fransay?*, in which virtually every sound is an English one substituting for its rather different French equivalent. The spelling *ay*, for example, stands here for a double vowel sound where the tongue glides from one position to another, as in English *play* or *stay*. While such *diphthongs* are common in English, they are rare in French: this one, *ay*, does not occur at all in French.

---

[4] The asterisks here and later indicate ungrammatical sentences or forms.

More commonly, transfer takes place at a more abstract level. For instance, a word's grammatical category might be assigned to its translated counterpart. Hakuta (1987, p. 42) reports that the five-year-old Japanese girl Uguisu said things like *I just mustake* (sic) and *You're mustaking* in English, assuming that English *mistake*, like its Japanese counterpart, is a verb. Swan and Smith (1987, p. 23) report that Scandinavian speakers typically say things like *She spoke to me quite polite.* Since Scandinavian languages make no overt distinction between adjectives like *polite* and their corresponding adverbs (here, *politely*), speakers of these languages seem to assume that a single form will suffice in English.

Slightly more subtle, yet still directly reflected in surface patterns, is the case where an L2 category is missing in the native language. Japanese, Thai, and Chinese have no category *article*, and thus have no words analogous to English *the* and *a*. This time, instead of putting similar elements in a different order, the speaker must learn a whole new type of word. This typically causes serious problems; even the most advanced speakers may have difficulty getting articles in all the right places. These examples were spoken by Chinese learners:

*He finished the school last year.

*He smashed the vase in the rage.

*Xiao Ying is a tallest girl in the class.[5]

Consider also a similar case drawn from semantics. In French and Spanish, when referring to parts of the body or very closely associated objects, the correct possessive form is *the*, not *my*, *your*, etc. Thus, one says "He broke *his* pencil," but (roughly) "He broke *the* arm" (meaning English "his arm"). Speakers of first languages where this distinction is not made seem to "transfer" the expectation that it does not exist: hence, they continue to use phrases like *his arm*, ignoring the correct form they hear from native speakers.

Unfortunately, most cases are not so clear-cut, even where first-language influence is undeniable. Consider, for instance, a recent study of English pronunciation by Brazilian Portuguese speakers. Roy Major (1987), puzzled by the extent to which the words *phonetics* and *fanatics* sounded alike in his students' speech, set out to examine the development of the vowel sounds in the words *bed* and *bad*, respectively. As the study progressed, Major found a puzzling fact: as students' pronunciation improved overall, their mastery of the sound [ɛ], as in English *bed* or *set*, became dramatically *worse*. This phenomenon was quite systematic, and unexpected, especially given that a very similar vowel sound exists in Portuguese. After careful study, Major concluded that a very subtle type

---

[5] Swan & Smith (1987), p. 231.

of error was being made early in the learning process. English has two vowels, [ɛ] as in *set* and [æ] as in *cat* or *sat*. Portuguese has only one vowel in the same range, pronounced more like the sound in English *set*. Confronted with this new complexity, the early learner concludes that a single phoneme, or sound, exists in English, just as in Portuguese. Furthermore, the sound adopted is the Portuguese vowel, which makes both of the above words sound rather like *set*. With intensive classroom practice on the new, "difficult" sound [æ], the student begins to improve. However, influenced by her original unconscious hypothesis that only one sound is involved, she begins to say words like *said* and *head* as if they were *sad* and *had*.

Hungarian college students provide another example of complex transfer.[6] These non-native English speakers tend to produce words like *cruelism, *deconcentrate, and *ignoration (substituting for correct *cruelty, dilute,* and *ignorance*). Again, the explanation is abstract. Hungarian cannot be said to have a direct equivalent for the deviant English words; nor could any Hungarian word-formation rules be equated to the ones underlying the English errors. But Hungarian *does* have many *affixes* which, like *-ism, de-,* and *-tion,* join to the beginning or end of an existing word to form a new one. In English this kind of affix attaches to only a small set of words: it is easier to find a bad formation with *-ism* than a good one (e.g., *stupidism, *redism, and *intelligentism versus *radicalism*). But in Hungarian, the situation is very different. Such affixes are highly productive: that is, they attach to just about any word of the right category, giving a new word with a predictably related meaning. Hungarian speakers seem to be transferring not a pattern, or even a rule, of their native language. They are transferring something even less tangible: the *expectation* that if you have an affix like *-tion,* you can add it to any eligible word.

To summarize, there are a great number of ways to define what a learner may "transfer": these include sounds, word order patterns (or more likely the rules that underlie them), abstract facts about individual words, plus a wide range of expectations about how language works and about what elements it includes.

But this fascinating diversity points to one of two major problems with the notion of "transfer": it is practically impossible to define. As originally conceived, transfer seemed to operate on actual sounds or strings of words. But even the limited list of examples above range far beyond that simple level. Is it principles a speaker transfers? Or word-patterns? Sounds, or "expectations"?

The second problem involves predicting transfer: in principle, interference from L1 to L2 should be equally likely at every point where the two languages differ. Unfortunately, it is not. In the early seventies, one

---

[6] Cited by Hatch (1983, p. 42), from work by Nemser.

study after another intending to document transfer by counting student errors yielded the same discouraging result: at best, only about half of the errors made by actual language students could be explained by interference from their native language. Most studies reported figures lower than that, one reporting numbers as low as five percent![7] Despite its intuitive appeal, contrastive analysis was a misleading basis for teaching, since it encouraged the idea that *only* first-language influence caused learner errors. To make the notion of transfer useful to teachers as well as to theoretical linguists, there must be some way to predict the places where L1 interference will occur, and where it will not.

Markedness

To see one way this might be done, return for a moment to the typewriter analogy. Suppose you learned to type on a rather idiosyncratic typewriter, where the letter *a* stood at the extreme top right of the keyboard, forcing you to stretch your right hand in an unnatural way every time you typed a word spelled with *a*. This would presumably take you some time to learn. Now, suppose you bought a computer whose keyboard placed *a* somewhere in the middle row, its "normal" position. Common sense suggests that you would adjust very easily to the new configuration. It seems equally obvious that you would find the opposite change (from midkeyboard to extreme top right) difficult to make. In general, one might assume that transfer of learning from an "unnatural" value to a more "natural" one would be expected, rather than transfer in the other direction.

The same commonsense argument applies to language. If very few languages have a given feature, and if children find it difficult to acquire, the feature is assumed to be universally "marked," or less natural, than its easier and more common counterpart(s). One might expect such a feature not to transfer — that is, not to be carried over from L1 to L2. Take, for instance, the French sound spelled *u* in words like *tu* or *plus*. Most English speakers learning French have special difficulty with this sound, using the vowel of English *food* or *moose* instead. The target sound in French involves a far-front tongue position *and* rounding of the lips. As it turns out, this is an unusual combination which gives the sound a "marked" status in comparison with the English sound. A summary look at the world's languages confirms this judgment: relatively few languages contain front, round vowels, whereas French, to the dismay of the potential learner, has three. In contrast, many languages have vowels similar to the offending English one.

Markedness considerations can greatly enrich the predictive power

---

[7] Study by Dulay and Burt (1974a), cited in Hakuta (1987), p. 38.

of the notion that transfer from L1 affects L2, provided that markedness itself can be defined adequately. Physical factors like tongue position and lip rounding may play a role in determining markedness for sounds; but they cannot be the determining factor elsewhere, such as when dealing with word order.

Some structures may be more natural because they are easier to process and understand. Children may learn a construction faster if it involves a clear one-to-one correspondence between sound units and meaning: thus, if the English progressive is analyzed as broken into two elements, *is* plus *-ing* as in *John is running*, it must be seen as relatively marked, or difficult. Persian, in contrast, has a single prefix, *mi-*, to mark the progressive, meaning ongoing action. However, the Persian form is itself marked on similar grounds, since it carries "progressive" meaning only in the past tense. If an element only *sometimes* signals a given meaning, it is semantically inconsistent, and a potential stumbling block for learners. For another example, compare English and German noun plurals. In English, plurals are almost always formed with the same ending *-s*, as in *books*; German, however, has several different plural forms. Obviously, the German situation must be more marked, since it requires that the learner associate a single "plural" meaning with several different forms, as well as keeping track of which plural type must go with each noun in the language.

One form which might be viewed as semantically consistent, hence easily learnable, is the little particle attached to nouns in some languages to show that the noun is "subject" or "object" of its sentence. In Japanese, for instance, a word can be immediately identified as "object of" the sentence, because it carries the particle *o* attached, as in *hon-o*, which means "book-object." English, in contrast, marks the "object" by its position: *book* in isolation is neither a "subject" nor an "object." Only in the whole sentence *My friend sold the book* can you see, from the position of *book*, that it is the object of the verb *sell*. But, in order to grasp the role of *book*, the English child must keep track of several words at once, whereas the Japanese child need only look at one word. So, as far as processing difficulty is concerned, the English-type object seems to be more marked.

Another example seems to involve rule systems and how they work, rather than processing difficulty. French and English differ in the way they encode direct object pronouns: English uses full pronouns, placed after the verb, while French places a special kind of stressless "clitic" pronoun before the verb, the form *le* below:

French: Je le vois.

      I it see

English: I see it.

In principle, if transfer occurred wherever languages differed, we would expect both French and English speakers to make mistakes like those given below:

French learners of English:

*I it see.

English learners of French:

*Je vois le.

As any French teacher will verify, the English learner makes the predicted error all too often. But, interestingly, it seems that the French learner does not. How can this be explained?

In terms of pronunciation, Romance clitics seem to act as if they were one with the verb they attach to: this combination of two words into one may in itself be marked. In addition, the clitic complicates the grammar of languages like French, at least on the surface, since it violates normal French sentence order (compare the sentence above with *Je vois le chat,* "I see the cat," where the object *le chat* comes after the verb). Thus, the French structure comes out as more marked on at least two counts. It is no wonder if transfer operates only in one direction here. We should expect the unmarked subject-verb-object of English *I see it* to transfer, but not its marked French counterpart.

A more subtle example comes from a Japanese learner of English:

> In Japan, industrial product is cheap. Because we have an economic growth. But vegetable is so expensive. Because we Japanese have a few lands.

The speaker used words and phrases like *industrial product* and *vegetable,* which require an overt plural ending *-s* in English. However, in Japanese, if plurality is clear from context, the plural need not be marked with the Japanese equivalent of the *-s* ending. If languages in general avoid redundant, or extra, markings, it is easy to see why Japanese speakers transfer this aspect of their language to English: one would expect English speakers to master the corresponding Japanese rule with relative ease.

Thus, markedness may result from physical difficulty, processing complexity, facts about the grammars of particular languages, or even universal features of human language. Linguists working in this area continue to search for a single, rigorous definition for this intuitively appealing notion.

Linguistic Distance

Whatever its ultimate definition, markedness clearly involves some inherent property of linguistic elements. We turn next to a rather different idea: that the relationship between L1 and L2, or more specifically the learner's perception of closeness between them, influences the likelihood of transfer.

Some believe that interference is more likely if the elements involved are perceived as similar in L1 and L2. For instance, consider the German sound normally spelled *ch*,[8] roughly like the sound you make when gargling (for a more precise description, see Callary's article in this volume). English speakers tend to substitute the English *k*. This results in the name *Bach*, which contains the unfamiliar sound, being pronounced something like English *Back*. However, when learning Bantu clicks, which clearly do not resemble any English sound, English speakers make a series of noises that (unfortunately) do not occur in either English or Bantu languages. The point is that they do not transfer the English sound. Major (1987) notes this, and attributes it to the closeness speakers perceive between *[ch]* and *[k]*.

To this he adds another surprising observation, again related to closeness. Recall that the French front, round vowel *u* (phonetically [y]) is difficult to pronounce for English speakers, who usually substitute the sound of English *food* instead. Amazingly enough, many an advanced English learner gives the impression of having an "accent" in French, not because of the difficult sound of French *tu*, but because of the relatively *easier* sound found in French words like *tout* and *fou*. Why? Learners sense from the start that the unfamiliar front, round vowel will be difficult. The totally new sound has one factor going in its favor: there is no native-language equivalent, almost but not quite identical, to provide a lasting source of interference. But with the easier sound, precisely the opposite is true. English [u] (as in *food*) is close enough to its French equivalent to pass as acceptable in the early stages when other major difficulties claim the beginner's attention. Later, lulled into thinking her version of that sound is correct, the learner never goes back to rectify it. Instead, she retains the English equivalent — which, as it turns out, differs subtly from the French target sound.

A similar observation comes from data by Jacqueline Schachter (1974), who recorded the use of relative clauses by speakers of four languages: Arabic, Persian, Japanese, and Chinese. The Arabic and Persian relative clause structure resembles, but is not identical to, the English pattern. For instance, where the English speaker says *the man that I talked to*, the Persian speaker simply inserts an extra pronoun, i.e., *the man that I talked to him*. In contrast, the Chinese and Japanese forms are radically different: the above phrase in Japanese corresponds roughly to *I talk man*.

Which group produces worse English relative clauses? As one might expect, the Japanese and Chinese speakers produce far fewer relative clauses than the other two groups, suggesting that they are uncomfortable

---

[8] A velar fricative, phonetically [x].

using the English form. But, interestingly, the ones they do form are *better* than those produced by Persian or Arabic speakers. Again, the same plausible explanation is at hand: the very closeness that should help learning actually hinders it: the Persian and Arabic structures look so similar to the English one that the learner is "tricked," as it were, into transfer. In contrast, the Japanese speaker perceives at the outset that his pattern is radically different, and avoids interference.

Roger Andersen (1983) has proposed yet another, possibly related condition that could help predict transfer. Called "transfer-to-somewhere," this principle claims that transfer will occur only if something the learner hears in the second language encourages it — if, in other words, some pattern in the second language looks enough like an L1 structure to trick the learner into transferring from L1 to L2. Of course, the problem here is: How do you identify a plausible "somewhere"? What does the learner have to hear in the second language to encourage L1 transfer?

In some cases, it may be no more than a similarity in sound between words in the two languages. One kind of interference that virtually never occurs by mistake is the borrowing of actual words. When one thinks of the phenomenal task of keeping two or more rather extensive mental *lexicons*, or word lists, separate, this is quite amazing, and has been a subject of wonder for psycholinguists. Such inadvertent word borrowing seems to be facilitated only when the two languages contain some identical or nearly identical word, as when the author's husband, accustomed to using Dutch, proclaimed that he had been recently *spitting* in his garden (the Dutch verb *spit* means "dig").

THE NATURE OF THE ADULT MIND

So far, it has become clear that a refined notion of first-language interference gives one answer to our original question: Why do people learn their first language so much better than any other? To set the stage for a second answer, which will involve biological and cognitive issues, it is important to look carefully at some central assumptions about language.

Language as Biological Endowment

First note that, in suggesting constraints on the possibility of transfer, we have implicitly assumed that human languages can be compared, or measured against one another by some kind of universal standard. It would make no sense to talk about concepts like "markedness" and "closeness" unless there were some valid way to define such notions — some way that, by definition, must be independent of any particular language. Without explicitly saying so, we have been gradually taking on ideas about language that were not part of the earlier descriptivist view, under which the concept of "transfer" arose.

Noam Chomsky's development of generative grammar in the sixties provided a new framework, better able to handle these ideas. Chomsky challenged the central assumptions of the descriptivist framework, casting serious doubts on the prevailing view of language. The most fundamental property of language, Chomsky pointed out, is *creativity*, not repetition. We are capable of uttering an infinite range of sentences we could never have heard or practiced. Thus, underlying language, there must be a system of rules and principles, *not* a list of habitually linked word patterns memorized by persistent drill.

In fact, Chomsky claims, humans could never learn systems as complex as natural language by simply hearing sentences. This he relates to what he called "Plato's problem": how do we know so much about things we never consciously study? In learning a language, a child comes to "know" much more than is available to him in the sentences he hears. The principles that have governed human language for thousands of years are so abstract and difficult that they have not yet been fully spelled out by linguists. Since no one consciously *knows* them, no one could deliberately learn them.[9] Yet, amazingly, children appear to absorb this complex maze of linguistic facts with no visible effort—and at a stage when their cognitive systems would be nowhere near mature enough to consciously grasp the system's underlying principles, even if they *were* understood by linguists or grammarians.

According to Chomsky, children can achieve this apparent miracle because, as a species, we have a biologically determined specialization for language. Current theory makes a very strong claim about the biological underpinnings of language: that the most central principles of language are available to us innately, as an automatic result of being human. A child need only grow, and have exposure to some language, to gain access to them. These are the principles of UG, or *universal grammar*.

Note that this does *not* mean that a baby can use innate linguistic principles to speak or understand language. Many biologically based behaviors do not show up at birth, even though they are part of our genetic code; although babies do not walk, we assume that they are genetically programmed to do so when the time comes. No one would deny that sexual traits and behavior are genetically determined, even though they do not show up for ten years or more after birth. As unfamiliar as the idea of genetically encoded knowledge may seem, it is not at all unrealistic.

Adults, Children, and UG

Of course, a theory that says that children have access to a special biologically based program for language acquisition provides an especially

---

[9] For discussion of the principles known thus far, see the article by F. Heny, this volume; also, for more detail, see Radford (1981).

neat answer to our original question: adults learn languages badly because they *are* adults, and not children. Thus, they have lost access to the principles of UG available to them in infancy.

Many believe that there is a "critical period," up to about adolescence, during which one's first language must be learned if it is to be learned at all. Once this critical period for language has passed, the brain's tissue loses its plasticity, and its capacity for acquiring language. Indeed, there is good evidence that a person with little exposure to language before puberty will suffer serious linguistic deficits.[10] Excited by the "critical period" concept, many have tried to extend it to second languages, to explain why adults virtually always learn a new language with some degree of foreign "accent." Proponents are quick to point out that, beyond the critical period, learning even a second language is much more difficult.

Unfortunately (or fortunately for those of us past adolescence), the evidence is not one-sided. Adults often learn the grammar and vocabulary of a language well, even faster than children, despite their tendency to speak with a foreign accent. So common is the phenomenon that it has been given its own name, dubbed the "Joseph Conrad" syndrome, after the famous novelist. Conrad always spoke English with a very heavy accent, despite the acclaimed mastery of his writing. At best, this suggests that the "critical period" strongly affects only the sound system of language: other aspects *can* be acquired effectively, even quite late in life. If they, too, are subject to a critical period in L2, it must occur much later than adolescence.

Still, adults do seem to find language learning much more painful than children, who often surpass adult learners after a few months of language study. All too often, the parents in an immigrant family in this country may continue for years to use a minimal version of English, while their children pass as native speakers within a few years. If a direct biological account does not explain this, perhaps a cognitive explanation is needed. The adult mind, of course, works in fundamentally different ways from that of a child. For one thing, the mature mind has higher-level cognitive abilities of the kind needed to learn science and math. Perhaps as these develop, the brain's special automatic capacity for processing language weakens. Or possibly these other processes simply overshadow its operation. We will now look a bit closer at this last possibility.

The Competition Model

The adult brain differs from the child's in the number and complexity of its abilities. Adults can, in principle, perform any number of tasks not possible for a child under five, such as solving complex mathematics problems, reading a map, and playing chess. These activities involve cognitive abilities that are relatively inactive in children. The very complex-

---

[10] Fromkin et al. (1974).

ity this implies may stand in the way of language acquisition for adults. In other words, the innate language faculty may still be present, intact in adults, but there may be so much other activity going on inside the older brain that the language faculty cannot function undisturbed, as it did in early childhood.

Such an idea can best be made plausible by looking at error types. If adult learning patterns differ in important ways from those of children, it suggests that the adult's mind may use different methods in learning language from those automatically available to children.

If Klein (1986) is right, adult learners *are* very different in some respects from children. Young children very seldom make errors in word categories: that is, they never act as though a verb were a noun, etc., as in *Daddy give goes.* In contrast, Klein cites as a typical L2 learner a Spanish migrant worker in Germany who used a single word *abai* to mean "job," "worker," and "(I) work." For this speaker, there seems to be no clear distinction between major word types like noun and verb. In fact, Klein is not alone in claiming that, in the early stages, it is virtually impossible to assign clear "structure" to the sentences of foreign speakers he has interviewed. At times, it almost looks as though, to communicate, the beginning adult learner is content to string out nouns in roughly the right semantic groupings, not worrying about form at all, as follows (these examples are translated from German, but they sound similar in both languages):

*This country, three year.

*But me study everybody more time, no?

*The schedule, the school, everybody more long, no?[11]

Sascha Felix, working in Germany and relying on evidence like this, suggests that the beginning adult learner unwittingly uses a mental faculty rather different from the child's UG-based principles in learning a second language. Felix claims that, in childhood, the brain's language-specific capacity can operate freely, since other major cognitive systems are not yet active. However, once we reach adulthood, the story is very different. We have, by that time, a highly developed "problem-solving" ability, which is so dominant that it "competes" with the mind's normal UG component, taking over some of the task of language learning—for which, unfortunately, it is not adequately suited. From this idea comes the name Felix coined for his theory: the "competition model."

Potential evidence for this model comes from a recent study of word order in adult learners of German (Clahsen and Muysken, 1986). In a careful comparison of child L1 learners versus adult L2 learners the re-

---

[11] Felix (1985), p. 60.

searchers found a number of subtle differences. These suggest that the adult learner's mind reacts to data in a way that can be fully explained neither by appealing to first-language interference nor to universal grammar. The authors conclude that the adult must indeed be using a mental faculty that is *not* the same as the one available to the child. Their claim awaits the test of further study.

Creative Construction

Notice that Felix's conception of second-language learning denies the "critical period" any direct importance as a reason for adult language-learning difficulties. Other linguists made similar claims over a decade ago, arguing that no major, biological change comes along at puberty to "turn off" the child's innate language capacity. But unlike Felix, these other researchers stressed the possibility that adults *can*, in principle, still use the innate mechanisms available to children. In fact, in the early seventies, as generative theory gained in popularity, it was natural to wonder whether one should emphasize not the *differences*, but instead the *similarities*, between first- and second-language acquisition.

If such a view is right, one should be able to see some trace of L1-like acquisition happening in adults. Trying to test this idea, several researchers working independently[12] made an interesting discovery. A famous study done at Harvard had shown that English-speaking children acquire elements like -*ing* (e.g., in *I am running*), past tense -*ed*, and about a dozen other forms in a definite order. All children follow roughly the same order, though they may start earlier or later. Many linguists agreed that this "natural order" of acquisition must reflect the operation of the child's innate linguistic capacity. If second-language learners showed a similar pattern, they reasoned, this could be taken as evidence that the same innate mechanisms mediate both first- *and* second-language acquisition.

The results were intriguing: it turned out that, even with first languages as different as Chinese and Spanish, learners of English seemed to progress through a fixed pattern of development, mastering forms like -*ed*, -*ing*, etc. in nearly the same order. At the same time it was found that foreign speakers often make the same mistakes in their English as monolingual English infants make, rather than the errors one would expect from looking at their native language patterns. For instance, Japanese and Norwegian both require that negative elements like *not* follow verbs. Given this, if transfer were to play a role, one would expect errors like the following in both groups:

---

[12] For instance, Dulay and Burt cited in Hatch (1983), Ch. 3.

Norwegian/Japanese transfer (predicted):

*He likes it not

*She likes not the dinner

In fact, these kinds of errors virtually never occur; instead, Japanese or Norwegian speakers use the same *developmental* pattern as English children, producing strings like those below, which have no possible source in Japanese or Norwegian:

*John no go here

*We not like this

This set of observations led to a new theory, called *creative construction*, or, informally, the "L2-equals-L1" hypothesis. As the second name suggests, the new theory claimed that second-language learners start from square one, just as do children. Creative construction seemed a refreshing new way to view foreign-language learning. When Dulay and Burt published a collection of learner errors called the *Gooficon* in 1974, they thought it unnecessary to mention the native languages of learners: facts about the first language seemed simply irrelevant to the process of acquiring a second.

There were of course some differences between "natural orders" in infants and later learners: but these were thought to come from differences in cognitive skills between younger and more mature learners. For instance, young children learn present tense before past tense (*he plays* before *he played*) because it is easier to talk about the here and now, rather than distant, past events. There is no reason for the second-language learner to do the same; her more advanced state of general knowledge should assure that past situations can be easily discussed. Likewise, children learn *in* before *between*, presumably because infants are naturally fascinated with containers, and because *in* encodes a simpler concept (note that *between* involves keeping track of the position of three objects at once). Again, adults who have mastered the concept once need not do so again.

Transfer or Development?

Clearly, the claims of creative construction clash with the approach of those who favor contrastive analysis and emphasize the importance of first-language transfer. One approach says that the first language is the *only* source of learner errors; the other says it *never* causes error. It is difficult to imagine that two views needing the opposite empirical evidence could both have been accepted and taken seriously. But one must remember that each theory arose from its own assumptions about the nature of language: for those who believed language learning was habit formation, transfer made undeniable, intuitive sense. But if innate mechanisms cause us to acquire our native language, it seems difficult to imagine that these mechanisms simply "turn off" once their job is done for the native language.

Besides, looking at learner data is often tricky: many errors are ambiguous, easily tossed under either "development" or "transfer," depending on which theory you are trying to support. For example, it is well known that German speakers produce unvoiced consonants like [p], [t], and [k] at the ends of English words that should end in voiced [b], [d], and [g]. This makes the word *bag*, for instance, sound like *back*. Since German has a rule of "devoicing," which ensures this pattern for these speakers in their own language, it is natural to assume that transfer has occurred: the learners are simply using a rule from L1 (inappropriately) in L2. However, a quick visit to an English-speaking two-year-old is likely to cause doubts: children learning English as a native language typically go through a stage in which they, too, devoice final consonants, pronouncing words like *bag* as *back*. Are German L2 learners transferring the German rule? Or are they returning to the language-learning process with a "clean slate" as it were, which just happens to lead them to produce words which sound like the output of the German rule? It is impossible to say for sure.

This kind of problem arises repeatedly. For instance, children learning a first language tend to simplify syllable structure, at the earliest stages even to a simple sequence of consonant plus vowel. At the age of two, the author's daughter had three uses for *ba*, one meaning "blanket," one meaning "banana," and the third meaning "baby"; later, "blanket" became *baba*. It has been assumed that children tend to simplify toward such a CVCV pattern, pronouncing all syllables as sequences of consonant-plus-vowel, the simplest possible form.

But what of a Polynesian speaker who produces the holiday greeting *meli kalisimasu* (to decipher this one, you need to remember that this speaker's first language makes no distinction between *l* and *r*). What of Japanese speakers, who have borrowed the English phrase for a woman one dates as *garu-firendu*? They too happen to speak a native language that tends naturally toward the *same* CV pattern as is typical in child speech. Again, is the error developmental, or a case of transfer? In such cases, it is impossible to separate the two, and in fact, both may play a role.

It seems sensible to think that in general, both transfer and development (i.e., first-language-like processes) contribute to language learning. And one important new trend in theoretical work has tried to reconcile insights from both earlier theories. We will look briefly at this research in the next section.

The Parametric Approach

Until now, we have not tried to specify how universal grammar is supposed to help a child learn language. To do so, we need to introduce the notion of *parameter*, common in recent theoretical work. A parameter is basically some linguistic value that can be assigned in one of several ways. It can be imagined, using Chomsky's analogy, as a kind of "switch" in the child's head, which has a small number of possible settings. To take just one example, languages tend to place verbs and prepositions in similar positions in their phrases: either consistently before, or after, their objects. In English, both prepositions like *to* and verbs like *want* precede their objects: *to the store, (I) want a new car.* In Japanese, just the reverse is true: both kinds of words come after the nouns they relate to. If this is seen as the result of some parametric setting, it will be predictable that verbs and prepositions behave in the same way. And from the child's point of view, the learning process is automatic: he simply sees the right data, sets the relevant parameter, and gets the major word-order facts of his language virtually free.

At this point, the reader may begin to see a possible connection between the notion of "markedness" discussed earlier, and the concept of universal grammar. If universal grammar refers to the total set of general principles shared by all natural languages, it might well provide a language-independent means for spelling out what is marked and what is not. One hopeful point of contact is just this notion of *parameter*.

By definition, a child must be born with any given parametric "switch" pointing somewhere, say to setting A. If the child happens to be learning type B language data instead of type A, the switch will automatically reset when he hears the crucial sentences and becomes (unconsciously) "convinced" that setting B is needed. A language requiring the basic "default" setting, of course (i.e., the setting the child is born with), could be argued to be the most natural one for a given parameter: the child has this setting available at birth, and need not take the trouble to "reset" it in the course of acquiring language. Although the use of parameters in L2 research is new, it is viewed as highly promising by some. Hence, it is worth taking a look at one example in detail.

One widely studied parameter determines *binding*, which, for now, we can define as a principle that tells a speaker how to interpret reflexive pronouns like *himself, herself,* and *themselves*. At one end is the English setting, which basically requires a reflexive pronoun to refer to the nearest subject noun phrase, as *Mary* in this sentence:

Joan said that Mary likes herself.

At the other extreme are Japanese and Korean, which would allow *herself* to refer to either *Mary* or *Joan*. No language goes farther than that option, allowing such an element to refer *outside* the sentence in which it occurs, say to someone just mentioned by another speaker.

For binding, the child is thought to begin with the English setting, and the switch simply automatically kicks into position for Japanese when the child hears Japanese sentences equivalent to the one that follows, which could not possibly make sense unless the reflexive pronoun can mean the same as *Dad* (for simplicity, an English analog is given instead of the Japanese sentence):

Dad wants to know if Mom will shave himself.

To summarize, there are two ways that a child learner can "set" or acquire parametric values: first, he could simply keep the one he is born with: in this case, the English one. Or, he could go through the natural resetting process that occurs when his brain has taken in the crucial *triggering* data (in this case, the Japanese equivalent of the sentence above). In neither case does the child have to puzzle out the principle, even subconsciously. Nor does he have to memorize anything. These are a special set of linguistic features that simply come packaged into our genetic makeup as human beings.

Now, if all this is true, then it is possible that these switches play some important role in second-language learning as well. Suppose the L1 position for a switch has been set, and L2 data come along requiring a changed setting. This may result in problems, especially when the native language uses setting A, the original or initial unmarked setting. If, on the other hand, L1 has chosen the *more marked* setting, it might be relatively easy for a speaker to "go back" to the initial state. One line of research in fact suggests that the latter is a possibility. Ellen Broselow and Dan Finer (1985) used cartoonlike pictures to test Korean students of English on their interpretation of reflexives in various patterns. In one such picture a person thinks of two possible interpretations of the sentence, "Mr. Short expects Mr. Tall to paint himself (him)." Two images of the sentence appear in a bubble above the person's head. One image is Mr. Tall brushing paint across Mr. Short's stomach. The other is Mr. Tall brushing paint across his own stomach. As mentioned above, Korean is like Japanese, in that the "long-distance" option, assumed to be more marked, operates. Since reflexive interpretation is too unconscious and obscure a feature to have been consciously taught in language classes, one might expect these learners of English to transfer their Korean long-distance pattern. Interestingly enough, they did not. Korean speakers assumed neither the English, highly restricted, initial setting, nor the broad Korean one. They chose instead a setting somewhere in between, less restrictive than English but more so than Korean. Broselow and Finer interpreted this as a move *toward*, if not *to*, the initial unmarked setting.

This area is complex, difficult, and very new; we obviously cannot do it full justice given the scope of this article. However, it should be clear that the parametric status of a feature might help explain the possibility that it will transfer from L1 to L2. For instance, why do speakers seem to switch so easily from one major word order to another, as happens when English speakers learn Japanese? If word order results, as many believe, from the setting of some parameter, this new approach could ultimately offer the needed explanation.

Conscious versus Unconscious Learning

Both creative construction and the later parametric approach embody the expectation that first- and second-language acquisition share important properties. Yet the context in which the two take place is radically different. One has only to spend one period in a typical college foreign-language classroom to see that a language student's experience has little in common with the child's first linguistic encounters. This might well lead us to yet another answer to our vexing problem: adults do not learn languages well because they are not taught in the right way. The formal, classroom situation is ill-equipped to duplicate the supportive, playful mood of parent-child interaction at its best.

Is there some way to make second-language teaching as "natural" as possible? Above all, should we not avoid teaching grammar rules, concentrating, just as mothers do, on *what* is being said, not *how* to say it? At least one outspoken scholar, Stephen Krashen, responds with a clear "yes." Influenced by the Chomskian framework, Krashen makes a distinction between "learning" and "acquisition." For him, "learning" occurs when we consciously memorize grammar rules. It is basically like the activity that goes on when one learns geographical or historical facts. "Acquisition," in contrast, is the result of innate processes, and happens naturally when a child, unconsciously and without concerted effort, mysteriously absorbs the principles of her native tongue. For Krashen, "learning" provides a speaker with a *monitor*, or a set of formal, consciously available grammatical rules. But, he claims, the monitor is of very little use: since it works at a speed much slower than normal speech, it can at best be used in written forms like essays or letters. Some learners seem to be aware of this rather clumsy apparatus while speaking a second language: they are aware of their mistakes, they "hear" them. But they cannot correct them and maintain reasonable fluency. Consciously memorized grammatical rules, for Krashen, play virtually no role in producing correct sentences. Some adults tend to feel that grammatical rules help them, but, for Krashen's followers, catering to this feeling would be misguided. Real mastery of a second language has its basis in acquisition, not learning. And to promote acquisition, the teacher must simply provide "comprehensible input": that is, sentences a learner can understand. The learner herself will do the rest.

Suspicion of conscious grammar rules as a teaching tool goes back as far as language teaching itself: St. Augustine favored an educational policy that generally allowed pupils to discover principles on their own. Applied to language teaching, this emphasized using a language, rather than memorizing the rules of its grammar.[13] But by the Middle Ages, this

---

[13] Kelly (1969), p. 35.

commonsense notion had lost ground, and the accepted method was to teach the rules of classical Latin and Greek. Still, some teachers resisted. In the sixteenth century, Georgius Haloinus Cominius drew a firm reproach from his famous mentor Erasmus when he advocated the complete abandonment of grammar in teaching, saying "The authority of a grammarian is, in itself, worth nothing."[14] Erasmus himself was suspicious of depending too heavily on grammar rules alone; but he advocated a middle course between using the language and teaching about it.

Though controversial, the revolt against formal grammar again became quite popular in the Renaissance: one particularly vocal opponent called it a "monstrous absurdity" to "bid [the students] give an account why they speake Latine right, before they can in any wise speake properly."[15] Grammar was seen by many as a boring complication to the real task of teaching language. This trend toward "inductive" language teaching could only be reinforced in the next century with the very important work of the educator Comenius, and with the need to teach modern languages, for which adequate grammars were not available. A French tutor of Mary Tudor expressed his frustration at this last problem: "I have nat neverthelesse founde rules infalibles, because it is nat possible to finde any suche."[16]

Gradually, this inductive idea grew into a "naturalistic" approach to language teaching, which tried to teach a second language in essentially the way a child learns his native language: by imitation and practice. The early nineteenth-century educator Lemare, heavily influenced by Rousseau's ideas, espoused this approach: no mother ever explains a grammatical rule or assigns a vocabulary list, reasoned Lemare. So why should the language teacher do so? Attractive and modern as this early "naturalistic" approach seems, its proponents still assumed that imitation and repetition are the basic ingredients of successful language learning. In the modern Chomskian era, naturalistic teaching approaches are again gaining ground, but within a greatly changed framework.

Interestingly enough, some quite recent trends almost seem to go against current naturalistic methods, encouraging teachers to explain principles on the grounds that consciously learned information can be made automatic, or subconscious in the way that linguistic knowledge must be.[17] This time, however, the emphasis is on other aspects of the learning process, not on grammatical rules. Some believe that it is helpful to point out cognates (words that are alike or nearly alike) in L1 and L2. Others claim that teachers could train students to use one learning strategy rather than another, as suggested later in section 3. This is, of course,

---

[14] Kelly (1969), p. 36.
[15] Kelly (1969), p. 37.
[16] Kelly (1969), p. 39.
[17] See the comments in Rubin (1987), p. 16, and the sources cited there.

a very different type of "conscious" control over the language process, and one worth pursuing, though it is too new to report on in detail here.

SOCIAL FACTORS

While looking so closely at the cognitive, biological, and pedagogical problems in L2 learning, we risk missing a crucial fact: in order to learn anything, you must *want* to learn. Children usually begin to talk in the nurturing warmth of parental care, and at a stage when their emotional needs are simple, if strong. Compare this with the situation an adult often faces. An adult who is learning among strangers, conscious of the fear of failure, embarrassed about making new and unfamiliar sounds, and suspicious about the unfamiliar customs and dress of a foreign culture may feel too threatened or uncomfortable to succeed. Thus, even if all other things were equal, emotional and social factors might often cause adults to learn language less perfectly than children. This is especially important in light of the fact that proper phrasing and sentence patterns do not in themselves make an effective speaker. The discussion that follows looks briefly at why this is so.

Communicative Competence

In 1972 Dell Hymes coined the term "communicative competence" to refer especially to those dimensions of language that are *beyond* formal grammar. Mastery of a language must ultimately be measured not by structures, but by one's ability to *use* those structures effectively in day-to-day situations: to get information, tease, tell jokes, persuade, suggest, or criticize. A recent, very strong trend in language teaching emphasizes this communicative competence as a central part of what must be called *proficiency* in a foreign language (see Figure 10.1). There are thousands of situations where a non-native speaker runs into trouble communicating effectively, but where grammar *per se* is irrelevant.

If you look carefully, you will see that two of the examples in this article's opening paragraph have nothing to do with rules: they are simply cases where a non-native speaker unknowingly used a phrase that happens to convey idiomatic meaning *(have a fit* and *if you think . . . you should see . . . !)* From the same source comes another sign with the same problem, this time from a Moscow hotel: "If this is your first visit to the U.S.S.R., you are welcome to it."

Almost every foreign-language learner will remember some embarrassing moment when she simply did not know the "right" thing to say, but where the problem was one of social patterning, not grammar. How does one greet a friend, begin a conversation, or get a stranger's attention in a new language? Should one make a request directly ("Please give me

Figure 10.1. Communicative Competence. A recent collection on classroom activities suggests the following game instead of traditional question-and-answer drills on a student's name and background. Each student draws a "mystery name tag" like the one shown here, encoding the personal information listed here. The cards are then put into a group. Each participant must draw one tag and find its owner by asking questions of the others present (from Klippel 1987, p. 15).

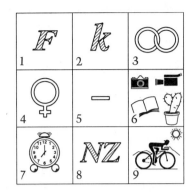

1. first name
2. surname
3. marital status
4. children
5. pets
6. hobbies
7. pet hates
8. favorite country
9. Where would you like to be now?

a brownie"), or chance an indirect hint ("Those brownies look great!"). What about accepting or refusing an offer? The English phrase *thank you* implies acceptance of something offered, while its French translation, *merci,* means just the opposite ("No, thank you"). In every linguistic situation there lurks the possibility of being misunderstood because of the social conventions a culture attaches to language use. These conventions are often quite unconscious. Have you ever stopped to think, for instance, that the sentence "We *must* have lunch together sometime soon" rarely leads to an actual lunch date? Or that "I'm home most evenings, just come anytime" is *not* to be automatically interpreted as an invitation in American culture?

The pitfalls of effective communication in L2 range from obvious to almost imperceptible. Before reading on, look at the two English questions below. On the surface, of course, they mean the same thing. But would you use them in the same situations?

Are you going to Baltimore next week?

You're going to Baltimore next week, are you?

Most speakers agree that the second question expects a positive answer, while the first is neutral. And, a speaker using the second form is subtly claiming a closer relationship with the hearer than the first, by asserting knowledge of the hearer's plans, and by the use of the familiar "tag question" *are you?* It is hard to imagine how a non-native speaker could "pick up" such nuances without extensive daily contact with English-speaking culture.

Even more difficult to become aware of are things we communicate by the rate or pitch of our voice. A recent study found that advanced Finnish learners of English speak more slowly than less advanced Swedish-speaking learners.[18] Does this mean that Finnish speakers are sluggish language learners? It certainly means that they risk being perceived as slow, unfriendly, or inarticulate by native English speakers. In fact, these speakers seem to be simply transferring the average *rate* of speech from their native languages.

This is a common phenomenon: German learners of English, and French learners of German, have been shown to follow the pause pattern of their native language when speaking their second language. This is neither surprising, nor is it an isolated, unimportant, fact. Perhaps the most "sticky" kinds of interference from L1 are those we never think about: intonation, pauses, hesitations, etc. Many an English-speaking learner of French hesitates by using the standard English *um* instead of repeating a word or producing the French filler-sound *euuu,* thus marking himself clearly as a non-native speaker. I vividly recall the baffled reaction of a native French speaker during an international telephone conversation several years ago: I had been speaking quite fluent French for some ten minutes, but inadvertently using Dutch "fillers" like *ja, ja,* instead of the expected French pause-noises cited above.

Second-language speakers are constantly faced with the danger of not "fitting in" socially: a woman from India working in a cafeteria is baffled to hear that she has been labeled "rude" by her customers. A friend tells you that she cannot deal with her Hispanic classmates, because they seem so obsequious. In each case, a perfectly fluent, but non-native, speaker of English has somehow given the wrong impression. Many Indian speakers of English tend to use higher pitches and faster rates of speech than Americans: this is often mistaken for a haranguing or irritable tone. Spanish speakers tend to apologize nearly twice as often as Americans in their own language, and in situations where an apology seems unnecessary to an English speaker. If they unconsciously carry this habit over into English, misconceptions may occur, and they may seem dishonest or obsequious.

Advocates of communicative competence as a basis for language testing sometimes claim that it is the *only* goal of second-language teaching, and hence that we can dispense with grammar altogether in teaching language. Perhaps the more common position, and the one closest to Hymes's original idea, is expressed by Jack Richards, when he defines grammar as "necessary, but not sufficient" for language proficiency.[19]

Teacher and Learner Strategies

The growing concern with communicative competence, coupled with the emphasis on creativity in generative grammar, has had a profound

---

[18] Cited in Faerch and Kasper (1983), p. 219.
[19] Richards (1985), p. 76.

impact on language teaching. Pedagogical experts are increasingly advocating the abandonment of the old-style, repetitious drill:

PATTERN: I'm holding a book.
CUE: Magazine
RESPONSE: I'm holding a magazine.
CUE: Banana
RESPONSE: I'm holding a banana.[20]

Disappearing, too, is the stylized question-answer format: "Where did you go last night?" "Last night I went to my home." Native speakers in real situations simply don't talk like that, the argument goes. Why should we teach the unfortunate learner to do so? Replacing traditional classroom dialogue is a wide range of activities from games to playacting. A recent collection of teaching activities, for example, suggests the following game, called "Lie Detector," for a small group of students: the group asks a series of questions of one student, who is instructed to lie on just one answer. Each student then tries to guess which answer was untrue, giving reasons for their suppositions.[21] For the beginner, there are guessing games centered on names; for the more advanced student, role-playing in tricky social situations ("You just remembered today is your best friend's birthday, but you have only one dollar to spend. What do you do?").

Studying the Learner

Again spurred by concern with communication in the broad sense, many educators are looking more closely at learner characteristics as well as teaching methods. What kind of person makes the best language learner? One goal has been to correlate character traits with successful language learning, and a commonsense profile has emerged of a good learner: willing to risk seeming foolish, positively disposed toward the language and identified with its speakers, and a user of multiple *strategies* that help the learner fully master linguistic input, rather that simply respond to it passively.

One might wonder whether this research, too, has some pedagogical implications. It may be difficult to change deep personality traits, like the extent to which a learner feels willing to appear foolish. But the strategies, or methods, a student uses may be relatively susceptible to molding by a good teacher. With this in mind, close analysis of learner behavior is being done, in the hope of better understanding the strategies and behaviors of language learners.

For instance, what does a person do when she doesn't know a word?

---

[20] Rivers (1983), p. 45.
[21] Klippel (1987), p. 35.

Elaine Tarone et al. (1983) identify a number of common behavior patterns. One important alternative is avoidance: if you don't know the word "election," don't discuss the presidential race; if you don't know how to phrase counterfactual conditionals, don't bother telling your native-speaking friend that you "would have gone with him if you could." If you can't pronounce, spell, or conjugate one French word, use another. Blum-Kulka et al. (1983) in Faerch and Kasper (1983) suggest that avoidance is a common phenomenon, extending farther than one might at first think: for instance, they claim that learners tend to avoid words for which no precise equivalent exists in their mother tongue. They cite Hebrew *silbec*, "to insert in a suitable place," which learners avoid in favor of *hixnis*, "insert," or *sim*, "place." Extensive avoidance behavior on the part of a learner on the level of sounds, words, and constructions probably exerts an important effect on the outcome of language teaching, and is thus a matter for serious concern.

Other strategies range from borrowing an L1 word or phrase, paraphrasing (saying "girls and boys" for "children"), or Tarone's (1983) more radical "message abandonment" (the speaker simply stops in midstream, leaving her sentence unfinished). These need little elaboration; readers who have learned a foreign language will invariably recall a distressing experience with at least one of them. It is too early to say how teaching might be improved by a deeper understanding of such strategies, but it is hoped that their study will yield useful suggestions.

A closely related set of strategies, of more immediate practical interest to the teacher, involves "negotiation of meaning": the methods a non-native speaker manages to build understandings and get his message across in the process of conversing. Strategies range here from hesitation and puzzled facial expressions to direct appeal to the native speaker (hinting for the correct word, or asking, "how do you say . . . ?").

Some believe that teachers could maximize their students' effectiveness as communicators if they could see clearly which strategies seem to work and selectively encourage them, even by overtly training students to use one strategy in favor of another. Abraham and Vann (1987), in a comparative case study of two learners, claim that the active use of a wide variety of learning strategies seems to have characterized the more effective learner. The following exchange shows their successful learner Gerardo persistently negotiating to grasp the meaning of a word; the investigator has just asked if Gerardo ever feels helpless in trying to learn English:

GERARDO: I think I don't understand exactly means of the "helpless."
INTERVIEWER: "Helpless" means . . .
GERARDO: No help.
INTERVIEWER: No help, yeah. You feel like you can't do anything about it.
GERARDO: All right, yeah. [pause] That is meaning, that I don't need help for example?

INTERVIEWER: No [gives more explanation].
GERARDO: I know "help." I know "less." L-E-S-S. Helpless. Helpless.
INTERVIEWER: Means nobody can help you. You feel like nobody can help you. There is nothing I can do to help you.
GERARDO: Yeah, Yeah.[22]

Behind the authors' discussion lies the question of whether other learners can be persuaded to adopt Gerardo's persistent tactics and use them successfully.

To summarize at this point, the adult faces yet another complex challenge beyond the existence of L1, and beyond biological or cognitive problems: how to master the extensive set of social conventions that will allow him to use the foreign language effectively, and often in a context where direct practice of those conventions is difficult.

THE BILINGUAL MIND

Given all the above, it comes as no surprise that people who begin studying a foreign language after puberty seldom achieve what has been called "balanced bilingualism," or equal fluency in two languages. Typically, even if they seem fluent, such speakers have a dominant, or stronger, language: they make much stronger grammaticality judgments, or fine linguistic distinctions, in their dominant language. They may read at a rate only about 60% or 70% as fast in their weaker language, and some recent research suggests that they may access words rather less efficiently in their nondominant language.[23] These dominance effects have not been studied in detail for children, but we can safely expect that they should be weaker the earlier language learning begins.

Until now, we have said nothing about second-language learning in childhood. But clearly, the maze of problems to which we have devoted this article emerges for the most part only in late childhood or at puberty. Of course, a young child will have a first language, and thus the potential of transfer; but the learning task should be, on every other count, much easier in childhood than later. The lesson to be drawn is clear: if second-language learning is desirable, parents and educators should provide every opportunity for children to learn language in early childhood. But one final worry remains: is second-language learning desirable in the first place?

Intelligence and the Second Language

Psychologists, parents, and educators have traditionally worried about the effect of bilingualism on general mental capacity. Does a person

---

[22] Abraham and Vann (1987), pp. 89–90.
[23] Segalowitz (1987).

who must keep track of knowledge of two languages necessarily give up mental space destined for some other kind of knowledge? Until quite recently, the generally accepted answer seemed to be "yes." Kenji Hakuta cites a popular psychology textbook from the fifties that associates words like "handicapped" and "retardation" with bilingualism.[24] Indeed, up until a decade after that text appeared, studies seemed invariably to conclude that bilingual children were at a cognitive disadvantage — and hence, bilingualism must be at fault. Of course, this causal link should have seemed suspect: the children being studied were from immigrant families who suffered from social and financial problems. Hence, any learning difficulties they may have had could have been caused by a very complex constellation of factors.

In the sixties the Canadian psychologist Wallace Lambert conducted a series of studies designed to test bilingual cognitive skills. Lambert expected to find learning disadvantages in bilingual children: his goal was not to question this but to yield some insight into the cognitive abilities of bilingual children, to learn how schools could best help them overcome their "handicap." The results came as a great surprise: in test after test, bilingual children came out, not behind or even equal to, but *ahead of* monolingual children on a wide variety of measures, both verbal and nonverbal, including both math and English (their *first* language). Since then, Lambert's positive findings have been replicated in societies as far apart as South Africa, Singapore, and Israel. To cite one result, a controlled study of French-English bilingualism in Montreal showed bilingual eighth graders scored higher on "divergent thinking," in a task asking them, for instance, how many uses they could think of for a paper clip.[25]

How did Lambert manage to turn the tide of scholarly opinion on this issue? In retrospect, the answer is easy. Without consciously trying to do so, he had identified a very different type of bilingual: Canadian middle-class children, who suffered from none of the handicaps of earlier subject populations. Thus, his results were bound to paint a more optimistic picture of the advantages of bilingualism.

In general, it is now believed that bilingual children are two or three years ahead of their monolingual peers in developing conscious linguistic sophistication. For instance, asked to play a game in which the word *moon* must be used for the word *sun* and vice versa, bilinguals perform significantly better than monolinguals. Similar advantages have been claimed for bilinguals in performing spatial tasks, and tasks which involve the separation of linguistic and nonlinguistic thinking.[26]

Thus, provided ongoing research continues to support these results,

---

[24] Hakuta (1986), p. 14.
[25] Lambert (1977), p. 17.
[26] For a recent summary, see Cummins (1987).

parents have little cause for worry based on popular fears that bilingual children are somehow deprived. There is no evidence that learning a second language hinders a child's learning in other areas, and one can safely pursue the optimistic hope that it will do just the opposite, at least in some domains.

BIBLIOGRAPHY

Abraham, Roberta G., and Roberta J. Vann. "Strategies of Two Language Learners: A Case Study." In Anita Wenden and Joan Rubin, eds., *Learner Strategies in Language Learning*. Englewood Cliffs, N. J.: Prentice-Hall, 1987.

Andersen, Roger W. "Transfer to Somewhere." In Susan Gass and Larry Selinker, eds. *Language Transfer in Language Learning*. Rowley, Mass.: Newbury House, 1983.

Blum-Kulka, Shoshana, and Eddie A. Levenston. "Universals of Lexical Simplification." In Claus Faerch and Gabriele Kasper, eds. *Strategies in Interlanguage Communication*. New York: Longman, 1983.

Broselow, Ellen, and Dan Finer. "Second Language Acquisition of Reflexive Binding." In *Proceedings of the New England Linguistic Society*, Vol. 16, 1985.

Clahsen, Harald, and Pieter Muysken. "The Availability of Universal Grammar to Adult and Child Learners — A Study of the Acquisition of German Word Order." *Second Language* 2, 1986, pp. 93–119.

Cummins, Jim. "Bilingualism, Language Proficiency, and Metalinguistic Development." In Peter Homel et al., eds. *Childhood Bilingualism: Aspects of Linguistic, Cognitive, and Social Development*. Hillsdale, N. J.: Lawrence Erlbaum, 1987.

Duff, Alan. *The Third Language: Recurrent Problems of Translation into English*. New York: Pergamon Press, 1981.

Dulay, Heidi, and M. Burt. "Natural Sequences in Child Second Language Acquisition." *Language Learning* 24, 1974, pp. 37–53.

Faerch, Claus, and Gabriele Kasper. "On Identifying Communication Strategies in Interlanguage Production." In C. Faerch and G. Kasper, eds. *Strategies in Interlanguage Communication*. New York: Longman, 1983.

Felix, Sascha W. "More Evidence on Competing Cognitive Systems." *Second Language Research* 1, 1985, pp. 47–72.

Fromkin, Victoria, Stephen Krashen, Susan Curtiss, David Rigler, and Marilyn Rigler. "The Development of Language in Genie: A Case of Language Acquisition Beyond the 'Critical Period.' " *Brain and Language*, vol. 1, no. 1. New York: Academic Press, 1974.

Hakuta, Kenji. *Mirror of Language: The Debate on Bilingualism*. New York: Basic Books, 1986.

———. "The Second-Language Learner in the Context of the Study of Language Acquisition." In P. Homel et al., eds. *Childhood Bilingualism*. Hillsdale, N. J.: Lawrence Erlbaum, 1987.

Hatch, Evelyn. *Psycholinguistics: A Second Language Perspective*. Rowley, Mass.: Newbury House, 1983.

Hymes, Dell. "On Communicative Competence." In J. B. Pride and J. Holmes, eds. *Sociolinguistics*. Harmondsworth: Penguin, 1972.

Kelly, L. G. *25 Centuries of Language Teaching.* Rowley, Mass: Newbury House, 1969.

Klein, Wolfgang. *Second Language Acquisition.* New York: Cambridge University Press, 1986.

Klippel, Friederike. *Keep Talking: Communicative Fluency Activities for Language Teaching.* New York: Cambridge University Press, 1987.

Lambert, Wallace E. "The Effects of Bilingualism on the Individual: Cognitive and Sociocultural Consequences." In Peter A. Hornby, ed., *Bilingualism: Psychological, Social, and Educational Implications.* New York: Academic Press, 1977.

Lo Bello, Nino. *English Well Speeched Here.* Los Angeles: Price Stern Sloan, 1986.

Major, Roy. "Phonological Similarity, Markedness, and Rate of L2 Acquisition." *Studies in Second Language Acquisition* 9, 1987: pp. 63–82.

McBee, Suzanna. "English: Out to Conquer the World." *U.S. News and World Report,* Feb. 18, 1985, pp. 49–52.

Radford, Andrew. *Introduction to Generative Syntax.* New York: Cambridge University Press, 1981.

Richards, Jack. "The Status of Grammar in the Language Curriculum." In Bikram K. Das., ed. *Communicative Language Teaching.* Singapore: Singapore University Press, 1985, pp. 64–83.

Rivers, Wilga M. *Communicating Naturally in a Second Language.* New York: Cambridge University Press, 1983.

Rubin, Joan. "Learner Strategies: Theoretical Assumptions, Research History and Typology." In Anita Wenden and Joan Rubin, eds. *Learner Strategies in Language Learning.* Englewood Cliffs, N. J.: Prentice-Hall, 1987.

Schachter, Jacqueline. "An Error in Error Analysis." *Language Learning* 24, 1974: pp. 205–214.

Segalowitz, Norman. "Skilled Reading in the Second Language." In Jyotsna Vaid, ed. *Language Processing in Bilinguals.* Hillsdale, N. J.: Lawrence Erlbaum, 1986.

Selinker, Larry. "Interlanguage." *International Review of Applied Linguistics* 10, 1974: pp. 209–231.

Swan, Michael, and Bernard Smith. *Learner English: A Teacher's Guide to Interference and Other Problems.* New York: Cambridge University Press, 1987.

Tarone, Ellen, A. D. Cohen, and G. Dumas. "A Closer Look at Some Interlanguage Terminology: A Framework for Communication Strategies." In C. Faerch and G. Kasper, eds., *Strategies in Interlanguage Communication.* New York: Longman, 1983.

FOR DISCUSSION AND REVIEW

1. What does Heny describe as "descriptivist?" Of what significance is it to the study of language acquisition?

2. Briefly describe the phenomena Heny refers to as "native language interference" in the acquisition of second languages.

3. What aspects of a learned L1 may be "transferred" to a learner's L2

during the process of acquiring a second language? Give examples in your discussion.

4. What characterizes "markedness"? Is this helpful to the study of second-language acquisition? Why is this theory not wholly accepted?

5. What does Chomsky mean by a language's fundamental property of creativity? How does this separate human language from other forms of communication?

6. What is universal grammar or UG? What is the "critical period"? According to the supporters of this belief, why is learning a second language more difficult after this critical period? What theories have been proposed to conflict with Chomsky's views? With which theory do you agree? Why?

7. What is Felix's "competition model"?

8. What is the creative construction theory? What observations fostered its development?

9. How does Stephen Krushen distinguish between "learning" and "acquisition"? What do each provide for language learners?

10. What is communicative competence? How might this notion create social expectations for language speakers? How can these expectations prevent the acceptance of second-language speakers in society?

11. What connections have scientists of the past made between bilingualism and intelligence? How have scientists tested this theory? What have been the results of the various studies done? Why must we keep in mind the context in which these studies were conducted?

Projects for "Language Acquisition"

1. Examine the following conversation between Eve, a twenty-four-month-old child, and her mother:

EVE: Have that?
MOTHER: No, you may not have it.
EVE: Mom, where my tapioca?
MOTHER: It's getting cool. You'll have it in just a minute.
EVE: Let me have it.
MOTHER: Would you like to have your lunch right now?
EVE: Yeah. My tapioca cool?
MOTHER: Yes, it's cool.
EVE: You gonna watch me eat my lunch?
MOTHER: Yeah, I'm gonna watch you eat your lunch.
EVE: I eating it.
MOTHER: I know you are.
EVE: It time Sarah take a nap.
MOTHER: It's time for Sarah to have some milk, yeah. And then she's gonna take a nap and you're gonna take a nap.
EVE: And you?
MOTHER: And me too, yeah.[1]

Compare the grammar of Eve's speech with that of her mother. What elements are systematically missing from the child's speech? Now, look at Eve's speech in a conversation with her mother that was taped only three months later:

MOTHER: Come and sit over here.
EVE: You can sit down by me. That will make me happy. Ready to turn it.
MOTHER: We're not quite ready to turn the page.
EVE: Yep, we are.
MOTHER: Shut the door, we won't hear her then.
EVE: Then Fraser won't hear her too. Where he's going? Did you make a great big hole there?
MOTHER: Yes, we made a great big hole in here; we have to get a new one.
EVE: Could I get some other piece of paper?
MOTHER: You ask Fraser.

---

[1] A transcription of a taped conversation from Ursula Bellugi, "Learning the Language," *Psychology Today* 4 (December 1970), 33.

EVE: Could I use this one?
MOTHER: I suppose so.
EVE: Is Fraser goin take his pencil home when he goes?
MOTHER: Yes, he is.[2]

What changes do you note in Eve's speech? Try to describe the "grammatical rules" that govern her speech in each passage. Although Eve could not tell us of the rules she learned during the three-month interval, what rules, as evidenced implicitly by her speech, has she internalized? What conclusions can you draw about the process of language learning among children? Write a short paper dealing with these questions.

2. Read Noam Chomsky's well-known review article "Review of B. F. Skinner's *Verbal Behavior*" (*Language* 35 [1959], 26–58). Prepare a report explaining the objections of Chomsky, a linguist, to the views of Skinner, a behaviorist psychologist, about language acquisition.

3. Prepare a report on how children acquire social skills in the use of language simultaneously with their acquisition of other language skills. Use as one source Susan Ervin-Tripp's "Social Backgrounds and Verbal Skills" in Renira Huxley and Elisabeth Ingram, eds., *Language Acquisition: Models and Methods* (New York: Academic Press, 1971).

4. One of the best texts on language acquisition is Jill G. de Villiers and Peter A. de Villiers, *Language Acquisition* (Cambridge, MA: Harvard University Press, 1978). Any single chapter in the book would provide enough material for a more detailed look at some stage or aspect of language acquisition than we could provide in this anthology, and the extensive bibliography will suggest additional topics.

5. Using the selected bibliography on pp. 193–195, prepare a report on feral or isolated children. Comparing the various cases with your classmates should clarify some of the problems earlier investigators have encountered.

6. We know that young children who are learning two or more languages at the same time use similar strategies to acquire the different languages. But it is not clear what effect, if any, being bilingual has on people. Using library resources, prepare a report in which you summarize opinions about the advantages or disadvantages of being bilingual.

7. The process of learning a second language is usually different for adults (and older children) than it is for young children, if only because the former group is likely to learn in a classroom setting. Using library resources, prepare a report in which you describe the difficulties that adult second-language learners encounter and the learning strategies they employ.

8. Throughout much of the world, people need to speak at least two languages in order to function in their societies. In the United States,

---

[2] Ibid., 33–34.

however, only about ten percent of Americans speak a language in addition to English. Proposals for curriculum reform in American schools often call for an increase in the teaching of foreign languages. As a group project, hold a debate on the subject, "American high-school graduates should be fluent in at least one language besides English."

Selected Bibliography

Note: Three of the six articles in this section include bibliographies (Moskowitz, Aitchison, and Heny). The reader should consult these for a more exhaustive listing of sources.

Anderson, Elaine S. *Speaking With Style: The Sociolinguistic Skills of Children.* New York: Routledge, 1990. [Describes the linguistic competence of children in conjunction with Chomsky's views.]

Bain, Bruce, ed. *The Sociogenesis of Language and Human Conduct.* New York: Plenum Press, 1983. [A large and eclectic collection of interesting essays.]

Bar-Adon, A., and W. F. Leopold. *Child Language: A Book of Readings.* Englewood Cliffs, NJ: Prentice-Hall, 1971.

Baron, Naomi S. *Growing Up With Language: How Children Learn to Talk.* Reading, MA: Addison-Wesley Publishing Company, Inc., 1992. [A look at the whys and hows of language development with a helpful reference section at the book's end to point readers in more specific directions.]

Bates, Elizabeth. *Language and Context: The Acquisition of Pragmatics.* New York: Academic Press, 1976. [Describes the development in children of knowledge of pragmatics.]

Bellugi, Ursula. "Learning the Language." *Psychology Today,* 4 (December 1970), 32–35, 66. [A nontechnical description of language acquisition and the grammar of children.]

Bickerton, Derek. *Roots of Language.* Ann Arbor: Karoma Publishers, 1981. [Develops the argument that Creole languages provide the key to understanding the nature of all human languages.]

Brown, Roger. *A First Language.* Cambridge, MA: Harvard University Press, 1973. [An important and classic work.]

———. "How Shall a Thing Be Called?" *Psychological Review,* 85 (1958), 145–154. [A discussion of how adults teach children the names of objects.]

Cox, Maureen V. "Children's Over-regularization of Nouns and Verbs." *Journal of Child Language* 16 (1989), 203–6. [A short and informative look at some patterns of child language development.]

Curtiss, Susan. *Genie: A Psycholinguistic Study of a Modern-Day "Wild Child."* New York: Academic Press, 1977. [A detailed analysis of Genie's linguistic and cognitive development.]

———. "Genie: Language and Cognition," *UCLA Working Papers in Cognitive Linguistics* 1 (1979), 15–62. [Genie's cognitive development and its relationship to her linguistic ability.]

———. "The Critical Period and Feral Children," *UCLA Working Papers in Cognitive Linguistics,* 2 (1980), 21–36. [A complete description of known cases of feral children; argues for the existence of a specific language faculty.]

de Villiers, Jill G., and Peter A. de Villiers. *Language Acquisition.* Cambridge, MA: Harvard University Press, 1978. [If you read only one book about language acquisition, choose this one. Thorough, complete, balanced; includes discussion of the language problems of deaf, retarded, dysphasic, and autistic children.]

Dromi, Esther. *Early Lexical Development.* New York: Cambridge University

Press, 1987. [An excellent guide to the study of language acquisition including helpful chapter outlines and summaries.]

Ferguson, Charles A., and Daniel I. Slobin, eds. *Studies of Child Language Development.* New York: Holt, Rinehart and Winston, 1973. [A valuable collection of hard-to-find papers; covers the acquisition by children of a number of different languages.]

Ferguson, Charles A., and Catherine E. Snow, eds. *Talking to Children: Language Input and Acquisition.* Cambridge: Cambridge University Press, 1977. [Focuses on the importance of mothers' speech to children; covers a number of different languages.]

Foster, Susan H. *The Communicative Competence of Young Children.* New York: Longman Inc., 1990. [An important source on language and communication that attempts to answer the question of how almost all children are able to learn a native language.]

Heatherington, Madelon E. *How Language Works.* Cambridge, MA: Winthrop Publishers, 1980. [Excellent introduction to the study of language; see Chapter 2 about language acquisition.]

Kagan, Jerome. "Do Infants Think?" *Scientific American*, 226 (1972), 74–82. [Argues that cognitive development is under way as early as nine months of age.]

Kess, Joseph, F. *Psycholinguistics: Introductory Perspectives.* New York: Academic Press, 1976. [See Chapter 3 for a detailed description of language acquisition.]

Larsen-Freeman, Diane, and M. H. Long. *An Introduction to Second Language Acquisition Research.* New York: Longman Inc., 1991. [A detailed study for anyone pursuing further research in the field.]

Lenneberg, Eric H. *Biological Foundations of Language.* New York: John Wiley & Sons, 1967. [A seminal and now classic work; technical investigation of the biological aspects of language.]

Levy, Yonata, and I. M. Schlesinger. *Categories and Processes in Language Acquisition.* Hillsdale, N.J.: Lawrence Erlbaum, 1988. [A thorough study that explores a variety of theories for language acquisition.]

"Love's Labors" (videotape). New York: Ambrose Video Publishing, Inc., 1991. (57 min.) [Explores the period between six months and three years to demonstrate how babies and infants are active participants in their linguistic worlds.]

Marcus, Gary F., S. Pinker, M. Ullman, M. Hollander, T. J. Rosen, and F. Xu. *Overregularization in Language Acquisition.* Chicago: The University of Chicago Press, vol 57, no. 4, 1992. [An excellent source of study for child language development with an interesting commentary on a comparative study between English and German.]

McNeill, David. *The Acquisition of Language: The Study of Developmental Psycholinguistics.* New York: Harper & Row, 1970. [A brief but technical discussion of language acquisition.]

Meier, Richard P. "Language Acquisition by Deaf Children" in *American Scientist*, January/February 1991, p. 60. [An intriguing article that explores how deaf children acquire linguistic skill in a manner similar to children who hear.]

Morehead, Donald M., and Ann E. Morehead, eds. *Normal and Deficient Language.* Baltimore: University Park Press, 1976. [Excellent studies of language acquisition by normal, deaf, dysphasic, and retarded children.]

Nilson, Don L. F., and Alleen Pace Nilsen. *Language Play: An Introduction to*

Linguistics. Rowley, MA: Newbury House Publishers, 1978. [A thoroughly readable book; see especially Chapters 2 and 4 for discussions of the behaviorist and innatist hypotheses of language acquisition and of the important role of playing with language.]

Radford, Andrew. *Syntactic Theory and the Acquisition of English Syntax*. Cambridge: Basil Blackwell Inc., 1990. [A helpful study meant for students with little familiarity in the field; devoid of unnecessary technical language.]

Schiefelbusch, Richard L., and Lyle L. Lloyd, eds. *Language Perspectives: Acquisition, Retardation and Intervention*. Baltimore: University Park Press, 1974. [An important collection; deals with a number of aspects of language acquisition by normal, deaf, retarded, and autistic children.]

Shipley, Elizabeth F., Carlota S. Smith, and Lila R. Gleitman. "A Study in the Acquisition of Language: Free Responses to Commands." *Language*, 45 (1969), 322–342. [Comprehension of speech exceeds ability to produce speech in children who are at certain stages of language development.]

Slobin, Dan I. *Psycholinguistics*. Glenview, IL: Scott, Foresman, 1971. [Still a good, brief introduction, especially helpful concerning language acquisition in children.]

———. "Children and Language: They Learn the Same Way All Around the World." *Psychology Today*, 6 (July 1972), 71–74, 82. [A nontechnical description of language acquisition by children of different cultures.]

Smith, Frank, and George A. Miller, eds. *The Genesis of Language: A Psycholinguistic Approach*. Cambridge, MA: The MIT Press, 1966. [Essays dealing with language development in children.]

Steinberg, Danny D. *Psycholinguistics: Language, Mind, and World*. New York: Longman, 1982. [Focuses on reading and second-language teaching; see especially Chapters 8 and 9.]

Teller, Virginia, and Sheila J. White, eds. "Studies in Child Language and Multilingualism." *Annals of the New York Academy of Sciences*, 365 (1980). [Contains four interesting articles on language acquisition.]

Walker, Edward, ed. *Explorations in the Biology of Language*. Montgomery, VT: Bradford Books, 1978. [Six difficult but important essays focusing on language as a biological manifestation of universal cognitive structure.]

Wood, David. *How Children Think and Learn*. New York: Basil Blackwell Inc., 1988. [A psychologist's account of the stages of children's language development.]

PART THREE

LANGUAGE AND THE BRAIN

During the last two decades, stimulated by what was learned from the split-brain operations of the 1960s, interest in and research about brain lateralization have increased dramatically. A number of popular books have appeared, most of them enthusiastic but not all of them entirely accurate. And, the field has attracted specialists from a variety of disciplines — psychology, philosophy, neurology, history, art, education, and most important from our point of view, linguistics. By the early 1980s, it had become clear that earlier ideas about the total dominance of the left hemisphere for language functions were major oversimplifications. The situation is far more complicated than early researchers believed, and we now know that the right hemisphere plays an important role in language processing.

In "Brain and Language," the first selection in Part Three, Jeannine Heny traces the development of research on the relationship of the brain to language and explores probable reasons for the development of brain lateralization. She then describes a variety of methods for measuring which hemisphere does what, and identifies the limitations of each method. The right hemisphere, Professor Heny explains, has a number of important functions, including some that are crucial to normal language-processing. In addition, she notes that linguistic tasks are not assigned identically in terms of hemispheres in all people, a point she makes clear in her discussion of bilinguals, deaf users of American Sign Language, literate people, speakers of certain languages, left-handers, and women.

Aphasia, or language impairment due to brain injury, is the subject of the second selection, Howard Gardner's "The Loss of Language." Approximately 400,000 Americans have a stroke every year. According to Gardner, because the probability of having a stroke increases with age, "if other causes do not intervene, it is from this condition that most of us will eventually die" (*The Shattered Mind*, p. 12). Although people do not usually survive severe strokes that destroy large parts of the brain, some strokes are so mild that individuals may not even be aware of them or may recover completely within a few days. Many strokes, however, fall between these extremes — they are "insufficient to kill the individual or reduce him to a vegetable state, yet serious enough to permanently affect his functioning" (ibid.). In "The Loss of Language," Gardner, who has worked extensively with brain-damaged patients, describes two major kinds of aphasia and suggests that further research in this area can yield valuable insight into how the human brain processes language.

In the third selection, linguist Elaine Chaika looks at how schizophrenic speech disintegrates and what it tells us about how the brain processes language. In attempting to unscramble the puzzle of this bizarre language, Chaika reviews the most salient features of the schizophrenic's speech and the possible reasons for such speech. She concludes, "If, as I think, schizophrenics who speak weirdly do so because of a linguistic problem caused by a biochemical imbalance, then the solution is biochemical."

In the fourth selection, "From Speaking Act to Natural Word: Animals, Communication, and Language," William Kemp and Roy Smith turn to a fascinating topic: the differences between animal communication and human language. Animal communication systems are interesting in themselves; in addition, by studying them we may learn more about how human language evolved. But of more immediate interest to many readers will be the question of human attempts to communicate with various animals, especially chimpanzees. The early 1970s brought what many people, scientists and nonscientists alike, believed was a real breakthrough: a number of chimpanzees had apparently learned forms of human language, ranging from American Sign Language, to a keyboard linked to a computer and used to make requests and respond to questions, to the rearrangement of plastic symbols so as to produce meaningful utterances. By the 1980s, however, some skeptics suggested that the problem of uncontaminated human-animal experiments designed to teach some form of human language to animals might be insoluble. Kemp and Smith survey the evidence thoroughly and objectively, concluding that the chimpanzee research achieved less than its extreme advocates claim but more than its severest critics allow.

Finally, in "The Continuity Paradox," the concluding selection in this section, Derek Bickerton explores the role evolution has played in the development of human language. If humans are the result of an evolutionary process, what then is the origin of language? According to Bickerton, "language must have evolved out of some prior system, and yet there does not seem to be any such system out of which it could have evolved" and therein lies the central paradox that Bick-erton discusses in this chapter from his book *Language and Species.*

There are still a great many questions about the relationships among the human brain, language, and cognition. It is clear, however, that research will continue and that, as it does, we will learn more about the functioning of the brain.

11

Brain and Language

Jeannine Heny

In the following selection, Jeannine Heny, professor of English at Indiana University of Pennsylvania, examines the evolution of the human brain and some possible causes of brain lateralization. She traces the sometimes halting progress of early research involving aphasia and the attempts to "map out" the language functions of the cortex. Describing the many contemporary methods of measuring hemispheric activity, Professor Heny demonstrates that both the left and right hemispheres of the brain are important in language processing, and that it is probably the type of processing, rather than the material being processed, that differentiates the two hemispheres. Curiously, though, people do not all use the same hemisphere for language tasks; in fact, the same person may process identical material differently at different times. As Professor Heny points out, our understanding of the complex relationship between language and the brain has increased enormously in recent years, but it is still tantalizingly incomplete.

About five million years ago, early hominid brain size began to increase dramatically. After about ten million years of relatively stable weight, the human brain was embarking on a growth phase that would see it more than triple its volume to reach today's proportions. Five million years may seem very long; but, as Figure 11.1 shows, it can represent a phenomenal rate of growth on an evolutionary scale.

At the same time, other changes were taking place as well: our forebears became predominantly right-handed, made use of increasingly sophisticated tools, and organized their culture in ever more complex ways. The result of this evolution, *homo sapiens*, looked rather unimpressive: a puny, almost hairless animal, with a bent windpipe that reduced breathing efficiency to nearly half of its original capacity. The creature's teeth were practically useless for chewing; it had nothing to match the sharp incisors of rats or the long canine teeth of wolves, lions, and other primates. Even inside the nervous system, the human species had taken risks, giving up a potentially useful insurance policy: the two halves of the brain were no longer identical, as in many lower species; thus, there was little chance of "backup" from one half of the brain if the other suffered damage. But the animal did have at least one feature that more

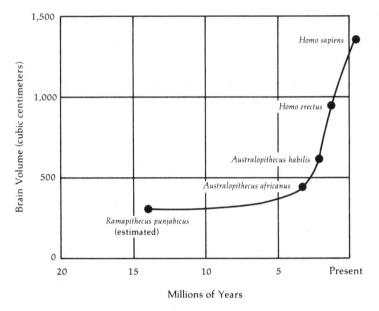

FIGURE 11.1. Human evolution: brain size.

than compensated for all it had lost: the most highly developed communication system on earth — human language.

In fact, human brain evolution involved much more than increased size, as Figure 11.2 reveals. In lower mammals such as the rat, the brain is almost wholly taken up with sensory and motor functions. In contrast, the primate brain has a greatly enlarged outer layer or *cortex*, resulting in a dramatic increase in "uncommitted" cortical tissue not needed for basic functions. A high degree of asymmetry, or hemispheric specialization, nearly doubles this available space in humans (by the way, one estimate suggests that the human cortex contains more nerve connections than there are people on earth!).[1] This essay focuses on the way in which the brain's powerful outer layer handles language.

DISCOVERING THE BRAIN

The Classical Language Areas

For centuries, the nature of the brain was shrouded in mystery. Aristotle is said to have thought it was a cold sponge, whose main task was

---

[1] Trevarthen (1983), p. 60.

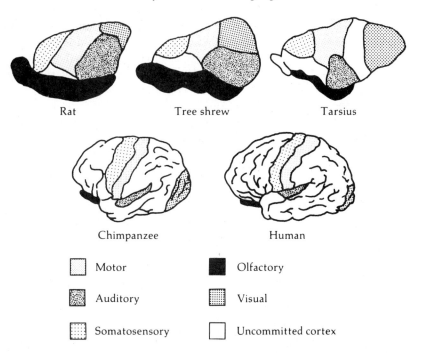

Rat   Tree shrew   Tarsius

Chimpanzee   Human

☐ Motor   ■ Olfactory

▨ Auditory   ▦ Visual

▨ Somatosensory   ☐ Uncommitted cortex

FIGURE 11.2.   Human evolution: brain function. These figures show the approximate space devoted to sensory and motor functions in various mammalian brains. The white areas, called *association* cortex, represent neural tissue not committed to basic functions. As shown, the increase in brain size is accompanied by a dramatic increase in the proportion of association cortex in humans.

to cool the blood.[2] Later, Leonardo Da Vinci represented the brain as a curious void filled by three tiny bulbous structures arranged in a straight line behind the eyeball, whose functions he defined according to commonly held assumptions of his time.[3]

Not all early theories were quite so misguided, however. From the first studies on language deficits in the Greco-Roman era, it was suspected that the brain played some direct part in language use. Still, modern scholarship on this question dates only to the early nineteenth century. At that stage, scientific opinion was divided; some believed that language resided in the frontal lobes, while Franz Gall, the founder of phrenology, drew language in Area XV on his now famous map of the brain. Neither theory contained any hint that language might be handled more actively in one hemisphere than the other.

In 1836, an obscure French country doctor, Marc Dax, attended a

---

[2] Comment (cited from work by Clarke and O'Mally) in Arbib, Caplan, and Marshall (1982), p. 6; this article provides an interesting overview of neurolinguistic history.
[3] Harth (1982), pp. 37–42. A copy of Leonardo's sketch appears on p. 43.

medical conference in Montpelier, France, and presented the only scientific paper of his life. Dax claimed that, in forty aphasic patients he had seen in his practice, loss of language ability always correlated with damage to the left half of the brain. The paper went unnoticed at the time, and its remarkable insight was soon forgotten.

It was the French surgeon Paul Broca who, in 1864, dramatically proved Dax's original claim (about which, by the way, he knew nothing). Broca described his patient "Tan," named after the only word he could say. Tan could write normally, and seemed to understand everything said to him; he could move his lips or tongue in any direction when asked to do so, but he was totally incapable of meaningful speech. Broca hypothesized that his patient suffered from a pure disturbance of language, resulting from left hemisphere injury. Soon, his claim was proven: at autopsy, patients like Tan were found to have brain damage in the rear portion of the left frontal lobe, just above the left ear. Equivalent damage to the right hemisphere seemed to have little effect on speech. The area Broca isolated, and the aphasia associated with it, now bear his name: the term "Broca's aphasia" (also called "nonfluent" or "motor" aphasia) has come to stand for a complex of symptoms, ranging from extreme difficulty in articulation to *agrammatic* speech, where a patient produces halting strings of words without grammatical markers (e.g., inflections on verbs) or function words (such as articles and prepositions). The passage below gives an example of speech by a patient with Broca's aphasia. The patient is trying to describe a picture showing a little boy stealing cookies from a cookie jar while his chair is tipping over; a little girl is helping him. Their mother stands at the window staring into space while the sink in front of her overflows.

> Cookie jar . . . fall over . . . chair . . . water . . . empty . . . ov . . . ov . . . [Examiner: "overflow?"] Yeah.[4]

Another agrammatic patient, asked to tell the story of Cinderella, responded as follows:

> Cinderella . . . poor . . . um 'dopted her . . . scrubbed floor, um, tidy . . . poor, um . . . 'dopted . . . si-sisters and mother . . . ball. Ball, prince um, shoe.[5]

Ten years after Broca's discovery, Karl Wernicke, a twenty-six-year-old researcher in Germany, made yet another startling breakthrough. The patients who especially attracted his interest had no damage to Broca's area. Nor did they have obvious physical difficulty producing speech: in some cases, they could produce a stream of speech with no trouble in pronunciation and no significant loss of grammatical morphemes. But the content of their utterances ranged from puzzling to meaningless.

---

[4] Cited from earlier work by Goodglass and Kaplan, in Blumstein (1982), p. 205.
[5] Schwartz, Linebarger, and Saffran (1985), p. 84.

The Wernicke's aphasic who produced the following passage was also trying to describe the cookie theft picture described above. His flowing speech contrasts sharply with the hesitant, ungrammatical answer of the first patient. Yet, despite his fluency, he seems to make very little sense of the situation he sees:

> Well, this is . . . mother is away here working out o' here to get her better, but when she's working, the two boys looking in the other part. One their small tile into her time here. She's working another time because she's getting, too.[6]

The symptoms of Wernicke's aphasia are diverse and complex: a particularly striking form, called *jargon aphasia*, is marked by super-fluent speech and *neologisms*, i.e., nonwords whose origin is unknown. The excerpt below is taken from a long spontaneous monologue:

> And I say, this is wrong, I'm going out and doing things and getting ukeleles taken every time and I think I'm doing wrong because I'm supposed to take everything from the top so that we do four flashes of four volumes before we get down low . . . Face of everything. This guy has got to this thing, this thing made out in order to slash immediately to all of the windpails . . . This is going right over me from there, that's up to five station stuff form manatime, and with that put it all in and build it all up so it will all be spent with him conversing his condessing . . .[7]

Wernicke's aphasics typically have great problems finding the simplest, everyday words, especially names for things. One patient, shown a knife, tried to tell what it was:

> That's a resh. Sometimes I get one around here that I can cut a couple regs. There's no rugs around here and nothing cut right. But that's a rug, and I had some nice rekebz. I wish I had one now. Say how Wishi idaw, uh windy, look how windy. It's really window, isn't it?[8]

As a result of studying such patients, the young Wernicke managed not only to isolate a new area, but also to present the first coherent model of language processing in the brain. According to Wernicke, a speaker first draws the words from Wernicke's area where meanings are stored, located near the primary auditory cortex (just above and behind the left ear). A bundle of nerves called the *arcuate fasciculus* then transmits the idea to Broca's area, where it picks up sound structure before being sent to the motor cortex. There, the message is encoded into commands to the tongue, lips, and other articulators, and emerges as speech. Wernicke's

---

[6] Blumstein (1982), p. 205.
[7] Brown (1981), pp. 170–171.
[8] Adapted from Buckingham (1981), p. 59.

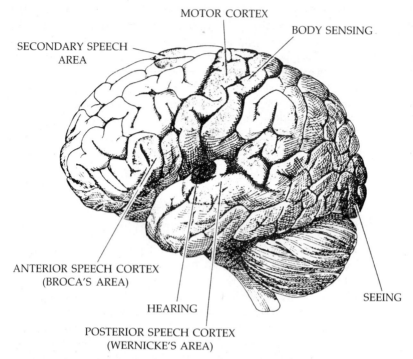

MOTOR CORTEX

BODY SENSING

SECONDARY SPEECH
AREA

ANTERIOR SPEECH CORTEX
(BROCA'S AREA)

SEEING

HEARING

POSTERIOR SPEECH CORTEX
(WERNICKE'S AREA)

FIGURE 11.3.   The classical language areas of the brain. Note the proximity
of Broca's area to the "motor cortex," where instructions to speech articulators
originate. The proximity of Wernicke's area to neural centers for sight and
hearing is also important, because this arrangement seems to allow the spoken
and written word to be available for semantic processing in Wernicke's area as
soon as they are perceived.

model, illustrated in Figure 11.3, still stands at the center of current research.

The discovery of Broca's and Wernicke's areas in the left hemisphere
soon inspired others to seek the remaining pieces of the neurolinguistic
puzzle. Scientists reasoned that all brain function must follow a clear, if
complex, mapping system. Indeed, a few striking cases turned up to fuel
the prevailing enthusiasm, where highly circumscribed damage caused
specific, clearly identifiable symptoms. In 1892, for example, the French
neurologist Dejerine observed a patient who could not read, although his
visual skills, writing, and speech were normal. On autopsy, it was found
that his left visual area was destroyed, along with the nerves connecting
visual regions in the two hemispheres. Thus, only the right, nonverbal
hemisphere could "see"—and it could not perceive what it saw as *language.* Hence, of course, it could not "read" what it saw. Nor could it
transmit the image it received to the language centers on the left for
interpretation.

But the diagram-makers ran into problems from the outset. For one thing, it had long been known that severe aphasics, with extensive left hemisphere lesions and with no ability to produce a normal spontaneous utterance, can often sing, curse, and produce fixed expressions such as "How are you?" This suggested that the right hemisphere (despite its absence on the neurolinguistic "map") might have some linguistic potential. More serious, however, was the elusive task of pinning down symptoms to points on the cortex. Exhaustive study by neurologists such as Henry Head in the 1920s showed that, at best, only a rough correlation could be found between symptom types and broad cortical areas. (Imagine a map of the United States in which the best one could do was place Boston "somewhere in the New England–New York State area." One could indeed capture the distinction between San Francisco and Boston with such a picture, but it could hardly be termed a useful guide for getting to Boston!)

These problems led many to abandon mapmaking altogether, on the grounds that language may be too complex to be broken down into discrete subprocesses, each assigned its own cortical territory. Now, the trend has again partially reversed, with recent research combining the spirit of both approaches. Scientists still search for the locus of specific verbal capacities, sometimes with painstaking accuracy, as in electrical stimulation research. Yet neurologists generally agree that this search is not likely to yield a one-to-one correspondence between units of grammatical knowledge and points on the brain's surface. The cortical areas that handle higher cognitive activity are too closely intertwined to be clearly teased apart and mapped out. And, within this system, linguistic and nonlinguistic capacity must be linked: a patient with a general impairment affecting, for example, memory or the ability to carry out purposeful actions, will have trouble speaking normally — but not because his grammatical knowledge is impaired.

Linguistics and Aphasia

When Broca and Wernicke made their discoveries about the brain, modern cognitive linguistics was unknown, and the terminology used to describe the functions of the language areas was vague; neurologists spoke of "sensory images" and "motor images" of words as being stored in Wernicke's and Broca's areas, respectively. Only now, after a century of brain research, has linguistic theory become rich enough to make a significant contribution to the understanding of aphasic syndromes. Three examples will help illustrate how this is happening.

First, consider the concept of "agrammatism." On the surface, it seems simple to describe. Take a sentence, like *A girl is playing in the yard*, and remove all the little particles, function words, and verb endings (*a, is, -ing*, etc.), and you have a plausible agrammatic sentence, right? (In this case, *girl . . . play . . . yard.*) Unfortunately, the answer is no. Broca's aphasics do not produce perfect language with a few predictable parts missing. For one thing, it may not be accurate to say that parts are *missing* at all: note that, in English, where both the bare stem *play* and the past tense *played* are fully acceptable forms, one *could* say that the aphasic simply chooses one form over another in saying *play* and not *played*. As it turns out, in languages where there is no "bare verb stem" form, such as *play*, this does seem to be what happens. In these languages, agrammatic speakers produce fully acceptable verb forms, but they use them in the wrong places. This suggests that the original "missing parts" description was prejudiced by the form of English, where the simple, unsuffixed verb form (e.g., *like*) happens to be the one agrammatics overuse most. This makes a critical difference in the linguistic interpretation of agrammatism. The earlier description implied that Broca's aphasics cannot form words properly; their *morphological*, or word-formation, rules for language do not function as they should. But under this new view things look very different: the rules that put elements like *play* and *-ed* together might be quite intact; it could be the *choice* of word forms, not their construction, that fails in these patients.

In fact, Broca's aphasic symptoms are not limited to word formation. Broca's aphasics produce too many nouns (recall the aforementioned sentence of *ball, prince um, shoe*). They often omit the verb altogether in a sentence, or use a related noun (e.g., *discussion* instead of *discuss*). Sentence patterns seem generally disrupted, as can be easily seen from agrammatic sentences cited in the literature, such as *the girl is flower the woman* and *the boy and the girl is valentine*. Researchers are now focusing on this question, trying to learn just how sensitive Broca's aphasics are to syntactic patterns, and where their attempts to put words together in the right order might be failing.

Other related work tries to interpret the classical description itself in linguistic terms. The trick is to characterize neatly the cluster of little elements lost: prepositions, articles, the *-ed* ending of the verb *walked*, the *'s* of *John's here*. What do all these have in common? Some represent whole words, and some represent parts of words. The preposition plays a major part in grammar, but articles don't. Just what part of linguistic *knowledge* would be missing in a patient whose only deficit was the omission of these elements? Mary-Louise Kean (1977) first proposed that these elements are all *unstressed*; hence, the agrammatic's problem, claimed Kean, is phonological (i.e., related to the sound system of the language). Since then, equally interesting suggestions have linked agrammatism to syntax, morphology, and language processing.[9] Although the final answer remains to be found, it is exciting that careful work on aphasic speech is finally able to yield such clear proposals.

---

[9] A detailed discussion and references to these theories can be found in Caplan (1987).

A second line of research suggests that Wernicke's aphasia, too, may have been described in overly simplistic terms: it has been assumed that a Broca's aphasic has access to the meaning of words, while a Wernicke's aphasic does not. One recent study challenges this notion, emphasizing the case of a Wernicke's aphasic who could neither read words nor identify pictures of an object, but could nevertheless say what category the object belongs to (girl's name, tool, animal, etc.). This suggests that a more careful view of "meaning" must be identified if Wernicke's aphasia is to be fully understood.[10] A similar note of caution comes from a recent study on meaning. When normal subjects are given series of letter-strings and asked to say whether they are real words, most respond more quickly if the current word is semantically related to one they have just heard. So, if the subject has just heard the word *barn*, he will react faster to, say, *horse* than to an unrelated word like *fry*. Amazingly enough, it is *Wernicke's* aphasics, and not Broca's, who react as normal subjects in this so-called "semantic priming" experiment,[11] suggesting that some kind of semantic access functions normally in these patients. Again, this kind of study can lead to important results, not only in defining aphasic types, but in understanding the nature of meaning itself.

A third exciting question being raised is this: is there a common denominator, some factor or cluster of factors that all aphasia types share? Goodglass and Menn (1985) found that *all* aphasics, regardless of type, had difficulty with sorting out the proper relationships between the underlined pairs of words in these sentences:

Point to the spoon with the pencil.
Point to the pencil with the spoon.

The trainer's dog is here.
The dog's trainer is here.[12]

Others have suggested that certain sentence patterns or even word forms may cause difficulty for virtually all aphasics. If such a common denominator can be found, it will obviously contribute a great deal to the task of defining classical aphasia types. And, again, it will help flesh out Wernicke's model of how the brain processes language.

TWO BRAINS OR ONE: HEMISPHERIC ASYMMETRIES AND THEIR ORIGIN

The realization that one important mental faculty seemed to belong to one side of the brain raised a host of intriguing questions from the

---

[10] Warrington and Shallice (1979), and later ongoing research cited in Caplan (1987).

[11] Milberg et. al. (1987).

[12] Goodglass and Menn (1985), p. 22.

TABLE 11.1   The Two Brains and What They Do.

LEFT BRAIN	RIGHT BRAIN
Analytic processing	Holistic processing (dealing with overall patterns, or "gestalt" forms)
Temporal relations	Spatial relations
Speech sounds	Nonspeech sounds
Mathematics	Music
Intellectual	Emotional

start. Does a human being have two consciousnesses or one? Is the mute right hemisphere teeming with unsatisfied desires and ideas that will never be expressed due to its dominant, talkative left twin? If the connections between the two halves were severed, would the result be a creature with two quite distinct personalities, each having its own thoughts, worldview, and feelings? The famous nineteenth-century psychologist William McDougall thought not. In fact, so deep was his conviction that he offered to have his brain anatomically split should he develop a terminal illness. He never did, and the experiment was left undone in his lifetime.[13]

To the more prosaic, however, other questions arose: what else does the left hemisphere do? And what, if anything, is the special domain of the right hemisphere? Hypotheses meant to capture the brain's left-right dichotomy have sprung up in abundance, especially in the past fifteen years. These include the short list given in Table 11.1.

At its most fanciful, the contrast implied in the last pair of terms has led to global claims about "Eastern" and "Western" modes of thought, which, fascinating as they may be, are unsubstantiated. This speculation often comes uncomfortably close in spirit to the now-discounted claims of phrenologists in the early nineteenth century that bumps on each person's skull mirror "bumps on the brain," which in turn reveal personality traits.

But serious scientific questions arise from Table 11.1 as well. First, what counts as "language"? Most would agree that the word *cow*, printed on a card, should be perceived as language, but what about the single letter *c*? Or, for that matter, what about groups of letters that don't spell a word? There is some evidence that we perceive sequences like *kug, zeb,* or *bem* as language, while sequences like *nku, lke,* and *okl* are perceived more as though they were simply geometric shapes (Young et al., 1984). Pronounceability seems to be the cue here; one could imagine Dr. Seuss creating a character called a *Zeb,* if he hasn't already done so, but a name like *Lke* would take some getting used to, even for the most imaginative child.

---

[13] Springer and Deutsch (1985), p. 26.

More puzzling still, the very same linguistic material presented in two forms may be handled differently. Subjects seem to use the left hemisphere to read text in standard print such as this, but the right hemisphere is called upon to handle elaborate lettering styles, which presumably require more visual skill (Bryden and Allard, 1976). Likewise, mirror-image writing, or blurred or incomplete text, seems to be processed on the right.

In fact, subtleties of this sort abound. Japanese readers show some tendency for right-hemisphere activity when reading in the *kanji* script, where each character represents a word. But in the phonetically based *kana* script, where a letter usually stands for a syllable, the expected left-hemisphere dominance reemerges. Aphasia types distinguish between the two writing systems as well. Japanese aphasics often seem to retain some ability to read *kanji* script, while no longer able to comprehend the sound-based *kana* system. This again suggests that the processing of *kanji* characters can be mediated by areas outside the normal language centers, possibly in the right hemisphere.

Thus, some seemingly verbal tasks may be handled by the right hemisphere. And the converse seems also to be true: some spatial work seems to be done on the left, especially if it involves comparison or association between pairs of shapes. To further complicate matters, in an interesting study done in 1980, Gur and Reivich found no hemispheric advantage for a spatial (gestalt completion) test, suggesting that it can be handled equally well by either hemisphere. But there was a significant difference in how well the job was done: subjects who "chose" to use the right, spatially adept, hemisphere performed with significantly greater efficiency. But those who used the left hemisphere also achieved reasonable results; this suggests that, in some cases, the unspecialized hemisphere may be like an untrained worker who manages to succeed at a job although he may not be the ideal person to do it.

In the light of these and similar findings, researchers now believe that it is the type of *processing*, not the type of *material* processed, that distinguishes the two hemispheres; in other words, the first entry in Table 11.1 can be thought of as the only true difference. The left hemisphere is called upon whenever detailed analysis is in order, whereas the right hemisphere goes into action if holistic processing is needed. Language and mathematics typically involve sequential analysis or other kinds of analytical thinking, whereas pictures and faces are usually taken in all at once, as are musical patterns.

Under this more subtle view of lateralization, the Gur and Reivich results can be more plausibly explained. If, for some reason, a task does not clearly identify itself as requiring a right or left hemisphere approach, the job might be shunted off to different halves of the brain in different people—or even in the same person at different times, depending on which hemisphere happens to be more active. But it is quite reasonable to expect that the hemisphere with a more appropriate approach to the task will get better results.

Interesting support for the "processing strategy" approach comes from several experiments showing that trained musicians (who analyze as they listen) actually process music in the *left* hemisphere. Only the musically unsophisticated layperson, who hears music as holistic patterns, shows the expected right-hemisphere dominance. Layperson and musician hear the same patterns, but their reaction, their *way of listening*, differs.

Finally, once lateralization is seen in this more abstract way, another seemingly unrelated fact may tie in as well: the ability for fine, sequenced hand movements, called *manual praxis*, is also linked to the left hemisphere. Although hand movement and language seem very different on the surface, it is reasonable to suppose that a similar type of neural mechanism might be needed to orchestrate fine hand movements and to fashion complex sentence patterns.

This last point brings us back to the opening theme of this article: where did brain asymmetry come from? Was language the first activity to move into the analytical left hemisphere? Some think not. As a species, they argue, we must have developed fine manual coordination before language as we now know it. The need to make a rock into a sharp arrowhead or scraping tool calls for complex techniques involving fingers, wrist, and hand; this, many believe, is the left hemisphere's original specialty. If so, language may have been drawn to the left hemisphere simply because the neural circuitry available there for complex tool use was somehow suited to take on linguistic calculations.

This hypothesis remains open for debate. But tantalizing pieces of evidence seem to support it. For instance, in aphasia, fine hand coordination is often impaired along with language. Furthermore, the human species has been overwhelmingly right-handed for a long time, suggesting that asymmetry for handedness came early in human evolution. Cro-Magnon hand tracings were virtually always of the left hand; thus, the artists must have been drawing with the right. The skulls of prehistoric animals provide mute evidence as well; archeologists tell us that the earliest hunting hominids must have used tools held in the right hand to slay game, judging from the position of fractures and marks on the skulls of ancient animals.

Other hints scattered along our evolutionary trail lead to a quite different view. Brain asymmetry has been found elsewhere in the animal kingdom — in rodents, in other primates, and especially in birds. Even the most imaginative of scientists has yet to suspect a song sparrow of being an effective tool user, yet sparrows and chaffinches have song strongly lateralized in the left hemisphere. Looking at such species makes it seem plausible to some scientists that tool use is not necessarily the answer. In fact, it may have been the right brain, not the left, that first specialized. In the struggle for survival, even a rat can use an acute eye and a quick emotional response to avoid becoming dinner for a hungry hawk. Some would argue that, for humans too, the demands of survival and the hunt preceded the impulse toward language. If so, the right hemisphere's visual and emotional roles may have taken their place *before* left hemisphere functions. Language may have simply migrated to the left hemisphere by default, as it were.

TESTING THE BRAIN

The careful reader will by now wonder how all the claims in Table 11.1 can be made with certainty. How do we know what a single hemisphere is doing? There are, of course, the aphasia studies, but studies of brain malfunction are not ideally reliable. Suppose you wanted to find out what a specific transformer does in a radio: would you remove the transistor or break it, turn the radio on, and see what happens? Relying on aphasia as an indicator of localized function comes remarkably close to this intuitively unsatisfactory method. In fact, matters are even worse than a simple analogy would suggest. It is well known that brain tissue (unlike radio components) can "reorganize." That is, if one area of the brain is damaged, especially at an early age, other areas may take over the original tissue's function. Clearly, information from aphasia must be treated with caution.

The "Split Brain"

A surgical technique known as *commissurotomy*, used to treat severe cases of epilepsy, seems at first sight to provide perfect subjects for studying brain lateralization. Commissurotomy involves severing the *corpus callosum*, the main bundle of fibers connecting the brain's two hemispheres, as shown on the following page in Figure 11.4. With patients who have undergone this operation, neurologists can communicate with each cerebral hemisphere separately. Thus, using specialized techniques, one can show a picture or a written text to a single hemisphere and see how it responds.

These patients have been studied intensely, and with interesting results; but the general implications of these studies are controversial. Epilepsy is clearly accompanied by abnormal brain activity, often from an early age. Thus, as with aphasics, the brain tissue of split-brain patients may have reorganized in ways that make them atypical. For decades, researchers have grappled with these problems by searching for tests that can be used with normal subjects.

Behavioral Tests

A widely used technique called *tachistoscopic presentation* represents one attempt to learn what one hemisphere does more efficiently or

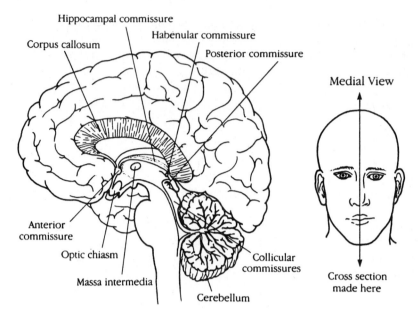

FIGURE 11.4.   The corpus callosum.

more accurately than the other. A subject is asked to fix her gaze on a central point directly in front of her. An image is then flashed to her right or left visual field. The subject does not know which side will display the image, and the flash is too brief (less than one-fifth of a second) to allow eye movement to one side or the other. Because of the human nervous system's organization, the image is perceived primarily by one side of the brain — the one *opposite* the visual field involved. If a subject handles stimuli presented on the right side of the screen better, she is assumed to be using the left hemisphere more actively.

Doreen Kimura at the Montreal Neurological Institute has adapted this principle to auditory stimuli in the *dichotic listening* test. The ear, like the eye, conveys messages most effectively via the so-called contralateral nerve pathway to the opposite hemisphere of the brain. Thus, if two different words are played to a subject's two ears, the left hemisphere will hear the word played to the right ear, and vice versa. As it turns out, many subjects consistently hear words more accurately with their right ear, but identify tunes played to the left ear more accurately. As with tachistoscopic data, dichotic listening results have played an important role in confirming the assumptions underlying Table 11.1.

The lateral eye movement (or LEM) provides a more indirect, and more controversial, way to look at brain activity via behavior. When answering a question, we tend to look left or right, rather than directly into the eyes of the asker. This sideways glance is said to show which hemisphere is providing the answer: activity on one side of the brain is said to trigger an automatic response to eye movement, in the opposite direction from the locus of mental activity. So, an emotional question should trigger an automatic eye shift leftwards; a verbal or intellectual question should cause the eyes to drift toward the right, while the analytical left hemisphere computes the necessary answer.

Unfortunately, behavioral tests have their drawbacks. A single subject tested twice with one week intervening may show different results. Furthermore, hemispheric activation at any given moment is fickle enough to be disrupted by seemingly minor factors, as in the phenomenon called "priming." Subjects are asked to memorize a list of words, thus presumably "turning on" the left hemisphere's circuits. If asked immediately afterwards to perform some spatial task that normally yields right-hemisphere dominance, they will often fail to show the expected result. Instead, they will perform the spatial task with the left hemisphere, presumably using the "wrong" processing strategy. To use a rough analogy, people seem to use the calculator which is already turned on, rather than the one specialized for the task at hand. Obviously, the success of lateralization tests demands control of such outside factors, which is no simple matter.

Physiological Measures

The cerebral cortex is highly asymmetrical, even to the naked eye. The Sylvian Fissure, a deep cleft running through the cortex, rises more sharply on the right, and is longer on the left. Its rear inner surface (called the *planum temporale*), which includes Wernicke's area, is usually larger on the left, even in fetal brains. In fact, the human skull, the brain's outer casing, protrudes noticeably in the left rear area, pushed out by the bulging left hemisphere. But despite a long and heated debate in the nineteenth century about the relationship between brain size and intelligence (Broca believed a large brain meant high intelligence), no detailed conclusions have resulted from gross measurement of brain tissue. More subtle methods are needed to deal with the brain in physiological terms.

Scientists have learned to observe chemical and electrical activity in different regions of the brain. Sophisticated devices for accomplishing this include computerized axial tomography (CT or CAT) scan, positron emission tomography (PET) scan, electroencephalogram (EEG), and measures of regional cerebral bloodflow (rCBF). Also useful is the famous Wada test, named after its developer, Juhn Wada.

In the Wada test, the powerful barbiturate sodium amytal is injected into the carotid artery leading to one hemisphere in patients about to undergo brain surgery, to determine whether language is affected. When the drug enters the language hemisphere, the patient's speech is arrested within seconds; thus, the surgeon can be sure which hemisphere should be protected during the operation. Yet another surgical technique involves direct stimulation of the brain. Pioneered in the 1950s by the surgeons Penfield and Wilder, this method has recently attracted renewed interest with the advent of improved techniques.

ARE WE ALL ALIKE?

What, the reader may ask, about *my* brain? Where do I store math, physics, music, or for that matter, language? Can one make a reliable guess for any individual brain as to how closely it approximates the classical model? The answer is "yes," — *but* only if you are a healthy monolingual, English-speaking, right-handed, hearing, adult male who can read. Beyond this class, caution is in order: some believe that the ideal classical pattern may apply to only about one person in four. The following sections show how populations may diverge from the picture given so far.

Babies

Babies, and even unborn fetuses, have physically enlarged language areas in their left hemisphere. Behaviorally, too, the very young show signs of asymmetry: by monitoring factors such as sucking response and changed heartbeat, one can determine the responses of infants to stimuli around them. Studies using such measures have found clear lateralization for speech sounds in the left hemisphere of infant brains, as opposed to chirps or nonspeech sounds, which the babies seem to process in the right hemisphere — this exists even in preterm babies born in about the thirty-sixth week of gestation.

However, until about age ten, child aphasia cases differ markedly from adult ones. Most young children show symptoms of something like Broca's aphasia regardless of where brain injury occurs within the left hemisphere. Thus, although language may be situated on the left by age five, localization within the left hemisphere may come later; hence, the classical diagram in Figure 11.3 may be only partially spelled out in children.

The question of infant asymmetry raises interesting questions. How can a brain that has no language be "specialized" for language? What kind of processing is the infant brain doing, and how does it assign a stimulus to a given hemisphere? Research on this intriguing topic may ultimately show which prelinguistic faculties lead to the development of language in children.

Bilinguals

A child's brain may in fact be like an electronic board with only some minimal (albeit highly significant) circuits provided at the outset. The details of the remaining circuitry may be up to the user to determine — in this case, the child, whose experiences in growing up "reconfigure" the brain's circuits. If so, different people may wire their neural boards in quite different ways, provided, that is, that they stay within the bounds imposed by the initial connections (which, in this case, ensure that some variant of wiring for human language emerges, and not binary code or birdsong).

Seen via this analogy, a bilingual speaker might be like a computer buff trying to do with one central processing unit the job normally done by two. Hence, one would expect the details of his processing machinery to be quite different. In fact, for some time, it has been noted that polyglot speakers (people with more than one language) produce unexpected aphasia types, perhaps because their experiences have led to special neural patterns. In about half the reported cases of polyglot aphasia, any recovery that takes place affects both (or all) languages at the same rate. Still, many patients recover one language earlier or more perfectly than others, and about one-fourth never regain one or more of their languages.[14] Physicians cannot predict which language will be recovered first or more fully, although some generalization is possible. The language best recovered is likely to be the last one used before injury, or the best known, or the one that is heard most during the recovery period.

Some rare cases pose especially perplexing challenges. One such case reported in 1980 involved a French-Arabic bilingual nun in Morocco who had a moped accident and became severely aphasic, losing speech altogether. Four days later, she could speak a few words of Arabic, but no French. After two weeks, she could speak French again fluently, but in the space of one day, her French fluency quite disappeared. She astounded observers by being able to converse fluently only in Arabic.[15]

The occurrence of bilingual aphasia suggests quite clearly that bilinguals have more right-hemisphere linguistic activity than monolinguals. Aphasia is about five times more likely to result from right-hemisphere damage in a polyglot speaker than in a monolingual: This can only be explained if some of a bilingual's linguistic ability is stored on the right side of the brain, or at least in areas not affected by damage to the classical language areas on the left. Research involving electrical stimulation of brain sites also gives some support for differential storage of two languages in a single brain: When the brain is stimulated at a given point, a patient may have trouble naming familiar objects. For bilinguals, naming difficulties in the two languages arise from stimulation at *different* points. Furthermore, electrical stimulation disturbs a patient's ability to name things in the less-proficient language over a broader range of sites, suggest-

---

[14] Grosjean (1982), p. 259.
[15] Grosjean (1982), p. 260.

ing that the second or nondominant language takes up more neural space than the first language.

Finally, some believe that the right hemisphere plays a major role in second-language learning, especially in the early stages when memory for stock phrases is essential to the learner. Can the very experience of learning a second language alter cerebral patterns in unexpected ways? Some early research suggests that bilingual children think differently — more independently and more creatively — and that this may extend to nonverbal areas. The significance of such intriguing findings has yet to be fully worked out.

The fact that languages can be stored, learned, or lost in different areas of the brain suggests strongly that the neural anatomy for two languages within a single brain can be different. Unfortunately, the relationship between gross anatomy and brain function remains mysterious. At best, we can turn to another analogy: Multilingual speakers may be telling us that the cerebral cortex is like a computer in some respects — highly complex, rigid in its basic setup, yet also versatile and subject to "programming" (here, unconscious) by the user.

Speakers Versus Signers

Users of American Sign Language (ASL or Ameslan) depend on manual activity, not speech, to encode basic meanings. If experience molds neural patterns, then the very nature of ASL raises some fascinating questions. Do the deaf generate and process signs in the left hemisphere? Can Broca's area, with its ability to interface with commands to the tongue and lips, also handle a system based on hand signals?

Early lateralization studies for ASL showed inconsistent results; some seemed to indicate right-hemisphere language processing, which could be explained by the visual nature of signing. Others concluded that signers had no cerebral asymmetry at all. The key may lie in the researchers' conception of signing: most early studies used static photographs to test asymmetry. But ASL signers do not communicate by flashing pictures at one another. In normal situations, signers deal with a number of dimensions at once: hand position, orientation, and crucially, *movement*. It makes intuitive sense to claim, as some have done, that signers in action *do* indeed make crucial use of the traditional left-brain language centers; we simply need more sophisticated techniques to verify this hypothesis.

Recent studies of impaired signers (see Bellugi, 1983) yield important evidence for the claim that signers may process language as oral speakers do: injury to the classical language areas on the left has been found to produce strikingly similar aphasia types in ASL and oral languages.

Here too, experience may be crucial. Deaf people whose schools used different training methods show consistently different patterns in the usual asymmetry tests. In fact, one startling finding about signers suggests that experience may be an even more potent force on the brain's map than previously suspected. Neville (1977) reported that he observed evoked potential (that is, electrical activity) in the *auditory* cortex of native signers in response to flashes of light. For oral speakers, the auditory cortex is the center, near Wernicke's area, where sound is first perceived. If Neville's claim is substantiated, the term "auditory cortex" may prove quite inappropriate for signers.

Readers, Japanese, and Others

The theme of experience leads neatly to the next point, which has implications for anyone reading this article. Where signing and multiple languages may cause a person's brain to diverge from the classical pattern, some believe that the experience of literacy may have a significant effect in *reinforcing* left-hemisphere dominance for language. Some studies report that illiterates show a much lower incidence of aphasia following left-hemisphere brain damage, and may even develop aphasia from right-hemisphere injury. If this is true, it suggests that language ability is more symmetrical in this group. Dealing with the written word may involve the left hemisphere's analytical techniques in such an intense way as to strengthen the ties between language and the left brain. This claim, however, has been controversial (it is challenged in Caplan 1987), and the aphasia data have proven difficult to confirm.

Yet another suggestion about early experience comes from Japanese. Normally, Americans tend to treat pure vowel sounds as "nonlanguage" in dichotic listening tests (sounds like *ah* and *ooooh* are likely to be interpreted as emotional utterances rather than as words). Japanese speakers, in contrast, seem to process single-vowel sounds on the left, as normal linguistic material. Professor Tadanoku Tsunoda of Tokyo's Medical and Dental University blames this on the "vowel dominant" nature of his language, which may influence the way Japanese children perceive the boundary between language and other sounds.[16]

This recalls a widely accepted claim about tone languages, based on lateralization for tone in Thai. Native speakers of Thai, who must make use of the pitch levels in a word to understand its meaning, tend to perceive tone as linguistic material. To most English speakers, the complex pitch patterns of a tone language like Thai or Vietnamese simply sound like some kind of puzzling singsong effect overlaid on speech; hence, they are likely to filter out the tone and send it off to the right hemisphere. Given this, it is not surprising that English speakers have substantial difficulty in learning tone languages!

---

[16] Brabyn (1982) p. 11.

Left-Handers and Women

Two more groups stand out as neurologically "different": left-handers and women. This time, the difference obviously cannot be linked to experience: genetics must play an important role.

This history of left-handers is fraught with myths and misleading ideas. In some societies, left-handed people have been viewed as clumsy and awkward, *gauche* if not downright *sinister*, to cite two words owing their origin to French and Latin forms meaning "left." In China, India, and in Arab countries, left-handers are said to have been banned from the dinner table. To many, however, reversed hand preference is seen as a sign of eminence: Michelangelo, Benjamin Franklin, Alexander the Great, and Einstein are cited as examples.

In their widely read book *Left Brain, Right Brain*, Sally Springer and Georg Deutsch include one chapter entitled "The Puzzle of the Left-Hander." They point out that it is difficult to even identify a left-hander for sure, since many people use the left hand for some activities and the right for others. Even supposedly unconscious tests for handedness (e.g., how a person crosses his arms, or draws a horse in profile, etc.) invariably yield mixed results.

Springer and Deutsch go on to trace opposing claims on the cause of handedness (genetic versus environmental), and many claims of smaller scope, such as the notion that the characteristic "inverted" writing position found in some left-handers may indicate left-hemisphere language, and that this may be part of a more general pattern for detecting "like-hemisphere" language and handedness. Supporters point to one isolated right-handed "inverter" who showed right-hemisphere language dominance.

But the puzzles of handedness remain. Scientists no longer believe that the left-handed person is simply a mirror image of a right-hander, with speech on the right and spatial abilities on the left. As many as 70 percent of left-handers have a dominant left hemisphere for language, just as do right-handers. Of the rest, half are thought to have bilateral language representation, with no clearly dominant hemisphere. This leaves a mere 15 percent of left-handers with language dominant on the right. Even this picture may not be accurate; one recent study reanalyzes data from aphasia and concludes that bilateral speech representation may be more common than previously believed, perhaps occurring in as high as 40 percent of all left-handed people (cited in Segalowitz and Bryden 1983, p. 348).

Aphasia tends to be less severe and to last a shorter time for left-handers, and even for right-handers in families with left-handed members. Moreover, left-handed speakers are eight times more likely than right-handers to suffer from aphasia after damage to the right hemisphere only. This must mean that they store more linguistic knowledge in the non-dominant hemisphere than do right-handers. Since there is no clear evidence for bilateral speech in right-handed monolinguals, this points to handedness as a clear indication of cerebral difference.

On women, our last interesting population, in 1879 the then-eminent social psychologist Gustave LeBon wrote:

> In the most intelligent races, as among the Parisians, there are a large number of women whose brains are closer in size to those of gorillas than to the most developed male brains . . . All psychologists who have studied the intelligence of women . . . recognize that they . . . represent the most inferior form of human evolution and that they are closer to children and savages than to an adult, civilized man.[17]

LeBon, following Broca, felt that bigger meant better in cerebral terms, and thus justified his sexist views by biological argument.

None but the most irrational antifeminist would today accept LeBon's comments. But we do know that women's brains are distinctive. For one thing, the gross physiological differences noted between the hemispheres are less obvious in women than in men. And other strong indicators of cerebral asymmetry are equally hard to confirm in women. Like left-handers, women may tend toward more symmetrical, evenly balanced, language capacities in the two hemispheres. Again, the aphasia statistics are revealing: women are less likely than men to become aphasic from unilateral damage to the left hemisphere. This suggests that, at the very least, the right hemisphere in women can take over language functions readily if the language centers on the left become disabled. More likely, the right hemisphere in women takes a more active role in language processing even in the absence of injury.

Behavioral tests yield supporting evidence. In dichotic listening tests, men outnumber women nearly 2–1 in showing right-ear advantage for verbal material. In fact, some early attempts to find cerebral asymmetries seem to have failed simply because they included too many female subjects! It is clear that neurological lateralization patterns must be considered in understanding the biological distinction between the sexes. Hopefully, further research will clarify and explain these differences.

WHERE DO WE GO FROM HERE?

The human brain still shelters the fundamental mystery of our existence: what does it mean to be human? Clearly, language must be an important part of the answer, and we have come a long way from the Egyptian physicians who attributed language disorders to the "breath of an outside god."[18] As this essay shows, much progress has been made in finding the answers to an ancient and fundamental question: how does

---

[17] Gould (1980), p. 155.
[18] Arbib et al. (1982).

the *homo sapiens* in Figure 11.1 differ from his Australopithecine ancestors? How does this creature manage to handle such a highly complex
communication system in the three pounds or so of gray matter lodged
in the human skull?

To fully understand the neurology of language, researchers will have
to answer the questions raised above, and many more not yet even hinted
at. How is language related to other cognitive skills? What goes on behind
the scenes, in the subcortical tissue beneath the language areas? (It is
clear that the thalamus, for instance, plays an important role in language.)

The complexity of the issues involved, and the way they touch on
many disciplines at once, is clearly reflected in recent publishers' lists:
two titles released in 1983 include the relatively new terms *neuropsychology* and *psychobiology. Neurolinguistics* has become a familiar term only
in the past decade. And a 1987 text cited in this essay provides an introduction to the new field of *linguistic aphasiology.* The next decade is
sure to see an ever-increasing crop of fascinating titles, as scholars from
many different areas together probe the mysteries of language, brain, and
cognition.

BIBLIOGRAPHY

Arbib, M. A., D. Caplan, and J. C. Marshall. "Neurolinguistics in Historical Perspective." In *Neural Models of Language Processes,* ed. M. Arbib, D. Caplan,
and J. Marshall. New York: Academic Press, 1982.

Bellugi, U. "Language Structure and Language Breakdown in American Sign Language." In *Psychobiology of Language,* ed. M. Studdert-Kennedy. Cambridge,
MA: MIT Press, 1983.

Blumstein, S. E. "Language Dissolution in Aphasia: Evidence for Linguistic Theory." In *Exceptional Language and Linguistics,* eds. L. Obler and L. Menn.
New York: Academic Press, 1982.

Brabyn, H. "Mother Tongue and the Brain." *UNESCO Courier,* Feb. 1982, 10–13.

Brown, J. W. "Case Reports of Semantic Jargon." In J. W. Brown, ed., 1981.

Brown, J. W., ed. *Jargonaphasia.* New York: Academic Press, 1981.

Bryden, M. P., and F. Allard. "Visual Hemifield Differences Depend on Typeface."
Brain and Language 3, 41–46, 1976.

Buckingham, H. "Where do Neologisms Come From?" In J. W. Brown, ed., 1981.

Caplan, D. *Neurolinguistics and Linguistic Aphasiology: An Introduction.* New
York: Cambridge University Press, 1987.

Caramazza, A., J. Gordon, E. G. Zurif, and D. DeLuca. "Right Hemisphere Damage
and Verbal Problem Solving Behavior." *Brain and Language* 3, 41–46, 1976.

Dennis, M. "Language Acquisition in a Single Hemisphere: Semantic Organization." In *Biological Studies of Mental Processes,* ed. D. Caplan. Cambridge,
MA: MIT Press, 1980.

Gardner, H., J. Silverman, W. Wapner, and E. Zurif. "The Appreciation of Ant-
onymic Contrasts in Aphasia." *Brain and Language* 6, 301–317, 1978.

Goodglass, H., and L. Menn. "Is Agrammatism A Unitary Phenomenon?" In M.-
L. Kean, ed. 1985.

Gould, S. J. *The Panda's Thumb: More Reflections in Natural History.* New York: W. W. Norton, 1980.

Grosjean, F. *Life With Two Languages.* Cambridge, MA: Harvard University Press, 1982.

Gur, R. C., and N. Reivich. "Cognitive Task Effects on Hemispheric Blood Flow in Humans: Evidence for Individual Differences in Hemispheric Activation." *Brain and Language* 9, 78–92, 1980.

Harth, E. *Windows on the Mind: Reflections on the Physical Basis of Consciousness.* New York: Morrow, 1982.

Kean, M.-L. "The Linguistic Interpretation of Aphasic Syndromes: Agrammatism in Broca's Aphasia, an Example." *Cognition* 5, 9–46, 1977.

Kean, M.-L., ed. *Agrammatism.* New York: Academic Press, 1985, 1977.

Milberg, W., S. Blumstein, and B. Dworetzky. "Processing of Lexical Ambiguities in Aphasia." *Brain and Language* 31, 138–150, 1987.

Neville, H. J. "Electroencephalographic Testing of Cerebral Specialization in Normal and Congenitally Deaf Children: A Preliminary Report." In *Language Development and Neurological Theory,* eds. S. Segalowitz and F. Gruber. New York: Academic Press, 1977.

Schwartz, M., M. Linebarger, and E. Saffran. "The Status of the Syntactic Theory of Agrammatism." In M.-L. Kean, ed. (1985).

Segalowitz, S., and M. Bryden. "Individual Differences in Hemispheric Representation of Language." In *Language Functions and Brain Organization,* ed. S. Segalowitz. New York: Academic Press, 1983.

Springer, S. P., and G. Deutsch. *Left Brain, Right Brain.* San Francisco: W. H. Freeman and Company, 1985, rev. ed.

Trevarthen, C. "Development of the Cerebral Mechanisms for Language." In *Neuropsychology of Language, Reading, and Spelling.* New York: Academic Press, 1983.

Wapner, W., S. Hamby, and H. Gardner. "The Role of the Right Hemisphere in the Apprehension of Complex Linguistic Materials." *Brain and Language* 14, 15–33, 1981.

Warrington, E. K., and T. Shallice. "Semantic Access Dyslexia." *Brain* 102, 43–63, 1979.

Winner, E., and H. Gardner. "The Comprehension of Metaphor in Brain-Damaged Patients." *Brain* 100, 719–727, 1977.

Young, A. W., A. W. Ellis and P. L. Birn. "Left Hemisphere Superiority for Pronounceable Nonwords, But Not for Unpronounceable Letter Strings." *Brain and Language* 22, 14–23, 1984.

=

FOR DISCUSSION AND REVIEW

1. What is the difference between Broca's area and Wernicke's area? How does each area seem to contribute to language production or understanding? How do relationships between these areas and cortical centers for sight, hearing, and motor function play an important role in Wernicke's overall model of how the brain works in terms of language?

2. Why might studies done on aphasics and split-brain subjects yield misleading information on brain lateralization?

3. Why is it difficult to clearly label a person as left- or right-handed? Do you know of any people who use different hands for different tasks? If so, list which hand is used for specific tasks. What pattern(s), if any, can you suggest?

4. Divide the following activities into two columns (*left* and *right*), according to which hemisphere you think is likely to be dominant for performing each. In cases where you are unsure, explain the aspects of the task that led you to list it tentatively on one side rather than the other:

    a. distinguishing between the syllables *ba* and *pa*
    b. choosing the right answer in a multiplication problem
    c. defining the word *independence*
    d. recognizing a friend's face
    e. singing the "Star Spangled Banner"
    f. deciding whether your employer is in a good mood
    g. recognizing the string of letters *ZBQ*
    h. playing the guitar
    i. recognizing a grasshopper's chirp
    j. understanding the utterance: "The girl was bitten by the dog."
    k. finding a word to rhyme with *inch*

5. There is some uncertainty about how blind people process Braille characters. In tests, it seems that subjects with good vision, when they first encounter the raised characters, can make them out best with their left hand. But it is very difficult to get clear-cut results for experienced Braille readers. How do you explain this? Discuss how this situation might be comparable to how trained and untrained people process music. What is the relationship to Heny's discussion of sign language? How would nonsigners be likely to process signs?

6. Would you expect a measure of electrical impulses from the brain of a sleeping person during an active dreaming session to reveal left or right hemispheric activity? Why? What kind of mental activity seems to be going on when a person dreams?

7. How do dichotic listening and tachistoscopic tests work? If a subject sees or hears more accurately on the left, which cerebral hemisphere must be involved? Why?

8. In general terms, how do women and left-handers seem to differ from other individuals in terms of brain asymmetry?

9. Suppose you constructed an experiment in which you asked people to choose a picture that matches the sentence: "He's really gotten himself into a nice pickle now!" Their choices include illustrations of:

a. A man who has just dug his way into a giant pickle.
b. A man with a bewildered look on his face standing near a disabled car on an isolated road. His clothes are covered with grease, and strewn around him on the ground are what appear to be the parts of his engine.
c. A man sitting in an armchair reading a book.

What performance would you expect on this test from each of the following groups, and why?

a. Broca's aphasics
b. Wernicke's aphasics
c. right-hemisphere–damaged patients
d. normal "control" subjects

12

≡

The Loss of Language

Howard Gardner

The limitations of handicapped people often give us a better understanding of the normal. We can also learn a great deal from the many people who suffer from aphasia, *the loss of language skills resulting from damage to the brain, usually from a stroke or traumatic head injury. In the following selection, Howard Gardner, author of* The Shattered Mind, The Quest for Mind, Frames of Mind, *and* Art, Mind, and Brain, *describes the symptoms of two major kinds of aphasia. The first is* Wernicke's aphasia, *whose victims speak fluent nonsense and have great difficulty both in uttering words that refer to specific objects and people and in understanding others' speech; the second is* Broca's aphasia, *whose victims can speak only slowly and imperfectly and have difficulty understanding speech in which word order, inflections, and other grammatical signals are especially important. Gardner suggests that linguists, as well as physicians and psychologists, have an important role to play in understanding aphasia, and that aphasia in turn can test linguists' assumptions about their subject, perhaps even offering an approach to some long-standing psychological and philosophical questions about language and thought.*

Skill in language develops so quickly and operates so smoothly that we take our linguistic capacities largely for granted. Most three-year-olds can speak simple grammatical sentences and execute simple commands. Nearly every 10-year-old in our society can read and write at the primer level and most adults can read a novel in an afternoon or write several letters in an evening.

Our linguistic potentials are even more impressive. Placed in a foreign culture, particularly as children, we readily learn the basic phrases of another language; and all of us, bilingual or not, have mastered various language-related codes — the number system (Arabic or Roman), musical notation, Morse code, or the familiar trademarks for commercial products.

The loss of various language abilities in the otherwise normal adult is tragic, and the consequences are as devastating as those of blindness, deafness, or paralysis (which often accompanies it). Deprived of the power to communicate through language and language-like channels, the individual is cut off from the world of meaning. . . . Though loss of language is relatively rare among young persons, it becomes increasingly common with age—about one quarter of a million individuals suffer linguistic impairment each year. The extent and duration of language disability vary greatly, but a significant proportion of the afflicted individuals are left with a permanent impairment. Those who suffer language loss as a consequence of damage to their brains are victims of the strange condition called aphasia.

Aphasic individuals are not always immediately recognizable. One patient whom I recently interviewed appeared to be normal when he entered the room: a nice-looking, well-groomed, sixty-two-year-old, re- tired bookkeeper. He answered my first questions appropriately and with a speed that suggested nothing was amiss. Asked his name, the gentleman responded, "Oh, my name, that's easy, it is Tuh, Tom Johnson and I. . . ." It was only when I gave Mr. Johnson a chance to speak a bit more that the extent and nature of his aphasia became clear:

"What kind of work have you done, Mr. Johnson?" I asked.

"We, the kids, all of us, and I, we were working for a long time in the . . . you know . . . it's the kind of space, I mean place rear to the spedwan. . . ."

At this point I interjected, "Excuse me, but I wanted to know what work you have been doing."

"If you had said that, we had said that, poomer, near the fortunate, forpunate, tamppoo, all around the fourth of martz. Oh, I get all con- fused," he replied, looking somewhat puzzled that the stream of language did not appear to satisfy me.

Mr. Johnson was suffering from a relatively common language disor- der called Wernicke's aphasia. Patients with this disorder have no trouble producing language—if anything, the words flow out too freely and it sometimes proves difficult to silence them. Nor do Wernicke's aphasics have any trouble producing the words that structure and modulate speech—"if," "and," "of," and the like. But when they try to come up with specific substantives—nouns, verbs, and adjectives that specify per- sons, objects, events, and properties—these patients have great difficulty. As Mr. Johnson exhibited several times, aphasics frequently cannot issue the precise words they want to say, and they frequently wander from the stated topic to another, the meaning of which remains obscure to the listener.

From my description of the interview, it may seem that Mr. Johnson understood what I was saying but was simply encountering trouble in responding appropriately. This supposition was quickly and dramatically dispelled when I took a key and a pencil from my pocket and asked him to point in turn to each one. These two simple words, known to any child, eluded him. When asked to point to other objects and to body parts, he also fared poorly, as he had when trying to name certain objects. He could not read words aloud correctly, nor could he understand most written commands, though he did read letters and numbers aloud. Any by-stander would have inferred that Mr. Johnson's understanding was very limited (as indeed it was).

One fascinating island of preserved comprehension remained, how-ever. Toward the close of the interview I said, almost out of the blue, "Oh, Mr. Johnson, would you please stand up and turn around twice?" Suddenly, as if his comprehension had been magically restored, Mr. John-son stood up and proceeded to rotate in just the way I requested. He was also able to carry out several commands that involved his whole body (like "Lean forward" or "Stand at ease"). However, this preserved compre-hension could not be elicited in any other manner.

Mr. Johnson, a Wernicke's aphasic, can be instructively contrasted with another patient whom I recently met. Mr. Cooper, a forty-seven-year-old former Army officer, was seated in a wheelchair, obviously para-lyzed on the entire right side of his body. A slight droop on the right side of his face became more noticeable when he opened his mouth or smiled. When I asked what was wrong with him, Mr. Cooper immediately pointed to his arm, his leg, and his mouth. He appeared reluctant to speak at all. Only when I pressed him did he point again to his mouth and with obvious effort blurt out the sound "Peech."

I posed Mr. Cooper a number of questions that could be answered by "yes" or "no," and in each case he nodded appropriately. I then said that it was important that he try to speak. Noting his wedding ring, I asked, "How many children do you have?" Mr. Cooper looked blank for a time. Then he peered at his fingers and began to raise them, accompanying the motion with low and strained sounds: "one, two, tree, pour, no pive . . . yes pive," he said triumphantly.

Next, I asked him to tell me about the kind of work he had been doing.

"Me . . . build—ing . . . chairs, no, no cab—in—nets." The words came out slowly, taking him forty seconds to finish.

"One more question," I said. "Can you tell me how you would go about building a cabinet?"

Mr. Cooper threw up his left hand in frustration, and after I gently insisted that he attempt a verbal explanation, he said, "One, saw . . . then, cutting wood . . . working. . . ." All of this was said with great effort and poor articulation, which left me (and Mr. Cooper) unprepared for a sudden oath, "Jesus Christ, oh boy." This was uttered effortlessly, as if another language mechanism—an island of preserved production—had tempo-rarily been stimulated.

During the rest of our examination, Mr. Cooper performed well on tasks that required little language production. On request he pointed eas-ily to objects around the room and even to a series of objects placed in front of him. He read simple commands silently and carried them out clumsily but properly. He could name some familiar objects and read aloud some names of objects, though he failed at reading aloud letters of

the alphabet and small grammatical words such as articles and prepositions. He could read aloud the word "bee," but not "be," though the latter
occurs more frequently in spoken and written language. He could carry
a melody and sing lyrics to familiar songs more readily than he could
recite those same lyrics.

But Mr. Cooper had definite difficulties in understanding. Although
he could designate a series of two objects, he sometimes failed at three
and he never succeeded at four—the level of success achieved by most
normal adults. He caught the drift of nearly all questions in casual conversation, and could almost always produce at least a minimally appropriate
response, but he experienced significant problems with questions that
involved careful attention to word order and inflection. I could stump
him with sentences like "Do you put on your shoes before you put on
socks?" or "The lion was killed by the tiger: Which animal is dead?" or
"With the pen touch the pencil." Just as Mr. Cooper's spontaneous speech
was limited largely to nouns and verbs and virtually devoid of words that
modulate meaning, so too he often failed on questions and commands
that required him to note the order of words and the meanings of prefixes,
suffixes, and other grammatical fixtures.

Mr. Johnson and Mr. Cooper illustrate two of the most common
forms of aphasia. In six years of work with aphasic patients, I have seen
dozens of patients whose symptoms closely resemble those of one or the
other man. Mr. Johnson is a victim of Wernicke's aphasia; as a result of
damage to the left temporal lobe of his brain his auditory comprehension
has become severely impaired, but he remains able to produce long, often
obscure, strings of speech. Mr. Cooper has Broca's aphasia, a condition
caused by damage to the left frontal lobe. He understands language, although not perfectly; his chief difficulty is in producing words, specifically those that modify nouns and verbs. The language of the Broca's
aphasic is called agrammatic (or telegrammatic), and such a patient's understanding suffers from some of the same limits that affect his spontaneous speech.

These and other aphasic syndromes are the regular and nearly inevitable consequences of significant damage to the left hemisphere of the brain
in normal right-handed individuals. As a result of a stroke, head injury,
or brain tumor, cortical (or surface) tissue is destroyed in this half of
the brain. Such lesions impair linguistic functions and frequently cause
paralysis and loss of sensation in the opposite (right) side of the body.
(The situation is somewhat different, and much more complex, in left-
handers.)

The precise location and extent of the brain damage determine the
nature of the linguistic disorder. There are forms of aphasia (called alexia)
in which an individual's ability to read is most severely impaired;
agraphia, in which disorders of writing are most pronounced; anomia,
in which most language functions are preserved but there is magnified
difficulty in naming objects; conduction aphasia, in which speech and

understanding are relatively intact but the patient experiences enormous difficulty in repetition; and a bizarre complementary condition called mixed transcortical aphasia, in which both conversational speech and comprehension are almost entirely destroyed, yet the patient retains the capacity to repeat, and even to echo, long strings of meaningful or meaningless words (it makes little difference which). The striking predictability of these syndromes reflects the uniformity with which language functions are organized in normal right-handed individuals.

Each of these conditions cries out for explanation. There are alexics who can read numbers, including Roman numerals, but not words or letters; transcortical aphasics who understand nothing but who will, in their repetitions, spontaneously correct ungrammatical phrases; anomic aphasics who cannot produce a familiar word (e.g., nose) but will readily produce a highly improbable substitute (proboscis). To be sure, not all aphasics show such clear syndromes; the syndromes are most likely to occur in individuals of middle age or older, who are fully right-handed, and who have suffered a stroke. Yet nearly every aphasic patient exhibits some bizarre combination of symptoms, and many exemplify the textbook descriptions in the preceding paragraph.

A first meeting with aphasic patients is often dramatic; their symptoms are frequently fantastic and disturbing. A person's first impulse is to aid these victims of brain disease in any way possible. But the study

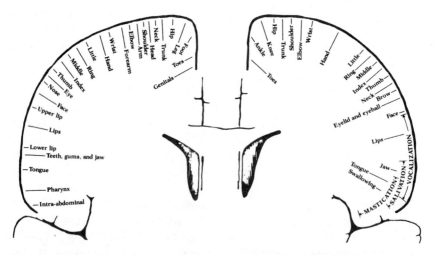

FIGURE 12.1.   Once Paul Broca and Carl Wernicke had linked two varieties of aphasia to specific areas in the brain, neurologists began trying to locate all intellectual functions. Although they failed, they did succeed in identifying the areas connected with most motor and sensory functions. This figure locates the relative amount of brain space devoted to various functions. On the right are the areas that control motor functions; the fine muscles that control the lips and hands take up the most space. On the left are the areas that receive sensory input from skin receptors.

of their condition has an importance that goes beyond helping victims of aphasia; it holds the promise of clarifying a host of philosophical and psychological issues about the nature of language and the mind.

Reports of aphasia can be found in many classical writings and even in the Bible. Yet the serious scientific study of aphasia began just over a century ago when Pierre Paul Broca, a French anatomist, described two cases whose symptoms resembled Mr. Cooper's. Broca's cases were important not because of the way he described their behavior patterns but because he made an analytic leap. Noting that both of these cases had brain damage in the anterior portion of the left hemisphere, Broca proposed that this part of the brain played a special role in language. Besides immortalizing his name (Broca's aphasia, Broca's area), this discovery laid the groundwork for all aphasia research.

The reason for this breakthrough was simple but instructive. Until Broca's time, nearly all scientists assumed that the two halves of the brain, which on casual inspection look alike, carried out the same functions. It had often been observed that aphasia accompanied strokes and paralysis, but Broca was the first to argue publicly that language disorders are linked to the left portion of the brain. Though his announcement provoked controversy, supporting cases were quickly reported. Thirteen years later Carl Wernicke, a German neuropsychiatrist, described another set of symptoms, this time primarily affecting comprehension. He linked them to the left posterior (particularly temporal) lobe of the brain, thereby contributing his name to another brain area and another type of aphasia. Even more than Broca's discoveries, Wernicke's work stimulated scientists to construct models of language based on the behavior of brain-injured patients. [See Figure 11.3, p. 206.]

Broca and Wernicke gave impetus to a group of neurologists who have been called localizers. Adherents of this approach carefully investigated the anatomy of the human brain, the structure of the cortical tissue, and the connections between the different parts of the nervous system. Building on this refined knowledge of human neuroanatomy, they sought to discover the functions that were governed by each part of the brain. Their first step was to locate the motor functions (or voluntary actions), which are associated with sites in the frontal lobe, and the sensory functions, associated with sites in the parietal, temporal, and occipital lobes. But the localizers went beyond these relatively elementary processes and tried to apportion even the highest intellectual and emotional functions to specific regions of the brain.

Findings about language function spurred them on. Researchers had discovered an indisputable "high" human function — one denied all other animals — occupying specific regions in the brain. The type of aphasia discovered by Broca and the startlingly different one described by Wernicke were but the first manifestations of this line of analysis. Within twenty years, a gaggle of aphasias had been described, each traced to a specific area in the brain, each exhibiting its own enigmatic symptoms.

Researchers transcended these correlations between brain and behavior to propose models of language function. In one popular version the language signal entered Wernicke's area, where it was comprehended; then a return message was fired forward to Broca's area, where it was fitted out with grammatical trimmings and ultimately spewed forth to the world. It naturally followed that a lesion confined to Broca's area allowed comprehension at the cost of grammatical speech, whereas destruction of Wernicke's area impaired comprehension but allowed a stream of grammatically rich, but often meaningless speech.

The localizers probably went too far in their approach. In the early part of this century, a rival school reanalyzed Broca's original cases and announced that there was but one type of aphasia, the form stemming from lesions in and around Wernicke's area. Broca's aphasics, they said, were linguistically intact individuals who suffered only from problems in articulating their speech. Followers of this theory pointed out that not even textbook cases of Broca's aphasia showed all the observed symptoms and that some displayed additional symptoms. In their view, lesions anywhere in the left hemisphere could produce aphasia, and its severity reflected primarily the size of the lesion rather than its site. These partisans went on to argue that every aphasic exhibits difficulties in all language functions. Differences among the so-called syndromes, they said, are differences in degree (a little more reading difficulty in one case, a little more repetition difficulty in another) rather than in kind.

Today, after a century of research, there is little sympathy for either of the conflicting theories. Due in large measure to the efforts of Norman Geschwind, professor of neurology at the Harvard Medical School, the genuine contributions of the localizers are again appreciated. At the same time, a range of factors that modulate the classic syndromes — such as the nature of the brain disease, the age of the patient, or the situation of testing — are also recognized. The classic syndromes are seen as useful signposts for describing patients rather than as fixed descriptions of what a patient with a given lesion can and cannot do.

Progress has been stimulated by a number of factors. In the wake of this century's wars, researchers have seen hundreds of patients with aphasia. The publication of numerous cases and countercases has clarified our knowledge of the incidence of full-blown examples of the classic syndromes and produced precise descriptions of the symptoms of aphasia.

But perhaps the biggest contribution has come from interactions among specialists from diverse disciplines, each of whom had approached aphasia from a different perspective. In my own view, the most important infusions have come from linguists, who have brought to the study of aphasia logical and well-conceived categories for the analysis of language, and from psychologists, whose accurate experimental techniques have supplemented the important but necessarily superficial methods of bedside examination evolved by attending physicians.

Issues raised by routine bedside testing often stimulate research by interdisciplinary teams. Consider, for instance, Mr. Cooper's apparent success at understanding spontaneous conversation. Such observations have led many neurologists to conclude that a patient with Broca's aphasia has no difficulties in comprehending language. Teams of linguists and psychologists noted, however, that when such patients were tested, they received multiple cues from the context in which a question was posed and from redundancies within the message. Accordingly, they devised questions that could be understood only if one were processing grammatical inflections and exploiting cues of word order. Deprived of the redundancy of ordinary conversational speech, individuals with Broca's aphasia showed only meager comprehension.

Turning to issues raised by Mr. Johnson, experimenters have also clarified the nature of the comprehension defect in Wernicke's aphasia. Because these patients have difficulty understanding auditory messages and decoding single isolated words, some aphasiologists concluded that the primary impediment for the Wernicke's aphasic lay in his inability to decipher individual phonemes — the smallest discrete sounds of language, such as "th," "p," and "b." Careful experimental studies have documented, however, that Wernicke's aphasics can readily discriminate between individual phonemes; they may surpass Broca's aphasics at this task. Their difficulty in understanding occurs at a higher level of semantic interpretation.

Not all the contributions have come from research scientists. Demonstrations by clinicians sometimes challenge — and even undermine — the workaday categories embraced by researchers. None of the categorical distinctions honored by psychologists or linguists can explain Mr. Johnson's curious ability to carry out commands that use the whole body. If, however, one takes into account certain anatomical considerations, this behavior becomes clarified. Unlike commands using the face or individual limbs, which are carried out by the major pyramidal motor pathways running from the cortex to the spinal cord, these commands are executed by the alternative nonpyramidal tracts of the nervous system. A lesion in Wernicke's area usually spares these tracts. Here is a case where an anatomical point of view advances the explanation of aphasic behavior.

Constant interplay between bedside testing and experimental work proves crucial, since experimenters tend to devise careful but artificial test situations. When a patient fails on such a test, it becomes difficult to determine whether the patient lacks the ability in question or is simply confused by the instructions or by the task itself. Sometimes a patient fails on an experimenter's test only to demonstrate the skill in question when a natural situation arises in his life. A patient may fail to repeat an arbitrary set of phrases spoken by an experimenter and yet produce just these phrases in situations where they are warranted. Thus, in a curiously productive way, clinicians and experimenters keep one another honest.

It is impossible to understand the mind without considering its linguistic capacities. Yet both linguists and psychologists face a fundamental problem: the categories, distinctions, terminology, and levels of linguistic competence are based on the study of individuals in whom all linguistic capacities are operating efficiently. These individuals can produce the proper sounds, combine words according to the structure of a language, understand the meaning of the words they use, and use language appropriately in natural situations. Scholars have divided the study of language in the same way, analyzing it in terms of its phonological, syntactic, semantic, and pragmatic levels. No independent means exists for examining the validity of these categories, for determining whether another means of slicing the linguistic pie might not prove more comprehensive and accurate.

Here is where aphasia can make a unique contribution. Were it the case, as some researchers once implied, that all language skills break down simultaneously in aphasia, this pathological condition would hold little scientific interest. But aphasia proves remarkably selective in its damage. A patient may have an impaired ability to read while still being able to write, fail to comprehend and yet speak, fail to understand and yet repeat accurately. These and numerous other dissociations can demonstrate the validity of certain categories of analysis. For example, both Broca's aphasia and transcortical aphasia provide evidence for a separate level of syntactic analysis in the brain.

At other times the dissociations call into question some of the distinctions made by linguists. Aphasia gives little support for the linguist's distinction between competence and performance. Symptoms that violate our expectations can suggest new distinctions and categorization that linguists have ignored, as in the case of the dichotomy in the brain's response to "whole-body" and other kinds of commands. Aphasia provides a testing laboratory for the distinctions made by those who study human languages — the primary window to the mind.

The study of aphasia may help to clarify several long-standing philosophical questions. Is language the ultimate symbol system on which all other modes of symbolization are parasitic? Or do other symbol systems exist that are relatively autonomous of language? Results from the study of aphasia indicate that language is but one of man's symbolic competences. Once a person's language ability is impaired, he ordinarily shows a lessened capacity to "read" other symbols. Yet this is not always the case. Many severely aphasic patients can carry out calculations, gesture meaningfully, or read musical notation.

Research on aphasia also pertains to another philosophical chestnut: the extent to which thought depends upon language. Aphasia exacts tolls on performance in various concept-formation tasks, as do all forms of brain damage. Yet it is by no means uncommon to encounter a severely aphasic individual who can solve a difficult maze or puzzle, play a game of chess or bridge, or score above normal on the nonverbal section of the Wechsler Adult Intelligence Scale. Other aphasic individuals have continued to paint, compose, or conduct music at a professionally competent level.

Mental functioning in aphasia is relevant to an issue of great current interest: the functions of the left and right hemispheres of the brain. In nearly all right-handers, the left hemisphere of the brain is specialized for language; lesions there will result in significant impairment of language. Such an injury spares right-hemisphere functioning and the aphasic patient remains relatively skilled in those functions for which the right hemisphere is superior — visual-spatial orientation, musical understanding, recognition of faces, and emotional balance.

In working with hundreds of aphasic patients I have been struck by the extent to which they seem to be well oriented, generally aware of what is going on around them, and appropriately attuned to emotional situations. And I have been struck, in contrast, by the frequently inappropriate and disoriented behavior of patients with right-hemisphere lesions, individuals whose language remains essentially intact but whose intuitive understanding of the world seems to have gone awry. In these areas, which have remained recalcitrant to formal testing, one may secure the best evidence that common sense does not depend on competence in language.

Anyone who has spent time with aphasic individuals will recognize the need to help these victims; their personal frustration is so glaring. In the wake of experiments by aphasiologists, speech pathologists have been able to begin rehabilitation with a greater understanding of the processes (and limitations) of language function, and with a heightened ability to exploit those mental powers ordinarily spared in aphasia. To be sure, no rehabilitation can fully compensate for destroyed brain tissue; the best healers are still time, youth, and — at least in matters of language — the degree of left-handedness in one's family.

Research on brain function has led to certain significant breakthroughs in aphasia therapy. Speech pathologists at the Boston Veterans Administration Hospital have devised a training program that significantly boosts language output. Their work is based on the clinical observation that Broca's aphasics can often sing well, and on experimental findings that musical and intonational patterns are mediated by structures in the right hemisphere. During the first phase of this rehabilitation program, called Melodic Intonation Therapy, patients sing simple phrases; in ensuing phases, they learn to delete the melody, leaving only the words. Mr. Cooper, who could sing lyrics to songs but had difficulty reciting them, would seem a likely candidate for this therapy. If he succeeds as well as other patients, in about three months he should be able to produce short but grammatical and appropriate sentences.

The study of aphasia is still in its infancy, but interest in this field has grown so rapidly that advances in understanding and rehabilitation are likely. Few areas of study feature as close a linkage between the medical and the scientific, the clinical and the experimental, the concerns of the theorist and the practitioner. And the mysteries to be solved are inextricably linked with the vast enigmas of language, brain, and mind. It is paradoxical — yet in a strange way heartening — that those who can say little may help us answer questions that have until now eluded even the most eloquent philosophers.

BIBLIOGRAPHY

Gardner, Howard, *The Shattered Mind.* New York: Knopf, 1975.

Goldstein, Kurt. *Language and Language Disturbances.* New York: Grune & Stratton, 1948.

Goodglass, Harold, and Norman Geschwind. "Language Disorders, Aphasia." *Handbook of Perception*, Vol. 7, ed. Edward Carterette and Morton Friedman. New York: Academic Press, 1976.

Goodglass, Harold, and Edith Kaplan. *The Assessment of Aphasia and Related Disorders.* Philadelphia: Lea & Febiger, 1972.

Luria, A. R. *Traumatic Aphasia: Its Syndromes, Psychology, and Treatment.* New York: Humanities Press, 1970.

===

FOR DISCUSSION AND REVIEW

1. What is the general definition of aphasia? How common a phenomenon is it? Who are its most frequent victims?

2. Describe the symptoms of Wernicke's aphasia. Reread the interview with Mr. Johnson, and give specific examples of these symptoms. Is he equally capable of dealing with nouns, verbs, and adjectives (content words) and with words like *if* and *of* (function words)? Note that Gardner states that "Mr. Johnson's understanding was very limited."

3. Examine the chart of the homunculus on p. 230, and consider the relative amount of brain space devoted to various motor functions and to sensory input reception from the skin. What conclusions can you draw? (Compare, for example, the amount of brain space devoted to motor functions of the mouth and that devoted to the trunk of the body, or compare the space allocated to the hands versus the feet. In terms of sensory input, which body areas use the most brain space? Why?)

4. Describe the symptoms of Wernicke's aphasia, and show how they are manifested in Mr. Cooper's behavior. Note the extent of his ability to deal with function words and with complex syntactic constructions (e.g., the passive). What similarities, if any, do you see with certain stages of language acquisition?

5. Compare and contrast Mr. Johnson and Mr. Cooper (or the symptoms of Broca's aphasia and Wernicke's aphasia).

6. There is not complete agreement on the names for all types of aphasia. Explain each of the following, which are in general use, as Gardner defines them: *alexia, agraphia, anomia, conduction aphasia,* and *mixed transcortical aphasia.*

7. Drawing on the previous article by Jeannine Heny (pp. 201–23), explain Gardner's statement that "The striking predictability of [the various types of aphasia] reflects the uniformity with which language functions are organized in normal right-handers."

8. How, today, have the extreme forms of the "localizers'" theory been modified? Describe four specific contributions to the understanding of aphasia made by linguists and psychologists (e.g., comprehension in Broca's aphasia, decipherment problems in Wernicke's aphasia).

9. What are three important implications of the fact that "aphasia proves remarkably selective in its damage," that not all language skills are damaged equally or simultaneously?

10. How can the study of aphasia increase our understanding (1) of the human use of symbols; (2) of *what* thought, if any, is possible without language; and (3) of hemispheric specialization?

13

Crazy Talk

Elaine Chaika

Scientists have long been baffled by the unusual things schizophrenics say. Their odd speech seems to come and go with the illness itself. Recently linguists have shed new light on the hotly debated issue of why schizophrenic speech occurs. In this selection from Psychology Today *Elaine Chaika, professor of linguistics at Providence College, studies the characteristics of schizophrenic speech in an attempt to offer insight into the mysteries of language in general. Chaika gives an overview of the characteristics of schizophrenic speech together with several current psychiatric theories on the subject. She examines differences between normal and schizophrenic speech patterns in an attempt to uncover specific areas of the brain, such as those controlling creativity, word association, and filtering techniques, that are affected by the disorder. As a linguist, Chaika suggests some causes of schizophrenic speech, and she offers several solutions for treating it.*

"My mother's name was Bill . . . and coo? St. Valentine's Day is the start of the breedin' season of the birds. All the buzzards can coo. I'd like to see it pronounced buzzards rightly. They work hard. So do parakeets."

Who would say such strange things, and why? The who is easy to answer. Some schizophrenics talk this way, but not all. And even among those who do, the odd speech comes and goes with the illness.

The question of why has been hotly debated for decades and has received a variety of answers. We are all creatures of our training. Psychiatrists are trained to look at humans in terms of stimulus and response. And linguists, like me, are trained to examine language in terms of levels of production and failures to apply linguistic rules—an approach that I believe has a special contribution to make in understanding schizophrenic speech. But first, let's look at other explanations.

The psychiatric resident who introduced me to the vagaries of schizophrenic speech subscribed to an idea that no longer has much support—Bateson's Double Bind theory. The schizophrenic's mother hates her child, the theory holds, but cannot accept the idea. When the child protests, the mother not only insists that she does love him or her but punishes the child for saying she doesn't. Or the child attempts to kiss the mother, who subtly rebuffs him and then later says, "Why don't you ever kiss me?" The child is caught in a double bind, unable to resolve or escape the contradictory demands, and never learns to communicate properly.

There are several problems with this interpretation. For one thing, children do not learn to speak solely from their parents, but also from playmates, teachers and other adults. Furthermore, there is little solid evidence that many adult schizophrenics were caught in a double bind as children or for that matter, that many normal people were not.

Some clinical psychologists and psychiatrists suggest that the strange speech helps schizophrenics avoid the therapeutic situation. A related theory is that schizophrenics speak strangely to express and at the same time hide socially unacceptable feelings, such as homosexual tendencies.

If we adopt these explanations, we are still left with a mystery. Normal language skills allow us to think one thing and say something else or nothing at all. Why would schizophrenics choose to produce such bizarre speech to avoid therapy or hide feelings? Its very strangeness draws attention, not the best situation for someone wanting to hide ideas or avoid a situation.

There is also the question of why schizophrenics speak this way only during their psychotic episodes. It seems reasonable to assume that the speech is a symptom of the illness rather than a learned response. What we really need to establish is how or why the illness causes the peculiar speech.

David V. Forrest and other psychiatrists suggest that these strange utterances are poetic. Schizophrenics use strange, even bizarre, speech to describe what it is to be schizophrenic. Forrest maintains that all speech is metaphorical, and that the psychiatrist's task is to interpret its deep meaning. For example, we all know about Freudian slips. If someone says "no" instead of "yes," a Freudian analyst would say that the person subconsciously really meant no. Psychiatrists look for this kind of meaning everywhere. Schizophrenic speech, more complex than a simple slip, requires even more skillful interpretation.

Forrest illustrates his point by citing the patient who said: "Doctor, I have pains in my chest, and hope and wonder if my box is broken and heart is beaten for my soul and salvation and heaven, Amen."

This means, Forrest says, "Doctor, I am heartbroken and hopeless and I pray you will save me."

Why didn't the patient just come out and say so? Because, according to Forrest, poetic speech is more powerful, more moving. He is telling what it is like to be schizophrenic. He is indulging in poetry.

To test the idea that schizophrenic speech is really poetic language, let us analyze another example, this one reported by a psychologist who had asked the patient to identify a color chip:

"Looks like clay. Sounds like gray. Take you for a roll in the hay. Hay Day. Mayday. Help. I need help."

This certainly rhymes and we associate poetry with rhyme. But in most poetry, rhyme and imagery are subordinate to meaning. In the above example, the first phrase in the sequence is correct; the chip was clay-colored. The rest of the rhyming, however, is an out-of-control associating of words that happen to end with the same final sounds. There seems no other reason for "sounds like gray." "Roll in the hay" is yet another chance rhyme. "Hay day" and "Mayday" continue the rhyme, and perhaps share the meaning of "fun" with the preceding phrase. Finally, "Help!" is what "Mayday" means.

Perhaps the patient really did feel in need of help, but it seems unlikely that the entire sequence was deliberately chosen to lead to "Help!" If it were, we would then have the problem of explaining why someone would ask for help in such a bizarre fashion.

Poetic rhymes and imagery ordinarily don't show this almost random going from one word or phrase to another. The words, bizarre or otherwise, are chosen with final sounds that are alike but which fulfill the larger meaning of the poem. Robert Frost's humorous "The Span of Life" is a good example:

> "The old dog barks backward without getting up,
> I can remember when he was a pup."

The unusual choice of wording gives an image of a dog barking backward in time, as well as of turning his head to bark at something behind him. Both the rhyme and word choice fit in with the second line, which reinforces the idea that he is now an old dog. The deviation from normal speech is based on meaning, not chance similarity between words.

Our everyday language skills let us create sentences and comprehend the words of others, linguist Noam Chomsky has shown, even when we never before have seen or heard those words in that order. We understand even complex poetry by using the same skills. But we don't understand schizophrenics' poetry, because they don't follow the same rules of language.

There is yet another difference between normal and schizophrenic creativity. If we have trouble understanding normal speech, the speaker can rephrase it until we do. "The schizophrenic," according to Forrest, "gets in trouble by trying to press on others the private linguistic connections he or she has found as the order of things they should accept; social manners demand more reactivity of viewpoint than that." We can accept this assumption, or we can assume that schizophrenics don't explain further because they don't realize that what they said is not what they thought they said.

My own training and experience lead me to accept the second explanation. To give just one example, I observed one patient, who exhibited especially severe speech disruption during psychotic episodes, as he watched a videotape of himself speaking in this disoriented way. Astonished, he said that he had never realized he spoke like that, and that it was no wonder people couldn't understand him. He had heard himself on audiotapes before, but explained, "I thought they were distorted."

We all monitor our speech as we talk; that's how we usually catch our slips of the tongue. Even if we occasionally miss one, we agree when someone points it out. If you're setting up a lunch date with a friend and say, "I'll meet you on the corner just after lunch," she might respond, "You mean 'before?'" To which you would probably answer, "Oh, yeah, sorry, 'before.'" Schizophrenics don't seem to monitor their speech in this way. They don't acknowledge their speech errors, either by correcting themselves or by agreeing when others correct them.

The psychologists who reported the "looks like clay" example explained it in behaviorist terms, saying the patient was trying to avoid a response that was wrong, hence punishable, by trying out a variety of responses. The problem with this explanation is that the first statement, "Looks like clay," is the most accurate. And the more the patient speaks, the more incorrect and bizarre his speech becomes. Even if we could prove that the patient was afraid he would be punished for a mistake, we would then still have to explain why he went on to say more and more wrong (punishable) things.

To linguists, these and other features of schizophrenic speech share a bond. When I compare it to normally structured speech, it seems clear that there is something wrong with the schizophrenics' verbal productions. Closer examination makes it evident that the deviations result from one basic process gone awry: retrieval of words and grammar.

A linguist is trained to look at language in terms of levels of production. Eugene Nida, a pioneer in modern linguistics, told me that what struck him most about a schizophrenic friend's speech was that it appeared to be disrupted at different levels, singly or in combination. He could almost tell how many days his friend had neglected his medication by noticing to which level his speech had disintegrated.

The lowest level consists of sounds that are put together by rules into syllables. For instance, in English we have the sounds "m," "b," "w," and "a," but we cannot form a syllable "mbwa," although one can be found in Swahili. Sounds and syllables form morphemes, the smallest units of language which have meaning. "Dis" is a morpheme in English. So is "temper." We combine morphemes to form words, words to form sentences, and sentences to form discourses such as jokes, conversations, sermons, reports, and books.

Nida found that his friend's speech disintegration proceeded from the top down. Rules of organized discourse were the first affected, then rules for sentences, as he started to chain words on the basis of associations rather than sense. This was followed by inappropriate choice of words and, finally, gibberish, as even the minimum ability to form words broke down. The progression seems to be generally true of schizophrenic speech dysfunction, although many patients cycle through the levels more than once in a single monologue.

Disintegration takes place when schizophrenics get sidetracked, so to speak. They may speak a coherent phrase or even a sentence, but then a word triggers another that rhymes or shares some meaning with it and they are off on a tack that has no relation to the original thought. Normal people control which words they choose to say what they want; schizophrenics lose this control and cycle through their mental dictionaries, producing associational chains or rhymes. As they lose control still further, they fail to match sounds to words or words to grammar, producing the gibberish or word salad I will discuss later.

Psychologists have advanced several other theories for schizophrenic speech based on the way people associate words. Some claim that schizophrenics "pigeonhole" the meanings of words rigidly. Psychologists Loren and Jean Chapman, for example, have found that schizophrenics tend to use the most dominant meaning of a word, the one most people ascribe to it in word-association tests. An opposing theory says that the meanings of words have become weakened for schizophrenics so that they associate words erroneously.

Neither of these contradictory theories explains schizophrenic speech very well. The fact that the erroneous associating takes place at all is what is deviant about such speech. The pathology lies in the fact that sentences are produced on the basis of associations between words that just happen to sound alike or share some meaning.

In normal speech, we select words according to the topic at hand, not random association. For instance, we wouldn't start to talk about cats and then in midspeech start to talk about dogs just because we associate the word "cats" with the word "dogs." We inhibit such random associations.

Here is a longer example, in which a schizophrenic is talking about her medication:

> "Speeds up your metabolism. Makes your life shorter. Makes your heart bong. Tranquilizes you if you've got the metabolism I have. I have to distemper just like cats do, 'cause that's what we all are, felines. Siamese cat balls. They stand out. I had a cat, a Manx, still around somewhere. His name is GI Joe; he's black and white. I had a little goldfish too like a clown. Happy Halloween down."

First she talks of the effects of the medicine. Then she erroneously picks the word "distemper" to refer to her mental illness, perhaps because "dis" means not and "temper" refers to the mind. Also, women in our society are often referred to as if they were felines: cats, pussies, kittens. The apparent pun on cat balls (fur balls in their stomachs, or testicles) may be motivated by the sexual connotations of these terms. Next she goes from cats as humans to cats as pets, then leaps to a goldfish as a pet. Next, "clown" used to describe the fish evolves another association with clowns: "Halloween," when children dress up as clowns. Then she gives the chance rhyme of "down" to "clown."

Examples like this have caused some observers to suggest that schizophrenics suffer from a filtering defect. They simply cannot screen out inappropriate matters. This certainly explains the associational character of the examples given so far. But schizophrenic speech abounds in other kinds of peculiarities. Among those that filtering doesn't explain are gibberish and word salad.

In the following example of gibberish, a schizophrenic was explaining to me a videotape he had just seen about a girl who wanted ice cream. The gibberish is in brackets:

> "a little girl. She's uh, she's on her own. She's so [weh] she get her [ous ow] after she ask her own father if she can go out for ice cream and he says uh answers her [shi] dunno and get ice cream for herself and [es] pass by [sh wu] and so it happened they're all happy."

Stretches of gibberish like this mimic the structure of English so well and blend in so smoothly with the rest of the narrative that at first listeners may think they have simply failed to catch what was said. I always go over passages of schizophrenic gibberish dozens of times and then have colleagues listen to them many times before conceding that the patient didn't say the words. The example above was English gibberish, but still gibberish.

Another patient, describing his neighborhood, produced this word salad, a string of words put together without any recognizable grammatical frame. Poor filtering can't explain ". . . when I'm not sure it's possible about the way I could read people mind about people's society attitude plot spirit . . . their thought of how I read think."

Another important feature of schizophrenic speech that filtering doesn't explain is perseveration, a major reason schizophrenic speech becomes more disorganized as it goes along. Once an intrusion of sound or meaning occurs, the schizophrenic perseveres along the new track rather than going back to the original topic.

The strange rhyming in the "looks like clay" sequence is caused by persevering first in rhymes with "clay" and then with the meaning of "Mayday." The mention of "St. Valentine's Day" after "bill and coo" is a perseveration of the meaning of love. This gets compounded with the image of birds in "bill and coo," explaining the following sequence about parakeets and buzzards.

Schizophrenic speech also features repetition, a form of perseveration. For example, the patient who described his neighborhood kept returning to this sequence of words and phrases:

> "will I see Paradise will I not see Paradise"
> "should I answer should I not answer"

He would lead into it in many ways, such as:

> "so I think I could read their mind as they drive by in the car sh-will I see Paradise"

Sometimes he would pick up the refrain in the middle, as in:

"... I just correct them for having me feel better about myself not answer will I should I answer should I not answer. . ."

From a linguistic point of view, schizophrenic speech is caused by an impairment, usually temporary, in the ability to control language on one level or more. This results in errors ranging from small intrusions to complete gibberish. The intrusions resemble the kinds of associations one finds among normal people in tests of word association and in slips of the tongue. The difference is that in schizophrenics, the slips are far more severe. Schizophrenics also combine slips with perseveration down the path opened by their association with words.

Gibberish and word salad, symptoms that show the most complete disintegration of language, are rare today. The drugs, such as Thorazine, that are used to treat schizophrenics lessen many psychotic symptoms, including disordered speech. While no one knows precisely why the drugs have this result, many researchers believe one key is their effect on the neurotransmitter dopamine.

How we view the weird speech of some schizophrenics affects how we treat them. If the speech is a way of avoiding therapy, patients must be persuaded or conditioned to accept therapy. If schizophrenics are merely being poetic or creative, then we must analyze every utterance to uncover its true meaning. If, as I think, schizophrenics who speak weirdly do so because of a linguistic problem caused by a biochemical imbalance, then the solution is biochemical. Find the proper medication and you alleviate the source of the problem.

≡

FOR DISCUSSION AND REVIEW

1. The question of why schizophrenics use such strange speech "has been hotly debated for decades and has received a variety of answers." What solutions have been proposed to answer the "why"? For what reasons have such theories as "Bateson's Double Bind" theory been disputed?

2. Chaika asserts: "What we really need to establish is how or why the illness causes the peculiar speech." What do David V. Forrest and other psychiatrists offer as explanation for this question?

3. What are some characteristics of schizophrenic speech? Why do schizophrenics use such forms of speech?

4. Given that we can understand poetry as "productive speech" (Chomsky's views) why are we unable to decipher schizophrenic poetry? What are the differences between normal and schizophrenic creativity?

5. What produces the deviations in schizophrenic speech? Are there any processes to the deviations?

6. Disintegration in schizophrenic speech occurs when schizophrenics become "sidetracked." What prevents normal speakers from becoming "sidetracked"?

7. What differences exist between the use of word association for sentence production in normal speakers as opposed to word association used in schizophrenic speech?

8. In the passage in which a patient speaks about her medication that begins, "Speeds up your metabolism. . ." examine the process of disintegration in the speech. What patterns do you observe? How are each of the sentences associated?

9. Chaika observes that "schizophrenics suffer from a filtering defect. They simply cannot screen out inappropriate matters." Many examples demonstrate the filtering defect of schizophrenic speech; however, there are conditions that are not explained by this filtering problem. What are some of these conditions?

10. From a linguistic point of view, what are the causes of schizophrenic speech?

11. What solutions exist, if any, for schizophrenic speech disorders?

14

$\equiv$

From Speaking Act To Natural Word: Animals, Communication, and Language

William Kemp and Roy Smith

For many years human beings have studied a variety of animal communication systems—and for many reasons. Just as the possibility of life somewhere in space has long fascinated people, so too has the possibility of finding that some animal here on earth can learn a form of human language. People have studied "talking" horses, dolphins, bees, whales, monkeys, and chimpanzees, all in an effort to discover if we alone possess language. Other researchers, especially ethologists, have studied animal communication systems because of their intrinsic interest and because such study helps us to understand both the similarities and differences between animal communication and human language. This research has revealed a great deal about the complexity of animal communication systems; it has also shown that human beings "share with other species an impressive degree of nonlingual communication." In the following selection, Professors William Kemp and Roy Smith, both of Mary Washington College, survey the research on animal communication. They explain the difficulties of such research, as well as its importance to understanding human language. They also describe the elaborate communication systems of bees, birds, and mammals, especially the nonhuman primates. Discussing the extensive work with chimpanzees and gorillas that was done in the 1970s and 1980s, they argue convincingly that these experiments have "demonstrated that apes can learn to use semantically a large number of arbitrary symbols. That achievement is more than the most hostile critics will allow. But it is also considerably less than human semantic abilities."

> The sound of the waterfall
> has for a long time
> ceased,
> yet with its name
> we can hear it still.
> — FUJIWARO NO KINTO, D. 1041

Haiku are instances of human language at its peak, creating stunning images with a few carefully chosen syllables. Despite claims for remarkable communication and even language among the many animals around us, no one has offered an example of a haiku from a humpback whale or a chimpanzee. This is not to say that animals do not communicate effectively; they certainly do. Still, most humans use language as something qualitatively different from other forms of communication, at least some of the time.

What are the differences between human language and nonhuman communication? This seemingly simple question has been the subject of considerable research and discussion among linguists and ethologists (specialists in animal behavior). An easy answer might be that language is the form of communication humans use, while animal signaling is what nonhumans use. Unfortunately, this view implies that a loving glance from your mother is part of language while a loving glance from your dog is not. Humans use language layered atop other forms of communication, and sometimes the nonlanguage signals contain the more important messages. At the very least, we share with other species an impressive degree of nonlingual communication. Examining the types of animal communication allows us to see the important ways in which language differs from communication in other animals. It also suggests that language is not an aberration that appears suddenly, without evolutionary precursors, in humans.

Ethologists treat animal communication under three headings (Smith, 1977a). The first of these is *form*. For an animal's behavior to have value as a signal, it must be in a constant form that others can recognize and connect reliably to some future behavior by the signaler. Ethologists call such stereotyped behavior a *display*. The second part of animal communication is *context*; it includes the general environment in which an animal is displaying as well as simultaneous displays it sends through other sensory modes or channels. Thus, a dog's bark conveys one message about future behavior when its tail is wagging, another when its tail is stiff. Context usually resolves such ambiguities. The third part of animal communication is the *response* to the signal. Communication is valuable because it increases the likelihood of one animal's choosing behavior that fits with the behavior of others. We must see the choice by the receiving animal to be sure communication has actually happened. Otherwise, we can't tell the difference between ruffling feathers to get them straight and ruffling feathers to signal an impending conflict.

You may have seen one of the elaborate prairie dog cities on the western plains. Alarm calls announce your approach and send nearby animals scurrying to holes from which they cautiously examine you. Can there be any doubt that sentries are telling their comrades about the intruder? Patient observation and careful analysis suggest that this alarm display, like other prairie dog vocalizations, is just that — a display about the state of alarm of the caller (Smith et al., 1977). Prairie dogs apparently give this signal whenever they become aroused enough to stop and scan the environment, but not scared enough to run for cover immediately. They give the same call during territorial disputes when the caller is unsure whether to attack or retreat. Other prairie dogs, upset by the signaler, give their own version of the display, spreading agitation through the colony. The alarm system works very effectively; knowing that your neighbor is aroused is important. But the prairie dog's behavior is a display containing information about the caller, not a word or sentence about the source of the alarm. Each prairie dog must sit up and look for himself.

Distinctive behavior reliably indicating what an animal will do promotes cooperation and reduces conflict, because it allows neighbors to adjust their actions according to what the display predicts. Few animals seriously injure one another in disputes over territory, food, or mates, because displays allow rivals to establish which one is dominant without resorting to real combat. Crudely put, the meaning of an agonistic display is, "I feel like attacking you ferociously very soon." The individual whose display is more convincing will usually win. We need not imagine animals computing the combat odds as they respond to each other, or planning their own displays. Sending and comprehending displays are parts of each animal's (and human's) automatic behavior. In human interactions, smiling usually elicits a responding smile and a frown prompts a frown, without any planning by anyone.

In discussing human language, linguists use concepts similar to the ethologist's form, context, and response. They work with *syntax*, which emphasizes form; *semantics*, which emphasizes meaning (defined partly by context); and *pragmatics*, which emphasizes how context modifies or replaces the meaning of an utterance. Linguists also analyze human speech into *morphemes* and *phonemes*, units that seem unique to spoken language. But particular manifestations of phonemes (called *allophones*) share with displays an invariant surface form guided by a stable program in the central nervous system. Both allophones and displays are examples of unvarying sets of motor movements that ethologists call *fixed action patterns* (Hinde, 1970).

As displays become language, several things change. The form of communication shifts from a limited number of lengthy, stereotyped displays to a very large number of very short displays (allophones) that can be combined in many ways according to hierarchical rules. The importance of context also changes. Displays begin as indications of an animal's probable response to its environment or context; they are more about the animal itself than about the world. In contrast, humans frequently use language to describe environment(s), while their displays signal much of the accompanying affective content. Although the context in which a sentence appears usually colors its meaning, the sentence has its own meaning independent of context. Displays have only contextual meaning.

While the response to a display is the indication of its meaning, the response of others to language may be unimportant. Although Fujiwaro wrote his haiku for others to read, and probably would be delighted to know that people are reading and appreciating it nine hundred years after his death, he must have written it partly or perhaps chiefly for the delight of capturing his experience in words. We have no clear evidence that nonhumans play with their communication systems simply to revel in the workings of the system itself.

Language is also capable of abstraction, a power that seems to have no natural parallel in animal communication. Of course, many animals can create general concepts (Griffin, 1981); some dogs understand that *all* cars are to be chased. And some higher primates, having learned artificial sign systems from humans, clearly use and understand some abstract signs (Walker, 1983). But even in the cleverest animals, natural displays have no way of presenting abstract propositions about either the animal or its world. The abilities conferred by language to plan for the future and control our environment are without parallel in other species. Language is far removed from the simple fixed action patterns of affective displays. A hierarchy of rule systems, from phonetics to semantics, transforms language from a set of environmental responses to a self-contained, generative symbol system operating simultaneously on several independently structured levels. Thus our thoughts are at least partly dissociated from our feelings.

Despite clear differences, animal communication systems have a lot to tell us about language. For one thing, displays have evolved in every other species out of environmental demands and animals' adaptations to meet those demands. The more carefully we study how other animals exchange signals, the more clearly we see how closely communication systems connect to other elements of behavior. We also find that many creatures are a good deal more clever than we suppose.

For example, we usually regard insects as just barely sentient, doing their business by instinct and incapable of significant mental activity, but we marvel at the architectural achievements of social insects (ants, bees, termites, and wasps). In fact, the architecture of a termite mound or an ant nest is genetically designed; these insects are no more likely to change the plans of their nests than they are to grow eight legs apiece. Each insect responds to the chemical and tactile signals around it with a set of fixed action patterns programmed into its simple brain. In a real sense no member of this miniature corps of engineers has any plan at all; the genetic repository of the whole community contains the blueprint for building the nest, and for other activity besides. More marvelous still are the systems of communication by which social insects manage their collective lives, using emitted chemicals (called *pheromones*), sound, and physical activity to exchange information and coordinate their behavior.

The best understood insect communication system is the dance of the honeybee *(Apis mellifera).* Because honey is delicious, humans have been interested for centuries in the bees that make it. But until the 1920s no one noticed that bees returning from a successful foray convey to hivemates important information which concentrates hive activity on the best sources of nectar. In 1919 Karl von Frisch set out to discover how hundreds of foraging bees could arrive as if by magic at a rich food source recently discovered by a single bee. The result of his experiment was striking:

> I attracted a few bees to a dish of sugar water, marked them with red paint and then stopped feeding for a while. As soon as all was quiet, I filled the dish again and watched a scout which had drunk from it before after her return to the hive. I could scarcely believe my eyes. She performed a round dance on the honeycomb which greatly excited the marked foragers around her and caused them to fly back to the feeding place. (von Frisch, 1967, pp. 72–73)

In a series of elegant experiments over the next twenty years, von Frisch established that the round dance conveys three pieces of information: the presence of a food source, its richness, and the type of food available (see Figure 14.1). The scent clinging to the dancer's body, along with droplets of nectar regurgitated from her honey stomach, tell nearby bees of her find. If she dances vigorously, other recruits follow her dance, then

FIGURE 14.1.   Round dance.

promptly leave the hive and search busily for the odors she carries, completely ignoring all other food sources. They may also be guided by a "Here it is!" pheromone the scout releases as she visits the source a second time. Returning to the hive, the recruits will also dance vigorously and spread the odor. Soon, hundreds of hivemates will be exploiting the recently discovered trove.

In 1944 von Frisch began exploring how honeybees deal with food sources far from their hive. The results were even more exciting, for he discovered that bees use a "tail-wagging" dance to communicate the distance and direction of remote food sources (see Figure 14.2). "In the tail-wagging dance," he reported (1967), "they run in a straight line wagging their abdomen to and fro, then return to the starting point in a semicircle, repeat the tail-wagging run, return in a semicircle on the other side, and so on." Bees responding to this dance would completely ignore food sources near the hive — even those with identical odors — in their flight to the distant goal.

Von Frisch also discovered that the tail-wagging dance tells the recruit bees which direction to fly and how far to go before starting their search. The scout bee does her dance on a vertical comb inside the dark

FIGURE 14.2.   Tail-wagging dance.

hive. The angle between an imaginary vertical line running up the comb surface and the tail-wagging run of her dance corresponds to the angle between the sun and the food source (see Figure 14.3). So if the food source is twenty degrees to the left or right of the sun as seen from the opening of the hive, her waggle run will be offset twenty degrees to the left or right of the vertical. If the food source is directly away from the sun, she will start at the top of the comb, dancing straight down, and so on. Later experiments established that this directional information is extremely accurate. In a typical trial lasting fifty minutes, 42 of 54 bees (78%) found the target food source, 7 missed by an angle of fifteen degrees to the right or left, 4 by thirty degrees, and 1 by forty-five degrees. The scout bees also compensate for detours, directing hivemates to fly straight toward the goal. Having reasonably accurate internal clocks, they can even adjust their waggle dance for the sun's movement across the sky (von Frisch, 1971). While the angle of the waggle run indicates the direction of the goal, its tempo indicates the distance; the farther the source, the more waggle runs the dancer makes per unit of time.

Not all honeybees use exactly the same language. Von Frisch's students have established that different honeybee strains set the boundaries between the round and tail-wagging dances at different distances, and encode like distances by different tempos. For example, Italian bees *(Apis m. ligustica)* dance slower for any given distance than do the Austrian bees *(Apis m. carnica)* von Frisch used. When Boch put both kinds of bees into one hive, miscommunication ran rampant. In response to Italian bees, the Austrian ones flew too far; in response to Austrian scouts, Italian

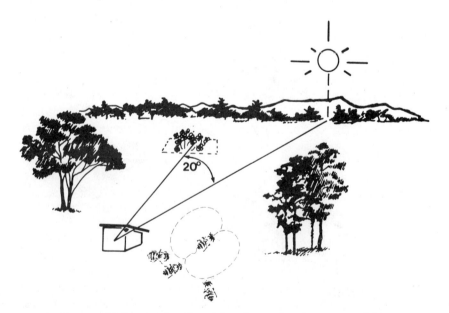

FIGURE 14.3.   Angle of wagging dance showing sun position.

bees did not fly far enough (Lindauer, 1961). One can accurately say that the bee "language" has genetic dialects.

But is the bee dance really language? It certainly conveys information in an arbitrary code about parts of the world outside the bee herself and remote from where she dances. The dance thus satisfies several of the design features by which Hockett and Altmann (1968) attempted to distinguish between animal communication and human language. But von Frisch himself found significant limits to the bee's communication system. He put a hive beneath a radio tower, placed a very rich sugar water solution high up in the tower, and showed several scouts where it was. After they returned to the hive and danced heroically, their mates searched busily all around the hive—but not up the tower (von Frisch, 1966). Evolved for foraging across horizontal landscapes, the powerful communication system of honeybees has no way of indicating up or down (von Frisch, 1971; Wilson, 1971). Unlike human language, bee displays are not productive; they do not recombine bits of the code to produce novel messages. Bee messages are essentially the same message, differing only in a few details, uttered almost mechanically, over and over again in response to a narrow band of stimuli. This rigidity prevents the bees in mixed hives from learning each others' dialects, despite repeated attempts to communicate.

Assessing not only the honeybees' communication system but their ability to create mental maps of the territory around their hive and remember what flower they are seeking, Gould and Gould (1983) observe, "these hard-working insects appear simply to be well-programmed learning machines, attending only to the cues deemed salient by evolution (and then only in well-defined contexts and often during precise critical periods)—and then filing the information thus obtained in pre-existing arrays." Of course, as Gould and Gould conclude, much of the same can be said of humans.

Because birds are larger and interact over longer distances, one might suppose they use even more complicated communication systems. Their behavior certainly seems more varied than that of insects, and more vocal. Calls and songs are embedded in a rich context of elaborate visual displays; no bird sits like a lump and sings. Its message to mate, rival, or neighbor arises from a coordinated package of activities, not any single element within the package (Smith, 1977b). Still, to linguists the sounds birds make are the most interesting part of their behavior because, like humans, birds are physiologically and behaviorally specialized to produce and respond to streams of meaningful sound.

Ornithologists divide bird vocalizations into two categories: *calls* and *songs*. Calls tend to be brief, simple in structure, and confined to a particular context. As a result, some calls elicit sharp reactions from nearly every bird hearing them. The contrasting *alarm* and *mobbing* calls that many birds produce when they spot a predator are often shared across species; many birds make similar acoustic distinctions between the two calls.

Alarms, given when the predator is airborne and thus able to strike promptly, have acoustic properties which make it difficult for the predator to find the bird emitting them (Marler, 1955, 1957; Konishi, 1973). In contrast, mobbing calls, which summon neighbors to attack a stationary predator, have different acoustic features which make the sound easy to locate, so that every bird responding will know where to attack. The survival value of differing calls is obvious.

But only a predator, rival, or prospective mate shows any interest in the information contained in bird song. Song is usually loud, sustained, complex in structure, seasonal, confined to males, and prompted by mating or territorial concerns. Some species, of course, sing no songs at all, using calls instead for territorial and breeding information; in strictest terms a song is simply an especially elaborate call. Still, the distinction between the two has a practical value because song seems musical to us and calls do not. Certainly, if a male songbird is to breed, he must learn to sing the right tune: it attracts females and keeps rival males away. And if a female is to breed, she must know the tune a proper male should sing.

A major function of bird song is to establish and maintain breeding territories. Each resident male spends much of his time patrolling his boundaries and declaring his presence in song. The "message" of the song indicates the singer's probable behavior. Roughly translated, a territorial song says that the singer will attack any adult male of the same species entering his territory. But as the singer's probable behavior changes across the spring, so does the meaning of the song. Early in the season, when pairs are still forming, a male chaffinch (Fringilla coelebs) will not attack adult females entering his territory. At that time of year, his song is all invitation. But later on, when eggs are incubating, he will attack strange females. The song does not change, but its meaning does (Nottebaum, 1975). Other birds know the meaning from the time of year.

Of even greater interest to linguists than what birds sing about is how they learn to repeat sometimes long and complex songs with great precision. In fact, most do not *learn* their songs in the strict meaning of the word. Only four of the twenty-nine avian orders have complex song repertoires or dialects and clearly must acquire their songs after birth (Nottebaum, 1975). In the other twenty-five orders, the appropriate calls or songs appear to be part of each bird's genetic heritage.

Even within the largest family of songbirds, learning strategies differ sharply from one species to the next. Young song sparrows (Melospiza melodia), for example, must hear themselves sing to produce their full repertoire; individuals deafened when young fail to develop normal song, unlike individuals merely isolated when young (Konishi and Nottebaum, 1969). In contrast, young finches of several species learn the song of the adult male who helps care for them, even if he is of another species (Immelmann, 1969). White-crowned sparrows (Zonotrichia leucophyrs) and chaffinches must hear adults of their own species sing during the first spring of their lives; individuals raised in isolation until their second spring never perform properly, even after hearing adult song (Thorpe, 1958; Marler and Tamura, 1964). In such species, each male appears to be born with a generalized template for his species song. The length and timing of his critical learning period differ according to species, but the general pattern is similar (Konishi and Nottebaum, 1969; Nottebaum, 1975). The point of crystallization, when the template has become rich enough to support full adult song during the coming year, varies with the species, but the necessity of a passive learning period does not. The analogy between this template and Chomsky's hypothesis of a genetically supported universal grammar in humans is obvious.

While the dialect differences in bees are genetically fixed, learning appears to produce regional dialects in birds just as it does in human speech. In many species, birds of one area will develop shared variations on the species song (Thielcke, 1969; Krebs and Kroodsma, 1980). These variations persist for several generations at least, and are clearly differences in learning rather than in the genetic template; fledglings from one area transported to another will sing the new dialect, not that of their parents.

Are we right in supposing that because birds are more like us than bees they are closer in communicative ability as well? Probably not. Insect communication and behavior are in many ways as complex as our own. The impressive achievements of insect communities depend on reliable communication systems coordinating the behavior of thousands, even millions. In contrast, bird vocalizations seem ambiguous. It may even be useful to see bird song as a simpler form of communication than either the stereotyped, meaning-packed movements and chemical signals of bees or the more variable multi-channel displays of some mammals.

But the complexity and variability of mammalian signaling may disguise the rather limited range of subjects about which mammals signal (Smith et al., 1977; Peters, 1980). If most mammals communicate about the same limited set of subjects, and if those subjects are part of an environment shared by humans, it is not really surprising that humans understand their mammalian pets — or that the pets appear to understand humans. It would be somewhat more difficult to share the world of a pet slime mold.

Four activities account for almost all the displays seen in mammals: mating, rearing young, resolving conflict, and maintaining group organization. In many species, from insects to birds, elaborate courtship rituals supplement the basic chemical signals of sexual readiness. Still, the rituals give only redundant information about the sexual condition and identity of the displaying animal. Mammals are no different, although their sexual displays are rather ordinary compared to the courtship of ducks. In contrast, the other three display categories show extensive expansion, reflecting specific mammalian adaptations.

Communication between mother and offspring is unimportant in sea turtles, which abandon their newly laid eggs and return to the sea. Even birds, many of which are good and faithful parents, communicate with their young through a simple set of calls and several kinds of specialized physical contact until the young are ready to fly. Then the fledgling is on its own to find food, avoid predators, and maybe even navigate from Great Britain to central Africa without ending up in Iowa by mistake. Young turtles are genetically programmed to run for the sea as soon as they hatch. In ways we are only beginning to understand, migratory birds are programmed to find their way accurately across immense distances. Neither turtles nor birds learn much from their parents. So it is hardly surprising that all turtles and most birds produce multiple offspring as insurance; although the casualty rate may be high, some are bound to solve their life tasks successfully and keep the species going.

In contrast, most mammalian parents invest a remarkable amount of energy and time in a few offspring, so maternal care over a long period involves elaborate and sustained interaction between mothers and their young. The displays guiding this interaction are no more complex than those controlling mating. In fact, to a casual human observer they may not seem to be displays at all, because we behave very similarly in caring for our own infants: feeding, cleaning, restraining, warning, punishing, and petting.

Young predatory mammals in particular must learn a good deal, so they spend much time imitating adults and playing with each other. Imitation is a way of acquiring complex skills such as finding food, reproducing, or caring for offspring. Adult nonhumans don't deliberately describe the environment to their offspring in symbolic terms or offer lessons in infant care, but many young mammals watch closely and copy diligently what their elders do. Long-lived social mammals in particular must learn not only skills but a large number of individual identities and interaction signals. Wolves (Mech, 1970), lions (Schaller, 1972), chimpanzees (de Waal, 1982; Goodall, 1971, 1986), and gorillas (Schaller, 1963; Fossey, 1983) form relatively stable social groups in which each individual must know and recognize the other members. Encounters will be highly reciprocal, consisting of very rapid interchanges; and although the messages will be about very few things, they will come frequently and in great numbers. Because different adults will respond in somewhat different ways, each animal must know not only the group members' identities but their temperaments. For example, adult gorillas in repose tolerantly let young ones climb all over them, but some adults are more tolerant than others. It is well for young gorillas to learn tolerance levels rapidly.

Still, the fundamental feature of animal communication persists in even the most social mammals: the value of displays does not depend on a desire to tell another animal something. And even the most highly social mammals send messages with great redundancy. Such redundancy, together with a fairly limited number of messages, perhaps only a couple of dozen, is important because it means that pulling one sensory channel from the display for some other purpose need not seriously disrupt the message. In developing language, humans appear to have done exactly that with the acoustic channel. But the original display system still functions in human behavior, as the expanding literature on kinesics testifies.

Representatives of another mammal group, the cetaceans, have also adapted the auditory channel for special communication. Water as a medium for chemical, visual, or acoustic signals is considerably different from air. Because we pierce only with difficulty the liquid blanket which shields the individual and social lives of water-based vertebrates from casual observation, we lack much of the behavioral context which helps us understand the communication systems of other animals (Caldwell and Caldwell, 1977). For years scientists studied the sonar signals of dolphins as a model for our own artificial sonar systems (Kellogg, 1961; Wood, 1973); various explanations for dolphin sonar have included stunning or killing prey, forming acoustic images of their surroundings, identifying individuals, and, according to one author, deliberately communicating with each other and with humans (Lilly, 1975). A decade of intensive work with captive dolphins showed both the refinement of dolphin sonar and the flexibility with which the animals apply it to solving problems (Kellogg, 1961). Early behavioral studies using trained animals also suggested that dolphin problem-solving ability stems from a high level of intelligence, but failed to find a useful way of measuring their cognitive skills (McBride and Hebb, 1948).

A particularly important study by Bastian (Wood, 1973) examined apparent intentional communication between two captive dolphins, Buzz and Doris. After training Buzz and Doris using two signals which indicated whether food would or would not be available if they pushed a lever, Bastian introduced a twist to the task: only Buzz could press the lever, and only Doris could see which signal was on. Further, the two dolphins were visually isolated and could only communicate using vocal signals. Buzz quickly learned when to press the lever to provide both dolphins with a fishy reward. After remarkably patient and painstaking analysis of a massive amount of data, Bastian concluded that the animals were indeed communicating, but not intentionally. Instead, he felt that Buzz was reacting to Doris's differing responses to the two signals; she revealed more excitement via her clicks and whistles when the "good" signal came on than when the "bad" signal did. These results are remarkably similar to the analysis of the prairie dog work summarized earlier (Smith et al., 1977).

More recently, Herman and his colleagues (1984) have shown that dolphins are capable of responding to unique sequences of previously learned signals that identify various objects and actions; his subjects can execute accurately an interesting range of novel instructions. While the resulting claims for dolphin syntax and sentence comprehension (Herman, Richards, and Woltz, 1984) are based on linguistically questionable definitions, this carefully described work illustrates again the remarkable cognitive capacities of the animals.

Another group of cetaceans, the Pacific humpback whales *(Megaptera novaeangliae)*, have been extensively studied in their breeding grounds off Hawaii and Baja California, and in their Alaskan hunting grounds (Herman, 1980; Baker and Herman, 1985). The animals seem to live in loose social aggregations without discernible structure. During their summer feeding season off Alaska, stable groups (most often chiefly female) sometimes hunt together in clearly coordinated ways, and even in the same areas from one year to the next (Baker and Herman, 1985). But during the winter breeding season, when the animals do little if any hunting, the only stable social groups are pairs of cows and calves, often followed by an interested adult male or three.

Like other cetaceans, humpback whales make a variety of sounds, but they are famous for singing; shortly after the discovery of this behavior in the 1960s, an album of whale songs was briefly popular. In several ways whale and bird songs are similar: males do the singing only during the breeding season, and the whale song is learned. Each song consists of several discrete *themes*, usually sung in the same sequence; the themes in turn contain *phrases*, the phrases contain *subphrases*, and the subphrases contain *units* (Frumhoff, 1983). Complex bird song can be analyzed using the same concepts. Whale song is also dialectical; Atlantic and Pacific humpbacks sing clearly different songs.

The most interesting feature of whale song is that within a given breeding population it changes rapidly over time. Analyzing the singing of Pacific whales for two breeding seasons, Payne, Twack, and Payne (1983) found "dramatic monthly evolution following set rules of change. Substitution, omission, and addition occur at different rates in different times, but at any one time all songs are similar." We know almost nothing about what constitutes "good" whale singing; since no one has been able to identify the offspring of any male humpback, we cannot correlate any specific performance of a whale song with success at breeding. But it appears that a singing male must do two things simultaneously: produce the complex song, and listen to the songs of his competitors. Nothing else can explain the fact that although the song changes steadily, nearly all males sing the same song all the time (Guinee, Chu, and Dorsey, 1983). The acoustic transactions among humpbacks exemplify a special kind of reciprocity in which the singing of each animal simultaneously shapes and is shaped by the singing of his neighbors.

Unfortunately, we do not know what to make of this behavior. Since nearly all males seem to be singing the same song, females may choose mates on the basis of their troubadorial gifts. Possibly the songs are addressed entirely to other males as a way of spacing out individuals within the breeding territory. Given our ignorance about how aquatic creatures spend their time, we might construct several models to explain whale singing, based on the behavior of various land creatures.

While interest in whales and dolphins has dominated communication research on marine mammals, another group, the pinnipeds, has attracted some scientists' attention (Wood, 1973). While seals, sea lions, and walruses lack the sonar and underwater vocalization systems of cetaceans, they too have acute visual and auditory capacities and an aptitude for training. Schusterman (1981) has conducted a series of studies on the language capacity of a pair of California sea lions, closely paralleling Herman's work with dolphins. He reports behavior that he interprets as indicating semantic and sentence comprehension skills similar to those claimed for dolphins (Schusterman and Kreiger, 1984, 1986). Unlike some other workers, Schusterman is open about the importance of traditional training techniques *(operant conditioning)* in producing the behavior he observes (Schusterman, 1967). But he argues that his animals eventually display more than complex behavior learned by rote. Instead, he believes, they are using complex cognitive strategies in responding to novel signal combinations in order to obtain rewards (Schusterman and Kreiger, 1986).

But in studying the ability of "bright" animals to execute complex commands, we may be looking at the wrong explanation for what we see. David Premack (1986) has suggested that we tend to find language skills in all animals that analyze the world (as we ourselves do) into agents, actions, and results of those actions. The intricate "go fetch" commands characteristic of the dolphin and sea lion experiments may work not because the animals have sophisticated communication systems but because they are genetically equipped to analyze the world using cognitive patterns which for humans are easily coded into syntax.

These cognitive patterns may result from selection for cooperation in obtaining and distributing food — behavior characteristic of large carnivorous mammals but unusual in herbivores. Certainly cooperative hunting and/or food sharing are characteristic of the mammals that seem to us to display high intelligence and the ability to use complex communication systems: cetaceans, primates, and social carnivores. And our failure to find languagelike cognitive skills in other animals may simply indicate that we haven't found what we have not looked for. Anecdotal evidence for the intelligence and comprehension of domestic animals such as cats and dogs abounds, and several kinds of wild carnivores have long been championed for their cleverness (North, 1966), and even for their complex vocal "songs" (Mowat, 1967).

But if we wish to understand the basis of human language in animal communication we are safer studying our closest surviving biological relatives, the other primates. While their similarity holds obvious promise for advancing our understanding, it makes research with primates difficult. Anne Premack (1976, p. 17) writes,

> Aside from a human baby, I can think of no creature which can arouse stronger feelings of tenderness than an infant chimpanzee. It has huge round eyes and a delicate head and is far more alert than a human infant

of the same age. When you pick up a young chimp, it encircles your body with its long, trembling arms and legs, and the effect is devastating — you want to take it home!

Being objective about any experimental work with such an appealing animal is extremely difficult, and the study of language capacity in primates presents a special problem.

Early studies, some using human infants as controls, investigated whether raising chimpanzees in a completely human environment *(cross fostering)* would produce humanlike behavior, including spoken language. While the chimps learned rapidly to respond to a variety of spoken commands, none acquired speech, or even clearly intelligible word sounds (Hayes, 1951; Kellogg, 1980). The possibility that primates are physically incapable of producing and controlling the speech sounds of human language led investigators to consider other means of communicating with the animals. Allen and Beatrice Gardner decided that American Sign Language (Ameslan or ASL) was not only a true language, but an appropriate way to test the language capability of chimps. Ameslan is a complex, flexible system of hand signs developed for the deaf. A language in its own right rather than a facsimile of English, it uses the shape of the hand(s), their relative position, and their movement to convey ideas (Wilbur, 1979). Since previous home-raised chimps had shown excellent motor control at an earlier age than human infants, the Gardners felt confident that chimps could master Ameslan.

They began their work in 1966 with a female chimp about one year old whom they named Washoe, after the Nevada county where their lab was located. Certain that a chimpanzee could readily learn arbitrary signs to obtain food, drink, and other things, they set a larger goal: "We wanted Washoe not only to ask for objects but to answer questions about them and also to ask us questions. We wanted to develop behavior that could be described as conversation" (Gardner and Gardner, 1969). Reasoning that an environment rich in emotional support and varied experiences was important for human language learning, they deliberately created one for Washoe. She lived in a furnished (though chimp-proofed) trailer, with numerous toys, books, and magazines to provide topics for signing. She also had human companions during her waking hours, all trained to some degree in Ameslan. To avoid uncertainty about what Washoe was responding to, vocal communication with and around her was prohibited.

The Gardners taught Washoe signs in several ways. Early in the experiment they made regular activities such as bathing, going to bed, and using the potty highly ritualized events involving specific signs. This provided Washoe with plentiful material to imitate, but these efforts produced few signs. Using the instrumental technique of shaping, in which they rewarded successive approximations to the desired sign, the Gardners began helping Washoe acquire a stable vocabulary. Later on, they deliberately taught her some signs by physically molding her hands into the desired conformation. Before recording data on how frequently Washoe used a given sign, they required reports from three different observers that she had used it spontaneously and in an appropriate context. After Washoe had done so on each of fifteen successive days, they regarded the sign as a stable part of her vocabulary. Just under two years into the project, Washoe had acquired 34 signs. By the end of the third year, she knew 85 signs. Her current mature vocabulary is approximately 180 signs (see Figure 14.4).

In later years the Gardners acquired other animals and offered them similar training, with similar results. Changes in funding transported this small colony of signing chimpanzees from Nevada to the University of Oklahoma for several years and finally to Central Washington University, where Roger Fouts, who began working with the animals as a graduate student of the Gardners, presides over five chimps living in a laboratory approximation of a natural group. Independently of the Gardners, though inspired by their work, Patterson (1978; Patterson and Linden, 1981) carries on a similar project with two gorillas, Koko and Michael, as did Miles (1983) with an orangutan named Chantek.

Even before the Gardners' first reports, Ann and David Premack (1972) had begun training a chimp named Sarah to answer simple ques-

FIGURE 14.4. Washoe signing "tickle."

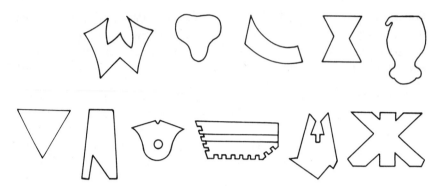

FIGURE 14.5. Sarah's symbols.

tions using plastic tokens instead of words, and their first publications nearly coincided with the Gardners'. Sarah's tokens were completely arbitrary shapes and colors (a blue triangle meant "apple," for instance), and the Premacks gave her very elaborate, step-by-step training in both definitions and sequence of tokens within a statement (see Figure 14.5), much as Herman and Schusterman later trained dolphins and sea lions.

Inspired by both the Gardners and the Premacks, Rumbaugh developed an arbitrary language called Yerkish (after the Yerkes Primate Center in Atlanta) to communicate first with a female chimp named Lana, then with two males named Sherman and Austin (Rumbaugh, 1980; Savage-Rumbaugh, 1986). Its symbols, called lexigrams, are arbitrary designs displayed on the backlit keys of a large, computer-controlled keyboard (see Figure 14.6). They are moved from key to key randomly so the animals will learn to select the designs rather than locations on the board. The lexigrams of the current message appear on a screen above the board, and the computer records all input.

Terrace (1979) directed a Gardner-like program with one animal, Nim Chimsky. The Gardners themselves no longer work with chimps. The Premacks' project continues, focused on the cognitive rather than linguistic abilities of their animals. Rumbaugh has extended his lexigram system to work with profoundly retarded humans and achieved very interesting results (Romski and Rumbaugh, 1981; Savage-Rumbaugh, 1986). Fouts and Patterson continue their Ameslan research programs. Fouts has given

FIGURE 14.6. Yerkish: sample lexigrams.

Washoe an adopted son, Loulis, and studies the transfer of signing from one generation to the next (Fouts, Hirsch, and Fouts, 1982).

Each of these experimenters wrestled with the problem Ann Premack explained: the animals are so engaging that workers may interpret results according to extensive informal interaction as well as formal tests. Science, however, requires the results of an experiment to be always the same, even if it is repeated by someone who does not share the theoretical position of the original observer, in this case someone not already enamored of primates. To avoid allowing their expectations or their affection for their subjects to influence the outcome of their experiments, some researchers borrowed the *double-blind* design developed by social psychologists to control the influence of extraneous information on the behavior of human subjects.

This influence arises because subjects often try to "help" the experimenter, modifying their behavior to fit the experimenter's expectations. Even if the experimenter tries to avoid revealing a study's hypothesis, subjects can usually detect from contextual or unintentional kinesic signals what behavior the experimenter expects to find. Animals too detect kinesic cues, and intelligent, observant animals may do it very well. This ability to respond to unintentional signals rather than to the intended stimuli of an experiment has been dubbed the *Clever Hans effect,* after a horse that seemed to do arithmetic (Sebeok and Rosenthal, 1981). Given a problem, Hans would count out the answer by tapping his hoof the appropriate number of times. Careful testing revealed that he could answer correctly only when he could see people who knew the answers. He would faithfully tap his hoof until he saw a nearly imperceptible relaxation in his trainer; then he would stop tapping. The trainer, of course, would unconsciously relax just as Hans got to the right answer. When his trainer was not present, Hans would read his cues from any human who was paying attention. Oskar Pfungst (1911), the psychologist who unraveled Hans's behavior, found that he himself could not avoid cuing the horse, even after he had figured out what was going on. In other words, Hans was reading fixed action patterns, which are normally unconscious and nearly unalterable. Both sending and receiving nonverbal signals is so fundamental a part of behavior that experiments with living subjects can be seriously distorted by inevitable kinesic communication between researcher and subject.

In a double-blind design, no one in direct contact with the subjects knows which experimental condition is in effect at any time. Consider, for example, a study to test for the effects of hypnosis on suggestibility. The chief experimenter decides on the design of the experiment but does not interact with the subjects. Having been told, perhaps, that the experiment is about pain perception, the hypnotist is blind to the hypotheses, so neither the hypnotized nor the control subjects can gather relevant cues from someone who does not know what behavior the experiment is measuring. And the experimenter gathering data, not knowing which of the subjects have been hypnotized, is blind to the experimental manipulation and cannot provide distorting cues either.

Obviously, the double-blind design can minimize both unconscious cuing and the tendency to anthropomorphize of anyone who works with higher primates. However, double-blinds are more difficult to use than other experimental designs. Either more than one person must help with the experiment, or the experimenter must develop a mechanical way of presenting stimuli, recording responses, or both. In any case, those involved must restrain their natural tendencies to interact freely with each other and with their very engaging subjects. Scientists who do not use such cumbersome methods are not attempting to produce misleading reports; in fact, few studies of language development in children have satisfied the requirements of objectivity that lead experimenters to use the double-blind method. But researchers working in an area as controversial as the language capability of primates must anticipate skepticism from those who have not had the sort of contact with young primates that nearly everyone has with human infants.

As the Gardners and others began publishing accounts of symbol-learning experiments with chimpanzees, critics attacked their results as arising from the Clever Hans effect (Sebeok and Rosenthal, 1981; de Luce and Wilder, 1983). No one has doubted that the animals perform clearly arbitrary behavior, whether making gestures, manipulating plastic tokens, or punching computer keys. But several critics (Umiker-Sebeok and Sebeok, 1980; Pettito and Seidenberg, 1979: Seidenberg and Pettito, 1979) have charged that the animals are responding to unconscious cues rather than doing anything even remotely languagelike. This interpretation can be answered by successful double-blind tests; and the Gardners early established a reliable double-blind system for testing Washoe's vocabulary. The Gardners (1980) report that in a typical double-blind testing session Washoe correctly named 91 or 92 of 128 items.

The obvious meaning of these experiments, confirmed by the Premacks and Rumbaugh using different symbol systems, is that chimpanzees can make the conceptual link between an arbitrary sign and a referent. While some other animals can perform the same kind of feat, only another higher primate, the gorilla, has thus far mastered anything like the sheer quantity of arbitrary signs reported in the various chimp experiments (Walker, 1983).

Critics have rejected even this limited conclusion, arguing that the animals are simply using a learned maneuver—whether making a gesture, selecting a plastic token, or punching a computer key—to get something they want from the experimenters (Chomsky, 1980; Umiker-Sebeok and Sebeok, 1980). The charge, in other words, is that the animals are not performing a cognitive function even vaguely analogous to naming familiar objects and action; they are simply doing tricks for reward, just as a pet mynah bird will say "come in" when it hears a knock on the door. But workers on all the primate language projects report spontaneous signaling which sometimes names, instead of soliciting (Gardner and Gardner, 1969; Patterson and Linden, 1981). Finally, Savage-Rumbaugh, Rumbaugh, and Boysen (1978) have run elaborate experiments requiring Sherman and Austin to exchange information through lexigrams so they could use appropriate tools to extricate food from various containers. The animals were placed in different rooms, and one was allowed to watch a human put food into one of six different kinds of container. After the human left, whichever animal knew where the food was hidden could use the keyboard to ask his comrade for the appropriate tool. If they completed the transaction successfully, they could share the prize. Allowed to use lexigrams, each would readily ask for or give the appropriate tool; deprived of lexigrams, each would present the available tools in random order, or persistently offer the same tool. Having or not having access to the arbitrary symbols of Yerkish completely changed how they solved their problem. In a reductive sense, of course, Sherman and Austin were doing tricks, but so is any student who takes a test. Their different ways of solving the problem indicate that one trick they have is using a shared set of arbitrary symbols to represent things. The Premacks (1983) also found that Sarah's language training improved her problem-solving ability, even when word symbols were not involved. Whatever tricks Sarah performs, learning to represent things by arbitrary symbols has improved her cognitive skills.

The symbol systems used by Rumbaugh and the Premacks impose sequence on the signs — left to right for Rumbaugh, top to bottom for the Premacks. Lana, for example, had to begin each request with a lexigram interpreted as "start," end it with another interpreted as "stop," and use English active-voice word order for the symbols in between. Typical commands (transcribed) are, "start give banana stop"; "start trainer tickle Lana stop"; and "start machine make window open stop." Analogous arbitrary sequence rules govern the Premacks' token system; both projects treated misordered sign sequences as errors. So when Washoe began stringing Ameslan signs together, it became possible to ask whether the animals had learned something like syntax in human language. Initially, David Premack (1971) and the Gardners (1975) argued that they had. The Premacks' claim was based on Sarah's ability to carry out instructions such as these (reading top to bottom):

Sarah	Sarah	Sarah	Sarah
banana	chocolate	apple	cracker
		cracker	candy
			yellow
dish	dish	dish	dish
apple	chocolate	cracker	cracker
			blue
pail	pail	pail	pail
insert	insert	insert	insert

The commands required Sarah to put the first item(s) into the first recep-tacle, and the second item(s) into the second receptacle. First the Pre-macks taught her the simple type of command in the left column, then the progressively more complicated ones. Her high degree of success in carrying out these instructions — 80%, even for the most complex in-struction, involving grouped items and colored receptacles — indicated that she understood the importance of symbol sequence in the com-mands. And sequence, or word order, is certainly important in the gram-mars of many languages — including English, the native language of these researchers. But in every human language, a sentence has hierarchical as well as linear structure. The sentence "Sebastian has bound books," for instance, has two different meanings, each described by a different way of grouping words *(immediate constituent analysis)*. If *has bound* is the verb phrase, the sentence means that Sebastian has worked at binding books. If *has* is the verb phrase and *bound* an adjective modifying *books*, the sentence means that Sebastian owns books that are bound. Our ability to recognize such ambiguity demonstrates that we know something more about the possible structures of this sentence than the order of its words tells us. Because the rigidity of the arbitrary systems invented by the Premacks and Rumbaugh prohibits structurally ambiguous sentences, their animals' success does not indicate mastery of syntax.

In fact, a much simpler explanation is available. Straub (1979) trained pigeons to peck four colors in rigid sequence to obtain food. Labeling the four colors with words to produce English sentences like "please give me corn," "start give corn stop," "dammit, where's the corn" does not mean that pigeons have learned syntax. Although critics have argued that the chimpanzees have simply learned to put one symbol after another, the comparison to pigeons is unfair in the sense that Sarah and the Rumbaugh chimps learned to insert a variety of signs into the slots provided by their symbol systems. In fact, Sherman and Austin can reliably identify a number of lexigrams as belonging to the tool or the food classes, and Sarah clearly grasps the concept "name of." Still, the symbol systems themselves preclude any evidence of the hierarchical structure that is essential to syntax.

The Gardners (1980) have offered a similar analysis of the Premacks' and Rumbaugh's work, and argued that because they themselves did not deliberately teach word order to Ameslan signing chimps, the evidence for sequence roles in Washoe and her companions is significant. They claim, in fact, that the chimps' acquisition of sign-sequence regularities is analogous to that of very young children learning spoken or sign lan-guage. But one can tell little about syntax rules from two- and three-symbol utterances, even in children; the sequences are too short to indi-cate the hierarchical structure essential in syntax (Limber, 1980). We see firm evidence of syntax in children only with the development of tele-graphic speech.

In addition, Terrace (1979, 1983, 1984) found as he analyzed videotapes of Nim's signing sequences that often a query or prompt from the human teacher would intervene between Nim's signs. Because Ameslan is a visual language, two people can be "talking" simultaneously with much less confusion than arises in a verbal language. Terrace observed that Nim's teachers would often hold their first sign or begin another while Nim was making his first one. If Nim then made a second sign, his total performance could be transcribed as either a two-sign combination or as two unconnected signs, each responding to a different prompt from the teacher. The usual sort of written transcript, in which words represent the kinetic signs of Ameslan, disguises such overlap. Terrace also noticed that Nim's utterances did not steadily get longer; instead, they fluctuated in average length between 1.1 and 1.6 signs. While all the signing apes do occasionally produce long strings of signs, they do so by simple repetition. Nim's longest string, for example, was *give orange me give eat orange me eat orange give me eat orange give me you.* The string contains sixteen signs but is clearly not a syntactic unit. In contrast, as children progress from the two-word stage to telegraphic speech, the mean length of their utterances grows very rapidly, reaching about 4.0 by 43 months of age in hearing children (Brown, 1973) and somewhat less (2.8 to 3.1 by 50 months of age) in deaf children learning Ameslan (Klima and Bellugi, 1972; Terrace, 1979, p. 211). These numbers come from very small samples (two children in each category), and *mean length of utterance* is an extremely crude measure of development that favors speaking over signing subjects because it counts morphemes, in which spoken language is much richer than Ameslan. Even so, Nim's utterances did not increase significantly in average length, while those of children do get longer and longer as the children master morphemics and syntax.

Terrace's project suffered from clear limitations. Because Nim worked long hours in a comparatively sterile environment with a parade of more than fifty teachers, his performance may well be inferior to that of animals enjoying happier circumstances (Fouts, 1983; Terrace, 1983, 1984). Still, Walker (1983) seems right in rejecting the arguments for even elementary syntax in trained apes. Experimental designs such as those of the Premacks and Rumbaugh which insist on a rigid sequence of symbols cannot avoid the strong implication that the animals have simply learned arbitrary sequence. The Ameslan experiments are only slightly less susceptible to the same argument, and their sign sequence data is cloudy. Even if it were not, two-sign units do not contain enough material to imply hierarchical syntax.

What then have all the signing ape projects accomplished? They seem to have shown that apes do not have a latent capacity for *human* language, but that is hardly a significant finding. As Chomsky (1980, p. 433) observes, "it would be something of a biological miracle . . . to discover that some other species had a [language] capacity but had never thought to put it to use, despite the remarkable advantages it would confer, until instructed by humans." Only Patterson and to a lesser degree Fouts continue to claim that the animals have even quasi-human language capacity. Criticisms of the signing ape research are not groundless. Sometimes the animals did respond to inadvertent cuing. Every time the Premacks, for example, introduced some variation in procedure to decrease Sarah's access to cues, her performance declined, and David Premack (1976) faithfully reported that development. But mere speculation (Umiker-Sebeok and Sebeok, 1980) about the possibility of cuing does not negate the results (summarized in Fouts and Rigby, 1980; Gardner and Gardner, 1980) of experiments that control for it, such as the Gardners' double-blind vocabulary test. Clearly, a number of animals have learned the meanings of a large number of symbols.

Again, some of the animals' performance can be attributed to their learning an arbitrary string of actions that elicits prizes — as Schusterman and Kreiger (1986) believe their sea lions were doing early in their training. If we think of vocabulary testing for these animals as a game, we can never be sure that they are always playing exactly the same game we are; ours may involve word meanings while theirs involves blue triangles, scratching the top of one's left hand, or picking out the three wavy lines. The very strong implication is that the early stages of training consist of exactly such parallel games. But later developments suggest with equal clarity that the animals master the notion of symbolic meaning (Savage-Rumbaugh, 1986). The total body of experiments with plastic tokens, Yerkish, and Ameslan has demonstrated that apes can learn to use semantically a large number of arbitrary symbols. That achievement is more than the most hostile critics will allow. But it is also considerably less than human semantic abilities. No ape seems to have anything like the rich, interlocked network of semantic relationships characteristic of human vocabulary. The name of the waterfall does not appear to evoke its sound for them.

The expanding body of information on animal communication in general and the acquisition of symbol systems by primates in particular is valuable to students of human language in several ways. First, it helps us to understand, however vaguely, the mental worlds of animals we often consider mindless if not senseless. And for linguists particularly, the study of ape signing provides a rare contrast to normal human language competence. Parallels between teaching signs to chimps and to severely retarded humans have already proved instructive (Romski and Rumbaugh, 1981; Savage-Rumbaugh, 1986). Last, because language does not leave fossils in the ground, we are unlikely to resolve all our questions about how it evolved. But we might resolve some of them by examining the closest thing to language fossils we have: the communicative and cognitive capacities of our nearest relatives.

Whereas careful study has shown how much human communication takes place on the level of affective displays using fixed action patterns, the same studies have shown just how great a gap separates animal use of symbols from our own. Human language is an additional symbolic layer, extremely rich in hierarchical rule systems, superimposed on an existing pattern of communication that we share with other animals. This new layer has led to rapid alteration of every facet of our social structure and even to changes in the way we perceive the world.

As investigators acquire information about communication systems in a broad range of animals at an accelerating rate, the need to rethink older data, integrate new studies, and even re-examine some of our operating assumptions increases. Communication within social groups is a fundamental part of animal life, and particular features of a species' communication system have long been seen as defining that species' unique social and even biological nature (Schneirla, 1972; Schneirla and Rosenblatt, 1972). We ended an earlier version of this essay with the rather facile observation that, "Only another human can understand the symbolic levels in the statement, 'you can make a monkey out of a man, but you can't make a man out of a monkey.' (Kemp and Smith, 1985)" Without distorting the truth of that observation, we would add that this difference in appreciating the levels of meaning in a set of auditory or written signals clearly separates the cognitive worlds of humans and monkeys. Advances in fields as different as neurophysiology, paralinguistics, cognitive science, and comparative psychology seem to be converging on new and exciting conceptions that will challenge much of our understanding of the role language plays in human cognition and behavior. While current information does not show that any other animals have even a close approximation of formal language systems, we have become increasingly impressed at how small a role such formal language (as opposed to other verbal and nonverbal communication systems) plays in the majority of our everyday lives.

By changing the focus of primate research from the study of formal language skills to cognitive strategies, several investigators have shown that chimps do have much the same cognitive mapping skills we use (Menzel, Savage-Rumbaugh and Lawson, 1985; Premack, 1986). The differences in the basic perceptual skills of higher primates may be slight indeed; genetic data suggests that the physical differences are minimal (Gribben and Cherfas, 1986). The similarity of the cognitive world of chimpanzees and humans plus their seemingly absolute difference in syntactic ability suggest how decisive the world-constructing power of language is. The linguistic differences between human and animal may, in the case of higher primates, represent only small cognitive differences. The power of language, once unleashed, has magnified them into an unbridgeable gulf.

BIBLIOGRAPHY

Baker, C. C., and L. M. Herman (1985). "Whales That Go to Extremes," *Natural History*, 94(10): 52–61.

Brown, R. (1973). *A First Language: The Early Stages.* Cambridge, MA: Harvard University Press.

Caldwell, D. K., and M. C. Caldwell (1977). "Cetaceans," *How Animals Communicate,* ed. T. A. Sebeok. Bloomington, IN: Indiana University Press.

Chomsky, N. (1980). "Human Language and Other Semiotic Systems," *Speaking of Apes: A Critical Anthology of Two-Way Communication with Man,* ed. T. A. Sebeok and J. Umiker-Sebeok. New York: Plenum Press.

De Luce, J. and H. T. Wilder (1983), "Introduction," *Languages in Primates: Perspectives and Implications,* ed. J. de Luce and H. T. Wilder. New York: Springer-Verlag.

DeWaal, F. (1982). *Chimpanzee Politics: Power and Sex Among Apes.* New York: Harper and Row.

Fossey, D. (1983). *Gorillas in the Mist.* Boston: Houghton Mifflin Company.

Fouts, R. (1983). "Apes and Language: The Search for Communicative Competence," *Languages in Primates: Perspectives and Implications,* ed. J. de Luce and H. T. Wilder. New York: Springer-Verlag.

Fouts, R., A. D. Hirsch, and D. H. Fouts (1982). "Cultural Transmission of a Human Language in a Chimpanzee Mother-Infant Relationship," *Child Nurturance 3,* ed. H. A. Fitzgerald and others. New York: Plenum Press.

Fouts, R., and R. Rigby (1980). "Man-Chimpanzee Communication," *Speaking of Apes: A Critical Anthology of Two-Way Communication with Man,* ed. T. A. Sebeok and J. Umiker-Sebeok. New York: Plenum Press.

Frumhoff, P. (1983). "Aberrant Songs of Humpback Whales *(Megaptera novaeangliae):* Clues to the Structure of Humpback Songs," *Communication and Behavior of Whales,* ed. R. Payne. AAAS Selected Symposium Series. Boulder: Westview Press, Inc.

Gardner, B. T., and R. A. Gardner, (1969). "Teaching Sign Language to a Chimpanzee," *Science,* 165: 664–672.

——— (1975). "Evidence for Sentence Constituents in the Early Utterances of Child and Chimpanzee," *Journal of Experimental Psychology: General,* 104(3): 224–276.

Gardner, R. A., and B. T. Gardner (1980). "Comparative Psychology and Language Acquisition," *Speaking of Apes: A Critical Anthology of Two-Way Communication with Man,* ed. T. A. Sebeok and J. Umiker-Sebeok. New York: Plenum Press.

Goodall, J. (1971). *In the Shadow of Man.* Boston: Houghton Mifflin.

——— (1986). *The Chimpanzees of Gombi: Patterns of Behavior.* Cambridge, MA: Belknap Press.

Gould, J. L., and C. G. Gould (1983). "Can a Bee Behave Intelligently?" *New Scientist,* 98: 84–87.

Gribben, J., and J. Cherfas (1982). *The Monkey Puzzle: Reshaping the Evolutionary Tree.* New York: Pantheon Books.

Griffin, D. R. (1981). *The Question of Animal Awareness: Evolutionary Continuity of Mental Experience.* Los Altos, Calif.: William Kaufmann, Inc.

Guinee, L. N., K. Chu, and E. M. Dorsey (1983). "Changes Over Time in the Songs of Known Individual Humpback Whales *(Megaptera novaeangliae),*" Communication and Behavior of Whales, ed. R. Payne. AAAS Selected Symposium Series. Boulder, CO: Westview Press, Inc.

Hayes, C. H. (1951). *The Ape in Our House.* New York: Harper and Row.

Herman, L. M. (1980). *Cetacean Behavior: Mechanisms and Function.* New York: Wiley and Sons.

Herman, L. M., D. G. Richards, and J. P. Wolz (1984). "Comprehension of Sentences by Bottlenose Dolphins," *Cognition*, 16: 128–219.

Hinde, R. A. (1970). *Animal Behavior: A Synthesis of Ethology and Comparative Psychology*, 2nd ed. New York: McGraw Hill.

Hockett, C. F., and S. A. Altmann (1968). "A Note on Design Features," *Animal Communication*, ed. T. A. Sebeok. Bloomington, IN: University of Indiana Press.

Immelmann, K. (1969). "Song Development in the Zebra Finch and Other Estrildid Finches," *Bird Vocalizations*, ed. R. A. Hinde. Cambridge, UK: Cambridge University Press.

Kellogg, W. N. (1961). *Porpoises and Sonar*. Chicago: University of Chicago Press.

———— (1980). "Communication and Language in the Home-Raised Chimpanzee," *Speaking of Apes: A Critical Anthology of Two-Way Communication with Man*, ed. T. A. Sebeok and J. Umiker-Sebeok. New York: Plenum Press.

Kemp, W., and R. Smith (1985). "Animals, Communication, and Language," *Language: Introductory Readings*, ed. V. Clark, P. Eschholz, and A. Rosa. 4th ed. New York: St. Martin's Press.

Klima, E. S., and U. Bellugi (1972). "The Signs of Language in Child and Chimpanzee," *Communication and Affect*, ed. T. Alloway and others. New York: Academic Press.

Konishi, M. (1973). "Locatable and Non-Locatable Acoustic Signals for Barn Owls," *American Naturalist*, 107: 775–785.

Konishi, M., and F. Nottebaum (1969). "Experimental Studies in the Ontogeny of Avian Vocalizations," *Bird Vocalizations*, ed. R. A. Hinde. Cambridge, UK: Cambridge University Press.

Krebs, J. R., and D. E. Kroodsma (1980). "Repertoires and Geographical Variation in Bird Song," *Advanced Study of Behavior*, 11: 143–147.

Lilly, J. C. (1975). *Lilly on Dolphins*. Garden City, NY: Anchor Books.

Limber, J. (1980). "Language in Child and Chimpanzee?" *Speaking of Apes: A Critical Anthology of Two-Way Communication with Man*, ed. T. A. Sebeok and J. Umiker-Sebeok. New York: Plenum Press.

Lindauer, M. (1961). *Communication Among Social Bees*. Cambridge: Harvard University Press.

Marler, P. (1955). "Characteristics of Some Animal Calls," *Nature*, 176: 6–7.

————. (1957). "Specific Distinctiveness in the Communication Signals of Birds," *Behavior*, 11: 13–19.

Marler, P., and M. Tamura (1964). "Culturally Transmitted Patterns of Vocal Behavior in Sparrows," *Science*, 146: 1483–1486.

McBride, A. F., and D. O. Hebb (1948). "Behavior of the Captive Bottle-nose Dolphin, *Tursops truncatus*," *Journal of Comparative and Physiological Psychology*, 41: 111–123.

Mech, L. D. (1970). *The Wolf: Ecology and Behavior of an Endangered Species*. Garden City, NY: Natural History Press.

Menzel, E. W., S. Savage-Rumbaugh, and J. Lawson (1985). "Chimpanzee *(Pan troglodytes)* Spatial Problem Solving with the Use of Mirrors and Televised Equivalents of Mirrors," *Journal of Comparative Psychology*, 99: 211–217.

Miles, H. L. (1983). "Apes and Language: The Search for Communicative Competence," *Language in Primates: Perspectives and Implications*, ed. J. de Luce and H. T. Wilder. New York: Springer-Verlag.

Mowat, F. (1967). *Never Cry Wolf*. New York: Little, Brown and Co.

North, S. (1966). *Raccoons are the Brightest People.* New York: E. P. Dutton and Co.

Nottebaum, F. (1975). "Vocal Behavior in Birds," *Avian Biology V*, ed. D. S. Farner and others. New York: Academic Press.

Patterson, F. (1978). "The Gestures of a Gorilla: Sign Language in Another Pongoid Species," *Brain and Language*, 5: 72–97.

Patterson, F., and E. Linden (1981). *The Education of Koko.* New York: Holt, Rinehart and Winston.

Payne, K., P. Tyack, and R. Payne (1983). "Progressive Changes in the Songs of Humpback Whales *(Megaptera novaeangliae):* A Detailed Analysis of Two Seasons in Hawaii," *Communication and Behavior of Whales*, ed. R. Payne. AAAS Selected Symposia Series. Boulder, CO: Westview Press, Inc.

Peters, R. (1980). *Mammalian Communication: A Behavioral Analysis of Meaning.* Monterey, CA: Brooks/Cole.

Pettito, L. A., and M. S. Seidenberg (1979). "On the Evidence for Linguistic Abilities in Signing Apes," *Brain and Language*, 8: 162–183.

Pfungst, O. (1911). *Clever Hans, the Horse of Mr. van Osten.* Ed. R. Rosenthal. New York: Holt, Rinehart and Winston, 1965.

Premack, A. (1976). *Why Chimps Can Read.* New York: Harper and Row.

Premack, D. (1971). "Language in Chimpanzee?" *Science*, 172: 808–822.

——— (1972). "Teaching Language to an Ape," *Scientific American*, 227: 92–99.

——— (1976). *Intelligence in Ape and Man.* Hillsdale, NJ: Lawrence Erlbaum.

——— (1986). *Gavagai: Or the Future of the Animal Language Controversy.* Cambridge, MA: MIT Press.

Premack, D., and A. Premack (1983). *The Mind of an Ape.* New York: W. W. Norton.

Romski, M. A., and D. M. Rumbaugh (1981). "Computer Based Language Training," *Education and Training of the Mentally Retarded*, 16: 193–200.

Rumbaugh, D. M. (1980). "Language Behavior in Apes," *Speaking of Apes: A Critical Anthology of Two-Way Communication with Man*, ed. T. A. Sebeok and J. Umiker-Sebeok. New York: Plenum Press.

Savage-Rumbaugh, S. (1986). *Ape Language: From Conditioned Response to Symbol.* New York: Columbia University Press.

Savage-Rumbaugh, S., D. M. Rumbaugh, and S. Boysen (1978). "Linguistically Mediated Tool Use and Exchange by Chimpanzees, *(Pan troglodytes),*" *Behavioral and Brain Sciences*, 1: 539–554.

Schaller, G. B. (1963). *The Mountain Gorilla: Ecology and Behavior.* Chicago: University of Chicago Press.

——— (1972). *The Serengeti Lion.* Chicago: University of Chicago Press.

Schneirla, T. C. (1972). "The 'Levels' Concept in the Study of Social Organization in Animals," *Selected Writings of T. C. Schneirla*, ed. L. R. Aronson and others. San Francisco: Freeman.

Schneirla, T. C., and J. S. Rosenblatt (1972). "Behavioral Organization and Genesis of the Social Bond in Insects and Mammals," *Selected Writings of T. C. Schneirla*, ed. L. R. Aronson and others. San Francisco: Freeman.

Schusterman, R. J. (1967). "Attention Shift and Errorless Reversal Learning by the California Sea Lion," *Science*, 156: 833–835.

——— (1981). "Behavioral Capabilities of Seals and Sea Lions: A Review of Their Hearing, Visual, Learning, and Diving Skills," *Psychological Record*, 31: 125–143.

Schusterman, R. J., and K. Kreiger (1984). "California Sea Lions Are Capable of Semantic Comprehension," *Psychological Record,* 34: 3–23.

——— (1986). "Artificial Language Comprehension and Size Transposition by a California Sea Lion *(Zalophus californianus),*" *Journal of Comparative Psychology,* 100: 348–355.

Sebeok, T. A., and R. Rosenthal, eds. (1981). *The Clever Hans Phenomenon: Communication with Horses, Whales, Apes, and People.* Annals of the New York Academy of Sciences, vol. 364. New York: New York Academy of Sciences.

Seidenberg, M. S., and L. A. Pettito. (1979). "Signing Behavior in Apes: A Critical Review." *Cognition* 7: 177–215.

Smith, W. John (1977a). *The Behavior of Communicating.* Cambridge, MA: Harvard University Press.

——— (1977b). "Communication in Birds," *How Animals Communicate,* ed. T. A. Sebeok. Bloomington, IN: Indiana University Press.

Smith, W. John, S. L. Smith, E. C. Oppenheimer, and J. G. DeVilla (1977). "Vocalizations of the Black-Tailed Prairie Dog *Cynomys ludovicianus.*" *Animal Behavior,* 25: 152–164.

Straub, R. O. (1979). "Serial Learning in the Pigeon," *Journal of the Experimental Analysis of Behavior,* 32: 137–148.

Terrace, H. S. (1979). *Nim: A Chimp Who Learned Sign Language.* New York: Alfred A. Knopf.

——— (1983). "Apes Who 'Talk': Language or Projection of Language by Their Teachers?" *Languages in Primates: Perspectives and Implications,* ed. J. de Luce and H. T. Wilder. New York: Springer-Verlag.

——— (1984). "'Language' in Apes," *The Meaning of Primate Signals,* ed. Rom Harre and Vernon Reynolds. Cambridge, UK: Cambridge University Press.

Thielke, G. (1969). "Geographic Variation in Bird Vocalizations," *Bird Vocalization,* ed. R. A. Hinde. Cambridge, UK: Cambridge University Press.

Thorpe, W. H. (1958). "The Learning of Song Patterns by Birds, With Especial Reference to the Song of the Chaffinch *Fringilla coelebs,*" *Ibis* 100: 535–570.

Umiker-Sebeok, J., and T. A. Sebeok (1980). "Introduction: Questioning Apes," *Speaking of Apes: A Critical Anthology of Two-Way Communication with Man,* ed. T. A. Sebeok and J. Umiker-Sebeok. New York: Plenum Press.

Von Frisch, K. (1966). *The Dancing Bees.* New York: Harcourt, Brace and World.

——— (1967). *A Biologist Remembers.* Trans. Lisbeth Gombrich. Oxford, UK: Pergamon Press.

——— (1971). *Bees: Their Vision, Chemical Senses, and Language.* Rev. ed. Ithaca, NY: Cornell University Press.

Walker, S. (1983). *Animal Thought.* London: Routledge and Kegan Paul.

Wilbur, R. B. (1979). *American Sign Language and Sign Systems.* Baltimore: University Park Press.

Wilson, E. O. (1971). *The Insect Societies.* Cambridge, MA: Harvard University Press.

Wood, F. G. (1973). *Marine Mammals and Man: The Navy's Porpoises and Sea Lions.* New York: Robert B. Luce, Inc.

=

FOR DISCUSSION AND REVIEW

1. Explain why ethologists and linguists believe that studying different kinds of animal communication is important.

2. In analyzing animal communication, ethologists use the terms *form*, *context*, and *response*. Define each term, and give an original example illustrating each.

3. Kemp and Smith state that "distinctive behavior that reliably indicates what an animal will do promotes cooperation and reduces conflict, because it allows neighbors to adjust their actions according to what the display predicts." Drawing on your own experience, write brief descriptions of three situations involving animals that illustrate this principle.

4. Explain the relationship between the *allophones* of human speech and animal *displays*.

5. Review Hockett's "design features" discussed by W. F. Bolton (pp. 4–6). To what extent does animal communication embody these features? Be specific; you may wish to consider only bees, or birds, or mammals, etc.

6. Explain the differences between bird *calls* and *songs*; be sure to consider the functions of each.

7. Explain the implications for comparisons of human language and animal communication of Kemp and Smith's statement that "the fundamental feature of animal communication persists in even the most highly social mammals: the value of displays does not depend on a desire to tell another animal something."

8. Why are specialists from many disciplines especially interested in studying nonhuman primate communication?

9. Write a short description of a *double-blind* experimental design. Why is this an important technique?

10. In all human languages, sentences have both hierarchical and linear structure. What is the significance of this fact to conclusions based on the work done with nonhuman primates?

15

The Continuity Paradox

Derek Bickerton

Where and how did humans acquire language? What events took place among people that stimulated the development of language? What role has language played in the development of our species? Scientists and linguists have long been trying to answer these questions. In this selection, taken from his book Language and Species, *Derek Bickerton, professor of linguistics at the University of Hawaii, examines what he refers to as a "paradox" in the evolution of and examination of human language: the Paradox of Continuity. Bickerton asserts that if the theory of evolution is accepted, then language must be no more than an evolutionary adaptation. The paradox exists because language is far too complicated to have been the result of a genetic mutation or shift. Bickerton discusses innate differences between human and animal communication systems as he focuses on such specifics as "creativity" and the differences between "calls" and "words." He also examines "formalist" versus "antiformalist" views in his attempt to solve the paradox of the evolution of language. In his search for solutions, Bickerton clearly demonstrates how our ability to use language distinguishes us from all other species, and how language is an invaluable asset to human beings.*

Anyone who sets out to describe the role played by language in the development of our species is at once confronted by an apparent paradox, the Paradox of Continuity. If such a person accepts the theory of evolution, that person must accept also that language is no more than an evolutionary adaptation — one of an unusual kind, perhaps, yet formed by the same processes that have formed countless other adaptations. If that is the case, then language cannot be as novel as it seems, for evolutionary adaptations do not emerge out of the blue.

There are two ways in which evolution can produce novel elements: by the recombination of existing genes in the course of normal breeding, or by mutations that affect genes directly. Even in the second case, absolute novelties are impossible. What happens in mutation is that the instructions for producing part of a particular type of creature are altered. Instructions for producing a new part cannot simply be added to the old recipe. There must already exist specific instructions that are capable of being altered, to a greater or lesser extent. What this means is that language cannot be wholly without antecedents of some kind.

But what kind of antecedents could language have? Since language is so widely regarded as a means of communication, the answer seems obvious: earlier systems of animal communication. It has long been known that many species communicate with one another. Some, like fireflies, have blinking lights, others, like crickets, rub legs or wingcases together, while many exude chemical signals known as pheromones. Of course such means are limited in their range of potential meaning and may signal nothing more complex than the presence of a potential mate. But the more sophisticated the creature, the more sophisticated the means — from the dances of honeybees, through the posturing of sea gulls, to the sonar of dolphins — hence, the more complex the information that can be conveyed. Could not human language be just a super-sophisticated variant of these?

The trouble is that the differences between language and the most sophisticated systems of animal communication that we are so far aware of are qualitative rather than quantitative. All such systems have a fixed and finite number of topics on which information can be exchanged, whereas in language the list is open-ended, indeed infinite. All such systems have a finite and indeed strictly limited number of ways in which message components can be combined, if they can be combined at all. In language the possibilities of combination, while governed by strict principles, are (potentially at least) infinite, limited for practical purposes only by the finiteness of the immediate memory store. You do not get from a finite number to infinity merely by adding numbers. And there are subtler but equally far-reaching differences between language and animal communication that make it impossible to regard the one as antecedent to the other.

But the net result of all this is the Paradox of Continuity: language must have evolved out of some prior system, and yet there does not seem to be any such system out of which it could have evolved. Until now, arguments about the nature, origin, and function of language have remained inextricably mired in this paradox. Let us see if there is any way in which they can be released from it.

A WORD ABOUT FORMALISM

We can at least clean a little of the mud from our wheels if we begin by tackling what might seem at first an unpromising and unrelated issue: the role that formal structure plays in language. Some linguists will tell you that the formal structure of language is very important. Others will tell you that it is relatively unimportant. Who is right?

There are two very odd imbalances between the formalist and antiformalist groups. The first imbalance is in what they believe. No formalist believes that a purely formal approach is the only way to study language. Any formalist would agree that there are many aspects of language—meaning, use, interaction with other social and psychological domains—that are all worthy of study. If you ask formalists why they insist on studying formal structure in isolation from all these other factors, they will probably tell you that significant advances in knowledge have always involved focusing on particular aspects of things and abstracting away from other aspects. They can see no reason for the study of our own species to reverse this sensible procedure.

But if you ask antiformalists why they ignore the formal structure of language, you will sometimes hear a much less tolerant story. They may tell you that it is quite senseless to study the formal aspects of language in isolation from its mode of functioning in society. Quite possibly they will go on to say that since those aspects are merely uninteresting mechanisms, or superficial trimmings, or even artefacts of the method of inquiry, they can be relegated to an inferior position, if not dismissed altogether.

The second imbalance between formalists and antiformalists is that since formalists have ignored all issues involving the evolution of language, that field has been yielded without a blow to the enemies of formalism. Subsequently there has been no significant interchange between the two sides, indeed they are barely on speaking terms. This has left the antiformalists alone to grapple with the Continuity Paradox.

Now to tackle a paradox, or indeed any research issue, from a one-sided position is not the best recipe for success. In large part, failure to resolve the Continuity Paradox has resulted precisely from what one might call the "naive continuism" of the antiformalists, who have tried in a variety of ways to establish a direct line of development from animal communication to human language. Although all their efforts have signally failed to produce a convincing "origins" story, their rejection of more formal approaches has left them without any viable alternative.

Accordingly the present work tackles the Paradox from a rather different viewpoint. This viewpoint takes as basic the assumption that formal properties of language do exist and do matter, and that without the very specific types of formal structure that language exhibits, it could not perform the social and communicative functions that it does perform, and could not convey the wealth of peculiarly human meaning that it does convey.

Those functions and that meaning should not—and, indeed, in a work of this nature literally can not—be ignored or even minimized. However, it seems reasonable to stand the antiformalist position on its head and say that it is quite senseless to study the origins and functions of language without at the same time studying the formal structures that underlie those functions. For these formal structures, abstract though they may appear, are exactly what enable language to communicate so efficiently. Nothing else that we know of (or can imagine) could have given language the unprecedented power that it proved to have: power that gave to a single primate line the mastery of the physical world and the first, and perhaps only, entry into the world of consciousness.

THE GULF BETWEEN LANGUAGE AND ANIMAL COMMUNICATION

Having established this perspective, we can now look a little more closely at the ways in which animal communication differs from language. Perhaps the most obvious is that of productivity. The calls or signs of other creatures usually occur in isolation from one another. There are as yet few, if any, clear cases where they can be combined to form longer utterances whose meaning differs from the sum of their meanings in isolation, in the way in which *look out!*, for instance, differs from the sum of the meanings of *look* and *out*.

It is not impossible that future research will uncover such cases. But then, if we were to parallel language, we would have to look for cases where the same calls in a different order can mean different things, like *Dog bites man* versus *Man bites dog*. Even this far from exhausts the possibilities of human syntax, which can also place similar words in different orders to mean the same thing *(John gave Mary the book, Mary was given the book by John)* or the same words in almost the same order to mean quite different things *(The woman that saw the man kicked the dog, The woman saw the man that kicked the dog)*.

Note however that to achieve such effects we have to use elements like *-en, by, that*. Later on we shall look at such elements in more detail. For the moment it is sufficient to note that they differ from elements like *John* or *woman* in that the latter refer (if only indirectly) to some entity or class of entities in the real world, whereas the former do not really refer at all, but rather serve to express structural relations between items that do refer. The first class of elements can be described as *grammatical items* and the second, the class that refers, as *lexical items*. To which class of items do animal calls and signs belong?

Certainly there seems to be nothing in any animal communication system that corresponds even vaguely to grammatical items. But it is also questionable, in at least a large majority of cases, whether there is any true correspondence with lexical items either. We may find, for example, a particular facial expression, accompanied perhaps by a bristling of hair, that we might want to translate as *I am very angry with you*, or a peculiar cry that perhaps we would translate as, *Look out, folks, something dangerous is coming!* In other words, most elements in animal communication systems might seem to correspond, in a very rough and ready sense, with complete human utterances, rather than with single words per se. But note that the true correspondence is with utterance rather than sentence, because oftentimes a single-word utterance like *Help!* or *Danger!* would serve as well. The category *complete utterance*, however, is not a structural category in language, precisely because it can cover anything from a complex sentence (or even a series of such sentences) to a one-word exclamation.

It follows that, for the most part, the units in animal communication systems do not correspond with any of the units that compose human language. There is a good reason why this is so. Animal communication is *holistic,* that is to say it is concerned with communicating *whole situations.* Language, on the other hand, talks mainly about *entities* (whether other creatures, objects, or ideas) and *things predicated of entities* (whether actions, events, states, or processes).

The units of animal communication convey whole chunks of information (rough equivalents of *I am angry, You may mate with me, A predator just appeared*). Language breaks up those chunks in a way that, to the best of our knowledge, no animal communication system has ever done. In order to convey our anger, we must, as an absolute minimum, specify ourselves by a particular sign and the state in which we find ourselves by another sign (in English and numerous other languages we have, in addition, to use an almost meaningless verb in order to link ourselves with our current state, while in another set of languages, we would have to add a particle to indicate that our state was indeed current, not a past or future one).

If we think about it, this way of doing things may seem somewhat less natural than the animal way. Suppose that the situation we want to convey is one in which we have just seen a predator approaching. From a functional point of view, it might seem a lot quicker to let out a single call with that meaning, rather than *Look out! A lion's coming!* But the oddity is not just functional. In the real situation, it is simply not the case that we would see two things: an entity (the lion) and something predicated of that entity ("coming"). If we actually were in that situation, what we would perceive would be the frontal presentation of a lion getting rapidly larger. That is, we would experience a single intact cluster of ongoing perceptions. So the animal's representation of this would seem to be not merely more expeditious, but more in accord with reality than ours.

But there are, even in this limited example, compensating features. A generalized predator warning call, or even a specific lion warning call, could not be modified so as to become *A lion was coming* (as in the context of a story), *A lion may come* (to propose caution in advance), *No lions are coming* (to convey reassurance), *Many lions are coming!* (to prompt still more vigorous evasive measures), and so on. To achieve this kind of flexibility, any utterance has to be composed of a number of different units each of which may be modified or replaced so as to transmit a wide range of different messages. And after all, if we want a rapid response, the possession of language in no way inhibits use of the human call system. In a tight corner, we can still just yell.

Still, you might argue, language had to begin somewhere, and where is it most likely to have begun than in some particular call whose meaning was progressively narrowed until it now covers about the same semantic range as does some noun in a language? Once the species had acquired a short list of entities — lions, snakes, or whatever — it needed only to attribute states or actions to those entities and it would then already have the essential subject-predicate core of language, to which all other properties could subsequently have been added.

You might then point to creatures such as the vervet monkey which have highly developed alarm calls. The vervet, a species that lives in East Africa, has at least three distinct alarm calls that might seem to refer to three species that are likely to prey upon vervets: pythons, martial eagles, and leopards. That it is the calls themselves that have this reference, and not any other behavioral or environmental feature, has been experimentally established by playing recordings of the calls to troops of vervets in the absence of any of the predators concerned. On hearing these recordings, most vervets within earshot respond just as they would to a natural, predator-stimulated call. They look at the ground around them on hearing the snake warning, run up trees on hearing the leopard warning, and descend from trees to hide among bushes on hearing the eagle warning.

We might therefore think that these calls were, in embryo at least, the vervet "words" for the species concerned. But in fact, a warning call about pythons differs from a word like *python* in a variety of ways. Even though *python* is only a single word, it can be modified, just as we saw the sentence *A lion is coming!* could be modified. It can, for instance, be given at least four different intonations, each of which has a distinct meaning. With a rising intonation it can mean "Is that a python there?" or "Did you just say python?" With a neutral intonation, it merely names a particular variety of snake, as in a list of snake species, for example. With a sustained high-pitch intonation it can mean that there's a python right there, right now. With an intonation that starts high and ends low, especially if delivered in a sneering, sarcastic tone, it can mean "How ridiculous to suppose that there's a python there!"

Assuming that all these are used without intent to deceive, only in the third case is there a python there for sure. But with the vervet call, there is always a python there. At least, with one rare exception, the vervet involved genuinely believes there is a python there. (Just like human children, young vervets have to learn the semantic range of their calls, and again like children they tend to overgeneralize and sometimes give calls in inappropriate circumstances.)

In order to understand further differences between humans and vervets, certain aspects of meaning must first be clarified. We might suppose that any relation between events in the world and meaningful utterances could be characterized as a mapping relation, that is to say, an operation that matches features of the environment with features of a (more or less arbitrary) representational system. We might begin by saying that a python in the real world is matched with a particular call in the vervet system and a particular noun in a given human language. This would be not very far from Bertrand Russell's theory of meaning and reference, for Russell believed, and got into terrible difficulties through believing, that nouns referred directly to entities in the real world.

Linguists, at least since Russell's contemporary de Saussure, have known that this is not so for human language. As noted above, grammatical items do not refer at all, and lexical items refer to real-world entities only indirectly. This is because not one, but at least two mapping operations lie between the real world and language. First our sense perceptions of the world are mapped onto a conceptual representation, and then this conceptual representation is mapped onto a linguistic representation.

Indeed, even in the animal case there cannot be a direct relationship between external object and call. Every now and then, even adult vervets will use, say, an eagle call for something that is not an eagle. It is no help to say that the vervet merely made a mistake. Why did it make that mistake? Because it thought that what it saw really was an eagle. In other words, if the vervet is wrong, it is wrong because it is responding to its own act of identification, rather than to the object itself. But are we then to say that the vervet responds to its own identification when it happens to be wrong and to the real object when it happens to be right? Obviously not. Vervets respond to their own identifications under all circumstances. But in that case there cannot be a direct link between call and object. The call labels an act of identification: the placing of some phenomenon in a particular category. In some sense, vervets too must have concepts.

That the things words refer to are not external entities is even clearer in our own case. One piece of evidence is the very existence of expressions like *a unicorn* or *the golden mountain* that gave Russell so much trouble. Since such expressions cannot refer to real-world entities, they must refer to a level of representation that is to some extent independent of the real world.

Indeed, it is sometimes inescapable that linguistic expressions are referring not to real-world entities but to our conceptions of these. It is surprising that Russell never discussed sentences like *The Bill Bailey I love and respect is very different from the drunken monster you depict him as being.* Here, obviously, two concepts of the same person are in conflict. Nor can we escape the situation by pointing to the indisputable fact that one does not normally preface proper names with the definite article, and claim therefore that while *the Bill Bailey I love and respect* may refer to a concept of Bill Bailey, *Bill Bailey* alone can only refer to Bill Bailey the real-world individual.

Suppose I say *Bill Bailey is honest* and you say *Bill Bailey is a rascal.* Since both qualities cannot be simultaneously predicated of the same person, the referent for the first use can only be my concept of Bill Bailey while that for the second can only be yours. But what about *Bill Bailey left early?* If we say that the name here refers to a real-world entity, we are in the uncomfortable position of claiming that names sometimes refer to real entities and sometimes to concepts. It seems safer to say that they refer to concepts all the time.

Yet even though both calls and words refer indirectly, there is evidence that they do not do so in the same way. For instance, it's a safe bet that no animal system has calls for unicorns or golden mountains or anything else of which there is no sensory evidence.

Another way in which calls and words differ is that words can be, and usually are, used in the physical absence of the objects they refer to, whereas calls hardly ever are so used. There is one exception: numerous observers have reported, for vervets and other primate species, what look like deliberate uses of alarm calls in the absence of any predator, designed to distract other monkeys from aggressive intentions or to remove potential competitors for some item of food.

If these can be proven to be genuine cases of deception, would they serve to undermine the distinction between words and calls? The answer is no, for two reasons. First, the strategy would not work unless all the other vervets believed, and behaved as if, there was a predator there. That is, it would work only if the deceiving monkey could rely on other monkeys to respond in the appropriate fashion. Second, in such observed instances the deceiving monkey itself failed to respond appropriately to its own call, even when it was in plain view of other monkeys. This suggests that the animal is not truly "using a call in the absence of its referent" but simply exploiting one consequence of alarm calls (the disappearance of other animals from the vicinity) for its own personal ends.

Closely linked to these issues is the question of evolutionary utility. If human words were no more than the equivalents of animal calls, referring in the same way that animal calls referred, it would be remarkable that we have all the words we do. Vervets can "name" pythons, leopards, and martial eagles. They cannot "name" vultures, elephants, antelopes, and a variety of other creatures that do not have a significant impact on the lives of vervets. Why, in that case, is the human insect repertoire not limited to *fly, mosquito, locust,* and *cockroach* (plus any other insects that may significantly affect the lives of humans), and why is it that we have words—like *cockchafer, ladybird, earwig,* and *dung beetle*—for countless species that affect us minimally, if at all?

Here we differ from other creatures along a rather interesting dimension. All other creatures can communicate only about things that have evolutionary significance for them, but human beings can communicate about *anything.* In other words, what is adaptive for other species is a *particular set* of highly specific referential capacities. What is adaptive for our species is the *system* of reference *as a whole,* the fact that *any* manifestation of the physical world can (potentially at least) be matched with some form of expression. The fact that this difference is qualitative rather than quantitative (vervets could increase their repertoire by many orders of magnitude without even approximating the global scope of human reference) suggests again that quite different mechanisms are involved.

We should take account, too, of the fact that while animal calls and signs are structurally holistic, the units of human language are componential in nature. What this means is that animal calls and signs cannot be broken down into component parts, as language can. Words are, on one level, simply combinations of sounds. These sounds are finite and, indeed, small in number, not exceeding seventy or so in any known language.

Though in themselves the sounds of a language are meaningless, they can be recombined in different ways to yield thousands of words, each distinct in meaning. A word like *pat*, for example, can be broken down into three distinct sounds: /p/, /a/, and /t/. Those same sounds can be recombined to form *tap* and *apt*, two words of entirely different meaning. In just the same way, a finite stock of words (usually some tens of thousands, probably not much more than half a million even in the most "developed" language) can be combined to produce an infinite number of sentences. Nothing remotely like this is found in animal communication.

To those already convinced that human language and animal communication are wholly unconnected, the foregoing paragraphs may seem like overkill. Yet contrasting animal communication and language has a purpose beyond merely convincing continuists that naive continuism won't work. It has the purpose of clarifying exactly what it is that makes language look like an evolutionary novelty. For if we don't do at least this, our prospects of explaining the evolutionary origins of language are dim. After all, anticontinuists have failed even more dismally than continuists at providing a convincing history of language and mind. Until we cease to regard language as primarily communicative and begin to treat it as primarily representational, we cannot hope to escape from the Continuity Paradox.

THE NATURE OF REPRESENTATION

It may be advisable to begin by clarifying some aspects of the general nature of representations. What do we mean when we say that *X* represents *Y*? Normally that *Y*, an event or an entity in the real world, bears some kind of correspondence relation to *X*, such that *X* somehow recalls or expresses *Y*, but not necessarily vice versa. This definition is informal and crude, and there may be several things about it that are questionable, but it will do as a starting point.

The first point to note is that in fact everything that we or any other creatures perceive is a representation, and not in any sense naked reality itself. That is to say, no creature apprehends its environment except by means of sensory mechanisms whose mode of functioning is everywhere the same. Particular facets of the environment excite responses (in terms of variations from their unstimulated firing rate) from particular cells that are specialized to respond to just those facets and no others. These neural responses in themselves constitute a level of representation. The firing of such-and-such a collection of neurons at such-and-such frequencies corresponds to the presence, in the immediate environment, of such-and-such a set of features. Almost simultaneously, in all vertebrates and many invertebrates, the original responses are synthesized and their synthesis, if functionally relevant to the creature concerned, is assigned to its appropriate category. This can be regarded as a further level of representation, in which the category assignment corresponds to a particular set of neuronal responses.

We do not, for example, directly see our surroundings. What happens is that sets of cells in our retinas programmed to react to specific features of the environment (lines at various angles, motions of varying kinds, different qualities of light, and so on) respond to those features on an individual basis, and this information is then relayed electrochemically to the visual areas of the cortex, where it is automatically reconstituted to provide a fairly, but not always completely, accurate simulacrum of what there is around us.

If this were not so, if our visual system merely presented us with a direct image of reality in the way that a mirror reflects whatever is before it, there would be no optical illusions. Optical illusions arise when properties of the visual system are imposed on the raw data of the physical world. Nor can we dismiss such illusions as marginal phenomena. When we look around us we see an entirely colored world, but color is simply a property of the perceiving mechanism. All of us have seen mountains, gray or brown in the light of midday, turn to blue as the sun descends, then perhaps to pink or crimson as the last rays touch them, then finally to black as night falls. Of course the mountains have not really changed color, only the light reflected by them has changed, and these changes in turn interact with our means of perceiving and categorizing differences in wavelengths. But in that case, what are the mountains' *real* colors? Clearly they cannot have any.

We can now return to an earlier remark that may have seemed problematic at the time. In the previous section, it was stated that expressions such as *the golden mountain* must refer not to the real world but to "a level of representation that is to some extent independent of the real world." How can we, one might ask, have a level that represents the real world but contains entities that do not exist in that world? If we treat "representation" as meaning simply "re-presentation"—a wholly faithful one-to-one mapping from one medium to another—this seems absurd. But in fact, representation can never have such a meaning.

Consider the most basic facts about what a representation is and does. Although what follows applies to representations generally, let us, for the sake of concreteness, take as a particular example a painting of the Battle of Lepanto; and let us for ease of exposition ignore for the present any intervening layer(s) of representation (sensory, conceptual, or other) that may come between the actual Battle of Lepanto and the painting with that title. It should immediately be clear that there are many properties of the Battle of Lepanto that the painting cannot represent. It cannot enable us, for instance, to smell the gunpowder smoke, or the sea spray, or the stench of blood below decks. The time that passed for an observer of the battle was determined by the length of the battle, but the time that passes for an observer of the picture is determined only by the observer's will. And there are many more properties of the actual Battle of Lepanto that are not, and indeed cannot be, represented in "The Battle of Lepanto."

But the converse is equally the case: there are many properties of the painting that never belonged to its original. "The Battle of Lepanto," unlike the Battle of Lepanto, is made of paint and canvas, hangs on a wall, can be brought and sold, has properties of proportion that can be discussed by art critics, and so on. Yet even though "The Battle of Lepanto" lacks much that the Battle of Lepanto possessed, and possesses much that the Battle of Lepanto lacked, we do not balk or express our derision when we read its title, instead we are perfectly prepared to accept it as a representation. Indeed someone who was actually present at the battle might have realized what the painting was meant to represent even without its title, by virtue of those features (names, types, and positions of ships, flags displayed, actual incidents depicted, and so forth) that the battle and the painting did share.

The relationship between a real-world event and a painting may look like an extreme kind of example to choose, since the level of real events and the level of pictorial representations might seem excessively remote from one another. However, it is hard to see how they are more remote than the level of real events is from the level of processing units in the brain, or than the level of processing units in the brain is from the level of spoken or written utterance. Moreover, remote or not, similar principles must apply wherever representation exists.

Both the properties of the Battle of Lepanto that must be excluded from the picture and the nonproperties of battle that a picture must impose will be determined by the properties of static (as opposed to dynamic) representations, the properties of two-dimensional (as opposed to three-dimensional) objects, the properties of paint (as opposed to other media), and so on. In the same way, wherever representation exists, the properties of the medium in which the representation is made (or, to put it another way, the formal structures onto which the things to be represented are mapped) must both select from and add to the properties of the original.

In particular, the properties of neural systems, some of which are general but some of which are highly species-specific, and the properties of language, almost all of which are species-specific, must both add to and subtract from anything that they represent. Indeed, since everything we seem to perceive is in fact only a representation, these principles must apply universally. For there is not, and cannot in the nature of things ever be, a representation without a medium to represent in, any more than there can be a medium that lacks properties of its own.

Perhaps the only way in which pictorial representation might mislead us about the nature of representations in general is by suggesting that if any representation exists there must also exist someone to perceive it. Thus if we talk of nervous systems 'representing' reality in the brain, it seems natural to think of someone or something—ourselves, a little person, or the soul—who sits inside our head and looks at the representation. Such beliefs have been the cause of endless pseudoproblems. For the moment, all we have to do is note that a representation does not have to be perceived by any kind of discrete or conscious agent. If the particular set of neurons in a rabbit's brain that are triggered by the appearance of a fox should happen to fire, thereby representing a fox to a particular rabbit, that representation has only to be read by the motor neurons that control the rabbit's legs. If, under similar circumstances, we are somehow conscious of ourselves seeing the fox, that only appears to be a different story. . . .

How veridical are representations? How much difference does it make that we can only perceive through a series of representations, rather than somehow perceiving directly? One might argue, with some justice, that representation at a lower level—what our brain derives from immediate sensory input—cannot stray too far from the reality it represents. If it did, the result would surely be dysfunctional from an evolutionary point of view. We would be continually colliding with obstacles, falling from high places, consuming poisonous substances, and performing a variety of other behaviors calculated to shorten our lifespan or even extinguish ourselves as a species. Indeed, you might argue that evolution must actively select for more veridical representations by eliminating those creatures that have less veridical ones.

But this line of reasoning cannot be taken too far. There is no indication that colorblindness, astigmatism, or tone-deafness are being bred out of us, nor that the range of our hearing is gradually extending, over succeeding generations, so that it will eventually approximate that of the dog or the bat. The sense of smell has not improved but has steadily deteriorated throughout the development of primates. Moreover, creatures like frogs or cockroaches with sensoria far poorer than ours have survived for tens of millions of years without apparent problems. Evolution does not hone and fine-tune representation to some point of near perfection. Rather it provides creatures with representational systems that are just about good enough for their immediate evolutionary needs. So long as a species can get by on what it has, there will be no selective pressure to improve.

What was said in the previous paragraph applies with even greater force to representation at the second level—the mapping from concepts to language. It was noted in the previous section that what gave our species its evolutionary advantage was not a capacity to represent in language just those things that had evolutionary significance for us, but a capacity (potential, at least) to represent *anything at all* in language, whether it was significant or not. The advantage this gave us was so enormous that members of our species can produce a great deal of dysfunctional behavior and still survive. Thus we would expect that the series of representational mappings from sense data to concepts and from concepts to language might carry us some distance from the world of reality, even to the point of representing entities that do not exist in that world.

We could even predict that a representational medium with the particular properties that language has would inevitably contain entities of the type of *the golden mountain.* [One property] . . . is that, subject to the constraints of a Sommers-Keil predictability tree, any adjective can apply to any noun. This means that if there is an adjective, *golden,* it can apply without limit to any noun that represents the concept of a concrete object. If a mountain is such an object, *the golden mountain* becomes inescapable, regardless of the fact that there is no mountain made of gold anywhere in nature.

The remarkable thing is that the relationship between concepts and language is a two-way street. Normally we assume that a linguistic expression refers to a preexisting concept, but this is by no means necessarily the case. Linguistic expressions can equally well create concepts. Once we have heard of *the golden mountain,* we can imagine such a thing, and even what it might look like if it did exist. A friend once remarked, "To evaluate that speech you'd really need your oxometer." On being asked what an oxometer was, he replied, "It measures the percentage of bullshit." There is, alas, as yet no oxometer in the real world. But you can imagine what it would be like, and maybe wish that you had one, too.

REPRESENTATION AND CONTINUITY

Having reviewed some of the ways in which representational systems work, we can return to the issue with which this chapter began. We have seen that between language and animal communication there exist qualitative differences, differences so marked as to indicate that no plausible ancestry for language can be found in prior communication systems. Yet evolution still requires that language have an ancestry of some sort. Thus if there is to be continuity, it must lie in some domain other than that of communication.

Communication is, after all, not what language is, but (a part of) what it does. Countless problems have arisen from a failure to distinguish between language and the use of language. Before language can be used communicatively, it has to establish what there is to communicate about.

If we perceived the world directly, this might not be so. Language might then indeed involve no more than the slapping of labels on preexisting categories and the immediate use of those labels for communicative ends. But, as the last section showed, no creature perceives the world directly. The categories a creature can distinguish are determined not by the general nature of reality but by what that creature's nervous system is capable of representing. The capacities of that nervous system are, in part at least, determined by what the creature minimally needs in order to survive and reproduce. (They may also be influenced by what the creature's ancestors needed—but unneeded sensory powers tend to decay, witness the eyeless fish in subterranean caverns.) The categories distinguished by frogs, it would seem, do not extend very far beyond bugs they can snap at, ponds they can jump into, and other frogs they can mate with. The categories distinguished by vervets are more numerous, and those distinguished by our own species more numerous still, but the same principles apply.

Note that it is immaterial, for our purposes, how such categories are derived. They may be innate, they may be learned, or they may be acquired by the process of experience fine-tuning an innate propensity. There is good reason to believe, for instance, that some primates have an innate representation of snakes; when members of these species, raised in isolation, are first confronted by a stuffed snake, or by anything that looks like a snake, they show signs of alarm or avoidance (in contrast to the high curiosity they exhibit towards certain other kinds of objects). At the opposite extreme, our representations of automobiles and airplanes are obviously learned.

Vervet categories seem to occupy an intermediate position. They cannot be wholly learned, for there are certain mistakes that young vervets seldom if ever make. They may generalize the martial-eagle call to owls or vultures, but they very seldom, if ever, use the eagle-call for snakes, or the python-call for leopards. In other words, they seem innately capable of distinguishing things that creep, things that walk, and things that fly. Experience is needed only to narrow those categories—of creeping, walking and flying things—to just those species that prey upon vervets.

Perhaps a word should be said about innateness, since many people still find the term objectionable. It may seem less so when one considers that all representations, whether innate, learned, or of mixed origins, share a common infrastructure. The medium onto which representations are mapped consists of sets of interconnected neurons, such that when enough of these respond to external phenomena, a particular behavioral response is triggered (the monkey's avoidance, the vervet's alarm call). Almost all creatures possess sensory cells that substantially vary their firing rate when particular features of the environment are presented to them; and they do so without benefit of experience. Let us suppose that in monkeys one set of cells responds to wavy lines, another set to rounded objects, a third set to the quality of light reflected from very smooth objects, a fourth to motions, and so on. It follows that most, if not all, of those sets of cells will vary their firing rates simultaneously when presented with a snake or similar object.

So far, there is nothing in the least marvellous about this. No one supposes that neurons are acquired through experience, or that we learn, in the traditional sense of learning, the difference between straight and wavy lines or between shiny and dull surfaces. The capacity to make such distinctions is simply part of our genetic inheritance, and it appears, if not actually at birth, at least early on in the development cycle (provided of course that those distinctions are observable in the environment). Nor does anyone express surprise if, as a result of particular experiences, the firing of all the relevant sets of neurons should eventually trigger a particular response. Anyone would then be content to say that a learned response had developed.

Now it is true that learned responses cannot be transmitted to offspring. However, if, by sheer chance, one out of countless billions of monkeys should happen to be born with a mutation that directly linked the sets of snake-responding cells to the cells that activated avoidance behavior, then that monkey would enjoy a selective advantage over its fellows. That monkey alone could be guaranteed to react appropriately to its very first encounter with a snake, while a small proportion of its unmutated fellows in each generation might fail to survive that experience. Clearly, the genes that conveyed such an advantage would produce more offspring than those that did not. Thus, gradually, over time, the strain that lacked an automatic snake reaction would die out, leaving that reaction as a truly species-specific innate response.

On this analysis, it is hard to see what there could be to object to in the notion that there are innate concepts. Indeed, the issue would hardly need to be treated at such length were it not a fact that resistance to what are often rather oddly termed "innate ideas" tends to grow stronger as one approaches the central citadel of language. That aspect of the innateness issue will be addressed in due course. For the present, it may be noted that, on the conceptual level at least, internal representations constitute a mosaic of innate and learned forms. If language is indeed, primarily, an additional system of representation found in a particular mammalian species, there seems no principled reason why it too should not consist of a similar mosaic.

But is language really a system of representation? If it is, then we should be able to resolve the Continuity Paradox. We could search for the ancestry of language not in prior systems of animal communication, but in prior representational systems.

But before this can be done, two things are necessary. The first is to show that language may indeed be properly termed a representational system, and to describe the properties peculiar to it. The second is to survey the development of representational systems in evolutionary terms, in order to show that at least a good proportion of the infrastructure necessary for language antedated the emergence of the hominid line. If these things can be done, we can then turn to the development of hominids and determine, first, what other properties were required to create language as we know it, and second, whether it is plausible that just those properties could have been developed by the few speciations that separate us from speechless primates.

Before we begin this quest, one point in favor of the chosen course may be noted. No attempt to derive language from animal communication could hope to tell us anything significant about the origins of consciousness. If language were no more than communication, it would be a process; consciousness is a state. But if language is a representational system, it too is a state. Moreover, if consciousness too is a way of representing to ourselves ourselves and the world around us, then it may be that the origins of the two are closely linked, and that by uncovering the one we may also uncover the other.

FOR DISCUSSION AND REVIEW

1. How does Bickerton explain his "continuity paradox" with respect to the evolution of language? What is the paradox?

2. Discuss the terms *formalist* and *antiformalist*. What imbalances exist between these two different groups?

3. What is the formalist viewpoint on the evolution of language and its study? Why does Bickerton believe that one cannot ignore this viewpoint in studying his paradox?

4. Outline the differences Bickerton explores between animal communication and language. Include in your discussion the term *productivity* as well as the units of communication each group uses. To what do the terms *holistic* and *entities* refer in this comparative process?

5. Bickerton asserts that the things words refer to are not external entities but, rather, our perceptions of these. How has the study of vervets led to this conclusion? In what ways do we conform to this hypothesis in our language?

6. What is Bickerton's purpose for contrasting animal communication and human language, two obviously distinct and separate systems?

7. What is the importance of the "two-way street" that exists in the relationship between concepts and language?

8. What can be said about the ancestry of language? How does innateness play a part in this ancestry?

9. What solutions, if any, does Bickerton offer for this "continuity paradox"?

Projects for "Language and the Brain"

1. Some recent findings on neural asymmetry suggest that the kind of notation or code used in a given task influences how the task may be done. (Recall the comments in "Brain and Language" by Jeannine Heny on the two types of Japanese script, for example.) Using examples from your own experience, think of how using different codes might influence how you do a task. One example might be the use of Roman numerals versus Arabic numerals in multiplication: which can you process faster: "XIX times III" or "19 times 3"? Another example, if you know German, might be the use of familiar modern printing as opposed to the more elaborate script used in earlier German texts. Write a short essay in which you discuss how codes might affect your efficiency or the way you approach one specific task.

2. Lateral eye movement (LEM) is perhaps the most controversial and difficult to control of all behavioral tests for brain asymmetry. But it is also the most accessible to the lay person. Construct a list of six questions, each of which is either clearly emotional or clearly intellectual. Such questions might be expected to elicit left- or right-eye movements, respectively. An emotional (right-hemisphere) question might be, "What would you do if you saw a poisonous snake?" An intellectual (left-hemisphere) question might involve defining an abstract word or explaining how to compute taxes. Ask four people your questions, and watch their eyes as they answer. Do their LEMs seem to vary with question type? Or do you find (as some suspect) that each person looks relatively consistently in one direction? (Don't forget that a left-eye movement means right-hemisphere activity; you may find this confusing when facing a person in normal conversation.)

3. The nature and extent of therapy available to aphasics often make the difference between at least partial recovery and continued, severe language disability. Prepare a report on one of the different rehabilitation techniques now in use. You may wish to supplement library research by interviews with speech therapists and others who work with aphasic patients.

You may find particularly interesting a program called "Melodic Intonation Therapy," in which aphasics are first taught to sing phrases. Information about this technique can be found in the following two articles: (1) Albert, M. L., Sparks, R. W., and Helm, N. A. "Melodic intonation therapy for aphasia." *Archives of Neurology* 29 (1973), 130–31. (2) Sparks, R., Helm, N., and Albert, M. "Aphasia rehabilitation resulting from melodic intonation therapy." *Cortex* 10 (1974), 303–16. If you prepare your report on melodic intonation therapy, explain why it is helpful. If you know someone who has been helped by this technique, see whether he or she would be willing to discuss it with you.

A different therapy, designed for patients with another kind of aphasia, has been suggested by A. R. Luria. It is discussed in his book *Higher Cortical Functions* (New York: Basic Books, 1966).

4. In a recent journal article (*Neuropsychologia* 21, [1983], 669–678), a Japanese researcher, Takeshi Hatta, described an experiment in which he asked people to look at pairs of digits, comparing their relative physical sizes and their relative numerical values to see if they matched. If the subject saw a large 7 and a small 2, he was to say "yes." On the other hand, a large 4 and a small 8 required a negative answer. As expected, because the task involved analytical thinking (comparison and mathematics), the left hemisphere showed superior performance. But interestingly, even when he translated the task into some rare Ming-era *kanji* characters, the left dominance remained. This occurred despite the high visual complexity of the figures and the fact that people seldom use them (they did not even appear in an official *kanji* list published in 1850). His two types of pairs are illustrated here:

Arabic numeral pairs:

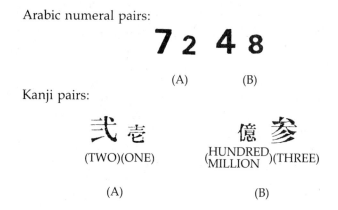

(A)   (B)

Kanji pairs:

(TWO)(ONE)   (HUNDRED MILLION)(THREE)

(A)   (B)

In an earlier study, Hatta had found that subjects read a watch (presumably a familiar "holistic" object) with the right hemisphere. Yet, when warned that the watch would be one hour slow or fast, the results reversed, and he found left-hemisphere superiority.

In both cases, the type of task seems more important than the visual stimulus: in the first case, the stimulus changes and hemispherical preference remains the same; in the second, the stimulus stays the same but hemispheric choice changes. What do the two tasks in the first experiment and the second time-telling task have in common that make them demand left-hemisphere processing space?

Design a hypothetical experiment similar in spirit and goal to one of those just cited. For example, think of a situation in which you see or hear the same material, but do two different things with it.

5. Elaine Chaika's article deals with a speech disorder associated with the brain: schizophrenic speech. Conduct research so that you may

present a report to the class on a different speech disorder associated with the brain. You might wish to begin your research with professional journals. Plenty of information can be found in journals such as *Journal of Speech and Hearing Research, Psychology Today, Perceptual and Motor Skills, Journal of American Academy of Child and Adolescent Psychiatry,* and *Journal of Speech and Hearing Disorders.* Include in your report issues such as the social and psychological effects these disorders cause their sufferers. Are there any treatments for the disorder you researched? What is the current research in your field? What areas of the brain are most commonly affected by these disorders or which areas of the brain are traumatized leading to the disorders?

6. The story of "Clever Hans," the extent of the belief in his near-human abilities, the variety of those abilities, and the long struggle to reveal the truth is a fascinating one. Prepare a report in which you review the events chronologically.

7. A number of films of the various chimpanzee experiments are available. Your media librarian should be able to help you compile a reasonably complete list. Watch at least one of these films in class. Can you detect any of the flaws in the experiments that are mentioned by Kemp and Smith? If so, describe them.

SELECTED BIBLIOGRAPHY

Note: The article by Jeannine Heny in Part Three contains an extensive bibliography, as do two of the books listed here: Segalowitz's Two Sides of the Brain *and Springer and Deutsch's* Left Brain, Right Brain. *The reader should consult these for a more exhaustive listing of sources.*

Bickerton, Derek. *Language & Species.* Chicago: The University of Chicago Press, 1990. [An interesting exploration of how language systems came to be, how they function, and what they accomplish.]

Blakeslee, Thomas R. *The Right Brain: A New Understanding of the Unconscious Mind and Its Creative Powers.* Garden City, NY: Anchor Press/Doubleday, 1980. [The title is accurate. Thorough exploration of the functions of the right hemisphere; excellent bibliography.]

Buck, Craig. "Knowing the Left from the Right." *Human Behavior,* 5 (June), 329–335, 1976. [Interesting collection of specific examples about what each side of the brain can do.]

Campbell, Jeremy. *Grammatical Man: Information, Entropy, Language, and Life.* New York: Simon and Schuster, 1982. [An extraordinary and fascinating book; see especially Parts Three and Four.]

Damasio, Antonio R. "Brain and Language" in *Scientific American,* Sept 1992, pp. 88–96. [An intriguing neurophysiological look at the brain and how it is used in language. Helpful diagrams are included.]

Farb, Peter. *Humankind.* Boston: Houghton Mifflin, 1978. [Readable and informative; see Chapter 15 for a broad discussion of a variety of aspects of the brain and its functioning.]

Fromkin, Victoria. "Slips of the Tongue." *Scientific American,* 229, 110–117, 1973. [Interesting in themselves, slips of the tongue offer clues to language processing in the brain.]

Gardner, Howard. *The Shattered Mind: The Person After Brain Damage.* New York: Alfred Knopf, 1975. [Chapters 2, on aphasia, and 9, on the brain's two hemispheres, are especially interesting.]

———. *Art, Mind, and Brain: A Cognitive Approach to Creativity.* New York: Basic Books, 1982. [A consistently interesting collection of thirty-one essays, almost all of which were originally published elsewhere.]

———. *Frames of Mind: The Theory of Multiple Intelligences.* New York: Basic Books, 1983. [An interesting synthesizing work; see especially II, 5, "Linguistic Intelligence," and II, 8, "Spatial Intelligence."]

Gardner, R. Allen, B. T. Gardner, and T. E. Vancantfort. *Teaching Sign Language to Chimpanzees.* Albany, NY: State University of New York Press, 1989. [An illustrative study of the processes of teaching sign language to chimps and the trends that parallel those in language development of human children.]

Gazzaniga, Michael S. "The Split Brain in Man." *Scientific American,* 217, 24–29, 1967. [A readable early report on the effects of split-brain surgery (commissurotomy).]

Geschwind, Norman. "Language and the Brain." *Scientific American,* 226, 76–83, 1972. [Discusses how aphasias and other kinds of brain damage help us understand how language is organized in the brain.]

———. "Specializations of the Human Brain." *Scientific American*, 241, 180–182, 186–187, 189–192, 196, 198–199, 1979. [Discussion of hemisphere specialization and of the specialization of particular areas of the brain.]

Jones, Gerald. "Clues to Behavior from a Divided Brain." In 1978 *Nature/Science Annual*, ed. Jane D. Alexander. Alexandria, VA: Time/Life Books, 1977. [A nontechnical summary.]

Macneilage, Peter F., M. G. Studdert-Kennedy, and B. Lindblom. "Hand Signals—Right Side, Left Brain and the Origin of Language" in *The Sciences*, January/February 1993, pp. 32–37. [A fascinating article that explores the relationships between left-hemisphere brain dominance and language origins.]

Ornstein, Robert E., ed. *The Nature of Human Consciousness: A Book of Readings*. San Francisco: W. H. Freeman and Company, 1973. [An interesting collection of forty-one articles; see especially Part II.]

Penfield, Wilder. *The Mystery of the Mind*. Princeton, NJ: Princeton University Press, 1975. [A personal account of the work of this renowned neurosurgeon.]

Perkins, William H. *Speech Pathology: An Applied Behavioral Science*, 2nd ed. St. Louis: C. V. Mosby, 1977. [Somewhat technical but very informative analysis of aphasia on pp. 131–133, 241–247, and 384–387.]

Pines, Maya. *The Brain Changers: Scientists and the New Mind Control*. New York: Harcourt Brace Jovanovich, 1973. [Fascinating chapters on many aspects of the brain; see especially Chapter 7, "What Half of Your Brain is Dominant—and Can You Change It?"]

Potter, Robert. "Language" (videorecording 30 min). New York: Insight Media, 1989. [An examination of the uniqueness of human language, its development, language and the brain, and a look at the topic cross-culturally.]

Premack, David. *Gavagai! or the Future History of the Animal Language Controversy*. Cambridge: MIT, 1986. [As controversial as its title, Premack offers insights as to whether human language is species- and/or task-specific.]

Restak, Richard M., M.D. *The Brain: The Last Frontier*. Garden City, NY: Doubleday & Company, 1979. [Readable, intriguing, and authoritative; hemispheric specialization, language acquisition, and much more. Good bibliography.]

Rieber, R. W., ed. *The Neuropsychology of Language: Essays in Honor of Eric Lenneberg*. New York: Plenum Press, 1976. [Although technical, the nine chapters are packed with information.]

Sagan, Carl. *The Dragons of Eden: Speculations on the Evolution of Human Intelligence*. New York: Random House, 1977. [Controversial but fascinating; worth reading.]

Sage, Wayne. "The Split Brain Lab." *Human Behavior*, 5 (June), 24–28, 1976. [An interesting and very readable summary of split-brain research.]

Samples, Robert E. "Learning With the Whole Brain." *Human Behavior*, 4 (February), 17–23, 1975. [Possible implications for education of our emphasis on the left half of the human brain.]

Scientific American, *The Brain*. San Francisco: W. H. Freeman, and Company, 1979. [The eleven articles originally appeared in the September 1979 issue of *Scientific American* and deal with a variety of topics related to the brain.]

Scientific American, *Mind and Behavior*. San Francisco: W. H. Freeman and Company, 1980. [Twenty-eight articles, mostly by psychologists, covering a diversity of interesting topics.]

Segalowitz, Sid J. *Two Sides of the Brain: Brain Lateralization Explored*. Englewood Cliffs, NJ: Prentice-Hall, 1983. [A very readable text by a distinguished researcher that discusses "the uses of the left-right distinction between the brain hemispheres" and gives "some perspectives on the limitations of [this] construct." Excellent bibliography.]

Smith, Adam. *Powers of Mind.* New York: Random House, 1975. [Popular and interesting account of the workings of the brain, TM, EST, Rolfing, and much more. See especially "II. Hemispheres," pp. 59–182.]

Springer, Sally P., and Deutsch, Georg. *Left Brain, Right Brain.* San Francisco: W. H. Freeman and Company, 1981. [An outstanding book that discusses most of the important research into the nature of hemispheric asymmetries. Excellent bibliography.]

Walker, Edward, ed. *Explorations in the Biology of Language.* Montgomery, VT: Bradford Books, 1978. [Six difficult but important essays focusing on language as a biological manifestation of universal cognitive structure. The second essay deals with aphasia.]

PART FOUR

PHONETICS, PHONOLOGY, AND MORPHOLOGY

The basic questions asked by any discipline vary over time. Such variation is taken for granted in a field such as chemistry, but it is less accepted in the study of language, or linguistics. And yet, in a mere seventy-five years, traditional grammar, largely unquestioned for centuries, has been fundamentally challenged, first by the proponents of structural grammar, and more recently by linguists advocating a generative approach to studying language. The basic goal of the latter group, who now dominate serious linguistic work in the United States, is to explain just what the speaker of a language, any language, knows. What does it mean, they ask, to know a language?

Most linguists agree that languages are best described in terms of their basic systems, or divisions:

1. *phonetics and phonology:* the sounds of a language, and the rules describing how they are combined
2. *morphology:* the ways in which the words of a language are built up from smaller units, and the nature of these units
3. *syntax:* the finite set of rules that enables native speakers to combine words in order to form phrases and sentences
4. *semantics:* the analysis of the meaning of individual words and of such larger units as phrases and sentences
5. *discourse:* the study of speech acts or of how language is used in various contexts

Each of these language components can be analyzed in terms of (1) the units that composed it and (2) the rules or patterns of each system that human beings follow when they speak.

Parts Four and Five deal with these basic systems of language. Part Four discusses the first two systems: phonetics and phonology, and morphology. There are good reasons to treat phonetics and phonology first. It is often helpful, for example, to use phonetic transcriptions or to refer to phonemes and phonological processes when discussing subjects such as syntax.

The first selection, "Phonetics," by Professor Edward Callary, deals with the important topic of phonetics, both articulatory and acoustic, and also with principles of phonetic transcription. Phonology is the subject of the next selection, "The Rules of Language," by Morris Halle. Professor Halle uses examples from a variety of languages to show that native speakers of a language possess a great deal of unconscious knowledge about the phonological rules of that language, knowledge that can be explained only by the existence of a genetic disposition to learn such rules. As he says, "our command of a language is genetically predetermined." Furthermore, the phonological rules of unrelated languages share a number of similarities, again pointing to our natural tendency to use rules and to the similarity of these genetically based rules.

Next, we turn to morphology. "The Minimal Units of Meaning: Morphemes," from the Ohio State University *Language Files,* focuses on the kinds of morphemes in English and the hierarchical way in which they combine to form words. The following selection, H. A. Gleason's "The Identification of Morphemes," uses data primarily from Hebrew to describe the analytical process for identifying morphemes. This discussion precedes "Morphology: Three Exercises," prepared by Professor Gleason, which involve the morphological analysis of samples of Swahili, Ilocano, and Dinka. In the final selection, Professor W. Nelson Francis examines the processes of word formation in English and explains which ones have been most important at different times. The concept of language as a rule-governed system recurs frequently in this anthology. It is stressed in Part Four, and it will be dealt with more extensively in Part Five. This repetition is warranted, for the concept is central to contemporary linguistics.

16

Phonetics

Edward Callary

Phonetics, which has been studied for many years, is one of the best known subfields of linguistics. Some knowledge of phonetics is an essential basis for further work in linguistics. In the following selection, written especially for this book, Professor Edward Callary of Northern Illinois University discusses some of the applications of current research in phonetics and clearly explains articulatory and acoustic phonetics. Then he explores two aspects of the "grammar of phonetics," aspects that are "known" by all native speakers of English: (1) some of the permissible sequences of sounds in English and how they can be described in terms of general rules, and (2) the regular changes in sounds made by speakers, changes that depend on the contexts in which the sounds occur. The exercises that appear throughout the article reinforce and clarify the author's points.

Phonetics — the science of speech sounds — is one of the best-known areas of language study, and perhaps the oldest as well. Descriptions of the sounds of speech date from at least the fifth century B.C., when Pānini, a Sanskrit grammarian, wrote an extensive series of rules describing the correct way to pronounce the Vedic hymns.

Apart from its intrinsic interest, phonetics is a field of language study with immediate and obvious practical value. A knowledge of phonetics is generally recognized as essential in foreign-language teaching and learning; in identifying and remediating communication disorders such as certain kinds of aphasia (the loss of language abilities) and stuttering; and in developing appropriate pedagogical and curricular materials for elementary- and secondary-school English language classes.

Recently, we have seen many technical applications of basic phonetic research. Work such as that done at Bell and Haskins Laboratories has been applied to the development and production of advanced communication systems, such as sending and receiving telephone messages, where phonetic knowledge has been crucial in determining the essential parts of the speech signal. Transmitting only relevant information and eliminating redundancies results in more efficient and less expensive communication. In the near future, we will undoubtedly see phonetic investigations contributing significantly to the general use of typewriters with microphones rather than keyboards and to security systems based upon voice analysis and recognition. Without fundamental knowledge of phonetics, these technological marvels would be impossible.

In this selection we will look at several aspects of phonetics. We will discuss first the physiology of sound production, that is, how speech sounds are produced by the human vocal mechanism; second, sounds as physical objects (acoustic phonetics); and third, we will look at how phonetics "fits" within the larger system of grammar. Finally we will consider a particularly sensitive and perennial question: What is "correct" pronunciation?

As a field of study, phonetics has several objectives. The first is to identify and describe the sounds of language. Ideally this would involve describing all the speech sounds found in all the world's languages; in practice, however, phoneticians usually confine their descriptions to the sounds of one or at most a few languages. Then using these descriptions, they aim to give a principled account (by "principled" we mean one that will reveal the abstract structure of the phonetic system that lies behind the observed sounds) of the way(s) these sounds are used in natural language; for instance, how sounds change when they are juxtaposed with other sounds, and how they are added to or deleted from strings of sounds.

Accordingly, we will begin our investigation of phonetics by identifying and describing the sounds of language. The examples will be drawn largely from English, since it is assumed that English is the language most familiar to readers of this book. Phonetic information from other languages will be brought in as needed to clarify some of the more important concepts.

Since speech sounds are used to convey information from one person to another, there are conceivably three perspectives from which we could view these sounds: first, as they are produced by a speaker, second, as they are transmitted through the air as sound waves, or third, as they are perceived and identified by a listener. These three perspectives are called *articulatory, acoustic,* and *perceptual* phonetics, respectively. They are complementary rather than competing points of view, and a full discussion of phonetics should make use of all three. Here, however, following the usual practice in introductory material, we will consider only the first two.

ARTICULATORY PHONETICS

The most obvious—and surely the oldest—approach to the study of speech sounds is through articulatory phonetics, so called because it deals with the ways in which the human vocal apparatus is manipulated as sounds are produced. The basic assumption of articulatory phonetics is that different sounds result from, and are best described in terms of, the different configurations of the vocal tract as different sounds are uttered.

Therefore, in order to understand the bases upon which articulatory phonetics rests, we must have at least a rudimentary knowledge of the anatomy and physiology of the human vocal tract. However, before we examine the vocal tract in detail, we need to introduce one of the most important concepts in phonetics: when we talk about the sounds of language, we mean just that—the *sounds* themselves and not the way they happen to be represented on a printed page. Phonetics is concerned with sound, not writing; to confuse the two, or to take the one for the other, is to confuse speech with its written representation. As literate people, we often make the (mistaken) assumption that writing is somehow the "real" language, and that speech is an attempt (and often a degenerate one at that) to express the sounds that letters inherently possess. The notion that letters have sound values, e.g., "the letter *c* has the sound of *s* or of *k*" is not only mistaken but terribly misleading as well. When we realize that, in the history of both the individual and the species, speech is considerably prior to writing, we can see that writing is an attempt to represent the transient sounds of language and not the other way around. Rather than saying the letter *c* has sometimes the sound of *s* and sometimes the sound of *k*, it is truer to the facts of language to say that, in the English spelling system, the sound [s] as well as the sound [k] is sometimes represented by the letter *c*.[1]

While the sound and the spelling systems of most (perhaps all) languages do not correspond exactly, the extent of misfit between sound and spelling in English is especially great. If you have studied a language such as Swahili or Spanish you know that the chances of your correctly pronouncing a word upon seeing it written for the first time are very good; conversely, upon hearing a word in Swahili or Spanish for the first time, you have a good chance of spelling it correctly. But this is not necessarily the case in English. Because of historical and cultural factors the relationship between sounds and their customary orthography (spelling) is often tenuous; yet, because we have grown up with an inadequate orthography and have become accustomed to such events as spelling bees (try to imagine a spelling bee in Spanish), learning long lists of "spelling demons," and hundreds of words with "silent letters," we tend too often to think in terms of letters rather than sounds.

Spelling inconsistencies are of three types: (1) there may be more (or fewer) sounds in a word than the spelling would suggest, (2) a single sound may be represented by a variety of spellings, and (3) a given spelling may represent several different sounds.

Most of the words with "silent letters" in English fall into the first category, and the majority of these can be explained by referring to the

---

[1] So as not to confuse sounds and letters, phoneticians have adopted the convention of using square brackets (sometimes slant lines) to enclose sound values. Thus, [s] refers to a sound and *s* refers to a letter of the regular alphabet.

history of the language. Most of the contemporary silent letters were not always silent; they were pronounced at one time (although this is little consolation to students struggling to master English spelling). The now quiet *gh* of *light*, *night*, and *fight* was once pronounced in English, as was the initial *k* of *knee* and *know*. In fact, five centuries ago (give or take a decade or two), English spelling matched English pronunciation quite well, but after spelling became formalized, the pronunciation of many words changed drastically, yet there was no accompanying change in spelling. Change in pronunciation continued (as it still does), and with the passing of the years spelling became ever more removed from pronunciation, and the "silent letters" kept piling up into the historical spelling baggage that we continue to carry with us today.[2]

EXERCISE 1

a. State the number of sounds in each of the following words (e.g., *lamb* has three sounds):

night	shack	watch	tax	check	knee
change	weigh	judge	itch	thought	which
thing	though	wrong	should	psalm	owe

b. The sound [e] (as in *ape* or *say*) is spelled in several different ways. List six words that illustrate six different ways of spelling this sound.

c. The letter *o* is ambiguous; it represents different sound values. List five words where *o* (spelled singly, not doubly) represents five different sounds.

In order to overcome the limitations imposed by the regular alphabet, phoneticians use a special *phonetic* alphabet, which maintains a one-to-one correspondence between sound and spelling.[3]

While phonetic alphabets differ from one another in terms of the

---

[2] There have been many attempts to reform English spelling, but, with few isolated exceptions, they have had no lasting effects. One of the more outspoken critics of English orthography was the dramatist George Bernard Shaw, who pointed out that English spelling is so confused one could spell *fish* as *ghoti* (take the *gh* of *laugh*, the *o* of *women* and the *t* of *nation*). Shaw provided in his will for an endowment to support research in spelling reform. Several revised spelling systems were proposed and one was given the monetary award. Although several literary works (including Shaw's own *Androcles and the Lion*) were published in the reformed script, the net effects on English spelling have been negligible. English speakers are apparently as reluctant to change their antiquated spelling as they are to adopt the metric system.

[3] There is no such thing as *the* phonetic alphabet; many phonetic alphabets have been devised over the years, each different from the others. To further complicate matters, several different phonetic alphabets, each using different sets of symbols, are currently in use. We will be using a modified version of the *International Phonetic Alphabet (IPA)*.

number and nature of the symbols they use, they share three characteristics: each symbol consistently represents one and only one language sound, each sound is consistently represented by one symbol, and the number of sounds is equal to the number of symbols.

Symbols used to represent the consonant sounds of English, along with some key words illustrating their sound values, are given [in the accompanying list].

PHONETIC SYMBOL	AS IN:	PHONETIC SYMBOL	AS IN:
p	pit, tip, stop	l	lit, till, slit
b	bat, tab	č	chew, hitch
m	mitt, ham, smoke	ǰ	gem, badge
f	fig, gift, muff	š	show, bush, chaperon
v	vat, save	ž	treasure, garage
θ	thin, bath	r	right, tire, shrimp
ð	thus, bathe	y	you, yew
t	tip, putt, stick	w	win, when
d	dip, pad	k	catch, back, skin
n	know, pan, snow	g	give, plague
s	sun, bus	ŋ	thing, tongue
z	zoom, fuzz	h	hot, who

Seventeen of the twenty-four consonant symbols are already familiar to you since they also occur in the regular alphabet. Seven of the symbols are unusual and deserve special consideration. Since the combination of letters *th* usually represents one or another of two different sounds (the first sound of *thick* and of *then*, for example), we need two unique symbols. We will represent the initial sound of *thick* with the Greek symbol *theta* [θ], and the initial sound of *thin* with the old English symbol called *eth* [ð].

Notice the special uses of the modified letters *č, ǰ, š,* and *ž*. The symbol [č] represents the initial and final sounds of *church* and [ǰ] represents the initial sound of *gem* or *Jim*. Without the diacritic wedge [s] and [z] represent the medial consonants of *Bessie* and *busy;* with the wedges, they represent the medial consonants of *masher* and *azure*.

The final sound of words such as *sing* and *thong* is usually spelled *ng*. But since this is a single sound, we want to represent it with a single symbol. We do this by using [ŋ]. (Think of it as an *n* with a tail.)

Because most of the consonant symbols are taken directly from the traditional alphabet and because their sound values vary so little across dialects and across speakers, they should not give you much trouble. The vowels, however, may pose some problems. They vary considerably from speaker to speaker and from one part of the country to another, so you should pay careful attention to the illustrations and become aware of any differences between your normal pronunciation and the key words given.

The phonetic vowel symbols and some words illustrating their sound values are given below.

PHONETIC SYMBOL	AS IN:	PHONETIC SYMBOL	AS IN:
i	see, each, machine	u	fruit, ooze, move
I	it, myth	U	book, full, could
e	able, weigh, great	o	flow, road, open
ε	said, says, guest	ɔ	raw, fought, taught
æ	at, plaid	a	tot, father
ə	about, son, cup, easily	ay	my, eye, buy
aw	out, cow, bough	oy	toy, boil, lawyer

When words are written in phonetic symbols, we say that they are transcribed phonetically. When doing phonetic transcription, one of the most important things to remember is to transcribe the words as you actually say them in normal conversational speech, not how you think they should be pronounced or how they are written in the regular alphabet. After you have determined your normal pronunciation, you must then select from the phonetic alphabet the symbols that represent that pronunciation.

Notice from the list of key words that I make a distinction between the words *tot* and *taught* (I would transcribe the first word [tat] and the second [tɔt]). Many people do not make this distinction; for them the two words are pronounced the same and should therefore be transcribed the same, i.e., [tat]. Do you make this distinction or not? On the other hand, while I do not merge [a] and [ɔ], I do merge *wail* and *whale, witch* and *which,* and other similar pairs. Many speakers do not. I would transcribe both *whine* and *wine* as [wayn], while speakers who distinguish them would probably transcribe the first as [hwayn] and the second as [wayn]. Neither pattern is right nor wrong; the important thing is to determine your own pronunciation and to transcribe the words accordingly.

Before using the phonetic alphabet, we must consider the question, "Which transcription should I record?" Many words have at least two standard pronunciations, an informal one that we use in general conversation, where we are more concerned with what we are saying than with how we are saying it, and a formal one that we use when there is a great deal of "static" (e.g., in a crowded room where many conversations are going on at the same time) or in a formal social setting (for instance, when giving a class report). Words such as *literature* or *education* have three or four regular pronunciations, strung out along the formal–informal continuum. Transcribe the words in the exercises below as you would pronounce them if you were speaking informally—with family or friends.

=====

EXERCISE 2

Transcription. Refer to the lists of phonetic symbols as necessary and
a. Transcribe the names of the letters of the alphabet—[e], [bi], [si], etc.
b. Refer to the phonetic symbols as necessary and transcribe the following words:

Group 1		*Group 2*	
ache	off	acne	fungus
choice	once	Aztec	Guam
coax	owe	bingo	gypsy
doubt	plague	biscuit	hygiene
ease	quick	bronco	jockey
eye	reach	buffet	many
guy	rhyme	busy	Maxwell
health	scheme	caffeine	menthol
inch	shook	champagne	honey
juice	squad	croquet	naive
junk	though	cyclone	onion
lounge	thrust	daisy	poncho
mouse	was	Duane	typhoid
numb	whose	equip	unique
of	wrench		value
	yacht		

Group 3: The schwa, ([ə]) as in Al*a*bam*a* and m*ou*stache, is one of the most frequent sounds used in English. Yet it is often difficult to recognize because it is spelled by all the vowel letters and there is often a competing form of the same word without a schwa that tends to deny its presence. For instance, in *symphony*, the second vowel is clearly a schwa, and the word should be transcribed [sImfəni]; yet there is a tendency to transcribe [sImfoni] both because of *o* in the spelling and the sound [o] in the related form *symphonious*. Each of the following words contains at least one occurrence of a schwa in informal American English. Relying on what you hear rather than what you see, transcribe each of the following words, paying particular attention to the schwa.

analytic	Gillette
Asia	giraffe
bonanza	Hiawatha
Canada	Messiah
colonial	Nevada
composition	statistics
crocodile	suppose
element	telegram
gallop	vanilla

Group 4: Transcribe each of the following words, paying particular attention to the pronunciation of the plural marker or past tense

marker of each word. Ideally you would put each in plural forms in the frame "the _____ are . . . ," e.g., the bags are . . . , the backs are . . . . In this way, the phonetic form of the plural will be brought out most clearly.

bags	paths
baked	raised
bluffed	raved
buzzed	ribs
caves	robbed
coughed	sacks
crashed	sighs
cuffs	spaced
gnats	tips
heads	toothed
hopes	traced
lacked	tripped
nagged	

Group 5: Further transcription practice:

accomplish	militia
Achilles	mosquito
Altoona	Odyssey
apostrophe	oxygen
Babylonia	physicist
camouflage	Sequoia
cathedral	silouette
dyslexia	sympathy
Honolulu	ukulele
Illinois	umbrella
kangaroo	unique
Macintosh	Venezuela
mayonnaise	zucchini

THE ARTICULATION OF SPEECH SOUNDS

Figure 16.1 shows an outline of the vocal tract indicating those areas that are especially important in speech production. Refer to this outline as often as necessary. You should be able to locate these anatomical features and explain their role in speech production.

Speech sounds are made by modifying a stream of air. In English, all speech sounds are made on the outgoing breath. (This is true for the great majority of speech sounds in all languages, although some—such as Sindhi, a language of India—make sounds on the incoming breath stream as well.) Air is pushed by the lungs through the trachea and into the oral or nasal cavity, or in some cases both. Different modifications

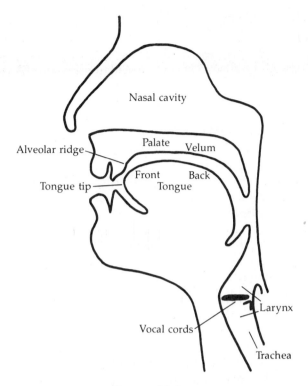

FIGURE 16.1.

of this flow of air cause different sounds to be articulated. While this seems trivial and self-evident, it is in fact a marvelously complex process; even the simplest act of articulation requires the coordination of hundreds of muscles, each working in harmony with the others in a display of coordination, timing, and precision rivaled only by the performance of the most accomplished ballet dancer. Our poor description of articulatory movements does not begin to do justice to the subtlety and grace of the acts themselves.

Since sounds are produced by modifying the breath stream, they can be described in terms of the kinds of modifications used to produce them. Characteristically, each speech sound is articulated at a particular place within the vocal tract and also with a particular kind of articulation. Each sound, then, can be described in terms of its characteristic point and characteristic manner of articulation. We will consider first the points of articulation, and then the various manners of articulation.

The first point at which the airstream from the lungs may be modified is at the larynx ([larInks], although often pronounced [larnIks]). Lying within the larynx are two sheets of elastic tissue called the vocal cords (also called the vocal bands or vocal folds). For speech, the vocal cords assume one of two basic positions: they are either relaxed and spread relatively far apart, or they are tensed and drawn close together so that there is only a narrow opening between them (this opening is called the *glottis*). The vocal cords are in the relaxed position when we make sounds such as [s] or [f], and in the tensed position when we produce the corresponding [z] and [v]. Also, when we articulate [s] or [f], the vocal cords remain relatively still, but for [z] or [v] they vibrate, and in so doing add a characteristic quality to the sound being uttered. This vocal cord vibration is called *voice*, and sounds produced with the vocal cords vibrating are called *voiced* sounds. The most noticeable difference between [s] and [z] or between [f] and [v] is vocal cord vibration for [z] and [v] but not for [s] or [f]. You can check for the presence of voice quite easily by placing your little fingers in your ears and articulating a sound. The buzzing you hear with some sounds but not others is vocal cord vibration. Try this first with [s] and then with [z]; then with [v] and [f].

The distinction between voiced and voiceless sounds is fundamental in phonetics since it is a feature found in all human languages. Most languages have pairs of sounds (such as [s] and [z]), which differ primarily in the fact that one member is voiced and the other is voiceless. English has eight such pairs:

Voiced: θ f s š p t k č

Voiceless: [ð] v z ž b d g ǰ

The voicing feature (voiced or voiceless) is one important way in which we may classify speech sounds. Another is by referring to the point of articulation. Consonant sounds are produced by obstructing the flow of air; the location of this obstruction can be used to describe and to classify these sounds. For English consonants, there are six major points of articulation:

1. *Bilabial* (literally, "two lips"). Bilabial sounds are [p], [b], and [m].
2. *Labio-dental.* Labio-dental sounds are made by bringing the lower lip into contact with the upper teeth. [f] and [v] are labio-dentals.
3. *Interdental.* As the name implies, interdental sounds are made by placing the tongue tip between the teeth. There are two interdental sounds in English; unfortunately, both are regularly spelled *th*. The *th* of *thin* and *teeth* is voiceless; its phonetic symbol is [θ]. The *th* of *then* and *the* is voiced and it is symbolized by [ð]. The interdentals have little acoustic energy and they are often hard to distinguish from one another, especially when they occur in the middle of words. Pay particular attention to the medial sounds of words such as *ether, father, bathing, neither, author* and *gather*.
4. *Alveolar.* The alveolar ridge is the bony protuberance located where the upper teeth join the palate. Six sounds are made in the alveolar area: [t] and [s], both voiceless, and [d], [z], [n], and [l], all voiced.
5. *Palatal.* The roof of the mouth is divided into two distinct parts: the hard anterior part, called the palate, and the softer posterior

part, called the velum. (By sliding the tip of your tongue back over the roof of your mouth, you can notice a sharp line which divides the palatal and velar areas.) Six sounds are articulated in the palatal region: the voiceless [č] and [š] and the voiced [ǰ], [ž], [r], and [y].

6. *Velar.* The velum is the soft, fleshy area lying directly to the rear of the palate. Velar sounds are articulated by bringing the back of the tongue into contact with the velum. There are three velars: [k], [g], and [ŋ].

We now have two ways to describe a speech sound: we may state its point of articulation or we may state the condition of the glottis (whether the sound is voiced or voiceless). In order to uniquely describe a speech sound, however, we must refer to a third dimension—the manner of articulation, a term that refers to the action of the vocal mechanism as a sound is produced. Several different actions are possible at most points of articulation. We have already seen that consonants are formed by obstructing the airstream; manner of articulation describes the way in which the airstream is obstructed. For English consonants there are six manners of articulation:

1. *Stops.* A stop is produced by completely blocking the breath stream. There are six stops in English, evenly distributed among three points of articulation: the bilabials [p] and [b], the alveolars [t] and [d], and the velars [k] and [g].

2. *Fricatives.* To produce fricatives, one of the articulators is brought close to one of the points of articulation, creating a narrow opening. When air is forced through this opening, a turbulence or friction is set up. Fricatives are therefore noisy sounds. As with stops, fricatives occur in voiced/voiceless pairs: interdental [θ] and [ð], labio-dental [f] and [v], alveolar [s] and [z], and palatal [š] and [ž].

3. *Nasals.* The velum serves several functions in speech. As we have seen, it provides the point of articulation for [k], [g], and [ŋ]. The velum can also be raised and brought into contact with the pharyngeal wall, thus closing off the nasal cavity, or lowered, thereby allowing the airstream to enter the nasal cavity. When the velum is lowered, air resonates in the nasal as well as the oral cavities, and the airstream exits the vocal tract through the nose rather than through the mouth. Sounds made with the velum lowered are called simply *nasals*. Since the action of the tongue and the velum are independent of one another, we can have nasals at various points of articulation within the oral cavity. [m] is a bilabial nasal, [n] is an alveolar nasal, and [ŋ] is a velar nasal. (We need not specify the state of the glottis when referring to nasals, since all nasals, at least in English, are voiced; they have no voiceless counterparts, as they do in some other languages. Burmese is the most

frequently cited example of a language having voiced and voiceless nasals.)

4. *Liquids.* The liquids are [l] and [r]. *Liquid* is not a satisfactory cover term for these two sounds, since it isn't descriptive like *stop* or *alveolar.* But it is traditional, so we will use it here. [l] and [r] are similar sounds in many respects, and they often have similar patterns in the world's languages. In fact, in some languages, such as Korean, [l] and [r] are phonetic variants of the "same sound." [l] and [r] are also among the sounds learned last by children. [l] is sometimes called a lateral liquid, since air flows around one or both sides of the tongue, and [r] is sometimes called a retroflex liquid, since the tongue tip is turned upward during its production. Although the specific points of articulation of [l] and [r] vary quite a bit depending upon the sounds which precede or follow, we will call [l] an alveolar liquid and [r] a palatal liquid.

5. *Affricates.* Affricates are complex sounds that result from pronouncing a stop and a fricative in rapid succession. Affricates appear initially in *chin* and *gin,* and finally in *itch* and *edge.* The affricate we represent with [č] consists of the stop [t] closely followed by the fricative [š]. The affricate symbolized by [ǰ] consists of the stop [d] plus the fricative [ž]. (If you say [t] and [š] rapidly, these sounds will lose their individual identities and will become the affricate [č].) The International Phonetic alphabet represents these two as a sequence of stop plus closely linked fricative; however, since these sounds function as single units in English, most American phoneticians use a single character to represent them.

6. *Glides.* Glides are sounds that provide transitions to or from other sounds. They are also called semi-vowels or semi-consonants, since at times they act like vowels and at other times they act more like consonants. While we can clearly recognize [y] and [w] initially in words such as *yet* and *wet,* it is less obvious that they occur finally in words such as *high* and *how.* Words like *my* and *cow* are even spelled with final *y* and *w*—further evidence of their vocalic quality.

Sounds such as [y] and [w] are difficult to classify using articulatory criteria. *Glide* (or *approximate*) seems the best choice, since in producing glides we normally bring one articulator near to a particular point of articulation, but not so near as to create friction; we approximate rather than attain a specific point of articulation. Since the approximation for [y] is in the palatal area, we call [y] a palatal glide. [w] presents more of a problem since it seems to have two simultaneous points of articulation: The tongue is bunched in the velar area, suggesting a velar glide, but at the same time, the lips are rounded, indicating that [w] has a labial quality as well. Some phoneticians call [w] a labio-velar glide. We will refer to it as velar.

TABLE 16.1. Consonants Arranged by Point and Manner
of Articulation and Voice.

| MANNER | POINT | LABIAL | | DENTAL | | | |
		Bilabial	Labiodental	Interdental	Alveolar	Palatal	Velar
Stop	Voiceless	p			t		k
	Voiced	b			d		g
Fricative	Voiceless		f	θ	s	š	
	Voiced		v	ð	z	ž	
Affricate	Voiceless					č	
	Voiced					ǰ	
Nasal		m			n		ŋ
Liquid					l	r	
Glide						y	w

To summarize briefly, we can describe any consonant by referring to its point of articulation, its manner of articulation, and the presence or absence of voice. A summary of English consonants arranged according to these features is given in Table 16.1.

The points of articulation shown on the chart are those we have been discussing, with several minor differences. The bilabials and labio-dentals (the "lip" sounds) can be brought together in the *labial* category. This allows greater flexibility of reference. If we want to refer to [p b m f v] as a group, we can use the more general term "labial"; while at the same time we can refer to such sub-groups as "bi-labial" ([p b m]) or "labio-dental" ([f] [v]). Likewise, the interdentals and alveolars can be described as separate groups or they can be identified together as the larger class of "dentals."

Note that [h] does not appear on the chart. Although some phoneticians call [h] a "glottal fricative" or "glottal glide," it seems to have no characteristic point of articulation; rather, [h] assumes the same point of articulation as the vowel or semi-vowel that follows it. We have not yet discussed the articulation of vowels, but notice that in a word such as *heat*, [h] is articulated with the tongue in the forward part of the mouth and with the lips spread, while in *hoot* [h] is produced with a retracted tongue and rounded lips. These tongue and lip positions are characteristic of the vowels [i] and [u], respectively. If you would like to add [h] to the consonant chart, make another column and label it "glottal." In the cell where this column intersects the "glide" row, put the phonetic symbol [h].

Notice, too, that the designation voiced/voiceless is relevant only for the stops, fricatives, and affricates (the class of "obstruents," to use the technical term). The "sonorants" (nasals, liquids, and glides) are all voiced; they have no voiceless counterparts.

Finally, you will also notice that the consonant chart contains many more unfilled cells than filled ones. At first glance, this may seem to indicate that our system of classification is at best uneconomical and at worst misleading. But such is not the case. Theoretically, a phonetic alphabet allows us to represent all the speech sounds of all the languages of the world. The large number of empty cells here results primarily from the fact that we have illustrated point and manner of articulation and voicing with English sounds only. If we had included sounds from other languages, many more of the cells would be filled.

Knowledge such as that summarized in this consonant chart is useful in many ways. One immediate application is in learning the correct pronunciation of a foreign language. For example, once you know what *fricative* or *voiceless* or *affricate* means, you can readily understand how these features are combined in a language to define a particular sound. Those of you who have studied Spanish may have had difficulty in correctly pronouncing the medial consonant of *lobo* or *Cuba* since this sound does not occur in English. However, if you know that it is a voiced bilabial fricative, you will be well on your way toward learning how to produce it. Similarly, modern Chinese (as well as many other languages) has a pair of sounds that do not occur in English. In the Chinese Pinyin (modern phonetic) writing system they are spelled *c* and *z*. They are respectively voiceless and voiced alveolar affricates. Many additional examples could be given, but they would only further illustrate the fact that all languages create sounds from the same phonetic material, but each language shuffles the phonetic cards a bit differently. This is what we would expect, of course, since the phonetic possibilities of languages are limited articulatorily by the nature of the human vocal tract and acoustically by the number and nature of sounds that can be easily identified.

Any consonant may be described by referring to its point of articulation, its manner of articulation, and whether it is voiced or voiceless. Conventionally, in describing one or a related group of speech sounds, the voicing feature (where relevant) is mentioned first, then the point of articulation feature, and finally the manner of articulation. Thus, we would describe [p] as a voiceless bilabial stop, [n] as an alveolar nasal (remember that all nasals are voiced, so it isn't necessary to mention voicing), [ž] as a voiced palatal fricative, and so on.

=

EXERCISE 3

a. Give the phonetic description of each of the following sounds. Refer to the consonant chart if necessary. Use the descriptions of [p], [n], and [ž] in the paragraph above as examples.

[m]   [ǰ]   [ŋ]   [f]   [k]   [θ]   [l]   [z]   [t]   [ð]   [y]

b. Features used to define individual sounds can also be used to describe sets of related sounds. For instance, the set consisting of [p t k b d g] would be described as those sounds sharing the feature [+ stop]. We can also use the features of manner of articulation, point of articulation and voice to subdivide larger sets of sounds. [p t k] would be described by the features [+ stop] and [− voice], [b d g] as [+ stop] and [+ voice], [p b] as [+ stop] and [+ bilabial], [t d k g] as [+ stop], [− bilabial], etc. Refer to the consonant chart and describe the following classes or subclasses of sounds:

[θ ð f v s z š ž]   [ð v z ž]   [v z ž]   [z ž]   [s z]

[p t]   [f v s z]   [m n]

VOWEL ARTICULATIONS

Vowels and consonants are produced in fundamentally different ways. While consonants are articulated by obstructing the oral cavity at some point, vowels are produced by modifying a relatively free-flowing airstream. Vowels are open rather than closed sounds, made primarily by shaping the vocal tract rather than interfering with the airstream. Since the tongue is the main instrument used to change the shape of the oral cavity, vowels are usually described in terms of the position of the tongue during their articulation.

Since they are made by shaping rather than obstructing the vocal tract, vowels have no discrete physical points of articulation, nothing as definite as *bilabial* or *alveolar;* rather they exist on several continua and individual vowels are best described as articulated with a greater or lesser degree of tongue position along a given dimension. Basically the tongue body can move along two dimensions: high-low (toward or away from the palate) and front-back. A vowel articulated with the body of the tongue relatively forward is classified as a front vowel, while one made with the tongue body relatively high is a high vowel, and so forth. Vowels produced with the body of the tongue neither high nor low are called mid vowels, and those made with the tongue body neither front nor back are central vowels. Table 16.2 uses the high-low and front-back dimensions to schematize the relative positions of articulation of English vowels.

We can describe any vowel in terms of its relative tongue height and tongue backness — distance from the palate. For instance, we can read from the chart that [i] is high front, [a] is low back and [ə] (schwa) is mid central.

The vowels shown in Table 16.2 are all *simple vowels;* that is, they retain their basic quality throughout their duration. Simple vowels contrast with diphthongs, which are complex sounds having different beginning and ending points. (The word *diphthong* comes from the Greek *di* meaning "twice" or "double" and *phthongos* meaning "sound" or "voice." So diphthongs are literally "two sounds.") Diphthongs are combinations of sounds, which is why we represent them with a sequence

TABLE 16.2. Vowels Arranged According to Tongue Height and Backness.

		Front	Central	Back
High	High	i		u
	Low-high	I		U
	Mid	e		o
	Low-mid	ɛ	ə	ɔ
Low	Low	æ		a

(vertical arrow labeled High at top and Low at bottom on the far left; horizontal arrow above table: Front ← → Back)

of symbols in our phonetic alphabet. The first symbol represents the approximate phonetic quality of the beginning sound, and the second represents the approximate ending quality. There are three regular diphthongs
in English: one occurs in words such as *my* and *sigh*, another in *now* and
out, and a third in *hoist* and *void*. The phonetic symbols for the diphthong
of *my* are [ay], indicating a sound close to [a] for the beginning element
and one close to [y] for an ending element. If you were to first pronounce
[a] and then glide to [y] you would approximate the vowel of *my*. Similarly
if you start with [a] and glide toward [w] you would approximate the
diphthong of *now* and *out*. The way [y] and [w] function in diphthongs
is one of the main reasons for calling them "glides."

The three English diphthongs are all "rising" diphthongs — they glide
from a low onset (nucleus) toward a high position — high and front for
[ay] and [oy] and high and back for [aw].[4]

ACOUSTIC PHONETICS

In recent years the science of articulatory phonetics has been comple-
mented handsomely by investigations into the physical properties of
speech sounds. These studies of *acoustic* phonetics have led to a variety
of technological advances, including improved radio and telephone communications and synthesized speech. (Synthesized speech, generated by
computer, is the disembodied voice you hear when your car tells you that
your seat belt isn't fastened, when computerized learning aids ask you
"How much is six times nine?", or when the copy machine warns, in its
monotone machine dialect, "Don't forget your original.") Research in
acoustic phonetics has increased our knowledge of speech properties so

---

[4] Some phoneticians symbolize the high front glide in diphthongs with [i] or [I]
rather than [y], and the high back glide with [u] or [U] rather than [w]. But the sound
is the same, whether *my* is transcribed [may] or [mai]. Both [y] and [i] are articulated
in the same palatal area, and [w] and [u] in the same velar area.

dramatically that today computer-generated speech is virtually indistinguishable from natural speech.

Acoustic phonetics relies on sophisticated equipment that analyzes a speech signal into its three primary components: frequency (expressed in hertz or cycles per second), intensity, and duration. The most commonly used instrument for this task is the sound spectrograph, which produces a sound spectrogram. Two spectrograms are shown below. The first displays the words *kit, coot,* and *kite,* spoken in isolation. Frequency is indicated along the vertical axis, duration along the horizontal axis (a single spectrogram can display approximately two and a half seconds of sound), and intensity by the relative darkness of the markings. These markings are the most important elements of acoustic analysis; they represent bands of energy and are called *formants.* Listeners are especially sensitive to the formant structure of speech sounds; they rely primarily upon the information contained in formant one (the formant lying closest to zero frequency) and formant two (the next highest) in identifying sounds.

Acoustically, vowels are the most clearly defined class of speech sounds; their formant structure is the cleanest and easiest to identify, as we can see from the spectrograms. The consonants are much more difficult to determine. In fact, perceptual studies have indicated that, not only do we identify individual vowels by the shape and relationship of the

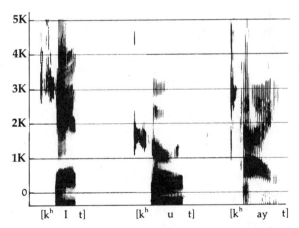

FIGURE 16.2. Spectrogram. The words *kit, coot,* and *kite,* spoken in isolation by an adult male. Note the differences among the vowels [I] and [u] and the diphthong [ay], keeping in mind that acoustically, vowels are the most clearly delineated class of sounds. In fact, the stops [p t k b d g] have no sound and do not usually show up in a spectrogram; we "hear" them because they affect the pronunciation of adjoining vowels. Since the dark areas of the spectrogram indicate the frequencies at which acoustic energy occurs, we can see that the front vowel [I] has two formants quite far apart, while the back vowel [u] has two formants that are much closer together.

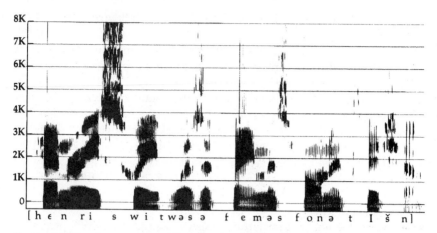

[h ɛ n   ri   s   wi   twəsə   f   eməs   fonə   t   ɪ š   n]

FIGURE 16.3.   Spectrogram. The sentence, "Henry Sweet was a famous phonetician," spoken by an adult male. What are the acoustic characteristics of the fricatives? How do these differ from the characteristics of the stops?

formants, we also use the vowel formants to determine the consonant(s) that precede or follow the vowels as well. This is to say that we apparently identify the initial consonant of *tea* not on the basis of the acoustic properties of [t] but rather on the shape of the formants of [i]. Speech perception and recognition are dynamic and vital areas of phonetic research and ones that hold great promise for increasing our understanding of the phonetic bases of human communication.

PHONOLOGY, THE GRAMMAR OF PHONETICS

Now that we have identified the phonetic inventory of English and have seen how sounds can be described by referring to their manner and place of articulation and voicing, we may begin to examine some of the ways these sounds are organized and altered in accordance with the rules of English grammar. We will consider two aspects of this "grammar of phonetics": first, permissible sequences of sounds, and second, the regular changes which certain sounds undergo when they occur in particular contexts. We will see that the grammar of English phonetics severely limits the numbers and kinds of sounds that can occur in sequence and that it also determines and specifies the different ways in which a given sound "changes" when it appears in different phonetic environments.

SEQUENCE CONSTRAINTS

All languages place restrictions on the numbers and kinds of sounds that can occur in sequence at various positions within a word. Chinese, for example, allows no consonant clusters at all, while Spanish does not allow sp-, st-, or sk- at the beginning of a word. If all possible combinations of one, two, or three consonants were allowed at the beginning of an English word, there would be more than 12,000 different possibilities. The number actually found, however, is fewer than 60; the other 11,900 or so are prohibited by the rules of English. In investigating these restrictions, we are interested first in determining which clusters are possible and which ones are ruled out, and second, we would like to go beyond a superficial listing of the combinations that can occur and state the principles that determine the permitted (and prohibited) clusters. In this way we can begin to understand how and why the English phonetic system works the way it does. To this end we will observe and then codify our observations of the workings of this one small part of English phonology.

Consider for the moment the words *brick*, *blick*, and *bnick*. As the linguist Noam Chomsky has pointed out, only the first occurs in English. However, and more importantly, the second might occur (it could be a new scientific term, or a detergent, or even the name of a new soap opera). But *bnick*? Never. There is a rule that blocks its becoming a fully integrated English word. We learned this rule and many other rules governing permissible sequences of sounds when we learned English.

We will begin by making a list of some possible consonant clusters. To simplify matters, for the present we will restrict ourselves to clusters of two consonants, to those that occur initially in English, and to those whose second member is [r]. In English only nine different clusters meeting these criteria are permitted. They are:

[pr] as in *prank*	[gr] as in *grain*
[br] as in *break*	[fr] as in *front*
[tr] as in *train*	[θr] as in *three*
[kr] as in *crane*	[šr] as in *shrimp*

(Remember, we are dealing with sound, not spelling.)

We could merely list the sounds that may occur before [r] at the beginning of an English word, i.e., [p t k θ š b d g f]. Such a list would indeed tell us which sounds may occur in this position, but it would tell us nothing about the underlying principles involved or the features shared by these sounds, nor would it explain why sounds such as [v], [l], or [m] are prohibited. Knowing these principles is part of knowing English, and it is this knowledge that we are attempting to describe.

When we examine these nine sounds further, we see that they are not a miscellaneous collection of phones, but rather they divide very neatly into two large groups: stops and fricatives. There are no nasals, liquids, glides or affricates. Thus we can see immediately why for instance a word such as [nro] is impossible in English: it violates the rule that says in effect that if there are two consonants at the beginning of a word, and the second of the two is [r], the first must be either a stop or a fricative.

There are other restrictions as well. While any stop can precede an [r] word, only certain fricatives can; we may have sequences of [fr], [θr], or [šr], but not [sr], [vr], [ðr], [zr], or [žr]. In order to describe this distribution, we need to write formal rules that will include [f], [θ], and [s], but exclude the other fricatives. To do this we must refer to the phonetic descriptions of the sounds involved. Note that all of the permitted fricatives are voiceless; thus [v], [ð], [z], and [ž] are ruled out because they are voiced. So far we have narrowed the class of fricatives to those which are voiceless, but we still have the problem of [s], a voiceless fricative which does not pattern with the other members of its sub-class.[5]

Since we have already referred to the manner of articulation (stops and fricatives) and voicing features (if fricative, then minus voice) we must refer to the point of articulation feature (since it's the only one of the three left) in order to exclude [s] from the permitted list. By looking at the consonant chart, we see that [s] and [s] alone among the prohibited fricatives is alveolar. The rules of English phonology will permit any voiceless fricative to precede an [r] word as long as it is not alveolar. A general statement summarizing these facts would be something like: "Any sound that is a stop may precede [r] at the beginning of any English word. So too may any fricative if it is also voiceless and not alveolar."[6]

EXERCISE 4

English sequence constraints.

a. Only six different consonants can precede [l] at the beginning of an English word. List them along with at least one example of each. Then, using the features of point of articulation, manner of articulation, and voice, group together the sounds that can precede [l] and describe the groups phonetically, much as we did for those sounds that can precede [r].

b. Following the same procedure as in Part a of this exercise, list and describe those sounds that can precede [w] (*twice, switch,* etc.).

---

[5] For some speakers, [s] rather than [š] occurs before [r], e.g. [srImp], [srIŋk], [srəb]; they have learned a rule that is slightly different from the one discussed here. For these speakers, the descriptive statements can be rewritten accordingly.

[6] We could state the rules more formally as follows:

[+ stop] or [+ fricative]
         [− voice]
         [− alveolar]

That is, any sound that has the feature [+ stop] or the combination of features [+ fricative], [− voice], and [− alveolar] may precede an [r] word. If you check the consonant chart, you will see that [p t k b d g] are described by the [+ stop] feature and that [f], [θ], and [s] are the only sounds sharing the features [+ fricative], [− voice], and [− alveolar].

c. An English word may begin with a maximum of three consonants. List as many examples of different three-consonant clusters as you can, then answer the following questions:

1. What must the first consonant be?
2. What two phonetic features must the second member of the cluster have?
3. What phonetic features must the third member have?

VARIATION IN SOUNDS

In addition to determining permissible sequences of sounds, the rules of a language also prescribe the different ways a sound is to be pronounced. Although we may feel that a sound is always pronounced in the same way, if we pay careful attention to English pronunciation, we will see that such is not the case. In fact, it is practically impossible to pronounce the same word twice in exactly the same way. Therefore, an incredible variety of speech sounds reaches our ears every day. And yet, we consistently recognize and interpret many of these physically different sounds as the "same" sound.

Why is there so much variety in the pronunciation of individual sounds? Basically, there are two reasons. One is that the size and shape of the vocal tract varies considerably from one speaker to the next. Because speech sounds are functions of anatomy, different anatomies produce different sounds. Because of differences in vocal tract size alone, any word will be pronounced differently by an adult male, an adult female; and a child. However, speakers of English ignore these differences when it comes to interpreting speech, and easily and unconsciously recognize *me* as *me*, and not as *see* or *tea* or *my*.

More important for our purposes than anatomical differences are differences that are part of the phonetic system of language and are therefore consistent from one speaker to the next. Variations of this type are generally determined by the phonetic environment in which a sound occurs. A given sound will have a number of different pronunciations, called *variants*; as speakers, we know which variant to use in a particular environment.

We will illustrate the concept of systematic or "rule-governed" variation with a sound that has a particularly large set of variants. Consider /t/ as it occurs in the words *top, stop, pit, mutton, eighth, startle*, and *city*. Functionally, all members of the set of [t] variants are the same in the sense that they distinguish one word from another (*top* is not *pop*, *pit* is not *pitch*, *stone* is not *scone*), but physically each [t] is different, both articulatorily and acoustically, from each of the others. To take the variants in turn: the [t] of *top* is produced with an accompanying puff of air (called aspiration), while the [t] of *stop* is unaspirated. (Aspiration is easy to detect. Place your fingertips against your lips and alternately pronounce *top* and *stop*. The burst of air you feel with the [t] of *top* is aspiration.)

The final sound of *pit* may be pronounced in several ways: it may be aspirated or unaspirated, or it may even be unreleased. [t] is unreleased when we make closure between the tongue tip and alveolar ridge, but stop articulation before the sound is released. Nonrelease of stops is an optional rule in English, unlike aspiration, which is obligatory whenever a stop appears at the beginning of a syllable.

We saw earlier that one function of the velum is to open or close the nasal cavity to airstream vibration. Usually, [m], [n], and [ŋ] are the only sounds released through the nose (with a lowered velum). However, when certain groups of sounds precede a nasal consonant, they too assume a nasal release. This is the case of the [t] in words like *mutton* and *rotten*. In articulating *mutton*, we close for [t] at the alveolar ridge, thus blocking egress of air from the oral cavity, but before breaking tongue contact we drop the velum and release both [t] and the following nasal through the nasal cavity. Other words having a nasally released [t] are *lighten, shorten, Latin,* and *kitten*.

The four variants of [t] that we have considered thus far are distinguished from one another by differences in their manners of articulation (presence or absence of aspiration, nasal release, nonrelease). The [t] of *eighth* differs from these in its point of articulation.[7] This [t] is made not at the alveolar ridge as are the [t]'s of *top, stop, pit,* and *mutton,* but with the tongue tip between the teeth. Since the teeth are involved, this sound has a dental articulation.

The second [t] of *startle* has two characteristic features. First, it is voiced rather than voiceless, making it more like a [d] than [t], and second, it is released through the position of the following [1]. In articulating this [t] we make contact between the tongue tip and the alveolar ridge, and drop one or both sides of the tongue. This articulation, known as "lateral release," occurs in normal speech whenever [t] precedes [1], for instance in the words *little, battle, turtle, bottle,* and *metal.*

The [t] of *city* is also voiced, but its manner of articulation is different from that of the [t] in *startle.* In *city* (and also in *party, water, notice,* and *butter*), the medial consonant is produced by bouncing the tip of the tongue off the alveolar ridge. Sounds articulated in this way are called "flaps" or "one-tap trills." In English, flaps are generally voiced; they most frequently occur between vowels for spelled *t* or *d* and create homophones (*homo* = same, *phone* = sound) such as *ladder-latter, atom-Adam,* and *utter-udder,* pairs of words that, in normal conversation for

---

[7] *Eighth* has two regular pronunciations in American English: [etθ] and [eθ]. The discussion is relevant to the [etθ] pronunciation only.

probably the majority of American speakers, are pronounced exactly alike.

We have seen that [t] has at least seven different variants in English: it is aspirated in *top*, unaspirated in *stop*, has a nasal release in *button*, a lateral release in *little*, may be unreleased in *pit*, has a dental articulation in *eighth*, and is a voiced flap in *city*. Such variation is not unique to [t]; all sounds have different variants and using the correct variants in the appropriate contexts allows a person to speak a language without an accent. In learning a second language as an adult, learning the basic sounds is far less a problem then learning the correct variants.[8]

Native speakers of a language know intuitively when to use each variant of a sound. This skill is part of our linguistic abilities, something we learned just as surely as we learned that a voiced labio-dental fricative is a sound of English but a voiced bilabial fricative is not. (A child learning a language, of course, has no use for terms like "fricative," "voice" or "stop." These are not part of language, but rather belong to the jargon linguists have developed to allow them to talk intelligently about the rules of language, which young language learners acquire effortlessly and elegantly.)

Even though we can accept intellectually the notion that any given sound has several distinct pronunciations, deep in our linguistic hearts we still believe that each of these different sounds is, in an important sense, the "same" sound. We can easily demonstrate that the medial sound of *atom* is voiced, making it more like a [d] than a [t], yet there is a part of our phonetic competence that says "It's still [t]," thus raising an apparent contradiction—that different sounds are the same sound.

The contradiction is more apparent than real, however, but to resolve it we must go beyond the physical description of speech sounds and into the minds of language users, specifically into the intentions of speakers and into the interpretations of sounds by listeners. We will see that the sounds intended by speakers do not always correspond directly to what they actually utter and, conversely, that the sounds listeners actually hear are not always those which they think they hear.

A basic tenet of modern linguistics is the notion that language exists on at least two levels. In phonetics, one level is the obvious level of physical phonetic facts, where we can describe, either articulatorily or acoustically, the properties of sounds as they are produced. This is what we have been doing to this point. The second level, which is more abstract and therefore less obvious, is the psychological or mental level, where

---

[8] Using the wrong variant of a sound results in a stilted, overcorrect, and artificial style of speech, or in a foreign accent. Surprisingly, "correct enunciation" has the same effects. Pronounce the following words using an aspirated [t]: *butter, brittle, party, stir, later, parting.* Although the words are recognizable, the pronunciation itself is forced and unidiomatic.

speech sounds are intended or interpreted. (These levels are analogous to the more familiar "surface structure" and "deep structure" of syntax.)

We can identify and describe the sound units of either level. In some instances, the two levels correspond quite closely, while in others they differ considerably. Thus we might have a mental picture of a sound or a word that is quite different from its phonetic reality.

The following example will show how the two levels are related. Suppose that an English speaker wanted to utter the phrase *top button* (not something you hear everyday, to be sure, but illustrative none the less). Speakers would feel (at the mental level, where language events are planned) that they would be producing [t] in each word—not any particular kind of [t], just [t]. At the mental level, one [t] appears to be the same as any other. However, between the planning of speech and its articulation, the rules of phonology intervene; each of these [t]'s must be different. You will remember that the [t] of *top* must be aspirated and the [t] of *button*, if it is to be idiomatic English, must be unaspirated and furthermore must be released nasally. Knowing these rules, English speakers unconsciously aspirate the first [t] and nasally release the second [t], resulting in the physical level of the speech event. Listeners, in their turn, hear physically different [t]'s in *top* and *button* (physical level), but ignore these differences and identify each sound as the same and assign each sound to the same conceptual unit (mental level).

It is important to realize that the mental and physical levels of speech are connected by the rules of language. In phonetics these rules in effect change to a greater or lesser degree an intended sound into a physical fact (for a hearer they change physical facts into mental facts). When we intend or interpret sounds, we apparently ignore such phonetic niceties as lateral or nasal release of stops. However, the rules of English phonetics force us to observe them (unconsciously of course) whenever we articulate speech sounds.

We mentioned above that, even though sound units occur on both the mental and physical levels, there is not an exact correspondence between the units of the two levels. Among other things, a single mental unit may have more than one corresponding physical unit. As we have seen, the mental unit /t/ has at least seven physical units corresponding to it. The technical term for the mental or underlying unit is phoneme (thus the abstract level is the phonemic level); the physical units are allophones, so the physical level is called the allophonic or simply the phonetic level. In English, there is one /t/ phoneme, but at least seven /t/ allophones.[9]

These two sets of units play different roles within the phonetic sys-

---

[9] The distinction between phoneme and allophone is an important one in phonetics and is reflected in our formalism. Phonemes are enclosed in slant lines and allophones are enclosed in square brackets.

tem of language. We apparently intend and interpret in phonemes but speak and hear in allophones. Furthermore, phonemes are contrastive units; they serve to distinguish different words. Substituting one phoneme for another will usually result in a different word, but substituting one allophone of a phoneme for another allophone of that same phoneme will not; although the pronunciation will be a bit strange, the word will still be recognizable. *City* spoken with an aspirated [t] will be recognized as *city* and not as *sissy* or *sicky* or something else.

There are more than functional differences between phonemes and allophones. Allophones are usually predictable while phonemes are not; that is, we can usually tell where a particular allophone will occur. A nasally released [t] is found only when /t/ occurs immediately before /n/; it does not occur elsewhere. Similarly, an unaspirated [t] occurs immediately following /s/ and this is the only allophone we use in this situation or environment. It is not correct English pronunciation to pronounce a word such as *spin* with an aspirated (or flap or unreleased) [t].

When members of a set of allophones occur in restricted environments (such as these variants of /t/), we say they are in complementary distribution. This means that certain allophones will occur only in certain environments and other allophones will occur only in other environments.

EXERCISE 5

a. The English phoneme /l/ has two major allophones—a front or "clear" allophone ([l]), and a back or "dark" allophone ([ł]), distributed as follows:

Clear /l/ in:	Dark /ł/ in:
lean	feel
lit	loot
lane	low
let	tell
latch	all
late	law

Front /l/ and back /ł/ are in complementary distribution; in these examples, front /l/ occurs in one environment and back /ł/ in two environments. Name them. Hint: You might want to transcribe each of the words above before determining their environments.

b. Sounds that are separate phonemes in some languages may be allophonic variants of the same phoneme in others. In Korean, /l/ and /r/ are allophones and are in complementary distribution. From the examples below, determine the environment(s) where each allophone is found. (Some of the data are from H. A. Gleason, *Workbook in Descriptive Linguistics*, page 57.)

1. mul	"water"	6. kiri	"road"
2. pal	"leg"	7. saram	"person"
3. ilkop	"seven"	8. kurəm	"then"
4. ipalsa	"barber"	9. irumi	"name"
5. səul	"Seoul"	10. rupi	"ruby"

It would seem that communication would be facilitated if sounds were pronounced consistently and uniformly. Yet we have seen that attempts to use the same variant in different phonetic environments result in unnatural speech. Since this is so, we must try to answer the related questions: Why is there so much variation within phonemes? Why do the allophones of a given phoneme assume their characteristic physical forms? Answers to these questions will go a long way toward explaining why the rules of language operate as they do.

As it turns out, phoneme variability is highly determined and we can explain much of the variability by referring to the phonetic descriptions of sounds. (I should mention at this point that, while there are many unexplained phonetic phenomena, we find the same kinds of rules operating in language after language, Eastern or Western, ancient or modern, which strongly suggests that phonetic rules have their basis in the human language faculty rather than in individual languages. Therefore, the discussions in the rest of this selection, allowing for differences in detail, illustrate general processes that may be found in all human languages.)

Let's return for a moment to the distribution of several allophones of the /t/ phoneme. Remember that the dental [t] occurs before dentals, the lateral release [t] occurs before [l], and the flap [t] (voiced) occurs medially, and is usually between vowels.

To explain why these allophones are distributed in this way, we must introduce a new term and a new concept: assimilation. In phonetics, assimilation refers to a change a sound undergoes in order to become more like another, often adjacent, sound. From the distribution of the allophones of /t/, there is a great deal of overlap between the phonetic description of the allophones and the description of their environments (the dental [t] before dentals, the nasally released [t] before nasals, etc.). These are cases in which the /t/ phoneme takes on features of articulation from its trailing sound in order to become more like (assimilate itself with) that sound. These are typical instances of assimilation in English; a sound usually (but not always) changes to become more like its trailing sound than the other way around.

Assimilation is a natural process found in all languages. The reason for assimilation is quite simple. As speakers we find that it's easier to pronounce some sequences of sounds and more difficult to pronounce others. In order to increase the ease of articulation, whenever possible we try to reduce our number of articulatory movements or "gestures." One way to do this is to extend one articulatory feature over a number of sounds. For example, instead of articulating the /t/ of *button* with an oral gesture (oral release) and the following /n/ with a nasal gesture, we anticipate the nasal release of /n/ and pronounce both the /t/ and the /n/ with nasal releases, thus extending the feature of nasal release over a group of sounds. This is an instance of assimilation in manner of articulation, since nasal release refers to how rather than to where a sound is produced.[10]

Now let's reconsider the medial /t/ of words such as *city*, *butter* and *water*. You will recall that this /t/ allophone was described as a voiced flap. Why should it be voiced, since we have characterized /t/ as a voiceless alveolar stop? The answer lies in the nature of the sounds that surround /t/ in these words. Note that in *wait*, *sit* and *light*, /t/ is voiceless when it occurs at the end of the word. But when it occurs between voiced sounds, as in the related forms *waiter*, *sitting*, and *lightest*, it becomes voiced. Again this change is motivated by the natural human tendency to decrease the articulatory effort. In each of these instances, instead of alternately producing voiced and voiceless sounds, we extend voicing over a sequence of sounds, thereby increasing the general ease of articulation. To pronounce *city* or *butter* or *waiting* with a voiceless medial consonant would require us to activate the vocal cords for the first vowel (all vowels are voiced in English), deactivate them for the /t/, and activate them once again for the following vowel. Very precise timing would be involved, and we find it easier to let the vocal cords vibrate through the articulation of /t/ as well as the vowels. Since /t/ takes on an articulatory gesture of another sound, this is again assimilation; but assimilation in voice since /t/, which is phonemically voiceless, becomes phonetically voiced when it occurs in voiced surroundings.[11]

---

[10] Assimilation is not confined to language; it is characteristic of many human endeavors. Consider another physical activity — typing. When typing, we try to keep our finger movements to a minimum; we anticipate upcoming keys and, wherever possible, "cheat" slightly in their direction. Those fingers not being used at the moment are free to approach their next striking position while, or even before, a preceding key is struck. This phenomenon is so frequent and regular that many typing errors can be explained, and even predicted, by its operation. Like the fingers, parts of the vocal tract that will be used in sounds yet to be uttered try, whenever possible, to assume phonating position before they are actually needed.

[11] The situation is a bit more complex than this discussion would suggest. Among other things, the other phonemically voiceless stops (/k/ and /p/) do not have voiced allophones intervocalically (we do not say [begɪŋ] for *baking*). Furthermore, stress (accent) and/or the syllable structure of a word may play a role in determining when the voiced allophone of /t/ will occur, e.g., *attack* is never [ədæk]. Finally, the rule of flap formation is sensitive to the formality of the speech situation. In less formal contexts, we are more likely to use the voiced flap, while in formal situations or for word identification, we more often use the voiceless (and aspirated) allophone. In response to the question "Did you say *Adam*?", if you did not, the answer would probably be "No, I said [ætəm]" with an aspirated and voiceless intervocalic /t/.

VARIATION IN MORPHEMES

To summarize briefly, we have seen that abstract units called phonemes appear in actual speech as a series of allophones. We have also seen that the occurrence of many of the allophones of a given phoneme can be predicted because they result from assimilation, assimilation in voice (e.g., the voiced flap allophone of /t/), assimilation in manner of articulation (the nasally or laterally released /t/), or assimilation in point of articulation (the dental allophone of /t/). In each of these cases the various allophones represent rather minor deviations from the basic phoneme; for the most part, the allophones are phonetically similar to one another, and nowhere (at least in the English examples we have considered) do we find a case where, for example, aspiration and nonaspiration constitute the only difference between words. However, there are instances where we want to include as allophones of a single phoneme sounds that in other circumstances function as phonemes in their own right. For example, consider the final sounds of the words *five* and *twelve* and the related words *fifth* and *twelfth*. Since we recognize intuitively that *five* and *fif* on the one hand and *twelve* and *twelf* on the other are phonetically different forms of the same word (or word element), we would like to capture this part of English speakers' knowledge by saying that *five* and *fif* (as well as *twelve* and *twelf*) are phonemically the same but phonetically different because a phonetic rule applies to *fif* and *twelf* but not to *five* and *twelve*. (We will not be concerned with the vowel differences in these words.) We will assume that both *five* and *fif* are phonemically /fayv/. Notice then what happens when a suffix beginning with a voiceless sound is added: the /v/ of *five* becomes the /f/ of *fifty* and *fifth*. While /v/ and /f/ contrast in many environments (e.g., initially *vine* is not *fine*), in other environments they are noncontrastive or allophones of a single phoneme (in this case allophones of /v/). From such examples we can infer that English has a phonetic rule that changes a voiced sound to the corresponding voiceless sound whenever it comes before an affix that begins with a voiceless sound. This is another example of assimilation in voice; the phonemically voiced labio-dental fricative /v/ becomes voiceless to assimilate itself with the voiceless quality of the first sound of the affix. (Note that assimilation in voice can go either way: phonemically voiceless sounds can become voiced or phonemically voiced sounds can become voiceless. In each case, assimilation is the motivation for the phonetic rules.)

This particular rule, which results in the de-voicing of a phonemically voiced sound applies to a large number of words in English and to a variety of different phonemes. Not only does the /v/ of *five* and *twelve* become the /f/ of *fifty* and *twelfth*, but the /d/ of *broad* and *wide* becomes the /t/ of *breadth* and *width*, and the final /b/ of *describe* and *absorb* becomes the /p/ of *description* and *absorption*.

EXERCISE 6

Listed below are several variants of one of the English prefixes meaning "not." Examine their distribution and explain the instances of assimilation.

Variant   *Found in:*

[Im]
immature
imperfect
imbalance
immaterial
implausible
imperfect

[In]
inoperative
indecent
intolerant
innocent
inedible
indelicate
interminable
inaudible

[Iŋ][12]
incomplete
ingrate
incorrigible
inglorious

[Ir]
irregular
irresponsible

[Il]
illegal
illegible

DISSIMILATION (SIMPLIFICATION)

As we have seen, assimilation is a natural process, at work in all languages, that tends to make neighboring sounds more alike. Many pho-

---

[12] The variant [Iŋ] occurs more frequently with some speakers than with others, and it is found more often in casual speech than in formal speech. However, most speakers use this variant at one time or another, and it is common enough to be considered part of the pronunciation patterns of American English.

netic rules are assimilatory rules; they operate in such a way as to mini-mize the articulatory differences between sounds, thus contributing to ease of articulation. Assimilation is probably the most widespread of all phonetic processes; it is found in languages throughout the world.

Given what we know about the phonetic bases of assimilation, it would seem that sequences of sounds that are most alike would be the easiest to pronounce. This appears to be true, however, only up to a point; sounds can be so much alike that they are difficult if not impossible to pronounce in sequence. Tongue-twisters are obvious examples. (Try say-ing "The sixth sick sheik's sixth sheep's sick," one of the worst tongue-twisters ever devised, according to the *Guinness Book of World Records.*) When faced with a sequence of very similar sounds, speakers frequently and systematically alter one or more of the sounds, making the sequence different from what it was originally. Examples abound in English, and not only in tongue-twisters. Compounds are especially prone to simplifi-cations of this sort, since the process of compounding words frequently juxtaposes sounds with similar articulations. When we compound *cup* and *board*, we get [kəbərd] and not [kəpbord]. This is because [p] and [b] are phonetically quite similar: both are bilabial stops, and this sequence has proved difficult for English speakers, who facilitate their articulation by deleting [p].

As a general rule, and depending upon the specific sounds involved, English speakers easily tolerate a cluster of two consonants in word-final position, even if they share a number of phonetic characteristics. How-ever, when affixation or compounding adds a third consonant, speakers tend to break up the three-consonant cluster, most often by deleting the middle consonant. We have no trouble with the final clusters of *friend*, *kind*, or *second*, even though [n] and [d] share point of articulation and voicing features. However, when another element is added, as in *friend-ship*, *kindness*, and *second time*, we have a problem. Our usual response is to delete the [d], giving us the conversational pronunciations [frenšɪp], [kaynnəs] and [sekəntaym].[13]

---

[13] Some phoneticians call the process we have just described "complete assimila-tion," arguing that the *d* has accommodated itself to the following sound so completely that, in effect, it has become that sound. Others call it "simplification." I prefer to think of it as a process that makes a sequence of sounds different from its original form. In the examples given above, original -nds- has become -ns-, -ndn- has become -nn-, and -ndt- has become -nt-. If assimilation is a process that serves to make a sequence of sounds more similar, then the reduction of consonant clusters such as those we have just examined should perhaps be called dissimilation, since it serves to make a string of similar items less similar. But the terminology is not important; what is important is an understanding of the forces at work shaping the sound systems of language.

EXERCISE 7

a. We mentioned earlier than many words have both a formal and an informal pronunciation. Transcribe the following words twice: first as you would pronounce them in a formal situation, and then as you would pronounce them casually, among friends. Comment on assimilations, dissimilations, and/or other changes that you find between your transcriptions of formal and informal pronunciation.

obvious	every	poem	strength
pumpkin	input	hundred	vegetable
today	county	suggest	banquet
library	candidate	almond	adjective

b. Explain, in terms of assimilation and/or dissimilation, the change(s) the items in column 1 undergo when they are combined with the words or affixes in column 2.

1	2
grand	pa
Christ	mass
clothe	s
truth	s
hand	ball
test	s
govern	ment
this	year
have	to
six	ths
horse	shoe
month	s
best	seller
has	you
won't	you

Together, assimilation and dissimilation (simplification) go a long way toward explaining why a certain word will appear in one phonetic form on one occasion and in other phonetic forms on other occasions. *Hand*, for instance, has at least three regular phonetic variants: [hænd] as in *hand, handout,* and *handle* (ignore the vowel differences in these words), [hæn] as in *handbag, handful,* and *handstand,* and [hæŋ] as in *handkerchief.* By considering the effects of assimilation and dissimilation we can see how (and to an extent why) *hand* assumes these different phonetic shapes. Of course, [hænd] itself needs no explanation, since in effect it does not change. [hæn] apparently results from dissimilation, since we have the final [nd] of *hand* immediately preceding a consonant in *handbag* and *handful*. The phonetic form of *handkerchief* requires a two-part explanation, because assimilation and dissimilation are both at work. Compounding *hand* and *kerchief* gives us three consonants in a row, and with interlocking phonetic characteristics. [n] and [d] are voiced alveolars, while [d] and [k] are stops. The [d] is dissimilated (deleted), resulting in the intermediate form [hænkərcIf]. The [n] is now free to assimilate to the point of articulation with the following [k], becoming the velar nasal [ŋ]. These two steps result in the usual phonetic form [hæŋkərcIf]. Note that the steps have to be ordered; dissimilation must precede assimilation. The change of [n] to [ŋ] cannot precede the deletion of [d], because before [d] is deleted, [n] is adjacent to an alveolar and not a velar.

Although they cannot account for all phonetic variation, assimilation and dissimilation, working separately or in concert, can explain many of the variant pronunciations of words. They are fundamental concepts in understanding how phonetic systems operate.

≡

EXERCISE 8

The English past tense marker, or morpheme, has three regular variants or allomorphs: /t/, /d/ and /əd/ (or [Id]). They are in complementary distribution, as shown below:

/t/ *as in:*	/d/ *as in:*	/əd/ *as in:*
coughed	saved	sifted
touched	judged	waded
passed	buzzed	heated
flapped	rubbed	bounded
marked	sagged	divided
mashed	sealed	coated
asked	dimmed	handed
dressed	pleased	directed
faked	played	sorted
moped	labored	provided

The distribution of these allomorphs can be largely explained by the processes of assimilation and dissimilation. Examine the words that take each variant and comment upon the effects of assimilation and dissimilation. You may want to transcribe the words before stating the rules involved.

"CORRECT" PRONUNCIATION

Faced with this abundance of variation, we might well ask: what is the "correct" pronunciation of a word? How, for example, should *hand* be pronounced? As [hænd], [hæn], or [hæŋ]? By now, it should be apparent that there are as many correct pronunciations of a word as there are phonetic rules that apply to the sounds of that word. There are no phonetic rules that would derive [hɪn] or [hæm] from /hænd/, but there are phonetic rules that derive [hænd], [hæn], and [hæŋ]. Many people find this kind of language variation disturbing; they believe that there is (or at least should be) one and only one way to pronounce a word, a way that is correct for all times and all places. For them, a particular pronunciation is either right or wrong, not right on some occasions and wrong on others. They would argue, for example, that the word *hand* has only the pronunciation [hænd], and should be rendered as such in all its forms, e.g., [haend], [hændbæg], and [hændkerčIf]. To pronounce it under any circumstances without the final [d] or with an [ŋ] rather than an [n] would only demonstrate the speaker's ignorance or stupidity (or perhaps both). Furthermore, they feel that it is the duty of those concerned with the purity of the language to codify and uphold the rules of correct pronunciation. However, as should be abundantly apparent by now, such attitudes are at odds with the facts of language. The language itself will ultimately define right and wrong pronunciation, just as it ultimately defines right and wrong syntax. The rules for correct pronunciation must be abstracted from within the language; they cannot be imposed from without.[14]

Many purists fail to appreciate contemporary variation in language. Much as we have different words and different patterns of syntax for different social occasions, we have different pronunciations when words occur in different phonetic environments. But this variation is not random; it is defined by the rules of the language. Consider a word such as *west*. Most American English speakers regularly use two forms of this word: [wɛst] and [wɛs]. The rules of English determine when each form is "correct." In learning English we learned that at the end of a word group or preceding a vowel, *west* is regularly pronounced [wɛst] (e.g., The Girl of the Golden West or West Australia), but when it precedes a consonant, the final /t/ is deleted, especially in less formal speech situations (West Texas or West Virginia). The pronunciation [wɛst tɛksəs] would be bizarre indeed, especially in Amarillo!

---

[14] Surely no one would seriously propose that we return to an earlier time when an initial [k] was pronounced in words such as *knee, knight,* and *know.* Yet we can easily imagine purists of centuries past warning against the "mispronunciation" of *knee* as [ni] and *knight* as [nayt]. The same warnings are now being raised about dropping the initial [h] in *human* and *humor,* a process that has been at work in English for centuries (cf. *honor* and *hour* vs. *head* and *hot*), and not pronouncing all the letters in words such as *sandwich* and *government.*

Assimilations in particular are frequently seized upon as indicators of sloppy or careless speech. However, learning to use assimilations (and dissimilations) is just as much a part of learning a language as learning individual words and sounds. To be effective users of a language, we must know the sounds that occur and the rules that define their actual pronunciations in different environments. Although it is true that the number of assimilations and dissimilations varies according to a number of social factors, including the context of the speech event, they are found among all speakers and in all situations. Far from being careless or sloppy, people who make appropriate use of assimilations and dissimilations are demonstrating their mastery of the phonetic component of their language.

CONCLUSION

In this chapter we have sketched only the barest outlines of phonetics and given only a sampling of the kinds of things that must be considered if we are to describe the sound patterns of language in a meaningful way. While phoneticians often disagree on the best way to describe phonetic phenomena, they generally agree that their descriptions must consider at least two levels of representation: (1) an abstract, phonemic level, which roughly corresponds to our mental impressions of speech sounds, and (2) a physical level, where speech sounds are produced and perceived. Linking these two levels are the phonetic rules of a language, which specify how the phonemic units are to be pronounced. Speakers' knowledge of the phonetic system of their language is marvelously complex, and quite mysterious, really. Like an iceberg, so much of it lies beneath the surface that its form and extent must be inferred from the few bits and pieces we can see. But in the end it is the hope of unraveling this mystery and understanding a significant part of human behavior that makes phonetics such a challenging and rewarding field of study.

FOR DISCUSSION AND REVIEW

1. Identify and explain the importance of the three characteristics shared by all phonetic alphabets.

2. Define the terms *point of articulation, manner of articulation,* and *voiced (sound).* Give two original examples of ways in which an understanding of these concepts could be helpful to you.

3. Examine the charts of English consonant and vowel phonemes. Explain why it is significant that not every slot (or cell) is filled.

4. Explain the relationship between phonemes and allophones and their differing roles within a language.

5. The terms *free variation* and *complementary distribution* are used to describe the occurrence of allophones. Define each term, and give two examples of each.
6. Both *assimilation* and *dissimilation* are important phonetic processes. Define each term, and give two original examples of each.

17

The Rules of Language

Morris Halle

When you talk, what do you say? When you listen to someone else talk, what do you hear? Words, of course — or so all speakers and listeners believe. But they are mistaken, according to Professor Morris Halle of the Massachusetts Institute of Technology. Native speakers do, however, share a great deal of largely unconscious knowledge about their language, and they acquire this knowledge without formal instruction. Drawing examples from a number of different languages, Halle illustrates some of the phonological rules and principles of various languages as well as some similarities among these rules and principles. Every language has its own set of rules, and all human beings have a natural tendency to look for and use rules when processing language. Our ability to learn these rules as very young children without instruction and our persistence in using them are attributable to our uniquely human genetic endowment.

The sounds that we hear when spoken to and that we emit when speaking are produced by complex gymnastics executed by our lips, tongue, velum, larynx, and lungs. The activities of these independent anatomical structures are coordinated with a precision that should be the envy of the most highly trained ballet dancer; yet this truly remarkable exercise is performed at the drop of a hat by even the clumsiest person. In contrast, even the most adroit primates have never been able to master it, despite intensive training. These facts suggest that the ability to speak is linked to our genetic endowment, that it is one of the aspects in which humans differ from all other mammals.

The gymnastic feats involved in speaking are clearly not the whole story. Speech is not just some noise that humans are capable of emitting; it is a noise that is produced to convey meaning. And how speech conveys meaning is surely one of the great puzzles that has intrigued thinkers for centuries.

Once the question of meaning is introduced, it is clear that we have to go beyond an analysis of vocal organ movements and of the acoustic signals these movements elicit. Such an analysis can tell us how the sounds of English differ from those of Finnish or Kwakiutl, but it cannot tell us why a sequence of sounds uttered by a speaker of English means something to us, whereas a sequence of sounds uttered by a speaker of Kwakiutl, or Finnish, usually means nothing. If we ask ourselves why most of us are able to understand a speaker of English but not a speaker of Finnish or Kwakiutl, the trivially obvious answer is that we know English but we don't know Finnish or Kwakiutl. But that answer leads naturally to a question with a much less obvious answer: What is the character of the specific knowledge that speakers of a particular language possess through which they are able to understand one another? Although not all linguists might choose to formulate it precisely in this fashion, this question has always been central to the science of linguistics.

WORDS: TO SAY AND TO HEAR

A striking fact about all speech is that all speakers—no matter in what language—are sure that they produce words, and all hearers are certain that they perceive utterances as sequences of words. When we pay attention to our own speech, we observe at once that we do not normally break up our utterances into words; rather, we run words together without intervening pauses. One can readily convince oneself of this fact by reading a text in a way so—as—to—pause—after— every—word and observing that the result is highly unnatural. The acoustical speech signal of an utterance thus differs from its representation in writing: the spaces between the written words are generally missing in speech. Does this mean that, because we do not pronounce utterances word by word, our perception that utterances are made up of words is a kind of illusion—that we perceive words even though they are not actually there?

I would argue that this is indeed the case, for what we hear is only partly determined by the physical signal that strikes our ears. For instance, we generally hear words in utterances of only our own language; we fail to hear words in equally clear utterances in an unfamiliar language. Moreover, many utterances, even when pronounced perfectly clearly, are ambiguous, in the sense that they can be perceived as either of two (or sometimes more) distinctly different sequences of words.

A recent incident illustrates this quite well. Somebody reported to me that he had met a person with the interesting name:

Me [lbə] tory,

in which ə represents the sound of *a* in *about*. "Oh, yes," said I, "this person has the same last name as a sixteenth-century Polish king, Stefan Batory, who fought against the Turks." As I began a minilecture on Turkey's role as a major military power for many centuries, I was interrupted with the information that the person in question was female and that her first name was *Melba* and her last name *Torrey*. Although this name also provided the basis for an erudite disquisition, the opportunity somehow had passed. Be that as it may, the point of the anecdote is that the utterance was ambiguous, and that its ambiguity was not located in the acoustical signal nor in the intention of the speaker. The hearer's misapprehension thus was due to the assumption (or illusion) that a particular sequence of sounds was divided into words in a way that did not coincide with the division intended by the speaker. Since knowing words is an essential component of every fluent speaker's command of language, an obvious topic to investigate is the form in which this knowledge is internalized by speakers: What do they know about the words of their language? At first blush it may appear that the answer is trivially simple. Speakers know that certain sound sequences have particular meanings; for example, the sound sequence [dɔg] refers to the animal otherwise known as man's best friend, whereas the sound sequence [tɔk] refers to the activity of speaking.

There is more to it, however. Speakers know not only the words of their language; they also know whether a given sound sequence could or could not be a word in their language. Consider the strings of letters in Table 17.1. Most readers have never encountered any of these "words" before. Yet there will be widespread agreement that some of these *might* be English words whereas others could not possibly be English. Furthermore, most readers will agree as to which "words" belong where; i.e., *thrim, snork, dramp, platch,* and *shripe* are likely to be judged English words, while *gnet, lgal, vrag, pfin, bdit,* and *nsip* are not English. Since none of the "words" was previously encountered, the judgment cannot be the result of checking through a list of memorized words. The explanation must be that we all share some basic information about the structural properties of English words—for example, that English words never begin with the consonant clusters gn and lg, whereas sn and pl are allowed. In other words, we all share some abstract principles of word structure such as those in the illustration.

It is unlikely that any readers will recall working out such principles in the course of learning English; in fact, few speakers will claim that they are even aware of knowing such principles. Yet their ability to judge "words" such as those cited above as English or not can only be explained

Some English "Nonwords"

thrim	lgal	dramp	pfin
platch	gnet	shripe	bdit
snork	vrag	chride	nsip

TABLE 17.1.   Readers whose mother tongue is English will recognize that some of these letter strings *might* be English words but some could not be. Abstract principles of word structure guide us subconsciously in our evaluation and use of these "nonwords."

by the assumption that speakers of English possess this type of knowledge. In other words, this suggests that we have knowledge about our native tongue of which we are not conscious. Like Moliere's M. Jourdain, we all speak prose, but we are totally unaware of doing so.

KNOWLEDGE: TAUGHT, LEARNED, AND INNATE

The existence of knowledge not directly accessible to our consciousness is not a particularly new discovery. One of the main purposes of Socrates' questions in Plato's writings was to demonstrate that even the most untutored among us possess knowledge of which we are totally unaware.

Many readers will accept this idea and yet be surprised that in passing on our language to our children we should be transmitting knowledge of which we ourselves are not consciously aware. Implicit in this surprise is the assumption that learning is always the result of overt teaching. But that assumption is false. Indeed, the acquisition of our mother tongue, I would argue, is a prime example of this kind of learning.

The fact that most of what we know about our native tongue is acquired without overt teaching raises a further question. All children are naturally interested in words and constantly inquire about them. But neither they nor their parents are the least bit curious about principles such as those illustrated in Table 17.2 that govern the distribution of initial consonant clusters. Yet somehow in the process of learning English we must have learned them. How can one explain this? How can one explain, in other words, that in the process of learning the words of English we incidentally learn principles of English word structure in which we have no conscious interest and to which nothing in our daily existence might plausibly draw our attention?

Some Principles of English Word Structure

1	m n	do not figure in any clusters except *sn* and *sm; snail* and *small* are words, *gnet* is not a possible word
2	m n l r w y	do not occupy the first position in a cluster; *platch* and *frith* are possible words, *lpatch* is not
3	b d g	do not occupy the last position in a cluster; *bdit* is not a possible word
4	p t k f o	may occupy either the first or the last position in a cluster, but not both; *thrim, sphere,* and *scare* are possible, but *pfin* is not

TABLE 17.2. **This list illustrates but a few of the abstract principles of English word structure. Although access to these (or similar) principles is necessary to account for English speakers' judgments about the "nonwords" above, few if any speakers will remember developing such principles in the course of learning the language.**

The only reasonable account of how speakers come to know these principles is to attribute them not to external factors but to innate mechanisms involved in memorizing words — that is, to assume that our minds are so constructed that when we memorize words, we automatically also abstract their structural principles. We might suppose that human memory for words is at a premium so that every word must be stored in a maximally economical form — i.e., in a form where every redundancy is eliminated. Since the principles noted in Table 17.2 capture an essential aspect of the redundancy inherent in English words, access to these principles is required to store English words in their most economical form. Different principles will, of course, be developed for different languages, but there is no language that lacks them altogether that does not place severe constraints on sequences of consonants and vowels in words. Thus the postulated mechanism that causes speakers to seek the abstract structural principles in their words will always produce a useful result.

It almost goes without saying that the propensity to search for structural regularities in the words we commit to memory is not something that we acquire from experience. Try to imagine, for instance, what sort of experiences might lead a child of average intelligence to grasp the fact that words contain redundancies that might be utilized for more economical coding. Moreover, these experiences must be common to children of all cultures, to Greenland Eskimos as well as to those whose parents are, for example, college professors. The only plausible explanation for the special way in which humans memorize words is innate: we do it in our particular way because for members of our species there is no other way.

There is of course nothing implausible in the suggestion that an organism is genetically constructed to perform particular tasks in particular ways. In fact, that is surely a major reason why a particular organism executes certain tasks very well and others poorly or not at all. Think, for example, of a kitten that shares a young child's every waking moment. At the end of a year or two the child will have acquired substantial mastery over its mother tongue, but the pet will fail to show any progress of this kind; instead, it will show great skill at catching mice and climbing trees. The reason for this is that humans are genetically different from cats, and part of that difference consists of the intellectual capacities that enable humans to acquire command of a language, presumably through special built-in features that determine, among other things, the way we memorize words.

UNIVERSALS OF LANGUAGE?

If the basis of our command of a language is genetically predetermined, then we should expect to find similarities among the principles and rules of all the different languages that are or have been spoken by humans. And we do.

The Special Roles of b, d, and g in Spanish

bajo	"low"	a[β]ajo	"below"
donde	"where"	a[ð]onde	"where to"
guardar	"to watch"	a[γ]uardar	"to wait for"

TABLE 17.3. The consonants b, d, and g are the subject of special rules in English (see Table 17.2) and Spanish (above). Though the rules are very different in the two languages, the fact that the same group of sounds figures in the rules of two distantly related languages points toward a single set of principles governing sound groupings in all languages.

In every language there are rules that affect groups of sounds rather than individual sounds, and the same groups of sounds figure in the rules of widely differing languages. For example, consider [b d g]. One of the most basic rules of Spanish phonetics states that these consonants are pronounced much as in English when they are the initial sound of a word and in certain other environments. However, they are pronounced very differently elsewhere, as shown in Table 17.3. We recall that clusters of consonants in this same class [b d g] are excluded from last position in English words (see Table 17.2). Thus, this class figures in rules of two such distantly related languages as English and Spanish.

Similarly, the class of consonants [m n l r w y] receives special treatment in the Papago language spoken by Indians native to Arizona, as shown in Table 17.4; here those consonants figure in compound nouns, the second element of which is [ʔ o o ʔ o o], meaning "bone." In compounding, as the illustration shows, nouns are simply adjoined. However,

Some Special Roles of Consonants in Papago

1	wawuk[ʔ]oo[ʔ]oo	"raccoon bone"
	[ʔ]u[ʔ]uhig[ʔ]oo[ʔ]oo	"bird bone"
	mawid[ʔ]oo[ʔ]oo	"mountain lion bone"
2	ba[ʔ]noo[ʔ]oo	"coyote bone"
	kaa[ʔ]woo[ʔ]oo	"badger bone"
	ceeko[ʔ]loo[ʔ]oo	"squirrel bone"

TABLE 17.4. In forming compounds, the Papago language of Indians native to Arizona treats nouns ending with m, n, l, r, w, and y differently (see Table 17.2) from other nouns (see Table 17.1). These consonants also figure in the principles of English (Table 17.2). That the same consonant groups—and few others—are involved in such rules in other languages suggests that to all humans, no matter what their linguistic heritage, certain sounds are naturally related and others unrelated.

adjoining consonants permute position, as in Table 17.4, when the first noun ends with a consonant from the set [m n l r w y] and the initial consonant of the second noun is a glottal stop [ʔ], a sound that in English we pronounce when we attempt to distinguish *an aim* from *a name*. Thus, when *wawuk* (raccoon) is adjoined to *ʔooʔoo*, the result is *wawukʔ-ooʔoo*, but when *ban* (coyote) is adjoined to *ʔooʔoo*, the result is not *banʔ-ooʔoo* but *baʔnooʔoo*.

The same group [m n l r w y] that figures in the Papago rule of noun compounding plays a role in English; the group is excluded from initial-consonant clusters in English words (see row 2 in Table 17.2).

These examples — and experienced linguists should have little difficulty in extending the list indefinitely — show that identical groups of consonants function in totally unrelated languages. Indeed, the same groupings of sounds reemerge in the rules of language after language, whereas other groupings of sounds — e.g., [n l b k] or [θ k r g m] — are never encountered. This observation suggests that to the human speaker there is something natural about certain groupings of sounds — that they somehow belong together — whereas other groupings are unnatural and therefore never encountered. The judgment as to what sounds naturally belong together probably derives from the design of our nervous system; and that, in turn, is determined by our genetic endowment.

FORMING WORDS FROM WORDS

Rules and principles of language are not at all something esoteric that only linguists and other pedants enjoy splitting hairs over. On the contrary, rules are the very stuff of which language is made, and speakers use them with the greatest ease, even abandon. Indeed, the rules and principles that determine the shape of the words in a language make up only a fraction of those regularly mastered by fluent speakers of the language.

To convey some impression of the exuberance with which languages use rules, let me briefly discuss part of the system of plural rules in Kasem, a language spoken by about 80,000 people in West Africa, primarily in Ghana. For the class of nouns shown in Table 17.5, the singular forms end with the suffix *a* and the plural forms end with the suffix *i*. The suffixes appear in this form in row 1 *(bakada-bakadi* and *fala-fali)*. The same suffixes are involved in the other examples, but their appearance there is masked by the effects of special rules.

For example, Kasem is subject to a rule that deletes the first in a sequence of identical vowels. Because of this Vowel Deletion Rule, the plural forms in row 2 are not *kambii* and *pii*, but *kambi* and *pi*.

A different rule — the Consonant Deletion Rule — accounts for the forms in row 3. This rule deletes stem-final [g] and [ŋ] in the plural. Consequently, in place of the expected *bugi* we get *bui*, and the plural of *diga*

The Plural Rules of Kasem

	Singular	Plural		Singular	Plural	
1	bakada	bakadi	"boy"	fala	fali	"white man"
2	kambia	kambi	"cooking pot"	pia	pi	"yam"
3	buga	bui	"river"	diga	di	"room"
4	mala	male	"chameleon"	kaba	kabe	"slave"
5	naga	ne	"leg"	la[ŋ]a	le	"song"

TABLE 17.5. For one class of nouns in Kasem, a language spoken by about 80,000 people in West Africa, the singular suffix is *a* and the plural suffix is *i* (see rows 1 and 2). But an elaborate set of rules obscures this simple state of affairs in many instances (see rows 3, 4, and 5).

is not *digi* but *di*. The form *di* is somewhat more complicated than is first apparent. We know that the Consonant Deletion Rule would delete the *g* in *digi*, turning it into *dii*, but that is not the correct form; the correct form is *di*. There is, of course, no difficulty explaining how *di* arose: *dii* was subject to the Vowel Deletion Rule.

In the derivation of *di*, the two rules were applied in a specific order. If the rules had been applied in the reverse order, the result would have been *dii*. Since the basic form *digi* does not contain a sequence of identical vowels it could not be subject to Vowel Deletion. The subsequent application of Consonant Deletion would then produce *dii*, but to this form Vowel Deletion can no longer apply since this rule has been ordered before (not after) Consonant Deletion.

A further complication arises in the case of *mala*, chameleon (row 4). The plural form should be *malai*; instead we find *male*. To a linguist this is not strange, because linguists know numerous languages where, as a result of the Monophthongization Rule, the diphthong [ai] is replaced by the monophthong [e]. In fact, English spelling still shows traces of this development; the letter sequence *ai* is pronounced *e* as in *pain, maim,* and *gain.* This process is even more general in Kasem, with not only [ai] becoming [e] but also [au] becoming [o]. Now we are in a position to explain the forms in row 5 of Table 17.5: they are the result of the interaction of the Consonant Deletion Rule with the Monophthongization Rule. Specifically, the basic plural forms *nagi* and *la[ŋ]i* are transformed by the Consonant Deletion Rule into *nai* and *lai*, respectively. They are then turned into *ne* and *le* by the Monophthongization Rule.

The fact that Kasem speakers use special rules to generate the plural forms of their nouns should not seem strange in light of what we have said. What may strike the layperson as implausible is the relative complexity of the procedure—outlined only incompletely in Table 17.6—that appears to be involved in the inflection of Kasem words. We might well wonder whether we really go to all this trouble just to say a few words.

Some Examples of Rules Operating on Kasem Plurals

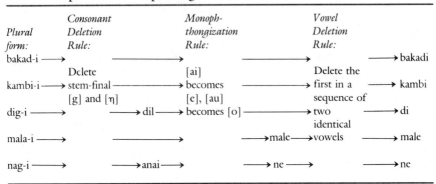

Plural form:	Consonant Deletion Rule:	Monoph- thongization Rule:	Vowel Deletion Rule:	
bakad-i ⟶	⟶	⟶	⟶	bakadi
	Delete	[ai]	Delete the	
kambi-i ⟶	stem-final	becomes	first in a	kambi
	[g] and [ŋ]	[e], [au]	sequence of	
dig-i ⟶	⟶ dil ⟶	becomes [o] ⟶	two	di
			identical	
mala-i ⟶	⟶	⟶ male ⟶	vowels	male
nag-i ⟶	⟶ anai ⟶	⟶ ne ⟶		ne

TABLE 17.6. A flowchart illustrating the application of three rules in the formation of plurals in Kasem, a West African language spoken in parts of Ghana. The
plurals of all words in this class are formed by adding the suffix *i* to the stem. But
a Consonant Deletion Rule, which applies first, eliminates stem-final [g] and [ŋ]
in the plural. Next, Monophthongization turns [ai] and [au] into [e] and [o],
respectively. Finally, Vowel Deletion eliminates one of two consecutive identical
vowels. If the rules were applied in a different order, the outcome would be quite
different for several forms. Unbroken arrows between rule blocks indicate that
the rules are not applicable to the form in question.

Implicit in this objection is the assumption that humans find it difficult to perform this sort of computation — that it would be easier to
memorize such facts as the plural of *naga* is *ne* and that of *diga* is *di* than
to postulate a single plural suffix *i* for all nouns in this class and to compute the different outputs according to the rules. The linguistic evidence
suggests that the converse is much closer to the truth, for the Kasem
example is the norm rather than the exception. Indeed, recourse to computation is so strongly favored over rote memory that speakers apparently
do not have the option of foresaking rules for memorization.

OWHAY ANCAY OUYAY EADRAY ISTHAY?

This natural bent for rules is expressed in a great many special uses
of language. Children frequently use secret languages such as Ablanguage
or pig Latin, both of which are nothing but normal English to which one
or two extra rules have been added. The rules for pig Latin, for instance,
consist of a permutation that moves the initial consonant cluster from
the beginning to the end of the word, to which the diphthong *ay* is then
adjoined. Thus, *pig* becomes *igpay* and *Latin* becomes *atinlay*. These simple rules produce words so greatly at variance with standard English that
children effectively possess a secret language quite impenetrable to their
teachers and parents, which is, of course, the main purpose. Though to

TABLE 17.7 **Rules of a Language Invented by Children**

	The Glottal Stop Rule			The Consonant Rule	
cake⟶		⟶ca[ʔ]⟶			⟶ca[ʔ]
	In words containing		Eliminate sounds		
full⟶	two identical sounds	⟶	in the group		⟶[p]ull
	from the group		[f θ s č š γ ð z j ž],		
did⟶	[p t k b d g], the	⟶di[ʔ]⟶	replacing them with		⟶di[ʔ]
	second occurrence		corresponding		
doze⟶	is replaced by a	⟶	stops—[p] for [f],		⟶do[d]
	glottal stop[ʔ].		etc.		

my knowledge the history of pig Latin has not been documented in detail, we know that it goes back many generations; today's speakers are not its inventors but have learned it from older children.

There are, however, numerous instances of secret languages invented by children. One such "language" was discovered about 20 years ago in Cambridge by Professor Joseph Applegate, then a member of the Department of Modern Languages at M.I.T.[1] A couple living in his building consulted Professor Applegate about their two younger boys who, they feared, were suffering from some neurological disorder. Although they appeared to understand English, the boys were speaking a jargon that the parents found quite incomprehensible. The third child in the family, who was a few years older than the two problem children, had apparently no trouble understanding his brothers and often acted as their translator. After listening to the children for a few evenings, Professor Applegate discovered that the children were using a secret language of their own devising: by adding two rules to standard English, they were rendering their language quite impenetrable to their parents — although not to their brother.

Specifically, Professor Applegate found that the children's speech was modified by two rules absent from their parents' English. In words containing two identical stops — i.e., two occurrences of a sound from the set [p t k b d g] — the children's speech was subject to a Glottal Stop Rule that replaced the second stop by a glottal stop [ʔ]. The children therefore pronounced words such as *cake, daddy,* and *paper* as shown in group 1 of Table 17.7.

Second, the children's speech lacked affricates and fricatives — i.e., sounds belonging to the set [f θ s č š γ ð z j ž] were not used. In the children's language, a Consonant Rule replaced these with the corresponding stops — [f] by [p], [θ s č š] by [t], [γ] by [b], and [ð z j ž] by [d]. As

[1] Applegate, Joseph R., "Phonological Rules of a Subdialect of English," *Word* 17 (1961): 188–193.

a result, the children pronounced alike words that are differentiated in adult speech, as shown in groups 2 and 3 of Table 17.8.

That was not all, however. The children differentiated the stop sound that arose by the Consonant Rule from all other stop sounds: only the latter were replaced by glottal stops as a result of the Glottal Stop Rule. (Additional examples are shown in group 3.) These rules, like those in the Kasem plural formation, were applied in a definite order, first the Glottal Stop Rule and then the Consonant Rule. Thus, *did* became *di*[ʔ] by the Glottal Stop Rule, and the Consonant Rule was not applicable. On the other hand, *doze*, to which the Glottal Stop Rule was not applicable, became *do*[d] by the Consonant Rule. Since the rules are ordered, it is impossible at this point to apply the Glottal Stop Rule again.

While this system may seem surprisingly sophisticated, both it and the rules of Kasem are instances of the human tendency to use rules—with sometimes unexpected results. In the case of the Cambridge children, the tendency was used to obstruct rather than facilitate communication.

LANGUAGE AS GENETIC ENDOWMENT

To summarize, the core of knowledge that fluent speakers have of their language has the form of rules, and these rules go well beyond what is directly observable in the movements executed by our vocal organs in speaking and the resulting acoustic signals. Each language has its own special set of rules, and these rules constitute the essence of what we learn when we acquire mastery of a given language. In learning these

Some Words In a Language Invented by Children

1	cake	ca[ʔ]	daddy	da[ʔ]y	paper	pa[ʔ]er
2	full	[p]ull	pays	pay[d]	walks	walk[t]
	pull	[p]ull	paid	paid	walked	walk[t]
3	suit	[t]uit	doze	do[d]	fife	[p]i[p]
	toot	too[ʔ]	did	di[ʔ]	pipe	pi[ʔ]

TABLE 17.8.   To give themselves a "secret" language, two children devised an elaborate set of transformations for common English words. Like the Kasem language of West Africa, the children's language was based on rules rather than rote memory—an indication, writes the author, that humans prefer even complex computation to rote memory. The relationship between the children's words and their cognates in adult varieties of American English is obvious in most instances, yet the differences were sufficient to block comprehension by adults. The [ʔ] is the phonetic symbol for a glottal stop, the sound that appears between the words *an aim* when the phrase is pronounced to differentiate it from the phrase *a name*.

rules, young children require no special instruction, and much of what they—or, for that matter, any language students—learn never enters their consciousness. Underlying these rules is a set of highly abstract hypotheses about language, including such propositions as these: Speech is made up of words; words, in turn, are made up of sequences of sounds subject to definite rules; the rules affect specific groups of sounds; the same groups of sounds figure in other rules in English as well as in other languages; and the rules of any given language interact in the fashion shown by the Kasem plurals and the children's secret language.

The highly sophisticated character of these propositions excludes the possibility that they are acquired through experience. Yet the attainment of fluent command of a language by a native speaker crucially implies access to these and similar propositions. The conclusion, therefore, is that these propositions are a special aspect of the human genetic endowment, that they are part of what makes our species distinct from all others.

BIBLIOGRAPHY

Chomsky, Noam, *Reflections on Language.* New York: Pantheon Books, 1975.
Chomsky, Noam, *Rules and Representations.* New York: Columbia University Press, 1980.
Halle, Morris, Joan Bresnan, and George A. Miller, eds. *Linguistic Theory and Psychological Reality.* Cambridge, MA: MIT Press, 1978.

FOR DISCUSSION AND REVIEW

1. How does Halle support his argument that "our perception that utterances are made up of words is a kind of illusion"?

2. Summarize four principles of English word structure. Describe when and how you learned them. If you know a language other than English, analyze whether or to what extent these same principles apply to it.

3. Why is it significant that the same groupings of sounds occur in the rules of many unrelated languages? Give two examples of such groupings. What kind of principle seems to govern the composition of these groupings? (Note: In answering the latter question, you may find it useful to review the preceding selection, "Phonetics" by Edward Callary.)

4. Halle refers to "the exuberance with which languages use rules" and illustrates his point with examples from Kasem, a language spoken in West Africa. Drawing on your own knowledge, give an example from another language. Explain how the Kasem example supports Halle's conclusion that "recourse to computation is so strongly fa-

vored over rote memory that speakers apparently do not have the option of foresaking rules for memorization."

5. Pig Latin and Ablanguage are only two of the many secret languages that children have developed. If you know another such language, write out an explanation of its rules. Describe how you learned the language.

18

The Minimal Units of Meaning: Morphemes

The Ohio State University Language Files

Phonemes by themselves have no meaning. However, as we have seen, one of the distinguishing features of human language is its duality of patterning, its multilayered quality. Thus, phonemes, in themselves meaningless, are combined to form units that do have meaning—morphemes. Not all languages use the same kinds of morphemes, but all languages do use various kinds of morphemes as building blocks to construct words, units larger than morphemes and harder to define. The first part of the following selection describes the kinds of morphemes that occur in English and identifies their various functions. The second part begins by examining the complex ways in which, in English, affixes combine with other units. It then explains the hierarchical internal structure of English words that results from these combinations.

A continuous stream of speech can be broken up by the listener (or linguist) into smaller, meaningful parts. A conversation, for example, can be divided into the sentences of the conversation, which can be divided up further into the words that make up each of the sentences. It is obvious to most people that a sentence has a meaning, and that each of the words in it has a meaning as well. Can we go further and divide words into smaller units which still have meanings? Many people think not; their immediate intuition is that words are the basic meaningful elements of a language. This is, however, not the case. Many words can be broken down into still smaller units. Think, for example, of words such as *unlucky, unhappy,* and *unsatisfied.* The *un-* in each of these words has the same meaning, loosely, that of "not," but *un* is not a word by itself. Thus, we have identified units — smaller than the word — that have meanings. These are called *morphemes.* Now consider the words *look, looks,* and *looked.* What about the *-s* in *looks* and the *-ed* in *looked?* These segments can be separated from the meaningful unit *look,* and although they do not really have an identifiable meaning themselves, each does have a particular function. The *-s* is required for agreement with certain subjects (*she looks,* but not **she look*), and the *-ed* signifies that the action of the verb *look* has already taken place. Segments such as these are also considered morphemes. Thus, a morpheme is the smallest linguistic unit that has a meaning or grammatical function.

Some words, of course, are not composed of other morphemes. *Car*, *spider*, and *race*, for example, are words, but they are also morphemes since they cannot be broken down into smaller meaningful parts. Morphemes that are also words are called *free morphemes* since they can stand alone. *Bound morphemes*, on the other hand, never exist as words themselves, but are always attached to some other morpheme. Some examples of bound morphemes in English are *un-*, *-ed*, and *-s*.

When we identify the number and types of morphemes a given word consists of, we are looking at what is referred to as the *structure* of the word. Morphology is the study of how words are structured and how they are put together from smaller parts. Morphologists not only identify the different classes of morphemes but also study the patterns that occur in the combination of morphemes in a given language. For example, consider the words *rewrite, retake,* and *relive.* Notice that *re-* is a bound morpheme that attaches only to verbs, and, furthermore, attaches to the beginning of the verb, not the end. Every speaker of English knows you can't say *write-re* or *take-re* (where *re-* is connected to the end of the free morpheme), nor can you say *rechoice* or *repretty* (where *re-* is connected to a morpheme that is not a verb). In other words, part of a speaker's linguistic competence is knowing, in addition to the meaning of the morphemes of a language, the ways in which the morphemes are allowed to combine with other morphemes.

Morphemes can be classified as either bound or free, as we have seen. There are three additional ways of characterizing morphemes. The first is to label bound morphemes according to whether they attach to the beginning or end of a word. You are most likely familiar with these terms. A *prefix* attaches to the beginning and a *suffix* attaches to the end of a word. The general term for prefixes and suffixes is *affix*, so bound morphemes are also referred to as affixes. The second way of characterizing morphemes is to classify bound morphemes according to their function in the complex words of which they are a part. When some morphemes attach to words, they create, or *derive*, new words, either by changing the meaning of the word or by changing its part of speech. For example, *un-* in *unhappy* creates a new word with the opposite meaning of *happy*. Notice that both *unhappy* and *happy* are adjectives. The suffix *-ness* in *quickness*, however, changes the part of speech of *quick*, an adjective, into a noun, *quickness*. Morphemes that change the meaning or part of speech of a word they attach to are called *derivational* morphemes. Other morphemes do not alter words in this way, but only refine and give extra grammatical information about the word's already existing meaning. For example, *cat* and *cats* are both nouns that basically have the same meaning (i.e., they refer to the same sort of thing), but *cats*, with the plural morpheme *-s*, contains only the additional information that there are more than one of these things referred to. The morphemes that serve a

TABLE 18.1   The Inflectional Suffixes of English

STEM	SUFFIX	FUNCTION	EXAMPLE
wait	-s	3rd per. sg. present	She waits there at noon.
wait	-ed	past tense	She waited there yesterday.
wait	-ing	progressive	She is waiting there now.
eat	-en	past participle	Jack has eaten the Oreos.
chair	-s	plural	The chairs are in the room.
chair	-'s	possessive	The chair's leg is broken.
fast	-er	comparative	Jill runs faster than Joe.
fast	-est	superlative	Tim runs fastest of all.

purely grammatical function, never creating a new word but only a different *form* of the same word, are called *inflectional* morphemes.

In every word we find that there is at least one free morpheme. In a morphologically complex word, i.e., one composed of a free morpheme and any number of bound affixes, the free morpheme is referred to as the *stem, root,* or *base.* However, if there is more than one affix in a word, we cannot say that all of the affixes attach to the stem. Consider the word *happenings,* for example. When *-ing* is added to *happen,* we note that a new word is derived; it is morphologically complex, but it is a word. The plural morpheme *-s* is added onto the word *happening,* not the suffix *-ing.*

In English the derivational morphemes are either prefixes or suffixes, but, by chance, the inflectional morphemes are all suffixes. Of course, this is not the same in other languages. There are only eight inflectional morphemes in English. They are listed below along with an example of the type of stem each can attach to.

The difference between inflectional and derivational morphemes is sometimes difficult to see at first. Some characteristics of each are listed below to help make the distinction clearer.

Derivational Morphemes

1. Change the part of speech or the meaning of a word, e.g., *-ment* added to a verb forms a noun *(judg-ment)*, and *re-activate* means "activate again."
2. Syntax does not require the presence of derivational morphemes. They typically indicate semantic relations *within* a word, but no syntactic relations outside the word (compare this with item 2 following), e.g., *un-kind* relates *-un* "not" to *kind,* but has no particular syntactic connections outside the word—note that the same word can be used in *he is unkind* and *they are unkind.*
3. Derivational morphemes are usually not very productive; they generally are selective about what they'll combine with. For example, the suffix *-hood* occurs with just a few nouns such as *brother,*

neighbor, and *knight,* but not with most others, such as *friend, daughter,* or *candle.*

4. They typically occur before inflectional suffixes, e.g., *government-s.* *-ment,* a derivational suffix, precedes *-s,* an inflectional suffix.
5. They may be prefixes or suffixes (in English), e.g., *pre-arrange, arrange-ment.*

Inflectional Morphemes

1. They do not change meaning or part of speech, e.g., *big, bigg-er, bigg-est* are all adjectives.
2. They are required by syntax. They typically indicate syntactic or semantic relations *between* different words in a sentence, e.g., *Nim love-s bananas.* *-s* marks the third-person singular present form of the verb, relating it to the third singular subject *Nim.*
3. They are very productive. They typically occur with all members of some large class of morphemes, e.g., the plural morpheme /-s/ occurs with almost all nouns.
4. They occur at the margin of a word, after any derivational morphemes, e.g., *ration-al-iz-ation-s.* *-s* is inflectional, and appears at the very end of the word.
5. They are suffixes only (in English).

There is one final distinction between types of morphemes that is useful. Some morphemes have semantic content. That is, they either have some kind of independent, identifiable meaning or indicate a change in meaning when added to a word. Others serve only to provide information about grammatical function by relating certain words in a sentence to each other (see item 2 about inflectional morphemes, above). The former are called *content* morphemes, and the latter are called *function* morphemes. This might appear at first to be the same as the inflectional and derivational distinction. They do overlap, but not completely. All derivational morphemes are content morphemes, and all inflectional morphemes are function morphemes, as you might have surmised. However, some words can be merely function morphemes. Examples in English of such free morphemes that are also function morphemes are prepositions, articles, pronouns, and conjunctions.

In this file, we have been using conventional spelling to represent morphemes. But it is important to realize that morphemes are pairings of *sounds* with meanings, not spellings with meanings, and representing morphemes phonetically reveals some interesting facts. We find that just as different free morphemes can have the same phonetic representations, as in *ear* (for hearing) and *ear* (of corn), the same is true of bound morphemes. For example, the plural, possessive, and third-person singular suffixes can all sound identical in English (e.g., *cats* [kæts], *Frank's* [fræŋks], and *walks* [waks]). These three suffixes are completely different morphemes, they just happen to be homophonous, or sound alike, in

English. Similarly, there are two morphemes in English which sound like [ɪn]. One means "not" as in *inoperable* or *intolerable,* and the other means "in" as in *intake* or *inside.*

One of the more interesting things revealed by transcribing morphemes phonetically is the interaction of phonological and morphological processes. For example, some morphemes have more than one phonetic representation depending on which sounds precede or follow them, but since each of the pronunciations serves the same function or has the same meaning, it is considered to be the same morpheme. In other words, the same morpheme can be pronounced differently depending upon the sounds which follow or precede it. Of course, these different pronunciations will be patterned. For example, the phonetic representation of the plural morpheme is either [s] as in *cats,* [z] as in *dogs,* or [əz] as in *churches.* Each of these three pronunciations is said to be an *allomorph* of the *same* morpheme because [s], [z], and [əz] all have the same function (making some word plural) and because they are similar phonetically. Note that this same phonological process that causes the plural morpheme /s/ to be pronounced as [s] after voiceless sounds, [z] after voiced sounds, and [əz] after sibilants also applies to the possessive morpheme /s/ and the third-person singular morpheme /s/. Consider the morpheme /ɪn/ that means "not" in the words *inoperable, incongruent,* and *impossible.* What are the allomorphs of this morpheme?

We now call your attention to a few pitfalls of identifying morphemes. First, don't confuse morphemes with syllables. A few examples will show that the number of morphemes and syllables in a word are independent of each other. Consider the word *coats.* It is a one-syllable word composed of two morphemes. *Coat* happens to be one morpheme and consist of a single syllable, but *-s* is not even a syllable, although it is a morpheme. Note that *syllable* is a three-syllable word composed only of one morpheme.

Secondly, note that a given morpheme has a particular sound or sound sequence associated with it, but not every instance of that sound sequence in the language represents that morpheme. For example, take the plural morpheme /s/. When you hear the word [karts] in isolation, you can't determine if the [s] is an instance of this plural morpheme *(the carts are back in the store),* or an instance of the possessive morpheme *(the cart's wheels turn funny)* or of the third-person singular morpheme *(he carts those books around every day).* That sound sequence may not even be a morpheme at all. The [s] in [sun], for example, is not a morpheme. Likewise, the [ɪn] of *inexcusable* is the morpheme that means "not," but the [ɪn] of *print* is not a morpheme.

Third, remember to analyze the phonetic representations of morphemes and not their spellings. A morpheme can have one or more allomorphs, and these allomorphs might be represented by the same or different spellings. The *-er* in *writer* is the same morpheme as the *-or* in *editor,* and the *-ar* in *liar,* since all three mean "one who," but they do not represent separate allomorphs since their pronunciations are identical, namely, [ɹ]. On the other hand, the -s in *Mark's*, *John's*, and *Charles's* are the same morpheme, but represent three different allomorphs, since each is pronounced differently.

Finally, we include below a summary list of criteria that might help you to identify the different types of morphemes.

Given a morpheme,

1. Can it stand alone as a word?

   YES → it's a *free* morpheme (e.g., *bubble, orange*)
   NO → it's a *bound* morpheme (e.g., *-er* in *beater*, *-s* in *oranges*)

2. Does it have the principal meaning of the word it's in?

   YES → it's the *stem* (e.g., *happy* in *unhappiness*)
   NO → it's an *affix* (e.g., *-or* in *contributor* or, *pre-* in *preview*)

3. Does it create a new word by changing the meaning and/or part of speech?

   YES → it's a *derivational* affix (e.g., *re-* in *rewind*, *-ist* in *artist*)
   NO → it's an *inflectional* affix (e.g., *-est* in *smartest*)

4. Does it have a meaning, or cause a change in meaning when added to a word?

   YES → it's a *content* morpheme (e.g., *-un* in *untrue*)
   NO → it's a *function* morpheme (e.g., *the, to, or, -s* in *books*)

THE HIERARCHICAL STRUCTURE OF WORDS

When we examine words composed of only two morphemes, we implicitly know two facts about the ways in which affixes join with their stems. First, the stems with which a given affix may combine normally belong to the same part of speech. For example, the suffix *-able* attaches freely to verbs, but not to adjectives or nouns; thus, we can add this suffix to the verbs *adjust, break, compare,* and *debate,* but not to the adjectives *asleep, lovely, happy,* and *strong,* nor to the nouns *anger, morning, student,* or *success.* Second, the words formed by the addition of a given affix to some word or morpheme also normally belong to the same part of speech. For example, the expressions resulting from the addition of *-able* to a verb are always adjectives; thus *adjustable, breakable, comparable,* and *debatable* are all adjectives.

These two facts have an important consequence for determining the way in which words with more than one affix must be formed. What it means is that words are formed in steps, with one affix attaching to a complete word, which can be a free morpheme or a morphologically complex word. Words with more than one affix are not formed in one single step with the affixes and stem just strung together. For example, consider the word *unusable*, which is composed of a prefix *un-*, a stem *use*, and a suffix *-able*. One possible way this morphologically complex word might be formed is all at once, as in: *un* + *use* + *able*, where the prefix and the suffix attach at the same time to the verb stem *use*. However, this cannot be the case, knowing what we know about how affixes attach only to certain parts of speech and create words of certain parts of speech. The prefix *un-*, meaning "not," attaches only to adjectives and creates new words that are also adjectives. (Compare with *unkind, unwise,* and *unhappy.*) The suffix *-able*, on the other hand, attaches to verbs and forms words that are adjectives. (Compare with *stoppable, doable,* and *washable.*) Therefore, *un-* cannot attach to *use*, since *use* is a verb and not an adjective. However, if *-able* attaches <u>first</u> to the stem *use*, then it creates an adjective, *usable*, and the prefix *-un* is allowed to combine with it. Thus, the formation of the word *unusable* is a two-step process whereby *use* and *-able* attach first, then *un-* attaches to the word *usable*.

Recall that what we are analyzing is the internal *structure* of words. Words, since they are formed by steps, have a special type of structure characterized as *hierarchical.* This hierarchical structure can be schematically represented by means of a "tree" that indicates the steps involved in the formation of the word, i.e., which morphemes joined together first and so on. The tree for *unusable* is:

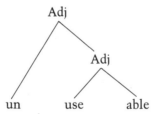

Now consider the word *reusable*. Both the prefix *re-* and the suffix *-able* attach to verbs, but we have already shown that one must attach first. Which is it? Notice that *reusable* cannot be regarded as the result of adding the prefix *re-* to the word *usable* since *re-* attaches only to verbs (compare with *redo, relive,* and *refuel*) and *usable* is an adjective. However, *-able* can attach to the verb *reuse* since *-able* attaches to verbs. Thus, our understanding of how the affixes *re-* and *-able* combine with other morphemes allows us to conclude that the verb *reuse*, but not the adjective *usable*, is a step in the formation of the adjective *reusable*.

Interestingly, some words are ambiguous in that they have more than one meaning. When we examine their internal structure, we find an explanation for this: their structure may be analyzed in more than one way. Consider, for example, the word *unlockable*. This could mean either "not able to be locked" or "able to be unlocked." If we made a list to determine the parts of speech the affix *un-* attaches to, we would discover that there are not one but two prefixes that sound like *un-*. The first combines with adjectives to form new adjectives, and means "not." (Compare with *unaware, unintelligent,* or *unwise.*) The second prefix *un-* combines with verbs to form new verbs, and means "do the reverse of." (Compare with *untie, undo,* or *undress.*)

Even though these prefixes sound alike, they are entirely different morphemes. Because of these two different sorts of *un-* in English, *unlockable* may be analyzed in two different ways. First, the suffix *-able* may join with the verb *lock* to form the adjective *lockable. Un-* may then join with this adjective to form the new adjective *unlockable,* with the meaning "not able to be locked." This way of forming *unlockable* is schematized in the following tree:

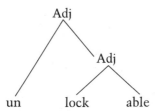

The second way of forming *unlockable* is as follows. The prefix *un-* joins with the verb *lock* to form the verb *unlock.* The suffix *-able* then joins with this verb to form the adjective *unlockable* with the meaning of "able to be unlocked." This manner of forming *unlockable* is represented by the following tree:

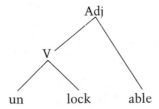

Some Suggestions

There are a few prefixes that do not attach exclusively to one part of speech. For example, consider the prefix *pre-. Pre-* attaches to verbs and does not change the part of speech, as the following examples show:

preexist

predecide

predetermine

predefine

premeditate

However, there are examples of words with the prefix *pre-* that do not follow the same pattern as those cited above:

preseason

predawn

prewar

pregame

In these words *pre-* attaches to a noun and forms an adjective *(the preseason game, the prewar propaganda, the pregame warmup)*. However, the meaning of the prefix is the same as in *preexist, predecide,* etc. (although its function is different). In addition, there are sets such as:

prefrontal

predental

preinvasive

prehistoric

In these words, *pre-* is attaching to an adjective, forming adjectives, and has the same meaning as in *preexist, predecide,* etc. So this is a bit problematic. We don't want to throw out the idea that a given affix attaches only to one part of speech, since the overwhelming majority of affixes adhere to this pattern. Apparently, some morphemes become so productive that their combinatorial possibilities can be extended. Such must be the case with *pre-*. Note, however, that its combinations are nevertheless rule-governed. When *pre-* attaches to verbs, it forms only verbs. When it attaches to nouns, it forms only adjectives, and when it attaches to adjectives, it forms only adjectives. So, it is advisable to consider many examples when attempting to determine the rules by which a given affix combines.

EXERCISES

1. Draw tree diagrams for each of the following words:

a. reconstruction	j. international	s. unmistakable
b. unaffordable	k. misunderstandable	t. insincerity
c. un-American	l. dehumidifier	u. dysfunctional
d. manliness	m. unrespectable	v. inconclusive
e. impersonal	n. nonrefundable	w. premeditatedly
f. irreplaceability	o. mismanagement	x. overgeneralization
g. oversimplification	p. underspecification	y. reformer
h. unhappiness	q. restatement	z. infertility
i. impotency	r. inflammability	aa. dishonesty

2. We said that polar opposite ("not") *un-* attaches only to adjectives, but two exceptions to this rule are *Uncola* and *Uncar*. Why are these exceptions? Why would advertisers have made them up in the first place when the words fail to follow the rule?

≡

FOR DISCUSSION AND REVIEW

1. Explain the difference between derivational morphemes and inflectional morphemes. Illustrate each difference with an example not in the text.

2. What is the difference between content morphemes and function morphemes?

3. Describe the relationship between morphemes and syllables.

4. Explain what an *allomorph* is. Give an example of an English morpheme, in addition to the regular noun plural, that has more than one phonetic representation.

5. Allomorphs, unlike allophones, need not be phonetically similar. The productive plural morpheme in English has the forms /-s/, /-z/, /-əz/; which one is used depends on the sound with which the noun to be made plural ends. These allomorphs are phonologically conditioned. Some nouns in English, however, do not form regular plurals. List as many "irregular" plurals as you can. Then try to divide them into groups (note: there are five types of morphologically conditioned plurals in English; four of them derive from Old English).

6. Explain the statement that "the internal structure of words is *hierarchical.*"

7. Explain the ambiguity of the words *bimonthly* and *biweekly*. Is it similar to or different from the ambiguity of *unlockable?* Explain.

19

The Identification of Morphemes

H. A. Gleason, Jr.

As native speakers of English, we usually do not find it difficult to iden-
tify the morphemes in English words. We are, of course, relying in part
on our unconscious knowledge of the rules of English and in part on our
familiarity with much of the English vocabulary. Therefore, in order to
begin to understand the complexity of morphemic analysis, we need to
examine data from a language that we do not know well. In the following
excerpt from his book An Introduction to Descriptive Linguistics, *Profes-*
sor H. A. Gleason uses some Hebrew verb forms to demonstrate the basic
analytical technique for the identification of morphemes: comparing
groups of utterances which are (1) partially identical in both expression
and content and (2) partially different in both expression and content.
Note that both conditions must be met: we are looking for the smallest
change in content (i.e., structure) that results in a change in meaning (i.e.,
expression). At the end of his analysis of Hebrew verb forms, Professor
Gleason introduces discontinuous morphemes, which do not occur in
all languages; the type of morpheme known as an "infix"; "replacives,"
which do occur in English; and the zero affix (Ø), which also occurs in
English.

The process of analysis [to identify morphemes] is best shown by detailed
discussion of an actual example. For this purpose we will use a series of
Hebrew verb forms. The data will be introduced a few words at a time.
This is an artificial feature of the presentation. The preceding step is
merely implied: namely that we have selected from the corpus those pairs
or sets of items that can be profitably compared. The order of presentation
is not necessarily that which is most efficient for the analysis of the data,
but that which most effectively illustrates the methods used.

1. /zəkartíihuu/   "I remembered him"
2. /zəkartíihaa/   "I remembered her"
3. /zəkartíikaa/   "I remembered thee"

Comparison of items 1 and 2 reveals one contrast in expression,
/-uu/:/-aa/, and one in meaning, as shown by translation, and hence presumably in content "him":"her." This may (tentatively!) be considered
as a pair of morphemes. However, comparison of 1, 2, and 3 suggests that

the first identification was wrong. The contrast now seems to be /-huu/ "him":/-haa/ "her":/-kaa/ "thee." We can be reasonably sure that the morpheme meaning "him" includes the sounds /-uu/ or /-huu/, but until we can identify the remaining parts of the word we cannot be sure how much else is included.

4. /zəkarnúuhuu/   "we remembered him"
5. /zəkarnúuhaa/   "we remembered her"
6. /zəkarnúukaa/   "we remembered thee"

Comparison of 4, 5, and 6 with 1, 2, and 3 reveals a contrast in expression and meaning between /-tíi-/ "I" and /-núu-/ "we." However, as before, we cannot be sure how much is to be included until the remainders of the words are identified. It is conceivable that the morphemes might be /-rtíi-/ "I" and /-rnúu-/ "we" . . . .

7. /qəṭaltíihuu/   "I killed him"
8. /qəṭalnúuhuu/   "we killed him"

Comparison of 7 and 8 with the foregoing gives us a basis for identifying /zəkar-/ "remembered" and /qəṭal-/ "killed." By so doing we have tentatively assigned every portion of each word to a tentative morpheme. We have, however, no reason to be certain that each portion so isolated is only a single morpheme. We have only reasonable assurance that by dividing any of these words in a manner similar to /zəkar-tíi-huu/ we have divided between morphemes, so that each piece consists of one or more essentially complete morphemes; that is, each piece is probably either a morpheme or a morpheme sequence.

The problem is somewhat simpler if one sample is identical with another except for an additional item of meaning and of expression:

/koohéen/   "a priest"
/ləkoohéen/   "to a priest"

There can be little doubt as to the most likely place to divide, and we can be rather confident in identifying two tentative morphemes /lə-/ "to" and /koohéen/ "priest." Nevertheless, there are significant possibilities of error, so that this sort of division must also be considered tentative. Consider the following English example:

/hím/   "a song used in church"
/hímnəl/   "a book containing /hímz/"

The obvious division is into two morphemes /hím/ and /-nəl/. Reference to the spelling (which is, of course, never conclusive evidence for anything in spoken language!), *hymn*:*hymnal* suggests that this is not very certain. Actually the two morphemes are /him ~ himn-/ and /-əl/, as may be shown by comparing additional data: *confession*:*confessional*, *hymnology*:*geology*, *hymnody*:*psalmody*.

9. /zəkaarúuhuu/   "they remembered him"
10. /zəkaaráthuu/   "she remembered him"

If we compare 9 and 10 with the foregoing we find /-huu/ "him,"
/-úu-/ "they," and /-át-/ "she." But where 1–6 have /zəkar-/, 9 and 10
have /zəkaar-/. There is an obvious similarity of form between /zəkar-/
and /zəkaar-/ and the meaning seems to be identical. We may guess that
they are two different allomorphs of one morpheme, and proceed to check
whether this hypothesis is adequate. . . . We must leave the question . . .
but must anticipate the result. /zəkar-/ and /zəkaar-/ will be shown to
be variants of one tentative morpheme.

But though we will proceed on the basis that the hypothesis can be
sustained, we must recognize that there are certain other possibilities.
(1) /zəkar-/ and /zəkaar-/ may be different morphemes. This seems unlikely because of the similarity of meaning, but we must always remember that English translation may be misleading. (2) A somewhat less remote possibility is that /zəkar-/ and /zəkaar-/ are each sequences of
morphemes and contain two contrasting morphemes. We can do nothing
with this possibility from the data at hand, because there is no evidence
of a contrast in meaning, but this may well be the kind of difference that
does not show up clearly in translation. (3) We may have divided wrongly.
Perhaps "I" is not /-tíi-/ but /-a-tíi-/ and "they" is similarly /-aa-úu-/.
This would mean that the morpheme for "remembered" would have to
be /zək-r-/. Our only present reason for rejecting this possibility is the
comparative rarity of discontinuous morphemes. We would ordinarily
assume that morphemes are continuous sequences of phonemes unless
there is cogent reason to believe the contrary.

11. /zəkartúunii/   "you remembered me"

We have as yet no item which forms a wholly satisfactory comparison
with 11. We may, however, tentatively divide it into /zəkar/ + /-túu-/
"you" + /-nii/ "me." We do this because we have come to expect words
similar to this to be divisible into three pieces, stem + actor + person
acted upon, in that order. A division on such a basis is legitimate if done
with caution, though obviously such an identification is not as certain
as it would be if based on contrasts for each morpheme separately.

12. /sə̃martúuhaa/   "you guarded him"
13. /ləqaaxúunii/   "they took me"

Even without providing minimal pairs, 12 and 13 pretty well corro-
borate the conclusion which was drawn from 11 [above]. They thus confirm the two morphemes /-túu/ "you" and /-nii/ "me." Words 11, 12, and
13 would be rather unsatisfactory words from which to start an analysis.
However, as the analysis proceeds, the requirements for satisfactory samples relax in some respects. This is because we are now able to make our
comparisons within the framework of an emerging pattern. This pattern

involves certain classes of elements, stems, actor affixes, and affixes stating the person acted upon. It involves certain regular types of arrangement of these elements. In short, the pattern we are uncovering is a portion of the structure of the language at a level a bit deeper than mere details of individual words.

14. /zəkaaróo/   "he remembered him"

This word cannot be analyzed by comparison with the foregoing only. We can easily identify the stem as /zəkaar-/, identical in form with that of 9 and 10. But the remainder /-óo/ neither seems to consist of the expected two parts (actor and person acted upon), nor to contain the morpheme /-huu/ "him" which meaning would lead us to expect. Since the pattern does not assist us here in the way it did with 11, we must seek some more direct type of evidence.

15. /zaakártii/   "I remembered"
16. /zaakárnuu/   "we remembered"
17. /zaakár/   "he remembered"

These three forms differ from all those examined before in that they do not express a person acted upon. If we compare these words with each other, and if we compare 15 and 16 with 1 and 4, we can easily identify the affixes expressing the actor. These are /-tii/ "I" and /-nuu/ "we," identical with those we found before except for a difference in the stress. In 17, however, there is no affix expressing actor. We will tentatively list Ø (zero) "he" with the other actor affixes. This is intended merely as a convenient notation for our conclusion that the actor "he" is expressed by the absence of any affix indicating some other actor. These three forms also show another variant of the stem: /zaakár/; we shall proceed on the hypothesis that like /zəkar-/ and /zəkaar-/, it is merely another conditioned variant. This proposal should be carefully checked by methods to be discussed later.

The analysis attained in the last paragraph suggests that item 14 can be considered as divisible as follows: /zəkaar-Ø-óo/. The zero is, of course, a fiction, but it does serve to indicate that the form does show a rather closer parallelism with the others than we could see at first. That is, it contains a stem and a suffix expressing the person acted upon, and these are in the same order that we have found before. Whereas the pattern we had found did not seem to fit this word, closer examination shows that it does fit in with only slight modification. The pattern is therefore valid.

One problem posed by item 14 is taken care of in this way, but the other remains. We have identified two forms meaning "him," /-huu/ and /-óo/. These are not so obviously similar in form as /zəkar-/ and /zəkaar-/, so the hypothesis that they are allomorphs of one morpheme is not so attractive. Nevertheless, the similarity in meaning, and certain peculiarities in distribution which would be evident in a larger body of data, should induce us to check such a hypothesis. It will be sustained; /-huu ~ -óo/ is one morpheme.

In the course of the discussion we have found four stems: /zəkar-/ "remembered," /qəṭal-/ "killed," /šəmar-/ "guarded," and /ləqaax-/ "took." Comparison of these forms reveals that they all have the same vowels and differ only in consonants. /ləqaax-/ is not an exception, since it compares directly with /zəkaar-/. More data would yield a much longer list of such forms. This similarity in vowels could be a coincidence, but that possibility is slight. Another hypothesis is that these forms consist of two morphemes each. This is very attractive, but there is no means of checking it without a contrast. The following will provide such:

18. /šooméer/   "watchman"
19. /zookéer/   "one who remembers"
20. /qooṭéel/   "killer"

By comparing these with some of the earlier samples we may identify the following morphemes: /z-k-r/ "remember," /q-ṭ-l/ "kill," /š-m-r/ "guard," /l-q-x/ "take," /-oo-ée-/ "one who," and /-ə-a- ~ -ə-aa- ~ -aa-á-/ "-ed." The first four of these are roots; the last two are some sort of affixes.

Note that we were wrong in considering /zəkar-/, /zəkaar-/, and /zaakár/ as allomorphs of a single morpheme. No damage was done, however, since these three forms, each composed of two morphemes, are distributed in exactly the same way as are allomorphs. What we assumed to condition the selection of one of these three (/zəkar-/ etc.) can just as well be considered as conditioning the selection of one of the allomorphs of the affix contained in these stems. Treating larger items as morphemes is, of course, wrong, but not seriously so at preliminary stages, provided the larger units consist of associated morphemes. Ultimate simplification is, however, attained by full analysis in any case like that just discussed.

That the [preceding] analysis . . . should yield morphemes such as /z-k-r/ and /-oo-ée-/ seems at first sight somewhat disconcerting. We expect morphemes to be sequences of phonemes. These, however, are discontinuous and interdigitated. Of course there is no reason why such morphemes cannot occur, as in fact our sample has indicated they do. They are much less common than compact sequences of phonemes, but they occur in a wide variety of languages and are quite common in some. Any combination of phonemes which regularly occur together and which as a group are associated with some point in the content structure is a morpheme. We need give no regard to any peculiarity of their arrangement relative to each other and to other phonemes. Rarely do morphemes consist of separate portions widely separated by intervening material. A linguist must always be prepared for such a phenomenon, however, rare as it may be.

Hebrew and related languages are unusual in the large number of discontinuous morphemes they contain. In fact the majority of the roots are similar to {zkr}, consisting of three consonants. Various allomorphs occur: /z-k-r/ in /zaakár/ "he remembered," /-zk-r/ in /yizkóor/ "he was remembering," and /z-kr-/ in /zikríi/ "my remembrance." The three consonants never occur contiguously in any utterance; such roots are discontinuous in all their occurrences.

In other languages, discontinuous allomorphs of otherwise quite usual morphemes occur. These commonly arise as a byproduct of a special type of affix not mentioned before, an infix. An infix is a morpheme which is inserted into the stem with which it is associated. In comparison with suffixes and prefixes, infixes are comparatively rare but of sufficiently frequent occurrence to warrant notice. An example is the common Greek stem formative /-m-/ in /lambanɔ·/ "I take" from the root /lab-/. Another is Quileute (Oregon) /-č-/ "plural" in /hočkʷat'/ "white men" from /hokʷat'/ "white person." Such infixes produce discontinuous allomorphs /la-b-/ and /ho-kʷat'/ of the root morphemes with which they occur.

An affix should not be considered as an infix unless there is cogent reason to do so. Of course, any affix which actually interrupts another morpheme is an infix. In Tagalog *ginulay* "greenish blue" is formed from the root *gulay* "green vegetables." The *-in-* is clearly an infix. But it is not justifiable to consider English *-as-* in *reassign* as an infix. This word is made by two prefixes. First *as-* and *sign* form the stem *assign*. Then *re-* is added. The alternative would be to consider *re-* and *sign* as forming a stem *resign* to which an infix *-as-* is added. The latter would be immediately rejected by any native speaker of English, since he would sense that *reassign* has a much closer connection with *assign* than with *resign*. It is always better, unless there is good reason to the contrary, to consider words as being constructed of successive layers of affixes outward from the root.

Most English verbs have a form that is made by the addition of the suffix *-ed* /-d ~ -t ~ -ɨd/. This is usually known as the past. The verbs which lack this formation do, however, have some form which is used in all the same syntactic environments where we might expect such a form, and in comparable social and linguistic contexts. For example, in most of the places where *discover* /dɪskə́ver/ can be used, *find* /fáynd/ can also. Similarly, where *discovered* /dɪskə́vərd/ can be used, *found* /fáwnd/ generally can also. *Found* must therefore be considered as the past of *find* in the same sense that *discovered* is the past of *discover*.

Most of the past tenses which lack the *-ed* suffix are clearly differentiated from the base form by a difference of syllable nucleus. We may express the facts by the following equations:

discovered = *discover* + suffix *-ed*
found　　 = *find*　　 + difference of syllable nucleus

When it is so stated, it becomes evident that the difference of syllable nucleus functions in some ways like the suffix. We may consider such a difference in phonemes (they are not restricted to nuclei; consider *send*: *sent*) as a special type of morphemic element called a *replacive*.

We will use the following notation for a replacive: /aw ← (ay)/. This should be read as "/aw/ replaces /ay/." The equation above can be stated in the following form:

found = find + ou ← (i)

/fáwnd/ = /fáynd/ + /aw ← (ay)/

If this is done, then we must consider /aw ← (ay)/ as another allomorph of the morpheme whose most familiar form is *-ed* and which we can conveniently symbolize {-D_1}. This morpheme has a number of replacive allomorphs. . . . All of them are morphologically conditioned. {-Z_1}, the English noun plural affix, also has replacives among its allomorphs.

It is, of course, possible to describe a language like English without recourse to replacives. Thus, *geese* /gíys/ can be described as containing a root /g-s/ and an infix allomorph of the plural morpheme {-Z_1} of the form /-iy-/. Then the singular would have to be described as containing an infix /-uw-/, an allomorph of a singular morpheme *{X}. Except for the cases under consideration, there are no infixes, nor discontinuous morphemes in the language. To consider plurals like *geese* as formed by an infix turns out to involve many more complications than the alternative of describing replacives. As is often the case, the simpler explanation accords more closely with the native speaker's feeling about his language.

With replacives it is not easy to divide a word into its constituent morphemes. Obviously /giys/ is two morphemes, but the four phonemes cannot be neatly apportioned between them. A morpheme does not necessarily *consist* of phonemes, but all morphemes are statable in terms of phonemes. A replacive must be described in terms of two sets of phonemes: those that appear when it is present (/iy/ in *geese*) and those that appear when the replacive is absent (/uw/ in *goose*). A morpheme can consist of any recurring feature or features of the expression which can be described in terms of phonemes, without restriction of any sort.

A further, and in some respects more extreme, type of morphemic element can be seen in the past of some other English verbs. Words like *cut* and *hit* parallel such forms as *walked* in meaning and usage. There is, however, no phoneme difference of any kind between the past and the nonpast form. Nevertheless, it is in the interests of simplicity to consider all English past verb forms as consisting of a stem plus an affix. Moreover, the description must in some ways note the lack of any overt marker of the past. An expedient by which both can be done is to consider *cut* "past" as containing a root /kət/ plus a zero affix. (Zero is customarily symbolized Ø to avoid confusion with the letter O.) Ø is therefore another of the numerous allomorphs of {-D_1}.

The plural affix {-Z_1} also has a zero allomorph in *sheep*. The reason that it is necessary to describe these forms in this way rests ultimately in English content structure. Native speakers feel that the dichotomy between singular and plural is a basic characteristic of nouns. Every individual occurrence of any noun must be either singular or plural. *Sheep* is ambiguous, but not indifferent to the distinction. That is, in any given utterance the word is thought of by speaker and hearer as either singular or plural. Sometimes they may disagree, plural being intended and singular being perceived, or vice versa. It requires conscious effort for a person accustomed only to English patterns to conceive of noun referents without consideration of number. To attempt to do so impresses many people as being "too abstract." Yet they feel under no such compulsion to distinguish the exact number if it is more than two.

In other words, there is a covert difference between *sheep* "singular" and *sheep* "plural," and this is linguistically significant as may be seen from the fact that it controls the forms of certain other words in *This sheep is. . . . : These sheep are. . . .* The recognition of a ∅ allomorph of {-Z₁} is merely a convenient device for entering all this into our description. . . .

FOR DISCUSSION AND REVIEW

Please see the following selection by Professor Gleason, "Morphology: Three Exercises."

20

≡

Morphology: Three Exercises

H. A. Gleason, Jr.

The following selection by H. A. Gleason, Jr., provides practice in morphemic analysis and will help you to assess your understanding of the concepts introduced in "The Identification of Morphemes." Believing that students of linguistics need to work with problems drawn from a variety of languages, Professor Gleason prepared a Workbook in Descriptive Linguistics *to accompany his textbook* An Introduction to Descriptive Linguistics, *from which the previous selection was excerpted. The following exercises have been taken from that workbook. In the preface to the workbook, Professor Gleason notes that although there is some inevitable distortion in presenting short samples of languages, "All the problems represent real languages" and "the complexities are all genuine" (p. 2).*

Swahili (East Africa)

1.	atanipenda	he will like me
2.	atakupenda	he will like you
3.	atampenda	he will like him
4.	atatupenda	he will like us
5.	atawapenda	he will like them
6.	nitakupenda	I will like you
7.	nitampenda	I will like him
8.	nitawapenda	I will like them
9.	utanipenda	you will like me
10.	utampenda	you will like him
11.	tutampenda	we will like him
12.	watampenda	they will like him
13.	atakusumbua	he will annoy you
14.	unamsumbua	you are annoying him
15.	atanipiga	he will beat me
16.	atakupiga	he will beat you
17.	atampiga	he will beat him
18.	ananipiga	he is beating me
19.	anakupiga	he is beating you
20.	anampiga	he is beating him

21.	amenipiga	he has beaten me
22.	amekupiga	he has beaten you
23.	amempiga	he has beaten him
24.	alinipiga	he beat me
25.	alikupiga	he beat you
26.	alimpiga	he beat him
27.	wametulipa	they have paid us
28.	tulikulipa	we paid you

Note: The forms glossed "he" could as well be glossed "she." The forms glossed "you" are all singular. The plural "you" is omitted from this problem because of a minor complication.

Give the morphemes associated with each of the following meanings:

subjects:	_____ I	objects:	_____ me
	_____ you		_____ you
	_____ he		_____ him
	_____ we		_____ us
	_____ they		_____ them
tenses:	_____ future	stems:	_____ like
	_____ present		_____ beat
	_____ perfect		_____ annoy
	_____ past		_____ pay

What is the order of the morphemes in a word?

Supply the probable forms for the following meanings:

_____ I have beaten them	_____ you have beaten us
_____ they are beating me	_____ we beat them
_____ they have annoyed me	_____ I am paying him

Supply the probable meanings for the following forms:

atanilipa	_____	walikupenda	_____
utawapiga	_____	nimemsumbua	_____

Ilocano (Philippine Islands)

1.	píŋgan	dish	piŋpíŋgan	dishes
2.	tálon	field	taltálon	fields
3.	dálan	road	daldálan	roads
4.	bíag	life	bibíag	lives
5.	nuáŋ	carabao	nunuáŋ	caribao
6.	úlo	head	ulúlo	heads

What type of affix is used to form the plural?

Describe its form and relationship to the stem. Be sure to make clear exactly how much is involved.

Given /múla/ "plant," what would be the most likely form meaning "plants"?

Given /tawtáwa/ "windows," what would be the most likely form meaning "window"?

Dinka (Sudan)

1.	pal	knife	paal	knives	_____
2.	bit	spear	biit	spears	_____
3.	ɣot	hut	ɣoot	huts	_____
4.	čiin	hand	čin	hands	_____
5.	agɔɔk	monkey	agɔk	monkeys	_____
6.	kat	frame	kɛt	frames	_____
7.	mač	fire	mĕč	fires	_____
8.	beñ	chief	bañ	chiefs	_____
9.	dom	field	dum	fields	_____
10.	dɔk	boy	dak	boys	_____
11.	gɔl	clan	gal	clans	_____
12.	tuɔŋ	egg	tɔŋ	eggs	_____
13.	muɔr	bull	mior	bulls	_____
14.	buɔl	rabbit	bial	rabbits	_____
15.	met	child	miit	children	_____
16.	ǰoŋ	dog	ǰɔk	dogs	_____
17.	yič	ear	yit	ears	_____

What type of affix is shown in [these] data? List the forms of the affixes in the spaces provided opposite the stems with which they are found. Do not attempt to find conditioning factors; the distribution of allomorphs is morphologically conditioned. This is very frequently true of this type of affix.

21

Word-Making: Some Sources of New Words

W. Nelson Francis

English has the largest vocabulary of any language in the world—over 600,000 words—in part, at least, because English has borrowed words from every language with which it has had any contact. (The rate of borrowing, interestingly, appears to be slowing; and English has become an exporter of words, much to the dismay of the French, among others.) But even without borrowing, English, like all other living languages, has a variety of ways of forming new words. Sometimes, of course, we use an old word with a new meaning, as when cool *("chilly") became* cool *("outstanding"). But many times we actually create new words; and when we do, we create them by very regular and predictable processes. In the following excerpt from his book* The English Language: An Introduction, *Professor W. Nelson Francis discusses the major ways, in addition to borrowing from other languages and semantic change, that new words are created and become a part of the vocabulary of English.*

Though borrowing has been the most prolific source of additions to the vocabulary of English, we acquire or create new words in several other ways. Those which will be discussed here, in descending order of importance, are *derivation, compounding, functional shift, back formation* and *clipping, proper names, imitation, blending,* and *original coinage.*

DERIVATION

The derivational process consists of using an existing word—or in some cases a bound morpheme* or morphemic structure—as a stem to

---

* Editors' note: Francis earlier tells us: "The smallest meaningful units of language—those which cannot be subdivided into smaller meaningful units—are called *morphemes.* In combinations like *rooster, greenness, lucky, widen,* and *strongly,* all of which are made up of two morphemes, one morpheme carries the principal part of the meaning of the whole. This is called the *base* (or sometimes the *root*). The bases in the examples are *roost, green, luck, wide,* and *strong.* These . . . bases are capable of standing by themselves and of entering rather freely into grammatical combinations.

which affixes are attached. Thus our imaginary word *pandle* might become the stem for such derivatives as *pandler, pandlette, depandle,* and *repandlize.* Affixes like these are called *productive;* all native speakers know their meanings and feel free to add them to various kinds of stems in accordance with analogy or the rules of English derivation. By this process any new word, whatever its source, may almost immediately become the nucleus of a cluster of derivatives. Thus *plane,* formed by clipping from *airplane,* had produced *emplane* and *deplane,* presumably by analogy with *entrain* and *detrain,* themselves formed by analogy with *embark* and *debark,* which were borrowed from French. When *telegraph* was formed by compounding of two Greek elements, it soon gave rise to *telegrapher, telegraphy, telegraphic,* and *telegraphist,* all of which were self-explaining derivatives.

So obvious is the process of forming derivatives with productive affixes that all of us probably do it much more frequently than we realize. The words we thus "create" in most cases have been frequently used before and are listed in the dictionary, but we may not know that. This process allows us to expand our vocabulary without specifically memorizing new words. But this reliance on analogical derivation may sometimes trap us into creating new words that are unnecessary because other derivatives already exist and have become standard. The student who wrote about Hamlet's *unableness to overcome his mental undecidedness* undoubtedly was familiar with *inability* and *indecision,* but under the pressure of an examination he forgot them and created his own derivatives instead.

COMPOUNDING

In a sense, compounding is a special form of derivation in which, instead of adding affixes (bound forms) to a stem, two or more words (or in some cases bound bases) are put together to make a new lexical unit. Compounding has been a source of new words in English since earliest times, and is particularly common in present-day English. Perusal of any daily paper will turn up countless examples of compounds that are new within the last few years or months: *launching pad, blast off, jet-port, freeway, ski-tow, freeloader, featherbedding, sit-in.* Our writing system does not indicate whether items like *weather satellite* are compounds or constructions. Many of them begin as constructions but then assume the

---

For this reason they are called *free bases.* Other bases cannot stand alone or enter freely into grammatical combinations but must always appear in close affiliation with other morphemes. These are called *bound bases.* We can recognize a common base *turb* in such words as *disturb, perturb,* and *turbulent;* it never stands alone as the *green* of *greenness* does, so it is a bound base."

characteristic stress patterns of compounds: some people still pronounce *ice cream* with the stress pattern of a construction (as in *iced tea*), but most treat it as a compound (as in *iceboat*). Some of the older compounds have gone through sound (and spelling) changes that have completely obscured their compound origin. Typical of these is *lord*, which began in early Old English as *hlāf-weard*, a compound of the ancestors of our *loaf* and *ward*, and passed through the stages of OE *hlāford* and ME *loverd* to its present monosyllabic form. Other examples are *woman,* originally a compound of the ancestors of *wife* and *man*, and *hussy*, from *house* and *wife,* hence etymologically a doublet of *housewife.*

The semantic relationships between the parts of compounds are very varied. If compounds are thought of as the product of a transformation process, this variety can be revealed by reconstructing the phrase from which the compound might have been created. This may range from a simple modification, in which the transformation involves only a change in stress pattern *(hot dog, blackboard, bluebird)*, to complete predication, where the transformation involves complicated reordering and deletion (as in *salesman* from *man who makes sales* or *movie camera* from *camera that takes movies*). Compounds may themselves enter into compounds to produce elaborate structures like *aircraft carrier* and *real estate salesman.* These must be considered compounds, since they have the characteristic stress pattern with the strongest stress on the first element *(aírcràft càrrier, réal estàte sàlesman),* in contrast to the stress pattern of modification constructions (as in *aírcràft desígner* or *rèal estàte invéstment).*

One special group of compounds, most of them of quite recent origin, includes those words — mostly technical and scientific terms — which are made up of morphemes borrowed from Greek. Many of the elements so used were free forms — words — in Greek, but must be considered bound bases in English. The practice of compounding them began in Greek: *philosophia* is compounded from *philos* "fond of" and *sophia* "wisdom." Words of this sort were borrowed into Latin in ancient times, and ultimately reached English by way of French. Renaissance scholars, who knew Greek and recognized the combining elements, began to make new combinations which did not exist in the original Greek. With the growth of scientific knowledge from the seventeenth century on, new technical and scientific terms were commonly invented this way.

Words created can be roughly divided into two groups. The first includes those which have wide circulation in the general vocabulary — like *telephone, photograph,* and *thermometer.* These are constructed out of a relatively small number of morphemes, whose meanings are well known:

tele	"far, distant"	*meter*	"measure"
phone	"sound"	*dyna*	"power"
photo	"light"	*hydro*	"water, moisture"
graph	"write, mark"	*bio*	"life"
thermo	"heat"	*morph*	"shape, form"

Inventors and manufacturers of new products often create names for their inventions from elements of this sort. Sometimes the Greek elements are combined with Latin ones, as in *automobile* (Greek *autos* "self," Latin *mobilis* "movable") and *television,* or even with native English elements, as in *dynaflow.* Recent creations in this group are *astronaut* and *cosmonaut,* from Greek *aster* "star," *kosmos* "universe," and *nautes* "sailor." Actually *cosmonaut* was first used in Russian, whence it was borrowed, but since both of its bases were already in use in English (as in *cosmology* and *aeronaut*), it might just as well have originated in English.

The second group of Greek-based compounds comprises the large number of technical and scientific terms whose use is almost wholly restricted to specialists. As in the case of *cosmonaut,* most of these words are readily interchangeable among the languages in which scientific publication is extensive. Since it is often difficult if not impossible to determine the language in which they were first used, the Merriam-Webster editors have recently made use of the term *International Scientific Vocabulary* (abbreviated ISV) to describe them. A few examples of wide enough circulation to be included in an abridged dictionary are the following:

hypsography: "recording *(graphy)* of elevation *(hypso)*"

telethermoscope: "instrument that perceives *(scope)* heat *(thermo)* at a distance *(tele)*"

electroencephalograph: "instrument that records *(graph)* electric current *(electro)* within *(en)* the head *(cephalo)*"

schizogenesis: "reproduction *(genesis)* by division *(schizo)*"

In all cases, since at least two of the combining elements are bases, these words must be considered compounds. They may also give rise to derivatives formed by the addition of affixes in regular patterns, such as *electroencephalography* and *schizogenetic.* It is in this way, rather than by direct borrowing, that Greek has made its great contribution to the English vocabulary.

FUNCTIONAL SHIFT

Since the late Middle English period, when most of the inflections surviving from Old English finally disappeared, it has been easy to shift a word from one part of speech to another without altering its form, at least in the unmarked base form. A verb like *walk* can be turned into a noun simply by using it in a syntactic position reserved for nouns, as in *he took a walk,* where the determiner *a* marks *walk* as a noun, direct object of *took.* This process, called *functional shift,* is an important concomitant of the historical change of English from a synthetic to an analytic language, and has greatly enlarged the vocabulary in a very economical way. Since the words so created belong to a different part of speech and hence have a different grammatical distribution from that of the original, they must be considered new words, homonymous in the base form with the words from which they were derived, rather than merely extensions of meaning. From another point of view, they may be thought of as derivatives with zero affixes. In some cases they may take a different stress pattern in their new use: the noun *implement*, with weak stress and the weak central vowel /ə/ in the last syllable, when shifted to a verb took secondary stress on the last syllable, whose vowel was changed to /ɛ/. Since there is overt change in pronunciation, this is true derivation rather than functional shift. But the two processes are obviously closely related.

Older instances of functional shift commonly produced nouns from verbs: in addition to *walk*, already cited, we might mention *run, steal, laugh, touch, buy, break*, and many others. In present-day English the shift from noun to verb is much in favor. In the past, short words like *brush* and *perch* were sometimes shifted from noun to verb, but today, longer nouns like *implement, position, process, contact* are often used as verbs. Even compound nouns get shifted to verbs; the secretary who said "I didn't back-file the letter, I waste-basketed it" was speaking twentieth-century English, however inelegant.

BACK FORMATION AND CLIPPING

Back formation and clipping are two modes of word creation which can be classed together as different types of *reduction*. In each case, a shorter word is made from a longer one, so that the effect is the opposite of derivation and compounding. Back formation makes use of analogy to produce a sort of reverse derivation. The existence of *creation, create*, and *donation* readily suggests that if there is not a verb *donate* there should be. This seems so natural to us that it is hard to believe that less than a century ago *donate* was considered an American barbarism by many puristically inclined British speakers of English.[1] Other words that have come into English by back formation are *edit* (from *editor*), *burgle* (from *burglar*), *enthuse* (from *enthusiasm*), *televise* (from *television*, by analogy with pairs like *supervise : supervision*), *automate* (from *automation*), *laze* (from *lazy*), and many more. Once pairs of words like these have become established, only the historical record proving prior use of the longer forms serves to distinguish them from normal derivational pairs.

---

[1] See H. L. Mencken, *The American Language*, 4th ed. (New York: Alfred A. Knopf, 1936), pp. 121, 165.

Clippings, on the other hand, are shortenings without regard to derivational analogy. They are frequent in informal language, especially spoken, as in the campus and classroom use of *exam, lab, math,* and *dorm.* They are possible because often a single syllable, usually the one bearing the main stress, is sufficient to identify a word, especially in a rather closely restricted context, so that the remaining syllables are redundant and can be dropped. Most of them preserve a colloquial flavor and are limited to the special vocabularies of occupational groups. Others, however — often over the objections of purists — attain wide circulation and may ultimately replace the longer forms on most or all levels of usage. Some that have done so are *van* (from *caravan*), *bus* (from *omnibus*), *cello* (from *violoncello*), *mob* (from Latin *mobile vulgus* "unstable crowd"), *piano* (from *pianoforte*), and *fan* (in sense "ardent devotee," from *fanatic*). Others which are in acceptable, though perhaps characteristically informal, use alongside the longer unclipped words are *phone* (for *telephone*), *taxi* and *cab* (from *taxicab*) and *plane* (for *airplane* or older *aeroplane*). A rather special form of clipping is that which reduces long compounds or idiomatic fixed phrases to one of their elements — often the modifying element rather than the head — as in *express train, car* from *motor car,* and *outboard* from *outboard motor (boat).* This process often accounts for what otherwise seem strange transfers of meaning.

An extreme form of clipping is that which reduces words to their abbreviations and longer phrases to their initials. Abbreviation is, of course, a standard device of the writing system to save space by reducing the length of common or often repeated words. Usually it is confined to writing, and to rather informal writing at that. But some common abbreviations have been adopted in speech and ways have been found to pronounce them. The common abbreviations for the two halves of the day — A.M. and P.M. — which stand for the Latin phrases *ante meridiem* ("before noon") and *post meridiem* ("after noon") are frequently used in speech, where they are pronounced /é: + èm/ and /pí:èm/. These must indeed be considered words, though their spelling is that of abbreviations. The same is true of B.C. and A.D. in dates, O.K. (which has become an international word), U.S., G.I., L.P., TNT, TV, and DDT. In all these cases the pronunciation is simply the syllabic names of the letters, usually with the strongest stress on the last: /yù: + és/, /dì: + dì: + tí:/, and so on.

If the initial letters of a phrase, used as an abbreviation, happen to make a combination that is pronounceable, what results is an *acronym* — a word whose spelling represents the initial letters of a phrase. Though very popular in recent times, acronyms are by no means an innovation of the twentieth century. The early Christians made a famous one when they took the initials of the Greek phrase {Ἰησοῦς Χριστὸς θεοῦ υἱὸς σωτήρ} ("Jesus Christ, son of God, Savior") to make the Greek word ἰχθύς ("fish") and adopted the fish as a symbol of Christ. Acronyms have become more frequent in English since World War II. Everyone talks about

NATO, UNESCO, and NASA, often without being able to supply the longer title whose initials created the acronym. In fact, acronyms have become so popular that some longer titles have been created by a kind of back formation from the desired initials. It was certainly more than a happy accident that led the Navy in World War II to call its feminine branch "Women Assigned to Volunteer Emergency Service," or WAVES. More recently an organization devoted to finding foster parents for orphan children from foreign lands has called itself "World Adoption International Fund" so its initials would spell WAIF.

PROPER NAMES

The giving of individual names to persons, geographic features, deities, and sometimes to animals is a universal human practice, apparently as old as language itself. A proper name, since it is closely restricted to a single specific referent, does not have the general and varied distribution and reference that characterize ordinary nouns. But there is frequent interchange across the line separating proper names from other words. Many proper names, such as *Taylor, Smith, Clark,* and *Wright,* are derived from common nouns describing occupations; others like *Brown, Strong,* and *Wild* derive from adjectives that may once have described the person so named. Placenames also frequently show their derivation from common nouns, as in *Northfield, Portsmouth,* and *Fairmount.*

There has also been interchange in the other direction, by which the proper name of a person or place becomes generalized in meaning, usually to refer to a product or activity connected with the referent of the proper name. One famous example is the name *Caesar,* originally a nickname coined from the Latin verb *caedo* "to cut" to describe Julius Caesar, who was cut from his mother's womb by the operation still called *Caesarian section.* The name was assumed by Julius's nephew Octavius, the first Roman emperor, and then by the subsequent emperors, so that it became virtually a synonym for *imperator* "emperor." In its later history it was borrowed into Germanic, ultimately becoming German *Kaiser* (there was also a Middle English word *kayser,* now obsolete), and into Slavonic, whence came *tsar.* Another interesting set of words derived from names are the adjectives *mercurial, saturnine,* and *jovial,* referring to temperaments supposed to be characteristic of people under the dominance of the planets Mercury, Saturn, and Jupiter. The corresponding *venereal* (from *Venus*) has been restricted in meaning almost entirely to medical use, but *venery* is still a rather high-flown word for love-making. Those supposed to derive instability from the changeable moon used to be called *lunatic* (from Latin *luna,* the moon). The punishment visited upon Tantalus, forever doomed to be within sight of food and water that receded when he reached for it, has given us the verb *tantalize,* formed by adding the productive suffix *-ize* (itself ultimately derived from Greek) to his name. Also ultimately Greek in origin are *hector* ("a bully, to bully") from the Trojan hero in the *Iliad* and *mentor* ("teacher" — now often used in the sports pages for "athletic coach") from the adviser of Telemachus in the *Odyssey*.

During the history of English since the beginning of the Middle English period, various words have been derived from proper names. Some earlier ones are *dunce* (from the scholastic philosopher Duns Scotus — used in ridicule of scholastic philosophy in the later sixteenth century), *pander* (from the character Pandarus in Chaucer's *Troilus and Criseyde*, c. 1385), *mawmet* (from Mahomet; at first it meant "idol," later "puppet, doll"). The Bible, widely read from Reformation times on and frequently discussed for its symbolic as well as its literal or historical meaning, has contributed many words of this sort, such as *jeremiad* ("a denunciatory tirade"), *babel*, *lazar* (from Lazarus; common for *leper* in Middle English), *maudlin* (from Mary Magdalen and her noted tears), and *simony* ("taking or giving money for church offices," from Simon Magus). On the border between proper and common nouns are names of Biblical and other personages taken in figurative meanings, though usually capitalized in writing, indicating that the transfer to common nouns is not complete: *the old Adam, raising Cain, a doubting Thomas, a Daniel come to judgment.*

Some proper names that have assumed general meanings have undergone pronunciation changes that obscure their origins. The adjective *tawdry* ("cheap and flashy") comes from a clipping of *Saint Audrey*, and presumably was first used to describe a kind of cheap lace sold at St. Audrey's Fair. *Bedlam*, which to us means "uproar, total confusion," was a proper name as late as the eighteenth century, when it was used as a short name for *St. Mary of Bethlehem*, a London insane asylum. The word *mawkin*, used dialectally in England for "scarecrow," comes from *Malkyn*, a girl's name, ultimately a nickname from *Mary*. The parallel nickname *Moll* gave rise to an American slang word for a criminal's girl. The history of *doll* is similar but more complicated; it passed from a clipped form of *Dorothy* to describe a miniature (usually female) figure, then to describe a small and pretty girl.

The names of historical characters — often those of unsavory reputation — have given us some rather common words. One of the most interesting of these is *guy*, from *Guy Fawkes*, used in England to describe the effigies of that notable traitor which are customarily carried in procession and burned on November 5, the anniversary of the discovery of his "Gunpowder Plot." The term came to mean "a figure of fun, a butt of scorn," and as a verb "to poke fun at, tease." In America it has become a universal colloquial term for any male not held in high respect. In phrases like *a nice guy* (when not used ironically) it has lost all of its original pejorative flavor.

Names of products derived from the names of their places of origin are rather plentiful in English. Textiles like *calico* (from *Calicut*, or *Calcutta*), *denim* (*serge de Nîmes*), *cashmere* (*Kashmir*), and *worsted* (from the name of a town in Norfolk, England) are well known. So are products like *china* (clipped from *chinaware* from *China ware*), *gin* (clipped from *Geneva*), *cognac,* and *cayenne.* Specialized and technical vocabularies are especially fond of words adapted from proper names. Skiing has its *telemark* and *christiania* (usually clipped to *christy*); librarians speak of *Dewey decimal classification* and *Cutter numbers;* horticulturalists of *fuchsia, dahlia,* and *wistaria;* physicists of *roentgen rays, curies,* and *angstrom units;* electricians of *ohms, watts,* and *amperes;* doctors of *rickettsia* and *Bright's disease.*

IMITATION

A relatively small number of words in English apparently owe their origin to attempts to imitate natural sounds. *Bow-wow, meow, baa, moo,* and other words for animal cries are supposed to remind us of the noises made by dogs, cats, sheep, and cows. They are not accurate imitations, since they are pronounced with sounds characteristic of the sound-system of English, which these animals, not being native speakers of English, do not use. Other languages have other, often quite different imitative words. Both *cock-a-doodle-doo* and *kikiriki* are supposedly imitative of a rooster's crow; unless we assume that English and Greek roosters make quite different sounds, we must attribute the difference between these words to the differing sound-systems of the two languages.

Related to imitation is the phenomenon sometimes called *sound symbolism:* the habit of associating a certain type or class of meanings with a certain sound or cluster of sounds. There seems to be in English an association between the initial consonant cluster *sn-* and the nose *(snarl, sneer, sneeze, sniff, snivel, snore, snort, snout,* and *snuffle).* When slang words referring to or involving the nose are coined they may begin with this cluster, as in *snook* and *snoop.* English speakers associate the sound-combination spelled *-ash* (/æš/) with a sudden loud sound or rapid, turbulent, or destructive motion, as in *crash, dash, flash, smash,* and *splash;* and a final *-er* on verbs suggests rapidly repeated, often rhythmic motion, as in *flicker, flutter, hover, quiver, shimmer, waver.* This last example is perhaps a morpheme in its own right, though to call it one would give us a large number of bound bases that occur nowhere else. But it is well on the way to the morphemic status which certainly must be accorded to the *-le* or *-dle* of *handle, treadle,* and *spindle.*

Imitation was once considered so important as to be made the basis for a theory of the origin of language—the so-called "bow-wow theory." This theory is commonly discounted nowadays.

BLENDING

Blending is a combination of clipping and compounding, which makes new words by putting together fragments of existing words in new combinations. It differs from derivation in that the elements thus combined are not morphemes at the time the blends are made, though they may become so afterward as a result of the blending process, especially if several blends are made with the same element and the phenomenon of *false etymology* is present.

The poem "Jabberwocky" in Lewis Carroll's *Through the Looking Glass* contains many ingenious blends, though only a few of them (called *portmanteau* words by Humpty Dumpty in the book) have passed into the general vocabulary. Thus *slithy* (from *lithe* and *slimy*) and *mimsy* (from *miserable* and *flimsy*) are not used outside the poem, but *chortle* (*chuckle* and *snort*) and *galumphing* (*galloping* and *triumphing*) are not uncommon words, though they are usually restricted to colloquial or facetious use.

The history of *-burger* illustrates the way in which blending can give rise to a new morpheme. The name *Hamburger steak* (varying with *Hamburg steak*) was given to a kind of ground beef in America in the 1880s. It was soon shortened by phrase-clipping to *hamburger*, losing its proper-name quality in the process. The *-er* here is simply the normal German suffix for making an adjective from a proper noun (as in *Brandenburger Tor* "Brandenburg Gate"). But to those who did not know German, the word looked (and sounded) like a compound of *ham* and *burger*. So the *-burger* part was clipped and combined with various words or parts of words to make *cheeseburger, deerburger, buffaloburger,* and many more. These have the form of compounds made up of one free base and a bound base *-burger.* Meanwhile by further clipping, *hamburger,* already short for *hamburger steak sandwich,* was cut down to *burger,* which now became a free form — a word. Thus what began as the last two syllables of a German proper adjective has become first a bound morpheme and then a full word in English.

Other morphemes which owe their origin to blending are *-rama,* *-orium, -teria,* and *-omat.* The first of these began with words of Greek origin like *panorama* and *cyclorama.*[2] The combining elements in Greek were *pan* "all," *kyklos* "circle, wheel," and *horama* "view," a noun derived from the verb *horan* "see." But the *-rama* part of these words was blended with *cine* (from *cinema*) to make *cinerama,* describing a type of wide-screen motion picture. Subsequently *-rama* was blended with various other elements to make new words like *colorama* and *vistarama,* as well as many trade and commercial names. It certainly must now be considered a separate morpheme, conveying a vague notion of grandeur and sweep (or so its users hope) to the words in which it is used. Similarly *-orium,* split off from *emporium* (a rather fancy Latin loan-word for "shop"), *-teria,* split off from the Spanish loan-word *cafeteria,* and *-omat,* split off from the trade name *Automat,* itself a clipping from *automatic,*

---

[2] See John Lotz, "The Suffix '-rama,'" *American Speech,* 39 (1954), 156–158.

have become separate morphemes, as in *lubritorium, valeteria,* and *laundromat.* The process of blending has thus produced not only new words but new morphemes capable of entering with some freedom into new compounds and derivatives. Many of the words thus coined never get any farther than their first application by an enterprising advertiser or proprietor, and those that do usually have a brief life. But a few seem to fill a real need and remain as part of the general vocabulary of English.

COINAGE

Very few words are simply made up out of unrelated, meaningless elements. The other resources for making new words and the abundant vocabularies of other languages available for borrowing supply so many easy ways of producing new words that outright coinage seldom suggests itself. The outright coinage — unlike the compound, clipping, derivative, and blend — is also hard to remember because it has no familiar elements to aid the memory. So wholly new coinages are both harder to make and less likely to be remembered and used. It is no wonder that they are relatively rare. Some words, however, are indubitable coinages, and others for which etymologists have found no source may be tentatively assumed to be. Words like *quiz, pun, slang,* and *fun* have no cognates in other Germanic languages, cannot be traced to other languages as loan-words, and, since they are monosyllabic, are not compounds or derivatives, though they might be blends to which we have lost the key. One can imagine that *slang* — an eighteenth-century creation — combined elements from *slovenly* and *language,* but this is pure guesswork. These, together with more recent words, most of them facetious or slangy, like *hooch* and *pooch, snob* and *gob* ("sailor"), most probably originated as free coinages, sometimes involving sound symbolism.

More elaborate coinages, having more than one syllable, are likely to combine original elements with various other processes of word formation, especially derivation. Thus the stems of *segashuate, sockdologer,* and *spifflicated* seem to be coinages, but the suffixes are recognizable morphemes. In fact, it would be exceedingly unlikely for a native speaker to coin a word of more than one syllable without making use of one or more of the word-forming devices we have been discussing.

As even this brief chapter must have made obvious, the vocabulary of English is large, complex, highly diversified in origin, and constantly changing. No dictionary, however large, can contain it all. Or, if such a dictionary should be prepared, it would be out of date by the time it was printed, since new meanings, new borrowings, and new creations are being added every day. Nor can any single individual know it all. Speakers of English share a large vocabulary in common, it is true, but every individual speaker has his own unique inventory of the less commonly used words and meanings, reflecting his unique experience with language.

Many people — perhaps most people — go through life with a vocabulary adequate only to their daily needs, picking up new words when some new facet of life makes it necessary, but never indulging in curiosity and speculation about words. Others are wordlovers — collectors and connoisseurs. They like to measure one word against another, trace their etymologies and shifts of meaning, use them in new and exciting or amusing combinations. They play word-games like *Scrabble* and *Anagrams*, they do crossword puzzles, they make puns and rhymes and nonsense jingles. Some make poems, which are the highest form of word-game. But even those who aspire no further than to the writing of good clear expository prose must become at least amateur connoisseurs of words. Only this way — not by formal exercises or courses in vocabulary-building — will they learn to make the best possible use of the vast and remarkable lexicon of English.

FOR DISCUSSION AND REVIEW

1. Why is an understanding of morphology important in the study of word formation?

2. What role does analogy play in the process of forming words by derivation?

3. Compounding is of particular importance in areas involving extensive technological development. One study found that 19 percent of the words in a series of NASA reports were in nominal compounds, compared to only 3 percent in articles published in the *American Scholar*. Why might this situation exist?

4. Keep a list of nominal compounds that you encounter in your reading during the course of a week. Where are you most likely to find them? What is the longest one you found? (The author of the study referred to in question 3 found a nominal compound that contained 13 words!)

5. Consider the order of importance of the various methods of word formation listed by Francis in the first paragraph of this selection. Discuss the possible causes of this particular ordering or of some of its components. Why, for example, are derivation and compounding so important? Why are imitation and blending so relatively unimportant?

6. Identify the process of word formation in the following words: *gas, contrail, happenstance, spa, diesel, flu, laser, smog, meow, syphilis.*

Projects for "Phonetics, Phonology, and Morphology"

Note: Since a large number of exercises are included for the readings in Part Four, and because short exercises are particularly useful for these topics, we have suggested fewer long projects than usual.

1. An excellent project, if you speak another language, is to compare the significant units of sound of the two languages. For example, German does not have the sound with which the English word *judge* begins and ends. As a variation of this project, you could make a similar comparison for two different dialects of English. In either case, try to make your data as complete as possible.

2. Examine the following: *"These foser glipses* have *volbicly merfed* the *wheeple* their *preebs."*[1] Although you do not know the meaning of any of the italicized words (How big is a "wheeple"? How does one "merf"? Are "glipses" good to eat?), you do know a great deal about them. What can you say about the form, function, and meaning of the words? On what basis?

3. Using either *The Barnhart Dictionary of New English Since 1963* or *The Second Barnhart Dictionary of New English*, choose a random sample of at least one hundred words and identify their source (e.g., borrowing, derivation, compounding). Prepare a report of your findings. Does your order of importance for processes of word formation coincide with that suggested by Francis? If not, try to suggest some reasons why it doesn't.

4. Read John Algeo's "Where Do All the New Words Come From?" in the Winter 1980 edition of *American Speech*. Prepare a report summarizing his findings. You may wish to compare them with what Francis says in his article in this section.

5. Many linguists and grammarians complain that our orthographic system contains too many ambiguities and too many uncertainties with regards to our pronunciations. One famous example is the spelling of "fish" by George Bernard Shaw as "g-h-o-t-i." The "gh" he takes from the word "enough," the "o" from the word "women," and the "ti" from the word "nation." Divide the class into groups of four or five and create your own lists of the names of the people in your class. How many of the names are decipherable by others? What does this tell you or reaffirm about our spelling system? What problems might this cause?

6. Select an article from your favorite magazine or journal and bring

---

[1] This example comes from Kenneth G. Wilson, "English Grammars and the Grammar of English," which appears in the front matter of Funk & Wagnalls Standard College Dictionary: Text Edition (New York: Harcourt, Brace & World, 1963).

a copy to class. In groups, select a paragraph or two and simplify the spelling of the words in the article. Feel free to eliminate unnecessary letters and to simplify as many consonant clusters as you wish. In order to further simplify the spelling you may choose to substitute letters for the ones in the printed words and do away with others altogether. After your "cleaning" is done, reinsert the paragraph in your article and exchange with another group. Are your classmates able to read the passage? Which sounds in our language appear to have the greatest variety of spelling? Which letter appears to represent the greatest variety of sounds? What would you propose as a revised English alphabet? What have you learned about our spelling system? As a result of this exercise, do you foresee any difficulties for foreign-language speakers trying to learn English?

Selected Bibliography

Adams, V. *An Introduction to Modern English Word Formation*. London: Longman, 1973. (A very thorough analysis.)

Anderson, Stephen R. *The Organization of Phonology*. New York: Academic Press, 1974. (Technical and comprehensive.)

Aronoff, Mark. *Word Formation in Generative Grammar*. Cambridge, MA: The MIT Press, 1976. (Excellent, but not for beginners.)

Chomsky, Noam, and Morris Halle. *The Sound Pattern of English*. New York: Harper & Row, 1968. (The first major application of transformational-generative theory to phonology.)

Cole, Ronald A., "Navigating the Slippery Stream of Speech," *Psychology Today* (April 1979).

Denes, Peter, and E. N. Pinson. *The Speech Chain*. Garden City, NY: Harper & Row, 1968. (A clear introduction to speech perception, speech production, and acoustic phonetics.)

Dyson, Alice Tanner. "Phonetic Inventories of 2- and 3-Year-Old Children" in *Journal of Speech and Hearing Disorders*, Feb. 1988, pp. 89–93. (A further detailed study into phonological acquisition of young children.)

Halle, Morris. "Knowledge Unlearned and Untaught: What Speakers Know About the Sounds of Their Language." In Morris Halle, Joan Bresnan, and George A. Miller (eds.), *Linguistic Theory and Psychological Reality*. Cambridge, MA: The MIT Press, 1978. (Very interesting; nontechnical.)

Halle, Morris, and G. N. Clements. *Problem Book in Phonology: A Workbook for Introductory Courses in Linguistics and in Modern Phonology*. Cambridge, MA: The MIT Press, 1983. (Contains an excellent introduction [pp. 2–25] and six sections with exercises based on a wide variety of languages.)

Hyman, Larry M. *Phonology: Theory and Analysis*. New York: Holt, Rinehart and Winston, 1975. (Important but difficult.)

Kenstowicz, M. and C. Kisseberth. *Generative Phonology: Description and Theory*. New York: Academic Press, 1979. (Technical but important.)

Ladefoged, Peter. *A Course in Phonetics*, 2nd ed. New York: Harcourt Brace Jovanovich, 1982. (An excellent introduction. The author writes, "This is a *course* in phonetics, not a book about phonetics.")

Matthews, P. H. *Morphology: An Introduction to the Theory of Word-Structure*. Cambridge Eng.: Cambridge University Press, 1974. (A comprehensive introductory textbook.)

Preisser, Debra A., B. W. Hodson, E. P. Paden. "Developmental Phonology: 18–29 Months" in *Journal of Speech and Hearing Disorders*, May 1988, pp. 125–130. (A detailed hands-on examination of the phonological processes of children.)

Schane, S. A. *Generative Phonology*. Englewood Cliffs, NJ: Prentice-Hall, 1973. (An introduction, but technical.)

Sommerstein, A. *Modern Phonology*. Baltimore: University Park Press, 1977. (Another very good introduction.)

Sproat, Richard. *Morphology and Computation*. Cambridge: Massachusetts Institute of Technology, 1992. (A useful overview of issues in morphology, computational morphology, and linguistics.)

PART FIVE

SYNTAX, SEMANTICS, AND DISCOURSE

As we stated in the introduction to Part Four, most linguists agree that languages are best described in terms of their basic systems or divisions. In this part, we focus on syntax, semantics, and discourse. Syntax involves the study of the largely unconscious finite set of rules that enables speakers to create and understand sentences, and of the relationships among the components of sentences. Although most people take it for granted, the ability of native speakers to comprehend sentences that they have never heard and to utter sentences that they have neither heard nor spoken previously is remarkable. We can do these things because all levels of language are rule-governed and because human beings are genetically predisposed to learn the kinds of rules characteristic of language. A discussion of syntax provides an excellent opportunity to reemphasize the concept of language as a rule-governed system.

Syntax is central to a description of a native speaker's knowledge of his or her language. What do native speakers know that enables them to create novel utterances and to understand sentences they have never heard? The first two selections in this part address this question directly. First, Roderick A. Jacobs and Peter S. Rosenbaum, in "What Do Native Speakers Know about Their Language?" point our four apparently trivial but actually complex and crucial skills possessed by all native speakers. Next, Frank Heny examines some important syntactic structures and rules, using mainly English examples to try to show the kinds of structures that are found in language and how some of these might relate directly to the way in which language is learned.

In the introduction to Part Four, we defined *semantics* as "the analysis of the meaning of individual words and of such larger units as phrases and sentences." However, this definition is too simple. As

George L. Dillon writes, "Most writers on semantics would agree that it is the study of meaning. This is probably the only statement about the subject that all would subscribe to, and disagreement begins with what is properly meant by *meaning*." Part of this disagreement arises because linguists and logicians tend to use the word *semantics* differently. Also, although semantics is currently a field of much interest to linguists (and also one characterized by much controversy), this interest developed only within the last twenty years as linguists realized that a complete description of what native speakers know about their language must include semantics.

The next two articles in this section deal with semantics. In the first, George L. Dillon presents one model for a description of the knowledge that native speakers have about semantics: (1) words can be ambiguous and can make sentences in which they occur ambiguous; (2) some combinations of words are anomalous, some are contradictory, and some are redundant; (3) some words share parts of their meanings, and there are special kinds of such relationships; and (4) just as words can have special relationships to other words, so too can sentences have specific relationships to other sentences, such as entailment and equivalency in truth value. Dillon argues that the best analysis of these facts will probably be the one that is the most general and explicit — and that is a long way from being completed. In the second article, "Bad Birds and Better Birds," Jean Aitchison explains the principles and uses of prototype theory. Drawing on such word categories as birds, vegetables, furniture, and lies, she shows how prototype theory works, "how humans are able to cope with word meaning when it is so fuzzy and fluid."

The final three articles in this section deal with *discourse*, the interaction between the speaker and the hearer and the dynamics of the context in which the conversation occurs. Linguists have increasingly realized that the context of an utterance plays an important part in determining its meaning, as do beliefs that are shared by a speaker and a hearer. In "Pragmatics," Madelon E. Heatherington briefly describes three basic kinds of speech-act principles. Not unexpectedly, these principles interact, and like the other basic systems of language, they are rule-governed and part of what native speakers "know" about their language. Interestingly, damage to the brain's right hemisphere often disrupts normal functioning of both perception and production of various aspects of language involved in pragmatics. As Sid J. Segalowitz writes, "some subtle characteristics [of language] are disrupted more by right-sided brain damage than by left-sided damage: expression of emotion and feelings, inference of others' feelings and motivations, and a sense of humor." (*Two Sides of the Brain.* Englewood Cliffs, NJ: Prentice-Hall, 1983, p. 42.)

In "Discourse Routines," Elaine Chaika offers specific examples of the ways in which social contexts often determine the meaning of what is said. In an abstract of "Discourse Routines," not included here, she writes:

> We control others and they control us by shared discourse routines. By saying certain things, the other party in a dialogue forces certain responses in us. Questions demand answers, and compliments elicit thanks, for instance. In order to understand these routines, one must understand the society in which they occur. Simply knowing the language is not sufficient, for the true meaning often lies not in the actual words uttered but in a complex of social knowledge. Examining such routines can help us understand the unspoken assumptions on which a society is based (*Language: The Social Mirror* [Rowley, MA: Newbury House Publishers, 1982], p. 69).

In the final article, "Girl Talk — Boy Talk," John Pfeiffer reviews the research in an exciting new field of discourse, the role of gender in speech. According to Pfeiffer, linguists are particularly interested in "how, under what conditions, and why the sexes talk differently." The research raises to a formal level issues that you have perhaps already intuitively sensed.

22

What Do Native Speakers Know about Their Language?

Roderick A. Jacobs
Peter S. Rosenbaum

In the following excerpt from their book English Transformational Grammar, *Professors Jacobs and Rosenbaum identify four kinds of knowledge that all native speakers of a language have about that language. These kinds of knowledge involve the ability to distinguish a grammatical utterance from an ungrammatical one, to understand utterances even though a portion or portions thereof may have been deleted, to recognize both lexical and syntactic ambiguity, and to recognize both lexical and syntactic synonymy. We take these abilities for granted; in fact, we usually do not even recognize that we have them. But trying to explain them, trying to account for these abilities of ours, raises fundamental questions. What is language? How is it learned? What is it that is learned? As the authors point out, "When we attempt to explain these skills, we are really seeking to explain an important part of what makes us human."*

The mysteries about language that will be discussed here [may] seem trivial and obvious at first sight. For example: Every normal human being is capable of distinguishing the sentences of his language from all other objects in the universe. Yet, how can this fact be explained? A sentence is a *string* of words, but not every string of words is a sentence. The following strings are English sentences:

1. the trains are most crowded during the holidays
2. aren't you thinking of a perambulator?
3. wash that car before breakfast!

Suppose the word order of these strings was reversed:

4. *holidays the during crowded most are trains the
5. *perambulator a of thinking you aren't
6. *breakfast before car that wash

Every speaker of English knows, without a moment's hesitation, that these strings are not English sentences, even though they contain English words. (An asterisk is always placed before a string which is syntactically or semantically deviant.) What is it that you know when you distinguish between strings of words which are sentences of your language and strings which are not sentences of your language? And where did you get this knowledge?

One possible answer to the latter question is that you memorized the possible sentences of your language while learning it in your infancy, much as you memorized the faces or names of classmates and friends. But this is not the way a human being learns his language. It is impossible to memorize *all* sentences possible in your language, and you frequently utter or hear sentences that do not duplicate any of your past experience. (In fact, the sentence you are reading now has probably not occurred previously in your experience.) Nonetheless, you have been able to distinguish between the grammatical strings and those strings made ungrammatical by reversal of word order. Obviously, you have not learned your language by memorizing its sentences. This, then, is one important human ability that needs to be investigated: How is a normal human being capable of deciding whether a string of words is a sentence in his language, and how is he able to do this for any of a potentially infinite number of strings he has never seen nor heard before?

But this is far from all that needs to be explained. For example, a speaker of a language can almost always tell whether a string is peculiar because of its meaning (i.e., its semantic interpretation) or because of its form (its "syntax"). In his first book on transformational grammar, Noam Chomsky pointed out that the following string is grammatical[1]:

*colorless green ideas sleep furiously.

However, it is nonsensical. It could be described as well-formed grammatically but ill-formed semantically.

Finally, the meaning of a string may be quite clear, but the string may be ungrammatical:

*John and I jumps over wall and we shoots he

*you don't can putting your feet on the table in here

*is reading your father this book.

Thus we are often able to understand foreigners and others who do not correctly use the rules of English.

Furthermore, what is left unsaid may also be very important in a normal sentence of English. You would not be able to explain the full meaning of the following ungrammatical string:

*so was Norbert Wiener

---

[1] *Syntactic Structures* (Gravenhage, 1957), p. 15.

but you would understand and be able to explain this string if it appeared as part of a grammatical string:

Yehudi Menuhin was a child prodigy and so was Norbert Wiener.

You understand the last four words to mean that Norbert Wiener was a child prodigy, although this is not stated in so many words. A speaker of a particular human language can often understand the full meaning of a sentence in his language without explicit statements in the words of the sentence. . . . Compare the following sentences:

1. Dr. Johnson asked someone to behave himself.
2. Dr. Johnson promised someone to behave himself.

When you read the first of these superficially similar sentences, you understood the person who was to behave to be "someone." But when you read the second sentence, you understood the person who was to behave to be "Dr. Johnson." In these two sentences, the items which you understood to refer to the person who was to behave were in different positions, although the sentences were identical on the surface except for one word. What is it that you know about English that enables you to understand the sentences correctly? How is it that you understand

finding the revolver in that drawer worried us

as meaning that *we* are the ones who found the revolver in that drawer? Your knowledge of your language includes the ability to reconstruct the full meaning of a sentence from a string of words which may not contain all the words necessary for an accurate interpretation if you were, say, a Thai learning English.

Frequently, a native speaker of English will understand a sentence as having more than one meaning, as being *ambiguous*. Sometimes just one word is ambiguous, as the word "bank" in

the police station was right by the bank.

Here "bank" could be either the bank where money may be deposited or the bank of a river. Sometimes, however, the ambiguity has to do with the grammatical structure of the sentence:

the lamb is too hot to eat.

This sentence means either that the lamb is so hot that it cannot eat anything or that the lamb is so hot that no one can eat it. Can you see the ambiguity in the following sentence:

visiting relatives can be a nuisance.

Sentences may be multiply ambiguous. Six possible interpretations of the following sentence are given below:

the seniors were told to stop demonstrating on campus.

1. The seniors were demonstrating on campus and were asked to desist.
2. The seniors were demonstrating and were asked, on campus, to desist.
3. The seniors were demonstrating and were asked to desist on campus (although they could demonstrate elsewhere).
4. People were demonstrating on campus, and seniors were asked to stop them.
5. People were demonstrating and seniors were asked, on campus, to stop them.
6. People were demonstrating and seniors were asked to stop them from doing this on the campus (although they could do it elsewhere).

This ability that you have to extract more than one meaning from some sentences of your language is matched by one other skill. You can usually tell when two or more sentences have the same meaning—when they are *synonymous*. Sometimes this synonymy arises from the existence of more than one word for a meaning, as in the joke translation of "Twinkle, twinkle, little star," which begins:

Scintillate, scintillate, diminutive asteroid,
How I speculate as to your identity.

Frequently the synonymy is a result of the way the sentences are structured, as demonstrated by the following sentences:

1. six out of seven salesmen agree that walruses have buck teeth.
2. that walruses have buck teeth is agreed by six out of seven salesmen.
3. it is agreed by six out of seven salesmen that walruses have buck teeth.

You have never seen nor heard these sentences before; yet you need little or no conscious thought to decide that all three of them have a common meaning—a meaning distinct from that of

six out of seven walruses believe that salesmen have buck teeth.

The simplest type of synonymy is word synonymy. As you saw in the alternative version of "Twinkle, twinkle, little star," different words may have the same meaning, though sometimes some alternatives may carry slightly differing connotations. Word synonymy is obviously responsible for the synonymy of the following pair of sentences:

oculists are expected to be well trained

eye doctors are expected to be well trained.

Anyone who speaks English as his native language understands these sentences to be synonymous because he has memorized the meanings of "oculist" and "eye doctor." Since these meanings are the same, he knows that the otherwise identical sentences must have the same meaning.

It is not as simple, however, to explain the native speaker's ability to detect synonymy in such sentences as:

1. the chicken crossed the expressway
   the expressway was crossed by the chicken
2. it is believed that the framers of the Constitution met in Philadelphia
   the framers of the Constitution are believed to have met in Philadelphia
3. economists claim that a recession is not inevitable, and economists are not noted for optimism
   economists, who are not noted for optimism, claim that a recession is not inevitable.

SUMMARY

When you use skills such as the four discussed in this article:

1. the ability to distinguish between the grammatical and ungrammatical strings of a potentially infinite set of utterances,
2. the ability to interpret certain grammatical strings even though elements of the interpretation may not be physically present in the string,
3. the ability to perceive ambiguity in a grammatical string,
4. the ability to perceive when two or more strings are synonymous,

you are making use of a kind of knowledge that can best be described as knowledge of the grammar of your language. This provides you with the grammatical information you need to understand and produce (or generate) the sentences of English. Although these four skills seem too obvious to bother with, they have never been satisfactorily explained. . . .

Language is a specifically human characteristic. Descartes noted in Part V of his *Discourse on Method:*

> It is a very remarkable fact that there are none so depraved and stupid, without even excepting idiots, that they cannot arrange different words together forming of them a statement by which they make known their thoughts; while, on the other hand, there is no other animal, however perfect and fortunately circumstanced it may be, which can do the same.[2]

The particular skills that human beings use when they speak and understand their own language are quite remarkable, especially when you realize that a language is basically an infinite set of sentences.

---

[2] Quoted in N. Chomsky, *Cartesian Linguistics* (New York, 1966), p. 4.

In a very real sense, then, the study of what a grammar must be like if it is to account for the sentences of our language is more than the study of the structure of English sentences and the processes which operate on these structures. The various linguistic skills reflect aspects of the intellectual abilities we possess by virtue of being human. When we attempt to explain these skills, we are really seeking to explain an important part of what makes us human.

FOR DISCUSSION AND REVIEW

1. Discuss the difference in the relationship between the italicized words in *a*, those in *b*, and those in *c* with respect to the phrase "to paint in Paris."

   a. *Whistler* persuaded *his mother* to paint in Paris.
   b. *Whistler* promised *his mother* to paint in Paris.
   c. *Whistler* left *his mother* to paint in Paris.

   Explain the ambiguity of *c*.

2. Explain the ambiguity of the following sentences:

   a. Eating apples can be enjoyable.
   b. She told me to leave at five o'clock.
   c. Could this be the invisible man's hair tonic?
   d. The old matron fed her dog biscuits.
   e. Every citizen may vote.

3. Describe the difference in the relationship of "Eberhart" to "please" in *a* and *b*:

   a. Eberhart is eager to please.
   b. Eberhart is easy to please.

4. Certain material has been deleted from the following sentences. Show what this deleted material must have been:

   a. She adopted forty-two cats simply because she wanted to.
   b. John likes Mary, Bill, and Sally.
   c. Oaks are taller than maples.
   d. Discovering the truth pleases scientists.
   e. Ladies wearing high heels are not welcome on tennis courts.

5. The following pairs of sentences are synonymous, but in a different way. Can you describe and explain the differences?

   a. My attorney specializes in copyright law.
      My lawyer specializes in copyright law.
   b. A proposal was made which bothered me.
      A proposal which bothered me was made.

23

Syntax: The Structure of Sentences

Frank Heny

A sentence is not just a string of words; it is a string of words in a certain order, a string that has structure. Thus, cat dog the the chased *is not a sentence; it is just a list of English words. But* the dog chased the cat *is a sentence (as is, for that matter,* the cat chased the dog*). A sentence, then, is more than the sum of its parts (i.e., its words); it is words ordered in a particular way, in this case according to the rules of English syntax. But how did we learn these rules, rules which to a large extent we don't know that we know?*

In the following article, Professor Frank Heny of University of Pittsburgh suggests an answer to this question, and then examines some of the basic syntactic rules of English that we all use every day of our lives. No single article can possibly treat English syntax in depth. But by drawing examples from two kinds of English questions and from several other familiar constructions, Professor Heny is able to illustrate some fundamental principles of syntax and to demonstrate that children come to language learning with an inborn mechanism that "severely limit[s] what the language learner needs to take into account," one of the crucial concepts in contemporary linguistic theory.

LEARNING LANGUAGE
IS LEARNING STRUCTURE

It is easy to think of your language as a vast collection of words — like *easy* and *think* and *language* and *vast*. But as soon as you try to take this idea seriously, you realize that it can't be the whole truth. String together the words of the previous sentence in another order:

1. you to that as take idea this try realize truth the be soon it but can't whole seriously you as

The obvious difference between (1) and *But as soon as you try to take this idea seriously, you realize that it can't be the whole truth* is the order of the words; and it is almost equally obvious that what happens when you change the order is that you change how the words themselves interact with each other. Certain words now form coherent groups, like *the whole truth* or *as soon as you try to take this idea seriously.* Saying or writing the words in a particular order structures them into groups: they stop being just isolated words and turn into real language.

English is not just a huge dictionary. Learning it is not simply committing a vast list of words to memory. This may be more obvious if you think about a foreign language. To be able to speak German or French you must do much more than just learn the sounds and meanings of a whole lot of words! Of course you have to know vocabulary, but you could learn dozens of German words from a dictionary every day for the rest of your life and still never approach being able to speak the language.

Despite this fact, that language is so much more than just a huge store of isolated words, what you remember of learning your own native language is likely to be limited to memories of just that — the learning of new words. Think back as far as you can, and see if you can recall starting to learn English. You may well remember occasions in which you learned what a new word meant — perhaps even as far back as when you were two years old. (Indeed, it is probably still an everyday occurrence to learn the meaning of a new word.) But you will not remember a thing about learning how to form the structures those words are set in, the structures that make your language what it is. No native speaker of English remembers learning how to make different kinds of sentences (questions, commands, passive sentences and so on) — or even how to form phrases like *the whole truth*. To a typical native speaker of English, the sentence structure, the way phrases are built up and joined together, seem often so natural that it is hard to conceive of putting words together in any other way — almost as if the structure of the language itself had never had to be learned.

It will take only a moment to verify this. There are kinds of sentences that we use every day yet have never thought about consciously. In the previous paragraph, the expression "passive sentences" appears. Here is a group of English sentences. Try to pick out all the passive ones and jot down the numbers. (Don't worry if you can't do this; just read on after you have tried.)

2. a. I watched the prisoner from the tower.
    b. The tower was where I watched the prisoner from.
    c. The prisoner was being watched from the tower.
    d. I was watching the prisoner.
    e. Who was watching the prisoner?
    f. Who was being watched from the tower?

Unless you happen to have studied traditional grammar, or some linguistics, it is not likely that you were comfortable with this task. The sentences are perfectly simple. You use sentences similar in form to all of them every day. Examples (c) and (f) in fact are passives — but you certainly didn't need to know that in order to use them or others like them.

The purpose of showing you the examples above was not to test your knowledge of traditional grammar. In fact, we assumed that the expression "passive sentence" might be a little unfamiliar, and wanted to show that even if you had no idea which of the examples were passives you would find the sentences perfectly ordinary: you would have absolutely no difficulty using and understanding such structures. If you happened to be familiar with the term "passive" you would not normally be at all conscious of the construction itself, even when you used it, and you would not be in any way helped in your use of passive sentences by being able to identify them. Furthermore, whether or not you picked out (c) and (f), many readers would have failed to do so — yet would not have been less able than you to use and understand passives. Conscious knowledge about the passive construction seems unrelated to the native speaker's ability to deal with passive sentences.

Do not confuse learning the basic structure of your language (which had taken place before you were five years old) with the attempts of teachers, for example, to get you to say "It is I" instead of "It's me" or to distinguish nouns from adjectives. That kind of learning *about* language was a collection of facts or opinions about your language and how it is used. Compared to your original achievement in learning the language itself, this added knowledge was really quite insignificant. Your high-school and college English teachers may have taught you a good deal about how to use the language effectively. In particular, they may well have contributed significantly to your ability to write effectively. Written language is an added, in part artificial, skill built upon the oral language that you developed for yourself. Writing you had to learn, consciously, just as you have had to learn math or music. In contrast, you had somehow mastered, quite unconsciously, and without any formal teaching, before you first went to grade school, a system so complex that linguists have still not figured out how it works — your native language itself. How did you do it?

At the present time no one really knows for sure. However, some very interesting ideas are now being explored, which seem to come rather close to the truth. It is likely that you developed the structures of your native language so easily because there was actually very little you had to *learn*. Even learning the words was not a matter of learning thousands of quite arbitrary items piece by piece. You learned the words as parts of structures and the structures you did not really have to learn at all. For they were already there before you learned the language — much as the eye is there, with all the appropriate structure, waiting within the womb for the light and the sights it will see.

The underlying patterns of language, any language, were waiting within you in some sense, and all you had to do was select from those internally stored structures the ones into which you could fit the sounds and words of the language you heard around you. By the time you were a year or so old, surrounded by English, the sounds of that language had already begun to form themselves into patterns in your mind—not as a result of your own individual attempts to "discover" the structure of English (surely too much for any toddler) but rather through a process in which those sounds began to clothe some of the preexisting structures, the ones matching English. From this perspective, your learning English was no miracle or mysterious feat of super intelligence! Indeed it would have been a miracle if you, as an ordinary, normal human being had not, under normal circumstances, and surrounded by English, become a fluent English speaker.

To repeat: it was not so much that you *learned* your language as that it simply *developed,* fleshing out certain of a number of possible language structures which were in effect already waiting to develop. The language around you merely determined the particular choices among those structures that had to be made. Had you grown up exposed instead to French or Navajo or Japanese, you would have been forced by the patterns made by the sounds and words to select a different set of options. To see what this idea amounts to we need to understand a little more about what kinds of systems languages are. Ideally, this would mean looking at a number of languages. Because that would take too long, this account will be based almost entirely on English. However, it will be aimed at demonstrating not what *English* is like, but what *language* is like.

STRUCTURE IS MORE THAN JUST WORD ORDER

Let us first be quite clear that sentences are not just strings of words in a particular order, but really do have a complex internal structure. In pointing out the rather obvious fact that a sentence is not just a string of words put together in any old order, we noted that when the words are in a particular order they acquire a certain structure—and in doing so fit together to make up a sentence. This structure is more than just order, for a single string of words strung together in just one order can have two quite different meanings. These two distinct meanings correspond to two sentences. An example follows; make sure that you see that (3) is really two quite distinct sentences, with two distinct meanings, before you go further. The bracketing in (a) and (b) should help you to distinguish these meanings clearly.

3. I watched the prisoner from the tower.
   a. I watched [the prisoner from the tower].
   b. I watched [the prisoner] [from the tower].

The first way of interpreting this string treats [*the prisoner from the tower*] as a unit: it is the [prisoner from the tower] who is seen by the speaker. This same group of words, [*the prisoner from the tower*], functions as a single unit, a *constituent*, in other, similar sentences. In such sentences, the words *the prisoner from the tower* act together to characterize someone as a prisoner from some tower:

4. a. [The prisoner from the tower] was what I saw.
   b. [The prisoner from the tower] was being watched carefully.
   c. [The prisoner from the tower], I watched carefully.

In each of these examples, the phrase [*the prisoner from the tower*] could be replaced by other constituents such as [*the prisoner from Siberia*], [*a visitor from Mars*], or [*three men in dark glasses*]. Each of these, too, would be acting as a single unit in such sentences. Under this first interpretation, the sentence has nothing at all to say about where the watcher was, but does imply something about the prisoner.

The other interpretation of (3), on the other hand, represented by (3b), does have something to say about where the watcher was, and has nothing to say about the prisoner. The words *from the tower* are not applied to *the prisoner* at all. The two phrases act quite independently, as separate units. This is suggested by the bracketing in (3b). This time, *from the tower* is much more closely associated with the verb *watched*, or with the pronoun *I* than with *the prisoner*. The sentence is not about a prisoner from a tower at all, but reports that the speaker *watched from the tower*. Given this fact, it is not surprising that (3b) is very similar in meaning to another sentence in which the phrase *from the tower* occurs right at the beginning, next to *I*:

5. [From the tower], I watched [the prisoner].

Constructed out of the same English words as (3), this string can be understood only as having a structure in which *the prisoner* and *from the tower* are separate, unrelated constituents. This is also the case in the following rather closely related sentence:

6. [The prisoner], I watched [from the tower].

This last example may seem a little stilted, but there are occasions when most of us use such forms. It is possible that you would more readily use something like: *It was the prisoner that I watched from the tower* or *As for the prisoner, I watched him from the tower* or perhaps even a passive: *The prisoner was watched from the tower by me — and my friend.* (That extra bit added on — *and my friend* — does not change the structure of the sentence and has been added just to help make the sentence sound more natural.) In all these cases, the phrase [*the prisoner*] is separated from [*from the tower*], and the two are quite independent of each other in meaning. Contrast the unambiguous interpretation of (5) and (6), where *from the tower* is not linked to *the prisoner* in any way, with the equally unambiguous interpretation of all the sentences of (4) — where the whole phrase [*the prisoner from the tower*] was always interpreted as a single constituent, i.e., where each sentence is about a prisoner from some tower.

In the examples of (4) the word order somehow forces us to interpret the words *the prisoner* and *from the tower* together as a single constituent whereas in (5) and (6) the word order splits the two parts of this string and they must be interpreted as two distinct, unrelated constituents. In contrast, the order of words in (3) permits either interpretation depending on how we take the words to be structured: as a single constituent or as two. The word order does not force us to choose, as it does in (4) or (5). In a particular instance, when we hear, or utter, a string of words like (3), we determine (generally quite unconsciously) which structure to assign to it and hence which sentence we will regard it as representing, (3a) or (3b). Thus there are two structures associated with that one order of words: word order sometimes forces words to be structured in a particular way, but it doesn't always do so. Structure and word order are not the same thing.

WAYS OF MARKING OUT PHRASES

All languages are built up from phrases; the phrases are small groups of words interacting with each other in various ways to produce sentences. In English, the order of the words limits the ways in which words can interact to form phrases, though as we saw in the case of (3), word order does not determine the phrase structure completely.

In many languages word order plays little role; in Warlpiri, for example, a language spoken in Australia, the words from a single phrase may be scattered around in a sentence. Thus in Warlpiri it is almost (but not quite!) as if one could say *The from watched I prisoner tower the* and mean (3a). Here is an actual Warlpiri sentence:

7. Wawirri   yalumpu   kapi-rna   panti-rni
   kangaroo   *that*   *spear*   NONPAST

   I will spear that kangaroo.

This sentence means roughly *I will spear that kangaroo*. There is no obvious word meaning *I*, but the meaning is implied. We are not interested in this aspect of (7), but in the order of the words that *do* appear in the sentence. First, let us focus on the words meaning *that kangaroo*. In (7), those two words are next to each other, as in English, but in the order *kangaroo that*. Thus far, Warlpiri might seem to require a different word order from English. Such an impression is consistent with the fact that the verb meaning *to spear* comes near the end of the sentence, whereas in English it would come before the phrase *the kangaroo*. So in English we would have *spear that kangaroo*, while in (7) we have the equivalent Warlpiri words in the order *kangaroo that spear*—with about the same meaning. There are many languages that differ from English in that the order of the words in the various phrases is not the same as the English order.

But Warlpiri is more radically different. The words of (7) (like those of other Warlpiri sentences) can be moved around in all sorts of ways without changing the essential meaning. Thus, the following means the same as (7):

8. Wawirri   kapi-rna   panti-rni   yalumpu
   kangaroo   *spear*   NONPAST   *that*

   I will spear that kangaroo.

This example contains just the same words as (7), but in a totally different order. Most striking is the fact that the word meaning *that* comes right at the end of the sentence, while the word meaning *kangaroo* is at the beginning—yet the two words are interpreted in such a way that together they form a phrase meaning the same as the English *that kangaroo*. Of course, a language like Warlpiri obviously must have some way of indicating which of the words of a sentence go together; Warlpiri speakers don't know by magic that in this example *wawirri* and *yalumpu* belong together! We cannot describe here how this is achieved because to do so would mean discussing numerous unfamiliar Warlpiri sentences.

Which words go in which phrases is by no means always signaled by word order. In Warlpiri, for example, as suggested by our examples, the order of the words is practically irrelevant. Other languages vary; the word order in French, like that of English, is quite rigidly fixed and serves to group the words into phrases and the phrases into sentences. Latin was quite free, and other devices signaled which words were grouped into phrases or where the phrases belonged in a sentence. Finnish, Russian, and German fall somewhere in between, with some freedom in word order, and a number of devices (patterns of agreement and case marking, for example) that show what belongs with what and where everything fits into a sentence. Still, Warlpiri sentences, and the sentences of all the other languages that we know about, are constructed out of phrases, and for the most part phrases are much the same as English ones, however they are marked.

A child hearing English or Warlpiri, or any other language, will therefore not need to "figure out" that the babble of noise around it consists of phrases. As far as we can tell today (though our knowledge about such matters is still rather fragmentary), the human infant automatically assumes that any noise it interprets as language consists of words grouped, by one of a small number of devices, into meaningful phrases and hence into sentences. Thus, the child has only to discover whether word order or one of those other methods (such as agreement patterns like those you may have met in Latin or German) signals how words group together into phrases.

There is much that we do not know for sure yet about how a child develops a knowledge of syntax. For example, we do not know just what it is that signals that word order is what matters in English, but that some other option must be relevant when Warlpiri is the language to be learned. One possibility is that certain options are, as it were, "favored" or "unmarked," which is to say that unless a child encounters specific indicators to the contrary, it automatically selects the "unmarked" option whenever there is a choice.

Assume for the sake of argument that word order is the "unmarked" way of grouping words into phrases. A child (no matter what language it will eventually acquire) assumes, until that assumption won't work on the language it hears, that it is hearing words grouped together in some fixed order. The child will expect to find words recurring in fixed, ordered patterns, with adjectives occurring consistently either before or after the nouns they go with and so on.

This expectation is met in the case of English. When the word *that* occurs as part of a phrase built up around the word *kangaroo*, as in *that kangaroo*, they have to appear together. In fact, *that* must appear before *kangaroo*. We can't even say *I want kangaroo that* and still be talking English. (An asterisk before a string of words indicates that that string is not a proper sentence in the language; we place it before *I want kangaroo that* to indicate that that string is not an English sentence.) So a child growing up hearing English merely needs to discover *which* order works for English. A child growing up hearing Warlpiri, on the other hand, will need to do more "figuring out" to discover how the phrases in that language are grouped together. (In regard to other aspects of language structure, it will be Warlpiri and not English that follows "unmarked" patterns.)

EXERCISE

1. Imagine you are a child. You hear some of the following words grouped together to form English phrases like *several monkeys* or *some gold:*

   books several yellow those that monkeys gold some inadequate little

   Try to form as many phrases as possible using various selections from these words (not all of them can occur together) and then try to give a general account of how the phrases are formed.

   To do this you will need to:

   a. Decide what orders are possible.
   b. Decide which words can occur at the same point in structure (for example, where *gold* can occur, *yellow* can generally occur

as well). You will thus be grouping the words into small classes that act alike.

c. Make up names for the word classes. If you have studied traditional grammar, it may be natural to call *little* and *gold* "adjectives," but what you call the classes matters little. You just need some way to refer to them. List the words that fall into each class.

d. Add several words to each of the word classes you have identified. Make sure that your examples act like the original members of the class.

e. Make up general rules for forming phrases that are built up out of the word classes you have named. Which words come before which other words? Are some word classes free to appear in alternative positions?

2. While continuing to deal only with phrases that seem to you to be very similar to those you have been dealing with, like *several monkeys*, add more and more *classes of words*, and decide what order they occur in. Is the order ever free? That is, can English words ever occur in alternative orders while still (as far as you can tell) occurring within these phrases? (Hint: think of strings of adjectives, like *old, sick*, or *tired*.) Can you find words that do not ever occur within phrases of the sort you are dealing with? For example, does the word *unfortunately* ever occur as part of one of these phrases? Try to explain precisely what you mean if you claim that it (or some other word) cannot occur within these phrases.

3. If you know another language that seems to have fixed word order, try to find instances where this is (a) the same as in English for some given pair of word classes (e.g., adjectives and nouns), and (b) where it is different.

SOME SIMPLE PHRASES: NP AND PP

So far we have seen that a string of words, like *the prisoner from the tower* may act as a single phrase or may be two independent phrases, *the prisoner* and *from the tower*, each a cónstituent adding its own meaning to the sentence—as in (3b). We have seen that English words, when occurring together in a sentence, are interpreted not just as *strings* of words, but as *structures*, i.e., phrases built up out of those words. The order of the words may determine completely how they group into phrases, as in (4), (5), and (6), or it may not, as in (3). It is the phrases rather than the words as such that form constituents of sentences: (3a) and (3b) contain the same words but different phrases—as suggested by the bracketing in those examples—and their distinct meanings. Phrases like [*the prisoner*], [*from the tower*], and [*the prisoner from the tower*] interact as units with the verb *watch* in a sentence like (3) to yield a meaningful sentence. Individual words like *from* or *the* or *prisoner* do not. Thus *the* was not watched, nor was *prisoner*, nor was the watching *from*. Rather it was [the prisoner] or [the prisoner from the tower] who was watched, and if we know anything about where the watching took place from, then we know that it was [from the tower].

We have seen that at the level of the sentence, it is not words but phrases that are significant, and have also seen how certain English phrases require that the words making them up occur in a fixed order. We have begun to build up a picture of how certain kinds of (so far undefined) phrases consist of various classes of words in certain specific orders. Only when those words occur together in a permitted order can they be grouped together to form a phrase. Now it is time to consider the structure of these phrases themselves, generalizing as precisely as possible about how they are constructed. In other words, we need to determine what may occur in such phrases. They can be very complex — or very short and simple. We could replace *the prisoner* in (5) by phrases of increasing complexity, without altering the essential structure of the sentence as a whole:

9. a. From the tower, I watched [*the prisoner with bare feet*].
    b. From the tower, I watched [*the prisoner in the yard with bare feet*].
    c. From the tower, I watched [*the prisoner in the yard with bare feet who was trying to run away*].

But we could also replace these complex phrases by just a single word:

9. d. From the tower, I watched [*John*].

A phrase does not have to be long, and in (9d) it consists of just that one word, *John*. In each example of (9), the phrase in square brackets refers to the person who is said to be being watched; thus the phrase in question, however long or short it may be, plays the same role in the meaning of the sentence as a whole. In (9c), for example, the prisoner is identified by a long and complex description: *The prisoner in the yard with bare feet who was trying to run away*. The length and complexity of this phrase in no way modifies the role of the phrase in the sentence, which is precisely the same as that of *John* in (9d); it identifies the object being watched.

The phrases of (9), despite their very different levels of complexity, are built up in essentially just one way. Each, no matter how complex (or simple), is constructed around a noun: *prisoner* in the first three, and *John* in the last. There are other nouns in these phrases, such as *yard* and *tower*. But these are just helping the main noun to build up the description, to identify precisely which thing or group of things the phrase refers to. We may call the phrase a noun phrase (NP). It is a phrase built up around a noun, the head noun of that phrase, which most directly identi-fies the kind of thing to which the phrase refers.

The word *John* is a noun that can act alone as a noun phrase. Most nouns can't. So we can't say **I was watching prisoner;* we have to say *I was watching the prisoner.* The noun *prisoner*, when it is in the singular, requires a determiner like *the* or *a*, though this is not always essential when the noun is plural, as in a sentence like *I was watching [prisoners] in the yard.* When *John* is used as the name of someone it does not gener-ally even permit a determiner, and if we said *From the tower I was watch-ing the john* we would probably want to spell the word *john* with a small letter — and mean something quite different from (9d)! Nouns differ in all sorts of ways regarding what they require or permit with them in their phrases; they are alike in that they allow an NP to be built around them, serving as its head.

Not every string of words containing a noun can act as an NP. In English (and this should now come as no surprise), the order of the words is significant. Whereas *the prisoner* is a perfectly fine NP, *prisoner the* is not. Nor is *from the tower the prisoner.* Hence a string like *from the tower the prisoner was watched carefully* can only be interpreted as a statement about how a prisoner, not further identified, was *watched from the tower.* Although right next to *the prisoner* and some distance away from the verb *watched*, the string *from the tower* goes unambiguously with *watched* and never with the NP *the prisoner.* There are many restric-tions on what can form a noun phrase. Some are general restrictions; others, as we saw in the previous paragraph, depend on the special proper-ties of the head noun.

Some strings simply cannot be rearranged in any way to form a single noun phrase. For example, there is no way at all to rearrange the words in the string **the suddenly prisoner* and end up with a single well-formed NP. Similarly with strings like **the run prisoner*, or **that the prisoner three.* Noun phrases, like all the parts of a sentence, have a very precise syntax: they are constructed according to exact formulas. Learning the language may consist in part of learning these, though it seems likely that many regular patterns in NPs do not have to be learned, since they derive from principles that determine the very process of language learn-ing in children. (One of the troublesome aspects of learning a language later in life is that we seem to have to learn far more of those word order rules than a young child does — something may be "blocking" our ability to make use of whatever linguistic principles are available to a young child.) How much of the syntax of noun phrases a child has to learn we do not yet know. If, as we have suggested may be the case, the "un-marked" way of grouping words into phrases is to have them occur in some fixed order, then all that an English-speaking child has to determine is the specific order in which the noun, adjectives, and so on have to be placed in the NP.

NPs do not constitute the only phrase-level building blocks of language. There are other phrases, for example, those like *from the tower.* Although not themselves noun phrases, these nevertheless contain noun phrases (*the tower* in this instance). In addition, they contain prepositions like *from.* Prepositions themselves vary greatly in behavior, just as nouns do. But just as the phrases built up around nouns have a great deal in common with each other, both from the point of view of what can occur inside them and from the point of view of where they can act in a sentence, so prepositional phrases (PPs), built up around prepositions, have a good deal in common. We will not deal in any detail with the syntax of prepositional phrases. We turn instead to the unit within which PPs and NPs have to occur — as do all other phrases and apparently isolated words that can occur in English, like *swiftly, perhaps,* or *as big as Peter.* This larger unit, which seems to be central in (virtually?) all languages, is the sentence.

BASIC ENGLISH SENTENCE PATTERNS

Phrases like NPs and PPs are very important constituents: they contribute a great deal to the structure of language. However, they do so only in interaction with verbs. Verbs, and the phrases built up around them, are what really determine the essentials of sentence structure. And ultimately a language consists of sentences rather than either isolated words or even just independent phrases. Sentences consist of phrases grouped together in certain specific ways, and these phrases consist of words grouped together in specific ways. It is sentence structure that we have to learn, over and above vocabulary, when we learn a foreign language. The syntax of our native language, English for most readers of this selection, is never consciously learned, and is often quite difficult for people to think about consciously. We are now attempting to do just that — to understand how sentences are constructed in language, using English as an example.

Generally it seems that a language will have one or two "normal" or "unmarked" sentence patterns, which are embodied in many of the commonest, most ordinary sentences. The verbs of the language are at the center of this structure, each verb occurring in some variant of the basic pattern. Here are some very simple examples of the English unmarked pattern:

10. a. [The cat] <u>slept</u>.
    b. [My friend] <u>likes</u> this puzzle.
    c. [The wanderer] <u>tramped</u> down the road.
    d. [The cat] <u>put</u> the mouse on the mat.

Each sentence in (10) contains a verb, which is underlined, and a phrase preceding it, the subject of the sentence, which is an NP (i.e., a noun phrase). The subjects are enclosed in square brackets.

Although every sentence in (10), and indeed every simple, "normal" English sentence, contains a verb preceded by a subject, there is a good deal of variation in what can *follow* the verb. Because of differences in the properties of the verbs, each sentence in (10) is forced to differ a little in structure from all the others — and these differences always concern what may, must or must not occur to the right of that verb. So, for example, (10a) cannot incorporate the phrase *this puzzle* after the verb.

11. *The cat slept this puzzle.

The asterisk is again used to indicate that the string *The cat slept this puzzle* is not a well-formed English sentence. The verb *sleep* differs from *like*; it does not permit the phrase *this puzzle* to appear to its right. In fact, it will not permit any other noun phrase to appear there.

Conversely, the verb *like* cannot appear *without* an NP after it, as suggested by the ungrammaticality of the following:

12. *My friend likes.

What can, must, or must not appear to the right of the verb depends directly on that verb. After *sleep*, no phrase like *this puzzle*, no NP, may appear at all, whereas after *like*, an NP must appear.

Those two verbs, *sleep* and *like*, represent the simplest cases. The first will not permit an NP to its right, while the second requires one. There is a name for verbs like *sleep*; they are called intransitive. Verbs like *like* are called transitive. A transitive verb is one that requires an NP directly to its right; an intransitive verb will not permit a plain NP in that position. An NP directly to the right of a verb is called a direct object. Thus, while transitive verbs require a direct object, intransitive verbs do not permit one.

These two classes of verbs are the most basic, but there are many variations in the way English verbs require or permit the presence or absence of NPs and PPs to their right. For example, *put* requires both an NP and a PP. This is shown by the ungrammaticality of both (11) and (12). (Compare these two with the grammatical [10d].)

13. a. *The cat *put* the mouse.
    b. *The cat *put* on the mat.

Likewise, the verb *tramp* seems very strange when used without a PP:

14. *The wanderer tramped.

Tramp at least arguably requires a PP to its right. (This does not mean that we call *tramp* intransitive, for that term is confined to verbs requiring a direct object, i.e., requiring an NP and not a PP to the right.)

In general, then, a verb is often closely associated with certain phrases that may or must appear to its right; these phrases, which include noun phrases and PPs, are called its complements.

Verbs that never permit any kind of complement at all are rare, and so are verbs which, like *put,* require more than one phrase to occur in their complement structure. Many verbs seem to *prefer* rather than absolutely *require* certain complements. For example, both of the following are perfectly acceptable:

15. a. Bob Dylan sings.
    b. Bob Dylan sings his own compositions.

The first of these examples suggests that *sings* is intransitive; the second that it is transitive — i.e., requires a direct object. Thus, the meaning of the verb *sing* appears to be such that the verb can permit but does not absolutely require an NP in its complement.

When we say that some phrase is a complement of a verb we are not concerned merely with whether it is absolutely required or excluded by that verb, but with whether the phrase in question goes with the verb in such a way that the meaning of the phrase is actually part of the meaning of the verb. When material to the right of the verb is not part of its complement at all, it is not required and, more significantly, does not interact directly with the meaning of the verb so as to form a part of that meaning. Take a sentence like the following:

16. Jane watched your father on the Paris metro.

What are the complements of *watch?* There are at least two quite distinct constituents after the verb. Each can "move around" independently, much as *the prisoner* and *from the tower* could in (3):

17. a. [On the Paris metro], Jane watched your father.
    b. [Your father] Jane watched on the Paris metro.

Of the two phrases *on the Paris metro* and *your father,* one seems to be part of the complement of *watched,* the other does not. Before we say which is which it would be a good thing to think about the meaning of sentence (16). Which of the two phrases interacts most closely with the verb, building up the meaning of *watched?* That will be the one that is its complement.

The answer is the NP *your father* rather than the PP *on the Paris metro.* The latter adds more detail about where the act of seeing occurred, but it is the *seeing of your father* which is the act of seeing. The PP *on the Paris metro,* a *locative adjunct,* adds information about where the seeing took place, its "location"; the NP *your father* fleshes out the meaning of the verb *watched:* the seeing is a seeing of your father.

This account might be confusing if not further supplemented. For there are all manner of adverbs, among them *quickly* and *carefully,* as well as PPs that can act like adverbs, which seem to be much more closely related to verbs than a locative phrase like *on the Paris metro:*

18. a. Jane watched *carefully.*
    b. Jim sang *in a crazy way.*
    c. Jack ate *noisily.*

These expressions are clearly neither direct objects nor locatives. In fact, they can occur with both:

> 19.　a.　Jane watched [NP your father] *carefully* [PP on the Paris metro].
> 　　　b.　Jim sang [NP the ditty] *in a crazy way* [PP in the bar].
> 　　　c.　Jack ate [NP the sausage] *noisily* [PP behind my back].

They add to the meaning of the sentence something about the manner in which the watching, singing, or eating was performed (and are often in fact called manner adverbials).

Why are such adverbials not part of the complement of the verb? To put the question another way, how does *eating a sausage* differ (structurally) from *eating noisily?* Consider the sausage. It is part of *eating*—in fact, it is consumed in the process. Nothing happens to "noisily." There is no "noisily" to take part in the eating process; only Jack and the sausages are involved in that. At least in the clear cases, it should be possible to see that the complements of a verb refer to things that participate in the verbal activity. They are the phrases (if any) that build up the core meaning of the verb, and along with that verb form part of a higher-level phrase, the verb phrase. So, in example (16), *your father* is part of the verb phrase, along with *watched*, while *on the Paris metro* is not. For *on the Paris metro* does not refer to anything that participates in the activity of watching, while *your father* does. *On the Paris metro* simply indicates where that activity takes place; it is a locative adjunct.

If we now put square brackets around the verb plus its complements in (10)—the verb phrase (VP)—then we see immediately that all four sentences have the same basic structure, an NP followed by a VP:

> 10'.　a.　[NP The cat]　　　　[VP *slept*].
> 　　　b.　[NP My friend]　　　[VP *likes* this puzzle].
> 　　　c.　[NP The wanderer]　　[VP *tramped* down the road].
> 　　　d.　[NP The cat]　　　　[VP *put* the mouse on the mat].

We can summarize what has been shown so far in this section in the following way: English sentences "normally" consist of an NP before the verb, i.e., a subject, followed by the verb itself and then the complements of that verb, if it has any. Whether a verb requires or permits complements, and if it does, then precisely how many—i.e., precisely how many NPs and/or PPs must or may follow it—is a property of the verb itself.

The complement structure of a verb depends largely on how complex the meaning of that verb is—how many distinct participants are involved in the relevant activity. Comparing the sentences of (10) with each other, it is easy to see how far the structure of each is directly dependent on the verb it contains and hence on the complements that must or may follow that verb. Sleeping is an activity that can involve only a single person; hence the verb *sleep* permits no complements in addition to the subject. You can't like without liking something, so there are two participants in the liking relationship. So *like* not only requires a subject (as do all verbs), but must also have an NP as its complement—a direct object. Wandering is an act that requires a place to wander in (or down, or whatever)—not just fortuitously but as part of what it means to wander. So *wander* more or less requires a PP as its complement. Notice that although *down the road* in (10c) is a kind of locative, somewhat like *on the Paris metro* in (16), it is not an *adjunct* but a *complement*. It does not *add* to our information about where some activity took place, for part of the core meaning of wandering is that it involves a relationship between a person and a place—it is in fact an activity in which the subject *changes its place*. Finally, the verb *put* requires both an NP and a PP in its complement, reflecting the fact that putting involves a change of place in something which unlike wandering is brought about by some other entity. The subject of sentence (10d) refers to the "putter." The direct object refers to the thing that is put—i.e., the thing that changes place. And the PP *on the mat* characterizes the location to which the thing is moved. Again, this is a locative phrase. In a sentence like *Jane hit Bill on the mat* it would be a locative adjunct. Put in (10d) it is a complement.

EXERCISE

In the text we said that (14), *The wanderer tramped, was not a possible English sentence, that *tramped* is a verb that requires a PP complement. That may well be true, but what about:

> The wanderer tramped on and on.
> Sam tramped wearily away.

What is *on and on?* What is *away?* Think of some other sentences based on verbs that seem to act somewhat like *tramp*, and think of other expressions that could occur instead of *on and on* or *away* in these examples. See if you can provide some kind of coherent account of what is happening. You are not likely to find a clear solution; the problem involves some borderline cases. You may find it interesting, nevertheless, to explore it.

BASIC ENGLISH SENTENCES:
A PHRASE STRUCTURE GRAMMAR

If there is a "normal" pattern that English sentences follow, and especially if it is true that the main lines of this pattern develop more or less automatically as a child constructs his or her own version of English, then it must surely be true that each of us who speaks English in some sense *knows* these basic sentence structures. This is one aspect of knowing the language that, in addition to a knowledge of the meanings of the words, is necessary in order to speak a language. Although, as with so much of language, we do not consciously know what the patterns are, it is clear (for example, when we try to learn another language) just how important that knowledge is.

It is still not clear how the patterns of language are stored in the mind. We know too little about how they develop, nor do we yet know exactly how the language user produces sentences that follow the stored patterns or recognizes that utterances conform to those patterns. Indeed it is still not certain what the crucial features of those patterns are. Structures like those in (10) can be represented in many ways, not all of them equivalent. The way of representing them that emphasizes those features that are truly significant is still subject to debate. That the patterns exist and are significant is perfectly clear, though, and linguists are now trying to find ways of representing these and other language patterns so their representations throw light on language development and use—and on other related aspects of human nature. To do this, they build models of sentence structures—much as a physicist builds models of atoms and molecules.

One of the most fruitful ways of modeling the basic structures of English has been by means of a phrase structure grammar. This is a way of directly representing the structure of every basic sentence of the language as a *tree*. Each tree corresponds to a particular sentence, being a model of (the structure of) that sentence. Some examples will help clarify this. The following trees might be assigned to the sentences of (10):

20. a.

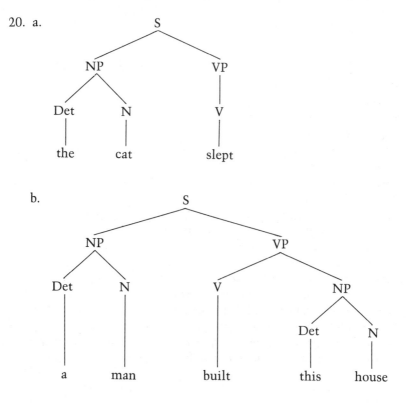

    b.

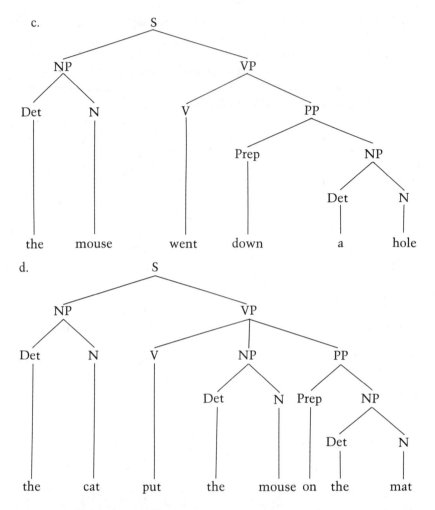

In principle, it is possible to imagine that we might store each sentence of our language independently in the mind, as a tree, like (20a–d), representing the structure of that sentence. However, a little reflection should be enough to make it clear that English cannot be represented in that way. Our knowledge of English cannot be thought of as simply a treelike structure stored with each sentence. We cannot store sentences individually in our brains. Apart from anything else, there are simply too many sentences. (In fact, there is an infinite number of possible sentences in the language, as in any human language.) Each of us deals effortlessly with hundreds of sentences every day that we have never heard before — every one not just a string of words but a structured string. Consequently, in learning English we must have acquired some way of assigning structure to *any* appropriate string of words.

This aspect of our language is represented in a phrase structure grammar by a set of rules that captures the main aspects of English sentence structure in the form of trees like those above, associated appropriately and automatically with every sentence of the language. For every (possible) sentence of English, the rules will construct a tree. The following set of rules would construct the trees of (20)—and others like them:

21. a. S → NP VP
    b. VP → V (NP) (PP)
    c. PP → Prep NP
    d. NP → (Det) N

These rules provide a "recipe" for building a number of related structural skeletons that English sentences of the "normal" pattern will flesh out once appropriate words are linked to the end symbols N, V, Prep, and Det. To yield a way of representing, automatically, a large class of English sentences, those like the sentences in (10), we need only add to the rules of (21) lists of nouns, verbs, prepositions, and determiners that can be linked to the lowest nodes of the trees built by these rules. Before we show precisely how the rules work, you should work through the following exercises.

———

EXERCISE

1. Make up lists of English words that would fall under the symbols N, V, Prep, and Det, and then draw several trees like those in (20), replacing the words in those trees by others from your lists.
2. Describe any problems that arose in completing the previous exercise.
3. If you know another language, try to make lists corresponding to those that you constructed for English, and then try to draw trees for comparable sentences to the ones given for English. Do you meet any problems in carrying out this assignment? If so, describe them.

———

Each rule in (21) may be thought of as building part of a tree. Let us start with the part built by the rule (21a): S → NP VP. In this tree (for each part of a tree is also itself a tree), the S to the left of the arrow in the rule in question is drawn above the NP and VP that appear to the right of the arrow, and it is linked directly to each of them. The symbols to the right of the arrow (i.e., *NP* and *VP*) appear in precisely the same order (from left to right) as they do in the rule itself. So, rule (21a) builds a little piece of structure that looks like this:

22.

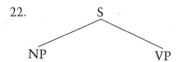

If you find it easier to think in terms of how *you* should interpret the rule, think of it as an instruction to write down the symbol to the left of the arrow and then to write, under it, and in the order in which they appear in the rule, all the symbols to the right of the arrow. And finally, link each of those lower symbols to the one above it. If you follow these instructions precisely, this should enable you to draw (22) as the structure (the *only* structure) resulting from the application of (21a) according to the interpretation we have just given to that rule. First you write down the "S." Then under it you write "NP VP." And finally, you link "NP" to "S," and "VP" to "S." The result is (22).

Now notice that this little tree forms a part of every one of the larger sentence trees given in (20). Make sure you follow this before going further. Either make a tracing of (22) and lay it over each of the trees given in (20), or simply look carefully at those four earlier trees and satisfy yourself that you *could* lay a tracing of (22) over each of them. (It would cover the S node at the top of each tree, and the NP and VP which are joined to it.)

This is not just a trivial fact, though at first you may not see why it is important. The real significance of having a rule like (21a) in our grammar of English — a rule that draws the sub-tree (22) as a part of every sentence — is that it directly represents an aspect of English structure that has been mentioned several times: the fact that all the "normal" sentence patterns of English contain a subject NP followed by a VP. This rule, (21a), contains NP + VP on the right-hand side, and is the only rule for S in the grammar, so it forces every tree to contain, below the S and connected to it, NP followed by VP. In this way, rule (21a) ensures that the language model of which it forms a central part will include only trees built with the structure NP + VP: every sentence will be associated with the structure NP + VP.

Although of itself quite a small point, it is a typical application of a basic methodology that is central to all current work in theoretical linguistics, and worth following closely for that reason. Let us look at it again from a slightly different angle: in order to discover just how language develops, we need to understand what kinds of structures may be included in a human language. In order to do that, we formulate hypotheses about the structure of language, representing these hypotheses by means of some clear formalism such as a phrase structure grammar. Put this way, the grammar (i.e., the set of rules) in (21) is a step towards understanding how we learn language and must be thought of as an attempt to build a model of the kinds of structure that we, as children, eventually assign to English sentences.

A linguist using the grammar of (21) in an account of English is thereby committed to the claim that a child ends up with a representation of the language that is essentially like that set of rules. The linguist is also committed to the representations for each of the sentences of (10) that are given in the trees drawn by those rules, namely (20a–d). It will be good to try and keep these underlying principles in mind as we proceed. The formal details are important, for it is only by understanding them that you can really grasp the significance of theoretical work on language, but it is all too easy to get bogged down in those formal details and to lose sight of the goals that give them their significance.

We can now fill in additional details, looking briefly at how the rules of (21b–d) provide "recipes" for drawing every aspect of the trees of (20). First, we must extend the sub-tree (22). Look at the diagram once again. One branch ends in the symbol "VP." This is the symbol on the left of rule (21b). So when we apply the general instructions for tree-building to this particular rule, "VP" will be the symbol we write down first, just as "S" was with respect to rule (21a). Then we will need to write down, under "VP," the symbols to the right of the arrow in the rule. And so on. In practice, since "VP" is already written down, in (22), we take that as our starting point. We don't write it again. Any time the left-hand symbol of a rule we are applying is already part of an existing tree we proceed in this way: we simply write down the symbols that are on the right of the arrow, placing them under the existing left-hand symbol. So, in this case, we may write down "V NP PP" (all of which appear on the right of the VP rule). We write them immediately under the existing VP in the tree in question, namely (22), in the order they appear in the rule, and we obtain (23):

23.

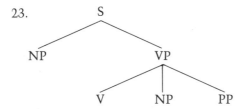

While it is perfectly true that application of rule (21b) to the VP in tree (22) does — and should — produce the above tree (which is a sub-tree of the tree given earlier in [20c]), we have ignored a small but quite significant property of rule (21b), which results in (23) being *not the only tree* drawn by that rule. In (21b) there are two symbols inside parentheses. These parentheses never appear in the trees at all; a tree never contains symbols inside parentheses. The parentheses are in fact not a part of the symbols themselves at all. They simply indicate, in the phrase structure rules, elements that *may* — but *need not* — appear in trees constructed by using those rules.

When we applied (21a), we had no choice but to write down both "NP" and "VP." There was no choice because there were no parentheses around either symbol; and the rule was written without parentheses around these symbols in order to represent English as a language in which every sentence has a subject NP followed by a VP. Rule (21b), on the other hand, allows us a number of choices when we apply it. This reflects the fact that the structure of VP differs from sentence to sentence — that is, not every VP has the same contents. In fact, as we emphasized early on, the structure of the VP of each sentence is dependent on what verb actually appears in it. Our general rules for constructing sentences must therefore permit the appropriate variation. The parentheses in rule (21b) are there, then, because a VP may contain an NP or a PP, both, or neither. Both the NP and the PP are optional, and this is marked by enclosing both symbols in parentheses. When we apply the rule, we have to make a choice; we do not need to write down "V NP PP" under the VP, but may leave out either NP or PP or both. So, under the VP, we may write down just "V NP," omitting the "PP." Or we may write down "V PP," or "V NP PP." Or just "V." We cannot leave out the "V" since that is not inside parentheses. But since everything else is, we may omit any or all of the other symbols.

The operation of the rule may be much easier to follow if we work through each of these possibilities one by one. First, here is the rule itself again:

VP → V (NP) (PP)

Omit both elements in parentheses and we obtain the shortest version of the rule — and, as suggested below, the simplest trees:

24. a. VP → V   VP
                     |
                     V

Omit only the NP and we have:

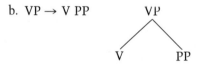

b. VP → V PP

Omit the PP and we have:

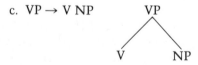

c. VP → V NP

If both NP and PP are selected in applying the rule, so that the longest possible version applies and the right-hand side includes the symbols "V NP PP," then the result is a tree like the one already shown in (23). Using the same format as (24a–c), we obtain:

d. V → V NP PP

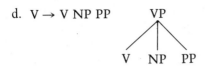

If, when we applied rule (21b) to the VP in tree (22), we had chosen just "V NP," instead of "V NP PP," then the result of applying that rule would not have been (23) but would instead have been:

25.

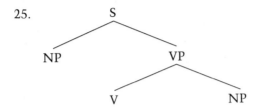

We could extend this figure so as to turn it into the tree shown in (20b). The structure we have in (25) is a "sub-tree" of (20b). That is to say, you could lay it over (20b) like a tracing, and (perhaps with a little stretching here and there) each symbol and line would match up precisely with a part of that larger, complete tree. To turn (25) into (20b) requires just two applications of rule (21d) to add the proper structure under NP — and then, of course, the right words have to be added at the ends of the branches. In a similar manner, all the sentences of (20) can be obtained from the rules of (21). It would be worth taking the time to try to derive each of these trees by applying those rules in proper order.

=

EXERCISE

1. Construct each of the trees of (20), using the rules in (21) in the manner described in the text.

2. Use the lists of words that you made for the exercise on page 411 to construct other trees for good English sentences having similar patterns to those of (20).

3. Describe briefly any difficulties you have encountered. If you are dissatisfied with the rules or with the way they work, state the problem briefly.

Notice that an un-English string of English words (like *on the mat the cat the mouse put*) will not be assigned a structure by any possible combination of the rules. We need to be clear about that. Why is it true? Here is one way of looking at it: Rule (21a), which starts each derivation off by getting the "S" for "sentence" in position, forces every sentence to consist of an NP followed by a VP. And the rule for VP insists that the verb appear at the beginning of the verb phrase — *followed* by NP or PP or both or neither. There is no rule that will get the verb to appear *preceded by* a string consisting of *on the mat the cat the mouse* since this string consists of PP *(on the mat)* + NP *(the cat)* + NP *(the mouse)*. None of the sub-rules of (21) will place PP + NP + NP in that order, let alone placing them before the verb. If English included sentences with such a pattern, we would need to add some rules to (21) to generate appropriate trees. For example, we might assign to this string a tree somewhat like the following:

26.

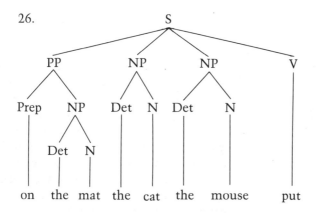

A rule that would generate (26) might, for example, be:

27. S → PP NP NP V

Since English does not permit these structures, of course, we don't add this rule to (21) and hence our grammar, correctly, never generates strings like *On the mat the cat the mouse put*. To that extent, it properly represents the English native speaker's internalized language, generating the sentences of (20) while excluding strings like that shown in (26).

BASIC SENTENCE PATTERNS IN THE MIND

We may regard the rules of (21) as a reasonable first approximation to the way the basic sentence structures of English eventually develop in the mind of a child. However, it is going much too far to conclude from this that rules like these do indeed represent how the English speaker stores those patterns. We cannot, without evidence from many sources, conclude that learning, or developing, a language is in part a matter of constructing a grammar like (21) to define trees for all the sentences of the language. To claim this, that a child acquiring English develops a phrase structure grammar like (21) as a mental representation of the basic patterns of the language, goes far beyond what can be concluded on the basis of the fact that those rules are a "reasonable first approximation" to the representation of English that the child must eventually develop. We have dealt thus far with only a very tiny part of English and there are many other ways of approximating the effect of rules like those in (21).

For a number of years, it seemed likely to most linguists that in learning a language a child does indeed build up a phrase structure grammar providing recipes for constructing all the sentences of the language. The grammar of English, according to this hypothesis about language, would include some rules very much like (21). Recently, it has become clear that a child probably never learns language in terms of rules like these. Rather than trying to discover a set of rules like (21), analyzing for this purpose the language it hears around it (which seemed for a time to be the most likely way for the child to learn language), it now seems probable that a young language learner engages in a much simpler task. To see what this might be, we must consider the task from the point of view of a young child.

Children learn languages other than English. In fact every child could just as well learn any language, and languages differ from each other in their basic sentence patterns — but not in infinitely many ways. The basic patterns of all languages have much in common. So when a child learns English it needs to determine that the verb goes between the subject and the direct object. Learners of Japanese or Persian need to determine that the verb goes last in the sentence. Young Irish speakers (there are now very few!) find the verb at the very beginning of the sentence. Whether the verb goes at the end or beginning of the sentence or, as in English, after the subject, is probably something that has to be learned. Since the verb is such an important part of every sentence, it needs to be identified.

The position of the verb undoubtedly helps the child to find it. In a language like Warlpiri, of course, where word order is not important, other signals must identify the verb, but generally verbs cannot appear at just any point in a sentence; there are just a very few positions where a verb can be expected to appear. It is likely that when a child begins trying to analyze the language around it, the limitations on word order, etc., which are included in every child's "instinctive" knowledge of what can constitute a language, greatly simplify the task of discovering the verbs of the language to which the child is exposed, and hence of determining those many aspects of structure that depend crucially on the verb.

There seems to be a link, for example, between the position in which the verb appears in a language (first in the sentence, last or after the subject) and the structure of PPs. A language with the verb in final position, which is to say one whose structure could be represented (in this respect) by a phrase structure rule something like (27), would not have prepositional phrases like those in English, with the preposition before the NP, but would place the preposition *after* the NP. (It would then be called a *postposition* by grammarians, but this difference in name does not reflect any real difference in the function of prepositions and postpositions.) A child exposed to a language in which the verb came last would quickly discover where the verb had to appear. The sentences of the language it heard would follow a rule with "V" on the far right, which we could represent by replacing rules (21a,b) with one like (27) (though probably with an NP in initial position), or perhaps replacing rule (21b) by a rule for VP like this:

VP → NP PP V

A child would not actually have to learn such a rule. Given the fact that language consists of sentences built around verbs having subjects, once the position of the verb was fixed there would be no need to learn, in addition, a specific rule like (27). Nor, given what has just been suggested about the linkage between the position of the verb and the position of prepositions/postpositions, there would be no need to learn a specific rule for PP. There would be only one rule available for PP (*post*positional phrase) in a language with the verb in final position: PP → NP Post. The Post would come last in its phrase, just as the verb comes last. And hence the rule would not need to be learned, let alone stored in the mind.

Now, whether this is indeed a case where the structure of human language is constrained by predetermined limitations built into the human mind is not yet certain. But it does seem very likely that specific rules directly corresponding to phrase structure rules do not often need to be learned by children developing language. In any case, the underlying point seems valid: the patterns of all human languages may well be derived by the application of a few deep, unlearned, "instinctive" principles that make it quite unnecessary to suppose that our native language is learned by constructing explicit grammars like the rules of (21).

Despite this fact, we will continue to present analyses of English in terms of phrase structure rules, just as if such rules really were how speakers of the language represented the patterns of their language. This is partly a matter of convenience: phrase structure rules provide the most transparent way known to us of characterizing the basic structures of a language as a whole. They are, as already pointed out, the best available approximation to those basic structures, even if in fact there is no explicit grammar of this sort that the language learner constructs.

SOME DEVIANT PATTERNS: AUXILIARIES IN ENGLISH QUESTIONS

Not all sentences of English follow patterns that are covered by the rules of (21). In the simplest cases, we would need only to extend those rules. For example, our account of English makes no provision for NPs containing adjectives, such as *little* in *the little cat*. Nor does it allow us to introduce a PP inside an NP, such as [NP *the prisoner* [PP *from the tower*]], one of the very first constructions we noticed, in (3). In both of these instances, it would be quite a simple matter to add extra optional elements at the appropriate points in the rule for NP, (21d). We might, for example, modify the present version, NP → (Det) N, to read NP → (Det) (Adj) N (PP), extending this rule even further to take care of complex NPs like *the man with a huge mouse in one of the three tiniest cages in the world* — and so on!

Among other words that must be introduced into the sentence in this way are the *auxiliaries*. These are the little verblike words that may appear between the subject NP and the VP in any ordinary English statement. When we introduced the idea that there are basic, unmarked patterns in English, we could perfectly well have added one or more auxiliaries to the sentences of (10), for auxiliary verbs are part of the basic sentence structure of the language. We could have used examples like the following (compare them with the corresponding sentences of [10]):

28. a. [The cat] *has* [slept].
    b. [A man] *could* [build this house].
    c. [The mouse] *is* [going down a hole].
    d. [The cat] *will* [put the mouse on the mat].

In each case, one auxiliary verb appears between the subject and the VP. This is perfectly normal. In fact up to three, and in passive sentences up to four auxiliaries can appear in this position. They always appear in a fixed sequence. The examples above could have been more complex: *The cat* may have been *sleeping,* or *The mouse* could be *going down a hole,* and so on.

In an exhaustive account of the basic structure of English we would need to allow for these auxiliaries. Just as we suggested expanding the rule for NP (i.e., [21d]) to include adjectives (when it would read NP → (Det) (Adj) N (PP)), so we might add an extra symbol, say "AUX," between the NP and the VP of rule (21a) to accommodate auxiliaries: S → NP AUX VP.

Adding such a node would allow us to draw trees like the following:

29.

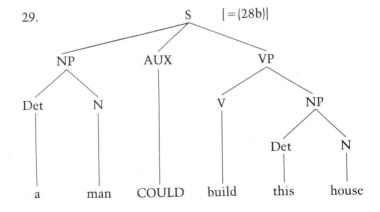

We cannot go into more detail about how to modify the basic structures of English so as to accommodate the auxiliaries in such sentences as these. For we are primarily concerned in this section with the fact that there are many English sentences whose structure differs from that of the "normal" patterns we have seen so far, and does so in ways that suggest that a grammar consisting only of rules like those of (21) does not adequately represent the full structure of a language like English—that human languages exhibit other kinds of structure in addition. The primary reason, therefore, for dealing with the auxiliaries is that in certain kinds of sentences they lead us on to structures that deviate in an interesting way from the "normal" patterns. Corresponding to each of (28a–d) there is a sentence which we may think of as its question counterpart. This question differs from the corresponding nonquestion only in that *the first auxiliary in the nonquestion appears before the subject NP in the question:*

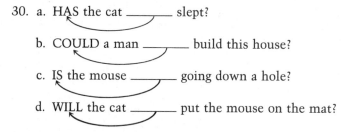

30. a. HAS the cat ———— slept?

    b. COULD a man ———— build this house?

    c. IS the mouse ———— going down a hole?

    d. WILL the cat ———— put the mouse on the mat?

Questions like these are often called "yes-no questions." Each is related to its nonquestion counterpart in a very regular fashion: the first auxiliary verb is not in its "normal" position, but appears to the left of the subject NP. This is suggested by the gaps and arrows in (30). (In fact, there is just a single auxiliary in each of these particular examples, just as there was in their statement counterparts; but it is clear from examination of pairs like *the mouse* could be *going down a hole* / could *the mouse* ———— be *going down a hole?* that when there is more than one auxiliary in a sentence, as there often is, then only the *first* auxiliary "moves" to the left of the subject.)

The arrows and gaps in (30), which suggest that the first auxiliary "moves" to a position to the left of the subject NP, imply that the order SUBJECT + AUXILIARY is in some sense normal, primary, or as it is often called, "unmarked," and that when the first of the auxiliaries appears before the subject in questions, this is a "deviation" from the normal order—a "marked" order. There are good reasons for thinking that something along these lines is indeed the case.

We take the order of the auxiliaries in statements as basic, and the order found in questions as in some sense derived from that basic order, because if we do so, then the order of the auxiliaries, and the way they are ordered with respect to the subject NP in a statement and in its corresponding question can be systematically related to each other. Both are taken care of in the basic trees—the ones that questions have before the first auxiliary has moved, which are identical to the trees for the corresponding statements. If we do not take the statement order as basic, then it is hard to relate statements and their corresponding questions in any systematic way. (We do not have the space to show this here, but it is not too difficult to show.) Of course, it could be the case that the order of the auxiliaries in English questions is totally unrelated to their order in statements. But that is rather unlikely; there are simply too many ways in which they can be systematically related—provided we derive the questions from the statements by a *movement rule,* along the lines suggested by the gaps and arrows in (30).

Given an account involving movement of the first auxiliary, a sentence like (28a), *The cat has slept,* would be defined directly by phrase structure rules like those of (21). But its question counterpart, (30a), *has the cat _____ slept,* would be defined in two steps: first, the phrase structure rules would yield a "normal" sentence, with *has* in the position it occupies in (28a), and then this word would be moved to its eventual position at the front of the sentence.

What stage have we reached in our account of syntactic structure? We began by developing a phrase structure grammar to represent the speaker's knowledge of the general patterns found in certain simple English sentences. We have just seen in outline how phrase structure rules would need to be supplemented by the addition of a movement rule in order to define the structure of English questions. However, we had already seen that there were good reasons for thinking that language learning is not a process by which a phrase structure grammar is constructed. In developing language, a child simply determines such things as the order of the verb and subject, of the verb and direct object, and so on. Speakers of English, Persian, Japanese, Irish and all other languages do not need to construct and store away phrase structure grammars to represent the basic sentence structures; those structures follow automatically once the correct choice is made between a limited number of alternative word orders such as the position of the verb. Now, what about movement rules? Does the English-speaking child learn a movement rule like "In order to form a question, move the first auxiliary in the corresponding statement to the left of the subject NP," and store this rule away in her mind?

The "movement" of the first auxiliary to the beginning of the sentence, which is so characteristic of English questions of all kinds (and occurs in a few other very minor constructions such as, "Boy, *can he* drink beer!"), is actually very rare in the languages of the world. There is probably no other language in which questions are marked by this auxiliary inversion rule—though the Germanic languages generally have the verb in initial position in yes-no questions, making them look superficially very much like (30a–d). It may be that at least certain aspects of this strange little construction do indeed have to be learned specifically by English speakers and stored away. However, there are other kinds of movement that seem so very widespread in the languages of the world that it is likely that they, like the phrase structure grammar which we eliminated as something that has to be learned, develop more or less automatically from general principles governing the structure of human language. In the next section, we look at one such widespread "movement" phenomenon as it appears in English.

WH-MOVEMENT

In addition to questions calling for "yes" or "no" as an answer, there are questions that ask for more detailed information; they are often called information questions. The following simple examples are quite typical:

31. a. Which cake *can* you make?
     b. What *has* Joe put on the table?
     c. Whose mouse *is* the boy looking for?

Like the examples of yes-no questions given earlier, each of these sentences exhibits subject-auxiliary inversion: each contains an auxiliary before the subject. This is perhaps easiest to see if we compare them to similar sentences that are statements rather than questions. Here are some examples that correspond directly to those of (31):

32. a. You *can* make this cake.
     b. Joe *has* put the book on the table.
     c. The boy *is* looking for his mouse.

In (31a) we find the sequence *can you* ("Which cake *can you* make?"); in the corresponding statement (32a), we find *you can* ("You can make this cake.)" Similarly we find *has Joe* in the question, (31b), but *Joe has* in the statement, (32b). In the third pair, we find *is the boy* in the question, but *the boy is* in the statement.

These information questions not only exhibit the rather rare, perhaps uniquely English, phenomenon of auxiliary fronting already discussed, but they also begin with a phrase containing a question word — which corresponds to nothing at the beginning of their nonquestion counterparts. It is "movement" of this sort that is so common: the movement of some phrase to the very front of the sentence. In English questions what moves is a phrase containing a special question word. In the following representation of (31) this "*Wh*-phrase" (as it is often called, for reasons that should be obvious) has been set in italic — and for clarity placed in square brackets.

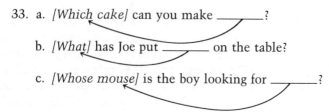

33. a. *[Which cake]* can you make _____?

     b. *[What]* has Joe put _____ on the table?

     c. *[Whose mouse]* is the boy looking for _____?

The representation in (33) of the sentences of (31) not only isolates the *Wh*-phrase for emphasis, but indicates by means of an arrow and an underlined "gap" where that *Wh*-phrase originated. In these examples, this gap has been placed in the position that would be occupied by an ordinary NP in a corresponding statement. Compare the verb phrases of (31a) and (32a):

> 34. a. [$_{VP}$ make _____]
> b. [$_{VP}$ make [$_{NP}$ *this cake*]]

What justification is there for representing the question (31a) in this way? Specifically, why must we think of the *Wh*-phrase as linked to that position in the VP, which in the statement (32a) contains the NP *this cake*? Why suppose that there is a rule that in some sense "moves" it from that position?

Intuitively, it seems clear that *which cake* in (31a) is the object of *make*, just as *this cake* is in (32a). There is, in each case, a sentence about some cake that can be made. This alone is not a very clear argument for the precise representation given previously involving movement to the beginning of the sentence from the direct object position. In fact there are clearer indications that the *Wh*-phrase must be regarded as in some sense a part of the verb phrase even though it is not actually inside that phrase in any of these questions. Recall how the verb of a sentence determines what can appear in the VP. The examples of (10–12) are relevant: whereas we can say *The cat slept*, we cannot say **The cat slept the milk*, and similarly, while we can say *A man built this house*, **A man built* is not acceptable. Now look again at the verb phrases of (31). This time, we will represent them as if they had no gap at all corresponding to the *Wh*-phrase:

> 35. a. Which cake can you [$_{VP}$ make]?
> b. What has Joe [$_{VP}$ put on the table]?
> c. Whose mouse is the boy [$_{VP}$ looking for]?

If we treat each of these verb phrases as a complete VP, as suggested by this last set of representations, then the VPs should be able to occur independently, forming acceptable sentences when they follow NP subjects. But this is simply not so, as illustrated in (36):

> 36. a. **You [$_{VP}$ made]
> b. **Joe [$_{VP}$ put on the table]
> c. **The boy [$_{VP}$ looked for]

If we try to use just the words *made, put on the table,* or *looked for* in an independent sentence without an initial *Wh*-phrase and *without a direct object*, the result is quite ungrammatical. This is comparable to ungrammatical examples like (11) and (12). It seems clear that in (31b), the verb phrase is not *put on the table* but *put [what] on the table*, and that the word *what* really is acting as the NP object of *put*. This is similar in the other two examples. So, the "real" structure of (31a) is *You can make [which cake]*. *And this is precisely the structure the sentence might have if it were generated directly by the phrase structure grammar of (21).* Wh-phrases, at least the ones we will look at here, are simply special kinds of NPs, which generally have to appear at the front of the sentence rather than in their "normal" position, for example, as part of the VP.

One way of analyzing such sentences follows closely the lines suggested by the representation in (32): the normal phrase structure rules (i.e., (21)) derive Wh-questions just as if they were ordinary statements, with the Wh-phrase in the position it would occupy if it were an ordinary NP. In each of our examples, it would be the object of the verb, inside the VP in the position indicated by the underline in (32). Then a rule of Wh-movement moves the phrase to the front of the sentence, as suggested by the arrows in those examples. So, for example, *Which cake can you make* starts out as something like *You can make which cake* and then the phrase *which cake* moves to the front, as in (32) — and the auxiliary moves, too, of course, though we are not concerned with that right now.

≡

EXERCISE

1. Use the phrase structure grammar of (21) to draw *basic* trees for each of the following sentences:
   a. What picture will you buy for Henry?
   b. Who was Jane talking about?
   c. Which preacher could Jack have seen in Boston?
   d. Whose father could he be thinking of?

2. Now show, by using arrows and gaps, as in the text, how the two movement rules that we have discussed apply to these basic forms to derive the final forms of the sentences.

(Hint: The first sentence should be in the form *You will buy what picture for Henry* when you use the rules of [21] to construct a basic tree for it. This is similar in the others as well.)

Now, how far should we suppose that a child has to learn specific movement rules of this sort in developing knowledge of English? A child must somehow discover that a Wh-phrase belongs in its "real" position in the sentence — and must be interpreted as if it still remained there. Yet there is no audible sign of the gap that we underlined in (32); a child simply has to use its knowledge of the language as a whole (in particular, of the basic sentence structures including the properties of verbs and what complements they permit or require) in order to determine where a gap exists. So far, this might not seem too great a feat. The Wh-phrase corresponds to one or other of the places where an NP could appear: the subject of the sentence, or somewhere inside the VP. That is all the learner needs to "discover." However, note that in English, and in many other languages, it is possible for the gap to be virtually any distance away from the *Wh*-phrase.

This comes about because sentences can function as parts of other sentences—which can in turn be parts of other sentences. Look at the example that follows:

37. Sam believes [$_{S1}$ (that) Bill can ride that horse].

The verb *believe* can appear with an ordinary NP object, as in *Sam believes [the child]*, but it can also appear with a whole sentence as its object, as in (37). There, the sentence *Bill can ride the horse* is the object of *believe*. (In [37] the word *that* may precede the embedded sentence, but it need not. It is shown in parentheses to suggest this. In subsequent examples *that* will often be omitted. This makes the sentences sound more natural to some speakers, though others may prefer to put it back in.)

Now we can repeat the process of embedding, setting (37) within another sentence as the object of yet another verb like *believe*. Let us use *think* in this case:

38. Sue will think [$_{S2}$ that Sam believes
    [$_{S1}$ that Bill can ride that horse]].

The process of embedding sentences inside others can go on indefinitely. The following example consists of (38) embedded as object of the verb *hope:*

39. Your friend hopes [$_{S3}$ that Sue will think
    [$_{S2}$ that Sam believes
    [$_{S1}$ Bill can ride that horse]]].

We could go on to say *I deny that my friend hopes that Sue will think that Sam believes that Bill can ride that horse.* There is no end.

Now look at what happens when we take complex sentences like these and "remove" one of the NPs, inserting a suitable *Wh*-phrase at the very beginning of the whole thing. Two examples will suffice:

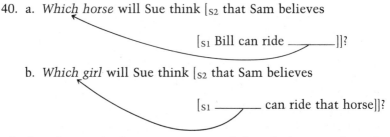

40. a. *Which horse* will Sue think [$_{S2}$ that Sam believes

    [$_{S1}$ Bill can ride _____]]?

    b. *Which girl* will Sue think [$_{S2}$ that Sam believes

    [$_{S1}$ _____ can ride that horse]]?

The fact that a *Wh*-phrase can appear indefinitely far away from the position in the sentence that it would occupy if it were an ordinary NP results in deviations from the unmarked NP AUX VP structure imposed by the phrase structure rules of (21) (as modified by the addition of AUX). One NP is not overtly present in its normal place, but appears at the beginning of some sentence, not necessarily even the one that it "really" belongs in.

A child learning the language would be better equipped to grasp the structure of such sentences if it did not have to discover from scratch that *Wh*-movement can occur in language—and better still if there were only certain places to which things could move. There is reason to believe that a child starts out with both advantages: the potential for *Wh*-movement is one of the devices that the learner takes for granted (as we have already suggested)—and there are very strict constraints on how phrases can be moved around. It seems very likely that these constraints are also not things a child has to discover but instead are limitations on the structure of human language that a learner can take for granted. These, at any rate, are the tentative results of recent work. We will now take a brief look at some of the limitations that appear to be placed on how a phrase can be moved.

It is striking that the moved *Wh*-phrase always ends up at the edge of a sentence. This is true not only in English but also in other languages, many quite unrelated to English. It would be strange if all languages had developed this constraint by chance, and there is every reason to believe that it results instead from some essential property of the human mind. This is even more true of some of the other constraints, which, although found in language after language in some form, are very complex and may even be in principle unlearnable.

Here is an example of a kind of structure that is excluded in English and many other languages:

41. **Which horse* did Sue ask

       [s2 whether Sam believes [s1 Bill can ride _____]]?

Any English sentence comparable in relevant ways to (41) will be ungrammatical. What are those "relevant" ways? There is just one difference between (41) and (40)—the latter of which was perfectly grammatical. The word *whether* occurs in the former, where *that* appears in the latter. *Whether* introduces a kind of question, and is in fact a special kind of *Wh*-word. It turns out that, in English, *Wh*-phrases, like *which horse* in (41), cannot be moved over a *Wh*-word. As suggested by the arrow in (41), this is precisely what would have to happen for this example to result from *Wh*-movement.

Now notice a very important implication of this fact. No child can learn that forms like (41) are ungrammatical by listening to the language around him. English speakers simply do not use these forms. There is no way, other than, for example, directly asking an adult, for a child to discover that the reason it never hears them is that they are ungrammatical, not part of the English language. Yet all of us know perfectly well that they are extremely bad: totally ungrammatical. And children have no tendency whatever to produce such forms as "mistakes." It is quite impossible that every child learning English is taught, explicitly, that such forms are not to be used; so the only possible explanation of the fact that we all feel them to be ungrammatical is that they are excluded by reason of some part of the inborn mechanism with which we approach the task of learning language. They reflect something quite deep, not learned but innate, which is part of our linguistic makeup.

As a matter of fact, the position is a little more complicated — and even more interesting. If no language permitted forms corresponding to (41), we might be inclined to say that the reason they are bad and never used by even children learning the language is that they simply make no sense. As speakers of English we are inclined to think that this is so. However, although many languages, including English, exclude forms like (41), there are others (those that form questions without making any use of *Wh*-movement) in which questions like (41) are perfectly well formed. Thus, despite our temptation, as native speakers of English, to think that such questions simply "make no sense," they not only make sense but are perfectly normal in languages that use slightly different constructions to form questions. (We can even approximate in English the meaning that [41] would have if it were grammatical, using a clumsy but grammatical sentence like *Of which horse is it true that Sue asked whether Sam believes Bill can ride it?*)

CONCLUSION

The structure of human languages is determined by the nature of the creatures that construct them: human children. Given this fact, we may hope to learn much of interest about human beings by examining the structure of their languages.

Human language consists of far more than just enormous collections of words; this is especially true if we think of words as limited to their meanings and sounds. Languages, including English, are highly structured, and words themselves are a part of that structure. English consists of sentences, which are built up around verbs, which in turn determine the kinds of phrases that make up the sentences. The structure of the sentences of a language is called the syntax of that language.

Every English sentence has a subject NP, but the verb determines what kinds of phrases must occur as its complement. Those phrases are generally NPs and PPs. The internal structure of NPs is determined (at least in part) by their head nouns — and in fact the structure of PPs is determined by the prepositions that head them, though we have not looked at these phrases in detail.

In English, but not, for example, in Warlpiri, word order largely determines the makeup of phrases. The grouping of words into phrases in basic English sentences can be modeled by a phrase structure grammar. There are, nevertheless, reasons for thinking that we do not store those basic patterns as a phrase structure grammar. Many aspects of language structure do not need to be learned. They are fixed, and a child merely has to determine, for example, the order of the verb and its direct object, or of the preposition/postposition and the NP that goes with it. It is these little language-specific facts about order, and not grammars consisting of rules, that have to be learned, and stored in the mind.

In addition to the basic sentence patterns that can be mimicked by a phrase structure grammar, there are patterns that involve the movement of constituents away from their basic positions. Many of these patterns probably do not have to be learned as separate rules. A child expects to find phenomena like *Wh*-movement in a language, and most of the characteristics of this phenomenon are universally constrained to follow set patterns. On the other hand, phenomena like the movement of the auxiliary in English may well have to be learned, assuming that they turn out not to follow solely from general linguistic principles in the way that *Wh*-movement does. There are idiosyncrasies in individual languages; the systematic study of syntax does not simply ignore them but attempts to set limits on them, at the same time concentrating on the universal principles that govern the structure of human language.

Although much remains to be learned about the syntax of human languages, some very significant facts have already been discovered, and syntactic research continues to throw new light on the nature of the mind.

FOR DISCUSSION AND REVIEW

1. Draw trees like those given in (20a–d) for the following sentences. As far as possible, use the same symbols as those used in the example trees (i.e., *PP, N, NP, VP,* and so on), but where you believe that a word does not fall into any of the classes for which symbols have already been given, feel free to invent new ones.
   a. Two beetles crawled over a little leaf.
   b. I can see several old men on the docks.
   c. The goats may eat your straw hat.
   d. Jane drove the new tractor into the barn.
   e. Someone may be asking for assistance.
2. a. Try to give detailed trees for the two interpretations discussed in the text for the string *I watched the prisoner from the tower*. That is, turn the marked sentences (3a and 3b) into proper tree representations. Your two trees should reflect the crucial differences be-

tween the two readings that are discussed in the text. (How should you represent *the prisoner from the tower* in [3a]?)

b. Do the rules given in (21) provide for trees like these you have constructed? If not, how do the rules need to be modified in order to do so? (Concentrate on [3a] and consider rule [21d], which draws NP trees.)

3. Your college library has introductory grammar texts for many languages, as do instructors in foreign-language departments. Look at the grammar of a language unfamiliar to you, preferably one very different from English. Where does the verb occur in statements? (At the end? At the beginning?) What is the structure of the NP? (Where does the N come, the Adj, and so on?) Try to formulate simple phrase structure rules for parts of the language you choose, along the lines of (21a–d) in the text, but with the symbols in the right place to draw appropriate trees for sentences in the language you have chosen. Draw a few trees for this language. Discuss problems that arise in deciding what the rules and trees should be like, and anything about language structure that this attempt has taught you.

4. Consider how information questions are formed in some language with which you are somewhat familiar. Use grammar books if necessary to supplement your knowledge, or ask a speaker of the language to help you find examples of these structures in it. Does the language use *Wh*-movement (as English does) for forming these questions? Give detailed arguments for or against your conclusion. (You will have to consider both the form of the questions and the form of ordinary statements in the language.)

5. Consider how far the development of language in children results from the imitation of what they hear and how far it results from factors that are purely internal to the children. Be as specific as possible in your discussion.

6. Summarize the structure of the grammar that, according to Professor Heny, English-speaking children must have internalized as a representation of their language. What kinds of "rules" does this grammar contain? Comment on aspects of sentence structure that seem to have been left out of this selection and that would need to be added for a complete account.

24

The Meaning of a Word

George L. Dillon

Semantics — the analysis of the meaning of individual words and of such larger units as phrases and sentences — is one of the basic systems of language. It is also a controversial area, with many unresolved problems, and an area in which a lot of research is being done. In the following essay from his book Introduction to Contemporary Linguistic Semantics, *Professor Dillon suggests a model to explain the kinds of semantic knowledge native speakers have. Speakers, he points out, know that some words are ambiguous and that their use can result in ambiguous sentences; that some combinations of words are anomalous or contradictory or redundant; that some words are related in meaning; and that sentences have certain kinds of logical relations to each other. He develops these central ideas with detailed examples, analyzing both the linguistic meaning of words (sometimes called* lexical semantics*) and the linguistic meaning of sentences* (sentence semantics).

THE DOMAIN OF SEMANTICS

Most writers on semantics would agree that it is the study of meanings. This is probably the only statement about the subject that all would subscribe to, and disagreement begins with what is properly meant by *meaning*. Nonetheless, a number of linguists have in recent years come to a shared understanding of what they would like to explain. . . . Essentially, they propose to explicate the knowledge speakers must have to be able to make the following judgments about words and sentences of the language:

(a) that many words are *ambiguous* over more than one *sense* and hence that some sentences containing them can be taken more than one way:

> He dusted the plants. ("put it on" or "took it off")
>
> She watered them. ("diluted" or "nourished")
>
> He is a tiger. (two- or four-legged)

(b) that various words in certain combinations are incongruous or *anomalous:*

They amused the tulips.

Green ideas sleep furiously.

(c) that certain combinations are *contradictory:*

colorless red fabric

accidentally chase

(d) that certain combinations are *redundant:*

intentionally murder

male uncle

scrutinize carefully

circumnavigate around

(e) that certain words share one or more elements of meaning — they are *related* in meaning:

chase, follow, pursue

embezzle, pilfer, filch, shoplift

(f) that a special case of relatedness exists where some words are more specific than more general words:

parent — father

cut — snip

take — steal — embezzle

(g) that sentences have logical relations to other sentences — some *entail* other sentences:

She killed him. He died.

some sentences are *equivalent* in truth-value:

The book is underneath the pillow. The pillow is on top of the book.

(h) that an element of meaning, while not strictly part of the meaning of a word, is usually *associated* with it, or sometimes associated with it:

Tigers are (usually) fierce.

One assumes that making these judgments draws on knowledge of the meanings of the words involved (plus knowledge about how these meanings are combined in sentences), and insofar as speakers agree in their judgments of particular cases (and they don't always) this knowledge is the same in the mind of each speaker.

Two facts about this knowledge are evident at the outset. First, word meanings cannot be unanalyzable wholes, each one arbitrarily different from every other, or judgments of relatedness and entailment could not be made. Second, judgments of anomaly and contradiction can be made with regard to whole classes of items: *colorless blue fabric* is as bad as *colorless red fabric, accidentally commit perjury* is as bad as *accidentally chase*. A major portion of modern linguistic semantics is devoted to finding the most general and explicit terms for analyzing this knowledge. A lot of it is represented in a scattered and implicit way in dictionaries — semantics aims at making it explicit and showing the general patterns. The most general and explicit analysis is not guaranteed to be psychologically the most real, however, for at least two reasons: one is that people undoubtedly differ in the degree to which they maximize the generality and simplicity of their codings of word meanings ("verbal aptitude" tests measure this); the other is that there may be alternative analyses that maximize generality in other areas of vocabulary, though not in the area in which we are looking. One person told me that she had always analyzed *telegraph* as "communicate a written message (electro)mechanically" (linking it with *write* and *telephone*) rather than "write at a distance" (linking it with *telephone, telescope, teletype*). Whether one analyzes *telegraph* her way or the other way does not affect the truth-value of *telegraph*. Both analyses, for example, can account for the contradiction in

I kept your location secret though I telegraphed it to the FBI.

Obviously one cannot make substantive claims about maximum generality and simplicity until whole vocabularies have been analyzed, and the accomplishment of this task lies very far in the future. The classic studies in descriptive semantics have been done in what appear to be fairly clearly bounded "fields" such as kinship terms, adjectival and prepositional meanings, causative and inchoative verbs, verbs of judging and verbs of cooking, and even with these there arise problems of psychological reality. Still, there is no question that the impulse to analyze and generalize is one very strong component in the human cognitive apparatus. . . .

SAMENESS AND DIFFERENCE OF MEANING

When people speak of the meaning of a word, they are usually speaking about one of its senses (corresponding roughly to the numbered subdivisions of a dictionary entry), usually what they believe is the primary or central sense. They do not mean to generalize on what all the senses have in common. It is not always obvious, however, how many different senses should be discriminated for a word, or whether a word in two sentences is being used in the same or different senses (or whether, indeed, it is the same word). . . . Linguists have developed "gapping" and "pronominalization" tests based on the fact that words can be gapped and pronominalized in conjoined sentences only when they are used in the same sense. When they are used in different senses, the effect is that of a pun. For example,

John watered the plants, and Mary watered the lawn.

can be gapped to

John watered the plants, and Mary, the lawn.

but the effect of

John watered the plants, and Mary, the drinks.

is mildly humorous, giving rise to the conclusion that *water* in *water the drinks* is used in a different sense ("dilute by adding water to") from that of the first *water* ("nourish by applying water to"). On the other hand, using *paint* to mean "protect by applying paint to" and to mean "decorate by applying paint to" would seem to be using the word in the same sense:

Mary painted the hall, and John, the downspouts.

Rather than say *paint* has two senses ("decorate" and "protect") we should say that it has only one ("apply paint to") with a certain range of purposes. The intention of protecting or decorating must be present, however: if a baby wiped paint-covered hands on the wall, we would not say that it painted the wall, except ironically. Actually, one might try to apply a different sense of *paint* here — "to produce in lines and colors on a surface by putting paint on something" — but the direct object of *paint* for this sense must be an object of art (mural, watercolor, etc.) or understood as a visual representation of the thing (*painted the tree in watercolors* — i.e., "a picture of the tree") — presumably the baby's smears would not amount to the representation of a wall, or anything else.

For another example, consider whether *suggest* has a different sense when used with a human subject from the sense it has when used with a nonhuman subject:

John suggested to Mary that she should get snow tires.

The skid suggested to Mary that she should get snow tires.

A slight variation of the gapping test yields the mildly humorous effect of a word being used in different senses:

John suggested to Mary that she should get snow tires and so did the skid. . . .

The definition of a sense of a word is the representation of the sense in terms of other words. That is, the definition *paraphrases* the sense or is *synonymous* with the word in the relevant sense (or should be). To explicate this basic notion of "sameness of sense" it is necessary to introduce some logical terminology. Briefly, for S_1 to be said to be a paraphrase of S_2, it is necessary that S_1 and S_2 be truth-functionally equivalent (i.e., that S_1 logically entail S_2 and vice versa). Entailment is basically the notion "follows from" and will be defined as follows:

S_1 *entails* S_2 if, over the whole range of possible situations truly described by S_1, S_2 would be true also.

For example, the sentence:

S_1: John got out of bed at 10 o'clock.

entails the sentence:

S_2: John was in bed immediately prior to 10 o'clock.

because there is no situation of which S_1 would be true but S_2 false. That is, if he got out of bed at 10 o'clock, then he *necessarily* was in bed to start with. Hence the conjunction of S_1 and *not-S_2* should be a contradiction (false in all possible worlds) (the X marks a contradiction):

XJohn got out of bed at 10 o'clock though he wasn't in it then.

Other examples of entailment pairs (the arrow → indicates "entails") are:

Jumbo is an elephant. → Jumbo is a mammal.
John stopped beating his wife. → John was beating or used to beat his wife.
John regrets beating his wife. → John beat his wife.

(Verbs like *stop* and *regret* are called "factive" verbs because they always entail the truth of their complements.)

Some reflection is often necessary to determine whether a relation between sentences is a true logical entailment. For example, the sentence:

S_1: He sharpened the knife.

might be said to entail:

S_2: The knife became sharp.

There are situations, however, of which S_1 would be true but not S_2, namely ones in which the knife became less dull but still not what one would want to call sharp.

If it happens also to be the case that S_2 entails S_1, then S_1 and S_2 are logically or truth-functionally *equivalent:*

S_1: John committed suicide.
S_2: John killed himself.

S_1: Not everyone came.
S_2: Some didn't come.

Again, the relation between two sentences may be close but fall short of full equivalence. *Forbid,* for example, entails *not permit,* but there are some cases where *not permit* does not entail *forbid*—where, that is, *not permit* would be true, but *forbid* false:

They didn't permit the crabgrass to spread.

One could argue, however, that there are really two senses of *permit*, one of which is equivalent to "grant permission to," the other equivalent to "allow to happen," and that, for the first of these, *not permit*₁ is equivalent to *forbid*. This still will not work, however, since the following is not a contradiction:

They didn't *permit*₁ him to leave, but they didn't forbid him to either.

Notice, by the way, that the *suicide* example is not quite right: suppose John were an anarchist who was working on a bomb and blew himself up by mistake—in that case, S_2 would be true but not S_1. If the word *deliberately* is added to S_2, however, the sentences are equivalent.

Logical entailment must be distinguished from what might be called factual entailment. As an example of the latter, S_1 might be said to factually entail S_2:

S_1: The batter hit a fly ball into center field which was caught.

S_2: The batter was out.

The "following" of S_2 from S_1 here depends on the rules of baseball rather than the meaning of *hit a fly ball* (and of course depends on the assumption that a game was in progress). This distinction is particularly hard to draw when the factual relation is one of natural cause and effect:

S_1: It began to rain.

S_2: The ground began to get wet.

This is a factual relation, however, not a logical one, because we can imagine circumstances in which the ground would not get wet when it rained (for instance, if it were covered with a tarpaulin).

TWO ASPECTS OF EXTRALOGICAL MEANING

Sentences may convey more than their logical content. Two aspects of extralogical meaning are easily confused with logical meaning and must be distinguished from it: shadings associated with the grammatical relations subject and direct object, and inferences arising from the pragmatics or "use" of sentences.

Shadings associated with what is subject appear in the following sets:

1. a. John met Harry.
   b. Harry met John.
   c. John and Harry met.

2. a. The truck collided with the bus.
   b. The bus collided with the truck.
   c. The bus and the truck collided.
3. a. The car is behind the bus.
   b. The bus is in front of the car.
4. a. The devil used to be frightening to the ignorant.
   b. People used to be afraid of the devil before the age of science.

There seem to be three relevant properties we associate with subjects: first, they are usually what the sentence is about (that is, the topic or *theme* under discussion). Thus (1a) seems to present the encounter as "what happened to John"—from his point of view, so to speak—but (1b) presents it from Harry's point of view and (1c) presents it as a mutual experience. So also in (3): one sentence is about the location of the car, the other about the location of the bus. Second, the subject is often assumed to be the instigator or "doer" even when the verb does not clearly refer to an action performed by someone on someone or something. Thus in (2), (a) would be preferred if the bus were stationary, (b) if the truck were stationary, and (c) if neither were. The same considerations apply in (1) if we imagine situations where one or the other is stationary. Third, referentiality is preeminently a property of subjects. Hence (4a) tends to suggest the existence (in at least the speaker's mind) of a referent for *the devil* more strongly than (4b) does.

The following sets have to do with what is the direct object:

5. a. They loaded the truck with furniture.
   b. They loaded furniture onto the truck.
6. a. They smeared the wall with paint.
   b. They smeared paint on the wall.
7. a. I teach the little monsters arithmetic.
   b. I teach arithmetic to the little monsters.
8. a. I am angry at Mary marrying that old man.
   b. I am angry at Mary's marrying that old man.
9. a. I expected Mary to support me.
   b. I expected that Mary would support me.

One might say that the direct object is assumed to be the most directly and completely affected participant. (5a) more strongly suggests a full truck than (5b), (6a) a covered wall. (7a) suggests more strongly than (7b) success at the teaching (i.e., they learn). In (8a) and (9a) the anger and expectation seem more directed at Mary than in the (b) sentences. . . .

Certain inferences that can be made from sentences appear to be based on how the sentence functions in actual speech situations. These are generally called *conversational implicatures* to distinguish them from logical entailments. One assumes that a speaker speaks in good faith, which means among other things that he is trying not to mislead his hearer, is trying to convey information he thinks his hearer wants to know or should know, and is not making unreasonable assumptions. For example, if you tell someone that something is possible, you conversationally implicate that it is not to your knowledge certain. If I said:

You may fail.

you would be justified in assuming that you have a chance to pass — such a statement from me after I had turned in an F would be highly misleading. . . .

ANALYSIS INTO COMPONENTS

The notion that the sense of a word can be expressed as a combination of the senses of other words is familiar to anyone who has used a dictionary. The goals of a semanticist and those of a lexicographer, however, differ considerably: one would like to make logical entailments and systematic relations of word senses clear, the other aims at giving clues to the common uses of words. In many cases it is possible to adapt a dictionary definition to semantic ends. For example, we can confirm the results of the gapping test with *water* by showing that the two different senses that the test indicated correspond to two different sets of entailments:

$water_1$: nourish by applying water to → nourish

→ put water on

$water_2$: dilute by adding water to → dilute

→ put water in

The senses of *water* here are not simply the sum of the two entailed parts, however, but include a causative or purposive relation between them. From here on, the term *component* will be used for these parts of meaning (other terms are *feature, sememe,* semantic *marker*), and they will be printed in block capitals to signify that they represent one sense of the word that they usually represent. The components may themselves abbreviate a complex of other components. . . .

The usefulness of componential analysis is perhaps most apparent when we consider the relations of words constituting an interlocking set, like kinship terms. With the components *male, female, parent* we can analyze the main senses of *father, mother, son, daughter, brother, sister.* For example:

X is father of Y: X parent Y + X male

X is brother of Y: $A + B$ parent $X + Y$ + X male. . . .

TAXONOMIC HIERARCHIES

It is not surprising that kinship terminology constitutes an interlocking set of contrasts along certain parameters. In general, terms referring to human institutions, artifacts, and actions can be defined at least roughly in this manner. The human instinct to classify and differentiate is most at home here—much less so in regard to natural objects and processes (e.g., *pear, thunder, wither*). There seems to be a human ability and tendency to arrange things into genus-and-species groupings, usually called *taxonomic hierarchies*, and these can be directly translated into componential definitions. For example, rifles, pistols, and shotguns can be classified as sidearms, differing in how they are held and the nature of the bore of their barrels. These contrasts can be represented in a branching tree:

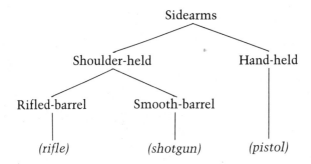

which translates into the analysis:

> *shotgun:* sidearm + shoulder-held + smooth-barrel
>
> *rifle:* sidearm + shoulder-held + rifled-barrel
>
> *pistol:* sidearm + hand-held

Notice that the components are entailed by the words:

> It is a shotgun. → It is smooth-barreled.
>
> → It is shoulder-held.
>
> → It is a sidearm.*

There are other attributes of shotguns, however, not represented in the definition. These would include: *pellet-firing, double-barrel, short range,* and *for shooting game.* These attributes differ from the preceding ones, however, in that they are not necessary properties of things called shotguns. That is, they are not entailed by the sentence *It is a shotgun;* rather, they are only *associated* components. The phrase *rifled shotgun* is contra-

---

* Editor's note: These are treated as *definitional* components and, as such, are entailed by the words.

dictory: there can be no object properly called a shotgun that is rifled. The phrases *slug-firing shotgun, single-barreled shotgun,* and so on are not contradictory: the modifiers block off components that are only associated. . . .

MORE ON ASSOCIATED COMPONENTS

Speakers not only discriminate definitional and associated components — they discriminate between closely and loosely associated components. George Lakoff (1972) has pointed out that hedge-words like *technically, strictly, loosely speaking, sort of, kind of, regular,* and *real* are sensitive to these discriminations. There are things that, while possessing the definitional attributes necessary to be referred to by an item, lack any of the associated attributes. In this case the hedge-word *technically* is appropriate:

Mae West is technically a spinster.

If the definitional attributes are present, and also some closely associated one or ones, but the more loosely associated ones are absent, the likely hedge-word is *strictly speaking:*

Strictly speaking, a whale is a mammal.

If we still want to refer to something that lacks the definitional attributes but has some of the associated ones, we can use *loosely speaking* or *in a manner of speaking:*

Loosely speaking, the whale is a fish.

In a manner of speaking, bats are birds.

Finally, if something has some attribute only loosely associated, and lacks the definitional and more tightly associated ones, the appropriate hedge is *real* or *regular:*

Harry is a regular fish.

Sam is a real tiger.

Notice that in the last examples the hedge-word can be omitted. . . .

HOW CHILDREN LEARN WORD MEANINGS

It is well known that younger children appear to overgeneralize the first words they learn, applying them to a wider range of things than they would be applied to in adult speech. A number of people, including Eve Clark (1973), have pointed out that these overgeneralizations can be viewed as underspecified senses. For example, if certain children use *apple* to refer to oranges, tennis balls, doorknobs, and paperweights as well as apples, one can conclude from their uses that they have for the sense of *apple* [*spherical* and *small*] and not much else. Their learning to restrict the term to the range of things that adults call apples would involve adding definitional components to that sense, and perhaps in some cases demoting a component previously taken as definitional to associated status, or dropping an associated component altogether. Demotion appears to be involved in children's learning of kinship terms, where the component *adult* seems definitional for *uncle* for younger children but of course must be demoted to associated status to get an adult's sense of *uncle.*

There is a fairly good basis (surveyed in Clark, 1973) for supposing that the components children initially make use of for definitions are those that refer to perceivable qualities like shape, sound, and texture rather than those that refer to more abstract properties like function (what something is used for). Since, for very many nouns, what it is used for, or functions as, is important in its definition, children will have to considerably reorganize their vocabularies as they come to recognize that at times a functional definition, rather than a physical one, gives a more coherent generalization about the things people call, e.g., *polish.* Some research by Elaine Andersen (1975) concerning the terms *cup* and *glass* explores the specification that children of different ages have of these terms by asking them to name and sort an array of objects as cups, glasses, or neither. Not all of the objects would be called either glass or cup by adults (i.e., there are some glass bowllike things in the array). The observer can infer the bases of the naming and the specificity of the terms. It appears that younger children (up to six years) take the physical shape and material as the predominant definitional components, and the older ones, like adults, rely more on probable function. Thus younger children will call a tall cylindrical plastic container a cup because it is made of plastic, especially if it is colored plastic, and a glass "bowl" a glass. There is a great deal more to be learned from this study, which the reader is urged to consult.

These terms are particularly tricky, because one term is also the name of a material *(glass)* but *cup* is not. This seems to induce us to call a thing that is a glass in shape and function a paper cup, though it may lack a handle. Having a handle is in general a good discriminator of a cup, but not a perfect one, and there are mugs to worry about as well as small bowls. In short, these terms "partition" the field of "drinking vessels" (notice the functionally defined term *drinking* has been smuggled in) but they do not constitute a discrete partitioning of the field — there are overlaps and conflicting criteria — and a taxonomic hierarchy like that set up for sidearms would be very difficult to construct. This situation is not uncommon: Adrienne Lehrer (1969) has noted that the set of verbs of cooking is not perfectly analyzable into a single hierarchy (*roast,* for example, overlaps *bake* and *broil*), and one might find similar results for *pot/pan,* etc. (see Lehrer, 1974). Older children and adults come to accept that the most natural and useful senses of terms may be neither inclusive enough to refer appropriately to any object we come across or conclusive enough to decide whether a given thing should be called by one or another term (consider *anxiety, fear, apprehension, uneasiness, . . .*). They learn to modify and hedge their applications and even to explain them: "You could call it a cup since it is cuppy in shape — bowls are wider and shallower"; "It's sort of a bowl"; and so on.

The shift that Andersen found from components based on form (in the broad sense of "all physical characteristics") to those of function is most interesting in regard to adult definitions of instrument and artifact nouns generally. Dictionary definitions often mention both form and function, sometimes giving more weight to form, sometimes to function. Consider the definitions of *hammer* and *polish* given in *[Webster's New Collegiate Dictionary]*.

$hammer_n$: 1a. A hand tool consisting of a solid head set crosswise on a handle and used for pounding.

$polish_n$: 3. A preparation that is used to produce a gloss and often a color for the protection and decoration of a surface.

Form and function are given about equal weight for *hammer*, but with *polish* function is the sole component. If children's definitions are heavy to the form side and weak to the function, one would expect them to generalize *hammer* to include axes and adzes and to have some trouble getting a stable sense for *polish*. I notice both phenomena in my daughter's speech at age three, who insisted on calling shoe polish, applied with a brush, *paint*, but rejected the term for an unpigmented polish squeezed from a tube and applied with a rag, suggesting with question intonation: toof-paste?! I do not know the degree to which adults vary in the amount of redefinition they have performed for individual words and the relative weight they give to form and function, but I suspect that it may be fairly great. Georgia Green (1972: 86) observed that for her "anything which could be used to paste with is paste, but not everything that you could 'glue' with is glue." For me, it is roughly the opposite: *glue* is the more functionally defined term, *paste* the more formally defined.

There is an apparent contradiction between the claimed priority of formal to functional definition and recent work by Katherine Nelson (1974) discussed by Judith Kornfeld (1975), though this turns on what is meant by *function*. Nelson argues that very young children (12 to 15 months) appear to class items as similar that can be acted upon in the same way: they will, for example, pick a cylinder as "like a ball" rather than a fixed sphere held in a frame because they can roll the cylinder but not the fixed sphere. This is a dynamic or "motor"-oriented classification, which may be reanalyzed in terms of "static" properties of form later. Obviously, *function* as we have been using the term is a far more abstract kind of coding involving typical or canonical or intended uses. Kornfeld reports cases of retarded and learning-disabled children (mental age two and a half to four years) who seem still to be functioning on this level, responding to a direction to "put the book on the chair" by taking the book and sitting on the chair. In effect, *chair* seems to be coded "for sitting on" whenever it turns up. Nelson observes that this sort of primitive, preconceptual "knowledge" of things (and relations) is important even in adulthood.

A final point is that functional properties are inherently relational, while form properties are not, and that words that involve relational components in their definitions (e.g., kinship terms, many adjectives) are not mastered in the exact adult sense until quite late in childhood (9 to 11 years). This suggests that relational components involve greater cognitive complexity than formal components. The reanalysis of, e.g., *X brother Y* from *[X male + X not adult]* to *[X male + A + B parent X + Y]* is not merely the substitution of one definitional component for another: it is the substitution of a relational for a nonrelational one and as such reflects a major step in cognitive development. . . .

This [discussion] has been about the structure of word senses. Analyzing the senses of words into configurations of components enables one to predict for a given sentence what its entailments will be, what other sentences will be equivalent to it, what sentences will be redundant, and what contradictory. These components constitute the definitional core of a sense. Other components appear to be present also, though not so centrally as to affect the truth-value of sentences containing the word. Speakers vary somewhat in their sorting of components into definitional, closely and loosely associated groups, and some of the variation may be a residue of incomplete reanalysis of previously learned senses.

The judgments not yet discussed are those of ambiguity and anomaly. The meanings of words are also reflected in the potential of the word for combining with other words. One of the things that speakers know about *amuse*, for example, is that it requires the noun that functions as its direct object to refer to a thing of a certain class, namely, a human or animal. Otherwise the sentence will be anomalous *(They amused the tulips)*. This is called a *selectional* (or *co-occurrence*) *restriction* of the verb *amuse*. The operation of selectional restrictions is reflected in the fact that words are generally more determinate in meaning when used in sentences than when cited in isolation. The word *water*, in isolation, might be thought of as a noun or a verb. In

She watered them.

it is clearly a verb because of its construction with a noun and a pronoun, but it is still ambiguous over at least two senses. But if the direct object is further specified:

She watered the plants.

the possibility of the "dilute" sense is cancelled. . . .

REFERENCES

Andersen, Elaine. "Cups and Glasses: Learning that Boundaries are Vague," *Journal of Child Language,* 2 (1975), 79–103.

Clark, Eve V. "What's in a Word? On the Child's Acquisition of Semantics in His First Language," in *Cognitive Development and the Acquisition of Language,* ed. T. E. Moore. New York: Academic Press, 1973.

Green, Georgia M. "Some Observations on the Syntax and Semantics of Instrumental Verbs," in *Papers From the Eighth Regional Meeting of the Chicago Linguistic Society,* ed. Paul M. Peranteau, Judith N. Levi, and Gloria C. Phares, 1972.

Kornfeld, Judith. "Some Insights into the Cognitive Representation of Word Meanings," in *Papers From the Parasession on Functionalism,* ed. Robin E. Grossman, L. James San, and Timothy J. Vance. Chicago Linguistic Society, 1975.

Lakoff, George. "Hedges: a Study in Meaning Criteria and the Logic of Fuzzy Concepts," in *Papers From the Eighth Regional Meeting of the Chicago Linguistic Society,* ed. Paul M. Peranteau, Judith N. Levi, and Gloria C. Phares, 1972.

Lehrer, Adrienne. "Semantic Cuisine," *Journal of Linguistics,* 5 (1969), 39–55.

———. *Semantic Fields and Lexical Structure.* New York: North Holland/American Elsevier, 1974.

Nelson, Katherine. "Concept, Word, and Sentence . . . ," *Psychological Review,* 81 (1974), 267–85.

=====

FOR DISCUSSION AND REVIEW

1. Make up an example of your own to illustrate each of the following points made by Dillon:
   a. "[M]any words are *ambiguous* over more than one *sense* and hence . . . some sentences containing them can be taken more than one way. . . ."
   b. "[V]arious words in certain combinations are incongruous or *anomalous.*"
   c. "[C]ertain combinations [of words] are *contradictory.*"
   d. "[C]ertain combinations [of words] are *redundant.*"
   e. "[C]ertain words . . . are *related* in meaning."
   f. "[A] special case of relatedness exists where some words are more specific than more general words."
   g. Some sentences "*entail* other sentences."
   h. "[S]ome sentences are *equivalent* in truth-value. . . ."
   i. "[A]n element of meaning, while not strictly part of the meaning of a word, is usually [or sometimes] *associated* with it. . . ."

2. Using original examples, explain why "word meanings cannot be unanalyzable wholes" and why "judgments of anomaly and contradiction can be made with regard to whole classes of items."

3. Try to arrange the following terms in an age sequence (oldest to youngest or youngest to oldest), and then write a brief explanation of your reasons for choosing the order upon which you decided:

baby girl	young girl
woman	little girl
girl	young woman

(It may help to try each word or phrase in a context such as: *Yesterday I saw a* _____ *at the beach.*) Would you use the same terms if the individual referred to were present? (Adapted from Dwight Bolinger, *Aspects of Language,* 2nd ed. [New York: Harcourt Brace Jovanovich, 1975], p. 231.)

4. Create two sentences that illustrate the "gapping" test and two that illustrate the "pronominalization" test.

5. Explain the difference between *logical entailment* and *factual entailment,* and give an original example of each.

6. According to Dillon, two reasons that "sentences may convey more than their logical content" are "shadings associated with the grammatical relations subject and direct object" and "inferences arising from the pragmatics or 'use' of sentences." Make up two sentences that illustrate each of these types of "extralogical meaning." Be prepared to explain how your examples work.

7. Explain the concept of "hedge words." Then make up a sentence in which each of the following hedge words could be used appropriately: *technically, strictly, loosely speaking, sort of, kind of, regular,* and *real.*

8. Explain what is odd or false about each of the following sentences. (Taken from George L. Dillon, *Introduction to Contemporary Linguistic Semantics.* Englewood Cliffs, NJ: Prentice-Hall, 1977, p. 24.)
   a. Strictly speaking the president is the chief executive.
   b. A beagle is sort of a dog.
   c. Loosely speaking, Peter is a skunk.
   d. A whale is a typical mammal.
   e. Strictly speaking, tomatoes are vegetables.

25

Bad Birds and Better Birds: Prototype Theories

Jean Aitchison

Which of the following list of colors most closely resembles the color blue: teal blue, peacock blue, sky blue, royal blue, navy blue, or midnight blue? How do we distinguish between such subtle differences in meaning? Semantics is the area of linguistics that analyzes the meaning of individual words and phrases. In this selection Jean Aitchison, from the Language Studies Center at University of London, examines a peculiar trait of our language that allows humans to cope with the ambiguities of word-meaning in English. Speakers of English use many words with slightly different meanings to represent similar messages, such as the use of the terms "happy, excited, jubilant, delighted, or elated" to represent a positive, pleasant, personal feeling. Aitchison refers to this ambiguous classification of word-meaning as "prototype theories." The question of how we determine which words are best suited to one specific thought is but one of the questions Aitchison attempts to answer in her exploration of our ambiguous system of word-meanings and how words are stored in the brain.

> The Hatter . . . had taken his watch out of his pocket, and was looking at it uneasily, shaking it every now and then, and holding it to his ear . . .
>
> 'Two days wrong!' sighed the Hatter, 'I told you butter wouldn't suit the works!'. . .
>
> Alice had been looking over his shoulder with some curiosity. 'What a funny watch!' she remarked. 'It tells the day of the month, and doesn't tell what o'clock it is!'
>
> — LEWIS CARROLL, *Alice's Adventures in Wonderland*

If words have a hazy area of application, we are faced with a serious problem in relation to the mental lexicon. How do we manage to cope with words at all? The quotation above from *Alice in Wonderland* gives us a clue. Alice appears to have some notion of what constitutes a "proper watch." This enables her to identify the butter-smeared object owned by the Hatter as a watch, and to comment that it is a "funny" one.

A feeling that some examples of words may be more central than others appears to be widespread, as shown by a dialogue between two small girls in a popular cartoon strip:

AUGUSTA: What colour did you say the Martians are?
FRIEND: Green.
AUGUSTA: What sort of green? I mean are they an emerald green or a pea green or an apple green or a sage green or a sea green or what?
FRIEND: Well I think they're a sort of greeny green.

Humans, then, appear to find some instances of words more basic than others. Such an observation may shed light on how people understand their meaning. Take birds. Perhaps people have an amalgam of ideal bird characteristics in their minds. Then, if they saw a pterodactyl, they would decide whether it was likely to be a bird by matching it against the features of a bird-like bird, or, in fashionable terminology, a "prototypical" bird. It need not have all the characteristics of the prototype, but if the match was reasonably good it could be labelled *bird*, though it might not necessarily be a very good example of a bird. This viewpoint is not unlike the check-list viewpoint, but it differs in that in order to be a bird, the creature in question does not have to have a fixed number of bird characteristics, it simply has to be a reasonable match.

This is an intriguing idea. But, like any intriguing idea, it needs to be tested. How could we find out if people really behave in this way? In fact, psychologists showed quite a long time ago that people treat colours like this (e.g., Lenneberg, 1967; Berlin and Kay, 1969). However, this type of study has only relatively recently been extended to other types of vocabulary items. Let us consider one of the pioneering papers on the topic.

BIRDY BIRDS AND VEGETABLEY VEGETABLES

Just over ten years ago Eleanor Rosch, a psychologist at the University of California at Berkeley, carried out a set of experiments in order to test the idea that people regarded some types of birds as "birdier" than other birds, or some vegetables more vegetable-like, or some tools more tooly.

She devised an experiment which she carried out with more than 200 psychology students: "This study has to do with what we have in mind when we use words which refer to categories" ran the instructions (Rosch, 1975: 198).

Let's take the word red as an example. Close your eyes and imagine a true red. Now imagine an orangish red . . . imagine a purple red. Although you might still name the orange red or the purple red with the term red, they are not as good examples of red . . . as the clear 'true' red. In short, some reds are redder than others. The same is true for other kinds of categories. Think of dogs. You all have some notion of what a 'real dog', a 'doggy dog' is. To me a retriever or a German shepherd is a very doggy dog while a Pekinese is a less doggy dog. Notice that this kind of judgment has nothing to do with how well you like the thing; you can like a purple red better than a true red but still recognize that the color you like is not a true red. You may prefer to own a Pekinese without thinking that it is the breed that best represents what people mean by dogginess.

The questionnaire which followed was ten pages long. On each page was a category name, such as "Furniture," "Fruit," "Vegetable," "Bird," "Carpenter's Tool," "Clothing," and so on. Under each category was a list of 50 or so examples. *Orange, lemon, apple, peach, pear, melon* appeared on the fruit list, and so did most of the other fruits you would be likely to think up easily. The order of the list was varied for different students to ensure that the order of presentation did not bias the results. The students were asked to rate how good an example of the category each member was on a seven-point scale: rating something as "1" meant that they considered it an excellent example; "4" indicated a moderate fit; whereas "7" suggested that it was a very poor example, and probably should not be in the category at all.

The results were surprisingly consistent. Agreement was particularly high for the items rated as very good examples of the category. Almost everybody thought that a *robin* was the best example of a bird, that *pea* was the best example of a vegetable and *chair* the best example of furniture. On the bird list, *sparrow, canary, blackbird, dove* and *lark* all came out high (Figure 25.1). *Parrot, pheasant, albatross, toucan* and *owl* came somewhat lower. *Flamingo, duck* and *peacock* were lower still. *Ostrich, emu* and *penguin* came more than half-way down the seven-point rating, while last of all came *bat*, which probably shouldn't be regarded as a bird at all. Similar results were found for the other categories, that is, *shirts, dresses* and *skirts* were considered better examples of clothing than *shoes* and *stockings*, which were in turn higher than *aprons* and *earmuffs. Guns* and *daggers* were better examples of weapons than *whips* and *axes*, which were better than *pitchforks* and *bricks. Saws, hammers* and *screwdrivers* were better examples of carpenters' tools than *crowbars* and *plumb-lines.*

Psychologists on the other side of America obtained very similar results when they repeated the experiment (Armstrong *et al.*, 1983), so the results are not just a peculiar reaction of Californian psychology students. And Rosch carried out other experiments which supported her original results. For example, she checked how long it took students to verify category membership. That is, she said, "Tell me whether the following is true," and then gave the students sentences such as "A penguin is a bird," or "A sparrow is a bird." She found that good exemplars (her name for examples) of a category were verified faster than less good exemplars, so that it took longer to say "yes" to "A penguin is a bird" than it did to "A sparrow is a bird" (Rosch, 1975).

The results of these experiments are fairly impressive. But there is one obvious criticism: were the students just responding faster to more common words? After all, people come across sparrows far more fre-

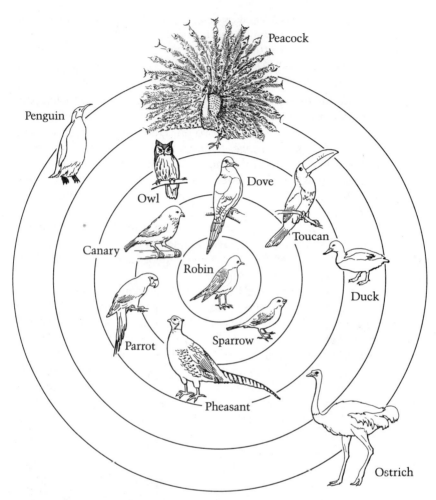

Figure 25.1. Birdiness rankings.

quently than penguins, and hammers more often than crowbars. Obviously, frequency of usage is likely to have some effect: in California nectarines and boysenberries are commoner than mangoes and kumquats, so it is not surprising that the former were regarded as "better" exemplars of fruit than the latter. However, the results could not be explained away solely on the basis of word frequency. On the furniture list, rare items of furniture such as *love seat, davenport, ottoman* and *cedar chest* came out much higher than *refrigerator,* which is a standard part of every American household. On the vegetable list, *pea, carrot* and *cauliflower* came out higher than *onion, potato* and *mushroom.* And on the clothes list, *pyjamas* and *bathing suit* came out higher than *shoe, tie, hat* and *gloves.* So people genuinely feel that some things are better exemplars of a category than others, a feeling which is not simply due to how often one comes across the word or object in question.

Furthermore, these judgments were not made primarily on the basis of appearance. Peas, according to Rosch, are prototypical vegetables. If people were simply comparing other vegetables to a visual image of a pea, then we would expect carrots to come out near the bottom of the list. In fact, they come very near the top. And if visual characteristics were important, we would also expect vegetables which look similar, such as carrots, parsnips and radishes, to be clustered together. But they are not. Nor were judgments made purely in terms of use. If this was so one would expect benches and stools to come out near the top, since they are closest in function to the prototypical piece of furniture, a chair. But in fact bookcases rank higher than either benches or stools. It is not immediately obvious, therefore, how people came to their conclusions. They were making some type of analysis, though its exact basis was unclear as the criteria used seemed to be heterogeneous.

To summarize, Rosch's work suggests that when people categorize common objects, they do not expect them all to be on an equal footing. They seem to have some idea of the characteristics of an ideal exemplar, in Rosch's words, a "prototype." And they probably decide on the extent to which something else is a member of the same category by matching it against the features of the prototype. It does not have to match exactly, it just has to be sufficiently similar, though not necessarily visually similar.

Prototype theory is useful, then, for explaining how people deal with untypical examples of a category. This is how unbirdy birds such as pelicans and penguins can still be regarded as birds. They are sufficiently like the prototype, even though they do not share all its characteristics. But it has a further advantage: it can explain how people cope with damaged examples. Previously linguists had found it difficult to explain why anyone could still categorize a one-winged robin who couldn't fly as a bird, or a three-legged tiger as a quadruped. Now one just assumes that these get matched against the prototype in the same way as an untypical category member. A one-winged robin who can't fly can still be a bird, even though it's not such a typical one.

Furthermore, the prototype effect seems to work for actions as well as objects: people can, it appears, reliably make judgements that *murder* is a better example of killing than *execute* or *suicide*, and that *stare* is a better example of looking than *peer* or *squint* (Pulman, 1983).

However, so far we have dealt only with assigning objects and actions to larger categories. We now need to consider whether this is the way in which humans cope with individual words.

DEGREES OF LYING

"Can you nominate in order now the degrees of the lie?" asks a character in Shakespeare's play *As You Like It* (V, iv), and the clown Touchstone responds by listing seven degrees of lying. Obviously the idea that some lies are better lies than others has been around for a long time, and still seems to be relevant today.

A "good" lie, it transpires, has several characteristics (Coleman and Kay, 1981). First, the speaker has to assert something that is untrue. However, people often utter untruths without being regarded as liars, particularly in cases of genuine mistakes: a child who argued that six and four make eleven would not be thought of as lying. So a second characteristic of a good lie is that a speaker must believe that what he is saying is false. But even this is insufficient, because a person can knowingly tell untruths without being a liar, as in: "You're the cream in my coffee, you're the sugar in my tea" (metaphor), "He stood so still, you could have mistaken him for a doorpost" (exaggeration or hyperbole), "Since you're a world expert on the topic, perhaps you could tell us how to get the cat out of the drainpipe?" (sarcasm). A third characteristic must therefore be added for a good lie, that the speaker must intend to deceive those addressed. In brief, a fully-fledged or prototypical lie occurs when a speaker:

1. asserts something false
2. which they know to be false
3. with the intention of deceiving.

A prototypical lie, therefore, might occur when a child denies having eaten a jam tart which it knows full well it has just scoffed. But consider a situation such as the following: "Schmallowitz is invited to dinner at his boss's house. After a dismal evening enjoyed by no one, Schmallowitz says to his hostess, 'Thanks, it was a terrific party.' Schmallowitz doesn't believe it was a terrific party, and he isn't really trying to convince anyone he had a good time, but is just concerned to say something to his boss's wife, regardless of the fact that he doesn't expect her to believe it" (Coleman and Kay, 1981: 31).

Did Schmallowitz lie? The 71 people asked this question were quite unsure. They had been told to grade a number of situations on a seven-point scale, from 1 (very sure non-lie) to 7 (very sure lie). For many people, Schmallowitz's situation lay just in the middle between these two extremes, at point 4, where they were unable to decide whether it was a lie or not. Another situation which lay in the middle was the case of Superfan, who got tickets for a championship game, and phoned early in the day to tell his boss that he could not come to work as he was sick. Ironically Superfan doesn't get to the game, because the mild stomachache he had that morning turned out to be quite severe food poisoning.

Both the Schmallowitz and Superfan cases broke out of the conditions of a good lie, though each broke a different condition. Schmallowitz was not trying to deceive his hostess, he was merely trying to be polite. Superfan did not tell an untruth. Lies, then, like birds, can be graded. Lies can still be lies even when they are not prototypical lies, and they shade off into not being "proper" lies at all.

The realization that individual words need not be used in their proto-typical sense can explain a number of puzzling problems, especially cases in which people are unsure of whether they are dealing with the "same" word or not. Consider the following sentences (Jackendoff, 1983):

I must have seen that a dozen times, but I never noticed it.

I must have looked at that a dozen times, but I never saw it.

Some people have argued that there are two different verbs *see*, one mean-ing "my gaze went to an object," as in the first sentence, and the other containing in addition the meaning "something entered my awareness," as in the second. But perhaps the first sentence contains an unprototypical usage of the verb *see* (Jackendoff, 1983). In prototypical instances of seeing, one's gaze goes to an object and the object enters one's awareness. But if the first characteristic is absent, one can stare at something without noticing it. If the second characteristic is absent, something can enter a person's awareness, such as a dream or hallucination, even though his gaze has not gone anywhere.

To take another example, look at the following sentences:

The staircase goes from top to bottom of the building.

The lift goes from top to bottom of the building.

The janitor goes from top to bottom of the building.

Some people might argue as to whether these are all instances of the same word *go*, since the janitor is clearly moving but the staircase is not. But a prototype approach allows one to treat this as all one word, *go* (Aitchison, 1985). In its prototypical use, *go* involves something moving from one point to another. However, the same word can be used untypi-cally, so that something can extend from one point to another, with no movement involved. Alternatively, something can leave one point but never get to another, as in:

The train goes at ten o'clock.

Judging something against a prototype, therefore, and allowing rough matches to suffice, seems to be the way we understand a number of differ-ent words. Furthermore, a general realization that this is how humans probably operate could be of considerable use in real-life situations, as in the example that follows.

MAD, BAD AND DANGEROUS TO KNOW

Some years ago a man who specialized in brutal murders of women was brought to trial. The Yorkshire Ripper, as he was called, divided public opinion sharply. Some people argued that he was simply bad, and therefore ought to be punished with a long term of imprisonment. Others claimed that he must be mad, in which case he should be admitted to a hospital and treated as someone who was not responsible for his actions.

Was he mad? Or was he bad? According to newspaper reports, the judge asked the jury to consider whether the Ripper had told the truth to the psychiatrists who examined him. The discrepancies and alterations in the Ripper's story made them conclude that he had told a considerable number of lies. This led them to classify him as "guilty"—bad, not mad. This judgement implies, therefore, that anyone who lies cannot be mad, a somewhat strange conclusion. Perhaps the situation would have been less confusing if the terms *mad* and *bad* had been considered in terms of prototypes (Aitchison, 1981a).

"To define true madness, What is't to be nothing else but mad?" asks Polonius, on observing the deranged Hamlet (II, ii). But contrary to Polonius's opinion, madness is not an all or nothing state. A prototypical mad person has several different characteristics. A mad person is, first, someone who thinks and acts abnormally. But this is insufficient, as it would categorize as mentally deranged such people as chess champions. Someone truly mad would, in addition, be unaware that he was thinking and acting abnormally, and furthermore, be unable to prevent himself from behaving oddly. A prototypical lunatic, therefore, might be someone who covers his head with tin-foil because he fears that moon men are about to attack, or someone who walks on her hands because God has supposedly told her not to wear out her feet. On this analysis, the Ripper was partially mad, because he acted strangely and seemed unable to prevent himself from doing so. Yet he was not prototypically mad, because he was perfectly aware that his actions were abnormal.

To turn to badness, someone bad commits antisocial acts, is aware that their actions are antisocial and could control their behaviour if they wished. So a prototypical villain might be the pirate Captain Hook in Peter Pan, or Shakespeare's character Iago. On this reasoning, the Ripper was partially bad in that he acted antisocially and was aware of it, but not entirely bad since he apparently could not control his actions.

To modify Caroline Lamb's statement about Lord Byron and reapply it to the Ripper, one could say that he is "Around two-thirds mad, two-thirds bad and certainly dangerous to know." No wonder the jury took so long to decide whether he was mad *or* bad, when he was neither prototypically mad nor prototypically bad.

THE ODDITY OF ODD NUMBERS

Prototypes seem to explain a lot. They show how people deal with the fuzziness of word meaning, and how new or damaged examples can be assigned to existing categories. Something could still be labelled a parrot if it was sufficiently like a prototypical parrot, even if it had one leg, pink and blue stripes and carried an umbrella. There remain, however, a number of unsolved questions. These will be discussed in the remainder of the chapter.

"The oddity of odd numbers" is perhaps the most puzzling problem. A group of researchers found that some odd numbers were felt to be "better" odd numbers than others (Armstrong *et al.*, 1983). The subjects they quizzed thought that 3 was a better example of an odd number than 23, which was in turn better than 57 or 447! How could people possibly think that 3 was better than 23 when both are equally odd? Furthermore, this result had nothing to do with the ambiguity of the word *odd* which can mean either "uneven" or "peculiar," because the researchers found a very similar result for even numbers: 4 was considered a better example than 18, which was in turn better than 34 or 106! So what's going on? Surely when they judge whether 57 is a good example of an odd number, people are not matching it against a prototypical odd number such as 3? Can we explain all this away, or is there some fatal flaw in prototype theory?

People are still arguing about these results, but a plausible explanation is that we need to make a distinction between identification criteria and stored knowledge (Osherson and Smith, 1981). In judging whether something is a good example of an odd number, people may be using easy recognition as their yardstick rather than basic knowledge. A clash between identification and knowledge is common in some areas. Take bulls. A farmer had trouble with people breaking down fences with the result that this cattle escaped, according to a newspaper report (*The Guardian*, November 1984). He therefore put a ring through the nose of one of the cows. Since a ring usually signifies a bull, which might be dangerous, he reckoned it would successfully keep people away. Within two days he had a telephone call from the local police:

> POLICE: You've got a bull in the park—it's illegal.
> FARMER: I'm sorry but we have no bull in the park.
> POLICE: I've seen it myself—I saw the ring in its nose.
> FARMER: You'd better go and look at the other end.

The moral is obvious. People know that bulls are male but they do not normally identify them by checking their genitalia—they identify them by something which could be quite extraneous to their basic make-up. The problems such cases raise in relation to prototypes is that we do not know exactly how identification criteria are interwoven with stored knowledge in the minds of speakers.

Of course, with many words identification criteria and stored knowledge might be the same, as perhaps with *rainbow* or *lamp-post*. But in a large number of others there may be a difference, even though the two will probably overlap to a considerable extent. How we perceive and identify things cannot be entirely removed from our stored knowledge of them: "Any sharp division between perception and conception seems questionable" (Miller and Johnson-Laird, 1976: 41). A further complication is that people sometimes have to interweave their own observations with information presented by others, since biological taxonomies and cultural beliefs may clash with instincts. For example, children often find it hard to believe that a spider is not an insect, a whale is not a fish and a bat is not a bird. And in Papua New Guinea, the Karam people of the upper Kaironk valley do not regard the cassowary as a bird, even though to us it obviously is one (Bulmer, 1967). It is unclear how such "facts" get integrated into a person's overall view of a word's meaning. This indicates that finding out the characteristics of a prototype is enormously difficult. Let us briefly summarize these difficulties.

FURTHER PROBLEMS WITH PROTOTYPES

There are basically three main problems which arise in specifying a prototype: first, the diversity of the characteristics which make up the prototype; second, the difficulty of arranging them in order of priority, since some are clearly more important than others; third, the problem of knowing where to stop. Let us briefly deal with each of these.

As we have seen, the properties of a prototype are heterogeneous, involving both identification criteria and knowledge. In addition, prototypes vary quite considerably in type from one another. For example, a birdy bird seems to be treated rather differently from a reddy red (Jackendoff, 1983). A birdy bird involves a cluster of "typicality conditions" relating to appearance and behaviour: it is likely to have feathers, wings and a beak, fly and lay eggs in a nest. But a reddy red is somewhat different in nature, unless one happens to be a physicist who can analyse the various properties of colours. For most people, a reddy red is likely to be characterized by "centrality conditions"—it will have a central place within a range of reds. To take another example, a *table* is likely to have a set of typical table features, but the term *adult* is usually understood with reference to a central example: a man of 25 would be a more adult-like adult than a 17-year-old.

So analysing the characteristics of a prototype turns out to be enormously difficult. A further problem is deciding how to arrange these characteristics in order of importance. Take birds. It is probably fairly important for a bird to have feathers. As the humorous poet Ogden Nash once noted:

> All I know about the bird:
> It is feathered, not furred.

But what comes next? Perhaps having wings. What then? Ability to fly? Egg laying? Nest building? There are unlikely to be clear answers, as suggested by the argument between the bird and the duck in Prokofiev's *Peter and the Wolf:*

Seeing the duck, the little bird flew down upon the grass, settled next to her and shrugged his shoulders:

"What kind of a bird are you, if you can't fly?" said he.

To this, the duck replied:

"What kind of a bird are you, if you can't swim?" and dived into the pond.

They argued and argued . . .

Furthermore, in trying to sort out the features of a prototype, where does one stop? There seems to be no end to the amount of encyclopaedic knowledge which people have about things, so does someone trying to model the mental lexicon have to go on for ever? In some cases this is particularly tricky, because it seems impossible to separate out the meaning of a particular word from the whole situation in which it occurs. Consider Gus, a character in Pinter's play *The Dumb Waiter*, who seems to have a clear idea of what a prototypical bowl of salad is like:

"They've probably got a salad bowl up there. Cold meat, radishes, cucumbers. Watercress, roll mops. Hardboiled eggs."

Gus's prototypical salad bowl seems to go way beyond the "meaning" of the word: his mind seems to have flipped up a whole "salad bowl situation," with particular ingredients in the bowl. Or consider the conversation between Ackroyd and Boothroyd, two characters who visit a ruined abbey in Alan Bennett's play *A Day Out:*

ACKROYD: There were Cistercian monks here . . .

BOOTHROYD: It's an unnatural life, separating yourself off like that . . . There wouldn't be any kids, would there? And allus getting down on their knees. It's no sort of life . . .

Here, the word *monk* has triggered not just the basic "meaning" of the word but a whole situation, in which he imagines silent corridors and monks praying. Are all these associated scenes part of our encyclopaedic knowledge of a word? To some extent, yes. In our memory we seem to have sets of stereotypical situations, "remembered frameworks" (Minsky, 1975), which we call up as necessary. These "frames" or "scenarios" provide a background into which one fits the details of the present situation. No one is quite sure how these frames might work and there have been several different proposals (for a useful summary see Brown and Yule, 1983). From the point of view of the mental lexicon, such stereotypical situations seem to be optional back-up material which is accessed if required. If a person was asked to define a *zebra*, they could do this quite efficiently without calling up a whole "zoo" or "safari" frame. But if they overheard someone talking about a zebra seen in London earlier in the day, then they could go deeper into their memory, and call up a zoo frame, which allowed them to fit the narrative into a predicted set-up, and be prepared for mentions of turnstiles, monkeys and elephant-rides.

This back-up information may work in two ways. Either the entries in the mental lexicon are organized so that the most important things pop up first, or, alternatively, the mind may automatically flip up considerably more information than is necessary, and humans may be very good at discarding or suppressing information that is not required. Or perhaps these two mechanisms work together. But whatever the mechanism involved, the activation of whole frames in the mind makes it even harder to specify the characteristics of individual prototypes since they interact with other elements present in the scene, and involve the optional use of a seemingly endless supply of back-up material from a person's memory.

In short, even though we suspect that humans work from prototypes when they deal with word meaning, the exact specification of the prototypes which apparently exist in a person's mind is still a long way beyond our current ability.

However, the fact that a prototype often calls up a whole scene, in which numerous other words are involved, indicates one important fact: words cannot be dealt with in isolation. We need to consider how they are stored in relation to one another.

SUMMARY

This essay has discussed how humans are able to cope with word meaning when it is so fuzzy and fluid. It seems likely that they analyse a prototypical exemplar of a word and then match any new example against the characteristics of the prototype. It does not have to be a perfect match, merely a reasonable fit. This explains how words can be used with slightly different meanings, and how people can recognize new or damaged examples of a category.

However, certain problems remain. It is extremely difficult to analyse the features of a prototype, since identification criteria are interwoven with stored knowledge. It is equally difficult to arrange the various features in order of importance. And it is unclear where a prototype stops, since humans have a seemingly endless amount of information about every word, and often seem to access whole situations or "frames" in order to understand them. All these problems do not invalidate prototype theory. They simply show that there is still a lot we do not know about the human word-store. However, the fact that humans do not deal with these prototypes in isolation from one another shows that we need to find out more about how words fit together in the mental lexicon.

FOR DISCUSSION AND REVIEW

1. What is a "prototype theory"? In what ways is this theory of word classification useful in our ongoing study of language?

2. How do we qualify "lie"? In what instances are untruths not classified as lies? What complications could this "qualification system" present for foreign language and ESL students?

3. How do verbs such as "see" and "go" adhere to the prototype theory? Compare your results with other prototypes.

4. How do English speakers learn to judge something against a prototype?

5. What are the differences between "identification criteria" and "stored knowledge"? How do we communicate successfully if we do not know how identification criteria are interwoven with stored knowledge in speakers' minds?

6. Aitchison explains "How we perceive and identify things cannot be entirely removed from our stored knowledge of them: 'Any sharp division between perception and conception seems questionable.'" What does Aitchison mean by this statement?

7. What difficulties exist in defining the characteristics of a prototype?

8. How and where must we place restrictions on the sorting of prototype features? Give examples to support your claims.

9. Aitchison says: "In our memory we seem to have sets of stereotypical situations, 'remembered frameworks,' which we call up as necessary. These 'frames' or 'scenarios' provide a background into which one fits the details of the present situation." How do these "frameworks" operate and when do you suppose we call on them the most?

10. Why must we not deal with words in isolation?

26

Pragmatics

Madelon E. Heatherington

Pragmatics, the study of speech acts or of how language is used in various contexts, is a relatively new subfield of linguistics. It is an important field because of the increasing recognition among linguists that the context of an utterance and the beliefs shared by a speaker and a hearer play an important role in determining meaning. Often people utter sentences that mean more than, or even something apparently different from, what they actually say, and yet listeners understand the additional or altered meaning. In the following selection from her book How Language Works, *Madelon E. Heatherington discusses (1) the various types of illocutionary force, or the communicative intent of the speaker; (2) conversational principles, or expectations that are shared by all participants in a conversation; and (3) presuppositions, the surprisingly large number of assumptions made by all speakers about what their listeners know. Although it is difficult to analyze, this complex of social knowledge that constitutes the rules of pragmatics must be included in any complete description of language.*

This field of study [pragmatics] deals with particular utterances in particular situations and is especially concerned with the various ways in which the many social contexts of language performance can influence interpretation. Pragmatics goes beyond such influences as suprasegmental phonemes, dialects, and registers (all of which also shape interpretation) and looks at speech performance as primarily a social act ruled by various social conventions.

Anyone who is not a hermit lives in daily contact with other human beings, learns the explicit and implicit codes by which human beings usually manage to keep from doing violence to one another, and responds to alterations in those codes with greater or lesser good nature and skill. We drive on the right-hand side of the road and expect other drivers to do so. When we write checks, we have the money to cover them, and we expect the bank to honor them. We assume that food will be forthcoming in a restaurant, haircuts in a barber shop, gasoline—maybe—from a service station. We know these contexts so well that we do not think much about them, nor do we often stop to list the expectations we have about the behavior of people in such contexts. Ordinarily, there is no need to be explicit, because ordinarily, everybody else is behaving as we would expect them to. The "unspoken rules" governing behavior work very well, most of the time.

Occasionally, however, they do not work, or someone is not aware of them, or they are deliberately violated. Then it becomes important to be explicit about the "rules," the silent expectations and conventions, in order to discover what they ask of us and whether they are worth saving or not. For example, many people in the past decade or so have come to question certain "rules" about what gentlemen should do for ladies (open doors, light cigarettes, carry packages, etc.), asking whether those behaviors are fixed for all time by generic requirements or perhaps are signs, in the semiotic sense, of role-playing and strategies for coping with conflict. Similarly, pragmatics attempts to identify the "rules" underlying the performance of speech acts, or language as it is uttered in conjunction with the many social conventions controlling what speaker and auditor expect from one another.

Pragmatics theorists have identified three kinds of speech-act principles: illocutionary force, referring to the speaker as interpreted pragmatically by his auditors; conversational principles, referring to the auditors' expectations of the speaker; and presuppositions, referring to assumptions held by both the speaker and the auditors. Each of the three principles, of course, influences the others and therefore influences the significance of the speech act as a whole.

ILLOCUTIONARY FORCE

This is the speaker's intention, so far as the auditors can discern it from the context. There are two major kinds of illocutionary force: implicit, below the surface and unstated, and explicit, on the surface and stated. The implicit forces are three: assertion, imperative, and question (sometimes called interrogative). Assertion is a statement about action or attitude ("He loves you," "He does not love you"). An imperative is a command for action ("Shut up!" "Will you please shut up!"). An interrogative is a request for information ("How much is that tie?" "What time is it?"). It is important to identify these implicit forces not only theoretically, but also as they appear in their various social contexts, for frequently the apparent intention of the speaker is not the same as the actual intent.

Social convention and good manners usually dictate, for instance, that a speaker will not use imperatives in polite company, perhaps at a party, at dinner, or when he is courting someone's favor. We are taught very early to say "please" as a way of disguising the illocutionary force of a command: "Please pass the biscuits"; "Give me the salt, please." It is even more polite to phrase the imperative as a question: "May I [or Can I] get through here?" "Would you like to go home now?" Most of us recognize that the implicit illocutionary force of these apparent questions is imperative, not interrogative, and we send the salt down or open a passageway without demur. We do not ordinarily respond to such implied commands by saying, "No" or by saying, "Yes" and not handing along the biscuits. We all understand that "May I have the biscuits?" is not a request for information, to be answered by "Yes" or "No," which would then have to be followed by another request for information—"Will you send them down here?"—which could then also be answered "Yes" or "No," and on and on while the biscuits stayed where they were and got cold.

Sometimes, however, the implicit illocutionary force of an utterance is not so clear, for it is often disguised by the surface-structure phrasing. When someone sitting outdoors on a cool evening says "I'm cold," that is phrased as a statement; it apparently requires neither information nor action. But if there is a wrap in the house, brought along for just this chilliness, and if the speaker's companion is attentive, the simple statement will probably be recognized as an implied command to bring the wrap out. Similarly, the statement "You're driving too fast" (assertion) may often carry the implicit illocutionary force of a command to slow down. "Do you love me?"—an apparent question—may carry many different implicit illocutionary forces: really a question, to be answered "Yes" or "No"; an assertion (perhaps "I love you" or perhaps "I am uncertain about your love for me"); or a command ("Tell me you love me"). Only context, linguistic or otherwise, will clarify this complex utterance.

It may be tentatively suggested that the more intimate the register, the more disguised the implicit illocutionary force in any given speech act. Conversely, the more formal is the register, the less disguised the force. Drill instructors in the armed forces do not suggest; they command. Their audience is presumed to be unfamiliar with the nuances of social convention that would instantaneously translate "Why don't we go for a walk?" into "Fifty-mile forced march, full packs, on the double!" Formalized situations tend to call for formalized utterances, so that an audience of varied backgrounds does not have to fumble with unfamiliar codes and levels of implied illocutions.

The other major kind of illocutionary force is explicit. Explicit illocutionary forces in speech acts take the form of statements in which the utterance itself is an action. "I tell you, it was awful!" performs the act of telling which the verb names. "I pronounce you man and wife" performs the act of pronouncing. "I promise I'll break your head" constitutes the act of promising. Statements like these, promising or pronouncing or telling (or asking or commanding), are called performative utterances; the utterance itself is the deed. There is an understood contract in such utterances, for assertions like these always carry the force of an unspoken command. The unspoken (implicit) command is that the auditor should believe the assertions to be true (should accept their truth value): it is true that something was awful; you are man and wife; your head will get broken.

Most of the time, we do accept such assertions as true, or we pretend to do so, but if the context is intimate enough, the implicit truth value may be questioned even here: "Oh, yeah? Who says it was awful? You wouldn't know 'awful' if it bit you!" Or "Oh, yeah? You and what army gonna break my head?" (But rarely, "Oh, yeah? Who says you're married?" for the context here is formal, not intimate.) When explicit and implicit intentions clash over a performative utterance, the auditors are challenging the speaker's capacity, not to *tell* the truth, but to *verify* the truth of the statements. The speaker is challenged to match the truth value of the utterance to some external referent or some action.

CONVERSATIONAL PRINCIPLES

This brings us to what the auditor can expect from a speaker, as opposed to the interpretive skills that a speaker can expect from his audience. In any speech act, the audience generally assumes that at least four conversational principles will apply to what a speaker says. The audience's first assumption is that the speaker is sincere, not saying one thing and meaning another, at least with no greater discrepancy between phrasing and intention than what we expect in the exercise of various illocutionary forces. The second assumption is that the speaker is telling the truth so far as he understands it, not deliberately telling lies. Third, the audience assumes that what the speaker has to say is relevant to the topic or general areas of concern. The final assumption is that the speaker will contribute the appropriate amount of information or commentary, not withhold anything important and not rattle on for an undue amount of time.

For example, if someone (speaker) asks, "What time is it?" we (auditors) usually assume that he does not know what the time is and that his request is a sincere one for information about the time. When we (now speakers) begin to reply, he (now auditor) will usually assume that we will answer with the correct time, not with a rambling discourse on the price of hamburger, nor with a scream of rage, nor with a lie. If any of those four assumptions prove incorrect, then discord immediately appears and one or the other of the conversants has to make a quick test of the assumptions, to discover which one has been violated and what the appropriate response should now be.

For example, should people be hurrying out of a burning building, a request for the correct time is presumed to be insincere and will elicit irritation or disgust: "You crazy? Keep moving!" But if someone begins a prepared speech on tax reform to the Lions Club with a joke about peanut butter, the audience will unconsciously recognize that the relevance of the joke is less to taxes than to the reduction of stress between strangers. It is understood here that the context of speech giving requires some preliminary establishment of shared concerns, even a sort of shared companionship, between the orator and the audience. Such a speaker is not expected to launch immediately into the technical points of his topic. But if that speaker's boss asks for a short telephone conversation on the same topic of tax reform, a joke would not be appropriate as an opening; it would be irrelevant in the context of a business discussion.

PRESUPPOSITIONS

Here, we move into what both speakers and auditors can expect of the content or information contained in an utterance,[1] that is, what a speaker and an auditor can suppose each other to know before a given speech act begins. For example, if I say, "But Jenny has never gone out with a married man before!" I presuppose (before I utter the sentence) that my listener knows at least these content items:

1. There is a person named Jenny.
2. Speaker and listener are both acquainted with Jenny.
3. Jenny goes out with men.
4. Jenny has just recently gone out with a married man.

Presumably, too, the listener and speaker both share the following bits of information, although these presuppositions are not so obvious nor so demonstrable from the utterance alone:

5. Jenny is female.
6. Jenny is not married.
7. Jenny does not usually go out with married men.
8. Jenny is adult.
9. Jenny is not so dependent upon speaker or listener that her behavior can be regulated by either of them.
10. Speaker and listener are surprised by Jenny's behavior.

Presupposition underlies a good deal of the unthinking adjustment we make from one speech situation to another, adjustment that helps ensure we are not (as speech-communication teachers say) "talking over our audience's head" or not "insulting our audience's intelligence." Presupposition is operating when we mutter secrets in hallways so that outsiders will not understand. All codes, jargons, cants, and deliberate use of elliptical or confusing language make use of presupposition.

It is very easy to misjudge presupposition when one does not know

---

[1] Since each of the three speech-act principles influences the other, it will be recognized that to separate presupposition from the other two is to be somewhat arbitrary. Presupposition about content will vary from one speech situation to another, depending on the influence of intention and expectation.

one's audience well, or when one thinks one knows them all too well. A good many people seem to sense this principle, as evidenced by the frequency with which they intersperse phrases like "You know," "I mean," or "Know what I mean?" in their conversation. For instance, if I tell you that I will meet you on the corner of Third and Main at noon today, I assume that you know what noon is, where Third Street makes a corner with Main Street, and which of the four points of that intersection I will be waiting on. If you are new in town, I may wait a long time. Conversely, if my husband tells me he wants his favorite meal for dinner and presupposes I will cook it, because we have been married a long time and I always know and cook what he asks for, then he may wait a long time. Presuppositions always require testing from time to time, to be sure that what the speaker and what the auditor assume or know are really the same.

An attentiveness to the unspoken and often unconscious "rules" or expectations inherent in speech acts can help to sharpen our awareness of what is really going on as we speak. The illocutionary force implicit in certain contexts, the active nature of performative statements, the conversational principles applicable to most speech situations, and the presuppositions all of us bring to conversations: these pragmatic contexts of language use shape our performance all the time. The more we understand them, perhaps the better we can control them. The same may be said of our control over individual meanings as well.

FOR DISCUSSION AND REVIEW

1. Develop the many implications of Heatherington's statement that pragmatics "looks at speech performance as primarily a social act ruled by various social conventions."

2. One of the three basic kinds of speech act principles is *illocutionary force,* a term that refers to the speaker's communicative intention to the extent that the hearer(s) can discern it. It is divided into *implicit illocutionary force* and *explicit illocutionary force.* Define these three concepts in your own words.

3. The three implicit illocutionary forces are assertion, imperative, and question (interrogative). Why is it important, in actual conversations, that the hearer identify these implicit illocutionary forces? Give an example from your own experience of an utterance or exchange involving a discrepancy between implicit and explicit illocutionary force. Did the social context make clear the actual intentions of the speaker? If so, describe how.

4. Heatherington suggests that "the more intimate the register, the more disguised the implicit illocutionary force in any speech act.

Conversely, the more formal is the register, the less disguised the force." Do you agree? Support your answer with specific examples.

5. Define "explicit illocutionary force" and supply two examples of your own. Why are these speech acts called "performative utterances"? In what sense is there "an understood contract" in performative utterances?

6. Just as speakers expect certain behavior on the part of their audience, so too audiences have expectations about speaker behavior called conversational principles. In general, Heatherington says, audiences assume (1) that a speaker is sincere; (2) that a speaker is telling the truth; (3) that what a speaker says will be relevant to the topic under discussion; and (4) that the speaker will neither withhold important information nor monopolize the conversation. (Actually, all the participants in a conversation share these expectations.) Describe a situation in which all the conversational principles were observed and one in which one or more was violated. What conclusions can you draw?

7. Presuppositions involve both speakers and hearers; and all utterances, even the simplest, involve a number of presuppositions. Examine the following sentences and list the presuppositions for each:
   a. Mary's husband works for IBM.
   b. Even though Bob promised never to lie to me again, he told me today that he didn't go to the movies with Sherry.
   c. That C− I got on the Psych quiz you missed is really going to hurt my average.
   d. Nonsmokers have rights too!

27

Discourse Routines

Elaine Chaika

In the following chapter from her book Language: The Social Mirror, *Professor Elaine Chaika examines a variety of ways in which the social rules of language, an aspect of pragmatics, control what we say and when and how we say it. We cannot fully understand the meaning of an utterance unless we understand its social context. And in order to understand the social context, we need to consider a complex set of interrelated rules, including speech events, intentions, speech acts, preconditions, presuppositions, utterance pairs, roles and social status, presequences, collapsing sequences, repairs by speaker or hearer, and more. All of these discourse routines play important roles in social interaction; all are rule-governed and largely unconscious behaviors, are learned as part of the language acquisition process, and are so important to people that "even when it makes no difference in a fleeting social contact . . . they demand that the right forms be chosen."*

A PARADOX

Language makes us free as individuals but chains us socially. It has already been demonstrated that we are not mere creatures of conditioning when it comes to language. We can say things we never heard before, as well as understand what we have not previously heard.

When we consider discourse rules, however, we find a strange paradox. The social rules of language often force us into responding in certain ways. We are far from free in forming sentences in actual social situations. Frequently we must respond whether we want to or not. Furthermore, we must respond in certain ways (see Givon 1979; Schenkein 1978; Labov and Fanshel 1977).

MEANING AND THE SOCIAL SITUATION

The actual meaning of an utterance depends partially on the social context in which it occurs.

Rommetveit (1971) gives a classic example of this. He tells a story about a man running for political office who is scheduled to give a talk in a school auditorium. When he arrives, he sees that there are not enough chairs. He calls his wife at home. Then he goes to see the janitor. To each, the candidate says, "There aren't enough chairs." To the wife, this means "Wow! am I popular," but to the janitor it means "Go get some more chairs." The full meaning evoked by the statement "There aren't enough chairs" is largely a product of the context in which it is said, including the relative social statuses, privileges and duties of the speaker and listener. The remainder of this chapter is concerned with the obligations society places upon us in discourse, as well as the real meaning of utterances in a social context.

SPEECH EVENTS, GENRES, AND PERFORMANCES

A speech event is the situation calling forth particular ways of speaking (Gordon and Lakoff 1975). *Genre* refers to the form of speaking. Usually, it has a label, such as *joke, narrative, promise, riddle, prayer,* even *greeting* or *farewell.*

Members of a speech community recognize genres as having beginnings, middles, and ends, and as being patterned. "Did you hear the one about. . .," for instance, is a recognized opener for the genre *joke* in our society. "Once upon a time. . ." is a recognized opener for the genre *child's story,* and the ending is "They lived happily ever after." The end of *joke* is the *punch line,* often a pun, an unusual or unexpected response to a situation or utterance, or a stupid response by one of the characters in the joke. Typically the stupid response to a situation is one that reveals that the character is lacking in some basic social knowledge or one in which the social meaning of an utterance is ignored and its literal meaning is taken instead. For instance, an old Beetle Bailey cartoon shows Sarge saying to Zero "The wastebasket is full." Instead of emptying the basket, Zero responds "Even I can see that." The joke is that Zero took the words at their face value rather than interpreting them as a command, which was their actual social force.

Sometimes the genre is the entire speech event but not always. Church services are speech events, for instance. *Sermons* are a genre belonging to church, but sermons do not cover the entire speech event. Prayers, responsive readings, hymn singing, and announcements also constitute the speech events of church services.

The way that participants carry out the demands of a genre is their *performance.* In some communities, this is more important than others. Also, performance is more important in some speech events than others. A professor's performance, for instance, is far more important than that of the students in the classroom. The exception would be those classes in which students have been assigned special speaking tasks.

Perhaps *important* is not quite the right word. The professor's performance will be judged more overtly than a student's and judged according to different criteria. These are the criteria judged in public performance, such as clarity of diction, voice quality, logic of lecture, and coherence. Correct performance in less formal speech events is just as important, but in those judgment is often confined to how appropriate the speech was to the situation. Everyday discourse routines are as much performances as are preaching, joke-telling, and lecturing.

Linguists often use the word *performance* in a more general sense than here. They use it to refer to one's actual speech, which may contain errors, such as slips of the tongue. Since people often realize that they have made speech mistakes, linguists say that there is a difference between *competence* and performance. In this chapter, performance will refer specifically to one's ability to carry out the requirements of a speech event in a given social situation. This, too, may differ from one's competence in that one can be aware of errors in one's performance of a genre. A professor may realize with a sickening thud, for example, that a prepared lecture is boring a class to sleep, or a party goer may be unable to think of any of the small talk or repartee called for at a party.

Performances in discourse routines are strongly controlled by turn-taking rules that determine who speaks when. Co-occurrence restrictions . . . operate stringently on genres. Often the speech event itself determines them. The genre of sermons occurs in the speech event of church services. Therefore, only features that go with formal style are usually used in sermons. Jokes, in contrast, occur in informal, play situations or as a means of helping someone relax and become more informal. Therefore, formal style features are inappropriate in jokes, so that they are included usually only in the reported conversation of a character in the joke.

INTENTION

In all interaction, the parties assume that each person means what he or she says and is speaking with a purpose. Esther Goody (1978) points out that people impute intentions to others. In fact, she notes, they "positively seek out intentions in what others say and do." What people assume is another's intention colors the meaning they get from messages. How often has someone suspiciously said to a perfectly innocent comment of yours, "Now what did you mean by that?" The question is not asking for literal meaning but for your intention in saying what you did. Presequences rely heavily on our perceiving a speaker's intentions or thinking we do. The child who hears an adult's "Who spilled this milk?" may rightly perceive the question as the precursor to a command "Wipe it up!"

Often, intentions are not perceived correctly, causing misunderstandings as harmless as hearing an honest question as a command or as serious as hearing an innocent comment as an insult. To illustrate the last, consider a man who, in front of his slightly plump wife, looks admiringly at a model, "Wow! what a body on that one!" The wife immediately bridles (or dissolves in tears, depending on her personal style) with a "I know I'm too fat. You don't have to rub it in."

The only time that we are freed from the obligation to carry out the socially prescribed roles in speech events is when the other party is incapable of acting with a purpose, as when drunk, stoned, or insane (Frake 1964). Perhaps one of the reasons that we get so angry when someone does not act or speak appropriately for the situation is that we cannot figure out his or her goals. Without knowing someone's goals, we do not know how to act ourselves when dealing with another person.

SPEECH ACTS

People usually think of speech as a way of stating propositions and conveying information. Austin (1962) also stressed the functions of speech as a way of "doing things with words." Sociolinguists and anthropologists have been very concerned with how people use language to manage social interactions. Threatening, complimenting ("buttering someone up"), commanding, even questioning can all be manipulative. Another person's behavior may be affected quite differently from what one might expect from the actual words used. "See that belt?" may be sufficient to restrain a child from wrongdoing. The words themselves are an action. The child, of course, imputes intention to the words. They are heard as a threat of a spanking with the belt.

A CASE IN POINT: THE TELEPHONE

The ritual nature of conversation as well as the role of social convention in determining meaning is easily seen in rules for the telephone (Schegloff 1968). The telephone has been common in American homes only for the past fifty or so years. Yet very definite rules surround its usage. Exactly how such rules arose and became widespread throughout society is not precisely known, any more than we know exactly how a new dialect feature suddenly spreads through a population. All we know is that whenever a social need arises, language forms evolve to meet the need.

The first rule of telephone conversation in the United States is that the answerer speaks first. It does not have to be so. The rule could as easily be that the caller speaks first. That makes perfectly good sense, as it means that the one who calls is identified at once. Of course, the American way makes equally good sense in that callers are ensured that the receiver is at someone's ear before they start to speak. There are often several equally logical possibilities in conversation rituals, but any one group may adopt just one of the possible alternatives. In other words, if we come across ways different from our own, we should not assume that "theirs" are any better or worse than "ours."

In any event, in the United States, the convention is that the answerer speaks first. If the call could conceivably be for the answerer because he or she is answering the phone in his or her home, the usual first utterance is "Hello."

In places of business or in a doctor's or lawyer's office, wherever secretaries or operators answer the phone, "Hello" is not proper. Rather, the name of the business or office is given, as in "E. B. Marshall Company," "Smith and Carlson," "Dr. Sloan's office" or "George West Junior High." Giving the name in itself means "This is a business, institution, or professional office." At one time it was appropriate for servants in a household or even neighbors or friends who happened to pick up the phone to answer "Jones' residence" rather than "Hello," unless the call might conceivably be for the answerer. Increasingly, however, it appears that people answer "Hello" to a residential phone even if the call might not be for them. This situation can lead to complications, especially since the callers seem to assume that whoever answers "Hello" belongs to that phone.

The British custom of answering with one's name, as "Carl Jones here," seems to be a very efficient solution. Many American callers get thrown off by such a greeting, however. Being impressed with the British rule, I have repeatedly tried to answer my own home phone with "Elaine Chaika here." The result is usually a moment of silence followed by responses like "Uh . . . uh. Elaine?" or "Uh . . . uh. Is Danny there?" The "Uh . . . uh" probably signifies momentary confusion or embarrassment, somewhat different from the "Uh" hesitation that precedes a request to a stranger for directions or the time, as in "Uh, excuse me. . . ." Predictably, answering my office phone the same way does not elicit the "Uh . . . uh," although the moment of silence still often occurs.

Godard (1977) recounts the confusion on both her part and callers' in the United States because her native French routine requires that callers verify that the number called is the one reached. Violation of discourse routines, like violations of rules of style, hinders social interaction at least a little even when the violations otherwise fit the situation just fine.

After the answerer says "Hello" or another appropriate greeting, the caller asks, "Is X there?" unless he or she recognizes the answerer's voice as being the one wanted. If the caller recognizes the answerer's voice but wishes to speak to someone else, he or she might say, "Hi, X. Is Y there?" Some do not bother to greet the answerer first. Whether or not hurt feelings result seems to depend on the degree of intimacy involved. Students in my classes report that their mothers often feel hurt if a frequent caller does not say the equivalent of "Hi, Mrs. Jones. Is Darryl there?" Sometimes callers wish to acknowledge the existence of the answerer (phatic communication), but do not wish to be involved in a lengthy conversation so they say the equivalent of "Hi, Mrs. Jones. It's Mary. I'm sorry but I'm in a hurry. Is Darryl there?" On the surface, "I'm sorry but I'm in a hurry" seems to have no relevance. It does, though, because it is an acknowledgment that the caller recognizes acquaintance with the answerer and therefore, the social appropriateness of conversing with her or him.

COMPULSION IN DISCOURSE ROUTINES

In terms of social rules, perhaps what is most interesting is that the person who answers the phone feels compelled to go get the one the caller wants. This compulsion may be so great that answerers find themselves running all over the house, shouting out the windows if necessary to get the one called.

One student of mine, John Reilly, reported an amusing anecdote illustrating the strength of this obligation. He called a friend to go bowling, and the friend's sister answered the phone. She informed John that her brother was cutting logs but that she would go to fetch him. John, knowing that the woodpile was 100 yards away, assured her it was not necessary. All she had to do was to relay the message. Three times she insisted on going. Three times John told her not to. Finally, she said, confusedly, "Don't you want to talk to him?" John repeated that she could extend his invitation without calling the friend to the phone. Suddenly, she just left the phone without responding to John's last remarks and fetched her brother.

As extreme as this may sound, it is actually no more so than the person who leaps out of the tub to answer the phone and, still dripping wet with only a towel for protection, proceeds to run to another part of the house to summon the person for whom the caller asked. It is the rare person who can say, "Yes, X is here, but I don't see her. Call back later." Indeed, there are those who would consider such a response quite rude. It seems as if the person who picks up the phone has tacitly consented to go get whomever is called, regardless of inconvenience, unless the called one is not at home. The sense of obligation, of having to respond in a certain way, is at the core of all social routines, including discourse.

MEANING IN DISCOURSE ROUTINES

Actually, if the one called on the phone is not at home or does not live there any more or never lived there at all, the semantically appropriate response to "Is X there?" should be "No." In fact, however, "No," is appropriate only if X does live there but is not now at home. For example:
If X once lived there, but does not now, an appropriate answer is

1. X doesn't live here any more.
2. X has moved.

or even

3. X lives at _____ now.

Although "no" has the correct meaning, it cannot be used if X no longer lives there.

If X has never lived there, one may answer

4. There is no X here.
5. What number are you calling?
6. You must have the wrong number.

Again "no" would seem to be a fitting response, but it cannot be used. "No" to "Is X there?" always means that X does belong there but is not there now. Notice that 4 semantically fits for a meaning of "X no longer lives here," but it never would be used for that meaning by someone socialized into American society.

In discourse routines, frequently an apparently suitable response cannot be used in certain social situations or the response will have a greater meaning than the words used. For instance, one apparently proper response to:

7. Where are the tomatoes? (in a store)

is

8. I don't know.

Most people would find such an honest answer rude, even odd. More likely is

9. I'm sorry, but I don't work here.

or

10. I'm sorry, I'll ask the manager.

If the one asked is an employee, then 10 is appropriate. As with the telephone, the answerer feels obligated. In this instance, the obligation is to supply the answer if he or she is an employee.

PRECONDITIONS

The response 9 would be bizarre except that we all know it is not actually the answer to "Where are the tomatoes?" Rather, it is a response to the preconditions for asking a question of anyone (Labov and Fanshel 1977). These are:

I. The questioner has the right or the duty to ask the question.

II. The one asked has the responsibility or obligation to know the answer.

Preconditions for speech acts are as much a part of their meaning as actual words are. If one asks someone in a store where something is, one probably has categorized that person as an employee, and employees have an obligation to know where things are in their place of work. Hence 9 really means "You have categorized me erroneously. I don't work here, so I am not obligated to know the answer."
Sometimes people answer

11. "I don't work here, but the tomatoes are in the next aisle."

The giveaway here is the *but*. It makes no sense in 11 unless it is seen as a response to precondition II. When *but* joins two sentences, it often means "although," as in 11, which means "Although I don't work here I happen to know that the tomatoes are in the next aisle." That is, "Although I am not responsible for knowing or obligated to tell you, since I do not work here, I will anyhow." Note that the statement "I don't work here" really adds nothing to the pertinent information. It is frequently said anyhow as a way of letting the asker know that he or she miscategorized by assuming that the answerer was an employee.

PRESUPPOSITION

Some meaning in discourse is also achieved by presupposition. This refers to meaning that is never overtly stated but is always presupposed if certain phrases are used. If one says "Even Oscar is going," the use of *even* is possible only if one presupposes that Oscar usually does not go, so that the fact of his going means that everyone is going. Both preconditions and presuppositions are part of the meaning of utterance pairs to be discussed shortly, and both may help constrain the kinds of responses people make to utterances.

UTTERANCE PAIRS

The phenomenon of responsibility which we have already seen as part of telephone routines and answering questions is part of a larger responsibility that adheres to the discourse rules that Harvey Sacks called *utterance pairs* (1968–72, 1970). These are conversational sequences in which one utterance elicits another of a specific kind. For instance,

- Greeting–greeting
- Question–answer
- Complaint–excuse, apology, or denial

- Request/command–acceptance or rejection
- Compliment–acknowledgment
- Farewell–farewell

Whoever is given the first half of an utterance pair is responsible for giving the second half. The first half, in our society, commands the person addressed to give one of the socially recognized appropriate responses. As with the telephone, these responses often have a meaning different from, less than, or greater than the sum of the words used.

Furthermore, the first half of the pair does not necessarily have to sound like what it really is. That is, a question does not have to be in question form nor a command in command form. All that is necessary for a statement to be construed as a question or a command is for the social situation to be right for questioning or commanding. The very fact that a speech event is appropriate for a question or a command may cause an utterance to be perceived as such, even if it is not in question or command form. As with proper style, situation includes roles and relative status of participants in a conversation. Situation, roles, and social status are an inextricable part of meaning, often as much as, if not more so than, the surface form of an utterance.

QUESTIONS AND ANSWERS

Let us consider questions and answers. Goody (1978) points out that questions, being incomplete, are powerful in forcing responses, at least in our society. . . . We have already seen that certain preconditions exist for questioning and that an answer may be to the precondition rather than to the question itself. In the following discussion, it is always assumed that the preconditions for questioning are fulfilled. We will then be able to gain some insights into how people understand and even manipulate others on the basis of social rules.

There are two kinds of overt questions in English, *yes–no* questions and *wh-* questions. The first, as the name implies, requires an answer of yes or no. In essence, if the *yes–no* question forms are used, one is forced to answer "yes," "no," or "I don't know." There is no way not to answer, except to pretend not to hear. If that occurs, the asker usually repeats the question, perhaps more loudly, or even precedes the repetition with a tap on the would-be answerer's shoulder (or the equivalent). Alternatively, the asker could precede the repeated question with a summons, like "Hey, Bill, I said . . ." or any combination of the three.

It is because members of our society all recognize that they must answer a question and that they must respond "yes" or "no" to a *yes–no* question that the following question is a recognized joke:

12. Have you stopped beating your wife?/your husband?

Since you must know what you do to your spouse, "I don't know" cannot be answered. Only a "yes" or a "no" will do. Either answer condemns. Either way you admit to spouse-beating.

Yes–no questions can also be asked by tags:

13. You're going, *aren't you?*
14. It's five dollars, *right?*

If the preconditions for questioning are present, however, as Labov and Fanshel (1977) point out, a plain declarative statement will be construed as a *yes–no* question, as in

15. Q: You live on 114th Street.
    A: No, I live on 115th.

The *wh-* questions demand an answer that substitutes for the question word. An "I don't know" can also be given. The *wh-* words are *what, when, why, who, where,* and *how* appearing at the start of a question. These words are, in essence, blanks to be filled in.

What has to be answered with the name of a thing or event; *when* with a time; *where* with a location; *why,* a reason; *who,* a person; and *how,* a manner or way something was done. There is actually yet another *wh-* question, "Huh?" which asks in effect, "Would you repeat the entire sentence you just said?" That is, the "Huh" asks that a whole utterance be filled in, not just a word or phrase.

The answer to any question can be deferred by asking another, creating *insertion sequences* (Schegloff 1971, p. 76). For instance,

16.   ┌─A: Wanna come to a party?
        │┌─B: Can I bring a friend?
        ││┌─A: Male or female?
        ││└─B: Female.
        │└─A: Sure.
        └─B: O.K.

Note that these questions are answered in reverse order, but all are answered. Occasionally, insertion sequences can lead conversationalists "off the track." When this happens participants may feel a compulsion to get a question answered even if they have forgotten what it was. Hence, comments like:

17. Oh, as you were saying . . .
18. Oh, I forget, what were we talking about?

Note that the "oh" serves as an indicator that the speaker is not responding to the last statement, but to a prior one. Such seemingly innocuous syllables frequently serve as markers in conversation.

USING THE RULES TO MANIPULATE

It is easy to manipulate people subtly by plugging them into the presuppositions and preconditions behind statements (Elgin 1980; Labov and Fanshel 1977). For example, a wife might try to get her husband to go to a dance by saying "Even Oscar is going" (p. 472). The presupposition is that if Oscar is going, then everyone is. There is a further presupposition that if everyone else is doing something, then so should the person being spoken to. If Oscar is going then everyone is going, ergo, so should the husband. Readers may recognize in this rather common ploy the childhood "Everyone else has one" or "Everyone else is going."

Elgin (1980) also discusses manipulations of the "If you really loved me. . ." variety. These are actually subtle accusations. What they mean is "You should love me, but you don't. The guilt you feel for not loving me can easily be erased, though, by doing whatever I want."

Another manipulation is the "Even *you* should be able to do that" type. Here we have *even* again, the word that tells someone that he or she is alone in whatever failing is being mentioned. Its use with *should* is especially clever because it implies that the hearer is stupid or some sort of gross misfit, but it backgrounds that message so that it is not likely to be discussed. Rather, the hearer is made to feel stupid and wrong, so that he or she will be likely to capitulate to the speaker's demands in an effort to prove that if all others can do it, so can the hearer.

One can achieve both manipulation and insult by preceding a comment with "Don't tell me you're going to _____" or "Don't tell me that you believe _____!" Notice that these are questions in the form of a command. They are actually asking, "Are you really going to _____?" or "Do you really believe. . . ?" However, the presuppositions behind these questions in command form are (a) "You are going to do _____" (or "You believe _____") and (b) "[your action or belief] _____ is stupid." For instance,

19. X: Don't tell me that you are going to vote for Murgatroyd!
    Z: Well, I thought I would, but now I'm not so sure.

The really clever manipulation is that Z is instantly made to feel foolish because of presupposition b. However, since X has not overtly accused Z of stupidity, argument is difficult. Z is not even allowed the luxury of anger at the insult, because the insult has not been stated. It is contained only in the presupposition. Z might become immediately defensive but still feel quite stupid because of the implied insult. Not only does X get Z to capitulate, but also X establishes that Z is the stupider of the two. As a manipulatory device, this one is a "double whammy."

Labov and Fanshel (1977) show that some people manipulate in even more subtle ways by utilizing common understanding of social and discourse rules. Using patient-therapist sessions which they received permission to tape, they describe the struggle of a woman named Rhoda for independence from a domineering mother. The mother finally leaves Rhoda at home and goes to visit Rhoda's sister Phyllis. Rhoda cannot cope, but neither can she ask her mother to come home, because that would be an admission that the mother is right in not giving Rhoda more freedom. Rather, Labov and Fanshel say that Rhoda employs an indirect request both to mitigate her asking her mother for help and to disguise her challenge to the power relationship between them. Rhoda calls her mother on the phone and asks,

20. When do you plan to come home?

Since this is not a direct request for help, Rhoda's mother forces an admission by not answering Rhoda's question. Instead, she creates an insertion sequence:

21. Oh, why?

This means "Why are you asking me when I plan to come home?" In order to answer, Rhoda must admit that she cannot be independent, that the mother has been right all along. Furthermore, as a daughter, Rhoda must answer her mother's question. Her mother has the right to question by virtue of her status, and Rhoda has the duty to answer for the same reason. So, Rhoda responds with

22. Things are getting just a little too much . . . it's getting too hard.

To which the mother replies:

23. Why don't you ask Phyllis [when I'll be home]?

Since, in our society, it is really up to the mother when she will come home, and also, since she has a prior obligation to her own household, "It is clear that Rhoda has been outmaneuvered," according to Labov and Fanshel. The mother has forced Rhoda into admitting that she is not capable, and she has, in effect, refused Rhoda's request for help.

It seems to me that this mother also has conveyed very cleverly to Rhoda that Phyllis is the preferred daughter and has said it so covertly that the topic cannot be discussed openly. Clearly it is the mother's right and duty to come home as she wishes. By palming that decision off on Phyllis, she is actually saying to Rhoda "No matter what your claim on me is, Phyllis comes first." That is, for Phyllis's sake, she will suppress her rights as a mother and allow Phyllis to make the decision. Notice that all of this works only because at some level both Rhoda and her mother know the rights and obligations of questioners and answerers.

INDIRECT REQUESTS AND CONFLICT WITH SOCIAL VALUES

All indirect requests do not arise from such hostile situations, although most are used when individual desires conflict with other social rules or values. Classic examples, spoken with an expectant lift to the voice, are:

23. Oh, chocolates.
25. What are those, cigars?

Assuming that 24 and 25 are spoken by adults who have long known what *chocolate* denotes and are familiar with cigars, these observations are perceived as requests. This is shown by the usual responses to either:

26. Would you like one?
27. I'm sorry, but they aren't mine. (*or*, I have to save them for X.)

Young toddlers just learning to speak do practice by going about pointing at objects and naming them. Once that stage is past, people do not name items in the immediate environment unless there is an intent, a reason for singling out the item. All properly socialized Americans know that one should never directly ask for food in another's household or for any possibly expensive goods such as cigars. That would be begging. Therefore, one names the items in another's home or hands so that the naming is construed as an indirect request. There is rarely another reason for an adult to name a common object or food. The responses to 24 and 25 make sense only if the hearer construes those as really meaning "I want you to offer me some of those chocolates/cigars."

COMMANDS

Requests for food are not the only discourse routines arising from conflicts between general social rules and the will of the individual. Both commands and compliments, albeit in different ways, run afoul of cultural attitudes.

Commands share virtually the same preconditions as questions.

I. The speaker who commands has the right and/or duty to command.
II. The recipient of the command has the responsibility and/or obligation to carry out the command.

The problem is that, even more than with questioning, the one who has the right to command is usually clearly of higher status than the one who must obey. The United States supposedly is an egalitarian society, but having the right or duty to command implies that some are superior to others. This runs counter to our stated ideals. Therefore, in most actual situations in American speech, commands are disguised as questions. The substitution of forms is possible because both speech acts share the same preconditions. Moreover, phrasing commands as questions maintains the fiction that the one commanded has the right to refuse, even when he or she does not. Consider.

28. Would you mind closing the door?

Even though it is uttered as a *yes–no* question, merely to answer "No" without the accompanying action or "Yes" without an accompanying excuse would either be bizarre or a joke. In the movie *The Return of the Pink Panther*, Peter Sellers asks a passerby if he knows where the Palace Hotel is. The passerby responds "Yes" and keeps on going. The joke is that "Do you know where X is?" is not really a *yes–no* question but a polite command meaning "Tell me where X is."

Direct commanding is allowed and usual in certain circumstances. For instance, parents normally command young children directly. For example,

29. Pick those toys up right away.

Intimates such as spouses or roommates often casually command each other about trivial matters, such as

30. Pick some bread up on your way home.

Often these are softened by "please," "will ya," "honey," or the like.

Direct commanding in command form occurs in the military from those of superior rank to those of inferior. During actual battle it is necessary for combatants to obey their officers without question, unthinkingly, and unhesitatingly. Direct commands yield this kind of obedience so long as those commanded recognize the social rightness of the command or the need. It is no surprise that direct commands are regularly heard in emergency situations, as during firefighting:

31. Get the hose! Put up the ladders!

A great deal of direct commanding is also heard in hospital emergency rooms:

32. Get me some bandages.
    Suture that wound immediately.

In situations that allow direct commands, the full command form need not always be invoked. Just enough has to be said so that the underling knows what to do, as in

33. Time for lunch. (meaning "Come in for lunch.")
34. Scalpel! Sutures! Dressings!

Note that such commands are contextually bound. They are interpretable as commands only if the participants are actually in a commanding situation. Similarly, Susan Ervin-Tripp's (1972) comment that

35. It's cold in here.

can be interpreted as a command works only in a specific commanding context. The speaker uttering 35 must somehow have the right to ask another to close a window, if that is the cause of the cold, or to ask another to lend his or her coat. In this situation, the fact that one person is closer to an open window may be sufficient reason for him or her to be responsible for closing it. The duty or obligation to carry out a command need not proceed only from actual status but may proceed from the physical circumstances in which the command has been uttered. That is why in the right circumstances ordinary statements or questions may be construed as commands, as in:

> 36. A: Any more coffee?
> B: I'll make some right away.
> A: No, I wanted to know if I had to buy any.

If it is possible to do something about whatever is mentioned, an utterance may be construed as a command. In 36, it was possible for B to make some coffee, and B must have been responsible for making it at least some of the time. Hence the question about coffee was misinterpreted as a command to make some. The same possibility of misinterpretation can occur in the question

> 37. Can you swim?

Said by a poolside, it may be interpreted as a command "Jump in," but away from a body of water, it will be heard merely as a request for information.

Although questions are often used as polite substitutes for commands, the question command can sometimes be especially imperious:

> 38. Would you mind being quiet?

Similarly, a command like the following may seem particularly haughty:

> 39. If you would wait, please.

I suspect that both 38 and 39 carry special force because the high formality signaled by "Would you mind" and "If you would . . . please" contrasts so sharply with the banality of keeping quiet and waiting that the effect of sarcasm is achieved.

COMPLIMENTS

Compliments are another utterance pair type that create conflict. This is because of general social convention and the rule that the first part of an utterance pair must evoke a response. Compliments call for an acknowledgment. The acknowledgment can properly be acceptance of the compliment, as in "Thank you." The problem is that to accept the compliment is very close to bragging, and bragging is frowned upon in middle-class America. Hence, one typical response to a compliment is a disclaimer, like

40. This old rag?
41. I got it on sale.
42. My mother got it for me.

An exception is special occasions when compliments are expected, as when everyone is decked out to go to a prom or a wedding. Then, not only are compliments easily received with "Thank you," but not to compliment can cause offense or disappointment.

Except for such situations, complimenting can lead to social embarrassment. If one persists in complimenting another, the other person often becomes hostile, even though nice things are being said. At the very least the recipient of excessive praise becomes uncomfortable and tries to change the subject. Often he or she becomes suspicious and angry or tries to avoid the person who is heaping praise. The suspicion is either that the complimenter is being patronizing or is trying to get something, to "butter the person up."

Once, I ordered a class to persistently compliment their parents, spouses, or siblings. The most common response was "OK. What do you want this time?" One of the students received a new suit from a friend who owned a men's clothing store, with the friend practically shouting, "OK. If I give you a new suit will that shut you up?"

Many of those complimented became overtly angry. Others quickly found an excuse to leave, and several students found that those on whom they heaped praise shunned them the next time they met. I suspect that the anger results from the social precariousness of being complimented. As with style, when a person is put at a social disadvantage so that he or she does not know how to respond, anger results. It is very uncomfortable to receive too much praise. It is tantamount to continually being asked to tread the line between gracious acceptance and boasting. Most people prefer to ignore anyone who puts them in that situation.

PRESEQUENCES AND SAVING FACE

An interesting class of discourse rules is what Harvey Sacks called *presequences* (lecture, November 2, 1967), particularly preinvitations. Typically, someone wishing to issue an oral invitation, first asks something like

43. What are you doing Saturday night?

If the response includes words like *only* or *just*, as in

44. I'm just washing my hair.
45. I'm only studying.

the inviter can then issue an invitation for Saturday night. If, however, the response is

46. I'm washing my hair.
47. I'm studying.

the potential inviter knows not to issue the invitation. Following a response like 46 or 47, the inviter signals a change in conversation by saying "Uh—" and then speaks of something other than Saturday night (or whatever date was mentioned). Issuing of preinvitations is an ego saver like the use of style to signal social class. Having been spared overt refusal, the inviter is able to save face (Goffman 1955).

COLLAPSING SEQUENCES

Sometimes utterance pairs are collapsed (Sacks, November 2, 1967) as in the following exchange at an ice cream counter:

48. A: What's chocolate filbert?
    B: We don't have any.

B's response is to what B knows is likely to come next. If B had explained what chocolate filbert is, then A very likely would have asked for some. Indeed, by explaining what it is, B would be tacitly saying that he or she had some to sell. In a selling situation in our society, explaining what goods or foods are is always an admission that they are available. Imagine your reaction, for instance, if you asked a waiter or waitress what some food was like, and he or she went into detail telling you about it. Then, if you said, "Sounds good. I'll have that," and the response were, "We don't have any," you would think you were being made a fool of.

Another common collapsing sequence is typified by the exchange:

49. A: Do you smoke?
    B: I left them in my other jacket.

Such collapsing sequences speed up social interaction by forestalling unnecessary explanations. They are used for other purposes as well, as when a newcomer joins a discussion in progress:

50. Hi, John. We were just talking about nursery schools.

This either warns John not to join the group or, if he is interested in nursery schools, gives him orientation so that he can understand what is going on.

REPAIRS

If a person uses the wrong style for an occasion, the other party(ies) to the interaction try to repair the error. Schegloff, Jefferson, and Sacks (1977) collected interesting samples of self-correction in discourse, people repairing their own errors. Sometimes this takes the form of obvious correction to a slip of the tongue, as in

51. What're you so *ha*—er un—un*ha*ppy about?

Sometimes speakers make a repair when they have made no overt error, as in

52. Sure enough ten minutes later the bell r—the doorbell rang.

Because such repairs do not show a one-to-one correspondence with actual spoken errors, Schegloff et al. preferred the term *repair* over *correction.* In both 51 and 52, for instance, neither repair was preceded by an error that actually occurred in speech.

Schegloff et al. found an orderly pattern in speech repair. Repairs did not occur just anywhere in an utterance. They occurred in one of three positions: immediately after the error, as in 51 and 52, or at the end of the sentence where another person would normally take the floor:

53. An 'en bud all of the doors 'n things were taped up—I mean y'know they put up y'know that kinda paper stuff, the brown paper.

or right after the other person speaks:

54. *Hannah:* And he's going to make his own paintings.
    Bea: Mm hm.
    Hannah: And—or I mean his own frames.

If the speaker does not repair an obvious error, the hearer will. Usually this is done by asking a question that will lead the speaker to repair his or her own error. Some examples:

55. A: It wasn't snowing all day.
    B: It *wasn't?*
    A: Oh, I mean it was.
56. A: Yeah, he's got a lot of smarts.
    B: *Huh?*
    A: He hasn't got a lot of smarts.
57. A: Hey, the first time they stopped me from selling cigarettes was this morning.
    B: From *selling* cigarettes?
    A: From buying cigarettes.

Often, the hearer will say "you mean" as in

58. A: We went Saturday afternoon.
    B: You mean Sunday.
    C: Yeah, uhnnn we saw Max . . .

In most of the repairs by hearers, it seems that the hearer knows all along what the intended word was. Still, it is rare, although not impossible, for the hearer actually to supply the word. This seems to be a face saver for the person who made the error. The hearer often offers the correction or the question leading to correction tentatively, as if he or she is not sure. That way, the speaker is not humiliated as he or she might be if the hearer in positive tones asserted that an error was made. Another reason that hearers offer corrections tentatively may be that in doing so, the hearer is in the position of telling someone else what must be going on in his or her mind.

Schegloff et al. (1977, p. 38) state that "the organization of repair is the self-righting mechanism for the organization of language use in social interaction." In other words, it maintains normal social interaction. We have already seen this in attempted repair of inappropriate style.

The importance of the self-righting mechanism is shown in the following almost bizarre interactions. These involve repairs in greetings and farewells collected as part of a participant observation by a student, Sheila Kennedy. While on guard duty at the door of a dormitory, she deliberately confounded greetings and farewells, with fascinating results.

To a stranger:
59. *Sheila:* Hi. [pause] Good night.
    Stranger: Hello. [pause] Take it easy.

Note that the stranger also gave both a greeting and a farewell, even matching the pause that Sheila used between them. . . .

To a female friend:
60. *Friend:* Bye, Sheila.
    Sheila: Hello.
    Friend: Why did you say hello? I said goodbye. [pause] Hi.

Even though the friend questioned the inappropriateness of Sheila's response, she still felt constrained to answer the greeting with a greeting.

To a male friend:
61. *Friend:* Hi!
    Sheila: So long.
        [Both spoke at the same time, so Sheila starts again.]
    Sheila: Hi!
    Friend: Bye. [laughs] Wait a minute. Let's try that again. Hi!
    Sheila: Hello.
    Friend: Bye.
    Sheila: So long.
    Friend: That's better. [laughs and leaves]

What is interesting here is the lengths the subject went to in order that the appropriate pairs were given. Note that he had to get both greeting and farewell matched up before he would leave. The degree to which we are bound by the social rules of discourse is well illustrated in 59–61. The very fact that people go to so much trouble to repair others' responses is highly significant. It shows the importance of discourse routines to social interaction, that one cannot be divorced from the other. Not only must style and kinesics be appropriate for social functioning but so must the discourse itself. Even when people know what the other must mean, as in 55–58, they ask that the discourse be righted. And, even when it makes no difference in a fleeting social contact, as in 59–61, they demand that the right forms be chosen.

NEW RULES OF DISCOURSE

New situations may involve learning new discourse rules. Anthony Wooton (1975, p. 70) gives an example from psychotherapy. Psychiatrists typically do not tell patients what to do. Rather, by asking questions, they try to lead the patient into understanding. The problem is that the questions asked and the answers they are supposed to evoke are different from those already learned as part of normal routines. As an example, Wooton gives:

> 62. *Patient:* I'm a nurse, but my husband won't let me work.
> *Therapist:* How old are you?
> *Patient:* Thirty-one this December.
> *Therapist:* What do you mean, he won't let you work?

Here, the patient answers the psychiatrist's first question as if it were bona fide, a real-world question. The psychiatrist was not really asking her age, however, as we can see by his next question. What he meant by that question was "You are old enough to decide whether or not you wish to work." His question was aimed at leading her to that conclusion.

The patient in therapy has to learn new discourse routines in order to benefit from the therapeutic situation. The therapist uses modes of questioning different from everyday discourse. This is not surprising, since the aim of psychotherapy is for the psychiatrist to lead the patient into self-discovery. Some patients become very annoyed by the questioning, feeling that the therapist is refusing to tell them anything. In traditional psychoanalysis it was accepted that there had to be a period during which the patient "fought" the analyst by refusing to dredge up the answers from the murky subconscious. It has occurred to me that this period may actually represent a time during which the patient must learn to respond to the new question and answer routines demanded by analysis.

It is very hard to gain insights into oneself by sustained self-questioning, perhaps because questioning is rarely used that way outside the therapeutic situation. Furthermore, repeated questioning in itself is threatening. In many societies, including our own, it is associated with accusation of wrongdoing and ferreting out the truth of one's guilt. It is used as a technique for teaching, to be sure, but even then it is often a way of ferreting out the pupil's lapses in learning.

TOPIC IN NORMAL AND PSYCHOTIC SPEECH

The first half of an utterance pair strongly limits what can come next. It limits both form and subject matter. These are intertwined virtually inseparably: a greeting is both a form and a subject matter. The response to a *wh-* question must use the same words as the question, filling in the missing word signaled by whichever *wh-* word was used. The answer to "Where did you go?" is "I went to [place X]." The answer to "Whom did you see?" is "I saw [person X]."

The larger conversation, beyond utterance pairs, is not so strongly constrained as to form. The entire syntax of the language can be drawn upon to encode new ideas, not just the syntax of greetings or compliments or invitation. The first sentence or so of an answer is predetermined by the question just asked, but the speaker becomes free as soon as an answer is given that fills in the *wh-* word or supplies the *Yes, No,* or *I don't know.* The constraints upon topic, however, remain very strong.

In normal conversation, everything has to be subordinated to topic, whatever is being talked about (see Van Dijk 1977). Schegloff (1971) likens this to co-occurrence restrictions such as we saw in style. Once a topic is introduced, it must be adhered to unless some formal indication of change is made. Paradoxically, in American English, this often is "Not to change the subject, but. . . ." This disclaimer always changes the topic. Other signals that change topic are "Oooh, that reminds me . . ." or "Oooh, I meant to tell you. . . ." The "Oooh" in itself, uttered rapidly on a high pitch with a tense throat, is a warning that an announcement about topic change is coming.

Adherence to a topic is so important that failure to do so is evidence of mental incapacity. A person's mind is said to wander if his or her words wander off topics with no warning. Many observers of patients diagnosed as schizophrenic have noticed peculiarities in their speech, peculiarities traditionally called *thought disorder* (TD). Since not all schizophrenics show these speech disorders, some are termed *nonthought disordered* (NTD). As a result of my own extensive analyses of speech termed TD, I think that such speech differs from normal or NTD speech mainly in that it does not stick to a topic. For instance,

63. My mother's name was Bill and coo. St. Valentine's Day was the start of the breedin' season of the birds.

CHAIKA 1974, 1977

64. Looks like clay. Sounds like gray. Take you for a roll in the hay. Hay day. May day. Help! I just can't. Need help. May day.

COHEN 1978

65. I had a little goldfish like a clown. Happy Hallowe'en down.

CHAIKA 1974, 1977

The greatest abnormality in such speech is that the patient is not sticking to a topic. Other than that, each part of the utterance is normal; grammar, word choice, and sounds are correctly used.

The words and phrases chosen do have a connection with one another in each of the samples just given. They are related on the basis of similarity of sound, especially rhyme, and on the basis of shared meaning. "Bill and coo" is an old metaphor for "love" based upon an image of lovebirds or doves, which bill and coo. Love is also associated with St. Valentine's Day. "Roll in the hay" means "(sexual) fun." "Hay day" not only rhymes with "hay," but if, as seems likely, the patient meant "heyday," it also refers to good times. "Hay day" rhymes with "May day," which is another way of saying "SOS" or "Help!" "Happy Hallowe'en" seems to be an association with "clown," with which "down" is a chance rhyme.

No matter how tightly such associations can be woven into the utterance, still 63–65 are obviously pathological speech. It is topic that determines normal speech, not other kinds of associations between words. Some people have suggested that schizophrenic speech is poetic, because, like poetry, it often rhymes. One major objection to this view is the high interjudge reliability when people are asked to distinguish schizophrenic utterances from others (Maher, McKeon and McLaughlin 1966; Rochester, Martin and Thurston 1977).

The schizophrenic rhyming and figurative speech occurs only because of chance association. Poetic rhyme and artistic language in general seem to be as constrained by a topic as any other kind of normal speech. Rhyming and other features of poetry, such as unusual associations and figurative language, are poetic when they are subordinated to a topic. . . .

In the twentieth century certain authors have deliberately set out to recreate stream of consciousness in their fiction, and some poetry is deliberately formless. Dr. Nancy Andreasen (1973) claims that James Joyce's *Finnegan's Wake* would appear to be schizophrenic to most psychiatrists. Even in such modern literature, however, form is usually subordinated to general topic.

WHAT TO MENTION

Besides adhering to a topic, a speaker is constrained to follow another related rule: "Say only what needs saying." Personal and cultural knowledge that speakers share is not mentioned but is assumed. This is why the speech between two intimates is often obscure to outsiders. For instance:

66. A: Saw Mary today.
    B: She better?
    A: Yeah, she went to Bob's last night.
    B: When's the date?

This works if both know the one Mary, that she has just been sick, that she is engaged to Bob, but the wedding has been postponed because of her illness. To reiterate what each of the speakers knows would be boring or insulting or both.

One kind of bore is the person who insists on telling you more than you have to be told about something. Also, if someone insists on being overdetailed in a explanation, it implies that the hearer does not know those details. This is why people feel insulted if someone tells them obvious facts.

A difficulty that grown children have in dealing with their parents is that the parents persist in "treating them as if they were children" — that is, telling them things they already know. It is hard for the children not to feel insulted and defensive. Often repairmen are guilty of insulting by mentioning the obvious. For instance, when taking my computer in to be repaired, I felt very put out when the technician said "It's probably your diskette. They're very fragile." Since the first thing one learns about such equipment is that the diskettes are fragile, the effect was insultingly condescending.

In conversation it is assumed that all parties are cooperating (Gordon and Lakoff 1975). It is also assumed that they mean what they say. If something is mentioned that is known, therefore, unless it is taken as a putdown it will be construed to be newly important. Searle (1975) says that mentioning of extraneous matters leads listeners down false trails, as they try to figure out how those matters fit the topic at hand. It seems to me that this is why our courts of law have such strong rules against introducing irrelevant matters. To do so clouds the issue for the jury.

Mentioning too much, even if it is related to the topic, can be as distracting as actual departures from the topic itself. People assume that anything known to all parties in a given conversation will not be overtly stated unless there is some special reason for so doing.

REFERENCES

Andreasen, N. 1973. "James Joyce, a portrait of the artist as a schizoid." *Journal of the American Medical Association.* 224:67–71.

Austin, J. L. 1962. *How to Do Things with Words*, 2nd ed. J. Urmson and M. Sbisa, eds. Cambridge, Mass.: Harvard University Press.

Chaika, E. 1974. "A linguist looks at "schizophrenic" language." *Brain and Language* 1:257–276.

———. 1977. "Schizophrenic speech, slips of the tongue, and jargonaphasia: a reply to Fromkin and to Lecours and Vaniers-Clement." *Brain and Language* 4:464–475.

Cohen, B. D. 1978. "Referent communication disturbances in schizophrenia." In S. Schwartz, ed. 1978. *Language and Cognition in Schizophrenia*. Hillsdale, N.J.: Lawrence Erlbaum., pp. 1–34.

Ervin-Tripp, S. 1972. "On sociolinguistic rules: alternation and co-occurrence." In J. Gumperz and D. Hymes, eds. 1972. *Directions in Sociolinguistics.* New York: Holt, Rinehart, and Winston, pp. 213–250.

Frake, C. O. 1964. "How to ask for a drink in Subanum." *American Anthropologist* 66:127–32.

Givon, T., ed. 1979. *Syntax and Semantics*, vol. 12, *Discourse and Syntax*. New York: Academic Press.

Godard, D. 1977. "Same setting, different norms: Phone call beginnings in France and the United States." *Language in Society* 6:209–220.

Goffman, E. 1955. "On facework." *Psychiatry* 81:213–231.

Goody, E. N., ed. 1978. *Questions and Politeness*. New York: Cambridge University Press.

Gordon, D. and G. Lakoff. 1975. "Conversational postulates." In P. Cole and J. Morgan, eds. 1975. *Syntax and Semantics*, vol. 3, *Speech Acts*. New York: Academic Press, pp. 83–106.

Labov, W. and D. Fanshel. 1977. *Therapeutic Discourse*. New York: Academic Press.

Maher, B., K. McKeon, and B. McLaughlin. 1966. "Studies in psychotic language." in P. Stone, D. Dumphy, M. Smith, and D. Ogilvie, eds. 1966. *General Inquirer*. Cambridge, Mass.: M.I.T. Press, pp. 469–501.

Rochester, S., J. Martin, and S. Thurston. 1977. "Thought process disorder in schizophrenia: The listener's task." *Brain and Language*. 4:95–114.

Rommetveit, R. 1971. "Words, contexts and verbal message transmission." In E. A. Carswell and R. Rommetveit, eds. 1971. *Social Contexts of Messages*. New York: Academic Press, pp. 13–26.

Sacks, H. 1964–1972. Lecture notes. Mimeo.

———. 1970. Discourse analysis. Untitled manuscript. Mimeo.

———. 1972. "An initial investigation of the usability of conversational data for doing sociology." In D. Sudnow, ed., 1971. *Studies in Social Interaction*. New York: The Free Press. pp. 31–74.

Schegloff, E. A. 1968. Sequencing in conversational openings. *American Anthropologist* 70:1075–1095.

———. 1971. "Notes on a conversational practice: Formulating place." In D. Sudnow, ed. 1971. *Studies in Social Interaction*. New York: The Free Press, pp. 75–119.

Schegloff, E. A., G. Jefferson, and H. Sacks. 1977. "The preference for self-correction in the organization of repair in conversation." *Language* 53:361–382.

Schenkein, J., ed. 1978. *Studies in the Organization of Conversation*. New York: Academic Press.

Searle, J. 1975. "Indirect speech acts." In P. Cole and J. Morgan, eds. 1975. *Syntax and Semantics*, vol. 3, *Speech Acts*. New York: Academic Press, pp. 59–82.

Van Dijk, T. 1977. *Text and Context: Explorations in the Semantics and Pragmatics of Discourse*. New York: Longman.

Wooton, A. 1975. *Dilemmas of Discourse: Controversies about the Sociological Interpretation of Language*. London: Allen and Unwin.

===

FOR DISCUSSION AND REVIEW

1. Explain the paradox described by Chaika: "Language makes us free as individuals but chains us socially."

2. Explain the relationship among speech events, genres, and performance.

3. Summarize the rules of telephone conversation in the United States. Then describe the rules of another culture, and compare them with those of the United States.

4. Drawing on your own experience, describe a situation (like Chaika's telephone-call and grocery-store incidents) in which a semantically appropriate response would not actually be used.

5. Explain the concept of "preconditions for speech acts." Illustrate it by an original example of such a situation.

6. Give an example of each of the utterance pairs listed by Chaika on pp. 472–73. Use examples in which the first half of the pair doesn't sound like what it really is.

7. Chaika states, "It is easy to manipulate people subtly by plugging them into the presuppositions and preconditions behind statements." Write a description of a real or imaginary instance of such manipulation.

8. Give two examples of conflicts between social rules and the wishes of an individual.

9. Test Chaika's description of people's reactions to persistent compliments by following the instructions she gave to her students (p. 480). Write a brief report summarizing your results.

10. Explain Chaika's statement, "In normal conversation, everything has to be subordinated to topic, whatever is being talked about."

28

Girl Talk — Boy Talk

John Pfeiffer

John Pfeiffer is a science writer whose works have appeared in such popular magazines as Science *and* Psychology Today. *The focus of the articles in this section is on how we arrange our words to create meaningful speech and how we use these combinations in conversation with one another. Pfeiffer's essay explores the active and rapidly expanding field of gender studies in language research. Pfeiffer examines differences between male and female speech patterns in conversation and the ways in which these patterns reflect our culture's image of the two sexes. His findings illustrate some of the myths that surround male and female speech patterns. At the same time, Pfeiffer presents new and surprising characteristics of conversations between the sexes and speculates about what these findings mean. That women ask more questions and men do most of the interrupting are two of the traits Pfeiffer discusses. He points out, furthermore, that as our attitudes about men and women change, the way we talk to each other changes, too.*

An investigator, pencil in hand, is transcribing two minutes of an "unobtrusively" recorded coffee-shop conversation between two university students, male and female — listening intently, making out words and pronunciations, noting hesitations, timing utterances. The tape whirs in reverse for a replay and then again, eight replays in all. Part of the final transcript:

> ANDREW: *It's about time uh that my family* really *went on a vacation* (pause) *y'know my father goes places all the time* (prolonged syllable) *but he y'know goes on business like he'll go ta' Tokyo for the afternoon 'n he'll get there at* (stammer) *at ten in the morning 'n catch a nine o'clock flight leaving* . . .
> (two-second pause)
> BETSY: *That sounds fantastic* (pause) *not everybody can jus' spend a day in someplace-* (interruption)
> ANDREW: *Well, we've already established the fact that um y'know he's not just* anyone.
> (eight-second pause)
> BETSY: *Don't you I* (stammer) *well it seems to me you you you proba-*

490

> *bly have such an um interesting background that you must y'know have trouble finding um people uh like to talk to if you-* (interruption)
> ANDREW: *Most definitely . . .*

Candace West and Don Zimmerman, the researchers who analyzed these recordings, were particularly interested in the interruptions. The pattern is typical. According to these University of California sociologists, it held for all 11 two-person, cross-sex conversations recorded mainly in public places: Males accounted for some 96 percent of the interruptions. In same-sex conversations males also cut off males and females cut off females, but in 20 recorded encounters, interruptions were equally distributed between the speakers.

This study is part of an active and rapidly expanding field of language research — the role of gender in speech, with the accent primarily on how, under what conditions, and why the sexes talk differently. A 1983 bibliography of relevant publications includes some 800 titles, compared with about 150 titles in a bibliography published eight years before. The boom started little more than a decade ago, inspired by the women's movement. A new generation of investigators began taking hard looks at some of the things that had been written about women's talk by earlier investigators, mainly male. They encountered a number of statements like the following from Otto Jespersen, a Danish linguist who has earned a prominent place in the feminist rogues' gallery: "[W]omen much more often than men break off without finishing their sentences, because they start talking without having thought out what they are going to say."

Such belittlement of female conversation may be somewhat less frequent nowadays. But it lives on in everyday contexts, hardly surprising since it involves attitudes imbedded in thinking that get passed on like bad genes from generation to generation. The latest issue of a women-and-language newsletter notes items involving sexism in everything from the *New England Journal of Medicine* and Maidenform bra ads to campaign speeches and government offices in Japan. Work focused on interruption contributes to understanding who controls conversations and how. To check on their original observations in a more casual context, West and Zimmerman conducted an experiment in which students meeting for the first time were told to "relax and get to know one another," with familiar results. Males again turned out to be the chief culprits, although they made only 75 percent of the interruptions, compared with that 96 percent figure for previously acquainted pairs — perhaps because they were more restrained among new acquaintances.

Men not only do the lion's share of the interrupting (and the talking) but often choose what to talk about. This can be seen in a study conducted by public relations consultant Pamela Fishman. Her subjects were three couples, a social worker and five graduate students, who consented to having tape recorders in their apartments, providing some 52 hours of conversation, 25 of which have been transcribed.

Fishman's first impression: "At times I felt that all the women did was ask questions . . . I attended to my own speech and discovered the same pattern." In fact, the women asked more than 70 percent of the questions. Dustin Hoffman put this speech pattern to use in the motion picture *Tootsie*, using the questioning intonation frequently when impersonating a woman and rather less frequently when acting unladylike.

In her study, Fishman discovered that a particular question was used with great frequency: "D'ya know what?" Research by other investigators had described how children frequently use this phrase to communicate with their elders. It serves as a conversation opener, calling for an answer like "What?" or "No, tell me," a go-ahead signal that they may speak up and that what they have to say will be heeded.

Pursuing this lead, Fishman found out why women need such reassurances when she analyzed the 76 efforts in taped conversations to start conversations or keep them going. Men tried 29 times and succeeded 28 times. That is, in all but a single case the outcome was some discussion of the topic broached. Women tried 47 times, sometimes for as long as five minutes, with dead-end results 30 times, an unimpressive .362 batting average. (It could have been worse. Each of the male subjects in this experiment professed sympathy for the women's movement.)

Other actions that control conversation (and often power) are more complicated, less open to statistical analysis. Cheris Kramarae, professor of speech communication at the University of Illinois in Urbana-Champaign, tells what happened when, as the only woman member of an important policy-shaping committee, she tried to communicate with the chairman before the start of a meeting. She suggested that certain items be added to the agenda, apparently to no effect. "He paid no attention to me, and I gave up." Once the meeting got under way, however, he featured her ideas in a review of the agenda and, turning to a male colleague, commented: "I don't remember who suggested these changes. I think it was Dick here."

Kramarae cites such instances of being heard but not listened to, "as if you were speaking behind a glass," as the sort of thing women must cope with every day. Other examples of everyday difficulties include being first-named by people who address males by last names plus "Mr." or "Dr.," hearing men discuss hiring a "qualified" woman, and looking a block ahead to see whether men are around who might make catcalls or pass out unwanted compliments.

These sorts of affronts lead women to a guarded way of life that fosters sensitivity to biases in the King's English. There is the intriguing record of efforts to abolish the generic masculine where *man* means not just males but all humans (as in "Man is among the few mammals in which estrus has disappeared entirely," from *Emergence of Man* by John Pfeiffer, 1978). *Woman* is used only in reference to a female, a rule established by male grammarians some 250 years ago.

At first the move to a more generalized language was widely opposed, mainly on the grounds of triviality and the inviolability of language. Critics included some feminists, the linguistic faculty at Harvard, and *Time* magazine, the latter exhibiting its usual delicate touch in an essay entitled "Sispeak: A Msguided Attempt to Change Herstory." Then a number of psychologists, among them Donald MacKay and Wendy Martyna of the University of California, ran tests showing that, whatever the speaker or writer intended, most people associate *man* and the matching pronoun *he* with a male image and that the generic masculine could hurt the way *boy* hurts blacks. Today it is common practice to edit such references out of textbook manuscripts and other writings.

Meanwhile research continues along a widening front, trying to cope with unconscious attitudes, sexist and otherwise, which distinguish women and men — "two alien cultures, oddly intertwined," in the words of Barrie Thorne of Michigan State University. Recent studies of the American male culture by and large support previous findings. Men spend considerable time playing the dominance game, either at a joking level or for real. The telling of a tall tale, followed by a still taller tale in an I-can-top-that atmosphere, seems to be typically male.

In this game, keeping cool commands the respect of the other players, with an occasional flash of emotion commended, providing it has to do with politics or sports or shop talk — practically anything but personal feelings. Elizabeth Aries of Amherst College, who has recorded 15 hours of conversation among newly acquainted male students, reports that certain males consistently dominated the conversation. Her subjects addressed the entire group rather than individuals at least a third of the time, nearly five times more often than women interacting under similar conditions.

Detailed studies of women's conversations are rare, mainly conducted in the past few years. Aries discovered that leaders in all-female groups tend to assume a low profile and encourage others to speak, while leaders among men tend to resist the contributions of others. Mercilee Jenkins of San Francisco State University studied the conversation of mothers in a discussion group over a five-month period. She was interested in subject matter as well as conversational style. She found that the young mothers discussed a broad range of subjects — much beyond domestic problems.

Storytelling makes up a large proportion of conversational encounters, with narrative styles that reflect other gender differences. "The universe is made of stories, not atoms," said poet Muriel Rukeyser, and linguistic analysis confirms her insight. As a rule, the women in the Jenkins study avoided first-person narratives. In 26 out of 57 transcribed stories, the narrator played no role at all, while men frequently shine in their own stories. The women listening became heavily involved in the incidents recounted and chimed in with stories supporting the narrator, challenging the preceding story in only about five percent of the cases.

Mixing sexes conversationally produces some interesting reactions, at least among newly acquainted Harvard students in the Aries study.

The men softened, competing less among themselves and talking more about their personal lives. (This may be a kind of instinctive mating or courting display, an attracting mechanism discarded upon closer acquaintance when the male usually reassumes his impersonal ways.) Women students responded with a pattern of their own, becoming more competitive. Aries notes that "the social significance of women for one another in a mixed group was low." They maintained a supportive style in talking with men, but it was every woman for herself as they spoke disproportionately more to the men than to each other.

The "music" of conversation may be as meaningful as the words. Women not only have higher voices, but the pitch is notably higher than can be explained solely by the anatomy of the female vocal apparatus. Moreover, Sally McConnell-Ginet of Cornell University finds that women's voices are more colorful — they vary more in pitch and change pitch more frequently than do men's voices. In one experiment, women immediately assumed a monotone style when asked to imitate men's speech. McConnell-Ginet regards speaking tunefully as an effective strategy for getting and holding attention, a strategy used more often by women than men, perhaps because they are more often ignored.

No one has a workable theory that accounts for all these differences. Even the longest running, most thorough searches for the root causes of differences between the sexes raise more questions than they answer. Carol Nagy Jacklin of the University of Southern California and Eleanor Maccoby of Stanford University have been tracking the development of 100 children from birth to age six. These children have been observed at several stages, in various settings. When this group reached 45 months of age, the researchers focused on how 58 of them interacted with their parents during playtime.

A surprising conclusion emerged: Discrimination by gender originates mainly outside the home. "Mothers do little behavior stereotyping," Jacklin summarizes. "They appear to treat [their own] little boys and little girls much the same." (While fathers tend to treat their children in more gender-stereotyped ways during playtimes, they ordinarily have less influence on childrearing and on actually creating the home environment.)

The implication is intriguing. If it is true that outsiders are largely responsible, and since most outsiders are also parents, it follows that parents have gender-based preconceptions more often about other people's children than about their own. In any event, school is one place where highly significant changes take place. In the beginning, teacher is "home base," a surrogate parent to whom children come for reassurance and support, and that holds for all children — until second grade.

At that point boys but not girls begin increasingly to turn away from teacher and toward one another. The stress is more and more on hierarchy, jockeying for position in speech as well as action, in talking as well as playing cowboy, soldier, Star Wars, and so on. All this is part of a constellation of changes. In playgrounds girls tend to go around in pairs, usually near teachers and the school building; boys form groups of half a dozen or so, usually as far away as possible. Boys may get more attention than girls because they are often more disruptive.

In discussing such patterns Thorne cites the classic psychoanalytic theory that boys, being raised mainly by women at home, feel the need at school to assert themselves as "not female." Also, teachers may have biased expectations about boys. But, according to Raphaela Best of the Montgomery County school system in Maryland, a high price may be paid for early male-male competition. She suggests that the resulting tensions may help account for the fact that reading disabilities are at least five times more frequent among boys than among girls.

Though the study of gender-based differences is relatively new, significant steps have been taken. Furthermore — a totally unexpected development — gender-related work has helped spark renewed interest in general language use. The ways in which men talk to men and women talk to women have come under scrutiny, as have the speech differences between people of different cultures and professional backgrounds.

West, for example, is currently interested in exchanges between doctors and patients. This work demands looking as well as listening, analyzing a kind of choreography of nonverbal as well as verbal behavior. Her raw data consist of videotapes complete with sound tracks. So far she has spent more than 550 hours transcribing seven hours of conversation in 21 patient-physician meetings at a family-practice center in the southern United States. Preliminary analysis indicates that doctors out-interrupt their patients, male and female, by a two-to-one margin — except when the doctor is a woman. In that case, the situation is reversed, with patients — both male and female — out-interrupting by the same margin.

Similar studies are tuning in on the finer points of speech and behavior. An outstanding and continuing analysis by Marjorie Harness Goodwin of the University of South Carolina shows that girls as well as boys form social groups, except that the girls tend to form exclusive "coalitions," whereas boys form all-inclusive hierarchies. With the girls not everyone gets to play, while with the boys everyone, even the nerds, can play as long as they respect rank. Girls also are far less direct in arguing with one another, and their debates may simmer for weeks, in contrast to male arguments, which generally end within a few minutes.

These findings are based on taped observations of black children at play in an urban setting. Other observations hint that the same points might apply more widely, a possibility that remains to be probed. What holds true for one culture or society may not for another. Male dominance in speech seems to be a global phenomenon. But the most notable exception cries for analysis: Sexism is probably at a lower level in Bali, where to vote or be otherwise active as a citizen, one must be part of a couple.

While most of the recent research has revealed conflict between the sexes, Carole Edelsky of Arizona State University has discovered a trend worth noting. She has studied five "very informal" meetings of a standing faculty committee consisting of seven women and four men — 7.5 hours of taped conversation. It started as a "fishing expedition" project — a search for sexisms, and there were plenty. As usual, men talked longer and interrupted more, appearing to hold the floor longer.

But Edelsky also recognized a second method of holding the floor. She identified short interludes, between the more formal addresses, that featured mutual support and "greater discourse equality." (These episodes were most informal and laughter-filled.) At first Edelsky had the impression that the women were doing most of the talking during these periods. But actual counts of words and time per turn revealed an equal-time situation (thus supporting the observation that a "talkative" woman is one who talks as much as the average man). These episodes made up less than 20 percent of total talk time, but such encounters as these may reflect a change in communication between the sexes.

The future may see great change in our current perception of a conversational gap between the sexes. It may also see a correction of imbalance in present-day research — a shift in the gender composition of the researchers. Today in the United States there are about 200 investigators of language and gender, and all but a dozen of them are women. Many of the researchers believe that as more men enter the field the "two alien cultures" will draw closer together.

FOR DISCUSSION AND REVIEW

1. What new discoveries are being made with regard to women's speech patterns and processes? What myths about women's speech are being disputed as a result of these discoveries?

2. In her study, Pamela Fishman discovered that, in conversation, women asked far more questions than men. What explanations are offered for this trend? What does this say about the differences between men and women in communication?

3. What are conversation-controlling actions? With respect to the research Pfeiffer cites, who utilizes more of these actions?

4. Can you think of any words in our language that are perceived of as "feminine," which if used to describe a mixed-sex group are not perceived as an insult? Are there any "masculine" terms that are applied to women without insult? What does this trend say about our language? Can you cite examples that suggest that our language might be undergoing change?

5. Pfeiffer explains that men spend considerable time playing the dominance game, either at a joking level or for real. This "I-can-top-that" atmosphere is a seemingly male communication trait. How does this differ from the atmosphere of women communicating? What possible

explanations can be offered for these two different styles besides the difference in gender?

6. What are the differences in the vocal patterns of women and men? How do scientists account for these differences?

7. Briefly discuss the differences in the socialization patterns of little boys and girls. In what ways do the methods of "play" differ for the two groups? How might these tendencies contribute to adult speech differences?

Projects for "Syntax, Semantics, and Discourse"

1. Briefly define the term *grammar*. Then ask at least five people, other than those in your class, to define the term. Jot down their definitions. Prepare a brief report in which you summarize your findings.

2. In "What Do Speakers Know about Their Language?" Roderick A. Jacobs and Peter S. Rosenbaum give examples of sentences illustrating native speakers' ability to recognize a grammatical English sentence, to interpret the meaning of a sentence, to perceive ambiguity, and to determine when sentences are synonymous. Using your own native-speaker knowledge, give at least one example of a sentence that illustrates each kind of knowledge, and write a brief explanation of how your example illustrates the knowledge.

3. This exercise is a class activity. Read the following paragraph:

> The hunter crept through the leaves. The leaves had fallen. The leaves were dry. The hunter was tired. The hunter had a gun. The gun was new. The hunter saw a deer. The deer had antlers. A tree partly hid the antlers. The deer was beautiful. The hunter shot at the deer. The hunter missed. The shot frightened the deer. The deer bounded away.

Without changing important words or the meaning, rewrite the paragraph so as to avoid the many short, choppy sentences. Then compare the re-written versions prepared by the different members of the class. Are the paragraphs alike? If not, describe the differences and account for the fact that passages that appear in such varying forms have the same meaning.

4. Prepare and circulate among five to ten people a short questionnaire designed to reveal (a) their experiences with grammar during their school years and (b) their attitudes toward grammar. Some information that you may want to obtain includes the grade(s) in which they were taught grammar, what was taught, how much time was devoted to grammar (compared, for example, to literature), the attitudes of the teachers and the students toward grammar, and the kind of grammar that was taught. Prepare a report summarizing your data. What conclusions can you draw?

5. Did your previous study of grammar enhance your understanding of English? Of other languages? If so, explain how; if not, explain why not. Be specific.

6. The study of English grammar has a long and interesting history. Write a paper or prepare an oral report on one of the following topics: the first English grammars; changing attitudes toward teaching grammar in schools; "prescriptive" versus "descriptive" grammars; the effect on students' writing abilities of studying grammar.

7. Based on library research, prepare a report analyzing the differing

opinions of Jean Piaget and Noam Chomsky about children's mental development.

8. As a native speaker of English, you have an internalized knowledge of the language — call it a "native-speaker intuition" if you will. For example, you can recognize a grammatical English sentence, you can interpret a sentence, you can perceive ambiguity, and you can determine when strings are synonymous. Examine the following groups of sentences. What can you tell about each group?

- a. 1. The bus station is near the bank.
  2. The soldiers were told to stop marching on the parade ground.
  3. The chicken is ready to eat.
- b. 1. That student continually sleeps in class.
  2. Student in class continually that sleeps.
  3. In class that student continually sleeps.
- c. 1. The Toronto Blue Jays beat the Atlanta Braves in the World Series.
  2. The ones that the Toronto Blue Jays beat in the World Series were the Atlanta Braves.
  3. The Atlanta Braves were beaten by the Toronto Blue Jays in the World Series.
- d. 1. Sam asked the students to build a display.
  2. Sam promised the students to build a display.
  3. Sam told the students to build a display.

Write a short paper describing your conclusions.

9. In "The Meaning of a Word," George L. Dillon notes, "The classic studies in descriptive semantics have been done in . . . fairly clearly bounded 'fields' such as kinship terms, adjectival and prepositional meanings, causative and inchoate verbs, verbs of judging and verbs of cooking." Prepare a report summarizing some of the descriptive semantic work that has been done in one of these areas.

10. Study the table on p. 500 from Dwight Bolinger's *Aspects of Language,* 2nd ed. (New York: Harcourt Brace Jovanovich, 1975, p. 207). Try to develop a similar grid or matrix for another well-defined semantic area.

11. In "Discourse Routines," Elaine Chaika briefly mentions certain peculiarities that often characterize schizophrenic speech (pp. 485–486). Using the references she cites, prepare a report on schizophrenic speech *(thought disorder,* or *TD).*

12. The *semantic differential* was developed originally by psychologists as a method for semantic differentiation and determination of the connotations of words, and was made well known, especially by Charles Osgood. Joseph S. Kess suggests marking your "impressions of a word on the [following] seven-point scale according to whether [you] view [it] as being, for example, extremely good, very good, good, neutral, bad, very bad, or extremely bad. Thus, if [you] had no feeling one way or the other about a word, [you] would mark the middle slot, indicating neutrality.

	Nonfat liquid	Fat	Direct heat	Vigorous action	Long cooking time	Large amt. special substance	Kind of utensil	Special ingredient	Additional special purpose	Liquids	Solids
								Other Relevant Parameters		*Collocates With*	
cook$_3$										+	+
boil$_1$	+	−								+	+
boil$_2$	+	−		+						+	+
simmer	+	−			−					+	+
stew	+	−			−	+			+ soften	−	+
poach	+	−			−				+ preserve shape	−	+
braise	+	−			−		+ lid			−	+
parboil	+	−			−					−	+
steam	+	−		+			+ rack, sieve, etc.			−	+
reduce	+	−		+					+ reduce bulk	+	−
fry	−	+					+ frying pan			−	+
sauté	−	+			−					−	+
pan-fry	−	+					+ frying pan			−	+
French-fry	−	+				+				−	+
deep-fry	−	+				+				−	+
broil	−	−	+							−	+
grill	−	−	+				?(griddle)			−	+
barbecue	−	−	+*					+ BarBQ sauce		−	+
charcoal	−	−	+*							−	+
plank	−	−	+				+ wooden board			−	+
bake$_2$	−	−	−							−	+
roast	−	−	±							−	+
shirr	−	−	−		−		+ small dish			−	+
scallop	−	−	−				+ shell	+ cream sauce		−	+
brown	−							°	+ brown surface	−	+
burn	−				+					−	+
toast	−	−	+						+ brown	−	+
rissoler	−	+				+			+ brown	−	+
sear	−	+			−				+ brown	−	+
parch	−	−			−				+ brown	−	+
flamber	−	−	+					+ alcohol	+ brown	−	+
steam-bake	+	−	−							−	+
pot-roast	+	−			−		(?) lid			−	+
oven-poach	+	−	−							−	+
pan-broil	−	−	+				+ frying pan			−	+
oven-fry	−	+			−					−	+

Culinary Semantics.

Source: Adapted from Adrienne Lehrer, "Semantic Cuisine," *Journal of Linguistics* 5 (1969): 39–55.

* "Hot coals."

Take, for example, the word *mother,* and mark it according to the way in which the word strikes you as being meaningful on the following sample semantic differential" (*Psycholinguistics: Introductory Perspectives* [New York: Academic Press, 1976], p. 161).

mother

good	____ : ____ : ____ : ____ : ____ : ____ : ____	bad
kind	____ : ____ : ____ : ____ : ____ : ____ : ____	cruel
weak	____ : ____ : ____ : ____ : ____ : ____ : ____	strong
beautiful	____ : ____ : ____ : ____ : ____ : ____ : ____	ugly
nice	____ : ____ : ____ : ____ : ____ : ____ : ____	awful
active	____ : ____ : ____ : ____ : ____ : ____ : ____	passive
positive	____ : ____ : ____ : ____ : ____ : ____ : ____	negative
heavenly	____ : ____ : ____ : ____ : ____ : ____ : ____	hellish
reputable	____ : ____ : ____ : ____ : ____ : ____ : ____	disreputable
large	____ : ____ : ____ : ____ : ____ : ____ : ____	small

Different informants will inevitably use different intuitive criteria when making judgments about the same words. It follows, therefore, that a high degree of subjectivity is inherent in the semantic differential, which, paradoxically, is both its principal strength and its major limitation.

Select two words, and ask two people to fill out a rating scale similar to Kess's. After tabulating the results, see what conclusions you can draw. For example, you could compare reactions to the words *sick* and *ill,* or *woman* and *lady.* If this exercise is done as a class (rather than individual) project, then class members themselves should fill out rating scales. After the results are tabulated, discuss the results and draw conclusions about the meanings of the words that were evaluated.

13. In his article, John Pfeiffer introduces us to at least three differences in the communication styles of boys and girls. In order to observe these differences on your own, visit a local school and conduct video sessions of girls and boys in a room with nothing other than two chairs. If you don't own your own video equipment, check with your department or with media services to obtain the use of a video camera.

Your task is to observe how girls at different ages communicate, how boys at different ages communicate, and how the two react in conversation with one another.

Select three ages to examine: age five, age ten, and age thirteen. Set your camera up in the room and send your couples in with no other instructions other than to talk to one another. When you have finished your recording, show the tapes to your class. Do you observe any distinct differences in the communication styles of little girls and boys? What happened in the mixed groups? What does this tell you about the styles of communication used by men and women?

14. An alternative method to use to observe the different communi-

cation styles of men and women is to record conversation groups in your class. Select a topic for debate, and have a tape recorder ready. After the discussion/debate has finished, listen to the tape, record your observations, and analyze your results, keeping in mind such things as length of time talking, interruptions, topics introduced in the conversation, and roles played by different members of the group. What do you expect to find? What do you find? Transcribe the tapes. Do you notice anything that went undetected in your initial observations? What do your results tell you about girls and boys, men and women in conversation?

15. In "Bad Birds and Better Birds," Jean Aitchison examines the trait in the English language in which we qualify lists or groups of words that refer to the same subject or are different types of the same class of words. She uses such examples as distinguishing which birds are most "bird-like," and which vegetables are most "vegetable-like." Create your own list of words that you feel may be subject to the same judgments about which Aitchison speaks. Organize your list into a questionnaire format that you may distribute to the class. Refer to the questionnaire forms that Aitchison describes in her article as your models. You may want to include pictures of the items on your list, or you may want to use pictures only in your results. What do your questionnaires tell you? Does everyone in your class have the same qualification scale? Why might the results differ from one person to the next?

Selected Bibliography

Akmajian, Adrian, Richard A. Demers, and Robert M. Harnish, *Linguistics: An Introduction to Language and Communication,* 2nd ed. Cambridge, MA: MIT Press, 1984. [A thoroughly revised edition of a very good text.]

Akmajian, Adrian, and F. W. Heny. *An Introduction to the Principles of Transformational Syntax.* Cambridge, MA: MIT Press, 1975. [An excellent introductory text.]

Austin, J. L. *How to Do Things With Words.* Cambridge, MA: Harvard University Press, 1962. [One of the classic works.]

Baker, C. L. *Introduction to Generative-Transformational Syntax.* Englewood Cliffs, NJ: Prentice-Hall, 1978. [Another excellent text; very thorough.]

Bierwisch, M. "Semantics." In John Lyons, ed., *New Horizons in Linguistics.* Baltimore: Penguin Books, 1970.

———. "On Classifying Semantic Features." In D. D. Steinberg and L. A. Jakobovits, eds., *Semantics.* Cambridge, Engl.: Cambridge University Press, 1971.

Bolinger, Dwight. *Aspects of Language,* 2nd ed. New York: Harcourt Brace Jovanovich, 1975. [A readable introduction to the study of language.]

Caplan, David, ed. *Biological Studies of Mental Processes.* Cambridge, MA: MIT Press, 1980. [Fifteen difficult but important essays.]

Chomsky, Noam. *Aspects of the Theory of Syntax.* Cambridge, MA: MIT Press, 1965. [The first major revision of TG theory as originally described in *Syntactic Structures.*]

———. *Syntactic Structures.* The Hague: Mouton & Company, 1957. [An essential but difficult study; where it all began.]

Cole, Peter, and Jerry L. Morgan, eds. *Syntax and Semantics, Volume 3: Speech Acts.* New York: Academic Press, 1975. [Excellent articles; see especially "Logic and Conversation" by H. Paul Grice and "Conversational Postulates" by David Gordon and George Lakoff.]

Cole, Ronald A. "Navigating the Slippery Stream of Speech," *Psychology Today* (April 1979), pp. 77–78, 82–94. [A fascinating discussion of how people segment and understand the constantly changing stream of sound that constitutes speech.]

Culicover, Peter W. *Syntax.* New York: Academic Press, 1976. [An excellent introduction to the study of the formal syntax of natural language; presupposes some previous work in linguistics.]

Davidson, D., and G. Harman, eds. *Semantics of Natural Languages.* Dordrecht, The Netherlands: Reidel, 1972. [Another fine collection of essays.]

Ellis, Donald G. *From Language to Communication.* Hillsdale, N.J.: Lawrence Erlbaum, 1992. [An informative book about language and how it relates to human communication.]

Fodor, J. D. *Semantics: Theories of Meaning in Generative Grammar.* New York: Crowell, 1977. [Important but difficult.]

Fromkin, Victoria, and Robert Rodman. *An Introduction to Language,* 5th ed. New York: Holt, Rinehart and Winston, 1993. [An outstandingly readable text for introductory courses in linguistics.]

Goodwin, Marjorie Harness. *He-Said-She-Said: Talk as Social Organization among Black Children.* Indianapolis: Indiana University Press, 1990. [A fascinating look at how speech is used to build social organization within peer groups and how the social lives of children are organized through talk.]

Grinder, John T., and Suzette Haden Elgin. *Guide to Transformational Grammar: History, Theory, Practice.* New York: Holt, Rinehart and Winston, 1973. [Marred by typographical errors, but still a valuable presentation.]

Gumperz, John J., and Dell Hymes, eds. *Directions in Sociolinguistics: The Ethnography of Communication.* New York: Holt, Rinehart and Winston, 1972. [Explores the components of the social context that determine linguistic behavior.]

Halle, Morris, Joan Bresnan, and George A. Miller, eds. *Linguistic Theory and Psychological Reality.* Cambridge, MA: MIT Press, 1978. [With nine main divisions that include material by eleven authors, this is a valuable collection; not for beginners.]

Hatch, Evelyn. *Discourse and Language Education.* Cambridge, Engl.: Cambridge University Press, 1992. [A thought-provoking examination of the ways in which we use language for communication in social contexts.]

Huddleston, Rodney. *An Introduction to English Transformational Syntax.* London: Longman, 1976. [Emphasis on syntax; little about semantics and phonology.]

Jackendoff, R. *Semantic Interpretation in Generative Grammar.* Cambridge, MA: MIT Press, 1972.

Jacobs, Roderick A., and Peter S. Rosenbaum, eds. *Readings in English Transformational Grammar.* Waltham, MA: Ginn and Company, 1970. [An anthology of theoretical and descriptive articles; excellent bibliography.]

Johnson, Nancy Ainsworth. *Current Topics in Language: Introductory Readings.* Cambridge, MA: Winthrop Publishers, Inc., 1976. [Essays with a practical orientation.]

Joos, Martin, ed. *Readings in Linguistics.* Chicago: University of Chicago Press, 1966. [Traces the development of linguistics in the U.S. since 1925.]

Katz, J. *Semantic Theory.* New York: Harper & Row, 1972.

———. *Propositional Structure and Illocutionary Force.* Cambridge, MA: Harvard University Press, 1980.

Kayser, Samuel Jay, and Paul M. Postal. *Beginning English Grammar.* New York: Harper & Row, 1976. [Stresses syntactic argumentation, not just assertion.]

Kempson, R. *Semantic Theory.* Cambridge, Engl.: Cambridge University Press, 1977.

Kess, Joseph S. *Psycholinguistics: Introductory Perspectives.* New York: Academic Press, 1976. [Good chapter on the relationship between the semantic differential and simpler versions of learning theory. Draws on the work of Charles Osgood.]

Langacker, Ronald W. *Language and Its Structure: Some Fundamental Linguistic Concepts,* 2nd ed. New York: Harcourt Brace Jovanovich, 1973. [Langacker cogently builds the case for universal principles of language organization in his chapter "The Universality of Language Design."]

Leech, Geoffrey N. *Principles of Pragmatics.* New York: Longman, 1983. [Argues that "grammar [in its broadest sense] must be separated from pragmatics"; excellent bibliography.]

Lehrer, Adrienne. *Wine and Conversation.* Bloomington, IN: Indiana University Press, 1983. [Fascinating; excellent bibliography.]

Lenneberg, Eric H. *Biological Foundations of Language.* New York: John Wiley,

1967. [A classic work that every student of linguistics should be familiar with.]

Lester, Mark, ed. *Readings in Applied Transformational Grammar.* New York: Holt, Rinehart and Winston, 1970. [Intended for a nontechnical audience and including articles about psycholinguistic questions and the applications of transformational grammar.]

Lieber, Justin. *Noam Chomsky: A Philosophic Overview.* New York: St. Martin's Press, 1975. [Chomsky says of this book, "It is the book that I would recommend to people who ask me what I'm up to."]

Lightfoot, David. *The Language Lottery: Toward a Biology of Grammars.* Cambridge, MA: MIT Press, 1982. [Highly recommended; not an introduction to the whole field of linguistics, but an exploration of the question "What is the genetic, internally prescribed basis of language structure?" Excellent bibliography.]

Lyons, J. *Semantics.* Cambridge: Cambridge University Press, 1977. [An important two-volume work.]

Lyons, John. *Introduction to Theoretical Linguistics.* Cambridge, Engl.: Cambridge University Press, 1968. [Still very useful despite its date; unusually complete.]

Lyons, John. *Noam Chomsky* rev. ed. New York: The Viking Press, 1978. [Clear and complete account of Chomsky's central ideas. Contains a bibliography of Chomsky's works to 1976.]

Miller, George. "Semantic Relations Among Words." In M. Halle, J. Bresnan, and G. A. Miller, eds., *Linguistic Theory and Psychological Reality.* Cambridge, MA: MIT Press, 1978.

Newmeyer, Frederick J. *Linguistic Theory in America: The First Quarter-Century of Transformational Generative Grammar.* New York: Academic Press, 1980. [An important work; traces chronologically and in detail the evolution of transformational-generative theory from the 1950s through the 1970s.]

Nilsen, Don L. F. and Alleen Pace Nilsen. *Semantic Theory: A Linguistic Perspective.* Rowley, MA: Newbury House Publishers, 1975. [Readable; excellent bibliographies, some of them annotated.]

Palmer, F. R. *Semantics: A New Outline.* Cambridge, Engl.: Cambridge University Press, 1976. [A very good introductory work.]

Piattellini-Palmarini, M., ed. *Language and Learning: The Debate Between Jean Piaget and Noam Chomsky.* London: Routledge and Kegan Paul, 1980. [Fascinating presentation of Piaget's ideas about developmental stages and his belief that the mind develops as a whole, and of Chomsky's thesis that various aspects of the mind develop in their own ways.]

Postal, Paul M. "Underlying and Superficial Linguistic Structure." *Harvard Educational Review* 34 [1964], 246–66; reprinted in Reibel and Schane, eds. [see below]. [A basic article.]

Pratt, Mary Louise. *Toward A Speech Act Theory of Literary Discourse.* Bloomington, IN: Indiana University Press, 1977. [An essential synthesizing work.]

Radford, Andrew. *Transformational Syntax: A Student's Guide to Chomsky's Extended Standard Theory.* Cambridge: Cambridge University Press, 1981. [One of the most up-to-date specialized texts; useful chapter bibliographies.]

Reibel, David A., and Sanford A. Schane, eds. *Modern Studies in English: Readings in Transformational Grammar.* Englewood Cliffs, NJ: Prentice-Hall, 1969. [An anthology of articles on the transformational analysis of English.]

Rosenberg, Jay F. and Charles Travis, eds. *Readings in the Philosophy of Language.* Englewood Cliffs, NJ: Prentice-Hall, 1971. [Includes sections on "Theories of Meaning," "Semantics," and "Speech Acts."]

Sadock, Jerrold M. *Toward a Linguistic Theory of Speech Acts.* New York: Academic Press, 1974. [A detailed discussion of illocutionary force and performative verbs.]

Saville-Troike, Muriel. "Bilingual Children: A Resource Document." *Bilingual Education, Series 2, Papers in Applied Linguistics.* Washington, DC: Center for Applied Linguistics, 1973. [Includes interesting discussion of eight components of the social context that affect linguistic behavior [pp. 9–11].]

Searle, John R. *Speech Acts: An Essay in the Philosophy of Language.* Cambridge, Engl.: Cambridge University Press, 1969. [A classic work.]

Soames, Scott, and David M. Perlmutter. *Syntactic Argumentation and the Structure of English.* Berkeley: University of California Press, 1979. [Difficult but valuable; focuses on syntactic argumentation and alternative hypothesis testing.]

Steinberg, Danny G. and L. A. Jakobovits, eds. *Semantics: An Interdisciplinary Reader in Philosophy, Linguistics, and Psychology.* New York: Cambridge University Press, 1971. [An excellent but difficult collection of articles.]

Studdert-Kennedy, Michael, ed. *Psychobiology of Language.* Cambridge, MA: MIT Press, 1983. [A collection of twenty essays; difficult but rewarding.]

Templeton, Shane. "New Trends in an Historical Perspective: Old Story, New Resolution — Sound and Meaning in Spelling" in *Language Arts,* October 1992, pp. 454–461. [A study of the reawakening of spelling and the ongoing controversy over the entire system including children's unique spelling systems.]

PART SIX

LANGUAGE VARIATION: REGIONAL AND SOCIAL

The language spoken in a country, or even in smaller areas — a town or city, for example — varies regionally and by social class. (It also varies over time, but chronological variation is the subject of Part Seven.) Regional and social dialects differ from one another because of (1) variations in vocabulary (*grinder, submarine, hoagie, hero, sub*); (2) pronunciation (/grisi/ or /grizi/, /krɪk/ or /krik/, /ant/ or /ænt/); and (3) grammar ("It's quarter [*to, 'til, of*] four," "He is not [*to, at,* Ø] home now"). Some variations are primarily regional; others are primarily social. Still others have more to do with an individual's age, sex, occupation, or particular circumstances. To the trained listener, individuals' speech reveals many things about them, and even untrained people often can tell a great deal about people based on how they speak.

The first selection in Part Six, Paul Roberts's "Speech Communities," explains that each of us belongs both successively and simultaneously to a number of different speech communities, some based on age, some on social class and education, and some on the places where we have lived. This article serves to introduce the concept of language variation.

The next selection, "Social and Regional Variation," reviews the study of regional and social dialects in the United States. The authors, Albert H. Marckwardt and J. L. Dillard, describe the first dialect research done in this country; it dealt with regional dialects and is best exemplified by works like the *Linguistic Atlas of New England* and the *Linguistic Atlas of the Upper Midwest*. They also identify a number of factors that have contributed to the various regional varieties of American English. And, explaining that in the 1960s the emphasis in dialect research shifted to the study of social dialects, they discuss some of the pioneering work that was done in this area. Next, Roger

Shuy's "Dialects: How They Differ" focuses on regional dialects and examines examples of American regional variations in pronunciation, vocabulary, and grammar. Shuy also provides extensive samples of questionnaires used in regional dialect research.

The last three selections in this part address the subject of "nonstandard" English. First, in "The Study of Nonstandard English," William Labov discusses the close relationship between standard American English and nonstandard dialects, making the important point that the latter are rule-governed and not just "corrupt forms" of the standard language. Next, in "Pidgins and Creoles," David Crystal discusses the dynamics of what happens when languages and cultures come into contact with each other. According to Crystal, "a pidgin is a system of communication which has grown up among people who do not share a common language, but who want to talk to each other, for trading or other reasons." He goes on to explain that "a creole is a pidgin language which has become the mother tongue of a community — a definition which emphasizes that pidgins and creoles are two stages in a single process of linguistic development." Finally, in "Language among Black Americans," Elizabeth Whatley looks at Black English Vernacular, analyzing its most significant phonological and syntactic features and discussing their relationship to those features of standard American English. Like Labov, she too stresses that all varieties of language are rule-governed. It should be understood that on the basis of linguistic criteria, Black English is one of the many dialects of English used in the United States. Although it shares many features with southern dialects, it is a distinct linguistic system and was recognized as such by a federal court in a July 1979 decision. The court ordered the Ann Arbor, Michigan, public schools to provide opportunities for teachers to learn about Black English so that they could incorporate this knowledge into their teaching methods in order to help children learn to read "standard" English.

29

Speech Communities

Paul Roberts

The concept of speech communities is basic to an understanding of regional and social variation in language, or dialects. In the following excerpt from his book Understanding English, *Professor Paul Roberts introduces this concept and discusses the diverse factors that contribute to the formation of speech communities and to the kinds of variation that occur within those communities. Speech communities, he argues, "are formed by many features: age, geography, education, occupation, social position." He might well have added that an individual's racial or ethnic identity and his or her sex often lead to membership in additional speech communities. In addition to variations in speech attributable to membership in speech communities, all speakers of a language also use a variety of jargons and a range of styles, the latter varying in terms of levels of formality. (For a discussion of these kinds of variations, see Harvey A. Daniels's "Nine Ideas about Language" in Part One.) Finally, Professor Roberts emphasizes that language variation is a natural phenomenon, neither "good" nor "bad," and that value judgments about language are often really value judgments about people.*

Imagine a village of a thousand people all speaking the same language and never hearing any language other than their own. As the decades pass and generation succeeds generation, it will not be very apparent to the speakers of the language that any considerable language change is going on. Oldsters may occasionally be conscious of and annoyed by the speech forms of youngsters. They will notice new words, new expressions, "bad" pronunciations, but will ordinarily put these down to the irresponsibility of youth, and decide piously that the language of the younger generation will revert to decency when the generation grows up.

It doesn't revert, though. The new expressions and the new pronunciations persist, and presently there is another younger generation with its own new expressions and its own pronunciations. And thus the language changes. If members of the village could speak to one another across five hundred years, they would probably find themselves unable to communicate.

Now suppose that the village divides itself and half the people move away. They move across the river or over a mountain and form a new village. Suppose the separation is so complete that the people of New Village have no contact with the people of Old Village. The language of both villages will change, drifting away from the language of their common ancestors. But the drift will not be in the same direction. In both villages there will be new expressions and new pronunciations, but not the same ones. In the course of time the language of Old Village and New Village will be mutually unintelligible with the language they both started with. They will also be mutually unintelligible with one another.

An interesting thing — and one for which there is no perfectly clear explanation — is that the rate of change will not ordinarily be the same for both villages. The language of Old Village changes faster than the language of New Village. One might expect that the opposite would be true — that the emigrants, placed in new surroundings and new conditions, would undergo more rapid language changes. But history reports otherwise. American English, for example, despite the violence and agony and confusion to which the demands of a new continent have subjected it, is probably essentially closer to the language of Shakespeare than London English is.

Suppose one thing more. Suppose Old Village is divided sharply into an upper class and a lower class. The sons and daughters of the upper class go to preparatory school and then to the university; the children of the lower class go to work. The upper-class people learn to read and write and develop a flowering literature; the lower-class people remain illiterate. Dialects develop, and the speech of the two classes steadily diverges. One might suppose that most of the change would go on among the illiterate, that the upper-class people, conscious of their heritage, would tend to preserve the forms and pronunciations of their ancestors. Not so. The opposite is true. In speech, the educated tend to be radical and the uneducated conservative. In England one finds Elizabethan forms and sounds not among Oxford and Cambridge graduates but among the people of backward villages.

A village is a fairly simple kind of speech community — a group of people steadily in communication with one another, steadily hearing one another's speech. But the village is by no means the basic unit. Within the simplest village there are many smaller units — groupings based on age, class, occupation. All these groups play intricately on one another and against one another, and a language that seems at first a coherent whole will turn out on inspection to be composed of many differing parts. Some forces tend to make these parts diverge; other forces hold them together. Thus the language continues in tension.

THE SPEECH COMMUNITIES OF THE CHILD

The child's first speech community is ordinarily his family. The child learns whatever kind of language the family speaks — or, more precisely, whatever kind of language it speaks to him. The child's language learning, now and later, is governed by two obvious motives: the desire to communicate and the desire to be admired. He imitates what he hears. More or less successful imitations usually bring action and reward and tend to be repeated. Unsuccessful ones usually don't bring action and reward and tend to be discarded.

But since language is a complicated business it is sometimes the unsuccessful imitations that bring the reward. The child, making a stab at the word *mother*, comes out with *muzzer*. The family decides that this is just too cute for anything and beams and repeats *muzzer*, and the child, feeling that he's scored a bull's eye, goes on saying *muzzer* long after he has mastered *other* and *brother*. Baby talk is not so much invented by the child as sponsored by the parent.

Eventually the child moves out of the family and into another speech community — other children of his neighborhood. He goes to kindergarten and immediately encounters speech habits that conflict with those he has learned. If he goes to school and talks about his *muzzer*, it will be borne in on him by his colleagues that the word is not well chosen. Even *mother* may not pass muster, and he may discover that he gets better results and is altogether happier if he refers to his female parent as his ma or even his old lady.

Children coming together in a kindergarten class bring with them language that is different because it is learned in different homes. It is all to some degree unsuccessfully learned, consisting of not quite perfect imitations of the original. In school all this speech coalesces, differences tend to be ironed out, and the result differs from the original parental speech and differs in pretty much the same way.

The pressures on the child to conform to the speech of his age group, his speech community, are enormous. He may admire his teacher and love his mother; he may even — and even consciously — wish to speak as they do. But he *has* to speak like the rest of the class. If he does not, life becomes intolerable.

The speech changes that go on when the child goes to school are often most distressing to parents. Your little Bertram, at home, has never heard anything but the most elegant English. You send him to school, and what happens? He comes home saying things like "I done real good in school today, Mom." But Bertram really has no choice in the matter. If Clarence and Elbert and the rest of the fellows customarily say "I done real good," then Bertram might as well go around with three noses as say things like "I did very nicely."

Individuals differ of course, and not all children react to the speech community in the same way. Some tend to imitate and others tend to force imitation. But all to some degree have their speech modified by forces over which neither they nor their parents nor their teachers have any real control.

Individuals differ too in their sensitivity to language. For some, language is always a rather embarrassing problem. They steadily make boners, saying the right thing in the wrong place or the wrong way. They have a hard time fitting in. Others tend to change their language slowly, sticking stoutly to their way of saying things, even though their way differs from that of the majority. Still others adopt new language habits almost automatically, responding quickly to whatever speech environment they encounter.

Indeed some children of five or six have been observed to speak two or more different dialects without much awareness that they are doing so. Most commonly, they will speak in one way at home and in another on the playground. At home they say, "I did very nicely" and "I haven't any"; these become, at school, "I done real good" and "I ain't got none."

THE CLASS AS A
SPEECH COMMUNITY

Throughout the school years, or at least through the American secondary school, the individual's most important speech community is his age group, his class. Here is where the real power lies. The rule is conformity above all things, and the group uses its power ruthlessly on those who do not conform. Language is one of the chief means by which the school group seeks to establish its entity, and in the high school this is done more or less consciously. The obvious feature is high school slang, picked up from the radio, from other schools, sometimes invented, changing with bewildering speed. Nothing is more satisfactory than to speak today's slang; nothing more futile than to use yesterday's.

There can be few tasks more frustrating than that of the secondary school teacher charged with the responsibility of brushing off and polishing up the speech habits of the younger generation. Efforts to make *real* into *really*, *ain't* into *am not*, *I seen him* into *I saw him*, *he don't* into *he doesn't* meet at best with polite indifference, at worst with mischievous counterattack.

The writer can remember from his own high school days when the class, a crashingly witty bunch, took to pronouncing the word *sure* as *sewer*. "Have you prepared your lesson, Arnold?" Miss Driscoll would ask. "Sewer, Miss Driscoll," Arnold would reply. "I think," said Miss Driscoll, who was pretty quick on her feet too, "that you must mean 'sewerly,' since the construction calls for the adverb not the adjective." We were delighted with the suggestion and went about saying "sewerly" until the very blackboards were nauseated. Miss Driscoll must have wished often that she had left it lay.

CONFRONTING THE ADULT WORLD

When the high school class graduates, the speech community disintegrates as the students fit themselves into new ones. For the first time in the experience of most of the students the speech ways of adult communities begin to exercise real force. For some people the adjustment is a relatively simple one. A boy going to work in a garage may have a good deal of new lingo to pick up, and he may find that the speech that seemed so racy and won such approval in the corridors of Springfield High leaves his more adult associates merely bored. But a normal person will adapt himself without trouble.

For others in other situations settling into new speech communities may be more difficult. The person going into college, into the business world, into scrubbed society may find that he has to think about and work on has speech habits in order not to make a fool of himself too often.

College is a particularly complicated problem. Not only does the freshman confront upperclassmen not particularly disposed to find the speech of Springfield High particularly cute, but the adult world, as represented chiefly by the faculty, becomes increasingly more immediate. The problems of success, of earning a living, of marriage, of attaining a satisfactory adult life loom larger, and they all bring language problems with them. Adaptation is necessary, and the student adapts.

The student adapts, but the adult world adapts too. The thousands of boys and girls coming out of the high schools each spring are affected by the speech of the adult communities into which they move, but they also affect that speech. The new pronunciation habits, developing grammatical features, different vocabulary do by no means all give way before the disapproval of elders. Some of them stay. Elders, sometimes to their dismay, find themselves changing their speech habits under the bombardment of those of their juniors. And then of course the juniors eventually become the elders, and there is no one left to disapprove.

THE SPACE DIMENSION

Speech communities are formed by many features besides that of age. Most obvious is geography. Our country was originally settled by people coming from different parts of England. They spoke different dialects to begin with and as a result regional speech differences existed from the start in the different parts of the country. As speakers of other languages came to America and learned English, they left their mark on the speech of the sections in which they settled. With the westward movement, new pioneers streamed out through the mountain passes and down river valleys, taking the different dialects west and modifying them by new mixtures in new environments.

Today we are all more or less conscious of certain dialect differences in our country. We speak of the "southern accent," the "Brooklyn accent," the "New England accent." Until a few years ago it was often said that American English was divided into three dialects: Southern American (south of the Mason-Dixon line); Eastern American (east of the Connecticut River); and Western American. This description suggests certain gross differences all right, but recent research shows that it is a gross oversimplification.

The starting point of American dialects is the original group of colonies. We had a New England settlement, centering in Massachusetts; a Middle Atlantic settlement, centering in Pennsylvania; a southern settlement, centering in Virginia and the Carolinas. These colonies were different in speech to begin with, since the settlers came from different parts of England. Their differences were increased as the colonies lived for a century and a half or so with only thin communication with either Mother England or each other. By the time of the Revolution the dialects were well established. Within each group there were of course subgroups. Richmond speech differed markedly from that of Savannah. But Savannah and Richmond were more like each other than they were like Philadelphia or Boston.

The Western movement began shortly after the Revolution, and dialects followed geography. The New Englanders moved mostly into upper New York State and the Great Lakes region. The Middle Atlantic colonists went down the Shenandoah Valley and eventually into the heart of the Midwest. The southerners opened up Kentucky and Tennessee, later the lower Mississippi Valley, later still Texas and much of the Southwest. Thus new speech communities were formed, related to the old ones of the seaboard, but each developing new characteristics as lines of settlement crossed.

New complications were added before and after the Revolution by the great waves of immigration of people from countries other than England: Swedes in Delaware, Dutch in New York, Germans and Scots-Irish in Pennsylvania, Irish in New England, Poles and Greeks and Italians and Portuguese. The bringing in of Negro slaves had an important effect on the speech of the South and later on the whole country. The Spanish in California and the Southwest added their mark. In this century movement of peoples goes on: the trek of southern Negroes to northern and western cities, the migration of people from Arkansas, Oklahoma, and Texas to California. All these have shaped and are shaping American speech.

We speak of America as the melting pot, but the speech communities of this continent are very far from having melted into one. Linguists today can trace very clearly the movements of the early settlers in the still-living speech of their descendants. They can follow an eighteenth century speech community west, showing how it crossed this pass and followed that river, threw out an offshoot here, left a pocket there, merged with another group, halted, split, moved on once more. If all other historical evidence were destroyed, the history of the country could still be reconstructed from the speech of modern America.

SOCIAL DIFFERENCES

The third great shaper of speech communities is social class. This has been, and is, more important in England than in America. In England, class differences have often been more prominent than those of age or place. If you were the blacksmith's boy, you might know the son of the local baronet, but you didn't speak his language. You spoke the language of your social group, and he that of his, and over the centuries these social dialects remained widely separated.

England in the twentieth century has been much democratized, but the language differences are far from having disappeared. One can still tell much about a person's family, his school background, his general position in life by the way he speaks. Social lines are hard to cross, and language is perhaps the greatest barrier. You may make a million pounds and own several cars and a place in the country, but your vowels and consonants and nouns and verbs and sentence patterns will still proclaim to the world that you're not a part of the upper crust.

In America, of course, social distinctions have never been so sharp as they are in England. We find it somewhat easier to rise in the world, to move into social environments unknown to our parents. This is possible, partly, because speech differences are slighter; conversely, speech differences are slighter because this is possible. But speech differences do exist. If you've spent all your life driving a cab in Philly and, having inherited a fortune, move to San Francisco's Nob Hill, you will find that your language is different, perhaps embarrassingly so, from that of your new acquaintances.

Language differences on the social plane in America are likely to correlate with education or occupation rather than with birth — simply because education and occupation in America do not depend so much on birth as they do in other countries. A child without family connection can get himself educated at Harvard, Yale, or Princeton. In doing so, he acquires the speech habits of the Ivy League and gives up those of his parents.

Exceptions abound. But in general there is a clear difference between the speech habits of the college graduate and those of the high-school graduate. The cab driver does not talk like the Standard Oil executive, the college professor like the carnival pitch man, or an Illinois merchant like a sailor shipping out of New Orleans. New York's Madison Avenue and Third Avenue are only a few blocks apart, but they are widely separated in language. And both are different from Broadway.

It should be added that the whole trend of modern life is to reduce rather than to accentuate these differences. In a country where college education becomes increasingly everybody's chance, where executives and refrigerator salesmen and farmers play golf together, where a college professor may drive a cab in the summertime to keep his family alive, it becomes harder and harder to guess a person's education, income, and social status by the way he talks. But it would be absurd to say that language gives no clue at all.

GOOD AND BAD

Speech communities, then, are formed by many features: age, geography, education, occupation, social position. Young people speak differently from old people, Kansans differently from Virginians, Yale graduates differently from Dannemora graduates. Now let us pose a delicate question: aren't some of these speech communities better than others? That is, isn't better language heard in some than in others?

Well, yes, of course. One speech community is always better than all the rest. This is the group in which one happens to find oneself. The writer would answer unhesitatingly that the noblest, loveliest, purest English is that heard in the Men's Faculty Club of San Jose State College, San Jose, California. He would admit, of course, that the speech of some of the younger members leaves something to be desired; that certain recent immigrants from Harvard, Michigan, and other foreign parts need to work on the laughable oddities lingering in their speech; and that members of certain departments tend to introduce a lot of queer terms that can only be described as jargon. But in general the English of the Faculty Club is ennobling and sweet.

As a practical matter, good English is whatever English is spoken by the group in which one moves contentedly and at ease. To the bum on Main Street in Los Angeles, good English is the language of other L.A. bums. Should he wander onto the campus of UCLA, he would find the talk there unpleasant, confusing, and comical. He might agree, if pressed, that the college man speaks "correctly" and he doesn't. But in his heart he knows better. He wouldn't talk like them college jerks if you paid him.

If you admire the language of other speech communities more than you do your own, the reasonable hypothesis is that you are dissatisfied with the community itself. It is not precisely other speech that attracts you but the people who use the speech. Conversely, if some language strikes you as unpleasant or foolish or rough, it is presumably because the speakers themselves seem so.

To many people, the sentence "Where is he at?" sounds bad. It is bad, they would say, in and of itself. The sounds are bad. But this is very hard to prove. If "Where is he at?" is bad because it has bad sound combinations, then presumably "Where is the cat?" or "Where is my hat?" are just as bad, yet no one thinks them so. Well, then, "Where is he at?" is bad because it uses too many words. One gets the same meaning from "Where is he?" so why add the *at?* True. Then "He going with us?"

is a better sentence than "Is he going with us?" You don't really need the *is*, so why put it in?

Certainly there are some features of language to which we can apply the terms *good* and *bad*, *better* and *worse*. Clarity is usually better than obscurity; precision is better than vagueness. But these are not often what we have in mind when we speak of good and bad English. If we like the speech of upper-class Englishmen, the presumption is that we admire upper-class Englishmen — their characters, culture, habits of mind. Their sounds and words simply come to connote the people themselves and become admirable therefore. If we heard the same sounds and words from people who were distasteful to us, we would find the speech ugly.

This is not to say that correctness and incorrectness do not exist in speech. They obviously do, but they are relative to the speech community — or communities — in which one operates. As a practical matter, correct speech is that which sounds normal or natural to one's comrades. Incorrect speech is that which evokes in them discomfort or hostility or disdain. . . .

≡

FOR DISCUSSION AND REVIEW

1. Identify the factors that, according to Roberts, bring speech communities into being and contribute to internal differences within each community. Trace the changing speech communities of an individual, considering age as the only variable.

2. Change has occurred less rapidly in American English than in British English; change also occurs more rapidly in both countries among the educated than among the uneducated. Identify three reasons why this is so.

3. Explain Roberts's statement that "Baby talk is not so much invented by the child as sponsored by the parent." Describe two examples of this phenomenon in your own family.

4. Roberts writes of the "enormous pressures" on people to conform to the speech of their age group and class, their speech community. Discuss the pressures that you felt while growing up.

5. Roberts believes that there are marked differences between the speech communities of one generation and the next. Observe and describe speech differences between students and faculty in your school. Compare your findings with those of your instructor. Is age the only factor here? What kinds of differences exist between your speech and that of your parents? Between your speech and that of your grandparents? What, in general, are people's attitudes toward these differences?

6. Explain the geographic basis from which American regional dialects

originated. Do you agree with Roberts's statement: "If all other historical evidence were destroyed, the history of the country could still be reconstructed from the speech of modern America"? Why or why not?

7. Roberts writes that "Language differences on the social plane in America are likely to correlate with education or occupation rather than with birth." Discuss the implications of this statement. Do your experiences support it? Explain your answer.

   (Note: Before answering questions 8 through 10, you should review Harvey A. Daniels's "Nine Ideas about Language" in Part One, pp. 17–34.)

8. Note three distinctive characteristics and/or functions of the consultative style.

9. In what ways does the casual style differ from the consultative?

10. Note five distinctive characteristics of the formal style. To what extent do you think most Americans have learned to speak in this style? Give specific examples — a professor lecturing to a class, for example, or an unrehearsed radio or television interview with a typical American.

30

Social and Regional
Variation

Albert H. Marckwardt
J. L. Dillard

In the following chapter from American English *by Albert H. Marck-wardt, revised by J. L. Dillard, the authors present an overview of the study of regional and social dialects in the United States. Regional dialects were the first to be studied. The methodology used was based largely on that developed in France by Jules Gilliéron and in Italy, Sicily, Sardinia, and Switzerland by Karl Jaberg and Jakob Jud. Beginning in the late 1920s, under the leadership of Hans Kurath, the original North American project called for a linguistic atlas of the United States and Canada. The first actual research, done in New England in the early 1930s, resulted in the publication of the multivolume* Linguistic Atlas of New England (LANE) *between 1939 and 1943 (reissued in 1972), the* Handbook of the Linguistic Geography of New England *(1939, 1972), and* A Word Geography of the Eastern United States *(1949). Linguistic atlases for other parts of the United States have been published or are in progress.*

In the 1960s, as Marckwardt and Dillard point out, emphasis shifted to the study of social dialects, the identification and analysis of dialect features that are significant indicators of social class. The authors describe some of the pioneering research in this area carried out by William Labov. Acknowledging the unique problems of working with dialects in the United States, they identify a few of the distinctive differences in the vocabulary, pronunciation, and grammar of various regional and social varieties of American English. As they write, "There is still some faith in the notion that understanding is the key to tolerance."

The English language is spoken natively in America by some two hundred million people, over an area of more than three million square miles, with a large number of minority subcultures offering proof that the "melting pot" was an ideal rather than a reality. For many groups found in all parts of the country, English is by no means the only — or even the first — language. Dialectologists are slowly coming to the realization that both class distribution of language variants, and prejudice against the users of "nonstandard" dialects are realities in twentieth-century America. Black English, the dialect of "disadvantaged" Black children, was recognized legally by a landmark Detroit court decision in July, 1979. Social dialect study was largely the product of the 1960s, but public awareness of social dialects may actually come about during the 1980s.

A pioneering sociologist, Glenna Ruth Pickford, began in 1956 to direct our attention to sociological factors like occupation and urban residence rather than to purely geographic factors in a paper published in that year but hardly noticed for ten years or so thereafter. The field of linguistics was, however, branching out into "hyphenated" disciplines like sociolinguistics, and works like William Labov's *Social Stratification of English in New York City* (1965) (though preceded by some important work on caste dialect in India), were perhaps most directly responsible for the new emphasis on social variation. [See Figure 30.1.]

Labov's influential work, although it contains much more highly technical data, is best known for its demonstration that certain variables of pronunciation like *that* and *dat* or *fourth floor* "with or without [r]" are socially and contextually distributed. Labov demonstrated that every speaker has some differing pronunciations: to do so, he ranked data col-

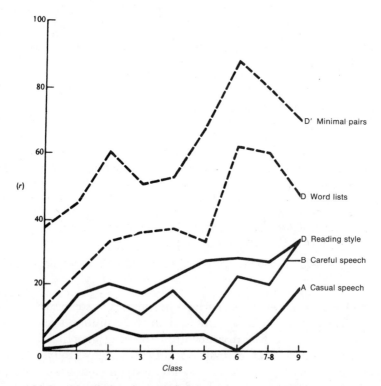

FIGURE 30.1. Detailed style stratification of *(r)*: nine classes. From William Labov's *Social Stratification of English in New York City*. Reprinted by permission of the Center for Applied Linguistics.

lected in casual speech, in the reading of a paragraph, in the reading of lists of unrelated words, and in the reading of paired words with something like minimal contrasts *(guard* and *god).* Not only did everyone pronounce "r" more often in the last context, but floorwalkers at posh Saks' Fifth Avenue put more "r" into *fourth floor* than did those at middle-class Macy's. S. Klein's, the poor man's haberdashery, trailed in the amount of "r" as well as in rank on the social scale.

Even more interesting than relative frequency across class, however, was the greater variability evidenced by the lower-middle class. These sociologically insecure people also indulge extensively, Labov found, in hypercorrection. Insofar as class goes (ignoring, for now, such other factors as the greater likelihood that a new biological generation will make changes), not the highest or the lowest but the class in between is the one most likely to foment linguistic change.

Research by others, as well as by Labov himself, indicates that *Social Stratification* slightly underemphasized social factors like ethnic group membership. Black English, with many of the same features in New York and Detroit as in Shreveport, Louisiana, has become one of the most thoroughly studied dialects of all time. Especially prominent has been work on the so-called zero copula *(He my main man),* and the demonstration that all speakers who use the "zero" also realize the copula in some positions *(Yes, he is),* and that non-use of the verbs *is* and *are* is not categorical with any speaker. Labov's 1969 paper on this feature developed the theory of inherent variability, with variable rules becoming the indispensable new tool of variation studies. Almost overlooked, unfortunately, were the grammatical implications of Black English forms like preverbal *been (You been know dat; He been ate de chicken)* marking a strongly past time (longer ago, for example, than *He done ate de chicken).*

Dialectology, before the criticism expressed by sociologist Glenna Ruth Pickford, followed the reconstructive lead of the *Atlas Linguistique de la France* and the *Sprachatlas des Deutschen Reichs.* The approach still dominates publications like the *Journal of English Linguistics* and *American Speech.* The nineteenth century had seen the beginning of the English Dialect Society (and publications like the *English Dialect Dictionary),* and the American Dialect Society was organized in 1889. Beginning in 1928, a group of researchers under the direction of Professor Hans Kurath undertook the compilation of a *Linguistic Atlas of the United States and Canada.* The *Linguistic Atlas of New England* was published over the period from 1939 to 1943. Considerably more field work has been completed since that time.

Pickford strongly criticized this work for including only three social groups (five in the closely related *Dictionary of American Regional English)* and for limiting, in practice, the interviews almost exclusively to rural informants. In the 1960s, partly in response to Pickford's criticism, dialectologists began to conduct studies in Washington, D.C., Detroit, Chicago, and New York.

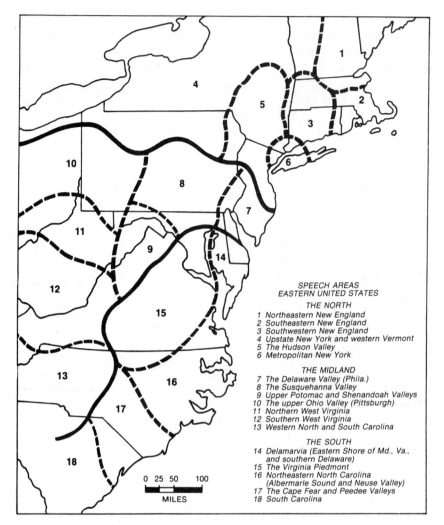

FIGURE 30.2

From the *Atlas* research procedures there seemed to emerge three major dialect boundaries, cutting the country into lateral strips and labeled by Kurath: Northern, Midland, and Southern. [See Figure 30.2.] This regional distribution had no place for either what Mencken had called the "American Vulgate" or for what others had called General American. Standardizing practices, often associated with the concept of General American, were dismissed as not really part of the informants' "natural" language.

What emerged in the dialect research of the 1960s, however, was something other than a picture of regional distribution. The "neutral" dialect concept of General American was replaced, especially in the research of certain psycholinguists, by that of Network Standard, the speech of television newscasters on the major networks and the kind of English which Americans clearly admired more than any other. They tended, however inaccurately, to form mental pictures of their own speech in terms of that prestige form. This regionally and socially neutral dialect clearly emerged as the ideal, if not the actuality, for most speakers of American English. Television, becoming really important as a medium in the 1960s, would permit relatively "nonstandard" usage from comedians and sportscasters, but anyone else had to disguise his dialect in order to work regularly for the networks. A nationally oriented and highly mobile population substituted this concept of a standard dialect for the older notion of prestige centers.

The older, geographically oriented type of research identified dialect areas for the essentially rural population in terms of predominantly lexical materials. For example, characteristic Northern expressions that were current throughout the area include *pail, swill, whiffletree* or *whippletree, comforter* or *comfortable* for a thick quilt, *brook, co-boss* or *come-boss* as a *cow call, johnny-cake, salt pork,* and *darning needle* for a dragonfly. When one considers how few cattle are called in New York City, or how few Manhattanites see a dragonfly during the course of a day, one realizes how irrelevantly quaint and rustic some of this research came to seem.

In the Midland area one found *blinds* for roller shades, *skillet, spouting* or *spouts* for eaves, a *piece* for food taken between meals, *snake feeder* for dragonfly, *sook* as the call to calves, *armload* for an armful of wood; and one *hulled* beans when he took off the shells. A quarter *till* the hour was a typical Midland expression, as [was] the elliptical *to want off,* or *out,* or *in.* The South had *lightwood* as the term for kindling, a *turn* of wood for an armful; stringbeans were generally *snap beans; low* was used for the sound cows make at feeding time; *hasslet* was the term for the edible inner organs of a pig, and *chittlins* for the small intestines. The last item above has now, of course, achieved nationwide spread in connection with the Black institution of soul food.

Subdialect areas were also found to have their characteristic forms. In coastal New England, for instance, *pigsty* was the normal term for a pigpen, *bonny clapper* for curdled sour milk, *buttonwood* for a sycamore, and *pandowdy* for a cobbler type of dessert. Some Eastern Virginians still have *cuppin* for a cow pen, and *corn house* for a crib. *Lumber room* survives as the term for a storeroom. *Hopper grass* competed with the national term *grasshopper,* and *batter bread* was used for a soft cornbread containing egg.

As far as the domains of the American lexicon which reflect regional differences are concerned, the matter is summarized in Kurath's *Word Geography,* where the author points out first of all that the vocabularies of the arts and sciences, of industries, commercial enterprises, social and political institutions, and even many of the crafts, are national in scope because the activities they reflect are organized on a national basis. He then goes on to say:

> Enterprises and activities that are regionally restricted have, on the other hand, a considerable body of regional vocabulary which, to be sure, may be known in other parts of the country, even if it is not in active use. The cotton planter of the South, the tobacco grower, the dairy farmer, the wheat grower, the miner, the lumberman, and the rancher of the West have many words and expressions that are strictly regional and sometimes local in their currency.

> Regional and local expressions are most common in the vocabulary of the intimate everyday life of the home and the farm — not only among the simple folk and the middle class but also among the cultured. . . . Food, clothing, shelter, health, the day's work, play, mating, social gatherings, the land, the farm buildings, implements, the farm stocks and crops, the weather, the fauna and flora — these are the intimate concern of the common folk in the countryside, and for these things expressions are handed down in the family and the neighborhood that schooling and reading and a familiarity with regional or national usage do not blot out.

In other domains of the lexicon, social differences are more strikingly important. Americans have, from the first, identified themselves much more by occupation than by region, and early commentators made much of the "jargon" of groups like the trappers ("mountain men") and the cowboys. Groups as diverse as hoboes, prostitutes, and advertising men have their own peculiar terminology and phraseology. In particular, American Blacks have had African or Afro-Creole survivals; these survivals came to national attention beginning around 1920, through the vocabulary of jazz and blues musicians. White musicians and then American teenagers made a shibboleth of the use of Black-associated "slang," and British rock groups like the Beatles and the Rolling Stones propagated it among the English youth.

It is not only in the vocabulary that one finds regional differences in American speech; there are pronunciation differences as well. Throughout the Northern area, for example, the distinction between [o] and [ɔ] in such word pairs as *hoarse* and *horse, mourning* and *morning,* is generally maintained; [s] regularly occurs in *grease* (verb) and *greasy* and *root* is pronounced with the vowel of *wood.* Within the Northern area such sub-dialects as coastal New England and Metropolitan New York also show many characteristic forms, although the extreme amount of variation found in the latter must not be forgotten. The treatment of the vowel of *bird* is only one of these, and words of the *calf, pass, path, dance* group constitute another. In the Midland area speakers fail to distinguish between *hoarse* and *horse* in many contexts. Rounding is characteristic of the vowels of *hog, frog, log, wasp,* and *wash,* and in the last of these words an *r* often intrudes in the speech of the rural and old-fashioned. The vowels of *due* and *new* will resemble that of *food* rather than that of *feud.* In the South and in eastern New England, there is a tendency to "lose" *r* except before vowels; but the former does not have the pronounced *Cuber* (for *Cuba*) and *idear of it* which John F. Kennedy carried from Massachusetts to the presidency. *R* is also "lost" in eastern New England and in New York City but not in the Northern area generally. Words like *Tuesday, due,* and *new* have a *y*-like glide preceding the vowel, and final [z] in *Mrs.* is the normal form. . . .

Regional variation in inflectional forms and syntax at the most superficial level can also be found, especially among older, relatively uneducated groups. *Hadn't ought* is a characteristic Northern double modal; *might could* and *may can* were perhaps exclusively Southern until Black speakers carried them into the Northern cities. Verb forms associated with the North have *been see* as a past tense form, *clim* for "climbed," *wa'n't* for "wasn't," uninflected *be* in such expressions as "How be you?" (much more limited syntactically than the superficially similar Black English form), and the choice of the preposition *to* in *sick to his stomach.* Associated with the Midlands were *clum* for "climbed," *seen* for "saw," *all the further,* and *I'll wait on you.* Characteristic Southern expressions, excluding Black English influence, were *belongs to be, heern* for "heard," *seed* as the past tense of "to see," and *holp* for "helped."

However quaint and rustic some of these forms may seem, and however unfamiliar to many other speakers of American English, they have been used, so far unsuccessfully, in attempts to trace the settlement history, particularly of the earliest immigrants. It has been hypothesized that, of ten families of settlers gathered in any one place, two might well have spoken London English, while three or four others spoke one of the southeastern county dialects. There might also have been a couple of families speaking northern English and another two or three employing a western dialect.

What would have happened to this hypothetical dialect mix is another matter. Recent studies emphasize the way in which children are influenced more strongly by the language of their peers than by that of their parents. Even if the parents retained the old regional dialect unchanged—and sociolinguistic research questions whether this is ever completely the case—children of the second generation would level the differences. Whatever compromises between British local dialects were worked out at various points on the Atlantic Seaboard would be supplemented by borrowings from the Indians and from other language groups. Other population groups which had extensive contacts with the children of the British immigrants, like the Black slaves of the Southern states, would also have strongly influenced their language.

Judging by the reports of observers, these influences became especially noticeable about the beginning of the nineteenth century. At about the same time, other changes occurred which were to have a profound effect upon the language situation in America. First, the industrial revolution resulted in the growth of a number of industrial centers, uprooting a considerable proportion of the farm population and concentrating it in the cities. The development of the railroad and other mechanical means of travel increased greatly the mobility of the average person. The large-scale migrations westward also resulted in some resettlement and shifting, even among those who did not set out on the long trek. All of this would have resulted in a general abandonment of narrowly local speech forms in favor of fewer, more accessible, varieties — even if there had not been prior forces leading toward the same end.

Some local speech forms have remained even to the present day. These are usually known as relics, particularly when they are distributed in isolated spots over an area rather than in concentration. *Open stone peach*, for example, is a relic for "freestone peach," occurring in Maryland. *Smurring up*, "getting foggy," survives as a relic in eastern Maine and more rarely on Cape Cod and Martha's Vineyard.

Even prior to the shifts in population and changes in culture pattern, certain colonial cities such as Boston, Philadelphia, and Charleston had acquired prestige by developing as centers of trade and immigration. They became socially and culturally outstanding, as well as economically powerful, thus dominating the areas surrounding them. As a consequence, local expressions and pronunciations peculiar to the countryside came to be replaced by new forms of speech emanating from these cosmopolitan centers. A fairly recent instance of this is to be found in the New England term *tonic* for soda water, practically coextensive with the area served by Boston wholesalers.

Little if anything of this sort has ever been observed for the influence of New York City on any large surrounding area. Nevertheless, Madison Avenue's influence on the advertising phraseology of the nation, along with the importance of New York City for radio, television, and publication, must have had a general, widely diffused influence. It has been suggested that the "Brooklyn" dialect of popular stereotype, particularly with its pronunciation of *bird, shirt, thirty-third*, etc. (imprecisely believed to be like "oy" of *Floyd*) resembles that of the same working-class people in New Orleans and elsewhere along the Atlantic and Gulf seacoasts because of the trade connections, particularly in cotton, between New Orleans and New York City.

Nor was the general process of dialect formation by any means completed with the settlement of the Atlantic seaboard. As the land to the west came to be taken up in successive stages (for example, western New York, Michigan, Wisconsin in the North; southern Ohio, Indiana, and southern Illinois in the Midland area), the same mixtures of speech forms among the settlers were present at first, and the same linguistic compromises had to be worked out. Although virtually every westward-moving group had to work out some way of dealing with the foreign-language groups in its language contact picture, the specific nature of the groups encountered varied at each stage.

The same processes occurred in the interior South, in Texas, and later on in the Far West. The complete linguistic history of the United States depends upon the formulation of what happened in each of those areas. We know, for example, from both surviving forms and historical sources that the Western cowboys used faro and poker terms *(in hock, pass the buck, deal from the bottom of the deck, four-flusher)*, and occupational terms *(little dogies, break the string, hand* for "worker"), many of which moved back toward the East.

Such environmental factors as topography, climate, and plant and animal life also played their part in influencing the dialect of an area, just as they did in the general transplanting of the English language to America. The complexity and size of the network of fresh-water streams affect the distribution and meaning of such terms as *brook, creek, branch,* and *river*—not to mention *wash* and *bayou.* In parts of Ohio and Pennsylvania, for example, the term *creek* is applied to a much larger body of water than in Michigan. It is even more obvious that in those parts of the country where snow is a rarity or does not fall at all, there will be no necessity for terms to indicate coasting face down on a sled. It is not surprising that those areas of the country where cows can be milked outside, for at least part of the year, will develop a specific term for the place where this is done: witness *milk gap* or *milking gap* current in the Appalachians south of the James River. The wealth of terms for various types of fences throughout the country is again dependent, in part at least, on the material which is available for building them, be it stones, stumps, or wooden rails. It is equally obvious that nationwide technological terms for television, like *commercial, station break, prime time, talk show,* and *situation comedy* should be the same in all parts of the country. Neither is it surprising that the increasingly nationwide distribution of major sporting events should lead to uniformity in *Super Bowl, Number One* ("We're Number One!"), *playoff, World Series,* and a host of other terms.

Before the days of radio, television, and national magazine advertising, a new invention or development introduced into several parts of the country at the same time would acquire different names in various places. The baby carriage, for example, seems to have been a development of the 1830s and '40s, and this is the term which developed in New England. Within the Philadelphia trade area, however, the article became known as a *baby coach. Baby buggy* was adopted west of the Alleghenies and *baby cab* in other regions throughout the country.

Within the last four decades, the building of large, double-lane, limited-access automobile highways has been undertaken in all parts of the country. In the beginning, there were many regional differences: *parkways* in eastern New York, Connecticut, and Rhode Island; *turnpikes* in Pennsylvania, New Jersey, New Hampshire, Maine, Massachusetts, Ohio, and Indiana. (The fanciest highway in Florida, from Miami to Gainesville, is, however, now a turnpike.) In New York *thruway* is used for what are *expressways* in Michigan and *freeways* in California. For a while—in the late 1950s—these seemed like regionalisms in the making, but a generation of car travelers has learned them all and uses them now synonymously, now with some specialization.

It is of interest also to look at the dialect situation from the point of view of various words which are employed for the same concept in different parts of the country. One of the most interesting and instructive distributions is to be found in connection with the terms used for *earthworm*. This word is used by cultivated speakers in the metropolitan centers. *Angleworm* is the regional term in the North, *fishworm* in the Midland area, and *fishing worm* in the coastal South. *Fish bait* and *bait worm* occupy smaller areas within the extensive *fishworm* region, but are also distributed over a wide territory.

In addition, there have been a large number of local terms, many of them used principally by the older and less-educated inhabitants. The Merrimack Valley, in New Hampshire, and Essex County, Massachusetts, have *mud worm*. *Eace worm* is used in Rhode Island. *Angle dog* appears in upper Connecticut, and *ground worm* on the Eastern Shore of Virginia. *Red worm* is used in the mountains of North Carolina, and an area around Toledo, Ohio, uses *dew worm*. Scattered instances of *rainworm* appear on Buzzards Bay in Massachusetts, throughout the Pennsylvania German area, and in German settlements in North Carolina, Maine, and Wisconsin. We have, thus, a wealth of older local terms, three distinct regional words, and the cultivated *earthworm* appearing in addition as a folk word in South Carolina and along the North Carolina and Virginia coast. Where and how did the various terms originate, and what can be determined about their subsequent history?

Earthworm itself is not an old word; it appears to have been compounded only shortly before the earliest English migrations to America. The earliest *Oxford English Dictionary* citation of the word in its present form is 1591; it appears also as *yearth worm* some thirty years earlier. The three regional terms all seem to have been coined in America; the dictionaries either record no British citations or fail to include the words at all.

The local terms have a varied and interesting history. *Mud worm* seems to occur in standard British English from the beginning of the nineteenth century on. *Eace worm*, as a combined form, goes back at least to Middle English; the first element was a term for "bait" as early as Aelfric; it is used today in a number of southern counties in England from Kent to Gloucester. *Angle dog* is used currently in Devonshire. *Ground worm*, through apparently coined in England, was transferred to North Carolina and Maryland in the eighteenth century. *Red worm* appears first in England in 1450 and continues through to the midnineteenth century, though chiefly in books on fishing, as does *dew worm*, which goes back even farther, to the late Old English period. *Rainworm*, though it appears in Aelfric as *renwyrm*, may be a reformation, even in British English, on the pattern of *Regenwurm* in German, for there is a gap of seven centuries in the citations in the *Oxford English Dictionary* and there is reason to believe that its revival in 1731 was influenced by the German form. Moreover, with but one exception, it has been cited for the United States only in areas settled by Germans.

Thus we have in the standard cultivated term one of relatively recent British formation. Apparently the regional terms were compounded in America, whereas the local terms represent survivals either of dialect usage or anglers' jargon and one loan translation. It is worth noting that the common Old English term, *angle twicce,* surviving as *angle twitch* in Cornwall and Devon, seems not to have found its way to America. There are, furthermore, such other English formations as *tag worm, marsh worm,* and *garden worm* which have not been recorded in America.

At times, too, changes in meaning seem to have entered into the dialect situation, as is illustrated by the development of the regional terms *skillet* and *spider,* the former current in the Midland and the Virginia Piedmont, the latter in the North and the Southern Tidewater area. *Frying pan* is the urban term and is slowly supplanting the others. *Spider,* once a nautical term for "the iron band around the mast to take the lower end of futlock rigging," was then applied to a cast-iron pan with short legs. It was later transferred to the flat-bottomed pan as well. The local term *creeper* is used in Marblehead, Massachusetts. *Skillet,* a term of doubtful etymology, first appears in English in 1403, when it was applied to a long-handled brass or copper vessel used for boiling liquids or stewing meat. It is still so used in dialects throughout England. The shift in meaning to a frying pan took place only in America, but an advertisement of 1790, offering for sale "bakepans, spiders, skillets," would suggest that even as late as this a distinction between the two was recognized.

The examples above have been offered only as a suggestion of the various language processes which have played a part in the distribution and meaning of some of our dialect terms. It is quite obvious that no definite conclusions about such matters can be reached on the basis of rather scant linguistic details. Such evidence as has been accumulated, however, seems to suggest that Kurath's original intuition was correct in that only home and farm terms give much evidence of regional or local distribution in the United States.

The question of social dialects or speech differences is quite another matter, with many scholars seeing much more profound grammatical differences between social — especially ethnic — groups. Black English, of which Gullah is the extreme case, comes immediately to mind; but the English of the Pennsylvania Germans also offers some grammatical constructions that are very strange to mainstream American English speakers.

Frequently, the matter of social dialect has been conceptualized in terms of "standard" and "nonstandard" dialects. H. L. Mencken believed in a so-called "American Vulgate" with reasonably uniform characteristics throughout the country — and with no special stated social distribution. Nonstandard dialects, however, do have many features in common, for whatever reason that may be.

One of the inflectional forms most characteristic of nouns in nonstandard American English is the unchanged plural after numbers: *six mile down the road, five foot tall,* and similarly applied to *month, year,* and *gallon.* In Black English it resembles the Afro-Creole nonredundant pluralization: *The boys* bears a plural inflection, but either *six boy* or *plenty boy* is plural without the final *s.* Any plural marking in the immediate environment, not just a numeral, may suffice, so that we sometimes find sentences like *Dem chair* for "Those are chairs."

The Mencken-type Vulgate may, in the case of some unmarked plurals, represent a preservation of linguistically older forms than those found in Standard English. It displays the opposite tendency, however, in the possessive pronoun in its so-called absolute form, which in the standard language represents a strange and inconsistent mixture of patterns. *Mine* and the archaic *thine* are derived from the adjectival form by adding *-n. Hers, ours, yours,* and *theirs,* on the other hand, add *-s* to the adjectival form. *His* and *its* are indistinguishable so far as their secondary and absolute forms are concerned. In contrast, the "Vulgate" possessive pronouns, *mine, yourn, hisn, hern, ourn, theirn,* present a perfectly regular pattern formed by an analogical extension of *mine* and *thine* to the third person singular and to the plural forms. The fact that Pidgin English probably had absolute *me one, you one, he one,* etc., may have contributed something to the leveling process of the Vulgate.

In the use of absolute possessives, Black English and other nonstandard dialects part company. In the most extreme form, which William Stewart calls *basilect,* Black English has *he book, you friend, they uncle.* In the "exposed" position, *It he book* becomes neither *It he* nor *It hisn.* Instead, basilect *It he own* alternates with a Standard-English influenced *It his.*

The reflexive pronouns give us another instance of a more regular operation of analogy on the nonstandard level than on the standard. In Standard English, *myself, yourself, ourselves,* and *yourselves* are combinations of the genitive pronoun plus the singular or plural of the *-self* form; *himself* and *themselves* employ the object form of the pronoun, whereas *herself* and *itself* could be either. Nonstandard English, in substituting *hisself* and *theirself* in the third person and adhering to the singular of *self* in *ourself* and *yourself* (plural), is not only more consistent but more economical in that the latter combinations signal the plural only once and avoid the redundancy of the plural *-selves.* The only ambiguity is in the second person, but the second personal pronoun has lost its distinctions between singular and plural anyway, except for nonstandard formations like the Southern *you all*—which never figures in the reflexive.

One curious feature of the nonstandard pronoun is the substitution of the object for the subjective form in such sentences as *Us girls went home, John and her was married, Me and him was late.* The use of the object form for the subject is normal in Black English basilect *(Me help you?)* and in Pidgin English. In Cajun English, of Louisiana, it can be used at the end of the sentence for emphasis: *I was late, me.* In the "Vulgate," however, it seems to occur principally when the subject is compound or when the pronoun is syntactically a modifier of the subject, as in *us girls* above. The schools have made such emphatic use of *we girls* and *It is I* (or *he, she*), that the result is a lot of overcorrection on the order of *between you and I* (or even *between he and I*); *She gave it to Mother and I; She took all of we children.*

A few typical nonstandard inflectional forms deserve mention. *Them* as a demonstrative adjective (*them* books) probably harks back to the days when the English article and the demonstrative *that* (dative *ðæm*) were one and the same form. *Dem* is the regular demonstrative adjective and noun pluralizer (*dem man* = "men") in Gullah, but postposed use as in Jamaican and other creoles *(man-dem)* is hinted at in the records of early Black English in one speech by newly imported African slaves and remembered by Frederick Douglass. The multiple negative was a regular and accepted feature of older English, but Black English negative concord *(It ain't no cat can't get in no coop)* has no such obvious earlier parallel. The adverb without the *-ly* suffix or other differentiation from the adjective *(He spoke quiet; You did real good)* may reflect very old practices in English.

The standard and nonstandard languages are undoubtedly farthest apart with regard to verb forms. Black English nonpassive preverbal *been (He been rub me the wrong way)*, and *be* in its negation by *don't*, and in contrast to "zero copula" are the most extremely different forms outside Gullah *de*. Less significantly, there is a tendency to dispose of the distinctive *-s* inflection for the third person singular, either by eliminating it in such forms as *he want, she write*, etc., or by extending the peculiar form of the third person to the first and second—*I has some good friends; You is in lots of trouble.* Black English makes widespread, often hypercorrective, use of these forms; the records tend to indicate that older varieties used (also hypercorrectively) *he am*, etc.

The overwhelming tendency in English verb development throughout the last seven or eight centuries has been toward an aggrandizement of the regular or weak inflection (*-ed* past tense) at the expense of the older minor conjugations. This is in effect a tendency toward a two-part verb, the infinitive or present stem opposed to an identical past tense and past participle. In general, this has been brought about through analogical processes. It is often impossible to know for certain whether nonstandard forms are the result of retention of an older preterite plural (*writ* as the past tense of *write*; or *begun* and *swum* in that function), or of analogies which have not operated in Standard English. Extension of the regular past inflections to such irregular verbs as *know* and *see* (*knowed, seed*) can only be analogical; as must the amalgamation of the strong preterite or past participle with the complementary form (*I taken, he done* as preterites; *have gave, have wrote, has went* as past participial forms).

The easy transition from one social class to another in the United States has resulted in a very hazy line of demarcation between what is acceptable and what is considered illiterate. According to the most rigorous textbook standard, some of the language employed in American legislative councils and in business life would not pass muster; one could not even be sure that what is spoken in college faculty meetings would always meet those same criteria. The awareness of this, combined with an unrealistic treatment of language in our schools, has resulted at times in a defiance of these questionable standards, in what could be called "dramatic low status assertion." More often it has given people guilt complexes about the language they use. The puristic schoolteacher for whom nothing is good enough, has been attacked in linguistics courses and textbooks since the 1940s. Some changes may have been made, but the prescriptive attitude, in one guise or another, lives on in our school systems and in handbooks of usage. On television's Public Broadcasting System, groups consisting of actors, drama critics, newscasters, and occasionally even a linguistics professor meet to discuss the "deplorable" state of the English language in America.

Consequently, many Americans, especially those who are socially mobile, lack confidence and assurance of the essential aptness and correctness of their speech. Fewer members of any class are able to switch comfortably between a nonstandard dialect and the standard—although this is by no means rare in other countries. Those educational programs that have called for use of children's home and peer group dialects in such educational activities as initial or remedial reading have generally met with scorn, even from many dialectologists. The Ann Arbor, Michigan, school district became in July, 1979, the first U.S. school system ordered to take Black children's dialect into account in planning its curriculum. Lawsuits similar to the one that elicited this decision have already been filed in Tampa, Florida, and Houston, Texas, and many others may follow.

Within professional dialectology, new developments like variation theory and inherent variability provide an even more solid foundation for acceptance of and interest in dialect and speech pattern differences. Popularization of the variable rule may be more difficult to achieve than was the case of regional and local differences; but there also seems to be less chance that the popularized knowledge will form the basis for invidious comparisons and linguistic snobbery. There is still some faith in the notion that understanding is the key to tolerance.

FOR DISCUSSION AND REVIEW

1. Explain the difference between regional (geographical) and social dialectology. Why has a great deal of work been done in the latter field in the last twenty-five years?

2. Carefully examine Figure 30.1 on p. 520. The vertical axis indicates the percentage of respondents using *(r)*; the horizontal axis indicates the frequency of occurrence of *(r)* by social class; the labels to the right of the chart show the increasing degrees of formality of speech. (The two top lines are broken rather than solid in order to indicate that these styles do not occur in normal connected speech.) Having studied the figure, explain Marckwardt and Dillard's statement: "Even more interesting than relative frequency across class, however, was the greater variability evidenced by the lower-middle class. These sociologically insecure people also indulge extensively, Labov found, in hypercorrection."

3. Identify the three major geographical dialect boundaries in the United States. How has the identification of these three areas modified earlier ideas about American regional dialects?

4. Explain the concepts of "General American" (dialect) and "Network Standard." Which, if either, is still important? Why or why not?

5. What, according to Marckwardt and Dillard, are the three aspects of American speech in which one finds regional differences? About which aspect do we have the most information? Why? Give three examples of each kind of regional difference.

6. Identify three areas of the lexicon in which regional differences are most important, and explain why this is so.

7. Explain the effects on American regional dialects of (a) the industrial revolution, (b) the development of the railroad, and (c) the large-scale migration westward.

8. List four reasons for the difficulty of doing research on American regional dialects.

9. Using examples not cited by Marckwardt and Dillard, explain how four environmental factors have influenced American regional dialects.

10. Marckwardt and Dillard state that the terms *parkway, turnpike, thruway, expressway,* and *freeway* for a while "seemed like regionalisms in the making, but a generation of car travelers has learned them all and uses them now synonymously, now with some specialization." Do you agree with their conclusion? Identify two other relatively recent inventions or developments that have acquired different names in various places.

11. Marckwardt and Dillard state that "Nonstandard dialects . . . have many features in common, for whatever reason that may be." Identify and describe four such features.

31

Dialects: How They Differ

Roger W. Shuy

We all speak a dialect; dialects are not things spoken by other people in other places. One often quoted definition of a dialect is that of Raven I. McDavid, Jr., who describes a dialect as "simply a habitual variety of a language, regional or social. It is set off from all other such habitual varieties by a unique combination of language features: words and meanings, grammatical forms, phrase structures, pronunciations, patterns of stress and intonation." Professor McDavid then points out that "No dialect is simply good or bad in itself; its prestige comes from the prestige of those who use it. But every dialect is in itself a legitimate form of the language, a valid instrument of human communication, and something worthy of serious study."* In the following excerpt from Discovering American Dialects, *Roger W. Shuy discusses, with many examples, regional variations in pronunciation, vocabulary, and grammar, and provides extensive samples of dialect questionnaires. These questionnaires are shortened versions of those used by field investigators in preparing the* Linguistic Atlas of New England (LANE) *and other regional atlases. The LANE questionnaire, for example, contained about 750 items. Shuy also explains the methods used by fieldworkers to collect dialect data and the importance of the "personal data sheet," and warns the would-be investigator that people are usually more self-conscious about their grammar than they are about either their vocabulary or pronunciation.*

Speakers of one dialect may be set off from speakers of a different dialect by the use of certain pronunciations, words, and grammatical forms. The frequent first reaction of a person who hears an unfamiliar dialect is that the strange sounds and words are a chaotic mess. This is similar to the feeling an American has when he sees British motorists driving "on the wrong side of the street," or to the bewildered feeling we have upon hear-

---

* "Sense and Nonsense About American Dialects" in *Dialects in Culture: Essays in General Dialectology* by Raven I. McDavid, Jr., edited by William A. Kretzschmar, Jr. University, AL: The University of Alabama Press, 1979, p. 70; originally published in *PMLA* 81 (1966) 2:7–17.

ing a foreign language for the first time. Surely, we feel, there is no system in that sort of behavior!

Mankind apparently views all unfamiliar human behavior as suspicious and unsystematic. If you have ever watched a bird build a nest on a window sill or in a bush within the range of any passing alley cat, you have probably not questioned the intelligence of the bird. Most people accept even apparently erratic animal behavior and assume that, no matter how foolish the act may seem, it probably makes sense to the animal. But as soon as a human being is seen to behave "differently," he is frequently considered foolish or uncooperative. Language, in this case a dialect, is also a form of behavior. That people speak different dialects in no way stems from their intelligence or judgment. They speak the dialect which enables them to get along with the other members of their social and geographical group.

DIFFERENCES IN PRONUNCIATION

Differences in pronunciation are of two types: totally patterned and partially patterned. A totally patterned difference is one in which the sound behaves consistently in a particular situation. For example, in some parts of the country, particularly in eastern New England, the pronunciation of *r* is lost before consonants and in word-final position. Thus, a Midwesterner's "park the car" becomes the New Englander's "pahk the cah." From the New Englander's point of view, it might be equally valid to say that Midwesterners insert *r*'s before consonants (park) and following a vowel at the ends of words (car). That the words in question have *r*'s in their spellings is really not important here, for spellings remain fixed long after pronunciations change, and letters may have different sound values in different dialects. But whether we say the New Englander *drops* an *r* or the Midwesterner *inserts* one, the fact remains that the difference is totally patterned in most speech styles. Recent dialect research has shown that a person may shift his pattern slightly, depending upon his relationship to his audience and on whether he is reading aloud or speaking impromptu. Professor William Labov of Columbia University has observed, for example, that New York working-class people tend to say *dis* for *this* and *dese* for *these* when they are talking about a bad accident or about a personal brush with death. They say *dis* and *dese* less frequently when talking with teachers and even less frequently when reading aloud.

The second kind of variation in pronunciation, a partially patterned difference, may occur in a few words or even in only one. The partially patterned sound is not consistent throughout the dialect. It was mentioned above that the eastern New Englander "drops" an *r* before consonants and in word-final position in a totally patterned way. Now let us cite the Midwesterner who inserts an *r* in certain words but in no particular phonetic pattern. In most of Ohio, Indiana, and Illinois (except for a few

FIGURE 31.1

northern counties), *wash* is pronounced *"worsh"* by a large number of speakers, particularly by those with no more than a high school education. If this were totally patterned, these speakers would also say "borsh" instead of *bosh* and "jorsh" instead of *josh* (many of them do say "gorsh" instead of *gosh*).

Other examples of partially patterned differences (still sticking with *r* problems) include "lozengers" for *lozenges,* "framiliar" for *familiar,* "quintruplets" for *quintuplets,* and "surpress" for *suppress.* This phenomenon, sometimes referred to as the "intrusive *r,*" is most noticeable in someone else's dialect. Midwesterners are amused at the Bostonian's pronunciation of "Cuber" and "Asiar" for *Cuba* and *Asia* before words beginning with vowels, failing to hear their own intrusive *r* in *worsh* and *lozengers.* Likewise, the Bostonian tends to hear the Midwesterner's intrusive *r*'s but not his own.

Our standard alphabet cannot record the many sounds in American English pronunciation. The dialectologist uses a highly detailed phonetic alphabet to record the most minute audible features of speech. The student can easily learn and use a simpler set of symbols to record the variations he meets in his dialect studies. [Here the author supplies a resumé of the phonetic alphabet like that included by Edward Callary in "Phonetics" (Part Four). He then suggests that readers practice transcribing how various speakers pronounce certain words.]

Remember that a good ear for sounds is not developed right away. You may wish to practice with other transcription exercises, or you may simply write phonetically the words used by teachers, classmates, television performers, or members of your family. If classmates or friends from a different part of the country are willing to serve as informants, have them pronounce the following words:

Word	Northern	Midland	Southern
1. cr*ee*k	ɪ and i	ɪ (north Midland) i (south Midland)	i
2. p*e*nny	ɛ	ɛ	ɪ–(Southwest)
3. M*a*ry	ɛ e (parts of eastern New England)	ɛ	e
4. m*a*rried	æ (east of Appalachians) ɛ (elsewhere)	ɛ	ɛ
5. c*ow*	ɑu	æu	æu or ɑu
6. s*i*ster	ɪ	ɨ (eastern)	ɨ (eastern)
7. f*o*reign	ɔ	ɑ	ɑ
8. *o*range	ɑ (east of Alleghenies) ɔ	ɑ and ɔ	ɑ and ɔ
9. tomat*o*	o	ə	o or ə
10. c*oo*p	u	u (NM), ʊ (SM)	ʊ
11. r*oo*f	ʊ	u and/or ʊ	u
12. b*u*lge	ə	ə or ʊ	ə or ʊ
13. f*a*rm	ɑ	ɑ or ɔ	ɑ or ɔ
14. w*i*re	ɑɪ	ɑɪ or ɑ	ɑ
15. w*o*n't	ə o (urban)	o ɔ	o ɔ
16. f*o*g	ɑ (New England) ɑ and ɔ (Midwest)	ɔ	ɔ
17. h*o*g	ɑ (New England) ɑ and ɔ (Midwest)	ɔ	ɔ
18. *o*n	ɑ	ɔ	ɔ
19. l*o*ng	ɔ	ɔ	ɑ (eastern Virginia) ɔ (elsewhere)
20. car*e*less	ɨ	ə	ɨ
21. stom*a*ch	ə	ɨ	ə

The vowels of these words are pronounced differently in the various parts of our country. The major variants are listed beside the words along with their general distributions.

Consonants sometimes will give clues to the dialect a person speaks. The following generalizations may be helpful:

Word	Northern	Midland	Southern
1. *hu*mor	hɪumər	yumər	hɪumər or yumər
2. wa*sh*	waš or wɔš	wɔrš or wɔɪš	wɔš or wɔɪš or wɑš
3. wi*th*	wɪð and wɪθ (N.Y., Chicago, Detroit = wɪt working class)	wɪθ	wɪθ
4. grea*sy*	grisɪ	grizɪ	grizɪ
5. b*a*rn	bɑrn (Eastern North = bɑn)	bɑrn	bɑrn (East Coast = bɑn)
6. *th*ese	ðiz (N.Y., Chicago, Detroit = diz working class)	ðiz	ðiz
7. *wh*ich	hwɪč	wɪč	wɪč
8. mi*ss*	mɪs	mɪs	mɪz
9. Mrs.	mɪsɨz	mɪsɨz	mɪzɨz or mɪz

With the mobility of the American population today, we are bound to discover exceptions to generalizations like these. Also, . . . settlement history has caused some curious mixtures of speech patterns in our country. On the whole, however, the generalizations may be useful in helping you to recognize the dialect of your informant.

One bit of advice as you get your informants to say these words — *try for a natural situation.* One way professional fieldworkers have done this is to ask, for example, for what the person calls a small stream of water that runs through a farm. *Creek* is a likely response. You can easily invent similar questions for other words. It might be interesting, furthermore, to compare a person's response in conversation with his pronunciation when he reads the word in a sentence or in a list of such words. You may discover that your classmates have different pronunciations for different occasions. . . .

DIFFERENCES IN VOCABULARY

Words are interesting to almost everyone. Through his vocabulary a person may reveal facts about his age, his sex, his education, his occupation, and his geographical and cultural origins. Our first reaction may be to imagine that all speakers of English use the same words. Nothing could be further from the truth; our language contains a vast number of synonyms to show different shades of meaning or reveal as much of our inner feelings as we want to. Some of these vocabulary choices are made deliberately. We use other words, however, without really knowing that our vocabulary is influenced by our audience.

Age

Certain words tell how old we are. For example, many people refer to an electric refrigerator as an *ice box* despite the fact that in most parts of our country ice boxes have not been in common use for many years. Older natives of some Northern dialect areas still may call a frying pan a *spider*, a term which remained in the vocabulary of the older generation long after the removal of the four legs which gave the descriptive title. Frying pans no longer look like four-legged spiders, but the name remains fixed in the vocabulary of certain people.

Sex

Our vocabulary may also identify whether we are male or female. Most high school boys, for example, are not likely to use *lovely, peachy, darling,* and many words ending in *-ie.* Adult males are not apt to know or use very many words concerned with fabrics, color shadings, sewing, or women's styles. Women of all ages are not likely to use the specialized vocabulary of sports, automobile repair, or plumbing.*

Education

A person also reveals his educational background through his choice of words. It is no secret that learning the specialized vocabulary of psychology, electronics, or fishing is necessary before one becomes fully accepted as an "insider," and before he can fully participate in these areas. Much of what a student learns about a course in school is shown in his handling of the vocabulary of the subject. It is also true, however, that a person's choice of words is not nearly as revealing of education as his grammar and pronunciations are.

Occupation

The specialized vocabulary of occupational groups also appears in everyday language. Truck drivers, secretaries, tirebuilders, sailors, farmers, and members of many other occupations use such words. Linguists who interview people for *The Linguistic Atlas of the United States and Canada* have found that the calls to certain animals, for example, illustrate what might be called farm vocabulary, particularly for the older generation of farmers (city dwellers obviously have no particular way of calling sheep or cows from pasture). Even within farming areas, furthermore, vocabulary will reveal specialization. Recent Illinois language studies showed that a male sheep was known as a *buck* only to farmers who had at some time raised sheep.

Origins

It is common knowledge that certain words indicate where we are from. Northerners use *pail* for a kind of metal container which Midlanders refer to as a *bucket*. *Pits* are inside cherries and peaches of Northerners; *seeds* are found by some Midlanders. It is amusing to some people, furthermore, that as a general rule horses are said to *whinny* or *whinner* in Northern dialect areas, whereas they *nicker* in some of the Midland parts of our country.

---

* Editors' note: Writing in 1967, Shuy could not have foreseen the many social changes that have occurred in the United States that necessitate some restriction of his generalizations in this area.

Customs are also revealed in our vocabulary. The *county seat* is relatively unknown in rural New England, where local government is handled at the town meeting.

The special names for various ethnic or national groups, whether joking or derogatory, are an indication of the settlement patterns of an area. If a person has the terms *Dago, Kraut,* or *Polack* in his active vocabulary, it is quite likely that he lives among or near Italians, Germans, or Polish people. Sometimes the nickname of a specific immigrant group becomes generalized to include most or all newcomers. Such a case was . . . noted in Summit County, Ohio, where some natives refer to almost all nationality groups as *Hunkies,* regardless of whether or not they come from Hungary. That this practice has been with us for many years is shown in a comment by Theodore Roosevelt that anything foreign was referred to as *Dutch.* One nineteenth-century politician even referred to Italian paintings as "Dutch daubs from Italy."[1]

Vocabulary Fieldwork

To show some of the ways a speaker's vocabulary may reveal his age, sex, occupation, or regional and cultural origins, let us do a dialect vocabulary project as it might be done by a linguist (called a fieldworker in this case) who interviews people (called informants) for *The Linguistic Atlas.*

The *Atlas* fieldworker gathers his information in face-to-face interviews. He may supplement his interview data, however, with questionnaires such as the one which follows. Sometimes these questionnaires are mailed; sometimes the fieldworker distributes them personally. Whatever method of distribution is used, one thing is certain: The questionnaires have been extremely helpful, reliable, and accurate indications of vocabulary in use.

A CHECKLIST OF REGIONAL EXPRESSIONS

Directions

1. Please put a circle around the word or words in each group which you ordinarily use (don't circle words you have heard — just those you actually use).
2. If the word you ordinarily use is not listed in the group, please write it in the space by the item.

---

[1] H. L. Mencken, *The American Language,* abridged and revised by Raven I. McDavid, Jr. (New York: Knopf, 1963), p. 371.

3. If you never use any word in the group, because you never need to refer to the thing described, do not mark the word.

Example:

Center of a peach: pit, seed, (stone,) kernel, heart

Household

1. *to put a single room of the house in order:* clean up, do up, redd up, ridd up, straighten up, tidy up, put to rights, slick up
2. *paper container for groceries, etc.:* bag, poke, sack, toot
3. *device found on outside of the house or in yard or garden:* faucet, spicket, spigot, hydrant, tap
4. *window covering on rollers:* blinds, curtains, roller shades, shades, window blinds, window shades
5. *large open metal container for scrub water:* pail, bucket
6. *of peas:* to hull, to pod, to shell, to shuck
7. *web hanging from ceiling of a room:* cobweb, dust web, spider's web, web
8. *metal utensil for frying:* creeper, fryer, frying pan, fry pan, skillet, spider
9. *over a sink:* faucet, hydrant, spicket, spigot, tap
10. *overlapping horizontal boards on outside of house:* clapboards, siding, weatherboards, weatherboarding
11. *large porch with roof:* gallery, piazza, porch, portico, stoop, veranda
12. *small porch, often with no roof:* deck, platform, porch, portico, step, steps, stoop, veranda, piazza
13. *devices at edges of roof to carry off rain:* eaves, eaves spouts, eavestroughs, gutters, rain troughs, spouting, spouts, water gutter
14. *rubber or plastic utensil for scraping dough or icing from a mixing bowl:* scraper, spatula, kidcheater, bowl scraper
15. *vehicle for small baby:* baby buggy, baby cab, baby carriage, baby coach
16. *to _____ the baby (in such a vehicle):* ride, roll, wheel, push, walk, stroll
17. *furry stuff which collects under beds and on closet floors:* dust bunnies, dust kittens, lint balls, pussies

Family

18. *family word for father:* dad, daddy, father, pa, papa, pappy, paw, pop

19. *family word for mother:* ma, mama, mammy, maw, mom, mommer, mommy, mother

20. *immediate family:* my family, my folks, my parents, my people, my relatives, my relations, my kin, my kinfolks

21. *others related by blood:* my family, my folks, my kind, my kinfolks, my people, my relation, my relatives, my relations, my kin

22. *of a child:* favors *(his mother)*, features, looks like, resembles, takes after, is the spitting image of

23. *of children:* brought up, fetched up, raised, reared

24. *the baby* moves on all fours *across the floor:* crawls, creeps

Automotive

25. *place in front of driver where instruments are:* dash, dashboard, instrument panel, panel, crash panel

26. *automobile device for making the car go faster:* accelerator, gas, gas pedal, pedal, throttle

27. *place where flashlight and maps may be kept:* glove compartment, compartment, shelf, cabinet

28. *automobile with two doors:* tudor, coupe, two-door

29. *the card needs _____:* a grease job, greased, lubrication, a lube job, to be greased, to be lubed, greasing, servicing, to be serviced

30. *large truck with trailer attached:* truck, truck and trailer, semi, rig, trailer-truck

Urban

31. *new limited access road:* turnpike, toll road, freeway, parkway, pay road, tollway, thruway, expressway

32. *service and eating areas on no. 31:* service stop, service area, oasis, rest area

33. *grass strip in the center of a divided road:* median, center strip, separator, divider, barrier, grass strip, boulevard

34. *place where fire engines are kept:* fire hall, fire house, fire station

35. *place where scheduled airlines operate:* airport, port, terminal, air terminal (by proper name), air field, field

36. *place where train stops:* station, railway station, depot, train stop, train station, railroad station

37. *place where firemen attach hose:* fire hydrant, fire plug, plug, hydrant, water tap

38. *grass strip between sidewalk and street:* berm, boulevard, bou-

levard strip, parking, parking strip, parkway, sidewalk plot, tree lawn, neutral ground, devil strip, tree bank, city strip

39. *call to hail a taxi:* taxi!, cab!, cabbie!, hack!, hey!, (wave arm), (whistle)
40. *policeman:* cop, policeman, copper, fuzz, dick, officer, bull
41. *the road is:* slick, slippery
42. *place where packaged groceries can be purchased:* grocery store, general store, supermarket, store, delicatessen, grocery, market, food market, food store, supermart
43. *a piece of pavement between two houses on a city block:* gangway, walk, path, sidewalk
44. *place where you watch technicolor features in a car:* drive-in, drive-in movie, outdoor movie, outdoor theater, open-air movie, open-air theater, passion pit

Nature

45. *animal with strong odor:* polecat, skunk, woodspussy, woodpussy
46. *small, squirrel-like animal that runs along the ground:* chipmunk, grinnie, ground squirrel
47. *worm used for bait in fishing:* angledog, angleworm, bait worm, eace worm, earthworm, eelworm, fish bait, fishing worm, fishworm, mudworm, rainworm, redworm
48. *larger worm:* dew worm, night crawler, night walker, (Georgia) wiggler, town worm
49. *dog of no special kind or breed:* common dog, cur, cur dog, fice, feist, mongrel, no-count, scrub, heinz, sooner, mixed dog, mutt
50. *insect that glows at night:* fire bug, firefly, glow worm, june bug, lightning bug, candle bug
51. *large winged insect seen around water:* darning needle, devil's darning needle, dragon fly, ear-sewer, mosquito hawk, sewing needle, snake doctor, snake feeder, sewing bug
52. *freshwater shellfish with claws; swims backward:* crab, craw, crawdad(die), crawfish, crayfish
53. *center of a cherry:* pit, seed, stone, kernel, heart
54. *center of a peach:* pit, seed, stone, kernel, heart
55. *hard inner cover of a walnut:* hull, husk, shell, shuck
56. *green outer cover of a walnut:* hull, husk, shell, shuck
57. *bunch of trees growing in open country (particularly on a hill):* motte, clump, grove, bluff
58. *web found outdoors:* cobweb, dew web, spider nest, spider's nest, spider web, web
59. *tree that produces sugar and syrup:* hard maple, rock maple, sugar maple, sugar tree, maple tree, candy tree, sweet maple

Foods

60. *melon with yellow or orange insides:* muskmelon, melon, mushmelon, lope, cantaloup, mussmellon
61. *a spreadable luncheon meat made of liver:* liver sausage, braunschweiger, liverwurst
62. *a carbonated drink:* pop, soda, soda pop, tonic, soft drink
63. *a glass containing ice cream and root beer:* a float, a root beer float, a black cow, a Boston cooler
64. *dish of cooked fruit eaten at the end of a meal:* fruit, sauce, dessert, compote
65. *peach whose meat sticks to seed:* cling, cling peach, clingstone, clingstone peach, hard peach, plum-peach, press peach
66. *food eaten between regular meals:* a bite, lunch, a piece, piece meal, a snack, a mug-up, munch, nash, nosh
67. *corn served on cob:* corn-on-the-cob, garden corn, green corn, mutton corn, roasting ears, sugar corn, sweet corn
68. *beans eaten in pods:* green beans, sallet beans, snap beans, snaps, string beans, beans
69. *edible tops of turnips, beets, etc.:* greens, salad, salat
70. *a white lumpy cheese:* clabber cheese, cottage cheese, curd cheese, curd(s), dutch cheese, home-made cheese, pot cheese, smear-case, cream cheese
71. *round, flat confection with hole in center, made with baking powder:* crull, cruller, doughnut, fatcake, fried cake, cake doughnut, raised doughnut
72. *bread made of corn meal:* cornbread, corn dodger(s), cornpone, hoe cake(s), johnnycake, pone bread
73. *cooked meat juices poured over meat, potatoes, or bread:* gravy, sop, sauce, drippings
74. *ground beef in a bun:* hamburg, hamburger, burger
75. *large sandwich designed to be a meal in itself:* hero, submarine, hoagy, grinder, poor-boy

Games

76. *children's cry at Halloween time:* trick or treat!, tricks or treats!, beggar's night!, help the poor!, Halloween!, give or receive!
77. *fast moving amusement park ride (on tracks):* coaster, roller coaster, rolly-coaster, shoot-the-chutes, the ride of doom
78. *call to players to return because a new player wants to join:* allie-allie-in-free, allie-allie-oxen free, allie-allie-ocean free, beebee bumble bee, everybody in free, newcomer-newcomer!

79. *call to passerby to return a ball to the playground:* little help!, ball!, hey!, yo!, ball up!
80. *to coast on sled lying down flat:* belly-booster, belly-bump, belly-bumper, belly-bunker, belly-bunt, belly-bust, belly-buster, belly-down, belly-flop, belly-flopper, belly-grinder, belly-gut, belly-gutter, belly-kachug, belly-kachuck, belly-whack, belly-whop, belly-whopper, belly-slam, belly-smacker
81. *to hit the water when diving:* belly-flop, belly-flopper, belly-bust, belly-buster
82. *to stop a game you call:* time!, time out!, times!, pax!, fins!

School

83. *to be absent from school:* bag school, bolt, cook jack, lay out, lie out, play hookey, play truant, run out of school, skip class, skip school, slip off from school, ditch, flick, flake school, blow school
84. *where swings and play areas are:* schoolyard, playground, school ground, yard, grounds
85. *holds small objects together:* rubber band, rubber binder, elastic binder, gum band, elastic band
86. *drinking fountain:* cooler, water cooler, bubbler, fountain, drinking fountain
87. *the amount of books you can carry in both arms:* armful, armload, load, turn

Clothing

88. *short knee-length outer garment worn by men:* shorts, bermuda shorts, bermudas, walking shorts, knee (length) pants, pants, knee-knockers
89. *short knee-length outer garment worn by women:* shorts, bermudas, walking shorts, pants
90. *outer garment of a heavy material worn by males as they work:* levis, overalls, dungarees, jeans, blue jeans, pants
91. *garment worn by women at the seashore:* swimsuit, swimming suit, bathing suit
92. *garment worn by men at the seashore:* swimsuit, swimming suit, bathing suit, swimming trunks, trunks, bathing trunks, swimming shorts

Miscellaneous

93. *a time of day:* quarter before eleven, quarter of eleven, quarter till eleven, quarter to eleven, 10:45

94. *someone from the country:* backwoodsman, clodhopper, country gentleman, country jake, countryman, hayseed, hick, hoosier, hillbilly, jackpine savage, mossback, mountain-boomer, pumpkinhusker, railsplitter, cracker, redneck, rube, sharecropper, stump farmer, swamp angel, yahoo, yokel, sodbuster
95. *someone who won't change his mind is:* bull-headed, contrary, headstrong, ornery, otsny, owly, pig-headed, set, sot, stubborn, mulish, muley
96. *when a girl stops seeing a boyfriend she is said to:* give him the air, give him the bounce, give him the cold shoulder, give him the mitten, jilt him, kick him, throw him over, turn him down, shoot him down, give him the gate, brush him off, turn him off, break up with him
97. *become ill:* be taken sick, get sick, take sick, be taken ill, come down
98. *become ill with a cold:* catch a cold, catch cold, get a cold, take cold, take a cold, come down with a cold
99. *sick ———:* at his stomach, in his stomach, on his stomach, to his stomach, of his stomach, with his stomach
100. *I ——— you're right:* reckon, guess, figger, figure, suspect, imagine

The preceding vocabulary questionnaire, frequently called a checklist, is only suggestive of what might be asked for in a particular community. Of the hundred items in ten general fields, you may find some questions more interesting and useful to study than others. Furthermore, you may add other words to this list, or you may find other answers to questions listed here.

Let us suppose, however, that you wish to make a vocabulary survey of your community using this checklist. If your school has ample facilities and supplies, you could reproduce all or part of this questionnaire, distribute it to various neighbors, let them fill it out at their leisure, and then have them return it to you for tabulation and analysis.

One last matter of data must be included, however, if the checklist is to be meaningful. The dialectologist needs to know certain things about the people who fill out the checklists. The following questions should be answered if the data are to be interpreted meaningfully.

Let us look for a moment at the personal data sheet. We note that dialectologists think it important to keep a record of the informant's age, sex, race, education, mobility, travel, ancestry, language skills, and occupation. People from the same general area may use different words, and this personal data sheet will help us find out why. In parts of Michigan, for example, the older generation may still use the term *spider* for what younger informants may call *frying pan.* This is an indication of current language change. It is never a surprise to us to hear that our parents' generation did things differently. Nor should we be surprised to note that they use different words.

Personal Data Sheet

Sex _____ Race _____

Have you filled out this same   Age _____ Highest grade level

questionnaire before? Yes __ No __ reached in school _____

State _____ County _____ Town _____

How long have you lived here? _____ years

Birthplace _____

                    (town)   (state)

Other towns, states, or nations you have lived in (please give approximate years for each place)

_____

_____

_____

Have you traveled much outside your native state? ____ (Yes or No)

If so, where? _____

_____

Parents' birthplace (state or nation):

Father _____ Grandfather _____

Grandmother _____

Mother _____ Grandfather _____

Grandmother _____

Do you speak any non-English language? ____ If so, which? _____

                                      (yes or no)

Occupation _____

If retired, former occupation _____

If housewife, husband's occupation _____

Name (optional) _____

There are any number of things you may be able to discover by making a vocabulary survey in your community. What you should remember as you gather your data is the principle of constants and variables, a principle familiar to you, no doubt, from mathematics. You may gather your data in any way you wish, but chances are you will not be able to get a representation of all ages, ethnic groups, religions, and occupations of the people in your area, especially if you live in an urban community. A somewhat narrower approach would be easier and more successful, for example:

1. *Age Contrast:* Collect checklists from three or four people who have lived all their lives in your community. This gives you two constants: the checklist and the native-born residents. The most interesting variables will be their age and education along with, of course, their answers. If you select older people and younger people of roughly the same education and social status, chances are that any vocabulary differences will stem from the contrast in ages.

2. *Education Contrast:* Collect checklists from three or four people who have different educational backgrounds. College graduates, for example, may be contrasted with people who have had less than a high school education. If your informants are of roughly the same age, and if their personal data sheets are otherwise similar, the differences which you note may be attributable to their contrasting educations.

3. *Describe the Local Dialect Area:* Collect checklists from three or four people who have lived all their lives in your community. Try to get older, middle-aged, and younger people who have educational backgrounds characteristic of your community (in some parts of our country, for example, college graduates are simply not frequently found). Then note the responses of these informants to some or all of the following questions: 1, 2, 3, 5, 8, 9, 10, 13, 24, 45, 46, 47, 50, 51, 53, 54, 64, 67, 69, 70, 71, 72, 87, 93, 97, 98, 99. For each of these questions there is a response which research has shown to be characteristic of one side of the dialect map (of course, the term may be used elsewhere, too, but not as generally). The following chart will indicate some of the words you may expect to find *in certain parts* of the Northern, Midland, and Southern dialect areas:

Word	Northern	Midland	Southern
1. *to put room in order:*		redd up ridd up	
2. *paper container:*	bag	sack	sack
3. *on outside of house:*	faucet	spigot spicket hydrant	spigot spicket hydrant
5. *container:*	pail	bucket	bucket
8. *metal utensil:* (frying pan common everywhere)	spider	skillet	skillet spider
9. *over a sink:*	faucet	spigot spicket	spigot spicket
10. *boards:* (siding common everywhere)	clapboards	weatherboards	
13. *devices at roof:*	gutters (ENE) eaves spouts eavestroughs	gutters spouting spouts	gutters
24. *baby moves:*	creeps	crawls	crawls
45. *animal:*	skunk	skunk polecat woodspussy woodpussy	polecat

Word	Northern	Midland	Southern
46. *animal:* (note: for some people, chipmunk and ground squirrel are two different animals)	chipmunk	ground squirrel	ground squirrel
47. *worm:*	angleworm	fish(ing) worm	fish(ing) worm
50. *insect:*	firefly (urban) lightning bug (rural)	lightning bug fire bug	lightning bug
51. *insect:*	(devil's) darning needle sewing bug dragon fly	snake feeder snake doctor dragon fly	snake feeder snake doctor dragon fly mosquito hawk
53. *cherry:*	pit stone	seed stone	seed stone
54. *peach:*	pit stone	seed stone	seed stone
64. *dish:*	dessert sauce fruit	dessert fruit	dessert fruit
67. *corn:*	corn-on-the-cob green corn sweet corn	corn-on-the-cob sweet corn roasting ears	roasting ears sweet corn
69. *tops:*		greens	greens salad salat
70. *cheese:* (cottage cheese common everywhere)	dutch cheese pot cheese	smear-case	clabber cheese curds
71. *confection:*	doughnut fried cake	doughnut	doughnut
72. *bread:*	johnnycake corn bread	corn bread	corn bread cone pone
87. *to carry:*	armful	armload	armload
93. *quarter* ——:	to of	till	till to
97. *become ill:*	get sick	take sick	take sick
98. *with a cold:*	catch a cold	take a cold	take a cold
99. *sick* ——: (at his stomach common everywhere)	to his stomach	on his stomach in his stomach	

Many of the suggested checklist items have not been surveyed nationally (the automotive terms, for example), and so we cannot show their regional distributions. This should not prevent you from checking them in your own community to discover what term is characteristic there.

4. *Contrast Regional Dialects:* Have two natives of your area and two newcomers from other parts of the country fill out all or part of the

checklist. Note the contrasts which are evidence of geographical differences. Your conclusions will be more certain if your informants are roughly the same age and have roughly the same educational background. This will help rule out age or education as the cause of the vocabulary difference.

DIFFERENCES IN GRAMMAR

In addition to pronunciation and vocabulary differences in dialects, there are differences which involve matters of grammar. In grammar we include such things as past tenses of verbs, plural nouns, and word order (syntax) patterns. For example, many people use *dived* as the past tense of the verb *dive*. Others use *dove*. Still others use both forms. Likewise, some people say *this is as far as I go*. Others habitually say *this is all the farther I go*. These forms are used by educated and respectable people, and their English is considered equally educated and respectable. If one or two of the above examples sound strange or wrong to you, then you are probably living in an area which uses the alternative form. This does not mean that your way is better or worse—only that it is different.

On the other hand, some variants of grammatical items are used by relatively uneducated people. For the past tense of *dive* they might use the forms *duv* or *div*. For the distance statement they might say *this is the furtherest I go* or *this is the fartherest I go*.

Thus we can see that grammatical items may indicate place of origin or social level. Table 31.1 shows how people in two theoretical areas differ internally, because of social class, and externally, because of where they live. Contrary to what some people think, even people of higher social classes do not make the same grammatical choices in different parts of our country. Well-educated natives of Wisconsin tend to say *dove;* their counterparts from Kentucky favor *dived.*

For determining social levels, grammatical choices are as important as pronunciation and vocabulary choices. Regional distributions of gram-

TABLE 31.1

AREA X		AREA Y	
Speaker	*Grammatical Item Used*	*Speaker*	*Grammatical Item Used*
higher social status	dove	higher social status	dived
middle social status	dove	middle social status	dived
lower social status	dove, duv	lower social status	dived, div

matical choice, however, are not as clearly marked as other differences. Of particular interest to American fieldworkers are the following items.[2]

1. *Prepositions*

    Trouble comes all _____ once. (to = N, at)

    It's half _____ six. (past, after)

    It's quarter _____ four. (of, to = N, till = M, before, until)

    It's _____ the door. (behind, hindside, in back of, back of)

    He isn't _____. (at home, to home, home)

    It's coming right _____ you. (at, toward, towards)

    Guess who I ran _____. (into, onto, up against, upon, up with, against, again, afoul of = NE, across)

    They named the baby _____ him. (after, for, at, from)

    I fell _____ the horse. (off, off of, offen, off from, from)

    I wonder what he died _____. (of, with, from, for)

    He's sick _____ his stomach. (to = N, at = M, S, of, on = M, in = M, with)

    He came over _____ tell me. (to, for to = SM, S, for = S)

    I want this _____ of that. (instead, stead, in room, in place)

    We're waiting _____ John. (on = M, for)

    The old man passed _____. (away, on, out, ϕ)

    He did it _____ purpose. (on, a, for, ϕ)

    I want _____ the bus. (off = M, to get off)

    He was _____ (singing, a-singing) and _____. (laughing, a-laughing)

    How big _____ (a, of a) house is it?

2. *Matters of agreement*

    Here _____ your pencils. (is, are)

    The oats _____ thrashed. (is = M, are = N)

    These cabbages _____ (is, are) for sale.

3. *Plural formations*

    I have two _____ of shoes. (pair = N, S, pairs = M)

    They had forty _____ of apples. (bushel = N, bushels = M)

    He has two _____ of butter. (pound = S, pounds = M)

    The fence has twenty _____. (posts, post, postis, poss)

    He likes to play _____. (horseshoe, horseshoes)

    Put your feet in the _____. (stirrup, stirrups)

    Let's spray for _____. (moth, moths, mothis)

    I bought two _____ of lettuce. (head, heads)

    That's a long _____. (way = N, ways = M)

    That's a short _____. (way = N, ways = M)

    It's nine _____ high. (foot, feet)

---

[2] Whenever ϕ appears, it signifies that nothing is added to the statement. N stands for Northern, M for Midland, NM for North Midland, S for Southern, SM for South Midland, and NE for New England.

We have three _____. (desks, desk, deskis, desses, dess)

4. *Pronouns*

It wasn't _____. (me, I)

This is _____. (yours, yourn)

This is _____. (theirs, theirn)

Are _____ (pl.) coming over? (you, youse, yuz, youns, you-all)

_____ boys are all bad. (Those, Them, Them there)

He's the man _____ owns the car. (that, who, what, which, as, φ)

He's the boy _____ father is rich. (whose, that his, that the, his)

"I'm not going!" "_____." (Me either, Me neither, Neither am I, Nor I either, Nor I neither)

It is _____. (I, me)

It is _____. (he, him)

He's going to do it _____. (himself, hisself)

Let them do it _____. (themselves, themself, theirselves, theirself)

I'll go with _____. (φ, you)

5. *Adjectives*

The oranges are all _____. (φ, gone)

Some berries are _____. (poison, poisonous)

6. *Adverbs*

You can find these almost _____. (anywhere, anywheres, any-place)

This is _____ I go. (as far as, as fur as, all the farther, all the further, the farthest, the furthest, the fartherest, the furtherest)

7. *Conjunctions*

It seems _____ we'll never win. (as though, like, as if)

I won't go _____ he does. (unless, without, lessen, thouten, douten, less, else)

I like him _____ he's funny. (because, cause, on account of, count, owing to)

Do this _____ I eat lunch. (while, whiles, whilst)

This is not _____ long as that one. (as, so)

8. *Articles*

John is _____ university. (in, in the)

She is _____ hospital. (in, in the)

I have _____ apple. (a, an)

John has _____. (flu, the flu)

Do you have _____? (mumps, the mumps)

9. *Verbs*

Past tense forms: began, begun, begin

blew, blowed

climbed, clim (N), clum (M)

came, come, comed

could, might could (SM, S)

<table>
<tr><td></td><td>dived, dove (N)</td></tr>
<tr><td></td><td>drank, drunk, drinked</td></tr>
<tr><td></td><td>did, done</td></tr>
<tr><td></td><td>drowned, drownded</td></tr>
<tr><td></td><td>ate, et, eat</td></tr>
<tr><td></td><td>gave, give (M)</td></tr>
<tr><td></td><td>grew, growed</td></tr>
<tr><td></td><td>learned, learnt, larnt, larnd</td></tr>
<tr><td></td><td>lay, laid</td></tr>
<tr><td></td><td>rode, rid</td></tr>
<tr><td></td><td>ran, run</td></tr>
<tr><td></td><td>saw, seen (M), seed (M), see (N)</td></tr>
<tr><td></td><td>sat, set</td></tr>
<tr><td></td><td>spoiled, spoilt</td></tr>
<tr><td></td><td>swam, swim</td></tr>
<tr><td></td><td>threw, throwed</td></tr>
<tr><td></td><td>wore, weared</td></tr>
<tr><td></td><td>wrote, writ</td></tr>
<tr><td>Past participles:</td><td>tore up, torn up</td></tr>
<tr><td></td><td>wore out, worn out</td></tr>
<tr><td></td><td>rode (M), ridden</td></tr>
<tr><td></td><td>drank, drunk</td></tr>
<tr><td></td><td>bit, bitten</td></tr>
<tr><td>Negative:</td><td>hadn't ought (N), ought not, oughtn't, didn't ought</td></tr>
</table>

Some of the preceding grammatical choices may seem appropriate to you; others may appear to be undesirable. But in unguarded moments you may find yourself using more than one of the choices. What is particularly interesting to linguists is the fact that many forces contribute to our shift from one variant to another.

Grammar Fieldwork

People tend to be much more self-conscious about their use of verb forms, prepositions, pronouns, and so on, than they are about their vocabulary or pronunciation. Consequently, no simple checklist will be given here. However, you can observe the above items in the casual conversations of your acquaintances, in the speech of television actors (especially those who portray Westerners, hillbillies, blue collar urbanites, farmers, well-heeled tycoons, and other special "types"), in the dialogue of novels or short stories, and in the speech of out-of-staters who have recently moved to your community. You must remember, however, that people are very sensitive about their grammar. The good fieldworker is tactful and objective. He does not ridicule the grammar of other areas or other social levels; in fact, he does not even seem to be especially interested in the grammar of his subject's responses. Much of the time he contents himself with getting details of grammar in conversation, without direct questioning.

=

FOR DISCUSSION AND REVIEW

1. As Shuy states, "That people speak different dialects in no way stems from their intelligence or judgment. They speak the dialect which enables them to get along with the other members of their social and geographical group." Despite this fact, many people consider dialects different from their own as "funny sounding," "strange," or even "wrong" — and these feelings about language are often transferred to the speakers of the different dialects. Drawing on your own experiences and attitudes, discuss the situation described above. For example, what are its implications for a family moving from, say, the South to New England?

2. Roberts describes two *types* of pronunciation differences. What are they, and how do they differ? Try to add to his lists of examples.

3. After reviewing the phonetic symbols provided by Callary (in "Phonetics," Part Four), carefully transcribe your pronunciation of each of the following words. Discuss any differences between your transcriptions and those of other members of the class.
   a. calm   f. judgment
   b. water   g. cushion
   c. horse   h. roof
   d. hoarse   i. parking
   e. wharfs   j. scent

4. Discuss, using your own specific examples, how vocabulary can reveal facts about a person's age, sex, education, occupation, and geographical and cultural origins.

5. Complete the vocabulary questionnaire. Compare your responses with those of other members of the class and with those provided in the article. Are the responses patterned? How do you account for any deviations from the patterns?

6. What is the importance of a "Personal Data Sheet" to a dialectologist?

7. Roberts states that "For determining social levels, grammatical choices are as important as pronunciation and vocabulary choices." Give three examples from your own experience that support or refute his assertion — that is, explain how grammatical constructions used by people, perhaps when you first met them, affected your opinion of them.

8. Why does Shuy believe that a checklist or questionnaire is inappropriate as the only means for determining the grammatical choices of informants? What are the alternatives to a direct questionnaire?

32

The Study of
Nonstandard English

William Labov

*William Labov, a research professor at the Center for Urban Ethnography
at the University of Pennsylvania, is well known for his many sociolinguistic studies, especially of New York City speech and of Black English.
In this condensed version of "The Study of Nonstandard English," he
explains the need, especially for teachers, to study and understand the
various nonstandard dialects of English. He also clarifies the relationship
between standard English and nonstandard dialects, showing the close
relationship between a number of their phonological and syntactic rules.
Most important, Labov emphasizes that nonstandard dialects of English,
like all human languages, are rule-governed; they are not "corruptions"
or "inferior versions" of standard English. In other studies, Labov has
advocated functional bidialectalism for speakers of a nonstandard dialect and has attempted to show how linguistic knowledge about Black
English Vernacular can be used to improve the teaching of reading to
BEV-speaking children.*

Since language learning does take place outside of the classroom, and the
six-year-old child does have great capacity for learning new language
forms as he is exposed to them, it may be asked why it should be necessary
for the teacher to understand more about the child's own vernacular.
First, we can observe that automatic adjustment does *not* take place in
all cases. Even the successful middle-class student does not always master
the teacher's grammatical forms; and in the urban ghettos we find very
little adjustment to school forms. Students continue to write *I have live*
after ten or twelve years in school; we will describe below failures in
reading the *-ed* suffix which show no advance with years in school. Second, knowledge of the underlying structure of the nonstandard vernacular
will allow the most efficient teaching. If the teacher knows the general
difference between standard negative attraction and nonstandard negative
concord, he can teach a hundred different standard forms with the simple
instruction: *The negative is attracted only to the first indefinite.* Thus
by this one rule we can make many corrections.

He don't know nothing	→ He doesn't know anything
Nobody don't like him	→ Nobody likes him
Nobody hardly goes there	→ Hardly anybody goes there
Can't nobody do it	→ Nobody can do it

Third, the vernacular must be understood because ignorance of it leads to serious conflict between student and teacher. Teachers in ghetto schools who continually insist that *i* and *e* sound different in *pin* and *pen* will only antagonize a great number of their students. The knowledge that *i* and *e* actually sound the same before *m* and *n* for most of their students (and "should" sound the same if they are normal speakers) will help avoid this destructive conflict. Teachers who insist that a child meant to say *He is tired* when he said *He tired* will achieve only bewilderment in the long run. Knowledge that *He tired* is the vernacular equivalent of the contracted form *He's tired* will save teacher and student from this frustration.

Granted that the teacher wishes to learn about the student's language, what methods are available for him to do so? Today, a great many linguists study English through their own intuitions; they operate "out of their own heads" in the sense that they believe they can ask and answer all the relevant questions themselves. But even if a teacher comes from the same background as his students, he will find that his grammar has changed, that he no longer has firm intuitions about whether he can say *Nobody don't know nothing about it* instead of *Nobody knows nothing about it*. He can of course sit down with a student and ask him all kinds of direct questions about his language, and there are linguists who do this. But one cannot draw directly upon the intuitions of the two major groups we are interested in, children and nonstandard speakers. Both are in contact with a superordinate or dominant dialect, and both will provide answers which reflect their awareness of this dialect as much as of their own. One can of course engage in long and indirect conversations with students, hoping that all of the forms of interest will sooner or later occur, and there are linguists who have attempted to study nonstandard dialects in this way. But these conversations usually teach the subject more of the investigator's language than the other way around. In general, one can say that whenever a speaker of a nonstandard dialect is in a subordinate position to a speaker of a standard dialect, the rules of his grammar will shift in an unpredictable manner towards the standard. The longer the contact, the stronger and more lasting is the shift. Thus adolescent speakers of a vernacular make very unreliable informants when they are questioned in a formal framework. The investigator must show considerable sociolinguistic sophistication to cope with such a situation, and indeed the teacher will also need to know a great deal about the social forces which affect linguistic behavior if he is to interpret his students' language.

NONSTANDARD DIALECTS AS "SELF-CONTAINED" SYSTEMS

The traditional view of nonstandard speech as a set of isolated deviations from standard English is often countered by the opposite view: that nonstandard dialect should be studied as an isolated system in its own right, without any reference to standard English. It is argued that the system of grammatical forms of a dialect can only be understood through their internal relations. For example, nonstandard Negro English has one distinction which standard English does not have: there is an invariant form *be* in *He always be foolin' around* which marks habitual, general conditions, as opposed to the unmarked *is, am, are,* etc., which do not have any such special sense. It can be argued that the existence of this distinction changes the value of all other members of the grammatical system and that the entire paradigm of this dialect is therefore different from that of standard English. It is indeed important to find such relations within the meaningful set of grammatical distinctions, if they exist, because we can then *explain* rather than merely describe behavior. There are many cooccurrence rules which are purely descriptive—the particular dialect just happens to have X′ *and* Y′ where another has X and Y. We would like to know if a special nonstandard form X′ *requires* an equally nonstandard Y′ because of the way in which the nonstandard form cuts up the entire field of meaning. This would be a tremendous help in teaching, since we would be able to show what sets of standard rules have to be taught together to avoid confusing the student with a mixed, incoherent grammatical system.

The difficulty here is that linguistics has not made very much progress in the analysis of semantic systems. There is no method or procedure which leads to reliable or reproducible results—not even among those who agree on certain principles of grammatical theory. No one has yet written a complete grammar of a language—or even come close to accounting for all the morphological and syntactic rules of a language. And the situation is much more primitive in semantics; for example, the verbal system of standard English has been studied now for many centuries, yet there is no agreement at all on the meaning of the auxiliaries *have . . . ed* and *be . . . ing*. The meaning of *I have lived here,* as opposed to *I lived here,* has been explained as (a) relevant to the present, (b) past *in* the present, (c) perfective, (d) indefinite, (e) causative, and so on. It is not only that there are many views; it is that in any given discussion no linguist has really found a method by which he can reasonably hope to persuade others that he is right. If this situation prevails where most of the investigators have complete access to the data, since they are native speakers of standard English, we must be more than cautious in claiming to understand the meaning of *I be here* as opposed to *I am here* in nonstandard Negro English, and even more cautious in claiming that the meaning of nonstandard *I'm here* therefore differs from standard *I'm here* because of the existence of the other form. Most teachers have learned to be cautious in accepting a grammarian's statement about the meaning of their own native forms, but they have no way of judging statements made about a dialect which they do not speak, and they are naturally prone to accept such statements on the authority of the writer.

There is, however, [much] that we can do to show the internal relations in the nonstandard dialect as a system. There are a great many forms which seem different on the surface but can be explained as expressions of a single rule, or the absence of a single rule. We observe that in nonstandard Negro English it is common to say *a apple* rather than *an apple*. This is a grammatical fault from the point of view of standard speakers, and the school must teach *an apple* as the written, standard form. There is also a rather low-level, unimportant feature of pronunciation which is common to southern dialects: in *the apple,* the word *the* has the same pronunciation as in *the book* and does not rhyme with *be*. Finally, we can note that, in the South, educated white speakers keep the vocalic schwa which represents *r* in *four*, but nonstandard speakers tend to drop it (registered in dialect writing as *fo' o'clock*). When all these facts are put together, we can begin to explain the nonstandard *a apple* as part of a much broader pattern. There is a general rule of English which states that we do not pronounce two (phonetic) vowels in succession. Some kind of semiconsonantal glide or consonant comes in between: an *n* as in *an apple*, a *"y"* as in *the apple*, an *r* as in *four apples*. In each of these cases, this rule is not followed for nonstandard Negro English. A teacher may have more success in getting students to write *an apple* if he presents this general rule and connects up all of these things into a single rational pattern, even if some are not important in themselves. It will "make sense" to Negro speakers, since they do not drop *l* before a vowel, and many rules of their sound system show the effect of a following vowel.

There are many ways in which an understanding of the fundamental rules of the dialect will help to explain the surface facts. Some of the rules cited above are also important in explaining why nonstandard Negro speakers sometimes delete *is*, in *He is ready*, but almost always delete *are*, in *You are ready;* or why they say *they book* and *you book* but not *we book*. It does not always follow, though, that a grammatical explanation reveals the best method for teaching standard English.

Systematic analysis may also be helpful in connecting up the nonstandard form with the corresponding standard form and in this sense understanding the meaning of the nonstandard form. For example, nonstandard speakers say *Ain't nobody see it*. What is the nearest standard equivalent? We can connect this up with the standard negative "foregrounding" of *Scarcely did anybody see it* or, even more clearly, the literary expression *Nor did anybody see it*. This foregrounding fits in with the general colloquial southern pattern with indefinite subjects: *Didn't anybody see it*, nonstandard *Didn't nobody see it*. In these cases, the auxiliary *didn't* is brought to the front of the sentence, like the *ain't* in the nonstandard sentence. But there is another possibility. We could connect up *Ain't nobody see it* with the sentence *It ain't nobody see it*, that is, "There isn't anybody who sees it"; the dummy *it* of nonstandard Negro English corresponds to standard *there*, and, like *there*, it can be dropped in casual speech. Such an explanation is the only one possible in the case of such nonstandard sentences as *Ain't nothin' went down.* This could not be derived from *Nothin' ain't went down*, a sentence type which never occurs. If someone uses one of these forms, it is important for the teacher to know what was intended, so that he can supply the standard equivalent. To do so, one must know a great deal about many underlying rules of the nonstandard dialect, and also a great deal about the rules of English in general.

NONSTANDARD ENGLISH AS A CLOSE RELATIVE OF STANDARD ENGLISH

Differences between standard and nonstandard English are not as sharp as our first impressions would lead us to think. Consider, for example, the socially stratified marker of "pronominal apposition"—the use of a dependent pronoun in such sentences as

My oldest sister she worked at the bank.

Though most of us recognize this as a nonstandard pattern, it is not always realized that the "nonstandard" aspect is merely a slight difference in intonation. A standard speaker frequently says the same thing, with a slight break after the subject: *My oldest sister—she works at the bank, and she finds it very profitable.* There are many ways in which a greater awareness of the standard colloquial forms would help teachers interpret the nonstandard forms. Not only do standard speakers use pronominal apposition with the break noted above, but in casual speech they can also bring object noun phrases to the front, "foregrounding" them. For example, one can say

My oldest sister—she worked at the Citizens Bank in Passaic last year.

The Citizens Bank, in Passaic—my oldest sister worked there last year.

Passaic—my oldest sister worked at the Citizens Bank there last year.

Note that if the foregrounded noun phrase represents a locative—the "place where"—then its position is held by *there*, just as the persons are represented by pronouns. If we are dealing with a time element, it can be foregrounded without replacement in any dialect: *Last year, my oldest sister worked at the Citizens Bank in Passaic.*

It is most important for the teacher to understand the relation between standard and nonstandard and to recognize that nonstandard English is a system of rules, different from the standard but not necessarily inferior as a means of communication. All of the teacher's social instincts, past training, and even faith in his own education lead him to believe that other dialects of English are merely "mistakes" without any rhyme or rationale.

In this connection, it will be helpful to examine some of the most general grammatical differences between English dialects spoken in the United States. One could list a very large number of "mistakes," but when they are examined systematically the great majority appear to be examples of a small number of differences in the rules. The clearest analysis of these differences has been made by Edward Klima (1964). He considers first the dialect in which people say sentences like

Who could she see?

Who did he speak with?

He knew who he spoke with.

The leader who I saw left.

The leader who he spoke with left.

What is the difference between this dialect and standard English? The usual schoolbook answer is to say that these are well-known mistakes in the use of *who* for *whom.* But such a general statement does not add any clarity to the situation; nor does it help the student to learn standard English. The student often leaves the classroom with no more than an uneasy feeling that *who* is incorrect and *whom* is correct. This is the state of half-knowledge that leads to hypercorrect forms such as *Whom did you say is calling?* In the more extreme cases, *whom* is seen as the only acceptable, polite form of the pronoun. Thus a certain receptionist at a hospital switchboard regularly answers the telephone: "Whom?"

The nonstandard dialect we see here varies from standard English by one simple difference in the order of rules. The standard language marks the objective case — the difference between *who* and *whom* — in a sentence form which preserves the original subject-object relation:

Q — She could see WH-someone.

The WH-symbol marks the point to be questioned in this sentence. When cases are marked in this sentence, the pronoun before the verb receives the unmarked subjective case and the pronoun after the verb the marked objective case.

Q — She (subjective case) — could — see — WH-someone (objective case).

The combination of WH, indefinite pronoun, and objective case is to be realized later as *whom.* At a later point, a rule of WH-*attraction* is applied which brings the WH-word to the beginning of the sentence:

Q—Whom—she—could—see.

and finally the Q-marker effects a reversal of the pronoun and auxiliary, yielding the final result:

Whom could she see?

Here the objective case of the pronoun refers to the underlying position of the questioned pronoun as object of the verb.

The nonstandard dialect also marks cases: *I, he, she, they* are subjective forms, and *me, him, her, them* are objective. But the case marking is done after, rather than before, the WH-attraction rule applies. We begin with the same meaningful structure, Q—*She could see* WH-*someone*, but the first rule to consider is WH-*attraction:*

Q—WH-someone—she—could—see.

Now the rule of case marking applies. Since both pronouns are before the verb, they are both unmarked:

Q—WH-someone (unmarked)—she (unmarked)—could see.

Finally, the question flip-flop applies, and we have

Who could she see?

The same mechanism applies to all of the nonstandard forms given above.

We can briefly consider another nonstandard grammatical rule, that which yields *It's me* rather than *It's I*. The difference here lies again in the rule of case marking. As noted above, this rule marks pronouns which occur after verbs; but the copula is not included. The nonstandard grammar which gives us *It's me* differs from standard English in only one simple detail—the case-marking rule includes the verb *to be* as well as other verbs. It is certainly not true that this nonstandard grammar neglects the case-marking rule; on the contrary, it applies the rule more generally than standard English here. But the order of the rules is the same as that for the nonstandard grammar just discussed: we get *Who is he?* rather than *Whom is he?* Like the other verbs, the copula marks the pronoun only after WH-attraction has applied.

In all of the examples just given, we can observe a general tendency towards simplification in the nonstandard grammars. There is a strong tendency to simplify the surface subjects —that is, the words which come before the verb. This is most obvious in pronominal apposition. The foregrounded part identifies the person talked about, *my oldest sister;* this person is then "given," and the "new" predication is made with a pronoun subject: *she worked at the Citizens Bank.*

A parallel tendency is seen in the nonstandard grammars which confine the objective marker to positions after the verb. But this tendency to simplify subjects is not confined to standard colloquial English. Sentences such as the following are perfectly grammatical but are seldom if ever found in ordinary speech:

For him to have broken his word so often was a shame.

Most often we find that the rule of "extraposition" has applied, moving the complex subject to the end of the sentence:

It was a shame for him to have broken his word so often.

In general, we find that nonstandard English dialects are not radically different systems from standard English but are instead closely related to it. These dialects show slightly different versions of the same rules, extending and modifying the grammatical processes which are common to all dialects of English.

Any analysis of the nonstandard dialect which pretends to ignore other dialects and the general rules of English will fail (1) because the nonstandard dialect is *not* an isolated system but a part of the sociolinguistic structure of English, and (2) because of the writer's knowledge of standard English. But it would be unrealistic to think that we can write anything but a superficial account of the dialect if we confine our thinking to this one subsystem and ignore whatever progress has been made in the understanding of [standard] English grammar.

FOR DISCUSSION AND REVIEW

1. According to Labov, why is it important for teachers to study "the child's own vernacular" (in this case, "the nonstandard vernacular")?

2. Granted that it is desirable for teachers to study the actual vernacular of children, what methods for doing so first suggest themselves? What, if any, are the problems with these methods? Explain your answer.

3. Labov argues that there is "a great deal that we can do to show the internal relations in the nonstandard dialect *as a system* [italics added]." Give some examples of what he means by this statement, and explain the importance of the phrase "as a system."

4. Labov argues that "nonstandard English is a system of rules, different from the standard but not necessarily inferior as a means of communication." What evidence does he present to support the first part of this claim? In your answer, explain some of the rules of nonstandard English and how they differ from those of standard English. What evidence does he present to support the second part? Do you agree or disagree? Defend your answer.

33

Pidgins and Creoles

David Crystal

In the seventeenth century a South American trader would have landed on the shores of Africa with wares to trade but no common language for communication. In order to conduct business, some means of communication had to be developed. A pidgin language incorporates vocabulary elements from two languages and simplifies grammatical forms from one or both languages. Typically used by speakers of two or more languages, pidgins are defined as rudimentary languages with simplified grammars and limited lexicons. Because people do not learn pidgins as native speakers, a pidgin language is called an auxiliary language. In contrast, "creoles," which develop from pidgins, are learned by native speakers and are considered fully developed languages. In the following selection taken from the Cambridge Encyclopedia of Language, *David Crystal of University College of North Wales examines the differences between pidgin and creole languages and points out that creole languages throughout the world exhibit remarkable structural uniformities. Although the number of creole speakers in the world continually diminishes and several misconceptions surround these languages, creole languages must be observed as valid and, more importantly, worthy subjects of our attention in the ongoing investigation of human language.*

PIDGIN LANGUAGES

A pidgin is a system of communication which has grown up among people who do not share a common language, but who want to talk to each other, for trading or other reasons. Pidgins have been variously called "makeshift," "marginal," or "mixed" languages. They have a limited vocabulary, a reduced grammatical structure, and a much narrower range of functions, compared to the languages which gave rise to them. They are the native language of no one, but they are nonetheless a main means of communication for millions of people, and a major focus of interest to those who study the way languages change.

It is essential to avoid the stereotype of a pidgin language, as perpetrated over the years in generations of children's comics and films. The "Me Tarzan, you Jane" image is far from the reality. A pidgin is not a language which has broken down; nor is it the result of baby talk, laziness, corruption, primitive thought processes, or mental deficiency. On the contrary: pidgins are demonstrably creative adaptations of natural languages, with a structure and rules of their own. Along with creoles, they are evidence of a fundamental process of linguistic change, as languages come into contact with each other, producing new varieties whose structures and uses contract and expand. They provide the clearest evidence of language being created and shaped by society for its own ends, as people adapt to new social circumstances. This emphasis on processes of change is reflected in the terms *pidginization* and *creolization.*

Most pidgins are based on European languages — English, French, Spanish, Dutch, and Portuguese — reflecting the history of colonialism. However, this observation may be the result only of our ignorance of the languages used in parts of Africa, South America or Southeast Asia, where situations of language contact are frequent. One of the best-known non-European pidgins is Chinook Jargon, once used for trading by American Indians in northwest U.S.A. Another is Sango, a pidginized variety of Ngbandi, spoken widely in west-central Africa.

Because of their limited function, pidgin languages usually do not last for very long — sometimes for only a few years, and rarely for more than a century. They die when the original reason for communication diminishes or disappears, as communities move apart, or one community learns the language of the other. (Alternatively, the pidgin may develop into a creole.) The pidgin French which was used in Vietnam all but disappeared when the French left; similarly, the pidgin English which appeared during the American Vietnam campaign virtually disappeared as soon as the war was over. But there are exceptions. The pidgin known as Mediterranean Lingua Franca, or Sabir, began in the middle ages and lasted until the 20th century.

Some pidgins have become so useful as a means of communication between languages that they have developed a more formal role, as regular auxiliary languages. They may even be given official status by a community, as lingua francas. These cases are known as "expanded pidgins," because of the way in which they have added extra forms to cope with the needs of their users, and have come to be used in a much wider range of situations than previously. In time, these languages may come to be used on the radio, in the press, and may even develop a literature of their own. Some of the most widely used expanded pidgins are Krio (in Sierra Leone), Nigerian Pidgin English, and Bislama (in Vanuatu). In Papua New Guinea, the local pidgin (Tok Pisin) is the most widely used language in the country.

CREOLE LANGUAGES

A creole is a pidgin language which has become the mother tongue of a community — a definition which emphasizes that pidgins and creoles are two stages in a single process of linguistic development. First, within a community, increasing numbers of people begin to use pidgin as their principal means of communication. As a consequence, their children hear it more than any other language, and gradually it takes on the status of a mother tongue for them. Within a generation or two, native language use becomes consolidated and widespread. The result is a creole, or "creolized" language.

The switch from pidgin to creole involves a major expansion in the structural linguistic resources available — especially in vocabulary, grammar, and style, which now have to cope with the everyday demands made upon a mother tongue by its speakers. There is also a highly significant shift in the overall patterns of language use found in the community. Pidgins are by their nature auxiliary languages, learned alongside vernacular languages which are much more developed in structure and use. Creoles, by contrast, are vernaculars in their own right. When a creole language develops, it is usually at the expense of other languages spoken in the area. But then it too can come under attack.

The main source of conflict is likely to be with the standard form of the language from which it derives, and with which it usually co-exists. The standard language has the status which comes with social prestige, education, and wealth; the creole has no such status, its roots lying in a history of subservience and slavery. Inevitably, creole speakers find themselves under great pressure to change their speech in the direction of the standard — a process known as *decreolization*.

One consequence of this is the emergence of a continuum of several varieties of creole speech, at varying degrees of linguistic "distance" from the standard — what has been called the "post-creole continuum." Another consequence is an aggressive reaction against the standard language on the part of creole speakers, who assert the superior status of their creole, and the need to recognize the ethnic identity of their community. Such a reaction can lead to a marked change in speech habits, as the speakers focus on what they see to be the "pure" form of creole — a process known as *hypercreolization*. This whole movement, from creolization to decreolization to hypercreolization, can be seen at work in the recent history of black English in the U.S.A.

The term *creole* comes from Portuguese *crioulo*, and originally meant a person of European descent who had been born and brought up in a colonial territory. Later, it came to be applied to other people who were native to these areas, and then to the kind of language they spoke. Creoles are now usually classified as "English based," "French based," and so on — though the genetic relationship of a creole to its dominant linguistic ancestor is never straightforward, as the creole may display the influences of several contact languages in its sounds, vocabulary, and structure.

Today, the study of creole languages, and of the pidgins which gave rise to them, attracts considerable interest among linguists and social historians. To the former, the cycle of linguistic reduction and expansion

TABLE 33.1

FRENCH	GUYANESE CRÉOLE	KRIO	ENGLISH
Mangez	Mãʒe	Chɔp	Eat
J'ai mangé	Mo mãʒe	A chɔp	I ate
Il/Elle a mangé	Li mãʒe	I chɔp	He/She ate
Je mange/Je suis en train de manger	Mo ka mãʒe	A de chɔp	I am eating
J'avais mangé	Mo te mãʒe	A bin chɔp	I ate/had eaten
Je mangeais	Mo te ka mãʒe	A bin de chɔp	I was eating
Je mangerai	Mo ke mãʒe	A go chɔp	I shall eat
Il/Elle est plus grand que vous	Li gros pas u	I big pas yu	He/She/It is bigger than you

which they demonstrate, within such a short time-scale, provides fascinating evidence of the nature of language change. To the latter, their development is seen to reflect the process of exploration, trade, and conquest which has played such a major part in European history over the past 400 years.

WHERE DO PIDGINS AND CREOLES COME FROM?

The world's pidgins and creoles display many obvious differences in sounds, grammar, and vocabulary, but they have a remarkable amount in common. Two opposed theories have attempted to explain these differences.

Many Sources?

A long-standing view is that every creole is a unique, independent development, the product of a fortuitous contact between two languages. On the surface, this "polygenetic" view is quite plausible. It seems unlikely that the pidgins which developed in Southeast Asia should have anything in common with those which developed in the Caribbean. And it is a general experience that these varieties come into use in an apparently spontaneous way—as any tourist knows who has faced a souvenir seller. Would not the restricted features of the contact situations (such as the basic sentence patterns and vocabulary needed in order to trade) be enough to explain the linguistic similarities around the world?

The view is tempting, but there are several grounds for criticism. In particular, it does not explain the *extent* of the similarities between these varieties. Common features such as the reduction of noun and pronoun inflections, the use of particles to replace tenses, and the use of repeated forms to intensify adjectives and adverbs are too great to be the result of coincidence. Why, then, should the pidginized forms of French, Dutch, German, Italian, and other languages all display the same kind of modifications? Why, for example, should the English-based creoles of the Caribbean have so much in common with the Spanish-based creoles of the Philippines? How could uniformity come from such diversity?

One Source?

The opposite view argues that the similarities between the world's pidgins and creoles can be explained only by postulating that they had a common origin (i.e., are "monogenetic"), notwithstanding the distance which exists between them. Moreover, a clear candidate for a "proto"-language has been found—a 15th-century Portuguese pidgin, which may in turn have descended from the Mediterranean lingua franca known as Sabir. The Portuguese are thought to have used this pidgin during their explorations in Africa, Asia, and the Americas. Later, it is argued, as other nations came to these areas, the simple grammar of this pidgin came to be retained, but the original Portuguese vocabulary was replaced by words taken from their own languages. This view is known as the *relexification* hypothesis.

There is a great deal of evidence to support the theory, deriving from historical accounts of the Portuguese explorations, and from modern analyses of the languages. For instance, every English-based pidgin and creole has a few Portuguese words, such as *savi* "know," *pikin* "child," and *palava* "trouble." In Saramaccan, an English-based creole of Suriname, 38% of the core vocabulary is from Portuguese. Early accounts of Chinese pidgin refer to a mixed dialect of English and Portuguese. And on general grounds, relexification of a single "proto"-pidgin seems a more plausible hypothesis than one which insists on a radical parallel restructuring of several languages.

The shift in approach, implicit in the relexification theory, is fundamental: it is not the case that English, and the other languages, were "creolized," but that an original (Portuguese) creole was "Anglicized." However, not all the facts can be explained in this way. Pitcairnese creole has no Portuguese influence, and yet has much in common with other varieties. What accounts for those similarities? Then there are several pidgins and creoles which have developed with little or no historical contact with European languages—Sango and Chinook, for instance. And there seem to be many structural differences between European and non-European pidgins and creoles, which the common origin hypothesis finds difficult to explain.

The evidence is mixed. Disentangling the structural similarities and differences between these varieties is a difficult task, and the evidence

TABLE 33.2.   Pidgins Compared.

ENGLISH	TOK PISIN	CHINESE PIDGIN	SANGO	CHINOOK JARGON
bell	bɛl	bell	ngbéréná	tíntin
big	bɪgfɛlə	big	kótá	hyás
bird	pɪǧɪn	bird(ee)	ndɛkɛ	kalákala
bite	kajkajɪm	bitee	tɛ	múckamuck
black	blækfɛlə	black	(zo)vɔkɔ́	klale
blood	blʊt	blood	méné	pilpil
cold	kilfɛlə	colo	dé	cole, tshis
come	kəm	li	ga	chahko
die	daj	dielo	kúi	mémaloost
dog	dɔg	doggee	mbo	kámooks
drink	drɪŋk	dlinkee, haw	yç	muckamuck
ear	ir	ear	mé	kwolánn
earth	grawn	glound	sése	illahie
eat	kajkaj	chowchow	kóbe, tɛ	múckamuck
fat	gris	fat, glease	mafuta	glease
feather	gras bɪlɔŋ pɪǧɪn	fedder	kɔ́á tí ndɛkɛ	kalákala yaka túpso
fish	fiš	fishee	susu	pish
give	gɪvɪm	pay	fú	pótlatch
green	grinfɛlə	gleen, lu	vɔkɔ́ kété	pechúgh
hair	gras bɪlɔŋ hɛd	hair	kɔ́á	yákso
hand	hæn	hand, sho	mabɔ́kɔ	le mah
head	hɛd	headee	li	la tet
heart	klak	heart	coeur	túmtum
know	save	savvy	hínga	kumtuks
man	mæn	man	kɔ́lĭ	man
no	no	na	non	wake
nose	nos	peedza	hɔ̃	nose
one	wənfɛlə	one piecee	ɔ́kɔ́	ikt
small	lɪklɪk	likki	kété	ténas
sun	sən	sun	lá	sun, ótelagh
talk	tɔk	talkee	tɛnɛ	wáuwau
two	tufɛlə	two	óse	mokst
warm	hɔtfɛlə	warm	wá	waum

Lexical similarities and differences between pidgins are clearly illustrated in this list of items collected by F. G. Cassidy in the 1960s, taken from the set of "basic words" used in glotto-chronology. The English element predominates in Tok Pisin and Chinese Pidgin; in Sango, the vast majority of the words are African; in Chinook, most words are from Chinook or other Amerindian languages (but note the influence of both French and English). French names for parts of the body have emerged in Sango and Chinook. Though there is no historical connection between the languages, note also the coincidences of thought which have produced the figurative phrases for feather *(grass-of-bird [Tok Pisin], hair-of-bird [Sango], and leaf-of-bird [Chinook]), and the words for* heart *in Tok Pisin and Chinook, both of which stress the notion of heartbeat.*

could be taken to support either a monogenetic or a polygenetic theory. Far more descriptive studies are needed before we rule out one view or the other.

Meanwhile, other theories have been proposed, in an attempt to explain these similarities and differences. Other forms of simplified speech have been noted, such as that used by children, in telegrams and headlines, and in talking to foreigners. It is possible that the processes underlying pidgins and creoles reflect certain basic preferences in human language (such as fixed word order, or the avoidance of inflections). In this connection, these languages provide fresh and intriguing evidence in the search for linguistic universals.

FOR DISCUSSION AND REVIEW

1. How does Crystal define pidgins and creoles?
2. What are the misconceptions that surround the study of pidgins?
3. How do pidgins and creoles develop? When is a pidgin said to become a creole? For this reason, which language is more likely to become extinct? How would the size of the population using the language influence the outcome? Give reasons for your explanation.
4. What does Crystal mean by "expanded pidgins"? At what point do pidgins became expanded?
5. How does a creole differ from a pidgin? What conflicts exist between creole and other language forms?
6. Define the terms *decreolization* and *hypercreolization*. How do these affect language change and tensions among languages? How have such events influenced the growth of such languages as BEV?
7. Crystal says, "The world's pidgins and creoles display many obvious differences in sounds, grammar, and vocabulary, but they have a remarkable amount in common." What are two opposing theories that attempt to explain these differences? Which theory do you favor? Why?
8. What is the relexification process that sometimes occurs in pidgin languages?
9. Why must we continue to study both pidgins and creoles? What value might they have for our ongoing study of language?

34

Language among Black Americans

Elizabeth Whatley

*One of the most active areas of dialect and sociolinguistic study today
is the language of Black Americans. In the past decade alone, countless
articles and a number of scholarly books have been written about Black
English Vernacular or "BEV." Some of these sources examine Black English Vernacular as a "deficient" type of "Standard English" while others
closely examine Black English grammatical structures. Still other works
on the topic are offered in an attempt to defend Black English as a separate and valid form of English. In this selection, taken from* **Language
in the U.S.A.,** *Elizabeth Whatley, professor of English at CUNY Queens
College, New York, presents a brief history of the origins of Black English
in the United States. Whatley demonstrates that differences exist between BEV and other forms of English, differences that are valid and
serve an important purpose in the language and speech communities of
Black Americans.*

The Afro-American experience in the United States has been different
from that of any other group, and the language situation of Black Americans is correspondingly different. Unlike other groups who came to America, almost all Africans were brought over as slaves, and up until the
Emancipation Proclamation, the overwhelming majority of Blacks in the
United States were still slaves. During the period of slavery, as well as
in the modern period, the patterns of communication between Blacks
and other Americans reflected the social distance between them. Also,
the Africans who reached American shores spoke many different African
languages and were, on the whole, unable to maintain viable speech communities based on the use of their mother tongues.

Thus, it is no surprise that Black Americans speak varieties of American English rather than African languages, and that the language of Blacks
will tend to differ from the language of other Americans in any community. Strong assimilatory forces have been at work and in some contexts
are becoming stronger, so that in many instances Blacks may speak to
all intents and purposes the same way as their neighbors. Just as complete
linguistic assimilation takes place with immigrant groups, so it can and
does with Blacks. On the other hand, several historical events have reinforced the tendency to differ. One was the early use of English-based

pidgins and creoles among slave populations. This had a tremendous effect on the kind of English which Black Americans have come to speak, not only in the surviving creole of the Sea Islands, but also in varieties of speech which have been called Black English Vernacular.

BLACKS IN URBAN LIFE

Another powerful historical event was the great exodus of Blacks from the Southeast to the Northeast and other parts of the country in the early twentieth century. This movement of people brought varieties of southern, often rural, Black English to urban areas of the North, where quite different kinds of English were spoken. The juxtaposition of northern and southern features made the separation of White and Black speech all the more evident and incontrovertible in these northern communities. The development of these speech communities was the result of a series of factors which created situations conducive to language maintenance on the one hand, and the development of a distinctive dialect on the other.

The evolution of predominantly Black urban areas in northern cities is traceable by an examination of the migratory patterns of Blacks from southern regions of the United States. From the 1790s to the early 1900s, 90 percent of the Black population lived in the South. In 1910, 89 percent continued to live in the South, but the percentage began to decrease in each succeeding decade to 85 percent in 1920, 77 percent in 1940, and 60 percent in 1960. Precise causes of the migration of Blacks to the North are unknown; however, certain social and economic factors influenced the movement. The first was the severe devastation of southern cotton by the boll weevil following on a series of bad crop years. The second was the development of labor needs in factories of the North. With the onset of World War I, the immigration of Europeans to the United States was abruptly curtailed. Industry, which previously provided hundreds of thousands of jobs each year for new immigrants, now had its labor supply curtailed during a period of great demand for labor. Many firms sent recruiters to the South to encourage Blacks to come North. Many Black southerners who migrated North later encouraged friends and relatives to join them, and the move became easier for those with someone at the other end to help find a job and a place to live. After World War I, immigration from Europe resumed, only to be curtailed permanently by restrictive legislation in the early 1920s. Black Americans then established a secure position in the northern industrial scene.

Most Blacks who migrated during this period were crowded into the ghettoes of New York, Detroit, Chicago, and Philadelphia, where reasonable housing was in extremely short supply. Initially, Blacks moved into neighborhoods inhabited by European immigrants who had not made sufficient economic gains to move out of these areas. But the increasing influx of Blacks created a major problem for northern inhabitants: competition for both living space and jobs. The slum areas of major cities absorbed thousands of Blacks between 1900 and 1914; however, the saturation point was reached shortly thereafter, and the demand for houses and living space produced dramatic increases in rents.

Every large city experienced a similar housing shortage as Blacks moved into previously White areas, took over the parks and playgrounds, and transformed White and mixed communities into solidly Black areas. It became quite clear that the territory of Black areas had to expand. The line was drawn. Urban Whites had nowhere to go in this presuburban period, and they attempted to create legally defined residential districts for Whites only. The courts struck down this attempt, and expansion of Black residential zones was halted through restrictive covenants and gentlemen's agreements between White homeowners and realtors. Explicit geographical boundaries were reinforced by explicit social boundaries in recreation, worship, and education. There were limited contacts between the diverse ethnic groups of the cities. The restricted social environment of Blacks fostered continuation of features of Black speech brought from the South and promoted the development of linguistic traits distinctive to urban life. The absence of sustained social and cultural contact with mainstream America created a linguistic situation in which Black speech was relatively free from White American English influences. By the end of the great Black migration, the speech forms of Blacks had changed considerably from southern variations.

Contributing to this change was the increasing participation of Black performers in public entertainment. In New York, Chicago, and Detroit, Black musicians played to White audiences whose responses helped promote the growth and development of blues and jazz. A network of entertainers traveled across the country, hitting small towns occasionally and giving distinctive character to portions of large cities: the French Quarter of New Orleans, Louisiana became synonymous with jazz and certain of its stars. The personnel connected with the entertainment world developed widespread communication networks connecting segments of Black populations in northern and southern cities. Innovations in music, dress, and language spread rapidly among these Blacks.

The constant contact among performers and agents and back-up personnel in the diverse locations led to some degree of homogenization of terms and styles of talking among Blacks in certain situations. Copping a plea and shucking, language performances used to get out of compromising situations with persons of authority, became familiar to Whites in their effects, if not their internal structures, as Black entertainers worked to provide themselves minimal comforts and opportunities in cities which allowed them highly restricted access to hotels and restaurants. Jiving, a style of talking in which both performer and audience know that the performance and not the content of the language is what counts, became widely recognized as a specialized language performance of

Blacks. Increasingly included as a humor form in comic interludes in musical performances and in vaudeville, jiving, shucking, and copping a plea became language styles expected of Blacks by Whites. Radio helped make the stylization of Black speech and language performances known to an even wider audience of Americans than that of the live entertainment circuit. Amos and Andy, and Rochester, Jack Benny's butler, helped develop stereotyped notions of the speech styles of Blacks and the ways they presented themselves to the world. Blacks were often forced to recognize it was to their advantage economically and socially to play to the images of them and their speech perpetuated through the entertainment world.

The result was some degree of homogenization in at least the speech structures and styles used by those who had roles which put them in daily association with Whites. Thus, the in-group communication of entertainers and the extension of some of these forms and styles promoted through the public media had a leveling and homogenizing influence on some styles of speech spoken by urban Blacks. Another homogenizing factor was the continuation of ties from northern urban communities to their home communities in the South. Funerals, homecoming celebrations at churches, and family reunions took northerners "down home" at least annually. In many urban centers, there developed communities in which a majority of members were from a particular southern state; for example, Philadelphia, in the 1970s, still had many neighborhoods whose residents maintained strong ties to South Carolina.

Ironically, widespread expectations of some language uses typical of interactions outside the community helped promote their maintenance within the community as well. In addition to those widely recognized aspects of language behaviors performed primarily for Whites were the highly distinctive language styles used almost exclusively within Black American communities. Black preaching styles, verbal games, and ritual insults of Black children, and vivid and allusive styles of street talk among adults had long been a part of Black community life. However, these speech styles used only among Blacks for in-group interactions were not displayed for public entertainment until the 1960s, when Black families were featured in television, theater, music, and cinema. For example, only after the Civil Rights movement of the 1960s did television situation comedies feature Blacks who ritually insulted family members and poked fun at each other for copping pleas, jiving, and using nonstandard language structures and "Black-only" styles of manipulating language. Even middle-class Blacks who had made it out of the ghetto were portrayed in situation comedies as occasionally "reverting" to the "talk and tricks" characterized as typical of "street talk."

Yet many aspects of expressive language use maintained by Black communities have not been flaunted for the entertainment of mass audiences. Many of these uses are certainly less distinctive but perhaps more significant in revealing the ways language is transmitted and evaluated in Black communities. Day-to-day interactions across community members of different age, sex, and status relations do not depend on the stylized speech performances which have been presented in the entertainment world. Workaday transactions within families and among friends are critical because they help maintain the social structure of the community as a whole. For communicative purposes, the eldest adults are the highest status members of the Black community. They have the privilege to initiate and maintain any or all types of communication with others regardless of their age. They can praise, fuss, tease, lie, joke, or preach. Other adults are high status members and can, without sanction, initiate almost as many types of communicative acts as can their elders. Nevertheless, they are restricted from using particular language behaviors with the elderly; a daughter may not fuss, preach, or lie to her "mamma" or any elder citizen. Both elders and other adults have nonreciprocal communicative rights when interacting with children. That is, there are many language behaviors which children cannot engage in with adults, yet they must acquire competence in these behaviors, because their power and prestige as adults depend on their facility with a wide range of styles and communicative acts. The age of conversational partners determines, in large part, the kind of language used. In this chapter a number of examples of verbal interaction will be given. They are all actual recorded events and they are transcribed here in a slightly modified form of ordinary orthography.

In the communicative event called fussing (a type of dispute or argument), whether a speaker fusses *at* or *with* another depends upon age and status relations. A fussing episode may be brief:

A: I told y'all not to do that!
B: Oh, stop fussing!

It can also be a more lengthy interaction. When speakers alternately state their disagreements, they are *fussing with* each other:

A: See what y'all did now, I told y'all 'bout messin' with stuff don't
 (be)long to y'all.
B: I ain't do it. He did.
C: No I didn't! You always sayin' I do stuff. You did it.
B: Yeah, I saw you, I saw you.

A *fussing at* interaction occurs when (a) two or more speakers talk simultaneously or (b) when a speaker directs disagreements to an interlocutor who either will not or cannot respond, because rules of language use related to age and status relations prevent doing so.

Among Black Americans, the eldest members of the community are given the widest latitude in the use of language. They can engage in all types of communication unless restricted by communicative norms related to the sex of the speaker. A female grandparent would not, for example, engage in ritual insults, toasts (epic-like tales), or other male-dominated communicative events. Pre-school-age children are also given wide latitude in language use. They too are permitted to engage in most communicative events with few exceptions. Latitude given to the very young provides the widest possible spectrum of communication for modeling. Adults can *fuss with* or *at* other adults of equal or comparable age. They can *fuss at* children but never *with* them. Similarly, adults do not *fuss with* or *at* elder members of the community. Children can engage in fussing interactions with peers or with younger siblings or relatives. They cannot engage in any type of *fussing with* adults or with the elders of the community.

Fussing is an example of one of the ways Black Americans structure the community for communicative purposes. Children are low-status members of the community and engage in communicative events primarily with other children. They are constrained by language use rules from initiating and maintaining certain types of interactions with adults. Interaction rules also require children to engage in particular kinds of language use; among these are formulaic greetings and other politeness forms, such as verbal responses to directives.

Children initiate greetings when they encounter familiar adults or when introduced to new ones. When accompanied by adults, they greet after adults have greeted each other. Community ways of interacting require equal-status members to greet each other first followed by greetings from high-status members (e.g., adults) to low-status members (e.g., children). When unaccompanied by adults, children are required to initiate the greeting when the addressee is a familiar or known member of the community. If children fail to offer a greeting, adults remind them of community expectations. They may offer a greeting, sometimes with intonation to show indignation; or they may accuse children of lacking knowledge, "You forgot how to speak?!" These verbal signals function as directives and compel children to assume their responsibility for initiating greetings.

A typical greeting is illustrated in the following interaction which occurred between three adults, A, B, and C, and two children, D and E. Speakers A and B are adults of equal age and status. Speaker C is an elder member of the community and the mother of A. Speakers D and E are 12 and 13 years of age, respectively. Speakers B and E enter the home where A, C, and D are waiting for them.

ADULT A: I saw you drive up. Come on in.	A $\xrightarrow{\text{1}}$ B
ADULT B: Hey, y'all, what's going on?	A $\xleftarrow{\text{2}}$ B
ADULT A: Ain't nothin' to it.	A $\xrightarrow{\text{3}}$ B
Hi E, how are you? (kisses E)	A $\underset{\text{4}}{\searrow}$ E
CHILD E: Fine.	A $\underset{\text{5}}{\nwarrow}$ E
ADULT B: Hello Miss C. How are you?	C $\underset{\text{6}}{\nwarrow}$ B

ADULT C: Jus' fine.

  Hello, E.

CHILD E: Hello.

ADULT B: (to D) Aren't you gonna speak?

CHILD D: (to B and E) Hello.

C ⟶ 7 ⟶B

C ⟶ 8 ⟶E

C ⟵ 9 ⟶E

10 ⟶B   D⟵

11 ⟶B   D ⟶E

Neither simultaneous greetings (i.e., one greeting exchange between the children and another among the adults) nor a generalized greeting to all is acceptable; the relative status of each member and acknowledgment of that status by greeting rituals must be marked. In groups of mixed ranks, such as the one illustrated here, exchanges between equals both open and close the greeting routine. Close analysis of the set of rules operating in this interaction reveals an unexpected complexity in the order of turn taking. The sequencing of the utterances is indicated by numbers; the directions of arrows indicates the relative rank of speakers. Several related rules are demonstrated in this interaction. First, the language used by speaker B to greet speaker C is less casual than the language used to greet speaker A; speaker C is high status, speaker A equal status. Secondly, both children maintained appropriate boundaries of language use and interaction rules. Whether accompanied or alone, children are not required to exceed the briefest form of greetings. "Hi," "Hello," or "Morning" are sufficient and appropriate forms of language use by children. Attempts to engage in an elaborate greeting — "Hello, Miss C. How are you? Nice day isn't it? How are your plants?" — is considered inappropriate for children. It is the act of greeting which carries communicative value in child–adult communications, not the extent of the verbal routine.

What may be a culture-specific form of politeness is the way in which children are required to show adults they are attentive listeners and they value adults' communications. One of the ways children indicate recognition of adults is to respond verbally when given directives or called. For example, if an adult tells a child to go downstairs and get the newspaper, the child must immediately respond verbally to the directive. Carrying out the task is not sufficient; a verbal acknowledgment of the directive is needed.

In child–child interactions, a wide range of the culture's rules of language use occurs. Interactions prohibited between children and adults or between adults take place among children. And, while these interactions are directly and importantly influenced by adult patterns of language use, there are aspects of language use which occur only in child–child interactions. The rules of language use are highly structured and follow intricate patterns of operation. They are rarely explicit, yet children learn what they are and when to apply them. Moreover, they learn how to punish those who break the rules and do not consistently mark their knowledge of how to keep boundaries.

For example, in boasting interactions, children use language skills to declare their achievements, attributes, and superiority over others. A boast may be a spontaneous speech act or a preplanned communicative event. Spontaneous boasts occur during children's everyday conversations and are usually outgrowths of immediately preceding utterances. Furthermore, they do not result in argumentative interactions between the speakers.

> A: Your mother feed you too much.
> B: Yeah, she feed me a whole lot and then she say "See how big I am." My mother's big.
> A: My mother's bigger.
> B: Yeah, well I guess I'll be going since I can't get in the door.

Spontaneous boasts show children's knowledge of appropriate ways of using language to interact with peers. Preplanned boasts indicate the strategies children know they will use when interacting. The goal of preplanned or purposeful boasting is to complete a sequence and win by receiving a closure from the other child. To fulfill this goal, the child must plan an entire series of responses to possible utterances from the opponent. Strategies used are frequently the result of collecting and organizing information into systematic and logical arguments. Most important, the underlying purpose of the interaction (i.e., to boast) must be disguised, often hidden behind an apparently innocent question.

> A: Do you know 'bout factors and all that stuff?
> B: Yea, I know all that.
> A: Well, how come you only made a 50 on that test?
> B: That test was tough — she ain't no good teacher anyway.
> A: But you been in the other Math class, the one dat ain't done factors like we have.
> B: We did too.
> A: No, you didn't. You only up to page 130. We on 165. You can't do factors. You can't do none of that stuff.
> B: Yea, but I can do spelling — and you can't.

It is clear in this boasting episode that child A had collected highly specific information to support his boast, and he set child B up to a challenge by a seemingly innocent question. The strategies and information to support these were planned out in advance. Child A wins this sequence, because child B must shift topic and begin another boast.

The boundaries of the primary speech community, which includes those recognized as members of the Black community, are marked by the situations and participants for these and other communicative events reserved for in-group associations. The means, purposes, and patterns of selection of all these events, those used by adults only and those used by children only, are reflections of the social structure. They are learned by children who listen to and observe adults and other children, practice these events among themselves, and thus gradually become competent language users by their community's standards. With the exception of works such as Labov, Cohen, Robins, and Lewis (1968), Mitchell-Kernan (1971), Kochman (1972), and Labov (1972a), relatively little scholarly attention has been devoted to description of these uses of language (and their contexts) in Black communities. Instead, much greater attention has been given to describing the structure and history of the language.

BLACK ENGLISH: A VARIETY
OF AMERICAN ENGLISH

In the early 1970s, the publication of *Black English: Its History and Usage in the United States* (Dillard 1972) brought to the attention of the American public a major question regarding the system of language used by Black Americans. Was it a separate system or was it part of the same system as other Englishes? The work of Labov *et al.* (1968) had shown that the vernacular (sometimes referred to as street talk) of Blacks had distinct rules of its own and was not, as had been the common misconception, a mass of random errors committed by Blacks trying to speak English. Labov (1972a), examining systematic relations between the rules of Black English Vernacular (BEV) and others and between different BEV rules, showed that the rules of BEV and Standard English did indeed form a single system for BEV speakers. Therefore, BEV could most accurately be considered a "subsystem within the larger grammar of English" (Labov 1972a: 64).

BEV has, therefore, come to be widely accepted as a rule-governed linguistic system. However, some parts of its phonology, morphology, and syntax and ways of speaking are neither produced nor fully understood by speakers of other English dialects. However, as a dialect of American English, many of its features and patterns are quite similar to those of Standard English. Some of the different or unique structural characteristics of BEV can be seen in the language used by two children engaged in a conversation with an adult in their neighborhood. Jimmy and David are 10 years of age.

> JIMMY: Hey Ms. Smith, d'ya evvah watch Kung Fu on TV wif dat dude
> . . . wha's his name?
> DAVID: He have my name, Jimmy. He David, too.
> JIMMY: Yeah, dat's right. Dat's duh dude's name.
> Ms. SMITH: Yes, I've watched it a few times. It's really an exciting
> show.

DAVID: Did you evvah see how he throw all dose dudes aroun', an'
how he use his legs?

JIMMY: Yeah. You know what? He can really fight. He don't fight to
be mean dough [though]. He fight to be good, and he'p people. An'
he always duh good guy.

DAVID: You know what? He one of dose pries' or somefin'. Hey Ms.
Smith, what is he? I can't remembah what dey call'.

MS. SMITH: Have you ever heard of the word "monk"?

JIMMY: No, what dat?

DAVID: It's one dose pries', I think, ain't it? Yea, it one dose pries'
dat live wif ovvah pries', dose monks. He live in a convent like.

JIMMY: In wha'? Wha's dat?

DAVID: Ah man, ain't you know what dat is? It's where dey have
people dat . . . people like pries' an' nuns live' dere.

JIMMY: No, but ain't he live in duh desert? He always be walkin' on
a desert on TV.

DAVID: No, but he ain't live in duh desert. He don't walk dere all duh
time. He don't live dere. He jus' be walkin' dere sometime'. He
move aroun' a lot, you know. He travel all different places.

JIMMY: I'm wonderin' where he learn everyfin'.

DAVID: He learn' in duh convent when he young, I think. Dat's where
dey say on TV one time.

On the phonological level, several features of Black English are evident in this interaction. One of the most obvious is the use of *duh, dat,
dose, dere*, and *dey*. Jimmy and David consistently use a *d* sound for the
voiced Standard English *th* sound at the beginning of words such as *the,
that, those, there* and *they*. The use of *d* for the voiced *th* (as in *that*) is
heard in other varieties of American English as well; for example, it is
common among New Yorkers. BEV differs from these other varieties in
having the *d* mostly at the beginning of words, but otherwise *v* for the
voiced *th*. For example, in this conversation David says *ovvah* for *other*,
where a white New Yorker might say *uddah*.

Another phonological characteristic of Jimmy and David's conversation is "*r*-lessness" or the dropping of *r*'s after vowels. This is not shown
consistently in the spelling used here, but at the end of words, where it
is especially noticeable, it is indicated by the spelling *-ah*, as in *evvah*
"ever" and *remembah* "remember." This dropping of the *r* is common
in many parts of the English-speaking world, and the prevalence of *r*-
lessness in the English of Black Americans in part reflects the southern
origin of many varieties of Black English.

A more characteristic feature of BEV is the simplification or weakening of consonant clusters at the end of words. All speakers of English
tend to reduce word-final consonant combinations such as *-st, -sk*, and
-nd by pronouncing the last consonant weakly or not at all (e.g., *las'* for
last, des' for *desk, han'* for *hand*), and the more informal, rapid, and casual

the speech is, the stronger this tendency is. In BEV the tendency is even stronger, and some words are regularly pronounced without the final consonant, such as *jus'* and *roun'* in this conversation.

Sometimes this weakening of final consonant clusters results in BEV plural forms which differ from the usual English plurals for particular words. Nouns that end in a cluster such as *-st, -sk,* or *-sp* may lose the final consonant and then make the plural as though the singular ended in *-s.* Since nouns ending in a sibilant in English add an extra syllable, spelled *-es,* to make the plural, as in *glass: glasses,* these BEV plurals will have an extra syllable. For example, many speakers of BEV will say *desses* as the plural of *des(k).* In the sentence *Sometime' dey even have contesses to see who bettah,* the plural *contesses* is based on the singular *contes'* in which the final *-t* has been dropped completely. In the conversation between Jimmy and David, the word *priest* is pronounced without the final *-t,* but some feeling of the final *-t* apparently persists because David seems to say *pries'* and not *priesses* for the plural. We cannot be completely sure, however, because the use of the plural ending is optional in BEV, and David may simply be using the singular.

The optionality of the plural is a grammatical feature of BEV, and another similar feature is the optionality of the past tense. Speakers of BEV sometimes use the same form of the verb for both present and past. Also, because of the weakening of final clusters as just described, it is often impossible to decide whether a verb form is the present tense used for the past or a past tense form with the final *-d* or *-t* dropped in pronunciation. In the last exchange of the conversation, when the boys use the verb *learn,* it is not clear whether it is the present tense or the past tense without the final *-d.*

Another grammatical feature characteristic of BEV is the omission of the *-s* ending which marks the third person singular in verbs. In place of Standard English *he learns,* the speaker of BEV often says *he learn.* This is not just the weakening of a consonant cluster, because the ending is also omitted after vowels, and in the case of words like *have* and *do* that have special forms for the third singular *(has, does),* BEV does not just drop the final *-s* of these forms but uses the full *have* and *do.* There are a number of examples of this phenomenon in the Jimmy and David dialogue: *He have my name. He throw all dose dudes aroun'. He fight to be good. He live in a convent. He move aroun' a lot. He travel all different places.*

One of the most often discussed grammatical characteristics of BEV is the use of the verb *to be.* It is often absent where Standard English would have it, the forms are different from those of Standard English, and there is at least one use of *be* in BEV which has no equivalent in Standard English. Omission of the verb *to be,* or "copula deletion," as it is usually called by linguists, is very characteristic of BEV. In all varieties of American English, speakers contract forms of *be* in some sentences; for example, in ordinary conversation, almost everyone would usually say *She's married*, instead of *She-is-married*. BEV takes the process a step further and lets the *is* be omitted completely. The boys' conversation has examples of both contraction and deletion.

Contraction	Deletion
Wha's his name?	He — David, too
Dat's right	He — always duh good guy
Dat's duh dude's name	He — one of dose pries'
Wha's dat?	What — dat?

In sentences where the *is* or other form of *be* is not contracted in general American English usage, it is not deleted in BEV. There are several examples in the dialogue:

What *is* he?

You know what dat *is?*

The special use of *be* which is found almost only in the English of Black Americans is illustrated toward the end of the boys' conversation. Jimmy says *He always be walkin' on a desert on TV*, and David in his rejoinder says *He jus' be walkin' dere sometime'*. This use of "invariant *be*," as it is often called by linguists, refers to repeated actions over a considerable extent of time, and the distinction between *he walk, he walkin'*, and *he be walkin'* has no exact parallel in Standard English. Incidentally, these three verb forms typically have different negatives.

He walk	He don't walk	[momentary]
He walkin'	He ain't walkin'	[progressive]
He be walkin'	He don't be walkin'	[habitual]

Another grammatical feature which has had a good deal of attention is the pattern of negation in BEV. Standard English generally requires just one negation in a clause, but BEV prefers the pattern of multiple negation where negation keeps being repeated throughout the clause or sentence. For Standard English *I didn't see anything like that anywhere*, BEV may have *I ain't see nothin' like dat no place*. Multiple negation was the rule in Old English, and examples are still common as late as Shakespeare, but the spread of the rule of single negation has gradually restricted multiple negation to nonstandard varieties of English. One factor in the change in English was the influence of Latin, which allows only single negation. Ironically, the modern Romance languages, such as French, Spanish, and Italian, which are the descendants of Latin, have all developed multiple negation as standard. Multiple negation, while typical of BEV, occurs in other dialects and registers of English, and is generally understood by speakers of Standard English. Some uses of the negative contraction *ain't* are, however, distinctive of BEV. For example, the use of *ain't* as a single past negative, as in the sentence just cited *I ain't see* for *I didn't see*, is pretty well limited to BEV, although the use of *ain't* for *isn't* or *hasn't* *(He ain't gonna do it, he ain't done it)* is common to many kinds of nonstandard English.

A number of other interesting phonological and grammatical features of BEV have been studied and several of them appear in our sample conversation, but one overall characteristic is apparent: the amount of fluctuation in forms and constructions which occurs in Black English. Almost every statement about BEV includes a qualification such as "may occur," "sometimes," "often," or "generally." Fluctuation of forms in the speech of the Black community tends to be greater than in other varieties of American English. The same speaker on one occasion will pronounce a plural ending and on another occasion will drop it. One sentence will have *ain't* for the past negative and the next one may have *didn't* or *ditn't*. The most plausible explanation for this fluctuation is the existence of two poles of language usage in the community — the most extreme form of creole-like English, what has been called *basilect,* and the model of educated Standard English, the *acrolect.* The fluctuating intermediate forms may represent different degrees of formality and different levels of competence in the polar forms. Someone who controls Standard English very well may prefer to relax into a more informal style or someone who is not very competent in Standard English may try to speak more formally. The fluctuation need not depend on the individual speakers' efforts to move back and forth between the extremes, since most American Blacks probably grow up in communities where they hear fluctuations in use on all sides, and the community has no well-codified norm of its own apart from the mainstream standard language.

One consequence of the considerable distance between basilect and acrolect and the great fluctuation in sounds and forms is that professional people in the Black community generally have a broader range of styles of speaking in their verbal repertoire than their White mainstream counterparts. A middle-class Black preacher in an urban church must be able to move back and forth among different levels of language use and different styles of preaching to maintain effective communication with his parishioners and his colleagues (Mitchell 1970). Unfortunately most of the linguistic research on Black English has been concerned with the varieties most divergent from Standard English and has paid little attention to the varieties of English spoken by educated Blacks in the varied settings and occasions of life in Afro-American communities. An earlier generation of dialectologists was interested in the continuity between British and American English and played down the distinctions of Black English (McDavid and McDavid 1971). The current generation of sociolinguists is interested in the linguistic analysis of the most informal and distinctive varieties of Black urban vernacular. Some ethnographers of communication are beginning to study the functional uses of different varieties of language in the daily life of Black American communities to give a balance to this perspective.

THE ORIGINS OF BLACK LANGUAGE

Coordinate with research on the uses and structures of the language of Black Americans has been an interest in the history of these speech forms. Where did they come from? How have they evolved? Current researchers generally agree that both structural and functional patterns have their roots in African traditional culture and in the social adjustments of the slave trade, and that they have taken their distinctive form in the evolution of Black American culture and social organization in New World settings, both rural and urban. There are, however, divergent views on the history of language contact situations which contributed to the development of particular structures or dialect features. During the period of Black migration and extending to the early 1960s, dialectologists believed that the language of Blacks was a direct descendant of the standard British regional dialects that existed in the colonial era of American history and that their language was largely the result of the influence of contact with southern White speech.

The views of dialectologists were seriously challenged by a group of scholars who proposed that the dialect spoken by Blacks is a pidgin-derived language, and not solely British and White in origin. Stewart and Dillard have been the leading proponents of this view. W. A. Stewart (1967) pointed out the need for African slaves to learn some kind of English and expressed his conviction that in almost all cases what they acquired was a pidginized variety of English. He and Dillard (see especially Dillard 1972) adduced historical evidence to show that a pidgin English existed in many places in West Africa in the sixteenth century. They both have tied the development of a pidgin English in Africa to the transformation of an earlier Romance-language-based pidgin by relexification, i.e., the replacement of the original Romance vocabulary by words taken from English. Although the exact origins of West Africa Pidgin English are still controversial, there can be no doubt of its existence at the time of the slave trade, and it is highly probable that many slaves acquired some kind of pidgin English either before they left Africa or in the course of their transportation to the New World and first experiences after arrival. The more interesting question is how much remained of their African mother tongues. Apparently very little remained of active use of the African languages comparable, for example, to the vestiges of Yoruba and other languages in Cuba, Brazil, and elsewhere. But Africanisms persisted in the English they spoke, some are still apparent in varieties of Black English, and a few have even entered the mainstream of American English.

An important early study which tends to support the maintenance of features of African languages is Turner's (1949) study of the communities of Blacks located on the Sea Islands and mainland of coastal South Carolina and Georgia. Prior to the 1801 Slave Trade Act nearly 100,000 slaves were brought directly from Africa to the Charleston, South Carolina region. It is assumed that these slaves had little or no knowledge of the English language and that the relative isolation of the Sea Islands allowed for the development of a language which was not of direct British descent. Turner found Africanisms in the sounds, morphology, syntax, vocabulary, and intonation of the region's dialect, and hypothesized numerous similarities between Gullah and the African languages. Turner's findings were originally rejected by dialectologists as an isolated phenomenon of "selective cultural differentiation" (Dillard, 1972: 117). Hall (1950), Dalby (1969, 1972), and Hancock (1970), however, supported Turner's thesis and showed additional instances of the spread and influence of Africanisms in languages, arts, music, and dance. Thus a number of scholars have come to agree that the creole of the Sea Islands is not an aberrant phenomenon of Afro-American language, but rather a remnant of speech situations which were probably widespread in the early days of slavery. There is little doubt that the language of Black Americans did and still does, to a certain extent, reflect aspects of the West African languages. Some scholars have posited retention of particular vocabulary items, some used exclusively by Black Americans, others widely known in other American English dialects (Dalby 1972; Dillard 1976a). *Bad* (often pronounced *ba-a-ad*) is an example often cited as showing the influence of West African languages. The use of negative terms to express positive values occurred in West African languages and appears today in the street or jive talk of young Black Americans in particular. Words common to other dialects of English, such as *banjo, tote* (for "carry"), *okay, jazz,* and *jam* (as in *jam session*), are also posited as being of West African origin, though there are debates surrounding each of these items. Somewhat less debated is the influence particular speech events or styles of talking developed by Blacks have had on the talk of young adults using almost any dialect of English. The words of American popular music sung by Whites and Blacks alike have double (sometimes multiple) interpretations; negative terms carry positive meanings; White and Black American teenagers, church organizations, and business executives have *rap* sessions. The latter, a term first used by BEV speakers to mean "greet, speak to, flirt with, con or fool," has been extended in meaning to convey a "down-to-earth talk."

The language of Black Americans, has, as have other dialects of American English, features unique to its subsystem as well as features of the general system of English grammar. In their communities and other primary groups, Black Americans have unique styles of talking and ways of structuring and communicating social relationships through particular uses of language, such as greeting and fussing. Likewise, many members are competent in engaging in speech events expected of them in interactions with outsiders and in exchanges with members of their own age and sex. In many ways, the Civil Rights movement of the 1960s and publicity over the educational crisis of Black students have helped to promote linguistic research on the language of Black Americans and to cause this variety's existence to be widely discussed by educators, journalists, and politicians. Such promotion has fostered two major misconceptions: the first is the view that Black English is entirely unique among dialects of American English. The second is that there are two major dialects of American English, that spoken by Whites and that used by Blacks. Neither of these views is accepted by linguists, but both have widespread acceptance by the man on the street. Research within communities of speakers of other varieties of American English, as well as continuing attempts to learn more about the similarities and differences of language structures and functions among Black Americans, may someday provide both a comprehensive and an accurate picture of the varieties of English in the United States.

FOR DISCUSSION AND REVIEW

1. In her examination of the differences between the English of Black Americans and other varieties of English, what explanations does Whatley give? Why is Whatley not surprised by these differences?

2. For what reasons did America witness a migration of Black Americans from the South to the North early in the twentieth century?

3. How was Black American speech created, in part, as a result of the social conditions during the period of Black migration?

4. Discuss the characteristics and uses of "copping a plea" and "shucking and jiving."

5. To what is Whatley referring when she speaks of the "homogenizing influences" on styles of speech used by urban Blacks?

6. What does Whatley mean when she refers to the "talk and tricks" and "street talk" of Black English?

7. What factors determine the types or kinds of speech used among Black speakers? What is the hierarchy involved in Black speech?

8. Describe the ways in which Black American speech structures the community for communicative purposes. Are you surprised by what Whatley refers to as the "unexpected complexity in the order of turn taking" used among Black speakers?

9. How do children somehow take advantage of language use in conversations with other children? What does this reveal about language acquisition among Black children?

10. How are the various kinds of language used among Black speakers? What are the purposes of "fussing" and "boasting"?

11. What are some current misconceptions with regard to the use of Black English Vernacular, or BEV? What arguments have been presented among current researchers to negate such misconceptions?

12. Briefly describe the unique grammatical features of BEV that Whatley examines. Include examples in your discussion.

13. What are the "fluctuations" that occur in Black English?

14. What is the significance of a "basilect" or an "acrolect"?

15. What theories exist to explain the origins of Black English? Why must we continue to refer to them as "theories"?

16. What evidence exists to support the notion that the language of Black Americans reflects, to a certain extent, aspects of West African languages?

17. What two major misconceptions surrounding Black English does Whatley describe?

Projects for "Language Variation: Regional and Social"

1. Prepare a report on the purposes and methods of the *Linguistic Atlas of the United States and Canada* project. Use the library card catalogue, Hans Kurath's *Handbook of the Linguistic Geography of New England,* Lee Pederson's *A Manual for Dialect Research in the Southern States,* and *Newsletter of the American Dialect Society,* the *PMLA Bibliography,* and the *Social Sciences Index* to locate materials for this project.

2. Collection of materials for the *Dictionary of American Regional English (DARE)* began in 1965; the goal was to produce by 1976 an American dictionary comparable to the *English Dialect Dictionary.* Prepare a report on the methodology and progress of the *DARE* project. A longer report could examine the similarities and differences in purposes and methods between the *Linguistic Atlas of the United States and Canada* and the *Dictionary of American Regional English.* As a starting point, read Frederic G. Cassidy's "The *Atlas* and *DARE,"* in *Lexicography and Dialect Geography,* ed. Harold Sholler and John Reidy (Wiesbaden: F. Steiner, 1973).

3. The names of cities, towns, rivers, and mountains often provide clues to settlement and migration patterns. Using a map of your area, list three local place names and discuss their significance. For example, you may wish to find out the meaning of each name and whether or not any of the names appear elsewhere in the country (and, if so, whether or not they are related). You will find the following references useful: Kelsie B. Hardner's *Illustrated Dictionary of Place Names* (1976) and George R. Stewart's *American Place-Names* (1970).

4. Study the history of your community so that you can write a report in which you discuss the ways in which settlement patterns, population shifts, and physical geography have influenced the speech of the area.

5. Bidialectalism is a highly controversial subject. Prepare a report (1) presenting the opposing views objectively or (2) after explaining the arguments, supporting one particular view. To start, reread Labov and consult O'Neil (1972), Pixton (1974), and Sledd (1969, 1972), plus more recent articles. Do you consider the sociologic and economic factors raised by the various authors important? What issues do not appear to be relevant? From an educational point of view, which argument is the strongest? Defend whatever position you take.

6. Prepare a report summarizing the history of Black English in America. (Note: Not all authorities agree on the origin and development of BE.) Consult Smitherman (1977) and Dillard (1972) both of which contain excellent bibliographies dealing with the subject.

7. As evidenced by Roger Shuy's discussion of methodology, word geography is a fascinating aspect of dialect study. Read E. Bagby Atwood's

"Grease and Greasy: A Study of Geographical Variation," *Texas Studies in English* 29 (1950), 249–60. Based on this reading, and using Shuy's "Checklist of Regional Expressions" and his "Personal Data Sheet," survey your class, your campus (or a random sample thereof), or your community (or a random sample). Before you actually collect any data, you will need to consider such matters as the size and nature of the population to be studied, the selection of reliable and representative informants, and possible significant influences in the history of the college or community. Tabulate your results. Do any local or regional patterns emerge? Do you find any other patterns (e.g., systematic differences by age, sex, educational level, etc.)?

8. In an article entitled "Sense and Nonsense About American Dialects" (*PMLA*, 81 [1966], 7–17), Raven I. McDavid, Jr., says that "the surest social markers in American English are grammatical forms." Collect examples of grammatical forms used in your community. What social classes are represented?

9. The concept of "standard English" has caused much misunderstanding and debate. For many Americans, "standard" implies that one variety of English is more correct or more functional than other varieties. Investigate the history of the concept of "standard English." How, for example, did the concept develop? How do various linguists define it? Is "standard English" a social dialect? What exactly is the power or mystique of "standard English"?

10. Select the work of an author whose characters speak a social or regional variety of English — e.g., William Dean Howells, *The Rise of Silas Lapham*; Mark Twain, *Roughing It* (particularly "Buck Fanshaw's Funeral"); Bret Harte, *The Luck of Roaring Camp and Other Sketches*; Sarah Orne Jewett, *The Country of the Pointed Firs*; Joel Chandler Harris, *Uncle Remus and Br'er Rabbit*; William Faulkner, *The Sound and the Fury*; Willa Cather, *My Antonia*; John Steinbeck, *The Grapes of Wrath*; or Henry Roth, *Call It Sleep*. Identify the dialect presented and discuss the devices that the author uses to represent dialect. Read a passage aloud; how closely does it approximate actual speech?

11. Dialect differences in pronunciation abound. Here are some words for which there are distinct regional pronunciations. Compare your pronunciation of these items with those of others in your class:

collar	cot	wash
car	apricot	paw
empty	dog	tomato
door	clientele	marry
garage	mangy	Mary
oil	house	roof
can	very	sorry
greasy	either	fog
lot	caller	water

caught	horse	almond
hurry	class	idea

What pronunciation differences do you note among the members of your class? Are any regional patterns of pronunciation evident? Compare your results with the regional pronunciations discussed by Roger Shuy.

12. The Ann Arbor, Michigan, decision in July 1979 about Black English and the schools received national attention and has been the subject of controversy and misunderstanding (*Martin Luther King Junior Elementary School Children, et al.* v. *Ann Arbor School District Board*, 473 F. Supp. 1371 [1979]). Using your library resources, prepare a report analyzing (a) the causes of the litigation, (b) the findings of the court, or (c) the effects of the decision on the Ann Arbor schools. One useful reference is *Black English: Educational Equity and the Law*, edited by John W. Chambers, Jr. (Ann Arbor, MI: Karoma Publishers, Inc., 1983).

13. Study the following information about the status of various United States linguistic atlas projects.

LAGS   *Linguistic Atlas of the Gulf States.* Lee Pederson, ed. In progress.

LAMSAS   *Linguistic Atlas of the Middle and South Atlantic States: Fascicles 1 & 2.* Raven I. McDavid and R. K. O'Cain. Chicago: University of Chicago Press, 1980.

LANCS   *The Linguistic Atlas of the North-Central States.* University of Chicago Library, 1977. (Basic materials on microfilm and microfiche.)

LANE   *Linguistic Atlas of New England.* Hans Kurath et al. Providence: Brown University Press, 1939–43; reissued 1972.

LAO   *Linguistic Atlas of Oklahoma.* (Fieldwork completed.)

LAPC   *Linguistic Atlas of the Pacific Coast (California–Nevada).* (Fieldwork completed.)

LAPN   *Linguistic Atlas of the Pacific Northwest.* (Fieldwork completed for Washington.)

LARMS   *Linguistic Atlas of the Rocky Mountain States.* (Fieldwork completed for Colorado.)

LAUMW   *The Linguistic Atlas of the Upper Midwest.* Harold B. Allen. Minneapolis: University of Minnesota Press, 1973–76.

Prepare two lists, one indicating states in which work is under way, the other indicating states in which no work has yet been done. What conclusions can you draw? Write a paragraph in which you argue for one of the following positions: (a) a linguistic atlas of the United States will probably be completed within the next twenty-five years or (b) the atlas will probably never be completed.

14. The readings in this section deal with differences in speech among people of different regions and social class. Among the students in your class, devise a list of what may be considered "slang" or "popular"

terms. Your list may or may not include words such as: "not" (an exclamation), "crunchy" (a type of person), "to dis" (verb), or "choice" (adjective). With your list of words, create some form of survey in which you
ask whether your subject has heard the term before, whether he or she
uses the term, what word if any the subject uses in this word's place,
what other words the person has heard that mean the same as your
"slang" term, and where your subject believes that your term originated.
You may wish to record your subject's age group and sex to help in the
analysis of your data.

Take your survey to your hometown, and prepare a report of your
results. Are there any distinct characteristics that you observe? Are there
words that may be considered masculine or feminine? Which terms are
new and which ones borrowed? Compare your results with others in class.
What does this tell you about American dialects or words geographies?

15. Following his selection, "Pidgins and Creoles," in *The Cambridge Encyclopedia of Language,* David Crystal lists one hundred different pidgin and creole languages of the world along with a map to illustrate
their locations. Some of the most prominent or most widely used of those
listed include:

1. Hawaiian Pidgin/Creole, est. 500,000 speakers
2. Gullah, est. 150,000–300,000 speakers
3. Louisiana Creole French
4. Papiamentu (Papiamento), est. 200,000 speakers
5. Haitian French Creole, est. four million speakers
6. Sranan, est. 80,000 speakers
7. Cocoliche
8. Bagot Creole English
9. Australian Pidgin
10. Cameroon Pidgin English, est. two million speakers
11. Tok Pisin (Neo-Malasian), est. one million speakers
12. Congo Pidgins

Select one of these pidgin or creole languages, or go to the selection and
pick one of your own. After some library research, prepare a report on
your language and share what you have discovered with the class. Where
did your pidgin or creole language originate? What other languages or
dialects does yours influence? What appears to be the future of your language? After your class has shared their reports, create a list of characteristics shared by all pidgins and creoles.

16. William Safire of the *New York Times* called *The Dictionary of
American Regional English* "the most exciting linguistic project going
on in the United States." To date, two volumes of this dictionary have
been published, bringing the project up to the letter *H.* Spend some time
familiarizing yourself with this work in preparation for writing a report
about it. Some questions you may wish to consider include: What is the
purpose of the dictionary? What kinds of information does it contain?
How was this information collected? How useful is this reference?

Selected Bibliography

The books by J. K. Chambers and Peter Trudgill, by Lawrence M. Davis, and by W. N. Francis contain excellent general bibliographies. Geneva Smitherman's book contains an excellent bibliography of works dealing with Black English. The journal American Speech *and the monograph series* Publications of the American Dialect Society (PADS) *regularly publish material of interest.*

Allen, Harold B. *The Linguistic Atlas of the Upper Midwest.* Vol. 1, "Regional Speech Distribution." Minneapolis: University of Minnesota Press, 1973; vol. 2, "Grammar." Minneapolis: University of Minnesota Press, 1975; vol. 3. "Pronunciation." Minneapolis: University of Minnesota Press, 1976. [An invaluable reference for study of speech in the Upper Midwest.]

———. "The Linguistic Atlases: Our New Resource." *English Journal,* 45 (April 1956), 188–194. [A discussion of *Linguistic Atlas* data and their applications.]

———. "The Primary Dialect Areas of the Upper Midwest." *Studies in Language and Linguistics in Honor of Charles C. Fries.* Ed. Albert H. Marckwardt. Ann Arbor: The English Language Institute, The University of Michigan, 1964. [A study of the lexical, phonological, and morphological features of the speech in the Upper Midwest region.]

———. "Two Dialects in Contact." *American Speech* 48 (Spring–Summer 1973), 54–66. [A study of dialect boundaries in the Upper Midwest based on *Atlas* materials.]

Allen, Harold B., and Gary N. Underwood, eds. *Readings in American Dialectology.* New York: Appleton-Century-Crofts, 1971. [An anthology of essays dealing with important regional and social aspects of American dialectology.]

"American Tongues" (videorecording, 57 min.). New York: International Production Center, 1986. [An invaluable illustration of various dialects of English in the United States.]

Ann Arbor Decision. Washington, DC: Center for Applied Linguistics, 1979. [Landmark decision requiring the Ann Arbor schools to take BE into account in planning curricula; Civil Action No. 7–71861, United States District Court, Eastern District of Michigan, Southern Division; Martin Luther King Junior Elementary School Children, et al., Plaintiffs, v. Ann Arbor School District Board, Defendant.]

Atwood, E. Bagby. *A Survey of Verb Forms in the Eastern United States.* Ann Arbor: University of Michigan Press, 1953. [A fundamental work in linguistic geography.]

Bailey, R. W., and J. L. Robinson, eds. *Varieties of Present-Day English.* New York: Macmillan, 1973. [An excellent collection of articles.]

Bentley, Robert H., and Samuel D. Crawford, eds. *Black Language Reader.* Glenview, IL: Scott, Foresman and Company, 1973. [A good selection of articles, emphasizing education.]

Brasch, Ila Wales, and Walter Milton Brasch. *A Comprehensive Annotated Bibliography of American Black English.* Baton Rouge: Louisiana State University, 1974. [An invaluable bibliography on the subject of Black English.]

Burling, Robbins. *English in Black and White.* New York: Holt, Rinehart and

Winston, Inc., 1973. [A thorough introduction to dialects, with emphasis on Black English; excellent for teachers.]

Carver, Craig M. *American Regional Dialects: A Word Geography.* Ann Arbor: The University of Michigan Press, 1987. [A broad, extensive survey of the dialect regions of the United States and their historical and cultural origins.]

Cassidy, Frederic G. *Dictionary of American Regional English.* Cambridge, MA: Belknap Press, Harvard University, forthcoming. [A long-awaited reference and research work.]

———. "A Method for Collecting Dialect." *Publication of the American Dialect Society,* no. 20 (November 1953), 5–96. [The entire issue is devoted to a discussion of field methods and the presentation of a comprehensive dialect questionnaire.]

Chambers, J. K. and Peter Trudgill. *Dialectology.* Cambridge, Engl.: Cambridge University Press, 1980. [Very complete in its coverage; British orientation; contains excellent bibliography.]

Chambers, John W., Jr., ed. *Black English: Educational Equity and the Law.* Ann Arbor, MI: Karoma Publishers, 1983. [A collection of seven interesting essays plus a forward, an introduction, and the text of Judge Charles W. Joiner's "Memorandum Opinion and Order."]

Christian, Donna, W. Wolfram, N. Dube. *Variation and Change in Geographically Isolated Communities.* Tuscaloosa: University of Alabama Press, 1988. [A closer look at language variation and change in America focusing on two specific language communities.]

Crawford, James. *Hold Your Tongue — Bilingualism and the Politics of "English Only."* Reading: Addison-Wesley Publishing Company, 1992. [This controversial look at the "official language" issue focuses on ethnic intolerance in the United States.]

Cullinan, Bernice E., ed. *Black Dialects & Reading.* Urbana, IL: National Council of Teachers of English, 1974. [Both theoretical and practical; all major positions are presented; includes an excellent 50-page annotated bibliography.]

Davis, A. L. "English Problems of Spanish Speakers," in *Culture, Class, and Language Variety,* ed. A. L. Davis, Urbana, IL: National Council of Teachers of English, 1972. [A detailed analysis of phonological contrasts between Spanish and English, with some discussion of grammatical contrasts.]

———. "Developing and Testing the Checklist." *American Speech* 46 (Spring-Summer 1971), 34–37. [A discussion of problems associated with developing a vocabulary questionnaire.]

———. "Dialect Distribution and Settlement Patterns in the Great Lakes Region." *The Ohio State Archeological and Historical Quarterly* 60 (January 1951), 48–56. [A study showing many interesting correlations between linguistic features and settlement patterns in the Great Lakes region.]

Davis, Lawrence M. *English Dialectology: An Introduction.* University, AL: The University of Alabama Press, 1983. [Intended as a text for courses in dialectology; surveys regional and social dialect work in the U.S. and Britain; contains excellent bibliography.]

Dillard, J. L. *American Talk.* New York: Random House, 1976. [Popular and interesting treatment of the development of a large variety of American expressions.]

———. *All-American English: A History of the English Language in America.* New York: Random House, 1975. [Stresses "Maritime English" and its influence on the American colonists.]

———. *Black English: Its History and Usage in the United States.* New York: Random House, 1972. [An investigation of the ways in which Black English differs from other varieties of American English.]

Drake, James A. "The Effect of Urbanization Upon Regional Vocabulary." *American Speech* 36 (February 1961), 17–33. [A study of regional dialect items and urbanization in Cleveland, Ohio.]

Duckert, Audrey R. "The Second Time Around: Methods in Dialect Revisiting." *American Speech* 46 (Spring–Summer 1971), 66–72. [Methods for studying areas previously surveyed by the *Atlas* project—with emphasis on New England.]

Fasold, Ralph W. "Distinctive Linguistic Characteristics of Black English." *Linguistics and Language Study: 20th Roundtable Meeting.* Ed. James E. Alatis. Washington, DC: Georgetown University Press, 1970. [An examination of the distinctive differences between the nonstandard speech of poor blacks and the speech of whites.]

Fasold, Ralph W., and Walt Wolfram. *Teaching Standard English in the Inner City.* Washington, DC: Center for Applied Linguistics, 1970. [Discussion of the problems of teaching Standard English—interesting chapter on "Some Linguistic Features of Negro Dialect."]

Fischer, J. L. "Social Influences on the Choice of a Linguistic Variant." *Word* 14 (1958): 47–56. [The pioneering study that may have influenced Labov.]

Fishman, Joshua A. *Sociolinguistics: A Brief Introduction.* Rowley, MA: Newbury House Publishers, 1970. [Still a very good brief introduction to the field.]

Francis, W. N. *Dialectology: An Introduction.* New York: Longman, 1983. [An excellent introductory text.]

Grant, Stephen A. "Language Policy in the United States," in *Profession 78.* New York: Modern Language Association of America, 1978. [An examination of both federal and state policies regarding, *inter alia,* foreign language training and use, bilingual education, cultural pluralism.]

Harder, Kelsie B., ed. *Illustrated Dictionary of Place Names: United States and Canada.* New York: Van Nostrand Reinhold Company, 1976. [An invaluable reference work for North American place names.]

Haskins, Jim, and Hugh F. Butts, M.D. *The Psychology of Black Language.* New York: Barnes & Noble Books, 1973. [A good, brief overview; extensive notes and bibliography, plus a glossary of BE words and phrases.]

Hendrickson, Robert. *American Talk: The Words and Ways of American Dialects.* New York: Viking Penguin, 1986. [Excellent for the student curious about American dialects—with plenty of dialect dialogue.]

Hoffman, Charlotte. *An Introduction to Bilingualism.* New York: Longman, 1991. [Focuses in detail with examples of European languages to demonstrate how truly normal and widespread the phenomenon of bilingualism is.]

Hoffman, Melvin J. "Bi-dialectalism Is Not the Linguistics of White Supremacy: Sense Versus Sensibilities." *The English Record* 21 (April 1971), 95–102. [An argument supporting the bidialectal approach to the teaching of Standard English and refuting James Sledd's position.]

Holm, John A. *Pidgins and Creoles,* Volume 1. New York: Cambridge University Press, 1988. [A comprehensive survey of the field for the general reader and early students of linguistics.]

Ives, Sumner. "Dialect Differentiation in the Stories of Joel Chandler Harris." *American Literature* 17 (March 1955), 88–96. [A study of the social implications of Harris's dialects.]

———. "A Theory of Literary Dialect." *Tulane Studies in English* 2 (1950), 137–182. [An essential reference for all students doing work in literary dialects.]

Kenyon, John S. "Cultural Levels and Functional Varieties of English." *College English*, 10 (October 1948), 31–36. [A classification of language that recognizes, first, levels having cultural or social associations and, second, formal and familiar varieties of language usage.]

Kretzschmar, William A., Jr., ed. *Dialects in Culture: Essays in General Dialectology by Raven I. McDavid, Jr.* University, AL: The University of Alabama Press, 1979. [A collection of 60 essays and reviews by one of America's best-known dialectologists.]

Kurath, Hans. *Studies in Area Linguistics.* Bloomington: Indiana University Press, 1972. [An examination of regional and social dialectology, American and foreign.]

———. *A Word Geography of the Eastern United States.* Ann Arbor: University of Michigan Press, 1949. [A basic book in linguistic geography.]

———. Miles L. Hanley, Bernard Block, et al. *Linguistic Atlas of New England.* 3 vols. in 6 parts. Providence, RI: Brown University Press, 1939–1943; reissued New York: AMS Press, 1972. [An indispensable research and reference work for the study of speech in New England and for comparative studies. Should be used with companion *Handbook*.]

Labov, William. *Language in the Inner City: Studies in the Black English Vernacular.* Philadelphia: University of Pennsylvania Press, 1972. [A definitive work; detailed study of BE and of its social setting; bibliography.]

———. "The Logic of Nonstandard English." *Linguistics and Language Study: 20th Roundtable Meeting.* Ed. James E. Alatis. Washington, DC: Georgetown University Press, 1970. [Refutes theories that Black English lacks logic and sophistication and reveals mental inferiority.]

———. *The Nonstandard Vernacular of the Negro Community: Some Practical Suggestions.* Washington, DC: Education Resources Information Center, 1967. [Some advice to teachers concerning bidialectalism for the speaker of a nonstandard dialect.]

———. *The Social Stratification of English in New York City.* Washington, DC: Center for Applied Linguistics, 1966. [A landmark sociolinguistic study of New York City speech.]

———. "Stages in the Acquisition of Standard English." *Social Dialects and Language Learning.* Ed. Roger W. Shuy. Champaign, IL: NCTE, 1964. [An investigation of the acquisition of Standard English by children in New York City.]

Labov, William, Paul Cohen, Clarence Robins, and John Lewis. *A Study of the Non-Standard English of Negro and Puerto Rican Speakers in New York City.* Final Report, Cooperative Research Project no. 3288, vol. 1. Washington, DC: Office of Education, 1968.

Lamberts, J. J. "Another Look at Kenyon's Levels." *College English* 24 (November 1969), 141–143. [A reassessment of John S. Kenyon's classification of cultural levels and functional varieties of English.]

McDavid, Raven I., Jr. See Kretzschmar, 1979.

McDowell, Tremaine. "The Use of Negro Dialect by Harriet Beecher Stowe." *American Speech* 6 (June 1931), 322–326. [A study in literary dialect.]

McMillan, James B. *Annotated Bibliography of Southern American English.* Coral Gables, FL: University of Miami Press, 1971. [A valuable reference work for the study of speech in southern states.]

Mencken, H. L. *The American Language: The Fourth Edition and the Two Supplements.* Abridged and ed. Raven I. McDavid, Jr. New York: Alfred A. Knopf, 1963. [A classic study of American English.]

Metcalf, Allan A. "Chicano English." *Language and Education: Theory and Practice* 2. Washington, DC: Center for Applied Linguistics, 1979. [Emphasizes that Chicano English is not an imperfect attempt by a native speaker of Spanish to master English.]

O'Neil, Wayne. "The Politics of Bidialectalism." *College English* 33 (1972), 433–438 [Argues that bidialectalism is aimed at maintaining the social status quo — the inequality of blacks in a predominantly white society.]

Pederson, Lee A. "An Approach to Urban Word Geography." *American Speech* 46 (Spring–Summer 1971), 73–86. [A presentation of vocabulary questionnaires suitable for urban testing — namely, in Chicago.]

———. "Negro Speech in *The Adventures of Huckleberry Finn.*" *Mark Twain Journal* 13 (1966), 1–4. [An examination of the literary representation of Negro dialect in Twain's classic novel.]

Pixton, William H. "A Contemporary Dilemma: The Question of Standard English." *College Composition and Communication* 5 (1974), 247–253. [Argues for the use of Standard English by blacks.]

Pyles, Thomas, *Words and Ways of American English.* New York: Random House, 1952. [An introduction to American English from colonial times to the present.]

Reed, Carroll E. *Dialects of American English.* 2nd edition. Amherst: The University of Massachusetts Press, 1973. [An introduction to dialect study with units devoted to sectional atlas studies and to urban dialect studies.]

———. "The Pronunciation of English in the Pacific Northwest." *Language* 37 (October–December 1961), 559–564. [A description of the pronunciation of vowels and consonants by residents of the Pacific Northwest.]

Schneider, Edgar W. *American Earlier Black English: Morphological and Syntactic Variables.* Tuscaloosa: The University of Alabama Press, 1989. [A detailed study of Black English Vernacular (BEV) through its history, terms, and grammatical structures.]

Shopen, Timothy and Joseph M. Williams, eds. *Style and Variables in English.* Englewood Cliffs, N.J.: Winthrop Publishers, 1981. [An excellent collection of essays.]

———. *Standards and Dialects in English.* Englewood Cliffs, N.J.: Winthrop Publishers, 1980. [A companion volume to the preceding one; accompanying tapes are available.]

Shores, David L. and Carole P. Hines, eds. *Papers in Language Variation.* University, AL: The University of Alabama Press, 1977. [A collection of 29 papers, almost all originally presented at an ADS or SAMLA meeting.]

Shuy, Roger W. "Detroit Speech: Careless, Awkward, and Inconsistent, or Systematic, Graceful, and Regular?" *Elementary English* 45 (May 1968), 565–569. [A discussion of nonstandard speech in Detroit, Michigan.]

———. "Some Useful Myths in Social Dialectology." The *Florida FL Reporter* 11 (Spring–Fall 1973), 17–20, 55. [Identifies several myths that, though oversimplifications, are useful to social dialectologists.]

Sledd, James. "Bi-Dialectalism: The Linguistics of White Supremacy." *English Journal* 58 (1969), 1307–1315. [Argues against linguists and teachers who advocate bidialectal programs.]

————. "Doublespeak: Dialectology in the Service of Big Brother." *College English* 35 (January 1972). [A trenchant argument against bidialectalism; a classic.]

Smith, Riley B. "Research Perspectives on American Black English: A Brief Historical Sketch." *American Speech* 49 (Spring–Summer 1974), 24–39. [A bibliographical essay with a historical perspective.]

Smitherman, Geneva. *Talkin' and Testifyin': The Language of Black America.* Boston: Houghton Mifflin, 1977. [Comprehensive study of Black English; includes an excellent bibliography of works dealing with the subject.]

Spolsky, Bernard, ed. *The Language Education of Minority Children.* Rowley, MA: Newbury House Publishers, 1972. [Fourteen essays; of interest especially to teachers.]

Stockton, Eric. "Poe's Use of Negro Dialect in 'The Gold-Bug.' " *Studies in Language and Linguistics in Honor of Charles C. Fries.* Ed. Albert H. Marckwardt. Ann Arbor: The English Language Institute, The University of Michigan, 1964. [An analysis of Jupiter's speech as an example of literary dialect used by pre-Civil War writers.]

Stoller, Paul, ed. *Black American English: Its Background and Its Usage in the Schools and in Literature.* New York: Dell Publishing Co., 1975. [An excellent collection of articles on the history and structure of BE, on BE and education, plus three literary excerpts illustrating use of BE; bibliography.]

Teschner, Richard V., Garland Bills, and Jerry R. Craddock. *Spanish and English of United States Hispanos: A Critical, Annotated, Linguistic Bibliography.* Washington, DC: Center for Applied Linguistics, 1975. [An invaluable research tool for studies in this area.]

Trudgill, Peter. *The Social Differentiation of English in Norwich.* Cambridge, Engl.: Cambridge University Press, 1972. [A model study; basic.]

————. *Sociolinguistics: An Introduction.* Penguin Books, 1974. [An excellent introduction by a leader in the field.]

Trudgill, Peter ed., J. K. Chambers. *Dialects of English: Studies in Grammatical Variation.* New York: Longman, 1991. [A helpful study of the history of American dialects and the British dialectical influences on American speech.]

Underwood, Gary N. "Vocabulary Change in the Upper Midwest." *Publication of the American Dialect Society* 49 (April 1968), 8–28. [An investigation of language change that utilizes four generations of informants.]

Williamson, Juanita V., and Virginia M. Burke, eds. *A Various Language: Perspectives on American Dialects.* New York: Holt, Rinehart and Winston, 1971. [An anthology of essential articles dealing with American dialects.]

Wolfram, Walt. *A Sociolinguistic Description of Detroit Negro Speech.* Washington, DC: Center for Applied Linguistics, 1969. [Thorough and detailed.]

————. *Sociolinguistic Aspects of Assimilation: Puerto Rican English in New York City.* Washington, DC: Center for Applied Linguistics, 1974. [A thorough study of the language problems encountered by Puerto Ricans in New York City.]

Wolfram, Walt, and Donna Christian. *Sociolinguistic Variables in Appalachian Dialects.* National Institute of Education Grant Number NIE-G-74-0026, Final Report. Washington, DC: Center for Applied Linguistics, 1975. [Definitive and informative.]

Wolfram, Walt, and Ralph W. Fasold. *The Study of Social Dialects in American English.* Englewood Cliffs, NJ: Prentice-Hall, 1974. [An introduction to the linguist's view of social variation in language — special attention given to possible educational applications.]

PART SEVEN

HISTORICAL LINGUISTICS AND LANGUAGE CHANGE

Any living language is in a constant state of change. We are not usually aware of the changes taking place in our language because most of them occur slowly over time. But if we look back at earlier forms of English — Chaucer's *Canterbury Tales*, for example, or, going back even further, the epic poem *Beowulf* — we can see that many significant changes have occurred. The study of the history and development of languages, which often involves comparing different languages, is called *historical* or *comparative linguistics*, and it was the earliest of the diverse areas of linguistics that have developed as fields of study.

The first selection, in this part, "Comparative and Historical Linguistics," introduces some basic concepts of historical linguistics: for example, the idea that some languages share a common ancestor, and the concepts of reconstruction and the comparative method. Using Grimm's Law as an example, Jeanne H. Herndon illustrates the systematic nature of language change and the key role that phonology plays in understanding such change. Next, Professor Paul Thieme explains how the reconstruction of the Indo-European language has given us a great deal of information about many aspects of the Indo-European way of life and culture. Thieme's selection, "The Indo-European Language," is followed by Herndon's chart of the Indo-European language family and its subdivisions, which details the large area over which these languages are now spoken. In "A Brief History of English," Professor Paul Roberts shows the relationship between historical events and the evolution of English, from the beginnings of Old English around A.D. 600, through Middle English to Early Modern English (1600), outlining the principal characteristics of the language during each of these periods.

The first four selections in this part emphasize the gradual, continuous changes that have taken place over the last six or seven thousand years in one language family, Indo-European, and during the last thirteen hundred years in English. In the last selection, "Language Change: Progress or Decay?" Professor Jean Aitchison concludes that language change is natural, inevitable, and continuous. Aitchison also discusses whether languages, as they change, are progressing or decaying, whether language change is evolutionary, and whether it is socially desirable and/or controllable.

35

Comparative and Historical Linguistics

Jeanne H. Herndon

Our Western grammatical tradition descends to us from the Greeks, via the Romans; and it was not until the late eighteenth century that language scholars broke away from traditional Western grammar and began to look at language in a different way — to study similarities and differences among many languages and to identify patterns of relationships among languages. Their work was entirely descriptive, and it should be noted that such objectivity was something new in the Western grammatical tradition. Unfortunately, the work of the great Indian grammarian Pānini (fourth century B.C.), who prepared a masterful descriptive grammar of Vedic Sanskrit, was unknown in the West until the beginning of the nineteenth century. In the selection which follows, excerpted from her book A Survey of Modern Grammars, *Professor Jeanne H. Herndon traces the beginnings of comparative and historical linguistics in the eighteenth century and, using Grimm's Law as an example, demonstrates the systematic nature of language change and that these changes can be most clearly traced through comparison of the sound systems of languages.*

In spite of the fact that most [of the early traditional] grammarians relied upon classical grammarians for method and classical languages for criteria of correctness, some new ideas were stirring in the field of language study in the eighteenth century. These new ideas were not to affect the work of school grammarians for several generations. But among these ideas are to be found the roots of a whole new approach to the problem of analyzing and describing language.

Many language scholars had noted similarities between various European languages; some languages had quite clearly developed from one variety or another of provincial Latin. It remained for an Englishman who was not primarily a language scholar to see relationships among the most widely dispersed of those languages that were later to be recognized as the Indo-European family of languages.

Sir William Jones had served in the colonial government of India and while there had studied Sanskrit. In 1786 he wrote of observing similarities between a remarkable number of vocabulary items in Sanskrit and their equivalents in European and Middle Eastern languages. He suggested that all these languages might have "sprung from some common source, which, perhaps, no longer exists."

Investigation of similarities and differences among languages is called *comparative linguistics.* As language scholars began to establish patterns of relationships among languages, their work came to be called *historical linguistics.* (These scholars were interested primarily in relationships among languages; they were concerned with matters of grammar only insofar as these might indicate relationships among languages and not as a matter of establishing rules of correctness.) Their research was simply a matter of gathering data, sorting, and analyzing it. Their view of change was totally objective. They were interested only in what kinds of changes had occurred, not whether these changes were "right" or "wrong," "good" or "bad."

Among the first linguists to make important comparative studies was a Danish scholar named Rasmus Rask, who compared Icelandic and Scandinavian languages and dialects. Another, Jacob Grimm, carried Rask's studies still further and proposed a theory to account for [some of the regular differences in certain sounds which] he found among languages. Out of these and many other, similar studies grew the theory that languages not only change gradually, over long periods of time, but that they change systematically and that the changes are best traced through comparison of the sound systems of languages.

The single most sweeping statement of this kind of sound relationship is often referred to as Grimm's Law or the First Germanic Consonant Shift. It is a systematic comparison of the sound systems of Indo-European languages, which both demonstrates the validity of the theory that these languages sprang from a common source and gives a wealth of information about how they are related.

Grimm concentrated, as had his predecessors, on written forms of words. Actually, he had no choice since he dealt with stages of language development long past. The differences he noted and compared were letters and spellings, but the spelling differences came to be recognized as representative of pronunciation or sound differences. Grimm went even further and, in addition to a simple listing and comparing of differences, he proposed an explanation of the orderly nature of the shift.

According to this theory, three whole sets of sounds in an ancestor of the Germanic languages had shifted from their earlier Indo-European pronunciation. [The accompanying chart shows] the original sounds and how they changed:

1. The sounds *b, d,* and *g* became *p, t,* and *k.* (There is only one *kind* of change here — three voiced sounds became silent, or voiceless, sounds.)

2. The sounds that began as *p, t,* and *k* became *f, th,* and *h.* (Again only one kind of change occurred — three "stops" became three "spirants," or sounds where the air is slowed down but not stopped completely.)

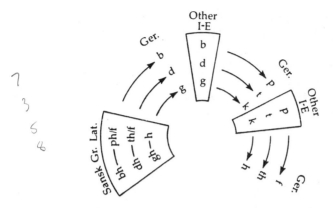

Chart of the first Germanic consonant shift.

3. The history of the third set of sounds is more complex. These had begun as the breathy voiced stops *bh, dh,* and *gh* in early stages of Indo-European language development and still remain in Sanskrit. They had developed into similar, but not quite the same, sounds *ph* or *f, th,* and *h* in later stages of Indo-European language development represented by Latin and Greek. As a part of the Germanic Consonant Shift, this group of sounds shifted to become the voiced stop consonants *b, d,* and *g.* The shift of all three sets of consonant sounds — for speakers of the Germanic parent language only — can be seen as something very like a game of phonetic musical chairs.

The boxed letters [in the chart] represent the sounds that remained in other Indo-European languages; the letters outside the boxes represent the sounds found in Germanic languages as a result of the consonant shift. These correspondences figure prominently in setting the languages derived from this Germanic parent language apart as a distinct branch of the Indo-European family of languages.

These shifts, to repeat, occurred gradually, over very long periods of time. They can be demonstrated by comparing words in a Germanic language, English, which developed after the shift occurred, with items taken from Latin and Greek, languages in which the sounds of these consonants did not shift.

Latin *turba* ⟶ English *thorp*
Latin *dentum* ⟶ English *tooth*
Greek *agros* ⟶ English *acre*
Greek *pous* ⟶ English *foot*
Greek *treis* ⟶ English *three*
Latin *cor* ⟶ English *heart*
Greek *phrater* ⟶ English *brother*
Greek *thygater* ⟶ English *daughter*
Latin *hostis* ⟶ English *guest*

Many words in these languages do not show precisely the same correspondences, but these can be shown to be the result of other shifts or to be related to other factors. Scholars such as Karl Verner noted additional complexities in the nature of the shift and differences resulting from later shifts and proposed theories to explain the apparent "exceptions," until it was possible to trace, in great detail, the development of Indo-European languages over vast stretches of history.

More language samples were gathered, examined, and analyzed; more comparisons were made and new theories proposed. Each new theory could be tested by gathering still more language data and making still more comparisons.

The area of inquiry had been greatly expanded with investigation of Sanskrit and the languages of the Middle East. Sanskrit provided an especially rich body of material for these historical linguists because of the nature of the records open to them. Sanskrit, a literary language of India, had been the subject of grammatical study centuries before Western European scholars had undertaken such investigation of their own languages. As early as the fourth century B.C., an Indian grammarian named Pānini had analyzed Sanskrit and had organized his analysis into a masterful codification of the grammatical units and possible combinations in Sanskrit. For students of historical linguistics, discovery and study of this work were profoundly valuable for two reasons. First, it was a full-fledged grammatical analysis as compared to the fragmentary records of some of the earlier languages they had studied and, second, it represented by far the earliest stage of development of any Indo-European language available to them for study.

Through most of the nineteenth century, linguistic scholarship concentrated primarily on comparative and historical studies. Methods of gathering, classifying, and analyzing data were tested, improved, or discarded, and the improvements tested again.

Comparison of the sound systems of languages was seen to account for only a part of the systematic changes in language. Word forms, inflections, and syntactic differences came to be recognized as important considerations in comparing different stages of the development of languages.

This study of the historical development of a language or languages is sometimes called *diachronic linguistics. Diachronic* is a combination of Greek stems, *dia-* meaning *across*, and *chronos* meaning *time*. For linguists it means that single features of language are traced over long periods of time with changes noted and related to changes in other features of languages over the same periods.

Language researchers gathered data from every nook and cranny of Europe including many dialects peculiar to very small, isolated villages and hamlets. This data led to a major shift of emphasis for some linguists. They moved from the study of historical developments into primary concentration on the similarities and contrasts between contemporary languages and dialects.

After two centuries of enormous amounts of language study, linguists have arrived at some very sweeping theories about the nature of the relationships among the many Indo-European languages. Stated in the simplest possible terms, the important points are these: (1) All these languages developed from a single language which no longer exists. (2) Differences developed when groups of people who spoke this language moved apart and were separated for long periods of time. That is, one group moved into India and their language developed and changed to become Sanskrit; another group moved into southeastern Europe and their language grew into the ancestor of Greek; another group broke off and moved into northern Europe and their language changed in some respects to become the parent language of German, English, Danish, and so on. (3) The fact that all these languages share a common heritage accounts for the fact that some similarities still exist in all of them.

FOR DISCUSSION AND REVIEW

1. What contribution to linguistics did Sir William Jones (1746–1794) make?

2. Describe the attitude of historical (or comparative) linguists toward language change. How does this attitude compare with that held by many popular contemporary writers about language usage (e.g., Edwin Newman and William Safire)?

3. What *kind* of change in language is the most useful to historical linguists? Why?

4. One of the most important characteristics differentiating the Germanic branch of Proto-Indo-European from the languages of all the other branches (see the chart on p. 601) is the set of sound changes called Grimm's Law. Its effects are most easily seen in word-initial sounds. Using the words *tooth, foot,* and *three,* show the effect of Grimm's Law in changing these words from their Latin equivalents.

5. Explain how the following sets of words do or do not illustrate Grimm's Law (note: do not consider *only* initial consonants):

	1	2	3
Sanskrit	pitar	bhinádmi	bhrátar
Greek	patèr	pheídomai	phráter
Latin	pater	findō	fráter
English	father	bite	brother

6. Why was Sanskrit of special importance to early historical linguists?

7. What were the major conclusions of historical linguists concerning the relationships among the many Indo-European languages?

36

≡

The Indo-European Language

Paul Thieme

Except for Basque, Finnish, Hungarian, and Estonian, all of the languages currently spoken in Europe belong to the Indo-European family of languages. So too, almost all of the languages spoken in Canada, the United States, and Central and South America are of Indo-European origin. (The exceptions are such surviving indigenous languages as Navajo, Cherokee, Eskimo, Quechua [in Peru], and Mazatec [in Mexico].) Therefore, given the importance of the Indo-European languages in today's world, it is only natural to wonder, who were the original Indo-Europeans? When and where did they live? What was their culture like? How did it happen that so many languages developed from this one source? In the following selection, Professor Paul Thieme uses the methods of comparative linguistics or philology to show how it has been possible to reconstruct a large part of the sound system, grammar, and even vocabulary of the Indo-European language, and from this reconstruction to learn a great deal about Indo-European culture and the original Indo-European homeland.*

Every educated person knows that French and Spanish are "related" languages. The obvious similarity of these tongues is explained by their common descent from Latin; indeed, we could say that French and Spanish are two dialects of "modern Latin," forms of the ancestral language that have grown mutually unintelligible through long separation. Latin has simply developed somewhat differently in these two fragments of the old Western Roman Empire. Today these dialects are called Romance languages.

The other great family of European languages is of course the Germanic. It includes English, Dutch, German and the Scandinavian

---

*Editor's note: Additional information about the Indo-European culture and homeland has become available since the original publication of this selection. See, for example, Calvert Watkins's "Indo-European and the Indo-Europeans" in *The American Heritage Dictionary.*

tongues, all descended from an ancient language—unfortunately unrecorded—called Teutonic [or Proto-Germanic].

Romance languages and Teutonic, plus Greek—these were once the center of our linguistic universe. During the past 200 years, however, linguistics has been undergoing a kind of prolonged Copernican revolution. Now the familiar European tongues have been relegated to minor places in a vaster system of languages which unites Europe and Asia. Known collectively as the Indo-European languages, this superfamily is far and away the most extensive linguistic constellation in the world. It is also the most thoroughly explored: while other language families have remained largely unknown, the Indo-European family has monopolized the attention of linguists since the 18th century. The modern discipline of linguistics is itself a product of Indo-European studies. As a result of these intensive labors we have come to know a great deal about both the genealogy and the interrelationships of this rich linguistic community.

If we look at the family as a whole, several questions spring to mind. Where did these languages come from? Every family traces its descent from a common ancestor: what was our ancestral language? What did it sound like? What manner of men spoke it? How did they come to migrate over the face of the earth, spreading their tongue across the Eurasian land mass?

Linguistics can now provide definite—if incomplete—answers to some of these questions. We have reconstructed in substantial part the grammar and sound-system of the Indo-European language, as we call this ultimate forebear of the modern Indo-European family. Although much of the original vocabulary has perished, enough of it survives in later languages so that we can contrive a short dictionary. From the language, in turn, we can puzzle out some characteristics of Indo-European culture. We can even locate the Indo-European homeland.

We can never hope to reconstruct the Indo-European language in complete detail. The task would be immeasurably easier if the Indo-Europeans had only left written records. But the Indo-Europeans, unlike their Egyptian and Mesopotamian contemporaries, were illiterate. Their language was not simply forgotten, to be relearned by archaeologists of another day. It vanished without a trace, except for the many hints that we can glean and piece together from its surviving daughter languages.

THE DISCOVERY OF THE LANGUAGE

The first clue to the existence of an Indo-European family was uncovered with the opening of trade with India. In 1585, a little less than a century after Vasco da Gama first rounded the Cape of Good Hope, an Italian merchant named Filippo Sassetti made a startling discovery in India. He found that Hindu scholars were able to speak and write an ancient language, at least as venerable as Latin and Greek. Sassetti wrote a letter home about this language, which he called *Sanscruta* (Sanskrit). It bore certain resemblances, he said, to his native Italian. For example, the word for "God" *(deva)* resembled the Italian *Dio;* the word for "snake" *(sarpa),* the Italian *serpe;* the numbers "seven," "eight" and "nine" *(sapta, ashta* and *nava),* the Italian *sette, otto* and *nove.*

What did these resemblances prove? Sassetti may have imagined that Sanskrit was closely related to the "original language" spoken by Adam and Eve; perhaps that is why he chose "God" and "snake" as examples. Later it was thought that Sanskrit might be the ancestor of the European languages, including Greek and Latin. Finally it became clear that Sanskrit was simply a sister of the European tongues. The relationship received its first scientific statement in the "Indo-European hypothesis" of Sir William Jones, a jurist and orientalist in the employ of the East India Company. Addressing the Bengal Asiatic Society in 1786, Sir William pointed out that Sanskrit, in relation to Greek and Latin, "bears a stronger affinity, both in the roots of verbs and in the forms of grammar, than could possibly have been produced by accident: so strong, indeed, that no philologer could examine them all three without believing them to have sprung from some common source, which, perhaps, no longer exists; there is similar reason, though not quite so forcible, for supposing that both the Gothick and the Celtick, though blended with a very different idiom, had the same origin with the Sanskrit."

Sir William's now-famous opinion founded modern linguistics. A crucial word in the sentence quoted is "roots." Jones and his successors could not have done their work without a command of Sanskrit, then the oldest-known Indo-European language. But they also could not have done it without a knowledge of traditional Sanskrit grammar. Jones, like every linguist since, was inspired by the great Sanskrit grammarian Panini, who sometime before 500 B.C. devised a remarkably accurate and systematic technique of word analysis. Instead of grouping related forms in conjugations and declensions — as European and U.S. school-grammar does to this day — Panini's grammar analyzed the forms into their functional units: the roots, suffixes and endings.

Comparative grammar, in the strict sense, was founded by a young German named Franz Bopp. In 1816 Bopp published a book on the inflection of verbs in a group of Indo-European languages: Sanskrit, Persian, Greek, Latin and the Teutonic tongues. Essentially Bopp's book was no more than the application to a broader group of languages of Panini's technique for the analysis of Sanskrit verbs. But Bopp's motive was a historical one. By gathering cognate forms from a number of Indo-European languages he hoped to be able to infer some of the characteristics of the lost language — the "common source" mentioned by Jones — which was the parent of them all.

In the course of time Bopp's method has been systematically developed and refined. The "affinities" which Jones saw between certain words in related languages have come to be called "correspondences," defined by precise formulas. The "Indo-European hypothesis" has been proved beyond doubt. And many more groups of languages have been found to belong to the Indo-European family: Slavonic, Baltic, the old Italic dialects, Albanian, Armenian, Hittite and Tocharian. The "family tree" of these languages has been worked out in some detail. It should be borne in mind, however, that when it is applied to languages a family-tree diagram is no more than a convenient graphic device. Languages do not branch off from one another at a distinct point in time; they separate gradually, by the slow accumulation of innovations. Moreover, we cannot be sure of every detail in their relationship. The affinities of the Celtic and Italic languages, or of the Baltic and Slavonic, may or may not point to a period when each of these pairs formed a common language, already distinguished from the Indo-European. Some Indo-European languages cannot be placed on the family tree because their lineage is not known. Among these are Tocharian and Hittite. These extinct languages (both rediscovered in the 20th century) were spoken in Asia but descend from the western branch of the family.

RECONSTRUCTION

Let us see how a linguist can glean information about the original Indo-European language by comparing its daughter tongues with one another. Take the following series of "corresponding" words: *pra* (Sanskrit), *pro* (Old Slavonic), *pro* (Greek), *pro* (Latin), *fra* (Gothic), all meaning "forward"; *pitā* (Sanskrit), *patēr* (Greek), *pater* (Latin), *fadar* (Gothic), all meaning "father." Clearly these words sprang from two words in the original Indo-European language. Now what can we say about the initial sounds the words must have had in the parent tongue? It must have been "p," as it is in the majority of the languages cited. Only in Gothic does it appear as "f," and the odds are overwhelmingly in favor of its having changed from "p" to "f" in this language, rather than from "f" to "p" in all the others. Thus we know one fact about the original Indo-European language: it had an initial "p" sound. This sound remains "p" in most of the daughter languages. Only in Gothic (and other Teutonic tongues) did it become "f."

Now let us take a harder example: *dasa* (Sanskrit), *deshimt* (Lithuanian), *deseti* (Old Slavonic), *deka* (Greek), *dekem* (Latin), *tehun* (Gothic), all meaning "ten"; *satam* (Sanskrit), *shimtas* (Lithuanian), *suto* (Old Slavonic), *he-katon* (Greek), *kentum* (Latin), *hunda-* (Gothic), all meaning "hundred." (The spelling of some of these forms has been altered for purposes of exposition. The hyphen after the Gothic *hunda-* and certain other words in this article indicates that they are not complete words.)

Certainly the "s," "sh," "k" and "h" sounds in these words are related to one another. Which is the original? We decide that "k" changed into the other sounds rather than *vice versa*. Phoneticians tell us that "hard" sounds like "k" often mutate into "soft" sounds like "sh." For example, the Latin word *carus* ("dear") turned into the French word *cher;* but the reverse change has not occurred.

Reconstruction would be much easier sailing but for two all-too-common events in the history of language: "convergence" and "divergence." In Sanskrit the three old Indo-European vowels "e," "o" and "a" have converged to become "a" (as in "ah"). In the Germanic languages the Indo-European vowel "e" has diverged to become "e" (as in "bet") next to certain sounds and "i" (as in "it") next to others.

Like most procedures in modern science, linguistic reconstructions require a certain technical skill. This is emphatically not a game for amateurs. Every step is most intricate. Some people may even wonder whether there is any point to the labors of historical linguists — especially in view of the fact that the reconstructions can never be checked by immediate observation. There is no absolute certainty in the reconstruction of a lost language. The procedure is admittedly probabilistic. It can only be tested by the coherence of its results.

But the results in the reconstruction of ancestral Indo-European are heartening. By regular procedures such as those I have illustrated, we have reconstructed a sound system for Indo-European that has the simplicity and symmetry of sound systems in observable languages. We have discovered the same symmetry in our reconstructions of roots, suffixes, endings, and whole words. Perhaps even more important, the Indo-European words we have reconstructed give a convincing picture of ancient Indo-European customs and geography!

THE INDO-EUROPEAN CULTURE

Consider the words for "mother," "husband," "wife," "son," "daughter," "brother," "sister," "grandson," "son-in-law," "daughter-in-law," all of which we can reconstruct in Indo-European. As a group they prove that the speakers lived in families founded on marriage — which is no more than we might expect! But we obtain more specific terms too: "father-in-law," "mother-in-law," "brother-in-law," "sister-in-law." Exact correspondences in the speech usage of the oldest daughter languages which have been preserved lead to the conclusion that these expressions were used exclusively with reference to the "in-laws" of the bride, and not to those of the groom. There are no other words that would designate a husband's "father-in-law," and so on. The inference is unavoidable that the family system of the old Indo-Europeans was of a patriarchal character; that is, that the wife married into her husband's family, while the husband did not acquire an official relationship to his wife's family as he does where a matriarchal family system exists. Our positive witnesses (the accumulation of designations for the relations a woman acquires by marriage) and our negative witnesses (the complete absence of designations for the relations a man might be said to acquire by marriage) are trustworthy circumstantial evidence of this.

The Indo-Europeans had a decimal number system that reveals traces of older counting systems. The numbers up to "four" are inflected like adjectives. They form a group by themselves, which points to an archaic method of counting by applying the thumb to the remaining four fingers in succession. Another group, evidently later arrivals in the history of Indo-European, goes up to "ten" (the Indo-European *dekmt-*). "Ten" is related to "hundred": *kmtom*, a word which came from the still earlier *dkmtom*, or "aggregate of tens." In addition to these four-finger and ten-finger counting systems there was a method of counting by twelves, presumably stemming from the application of the thumb to the twelve joints of the other four fingers. It is well known that the Teutonic languages originally distinguished a "small hundred" (100) from a "big hundred" (120). The latter is a "hundred" that results from a combination of counting by tens (the decimal system) and counting by twelves (the duodecimal system). Traces of duodecimal counting can also be found in other Indo-European languages.

Reconstruction yields an almost complete Indo-European inventory of body parts, among them some that presuppose the skilled butchering of animals. The Indo-European word for "lungs" originally meant "swimmer." We can imagine a prehistoric butcher watching the lungs float to the surface as he put the entrails of an animal into water. There is no reference in the word to the biological function of the lungs, which was presumably unknown. The heart, on the other hand, appears to have been named after the beat of the living organ.

So far as tools and weapons are concerned, we are not quite so lavishly served. We obtain single expressions for such things as "arrow," "ax," "ship," "boat," but no semantic system. This poverty is due partly to an original lack of certain concepts, and partly to the change of usage in the daughter languages. It is evident that new terms were coined as new implements were invented. We do find words for "gold" and perhaps for "silver," as well as for "ore." Unfortunately we cannot decide whether "ore" was used only with reference to copper or to both copper and bronze. It is significant that we cannot reconstruct a word for "iron," which was a later discovery. In any case we need not picture the people who spoke Indo-European as being very primitive. They possessed at least one contrivance that requires efficient tools: the wagon or cart. Two Indo-European words for "wheel" and words for "axle," "hub" and "yoke" are cumulative evidence of this.

THE INDO-EUROPEAN HOMELAND

Especially interesting are the names of animals and plants, for these contain the clue to the ancient Indo-European homeland. It is evident that our reconstructed language was spoken in a territory that cannot have been large. A language as unified as the one we obtain by our reconstruction suggests a compact speech community. In prehistoric times, when communication over long distances was limited, such a community could have existed only within comparatively small boundaries.

These boundaries need not have been quite so narrow if the people who spoke Indo-European had been nomads. Nomads may cover a large territory and yet maintain the unity of their language, since their roamings repeatedly bring them in contact with others who speak their tongue. The Indo-Europeans, however, were small-scale farmers and husbandmen rather than nomads. They raised pigs, which kept them from traveling, and they had words for "barley," "stored grains," "sowing," "plowing," "grinding," "settlement" and "pasture" (agros), on which domesticated animals were "driven" (ag).

We cannot reconstruct old Indo-European words for "palm," "olive," "cypress," "vine," "laurel." On the strength of this negative evidence we can safely eliminate Asia and the Mediterranean countries as possible starting points of the Indo-European migrations. We can, however, reconstruct the following tree names: "birch," "beech," "aspen," "oak," "yew," "willow," "spruce," "alder," "ash." The evidence is not equally conclusive for each tree name; my arrangement follows the decreasing certainty. Yet in each case at least a possibility can be established, as it cannot in the case of tree names such as "cypress," "palm" and "olive."

Of the tree names the most important for our purposes is "beech." Since the beech does not grow east of a line that runs roughly from Königsberg (now Kaliningrad) on the Baltic Sea to Odessa on the northwestern shore of the Black Sea, we must conclude that the Indo-Europeans lived in Europe rather than in Asia. Scandinavia can be ruled out because we know that the beech was imported there rather late. A likely district would be the northern part of Middle Europe, say the territory between the Vistula and Elbe rivers. It is here that even now the densest accumulation of Indo-European languages is found—languages belonging to the eastern group (Baltic and Slavonic) side by side with one of the western group (German).

That the Indo-Europeans came from this region is indicated by the animal names we can reconstruct, all of them characteristic of the region. We do not find words for "tiger," "elephant," "camel," "lion" or "leopard." We can, however, compile a bestiary that includes "wolf," "bear," "lynx," "eagle," "falcon," "owl," "crane," "thrush," "goose," "duck," "turtle," "salmon," "otter," "beaver," "fly," "hornet," "wasp," "bee" (inferred from words for "honey"), "louse" and "flea." We also find words for domesticated animals: "dog," "cattle," "sheep," "pig," "goat" and perhaps "horse." Some of these words are particularly significant. The turtle, like the beech, did not occur north of Germany in prehistoric times.

THE IMPORTANCE OF THE SALMON

It is the Indo-European word for "salmon" that most strongly supports the argument. Of all the regions where trees and animals familiar to the Indo-Europeans live, and the regions from which the Indo-Europeans could possibly have started the migrations that spread their tongue from Ireland to India, it is only along the rivers that flow into the Baltic and North seas that this particular fish could have been known. Coming from the South Atlantic, the salmon ascends these rivers in huge shoals to spawn in their upper reaches. The fish are easy to catch, and lovely to watch as they leap over obstacles in streams. Without the fat-rich food provided by the domesticated pig and the salmon, a people living in this rather cold region could hardly have grown so strong and numerous that their migration became both a necessity and a success.

The Indo-European word for "salmon" *(laks-)* survives in the original sense where the fish still occurs: Russia, the Baltic countries, Scandinavia and Germany (it is the familiar "lox" of Jewish delicatessens). In the Celtic tongues another word has replaced it; the Celts, migrating to the West, encountered the Rhine salmon, which they honored with a new name because it is even more delectable than the Baltic variety. The Italic languages, Greek and the southern Slavonic tongues, spoken where there are no salmon, soon lost the word. In some other languages it is preserved, but with altered meaning: in Ossetic, an Iranian language spoken in the Caucasus, the word means a large kind of trout, and the Tocharian-speaking people of eastern Turkestan used it for fish in general.

Several Sanskrit words echo the importance of the salmon in Indo-European history. One, *laksha,* means "a great amount" or "100,000," in which sense it has entered Hindustani and British English with the expression "a lakh of rupees." The assumption that the Sanskrit *laksha* descends from the Indo-European *laks-* of course requires an additional hypothesis: that a word meaning "salmon" or "salmon-shoal" continued to be used in the sense of "a great amount" long after the Indo-European immigrants to India had forgotten the fish itself. There are many analogies for a development of this kind. All over the world the names of things that are notable for their quantity or density tend to designate large numbers. Thus in Iranian "beehive" is used for 10,000; in Egyptian "tadpole" (which appears in great numbers after the flood of the Nile) is used for 100,000; in Chinese "ant," for 10,000; in Semitic languages "cattle," for 100; in Sanskrit and Egyptian "lotus" (which covers lakes and swamps), for "large number." Several words in Sanskrit for "sea" also refer to large numbers. In this connection we may recall the words in *Hamlet:* ". . . to take arms against a sea of troubles, and by opposing end them."

A second Sanskrit word that I believe is a descendant of the Indo-European *laks-* is *lākshā,* which the dictionary defines as "the dark-red resinous incrustation produced on certain trees by the puncture of an insect *(Coccus lacca)* and used as a scarlet dye." This is the word from which come the English "lac" and "lacquer." *Lākshā,* in my opinion, was originally an adjective derived from the Indo-European *laks-,* meaning "of or like a salmon." A characteristic feature of the salmon is the red color of its flesh. "Salmonlike" could easily develop into "red," and this adjective could be used to designate "the red (substance)," *i.e.,* "lac."

There is even a third possible offshoot: the Sanskrit *laksha* meaning "gambling stake" or "prize." This may be derived from a word that meant "salmon-catch." The apparent boldness of this conjecture may be vindicated on two counts. First, we have another Indo-European gambling word that originally was an animal name. Exact correspondences of Greek, Latin and Sanskrit show that the Indo-Europeans knew a kind of gambling with dice, in which the most unlucky throw was called the "dog." Second, in Sanskrit the gambling stake can be designated by another word, a plural noun *(vijas)* whose primary meaning was "the leapers." The possibility that this is another old word for "salmon," which was later used in the same restricted sense as *laksha,* is rather obvious.

By a lucky accident, then, Sanskrit, spoken by people who cannot have preserved any knowledge of the salmon itself, retains traces of Indo-European words for "salmon." Taken together, these words present a singularly clear picture of the salmon's outstanding traits. It is the fish that appears in big shoals (the Sanskrit *laksha,* meaning "100,000"); that overcomes obstacles by leaping (the Sanskrit *vijas,* meaning "leapers," and later "stake"); that has red flesh *(lākshā,* meaning "lac"); that is caught as a prized food *(vijas* and *laksha,* meaning "stake" or "prize").

THE AGE OF THE LANGUAGE

If we establish the home of our reconstructed language as lying between the Vistula and the Elbe, we may venture to speculate as to the time when it was spoken. According to archaeological evidence, the domesticated horse and goat did not appear there much before 3000 B.C. The other domesticated animals for which we have linguistic evidence are archaeologically demonstrable in an earlier period. Indo-European, I conjecture, was spoken on the Baltic coast of Germany late in the fourth millennium B.C. Since our oldest documents of Indo-European daughter languages (in Asia Minor and India) date from the second millennium B.C., the end of the fourth millennium would be a likely time anyhow. A thousand or 1,500 years are a time sufficiently long for the development of the changes that distinguish our oldest Sanskrit speech form from what we reconstruct as Indo-European.

Here is an old Lithuanian proverb which a Protestant minister translated into Latin in 1625 to show the similarity of Lithuanian to Latin. The proverb means "God gave the teeth; God will also give bread." In Lithuanian it reads: *Dievas dawe dantis; Dievas duos ir duonos.* The Latin version is *Deus dedit dentes; Deus dabit et panem.* Translated into an old form of Sanskrit, it would be *Devas adadāt datas; Devas dāt* (or *dadāt*) *api dhānās.* How would this same sentence sound in the reconstructed Indo-European language? A defensible guess would be: *Deivos ededōt dntns; Deivos dedōt* (or *dōt*) *dhōnās.*

═══

FOR DISCUSSION AND REVIEW

1. What do Filippo Sassetti and Sir William Jones have in common?
2. Thieme states that "a crucial word" in Sir William Jones's 1786 statement is *roots.* Explain (a) why this is so and (b) why the work of Pānini has been so important to historical linguists.
3. Summarize what the Indo-European vocabulary tells us about the way its speakers lived.
4. According to Thieme, where was the original Indo-European homeland? What evidence does he use to support this conclusion? Find this area on a map. In what country or countries is it now located?
5. The following are reconstructed Indo-European roots (as indicated by the asterisks) from which English words and words in cognate languages have developed: *māter-, *agh-, *eis-, *nekwt-, *dhē-, *kwon-. Identify one English word and at least one cognate word in a contemporary language that have developed from each of these roots. (Note: You will find *The American Heritage Dictionary* especially useful in doing this exercise.)

37

Relationships of Some Indo-European Languages with Detail of English Dialects

Jeanne H. Herndon

The Indo-European family of languages, of which English is a member, is descended from a prehistoric language, Proto-Indo-European, or Indo-European, which was probably spoken in the fourth millennium B.C. in a region that has not been positively identified. However, we have been able, through the comparative method, to learn a great deal about the phonology, morphology, syntax, and semantics of Indo-European, and — because language is an aspect of culture — about the kind of society that its speakers created. The following chart lists the principal branches of the Indo-European family and indicates the new languages that developed in each branch. The branches of Indo-European that are still represented today by one or more living languages are Celtic, Germanic, Italic, Hellenic, Balto-Slavic, Armenian, Albanian, and Indo-Iranian. In the lower left-hand corner of the chart, note the list of the various dialects of Old English (i.e., Mercian, Northumbrian, Kentish, and West Saxon) and the development of Mercian into some dialects of Middle English, Early Modern English, and finally Modern English.

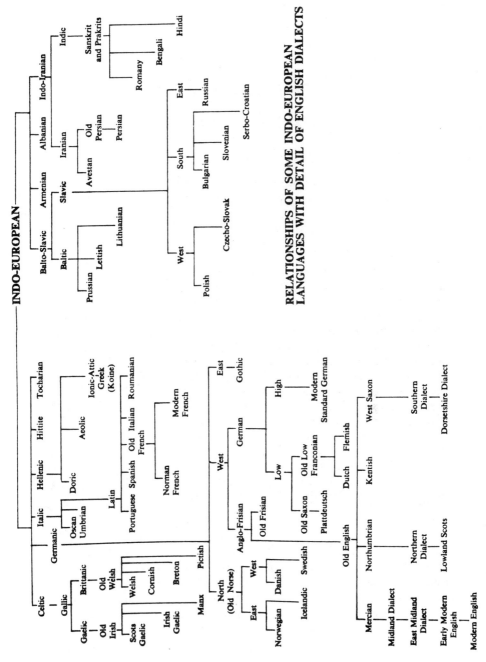

RELATIONSHIPS OF SOME INDO-EUROPEAN
LANGUAGES WITH DETAIL OF ENGLISH DIALECTS

FIGURE 37.1

38

A Brief History
of English

Paul Roberts

Earlier selections in this part have discussed how the existence of the Proto-Indo-European language was established through historical reconstruction, and have described the major branches of that language family. In this selection, the late Paul Roberts narrows the focus still more and traces briefly the history of the English language. He places its development in the context of historical events, showing their effects on the language. In general, the grammatical changes from Old English to Modern English have resulted in a change from a synthetic or highly inflected language (like Latin or Russian) to an analytic language, with few inflectional endings and heavy reliance on word order and function words to signal grammatical meaning. Roberts also discusses some of the major changes in pronunciation and vocabulary from Old English through Middle English to Modern English, commenting especially on the effects of the Great Vowel Shift and on the borrowing of large numbers of foreign words that increased the size of the English vocabulary.

No understanding of the English language can be very satisfactory without a notion of the history of the language. But we shall have to make do with just a notion. The history of English is long and complicated, and we can only hit the high spots.

The history of our language begins a little after A.D. 600. Everything before that is pre-history, which means that we can guess at it but can't prove much. For a thousand years or so before the birth of Christ our linguistic ancestors were savages wandering through the forests of northern Europe. Their language was a part of the Germanic branch of the Indo-European Family (see the previous selection).

At the time of the Roman Empire — say, from the beginning of the Christian Era to around A.D. 400 — the speakers of what was to become English were scattered along the northern coast of Europe. They spoke a dialect of Low German. More exactly, they spoke several different dialects, since they were several different tribes. The names given to the tribes who got to England are *Angles, Saxons,* and *Jutes*. For convenience, we can refer to them as Anglo-Saxons.

Their first contact with civilization was a rather thin acquaintance with the Roman Empire on whose borders they lived. Probably some of the Anglo-Saxons wandered into the Empire occasionally, and certainly Roman merchants and traders traveled among the tribes. At any rate, this period saw the first of our many borrowings from Latin. Such words as *kettle, wine, cheese, butter, cheap, plum, gem, bishop, church* were borrowed at this time. They show something of the relationship of the Anglo-Saxons with the Romans. The Anglo-Saxons were learning, getting their first taste of civilization.

They still had a long way to go, however, and their first step was to help smash the civilization they were learning from. In the fourth century the Roman power weakened badly. While the Goths were pounding away at the Romans in the Mediterranean countries, their relatives, the Anglo-Saxons, began to attack Britain.

The Romans had been the ruling power in Britain since A.D. 43. They had subjugated the Celts whom they found living there and had succeeded in setting up a Roman administration. The Roman influence did not extend to the outlying parts of the British Isles. In Scotland, Wales, and Ireland the Celts remained free and wild, and they made periodic forays against the Romans in England. Among other defense measures, the Romans built the famous Roman Wall to ward off the tribes in the north.

Even in England the Roman power was thin. Latin did not become the language of the country as it did in Gaul and Spain. The mass of people continued to speak Celtic, with Latin and the Roman civilization it contained in use as a top dressing.

In the fourth century, troubles multiplied for the Romans in Britain. Not only did the untamed tribes of Scotland and Wales grow more and more restive, but the Anglo-Saxons began to make pirate raids on the eastern coast. Furthermore, there was growing difficulty everywhere in the Empire, and the legions in Britain were siphoned off to fight elsewhere. Finally, in A.D. 410, the last Roman ruler in England, bent on becoming emperor, left the islands and took the last of the legions with him. The Celts were left in possession of Britain but almost defenseless against the impending Anglo-Saxon attack.

Not much is surely known about the arrival of the Anglo-Saxons in England. According to the best early source, the eighth-century historian Bede, the Jutes came in 449 in response to a plea from the Celtic king, Vortigern, who wanted their help against the Picts attacking from the north. The Jutes subdued the Picts but then quarreled and fought with Vortigern, and, with reinforcements from the Continent, settled permanently in Kent. Somewhat later the Angles established themselves in eastern England and the Saxons in the south and west. Bede's account is plausible enough, and these were probably the main lines of the invasion.

We do know, however, that the Angles, Saxons, and Jutes were a long time securing themselves in England. Fighting went on for as long as a hundred years before the Celts in England were all killed, driven into

Wales, or reduced to slavery. This is the period of King Arthur, who was not entirely mythological. He was a Romanized Celt, a general, though probably not a king. He had some success against the Anglo-Saxons, but it was only temporary. By 550 or so the Anglo-Saxons were firmly established. English was in England.

OLD ENGLISH

All this is pre-history, so far as the language is concerned. We have no record of the English language until after 600, when the Anglo-Saxons were converted to Christianity and learned the Latin alphabet. The conversion began, to be precise, in the year 597 and was accomplished within thirty or forty years. The conversion was a great advance for the Anglo-Saxons, not only because of the spiritual benefits but because it reestablished contact with what remained of Roman civilization. This civilization didn't amount to much in the year 600, but it was certainly superior to anything in England up to that time.

It is customary to divide the history of the English language into three periods: Old English, Middle English, and Modern English. Old English runs from the earliest records—i.e., seventh century—to about 1100; Middle English from 1100 to 1450 or 1500; Modern English from 1500 to the present day. Sometimes Modern English is further divided into Early Modern, 1500–1700, and Late Modern, 1700 to the present.

When England came into history, it was divided into several more or less autonomous kingdoms, some of which at times exercised a certain amount of control over the others. In the century after the conversion the most advanced kingdom was Northumbria, the area between the Humber River and the Scottish border. By A.D. 700 the Northumbrians had developed a respectable civilization, the finest in Europe. It is sometimes called the Northumbrian Renaissance, and it was the first of the several renaissances through which Europe struggled upward out of the ruins of the Roman Empire. It was in this period that the best of the Old English literature was written, including the epic poem *Beowulf.*

In the eighth century, Northumbrian power declined, and the center of influence moved southward to Mercia, the kingdom of the Midlands. A century later the center shifted again, and Wessex, the country of the West Saxons, became the leading power. The most famous king of the West Saxons was Alfred the Great, who reigned in the second half of the ninth century, dying in 901. He was famous not only as a military man and administrator but also as a champion of learning. He founded and supported schools and translated or caused to be translated many books from Latin into English. At this time also much of the Northumbrian literature of two centuries earlier was copied in West Saxon. Indeed, the great bulk of Old English writing which has come down to us is in the West Saxon dialect of 900 or later.

In the military sphere, Alfred's great accomplishment was his successful opposition to the viking invasions. In the ninth and tenth centuries, the Norsemen emerged in their ships from their homelands in Denmark and the Scandinavian peninsula. They traveled far and attacked and plundered at will and almost with impunity. They ravaged Italy and Greece, settled in France, Russia, and Ireland, colonized Iceland and Greenland, and discovered America several centuries before Columbus. Nor did they overlook England.

After many years of hit-and-run raids, the Norsemen landed an army on the east coast of England in the year 866. There was nothing much to oppose them except the Wessex power led by Alfred. The long struggle ended in 877 with a treaty by which a line was drawn roughly from the northwest of England to the southeast. On the eastern side of the line Norse rule was to prevail. This was called the Danelaw. The western side was to be governed by Wessex.

The linguistic result of all this was a considerable injection of Norse into the English language. Norse was at this time not so different from English as Norwegian or Danish is now. Probably speakers of English could understand, more or less, the language of the newcomers who had moved into eastern England. At any rate, there was considerable interchange and word borrowing. Examples of Norse words in the English language are *sky, give, law, egg, outlaw, leg, ugly, scant, sly, crawl, scowl, take, thrust.* There are hundreds more. We have even borrowed some pronouns from Norse — *they, their,* and *them.* These words were borrowed first by the eastern and northern dialects and then in the course of hundreds of years made their way into English generally.

It is supposed also — indeed, it must be true — that the Norsemen influenced the sound structure and the grammar of English. But this is hard to demonstrate in detail.

A Specimen of Old English

We may now have an example of Old English. The favorite illustration is the Lord's Prayer, since it needs no translation. This has come to us in several different versions. Here is one:

Fæder ure,
þu þe eart on heofonum,
si þin nama gehalgod.
Tobecume þin rice.
Gewurþe ðin willa on eorðan swa swa on heofonum.
Urne gedœghwamlican hlaf syle us to dæg.
And forgyf us ure gyltas, swa swa we forgyfað urum gyltendum.
And ne gelæd þu us on costnunge,
ac alys us of yfele. Soþlice.

Some of the differences between this and Modern English are merely differences in orthography. For instance, the sign æ is what Old English writers used for a vowel sound like that in modern *hat* or *and*. The *th* sounds of modern *thin* or *then* are represented in Old English by þ or ð. But of course there are many differences in sound too. *Ure* is the ancestor of modern *our*, but the first vowel was like that in *too* or *ooze*. *Hlaf* is modern *loaf*; we have dropped the *h* sound and changed the vowel, which in *hlaf* was pronounced something like the vowel in *father*. Old English had some sounds which we do not have. The sound represented by *y* does not occur in Modern English. If you pronounce the vowel in *bit* with your lips rounded, you may approach it.

In grammar, Old English was much more highly inflected than Modern English is. That is, there were more case endings for nouns, more person and number endings for verbs, a more complicated pronoun system, various endings for adjectives, and so on. Old English nouns had four cases — nominative, genitive, dative, accusative. Adjectives had five — all these and an instrumental case besides. Present-day English has only two cases for nouns — common case and possessive case. Adjectives now have no case system at all. On the other hand, we now use a more rigid word order and more structure words (prepositions, auxiliaries, and the like) to express relationships than Old English did.

Some of this grammar we can see in the Lord's Prayer. *Heofonum*, for instance, is a dative plural; the nominative singular was *heofon*. *Urne* is an accusative singular; the nominative is *ure*. In *urum gyltendum* both words are dative plural. *Forgyfaþ* is the first person plural form of the verb. Word order is different: "urne gedæghwamlican hlaf syle us" in place of "Give us our daily bread." And so on.

In vocabulary Old English is quite different from Modern English. Most of the Old English words are what we may call native English: that is, words which have not been borrowed from other languages but which have been a part of English ever since English was a part of Indo-European. Old English did certainly contain borrowed words. We have seen that many borrowings were coming in from Norse. Rather large numbers had been borrowed from Latin, too. Some of these were taken while the Anglo-Saxons were still on the Continent (*cheese, butter, bishop, kettle*, etc.); a large number came into English after the conversion (*angel, candle, priest, martyr, radish, oyster, purple, school, spend*, etc.). But the great majority of Old English words were native English.

Now, on the contrary, the majority of words in English are borrowed, taken mostly from Latin and French. Of the words in *The American College Dictionary* only about 14 percent are native. Most of these, to be sure, are common, high-frequency words — *the, of, I, and, because, man, mother, road*, etc.; of the thousand most common words in English, some 62 percent are native English. Even so, the modern vocabulary is very much Latinized and Frenchified. The Old English vocabulary was not.

MIDDLE ENGLISH

Sometime between the years 1000 and 1200 various important changes took place in the structure of English, and Old English became Middle English. The political event which facilitated these changes was the Norman Conquest. The Normans, as the name shows, came originally from Scandinavia. In the early tenth century they established themselves in northern France, adopted the French language, and developed a vigorous kingdom and a very passable civilization. In the year 1066, led by Duke William, they crossed the Channel and made themselves masters of England. For the next several hundred years, England was ruled by kings whose first language was French.

One might wonder why, after the Norman Conquest, French did not become the national language, replacing English entirely. The reason is that the Conquest was not a national migration, as the earlier Anglo-Saxon invasion had been. Great numbers of Normans came to England, but they came as rulers and landlords. French became the language of the court, the language of the nobility, the language of polite society, the language of literature. But it did not replace English as the language of the people. There must always have been hundreds of towns and villages in which French was never heard except when visitors of high station passed through.

But English, though it survived as the national language, was profoundly changed after the Norman Conquest. Some of the changes — in sound structure and grammar — would no doubt have taken place whether there had been a Conquest or not. Even before 1066 the case system of English nouns and adjectives was becoming simplified; people came to rely more on word order and prepositions than on inflectional endings to communicate their meanings. The process was speeded up by sound changes which caused many of the endings to sound alike. But no doubt the Conquest facilitated the change. German, which didn't experience a Norman Conquest, is today rather highly inflected compared to its cousin English.

But it is in vocabulary that the effects of the Conquest are most obvious. French ceased, after a hundred years or so, to be the native language of very many people in England, but it continued — and continues still — to be a zealously cultivated second language, the mirror of elegance and civilization. When one spoke English, one introduced not only French ideas and French things but also their French names. This was not only easy but socially useful. To pepper one's conversation with French expressions was to show that one was well-bred, elegant, *au courant*. The last sentence shows that the process is not yet dead. By using *au courant* instead of, say, *abreast of things*, the writer indicates that he is no dull clod who knows only English but an elegant person aware of how things are done in *le haut monde*.

Thus French words came into English, all sorts of them. There were words to do with government: *parliament, majesty, treaty, alliance, tax, government;* church words: *parson, sermon, baptism, incense, crucifix, religion;* words for foods: *veal, beef, mutton, bacon, jelly, peach, lemon, cream, biscuit;* colors: *blue, scarlet, vermilion;* household words: *curtain, chair, lamp, towel, blanket, parlor;* play words: *dance, chess, music, leisure, conversation;* literary words: *story, romance, poet, literary;* learned words: *study, logic, grammar, noun, surgeon, anatomy, stomach;* just ordinary words of all sorts: *nice, second, very, age, bucket, gentle, final, fault, flower, cry, count, sure, move, surprise, plain.*

All these and thousands more poured into the English vocabulary between 1100 and 1500 until, at the end of that time, many people must have had more French words than English at their command. This is not to say that English became French. English remained English in sound structure and in grammar, though these also felt the ripples of French influence. The very heart of the vocabulary, too, remained English. Most of the high-frequency words—the pronouns, the prepositions, the conjunctions, the auxiliaries, as well as a great many ordinary nouns and verbs and adjectives—were not replaced by borrowings.

Middle English, then, was still a Germanic language, but it differed from Old English in many ways. The sound system and the grammar changed a good deal. Speakers made less use of case systems and other inflectional devices and relied more on word order and structure words to express their meanings. This is often said to be a simplification, but it isn't really. Languages don't become simpler; they merely exchange one kind of complexity for another. Modern English is not a simple language, as any foreign speaker who tries to learn it will hasten to tell you.

For us Middle English is simpler than Old English just because it is closer to Modern English. It takes three or four months at least to learn to read Old English prose and more than that for poetry. But a week of good study should put one in touch with the Middle English poet Chaucer. Indeed, you may be able to make some sense of Chaucer straight off, though you would need instruction in pronunciation to make it sound like poetry. Here is a famous passage from the *General Prologue to the Canterbury Tales,* fourteenth century:

> Ther was also a nonne, a Prioresse,
> That of hir smyling was ful symple and coy,
> Hir gretteste oath was but by Seinte Loy,
> And she was cleped Madame Eglentyne.
> Ful wel she song the service dyvyne,
> Entuned in hir nose ful semely.
> And Frenshe she spak ful faire and fetisly,
> After the scole of Stratford-atte-Bowe,
> For Frenshe of Parys was to hir unknowe.

EARLY MODERN ENGLISH

Sometime between 1400 and 1600 English underwent a couple of sound changes which made the language of Shakespeare quite different from that of Chaucer. Incidentally, these changes contributed much to the chaos in which English spelling now finds itself.

One change was the elimination of a vowel sound in certain unstressed positions at the end of words. For instance, the words *name, stone, wine, dance* were pronounced as two syllables by Chaucer but as just one by Shakespeare. The *e* in these words became, as we say, "silent." But it wasn't silent for Chaucer; it represented a vowel sound. So also the words *laughed, seemed, stored* would have been pronounced by Chaucer as two-syllable words. The change was an important one because it affected thousands of words and gave a different aspect to the whole language.

The other change is what is called the Great Vowel Shift. This was a systematic shifting of half a dozen vowels and diphthongs in stressed syllables. For instance, the word *name* had in Middle English a vowel something like that in the modern word *father; wine* had the vowel of modern *mean; he* was pronounced something like modern *hey; mouse* sounded like *moose; moon* had the vowel of *moan.* Again the shift was thoroughgoing and affected all the words in which these vowel sounds occurred. Since we still keep the Middle English system of spelling these words, the differences between Modern English and Middle English are often more real than apparent.

The vowel shift has meant also that we have come to use an entirely different set of symbols for representing vowel sounds than is used by writers of such languages as French, Italian, or Spanish, in which no such vowel shift occurred. If you come across a strange word — say, *bine* — in an English book, you will pronounce it according to the English system, with the vowel of *wine* or *dine.* But if you read *bine* in a French, Italian, or Spanish book, you will pronounce it with the vowel of *mean* or *seen.*

These two changes, then, produced the basic differences between Middle English and Modern English. But there were several other developments that had an effect upon the language. One was the invention of printing, an invention introduced into England by William Caxton in the year 1475. Where before books had been rare and costly, they suddenly became cheap and common. More and more people learned to read and write. This was the first of many advances in communication which have worked to unify languages and to arrest the development of dialect differences, though of course printing affects writing principally rather than speech. Among other things it hastened the standardization of spelling.

The period of Early Modern English — that is, the sixteenth and seventeenth centuries — was also the period of the English Renaissance, when people developed, on the one hand, a keen interest in the past and, on the other hand, a more daring and imaginative view of the future. New ideas multiplied, and new ideas meant new language. Englishmen had grown accustomed to borrowing words from French as a result of the Norman Conquest; now they borrowed from Latin and Greek. As we have seen, English had been raiding Latin from Old English times and before, but now the floodgates really opened, and thousands of words from the classical languages poured in. *Pedestrian, bonus, anatomy, contradict, climax, dictionary, benefit, multiply, exist, paragraph, initiate, scene, inspire* are random examples. Probably the average educated American today has more words from French in his vocabulary than from native English sources, and more from Latin than from French.

The greatest writer of the Early Modern English period is of course Shakespeare, and the best-known book is the King James Version of the Bible, published in 1611. The Bible (if not Shakespeare) has made many features of Early Modern English perfectly familiar to many people down to present time, even though we do not use these features in present-day speech and writing. For instance, the old pronouns *thou* and *thee* have dropped out of use now, together with their verb forms, but they are still familiar to us in prayer and in Biblical quotations: "Whither thou goest, I will go." Such forms as *hath* and *doth* have been replaced by *has* and *does;* "Goes he hence tonight?" would now be "Is he going away tonight?"; Shakespeare's "Fie, on't, sirrah" would be "Nuts to that, Mac." Still, all these expressions linger with us because of the power of the works in which they occur.

It is not always realized, however, that considerable sound changes have taken place between Early Modern English and the English of the present day. Shakespearian actors putting on a play speak the words, properly enough, in their modern pronunciation. But it is very doubtful that this pronunciation would be understood at all by Shakespeare. In Shakespeare's time, the word *reason* was pronounced like modern *raisin; face* had the sound of modern *glass;* the *l* in *would, should, palm* was pronounced. In these points and a great many others the English language has moved a long way from what it was in 1600.

RECENT DEVELOPMENTS

The history of English since 1700 is filled with many movements and countermovements, of which we can notice only a couple. One of these is the vigorous attempt made in the eighteenth century, and the rather half-hearted attempts made since, to regulate and control the English language. Many people of the eighteenth century, not understanding very well the forces which govern language, proposed to polish and prune and restrict English, which they felt was proliferating too wildly. There was much talk of an academy which would rule on what people could and could not say and write. The academy never came into being, but the eighteenth century did succeed in establishing certain attitudes which, though they haven't had much effect on the development of the language itself, have certainly changed the native speaker's feeling about the language.

In part, a product of the wish to fix and establish the language was the development of the dictionary. The first English dictionary was published in 1603; it was a list of 2,500 words briefly defined. Many others were published with gradual improvements until Samuel Johnson published his *English Dictionary* in 1755. This, steadily revised, dominated the field in England for nearly a hundred years. Meanwhile in America, Noah Webster published his dictionary in 1828, and before long dictionary publishing was a big business in this country. The last century has seen the publication of one great dictionary: the twelve-volume *Oxford English Dictionary,* compiled in the course of seventy-five years through the labors of many scholars. We have also, of course, numerous commercial dictionaries which are as good as the public wants them to be if not, indeed, rather better.

Another product of the eighteenth century was the invention of "English grammar." As English came to replace Latin as the language of scholarship, it was felt that one should also be able to control and dissect it, parse and analyze it, as one could Latin. What happened in practice was that the grammatical description that applied to Latin was removed and superimposed on English. This was silly, because English is an entirely different kind of language, with its own forms and signals and ways of producing meaning. Nevertheless, English grammars on the Latin model were worked out and taught in the schools. In many schools they are still being taught. This activity is not often popular with schoolchildren, but it is sometimes an interesting and instructive exercise in logic. The principal harm in it is that it has tended to keep people from being interested in English and has obscured the real features of English structure.

But probably the most important force on the development of English in the modern period has been the tremendous expansion of English-speaking peoples. In 1500 English was a minor language, spoken by a few people on a small island. Now it is perhaps the greatest language of the world, spoken natively by over a quarter of a billion people and as a second language by many millions more. When we speak of English now, we must specify whether we mean American English, British English, Australian English, Indian English, or what, since the differences are considerable. The American cannot go to England or the Englishman to America confident that he will always understand and be understood. The Alabaman in Iowa or the Iowan in Alabama shows himself a foreigner every time he speaks. It is only because communication has become fast and easy that English in this period of its expansion has not broken into a dozen mutually unintelligible languages.

FOR DISCUSSION AND REVIEW

1. Roberts describes in some detail the relationships between historical events in England and the development of the English language. Sum-

marize the most important events and comment on their relationship to or effect on the English language.

2. What are the three major periods in the history of English? What are the approximate dates of each? On what bases do linguists make these distinctions?

3. During what period was the epic poem *Beowulf* written? Does Roberts suggest why this period was propitious for the creation of such a work?

4. How did the pronouns *they, their,* and *them* come into English? What is unusual about this occurrence?

5. List four important ways in which the grammar of Old English differed from that of Modern English. What was the principal difference between the vocabulary of Old English and that of Modern English?

6. When the Anglo-Saxons invaded England, their language became the language of the land, almost completely obliterating the Celtic which had been spoken by the earlier inhabitants. How do you account for the fact that French did not become the language of England after the Norman Conquest? Explain Roberts's statement that "English . . . was profoundly changed after the Norman Conquest."

7. How would you characterize in social terms the French words that were brought into English by the Norman Conquest? In what areas of life did French have the greatest influence?

8. Describe the changes the English language underwent as a result of the Great Vowel Shift. What is the importance of this linguistic phenomenon for modern English?

9. Identify two significant effects that the invention of printing had on the English language.

10. Early English grammars — indeed, almost all English grammars published before 1950 — were modeled on Latin grammars. Why was this the case? List four of the erroneous assumptions included in these Latin-based grammars.

39

Language Change: Progress or Decay?

Jean Aitchison

In this chapter from her book Language Change, *Professor Jean Aitchison of the London School of Economics asserts that language change is "natural, inevitable and continuous, and involves interwoven sociolinguistic and psycholinguistic factors which cannot easily be disentangled from one another." It is not, she points out, in any sense "wrong for human language to change." In view of these facts, Professor Aitchison raises three questions: "First, is it still relevant to speak of [language] progress or decay? Secondly, irrespective of whether the move is a forwards or backwards one, are human languages evolving in any detectable direction? Thirdly, even though language change is not wrong in the moral sense, is it socially undesirable, and, if so, can we control it?" In the following pages, she describes the difficulties of answering these questions and suggests some reasonable answers: (1) language is constantly changing, but it is neither progressing nor decaying; (2) languages are slowly changing (not "evolving" in the usual sense of the word) in different—indeed, sometimes opposite—directions; (3) language change is not wrong, but it may sometimes lead to situations in which speakers of different dialects of the same language have difficulty understanding one another; and (4) although it is impossible to halt such change by passing laws or establishing monitoring "academies," careful language planning can often help.*

> If you can look into the seeds of time,
> And say which grain will grow and which will not. . . .
> —WILLIAM SHAKESPEARE, *Macbeth*

Predicting the future depends on understanding the present. The majority of [the many objectors to language change, from the purists of the eighteenth century to today's self-proclaimed experts,] had not considered the complexity of the factors involved in language change. They were giving rise to a purely emotional expression of their hopes and fears.

A closer look at language change [indicates] that it is natural, inevitable and continuous, and involves interwoven sociolinguistic and psycholinguistic factors which cannot easily be disentangled from one another.

It is triggered by social factors, but these social factors make use of existing cracks and gaps in the language structure. In the circumstances, the true direction of a change is not obvious to a superficial observer. Sometimes alterations are disruptive, as with the increasing loss of *t* in British English, where the utilization of a natural tendency to alter or omit final consonants may end up destroying a previously stable stop system. At other times, modifications can be viewed as therapy, as in the loss of *h* in British English, which is wiping out an exception in the otherwise symmetrical organization of fricatives.

However, whether changes disrupt the language system, or repair it, the most important point is this: it is in no sense wrong for human language to change, any more than it is wrong for humpback whales to alter their songs every year (Payne, 1979). In fact, there are some surprising parallels between the two species. All the whales sing the same song one year, the next year they all sing a new one. But the yearly differences are not random. The songs seem to be evolving. The songs of consecutive years are more alike than those that are separated by several years. When it was first discovered that the songs of humpbacks changed from year to year, a simple explanation seemed likely. Since the whales only sing during the breeding season, and since their song is complex, it was assumed that they simply forgot the song between seasons, and then tried to reconstruct it the next year from fragments which remained in their memory. But when researchers organized a long-term study of humpbacks off the island of Maui in Hawaii, they got a surprise. The song that the whales were singing at the beginning of the new breeding season turned out to be identical to the one used at the end of the previous one. Between breeding seasons, the song had seemingly been kept in cold storage, without change. The songs were gradually modified as the season proceeded. For example, new sequences were sometimes created by joining the beginning and end of consecutive phrases, and omitting the middle part — a procedure not unlike certain human language changes.

Both whales and humans, then, are constantly changing their communication system, and are the only two species in which this has been proved to happen — though some birds are now thought to alter their song in certain ways. Rather than castigating one of these species for allowing change to occur, it seems best to admit that humans are probably programmed by nature to behave in this way. As a character in John Wyndham's novel *Web* says: "Man is a product of nature. . . . Whatever he does, it must be part of his nature to do — or he could not do it. He is not, and cannot be *un*natural. He, with his capacities, is as much the product of nature as were the dinosaurs with theirs. He is an *instrument* of natural processes."

A consideration of the naturalness and inevitability of change leads us to . . . three final questions which need to be discussed. . . . First, is it still relevant to speak of progress or decay? Secondly, irrespective of whether the move is a forwards or backwards one, are human languages evolving in any detectable direction? Thirdly, even though language change is not wrong in the moral sense, is it socially undesirable, and, if so, can we control it? . . .

FORWARDS OR BACKWARDS?

"Once, twice, thrice upon a time, there lived a jungle. This particular jungle started at the bottom and went upwards till it reached the monkeys, who had been waiting years for the trees to reach them, and as soon as they did, the monkeys invented climbing down." The opening paragraph of Spike Milligan's fable, *The Story of the Bald Twit Lion*, indicates how easy it is to make facts fit one's preferred theory.

This tendency is particularly apparent in past interpretations of the direction of change, where opinions about progress or decay in language have tended to reflect the religious or philosophical preconceptions of their proponents, rather than a detached analysis of the evidence. Let us briefly deal with these preconceptions before looking at the issue itself.

Many nineteenth-century scholars were imbued with sentimental ideas about the "noble savage," and assumed that the current generation was by comparison a race of decadent sinners. They therefore took it for granted that language had declined from a former state of perfection. Restoring this early perfection was viewed as one of the principal goals of comparative historical linguistics: "A principal goal of this science is to reconstruct the full, pure forms of an original stage from the variously disfigured and mutilated forms which are attested in the individual languages," said one scholar (Curtius, 1871, in Kiparsky, 1972: 35).

This quasireligious conviction of gradual decline has never entirely died out. But from the mid-nineteenth century onward, a second, opposing viewpoint came into existence alongside the earlier one. Darwin's doctrine of the survival of the fittest and ensuing belief in inevitable progress gradually grew in popularity: "Progress, therefore, is not an accident, but a necessity. . . . It is a part of nature," claimed one nineteenth-century enthusiast (Herbert Spencer, *Social Statics*, 1850). Darwin himself believed that in language "the better, the shorter, the easier forms are constantly gaining the upper hand, and they owe their success to their inherent virtue" (Darwin, 1871, in Labov, 1972: 273).

The doctrine of the survival of the fittest, in its crudest version, implies that those forms and languages which survive are inevitably better than those which die out. This is unfortunate, since it confuses the notions of progress and decay in language with expansion and decline. [But] expansion and decline reflect political and social situations, not the intrinsic merit or decadence of a language. For example, it is a historical accident that English is so widely spoken in the world. Throughout history, quite different types of language—Latin, Turkish, Chinese, for example—have spread over wide areas. This popularity reflects the military and political strength of these nations, not the worth of their speech. Similarly, Gaelic is dying out because it is being ousted by English, a language with social and political prestige. It is not collapsing because it has got too complicated or strange for people to speak, as has occasionally been maintained.

In order to assess the possible direction of language, then, we need to put aside both religious beliefs and Darwinian assumptions. The former leads to an illogical idealization of the past, and the latter to the confusion of progress and decay with expansion and decline.

Leaving aside these false trails, we are left with a crucial question: what might we mean by "progress" within language?

The term "progress" implies a movement towards some desired endpoint. What could this be, in terms of linguistic excellence? A number of linguists are in no doubt. They endorse the view of Jespersen, who maintained that "that language ranks highest which goes farthest in the art of accomplishing much with little means, or, in other words, which is able to express the greatest amount of meaning with the simplest mechanism" (Mühlhaüsler, 1979: 151).

If this criterion were taken seriously, we would be obliged to rank pidgins as the most advanced languages. . . . [However,] true simplicity seems to be counterbalanced by ambiguity and cumbersomeness. Darwin's confident belief in the "inherent virtue" of shorter and easier forms must be set beside the realization that such forms often result in confusing homonyms, as in the Tok Pisin *hat* for "hot," "hard," "hat," and "heart."

A straightforward simplicity measure then will not necessarily pinpoint the "best" language. A considerable number of other factors must be taken into account, and it is not yet clear which they are, and how they should be assessed. In brief, linguists have been unable to decide on any clear measure of excellence, even though the majority are of the opinion that a language with numerous irregularities should be less highly ranked than one which is economical and transparent. Note, however, that preliminary attempts to rank languages in this way have run into a further problem.

A language which is simple and regular in one respect is likely to be complex and confusing in others. There seems to be a trading relationship between the different parts of the grammar which we do not fully understand. This has come out clearly in the work of one researcher who has compared the progress of Turkish and Yugoslav children as they acquired their respective languages (Slobin, 1977). Turkish children find it exceptionally easy to learn the inflections of their language, which are remarkably straightforward, and they master the entire system by the age of two. But the youngsters struggle with relative clauses (the equivalent of English clauses beginning with *who, which, that*) until around the age of five. Yugoslav children, on the other hand, have great problems with the inflectional system of Serbo-Croatian, which is "a classic Indo-European synthetic muddle," and they are not competent at manipulating it until around the age of five. Yet, they have no problems with Serbo-Croatian relative clauses, which they can normally cope with by the age of two.

Overall, we cannot yet specify satisfactorily just what we mean by a "perfect" language, except in a very broad sense. The most we can do is to note that a certain part of one language may be simpler and therefore perhaps "better" than that of another.

Meanwhile, even if all agreed that a perfectly regular language was the "best," there is no evidence that languages are progressing towards this ultimate goal. Instead, there is a continuous pull between the disruption and restoration of patterns. In this perpetual ebb and flow, it would be a mistake to regard pattern neatening and regularization as a step forwards. Such an occurrence may be no more progressive than the tidying up of a cluttered office. Reorganization simply restores the room to a workable state. Similarly, it would be misleading to assume that pattern disruption was necessarily a backwards step. Structural dislocation may be the result of extending the language in some useful way.

We must conclude therefore that language is ebbing and flowing like the tide, but neither progressing nor decaying, as far as we can tell. Disruptive and therapeutic tendencies vie with one another, with neither one totally winning or losing, resulting in a perpetual stalemate. As the famous Russian linguist Roman Jakobson said fifty years ago: "The spirit of equilibrium and the simultaneous tendency towards its rupture constitute the indispensable properties of that whole that is language" (Jakobson, 1949: 336; translation in Keiler, 1972).

ARE LANGUAGES EVOLVING?

Leaving aside notions of progress and decay we need to ask one further question. Is there any evidence that languages as a whole are moving in any particular direction in their intrinsic structure? Are they, for example, moving towards a fixed word order, as has sometimes been claimed?

It is clear that languages, even if they are evolving in some identifiable way, are doing so very slowly—otherwise all languages would be rather more similar than they in fact are. However, unfortunately for those who would like to identify some overall drift, the languages of the world seem to be moving in different, often opposite, directions.

For example, over the past two thousand years or so, most Indo-European languages have moved from being SOV (subject-object-verb) languages, to SVO (subject-verb-object) ones. . . . Certain Niger-Congo languages seem to be following a similar path. Yet we cannot regard this as an overall trend, since Mandarin Chinese seems to be undergoing a change in the opposite direction, from SVO to SOV (Li and Thompson, 1974).

During the same period, English and a number of other Indo-European languages have gradually lost their inflections, and moved over to a fixed word order. However, this direction is not inevitable, since Wappo, a

Californian Indian language, appears to be doing the reverse, and moving from a system in which grammatical relationships are expressed by word order to one in which they are marked by case endings (Li and Thompson, 1976).

A similar variety is seen in the realm of phonology. For example, English, French and Hindi had the same common ancestor: nowadays, Hindi has sixteen stop consonants and ten vowels, according to one count. French, on the other hand, has sixteen vowels and six stops. English, meanwhile, has acquired more fricatives than either of these two languages, some of which speakers of French and Hindi find exceptionally difficult to pronounce. Many more such examples could be found.

Overall, then we must conclude that "the evolution of language as such has never been demonstrated, and the inherent equality of all languages must be maintained on present evidence" (Greenberg, 1957: 65).

IS LANGUAGE CHANGE SOCIALLY UNDESIRABLE?

Let us now turn to the last two questions. Is language change undesirable? If so, is it controllable?

Social undesirability and moral turpitude are often confused. Yet the two questions can quite often be kept distinct. For example, it is certainly not "wrong" to sleep out in the open. Nevertheless, it is fairly socially inconvenient to have people bedding down wherever they want to, and therefore laws have been passed forbidding people to camp out in, say, Trafalgar Square or Hyde Park in London.

Language change is, we have seen, in no sense wrong. But is it socially undesirable? It is only undesirable when communication gets disrupted. If different groups change a previously unified language in different directions, or if one group alters its speech more radically than another, mutual intelligibility may be impaired or even destroyed. In Tok Pisin, for example, speakers from rural areas have great difficulty in understanding the urbanized varieties. This is an unhappy and socially inconvenient state of affairs.

In England, on the other hand, the problem is minimal. There are relatively few speakers of British English who cannot understand one another. This is because most people speak the same basic dialect, in the sense that the rules underlying their utterances and vocabulary are fairly much the same. They are likely, however, to speak this single dialect with different accents. There is nothing wrong with this, as long as people can communicate satisfactorily with one another. An accent which differs markedly from those around may be hard for others to comprehend, and is therefore likely to be a disadvantage in job-hunting situations, as a number of recent immigrants have found. But a mild degree of regional variation is probably a mark of individuality to be encouraged rather than stamped out.

A number of people censure the variety of regional accents in England, maintaining that the accent that was originally of one particular area, London and the southeast, is "better" than the others. In fact, speakers from this locality sometimes claim that they speak English *without* an accent, something which is actually impossible. It is, of course, currently socially useful in England to be able to speak the accent of so-called Southern British English, an accent sometimes spoken of as Received Pronunciation (RP), which has spread to the educated classes throughout the country. But there is no logical reason behind the disapproval of regional accents. Moreover, such objections are by no means universal. In America, a regional accent is simply a mark of where you are from with no stigma attached, for the most part.

Accent differences, then, are not a matter of great concern. More worrying are instances where differing dialects cause unintelligibility, or misunderstandings. In the past, this often used to be the case in England. Caxton, writing in the fifteenth century, notes that "comynenglysshe that is spoken in one shyre varyeth from another" (Caxton, preface to *Erydos* [1490]). To illustrate his point, he narrates an episode concerning a ship which was stranded in the Thames for lack of wind, and put into shore for refreshment. One of the merchants on board went to a nearby house, and asked, in English, for meat and eggs. The lady of the house, much to this gentleman's indignation, replied that she could not speak French! In Caxton's words, the merchant "came in to an hows and axed for mete and specyally he axyd after eggys. And the goode wyf answerde that she coude speke no frenshe. And the marchaut was angry for he also coude speke no frenshe, but wolde haue, hadde egges and she vnderstode hym not." The problem in this case was that a "new" Norse word *egges* "eggs" was in the process of replacing the Old English word *eyren*, but was not yet generally understood.

Unfortunately, such misunderstandings did not disappear with the fifteenth century. Even though, both in America and England, the majority of speakers are mutually intelligible, worrying misunderstandings still occur through dialect differences. Consider the conversation between Samuel, a five-year-old [black] boy from West Philadelphia, and Paul, a white psychologist who had been working in Samuel's school for six months:

SAMUEL: I been know your name.
PAUL: What?
SAMUEL: I been know your name.
PAUL: You better know my name?
SAMUEL: I *been* know your name. (Labov, 1972a: 62).

Paul failed to realize that in Philadelphia's black community *been* means "for a long time." Samuel meant "I have known your name for a long time." In some circumstances, this use of *been* can be completely misleading to a white speaker. A [black] Philadelphian who said *I been mar-*

ried would in fact mean "I have been married for a long time." But a white speaker would normally interpret her sentence as meaning "I have been married, but I am not married any longer."

Is it possible to do anything about situations where differences caused by language change threaten to disrupt the mutual comprehension and cohesion of a population? Should language change be stopped?

If legislators decide that something is socially inconvenient, then their next task is to decide whether it is possible to take effective action against it. If we attempted to halt language change by law, would the result be as effective as forbidding people to camp in Trafalgar Square? Or would it be as useless as telling the pigeons there not to roost around the fountains? Judging by the experience of the French who have an academy, the Académie Française, which adjudicates over matters of linguistic usage, and whose findings have been made law in some cases, the result is a waste of time. Even though there may be some limited effect on the written language, spoken French appears not to have responded in any noticeable way.

If legal sanctions are impractical, how can mutual comprehension be brought about or maintained? The answer is not to attempt to limit change, which is probably impossible, but to ensure that all members of the population have at least one common language, and one common variety of that language, which they can mutually use. The standard language may be the only one spoken by certain people. Others will retain their own regional dialect or language alongside the standard one. This is the situation in the British Isles, where some Londoners, for example, speak only standard British English. In Wales, however, there are a number of people who are equally fluent in Welsh and English.

The imposition of a standard language cannot be brought about by force. Sometimes it occurs spontaneously, as has happened in England. At other times, conscious intervention is required. Such social planning requires tact and skill. In order for a policy to achieve acceptance, a population must *want* to speak a particular language or particular variety of it. A branch of sociolinguistics known as "language planning" or, more recently, "language engineering" is attempting to solve the practical and theoretical problems involved in such attempts (Bell, 1976; Würm, Mühlhäusler, and Laycock, 1977).

Once standardization has occurred, and a whole population has accepted one particular variety as standard, it becomes a strong unifying force and often a source of national pride and symbol of independence.

GREAT PERMITTERS

Perhaps we need one final comment about "Great Permitters"—a term coined by William Safire, who writes a column about language for the *New York Times* (Safire, 1980, from whom the quotations in this section are taken). These are intelligent, determined people, often writers, who "care about clarity and precision, who detest fuzziness of expression that reveals sloppiness or laziness of thought." They want to give any changes which occur "a shove in the direction of freshness and precision," and are "willing to struggle to preserve the clarity and color in the language." In other words, they are prepared to accept new usages which they regard as advantageous, and are prepared to battle against those which seem sloppy or pointless.

Such an aim is admirable. An influential writer-journalist can clearly make interesting suggestions, and provide models for others to follow. Two points need to be made, however. First, however hard a "linguistic activist" (as Safire calls himself) works, he is unlikely to reverse a strong trend, however much he would like to. Safire has, for example, given up his fight against *hopefully*, and also against *viable* which, he regretfully admits, "cannot be killed." Secondly, and perhaps more importantly, we need to realize how personal and how idiosyncratic are judgments as to what is "good" and what is "bad," even when they are made by a careful and knowledgeable writer, as becomes clear from the often furious letters which follow Safire's pronouncements in the *New York Times*. Even a Safire fan must admit that he holds a number of opinions which are based on nothing more than a subjective feeling about the words in question. Why, for example, did he give up the struggle against *hopefully*, but continue to wage war on *clearly*? As one of his correspondents notes, "Your grudge against clearly is unclear to me." Similarly, Safire attacks ex-President Carter's "needless substitution of encrypt for encode," but is sharply reminded by a reader that "the words 'encrypt' and 'encode' have very distinct meanings for a cryptographer." These, and other similar examples, show that attempts of caring persons to look after a language can mean no more than the preservation of personal preferences which may not agree with the views of others.

SUMMARY AND CONCLUSION

Continual language change is natural and inevitable, and is due to a combination of psycholinguistic and sociolinguistic factors.

Once we have stripped away religious and philosophical preconceptions, there is no evidence that language is either progressing or decaying. Disruption and therapy seem to balance one another in a perpetual stalemate. These two opposing pulls are an essential characteristic of language.

Furthermore, there is no evidence that languages are moving in any particular direction from the point of view of language structure — several are moving in contrary directions.

Language change is in no sense wrong, but it may, in certain circumstances, be socially undesirable. Minor variations in pronunciation from region to region are unimportant, but change which disrupts the mutual intelligibility of a community can be socially and politically inconvenient. If this happens, it may be useful to encourage standardization — the adoption of a standard variety of one particular language which everybody will be able to use, alongside the existing regional dialects or languages. Such a situation must be brought about gradually, with tact and care, since a population will only adopt a language or dialect it *wants* to speak.

Finally, it is always possible that language is developing in some mysterious fashion that linguists have not yet identified. Only time and further research will tell. There is much more to be discovered.

But we may finish on a note of optimism. We no longer, like Caxton in the fifteenth century, attribute language change to the domination of man's affairs by the moon:

> And certaynly our langage now vsed varyeth ferre from that which was vsed and spoken whan I was borne. For we englysshe men ben borne vnder the domynacyon of the mone, which is neuer stedfaste but euer wauerynge wexynge one season and waneth and dycreaseth another season. (Caxton, preface to *Erydos* [1490])

Instead, step by step, we are coming to an understanding of the social and psychological factors underlying language change. As the years go by, we hope gradually to increase this knowledge. In the words of the nineteenth-century poet, Alfred Lord Tennyson: "Science moves, but slowly slowly, creeping on from point to point."

REFERENCES

Bell, R. (1976), *Sociolinguistics: Goals, Approaches, and Problems*. London: Batsford.

Greenberg, J. H. (1957), *Essays in Linguistics*. Chicago: University Press; Phoenix Books edition, 1963.

Keiler, A. R., ed. (1972), *A Reader in Historical and Comparative Linguistics*. New York: Holt, Rinehart & Winston.

Kiparsky, P. (1972), "From paleogrammarians to neogrammarians." *York Papers in Linguistics* 2, 33–43.

Labov, W. (1972), *Sociolinguistic Patterns*. Philadelphia: University of Pennsylvania Press.

———. (1972a), "Where do grammars stop?" In R. W. Shuy, ed., *Sociolinguistics: Current Trends and Prospects*, 23rd Annual Round Table Meeting, Georgetown University School of Languages and Linguistics. Georgetown: University of Georgetown Press.

Li, C. N. and Thompson, S. A. (1974), "Historical change of word order: A case study of Chinese and its implications." In Anderson, J. M., and Jones, C., eds. (1974), *Historical Linguistics*. Amsterdam: North Holland.

———. (1976), "Strategies for signaling grammatical relations in Wappo." *Papers From the Twelfth Regional Meeting*. Chicago: Chicago Linguistic Society.

Mühlhäusler, P. (1978), "Samoan plantation pidgin English and the origin of New Guinea Pidgin." *Papers in Pidgin and Creole Linguistics*, I, 67–119.

Payne, R. (1979), "Humpbacks: their mysterious songs." *National Geographic* 155, 1, January, 18–25.

Safire, W. (1980), *On Language*. New York: Times Books.

Slobin, D. I. (1977), "Language change in childhood and history." In J. Macnamara, ed., *Language Learning and Thought*. New York: Academic Press, 1977.

Wurm, S. A., Mühlhäusler, P., and Laycock, D. C. (1977), "Language planning and engineering in Papua New Guinea." In S. A. Wurm, ed., *New Guinea Area Languages and Language Study*, vol. 3. Canberra: Pacific Linguistics, C–40.

≡

FOR DISCUSSION AND REVIEW

1. What point about human language does Aitchison make by describing the songs of humpback whales?

2. What was the attitude of the early historical linguists toward language change? How did Darwin's doctrine of survival of the fittest affect linguists' attitudes?

3. Explain three criteria that might be used to measure "progress" in language. Are these criteria completely satisfactory? Why or why not?

4. Describe four of the very slow changes that are occurring in the world's languages, noting especially instances in which languages seem to be evolving in different or opposite directions. In your description, consider such things as word order, inflections, and phonology.

5. Drawing upon your own experience, describe an instance in which "differing dialects cause[d] unintelligibility, or misunderstandings."

6. Summarize Aitchison's conclusions about the "Great Permitters."

Projects for "Historical Linguistics and Language Change"

1. The articles in Part Seven have dealt primarily with genetic classification of languages. Another type of classification, typological, was formerly popular and, much refined, is still useful. Prepare a report on typological classification that includes discussion of its earlier problems and its present status. You will want to read "A Quantitative Approach to the Morphological Typology of Language" by Joseph H. Greenberg and consult a text such as *Introduction to Historical Linguistics* by Anthony Arlotto (both are listed in the bibliography).

2. Prepare a report summarizing the development of the English dictionary. One useful source is the workbook *Problems in the Origin and Development of the English Language* by John Algeo (listed in the bibliography).

3. The *Oxford English Dictionary (OED)* is probably the finest historical dictionary ever prepared. Prepare a report describing its preparation and explaining the kinds of information that it contains.

4. The following passages are versions of the Lord's Prayer as they were written during different periods in the history of the English language. (a) Analyze the forms that the various words have in common, and consider how each word changes from the first to the last version and, also, from one version to the next (e.g., Faeder, fadir, father, Father). (b) Do the same kind of analysis on the various syntactical (i.e., word-order) changes that you discover (e.g., Tōcume þīn rīce; Thy kyngdom cumme to; Let they kingdom come; Thy kingdom come). (c) Write an essay in which you comment on the changes that you have discovered in these excerpts. Give as many examples of the various changes as you believe are necessary to support your conclusions. Finally, draw some conclusions about the evolution of the English language as it is revealed in the passages.

1. Eornostlīce gebiddaþ ēow þus Fæder ūre þū be eart on heofonum, sie þin nama gehālgod.
2. Tōcume þīn rice. Gewurþe þīn willa on eorþan swā swā on heofonum.
3. Ūrne daeghwæmlīcan hlāf syle ūs tōdæg.
4. And forgyf ūs ure gyltas swā swā we forgyfaþ ūrum gyltendum.
5. And ne gelæd þū ūs on costnunge ac ālys us of yfele.
6. Witodlice gyf gē forgyfaþ mannum hyra synna, þonne forgyfþ ēower sē heofonlīca fæder ēow ēowre gyltas.
7. Gyf gē sōþlīce ne forgyfaþ mannum, ne ēower fæder ne forgyfþ ēow ēowre synna.

Old English (ca. 1000)

1. Forsothe thus ʒe shulen preyen, Oure fadir that art in heuenes, halwid be thi name;
2. Thy kyngdom cumme to; be thi wille don as in heuen and in erthe;
3. ʒif to vs this day oure breed ouer other substaunce;
4. And forʒeue to vs oure dettis, as we forʒeue to oure dettours;
5. And leede vs nat in to temptacioun, but delyuere vs fro yuel. Amen.
6. Forsothe ʒif ʒee shulen forʒeuve to men her synnys, and ʒoure heuenly fadir shal forʒeue to ʒou ʒoure trespassis.
7. Sothely ʒif ʒee shulen forʒeue not to men, neither ʒoure fadir shal forʒeue to ʒou ʒoure synnes.

Middle English (Wycliffe, 1389)

1. After thys maner there fore praye ye, O oure father which arte in heven, halowed be thy name;
2. Let thy kingdom come; they wyll be fulfilled as well in erth as hit ys in heven;
3. Geve vs this daye oure dayly breade;
4. And forgeve vs oure treaspases, even as we forgeve them which trespas vs;
5. Leede vs not into temptacion, but delyvre vs ffrom yvell. Amen.
6. For and yff ye shall forgeve other men there trespases, youre father in heven shal also forgeve you.
7. But and ye wyll not forgeve men there trespases, no more shall youre father forgeve youre trespases.

Early Modern English (Tyndale, 1526)

1. Pray then like this: Our Father who art in heaven, Hallowed be thy name.
2. Thy kingdom come, Thy will be done, On Earth as it is in heaven.
3. Give us this day our daily bread;
4. And forgive us our debts, As we also have forgiven our debtors;
5. And lead us not into temptation, But deliver us from evil.
6. For if you forgive men their trespasses, your heavenly Father also will forgive you;
7. but if you do not forgive men their trespasses, neither will your Father forgive your trespasses.

Modern English (1952)

5. Roberts mentions that there was at one time interest in establishing an "academy" to monitor and purify the English language. One of those interested was Jonathan Swift (1667–1745). Prepare a report on the history of interest in such an academy and of the arguments for and against it.

6. A number of artificial languages have been developed with the aim of providing a universal language that would be acceptable to everyone and easily learned. The best known of these languages are Volapük,

Esperanto, and Interlingua. Basic English is also sometimes included in this group. Prepare a report on one of these languages; be sure to include samples of it, and argue for or against the concept of a universal language. The following works will be helpful: (1) Connor, George Alan, D. T. Connor, and William Solzbacher. *Esperanto: The World Inter-Language.* New York: Bechhurst Press, 1948. (2) Pei, Mario. *One Language for the World.* New York: Devin-Adair, 1961. (3) White, Ralph G. "Toward the Construction of a Lingua Humana." *Current Anthropology* 13 (1972), 113–23. (4) Hayes, Curtis W., Jacob Ornstein, and William W. Gage. *ABC's of Languages and Linguistics.* Silver Spring, MD: Institute of Modern Languages, Inc., 1977, especially Chapter X, "One Language for the World?"

7. The following words have interesting etymologies: *algebra, anaesthetic, assassin, caucus, crocodile, tawdry,* and *zest.* Look at their entries in the *Oxford English Dictionary* and then write a brief statement about each. If you have difficulty understanding the abbreviations and designations in the *OED,* consult the frontmatter.

8. Aitchison mentions the possibility and the importance of "language planning." A great deal has been written about this subject in recent years, and the material deals with a number of different countries (e.g., India, the Sudan, various African countries, Haiti, Papua-New Guinea, and the Scandinavian countries). Using the resources in your college library, investigate the particular problems faced in one country and the kinds of "language planning" that have been done. Evaluate the success (or lack of success) of the planning.

9. Modern English developed from the East Midland dialect of Middle English (1100–1500). Chaucer wrote in this dialect, which is one reason why his poetry is relatively easy to read. But *why* did Modern English develop from the East Midland dialect? Based on library research, write a brief paper explaining the various reasons for this development.

10. After briefly discussing the "Great Permitters" (pp. 634–635), Aitchison concludes that "attempts of caring persons to look after a language can mean no more than the preservation of personal preferences which may not agree with the views of others." After reading at least three articles or book chapters by such "Great Permitters" as William Safire, Edwin Newman, and John Simon, write a short paper in which you analyze the validity of Aitchison's statement. You may find two books particularly helpful: (a) Harvey A. Daniels, *Famous Last Words: The American Language Crisis Reconsidered* (Carbondale: Southern Illinois University Press, 1983) and (b) Jim Quinn, *American Tongue and Cheek* (New York: Pantheon, 1981).

11. As we have seen, English is a member of the Germanic branch of the Indo-European language family. Prepare a report on either the Indo-Iranian, Balto-Slavic, or Italic branch, indicating what contemporary languages have developed from it, where they are spoken, and, if possible, by how many people.

12. Of the world's approximately five thousand living languages,

only seventy are Indo-European. Some of the major non–Indo-European language families are the Afro-Asiatic, Altaic, Dravidian, Malayo-Polynesian, Niger-Congo, and Sino-Tibetan. Each of these families contains a number of different languages, each of which has more than a million native speakers. Choose one of these six non–Indo-European language families, and prepare a report describing it. For example, does the language family have subfamilies? What are they? What languages belong to it? Where are they spoken? By how many people? What features characterize these languages?

13. The majority of essays in this section touch on a belief that the English language, as well as the other European languages, have descended from an ancient common language: Indo-European. After conducting some library research, create a "family tree" of the language and the dialect that is spoken in your community, beginning with your oldest known ancestor, the Indo-European language. How did you come to speak the language you know? What historical events or migrations of people have given you your dialect?

14. The *Oxford English Dictionary* with all of its supplements comprises the most complete history of the English language we have. Find a word in the dictionary, familiar to you and still used today, that has at least five meaning changes. Describe the word's history and how the word meanings have changed over time. Can you easily trace the meaning changes and how they changed? What groups of people may have been responsible for the changes in meaning? Has the spelling of your word changed? What events in our language's history have led to the spelling changes? After you have finished your study, find a word in the dictionary that may already require an updated meaning. What classes of words are changing most rapidly? Why?

Selected Bibliography

Aitchison, Jean. *Language Change: Progress or Decay?* 2nd ed. New York: Cambridge University Press, 1991. [Explores the process of language change without confusing technical terms and attempts to answer all questions on the subject.]

Algeo, John. *Problems in the Origin and Development of the English Language,* 3d. ed. New York: Harcourt Brace Jovanovich, 1982. [An outstanding workbook; interesting and careful problems.]

Anttila, Raimo. *An Introduction to Historical and Comparative Linguistics.* New York: The Macmillan Company, 1972. [An excellent text; many examples; difficult but comprehensive.]

Arlotto, Anthony. *Introduction to Historical Linguistics.* Boston: Houghton Mifflin Company, 1972. [Very clear, readable, brief (243 pp.) introductory text.]

Baron, Dennis. *Declining Grammar and Other Essays on the English Vocabulary.* Urbana, IL: National Council of Teachers of English, 1989. [An accessible book about where the English language has been, where it is now, and speculations on where it is going.]

Baugh, Albert C., and Thomas Cable. *A History of the English Language,* 3rd ed. Englewood Cliffs, NJ: Prentice-Hall, 1978. [Long a standard, nontechnical text, the third edition is largely unchanged from the second.]

Bender, Harold H. *The Home of the Indo-Europeans.* Princeton, NJ: Princeton University Press, 1922. [The standard work on the subject.]

Bolton, W. F. *A Living Language: The History and Structure of English.* New York: Random House, 1982. [An excellent text; uncommon linking of the history of the language and the development of its literature.]

Breivik, Leiv Egil ed., E. H. Taylor. *Trends in Linguistics: Language Change — Contributions to the Study of Its Causes.* New York: Mouton de Gruyter, 1989. [An accessible collection of short essays on the subject of language change.]

Dillard, J. L. *All-American English: A History of the English Language in America.* New York: Random House, 1975. [Emphasizes influence of maritime English on American colonists and the later imports of Yiddish, Pennsylvania Dutch, and "Spanglish."]

Gordon, James D. *The English Language: An Historical Introduction.* New York: Thomas Y. Crowell Company, 1972. [A good text; useful bibliography.]

Greenberg, Joseph H. "A Quantitative Approach to the Morphological Typology of Language." *International Journal of American Linguistics* 26 (1960), 178–194. [Presents a number of criteria for typological classification of languages; an important article.]

Greenough, James B., and George L. Kittredge. *Words and Their Ways in English Speech.* New York: Crowell-Collier and Macmillan, 1901; paperback by Beacon Press, 1962. [An older book but still valuable especially on meaning changes and slang.]

Haas, Mary. *The Prehistory of Languages.* The Hague: Mouton, 1969. [The title of an earlier version describes the contents: "Historical Linguistics and the Genetic Relationship of Languages."]

Jeffers, Robert J., and Ilse Lehiste. *Principles and Methods for Historical Linguis-*

tics. Cambridge, MA: The MIT Press, 1979. [An excellent advanced text; numerous examples.]

Keiler, Alan R., ed. *A Reader in Historical and Comparative Linguistics*. New York: Holt, Rinehart and Winston, 1972. [Twenty essays, from 1902 on.]

King, Robert D. *Historical Linguistics and Generative Grammar*. Englewood Cliffs, NJ: Prentice-Hall, 1969. [A pioneering work; not for the beginner.]

Krapp, George Philip. *Modern English: Its Growth and Present Status*. Rev. by Albert H. Marckwardt. New York: Charles Scribner's Sons, 1969. [First published in 1909, it became a classic; now updated by the late professor Marckwardt.]

Lamb, Sidney M., E. D. Mitchel, eds. *Sprung From Some Common Source*. Stanford, CA: Stanford University Press, 1991. [An in-depth look at the origins of language with a short history of Indo-European languages.]

Lass, Roger, ed. *Approaches to English Historical Linguistics: An Anthology*. New York: Holt, Rinehart and Winston, 1969. [Thirty articles of general interest.]

Lehmann, Winfred P. *Historical Linguistics: An Introduction*, 2nd ed. New York: Holt, Rinehart and Winston, Inc., 1973. [An excellent standard text; annotated bibliography.]

Lloyd, Donald J., and Harry R. Warfel. *American English in Its Cultural Setting*. New York: Alfred A. Knopf, 1956. [Includes an excellent short history of the American dictionary plus sections ("Our Land and Our People" and "Our Language") interesting for the history of American English.]

Lodwig, Richard R., and Eugene F. Barrett. *The Dictionary and the Language*. New York: Hayden Book Companies, 1967. [A good section on the making of a modern dictionary.]

Markman, Alan M., and Erwin R. Steinberg, eds. *English Then and Now: Readings and Essays*. New York: Random House, 1970. [A collection of essays and excerpts arranged by language period.]

Marckwardt, Albert H. *American English*, 2nd ed. Rev. by J. L. Dillard. New York: Oxford University Press, 1980. [A fine revision and updating of a classic work.]

Myers, L. M. *The Roots of Modern English*. Boston: Little, Brown and Company, 1966. [See especially Myers's specimens of OE.]

Nunberg, Geoffrey. "The Decline of Grammar." *The Atlantic* (December 1983), pp. 31–46. [An excellent and entertaining essay about attitudes toward change in the English language.]

Pedersen, Holger. *The Discovery of Language: Linguistic Science in the Nineteenth Century*. Trans. by John Webster Spargo. Bloomington, IN: Indiana University Press, 1962. [A readable discussion of the principles of historical linguistics; many examples; originally published in Copenhagen in 1924.]

Pyles, Thomas. *Words and Ways of American English*. New York: Random House, 1952. [An introduction to American English from colonial times to the present.]

Pyles, Thomas and John Algeo. *The Origins and Development of the English Language*, 3rd ed. New York: Harcourt Brace Jovanovich, 1982. [An outstanding revision of an already fine text; the Algeo workbook *(supra)* accompanies this text.]

Renfrew, Colin. *Archaeology and Language: The Puzzle of Indo-European Origins*. New York: Cambridge University Press, 1987. [An excellent text on the origins of languages used in the world today.]

Roberts, Paul. "How to Find Fault With a Dictionary." *Understanding English*.

New York: Harper & Row, 1958. [Useful on both the history of dictionaries and how to use them.]

Sledd, James, and Wilma R. Ebbitt. *Dictionaries and THAT Dictionary.* Glenview, IL: Scott, Foresman and Company, 1962. [A casebook on the controversy concerning the publication of *Webster's Third New International Dictionary, Unabridged;* introductory section on the history of dictionaries.]

Watkins, Calvert. "The Indo-European Origin of English," "Indo-European and the Indo-Europeans," "Indo-European Roots," in *The American Heritage Dictionary of the English Language.* Ed. William Morris. Boston: American Heritage Publishing Co. and Houghton Mifflin Company, 1969. [The first two items are essays and are somewhat technical; the third item is an Indo-European root dictionary to which items in the dictionary proper are cross-referenced.]

Weinreich, Uriel. *Languages in Contact: Findings and Problems.* The Hague: Mouton, 1967. [A classic work; a revision of the original 1953 edition.]

Whitehall, Harold. "The Development of the English Dictionary," in *Webster's New World Dictionary of the English Language.* New York: The World Publishing Company, 1958. [A basic historical survey.]

Williams, Joseph M. *Origins of the English Language: A Social and Linguistic History.* New York: The Free Press, 1975. [Contains especially fine and numerous problems.]

Wilson, Kenneth G., R. H. Hendrickson, and Peter Alan Taylor. *Harbrace Guide to Dictionaries.* New York: Harcourt, Brace & World, 1963. [Thorough, but does not treat recently published dictionaries; good historical section.]

PART EIGHT

BROADER PERSPECTIVES

As linguistics as a discipline has developed and changed during the twentieth century, the number and variety of its subdivisions and areas of study have steadily increased. In this final part, we will examine four different topics, all of which have attracted a great deal of attention from linguists in recent years.

In the first selection, "Sign Language," George Yule points out that American Sign Language (ASL) is the third most commonly used non-English language in the United States. He traces the origin and history of ASL and discusses the structure and meaning of individual signs. In addition, Yule points out the linguistic similarities between ASL and spoken English.

The second selection, George A. Miller's "Nonverbal Communication," discusses the significant role of nonverbal signals in the communication process. When people think of language, they generally consider it in terms of the words they say or write — or, on a more sophisticated level, in terms of phonology, morphology, syntax, semantics, and pragmatics. To look at language in this way, however, is to ignore the importance of the role played by nonverbal communication. Ray L. Birdwhistell estimates that in a typical two-person conversation, more than sixty-five percent of the social meaning is conveyed by nonverbal signals. He also estimates that the average person spends only about ten or eleven minutes a day actually talking. Given the importance to communication of nonverbal cues, it behooves us to study them carefully. But nonverbal signals differ from culture to culture at least as much as one language differs from another. Thus, as Miller points out, knowledge of a language is woefully incomplete unless it extends to the nonverbal system of the culture in which the language is spoken.

With the third selection, John P. Hughes's "Languages and Writing," we shift our focus to a "secondary" form of language. By *secondary*, we mean that, whereas all normal children learn to speak their native language(s) without formal instruction, this is not the case with writing. We have to be taught to read and write; we are not genetically predisposed to acquire this form of language. Furthermore, many millions of the world's inhabitants are illiterate, and there are some languages that do not have a writing system. Nevertheless, the alphabet has been called the greatest invention since the wheel, and Hughes explains why. In doing so, he traces the variety of ways in which human beings, over the centuries, have attempted to represent the spoken language. He concludes that the alphabetic system is truly unique.

In the fourth selection, "Dictionaries, Change, and Computers," James Larkin demonstrates the incredible speed with which our language changes, how some words today mean something they didn't mean just twenty-five years ago. For example, the word *mouse* is now used to refer to a computer pointing device that has some mouselike physical characteristics. With such rapid changes in our language, dictionaries have become even more important, he argues. After tracing the brief two-hundred-and-fifty-year history of modern English dictionaries, Larkin predicts the roles computers will play in developing lexical databases and in facilitating the more rapid publication of dictionaries.

In the final selection, "Speaking with a Single Tongue," Jared Diamond looks at the social, economic, and political forces that are bringing thousands of languages to the brink of extinction. But why should anyone care if certain languages cease to exist; after all, isn't one language as good as another? Only now are linguists starting to give this subject serious attention because they realize that, as Diamond says, "each language is the vehicle for a unique way of thinking, a unique literature, and a unique view of the world."

40

Sign Language

George Yule

In January 1993 millions of people watched as the forty-second president of the United States was inaugurated. What was unique about this inauguration ceremony was that there was a person signing every word of the new president's address. As more and more attempts are made to make the world of the hearing readily accessible to the deaf, it is no longer uncommon to see a person signing to an audience at public events. In this selection George Yule, professor of speech, communication, and theatre at Louisiana State University, asserts the importance and necessity of the various forms of signed languages used among deaf speakers. Yule distinguishes between what is commonly known as American Sign Language (ASL) and the newer "Signed English" in order to introduce to his readers the communication world of the deaf. Both ASL and Signed English are commonly used in schools for the deaf today, and they facilitate interaction between the deaf and hearing communities with their use of gestures, facial expressions, and "icons." Although difficulties may arise with attempts to write and teach sign language to the hearing community, Yule believes the difficulties are minimal and must be accommodated. He explains that all the defining properties of language are present in ASL with equivalent levels of phonology, morphology, and syntax. Acceptance and knowledge of signed forms of language are essential for communication among deaf and hearing people and necessary for a more complete understanding of language in general.

> The deaf perceive the world through skilled and practiced eyes; language is at their fingertips. When I wanted to learn about silence and sign language, I went to talk to the deaf.
>
> —ARDEN NEISSER (1983)

In our consideration of the acquisition of language, we concentrated, for the most part, on the fact that what is naturally acquired by most children is speech. It would be a mistake to think that this is the only form a first language can take. Just as most children of English-speaking or French-speaking parents naturally acquire English or French at an early age, so the deaf children of deaf parents naturally acquire *sign language.* If those deaf children grow up in American homes, they will typically acquire American Sign Language, also known as Ameslan or ASL. With a signing population of almost 500,000, ASL is the third most commonly used non-English language (after Spanish and Italian) in the United States. The size of this number is quite remarkable since, until very recently, the use of ASL was discouraged in most educational institutions for the deaf. In fact, historically, very few teachers of the deaf knew anything about ASL, or even considered it to be a "real" language at all.

ORALISM

To be fair to those generations of teachers in deaf education, we must acknowledge that it is only in the last two decades that any serious consideration has been given to the status of ASL as a natural language. It was genuinely believed by many well-intentioned teachers that the use of sign language by deaf children, perhaps because it was "easy," actually inhibited the acquisition of speech. Since speech was what these children really required, a teaching method generally known as *oralism* was rigorously pursued. This method, which dominated deaf education for a century, required that the students practice English speech sounds and develop lipreading skills. Despite its resounding lack of success, the method was never seriously challenged, perhaps because of a belief among many during this period that, in educational terms, most deaf children could not achieve very much anyway.

Whatever the reasons, the method produced few students who could speak intelligible English (reckoned to be less than 10 percent) and even fewer who could lipread (around 4 percent). While oralism was failing, the use of ASL was surreptitiously flourishing. Many deaf children of hearing parents actually acquired the banned language at schools for the deaf—from other children. Since only one in ten deaf children had deaf parents from whom they acquired sign language, it would seem that ASL is a rather unique language in that its major cultural transmission has been carried out from child to child.

SIGNED ENGLISH

Substantial changes in deaf education have taken place in recent years. There remains an emphasis on the acquisition of English, written rather than spoken, and as a result, many institutions promote the learning of what is called *Signed English* (sometimes described as Manually Coded English). This is essentially a means of producing signs which correspond to the words in an English sentence, in English word order. In many ways, Signed English is designed to facilitate interaction between the deaf and the hearing community. Its greatest advantage is that it seems to present a much less formidable learning task for the hearing parent of a deaf child and provides that parent with a "language" to use with the child.

For similar reasons, hearing teachers in deaf education can make use of Signed English when they sign at the same time as they speak (known as the "simultaneous method"). It is also easier to use for those hearing interpreters who produce a simultaneous translation of public speeches or lectures for deaf audiences. Many deaf people actually prefer interpreters to use Signed English because they say there is a better chance of understanding the message. When most interpreters try to use ASL, the message seems to suffer, for the simple reason that few hearing people who didn't learn ASL in childhood are very proficient at it.

However, Signed English is neither English nor is it ASL. When used to produce an exact version of a spoken English sentence, Signed English takes twice as long as the production of the sentence in either English or ASL. Consequently, in practice, exact versions are rarely produced and a hybrid format emerges, using some word-signs and incomplete English word order. (In many cases, even the word-signs are "anglified" with, for example, a G letter-shape used to represent the English word *glad*, rather than the actual ASL sign for this concept.) It's sort of like producing messages with German word order, but containing French nouns, adjectives, verbs, and so on. The product is neither French nor German, but, it could be argued, it is one way of getting French speakers to learn how German sentences are constructed. The type of argument we have just noted is what has been used in support of teaching Signed English in deaf schools, since one of the major aims is to prepare students to be able to read and write English. Underlying that aim is the principle that deaf education should be geared towards enabling the deaf, for obvious economic reasons, to take part in the hearing world. The net effect is to make ASL a kind of underground language, used only in deaf–deaf interaction. As such, it continues to be poorly understood and subject to many of the myths which have existed throughout its history.

Origins of ASL

It would indeed be surprising if ASL really was, as some would have it, "a sort of gestured version of English." Historically, it developed from the French Sign Language used in a Paris school founded in the eighteenth century. Early in the nineteenth century, a teacher from this school, named Laurent Clerc, was brought to the United States by an American Congregational minister called Thomas Gallaudet. Clerc not only taught deaf children, he trained other teachers. During the nineteenth century, this imported version of Sign Language, incorporating features of indigenous natural sign languages used by the American deaf, evolved into what became ASL. Such origins help explain why users of ASL and users of British Sign Language (BSL) do not, in fact, share a common sign language.

ASL and BSL are separate languages and neither should be treated as versions of spoken English which happen to involve the use of the hands.

The Structure of Signs

The idea that natural sign languages involve simple gestures with the hands is a persistent fallacy. In producing linguistic forms in ASL, signers will help themselves to four key aspects of visual information. These are usually classified as shape, orientation, location and movement. In analogies with natural spoken languages, these four elements are sometimes called the *articulatory parameters* of ASL. These parameters can be illustrated by referring to the following representation of a clear, isolated use of the sign for THANK-YOU. To describe the articula-

tion of THANK-YOU in ASL, we would start with the *shape*, or configuration of the hand(s) used in forming the sign. In forming THANK-YOU, a "flat hand" is used and not a "fist hand" or "cupped hand" or other permissible shape. The *orientation* of the hand describes the fact that the hand is "palm-up" rather than "palm-down." In other signs the hand can be oriented in a number of other ways, such as the "flat hand," "palm towards signer" form used to indicate MINE. The *location* of the sign captures the fact that, in THANK-YOU, it is first at the chin, then at waist level, and the *movement* (in this case, out and downward) involved in the formation of the sign is the fourth parameter. These four general parameters can be analyzed into a set of *primes* (e.g., "flat hand" and "palm-up" are primes in shape and orientation respectively) in order to produce a full feature-analysis of each sign.

In addition to these parameters, there are very important functions served by nonmanual components such as head-movement, eye-movement and a number of specific facial expressions. For example, if a sentence is functioning as a question, it is typically accompanied by a raising of the eyebrows, widened eyes, and a slight leaning forward of the head.

If a new term or name is encountered, there is the possibility of *finger-spelling* via a system of hand configurations conventionally used to represent the letters of the alphabet.

It should be obvious from this very brief description of some of the basic features of ASL that it is a linguistic system designed for the visual medium. Signing is done in face-to-face interaction. The majority of signs are located around the neck and head, and if a sign is made near the chest or waist, it tends to be two-handed. One of the key differences between a system using the visual as opposed to the vocal—auditory channel is that visual messages can incorporate a number of elements simultaneously. Spoken language is produced with a structure determined by the linear sequence of sound signals. It is extremely difficult to produce or to perceive more than one sound signal at a time. In the visual medium, multiple components can be produced all at the same time. Thus, from a structural point of view, a spoken word is a linear sequence of sound segments, while a sign is a combination of components within spatial dimensions which occur simultaneously.

THE MEANING OF SIGNS

The signs of ASL are often, erroneously, thought to be clear visual representations or "pictures" of the objects or actions they refer to. Indeed, the language of the deaf is still considered by many to be some type of pantomime or mime in which EATING is represented by mimicking the act of eating or TREE is represented by "forming" a tree with the hands. This misconception is usually accompanied by the myth that a sign language like ASL consists of a fairly primitive set of gestures which can only really be used to refer to "concrete" entities and actions, but not to anything "abstract." Such misconceptions may persist because the hearing world rarely witnesses conversations or discussions in ASL, which range over every imaginable topic, concrete and abstract, and which bear little resemblance to any form of pantomime.

However, a visual communication system can avail itself of forms of representation which have an iconic basis. *Icons* are symbolic representations which are physically similar to the objects represented. (Pictograms and ideograms are types of iconic representation.) So, in using ASL, a signer can indeed produce an iconic representation to refer to something encountered for the first time, or something rarely talked about. A good example is provided by Klima & Bellugi (1979), in which several different signers produced a range of different forms to refer to a straitjacket. Interestingly, when you are told that a sign is used for referring to a particular object or action, you can often create some iconic connection. You may have seen the sign for THANK-YOU as some appropriately symbolic version of the action involved. However, most of the time, it does not work in the opposite direction — you may find it difficult to get the "meaning" of a sign simply on the basis of what it looks like. Indeed, you may not even be able to identify individual signs in fluent signing. In this sense, most everyday use of ASL signs is not based on the use and interpretation of icons, but on conventional linguistic symbols. Even if some signs have traceable iconic sources, their actual use in ASL does not depend on the signer thinking of the iconic source in order to interpret the sign. Here is an example of a common sign. This sign consists of rotating

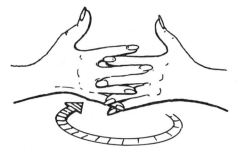

both hands with the fingers interlocked. Two quite different iconic sources have been suggested: that it represents the stripes which occur on a country's flag or that it derives from the union of a number of separate states together. To suggest that either of these images comes into the mind of a signer who, in conversation, uses this sign to refer to AMERICA is as absurd as saying that in hearing the word *America*, an English speaker must be thinking about Amerigo Vespucci, the sixteenth-century Italian whose name is reputed to be the source of the modern word.

WRITING IN ASL

The fact that a sign language exploits the visual medium in quite subtle ways makes it difficult to represent accurately on the page. As Lou Fant (1977) has observed, "strictly speaking, the only way to write Ameslan is to use motion pictures." One of the major problems is finding a way to incorporate those aspects of facial expression which contribute to the message. One partial solution is to produce one line of the manually signed "words" and over this line to indicate the extent and nature of the conventional facial expression which accompanies those words. Thus, the *q* in the following transcription shows that the facial expression indicated a question function and lasted throughout the word-signing of what would be translated as *Can I borrow the book?*

q
_____

ME BORROW BOOK

Other subtle aspects of meaning which can be conveyed by facial expression are still the subject of investigation. In one study, it was noted that a signer, in the middle of telling a story, produced a signed message such as MAN FISH CONTINUOUS, which we would translate as *the man was fishing*. However, other ASL users, watching the signer, would translate the message as *the man was fishing with relaxation and enjoyment*. The source of this extra information was a particular facial expression in which the lips were together and pushed out a little, with the head slightly tilted. This nonmanual signal was clearly capable of functioning as the equivalent of an adverb in English and was an integral part of the message. The notation *mm* was chosen as a way of incorporating this element and so a more accurate transcription of the message might look like this:

mm
_____

MAN FISH CONTINUOUS

A number of other such notations have been devised to capture major nonmanual elements in ASL communication. No doubt others will have to be introduced as other aspects of this subtle and rich communication system become better known.

ASL AS A LINGUISTIC SYSTEM

Investigations of ASL, from a linguistic point of view, are a relatively recent phenomenon. Yet it has become very clear that any feature which is characteristically found in spoken languages has a counterpart in ASL. All the defining properties of human language are present in ASL; there are equivalent levels of phonology, morphology and syntax; children acquiring ASL go through many of the recognized stages of children learning spoken language, though the production of signs seems to begin earlier than the production of spoken words; in the hands of witty individuals, ASL is used for a wide range of jokes and "sign-play"; there are different ASL dialects in different regions and historical changes in the form of signs can be traced since the beginning of the century (older versions are preserved on old films). In short, ASL is a natural language which is quite remarkable for its endurance in the face of decades of prejudice and misunderstanding. There is a very old joke among the deaf which begins with the question *What is the greatest problem facing deaf people?* Perhaps increased knowledge and appreciation of their language among the world at large will bring about a change in the old response to that question. The traditional answer was *Hearing people.*

FOR DISCUSSION AND REVIEW

1. For what reasons has ASL been dismissed as a natural language? What was used for deaf children in its place? Were these methods successful?

2. What are the differences between "ASL" and "Signed English"? What are the advantages of a system such as Signed English? Are there any disadvantages?

3. Given that Signed English is neither English nor ASL, what arguments have been presented for the necessity of Signed English use in deaf schools?

4. What are the major aims and uses of Signed English? How will these aims aid in the communication between deaf and hearing worlds?

5. What are the origins of ASL? Why should ASL not be treated as a "version of spoken English which happens to use the hands"?

6. Why is the idea that natural sign language involves simple hand gestures a "persistent fallacy"?

7. What are "articulatory parameters" of ASL? What are primes?

8. What is the purpose of nonmanual components in sign language? How can a nonmanual component function as a specific part of speech? Do you recognize any correspondence between spoken language "components" and those of Signed English?

9. What does Yule describe as one of the key differences between a system using visual as opposed to vocal-auditory channels of communication?

10. Yule repeatedly refers to misconceptions and erroneous assumptions the vocal-auditory world makes with respect to ASL and other signed languages. What are some of these misconceptions? Why might such assumptions exist?

11. Discuss the use of "icons" in ASL. How often are they used in sign language?

12. What difficulties arise in attempts to write sign language? How can we accommodate these difficulties?

13. "All the defining properties of human languages . . . are present in ASL; there are equivalent levels of phonology, morphology, and syntax." Discuss this statement, keeping in mind the reactions towards languages used by other minorities in our society.

41

Nonverbal Communication

George A. Miller

The famous linguist Edward Sapir once described nonverbal behavior as "an elaborate and secret code that is written nowhere, known by none, and understood by all." His statement is to a great extent still true. Nonverbal behavior has been studied extensively, but our understanding of it is far from complete. Unfortunately, most of the popular books and articles about nonverbal communication — usually referred to as "body language" — have drastically oversimplified the subject, suggesting that one can easily learn to "read" the nonverbal signals unconsciously "sent" by other people. In fact, however, the study of nonverbal communication is complex and subtle, far more than a kind of game that anyone can play. Returning to Sapir's phrase, "understood by all," the "all" refers to members of the same culture. Cross-culturally, people continue to misunderstand one another because they have different nonverbal systems — different acceptable postures, ways of moving, gestures, facial expressions, eye behavior, and use of space and distance. In the following selection, Professor George A. Miller uses a variety of examples to explain how necessary it is to understand the nonverbal systems as well as the languages of other cultures.

When the German philosopher Nietzsche said that "success is the greatest liar," he meant that a successful person seems especially worthy to us even when his success is due to nothing more than good luck. But Nietzsche's observation can be interpreted more broadly.

People communicate in many different ways. One of the most important ways, of course, is through language. Moreover, when language is written it can be completely isolated from the context in which it occurs; it can be treated as if it were an independent and self-contained process. We have been so successful in using and describing and analyzing this special kind of communication that we sometimes act as if language were the *only* kind of communication that can occur between people. When we act that way, of course, we have been deceived by success, the greatest liar of them all.

Like all animals, people communicate by their actions as well as by the noises they make. It is a sort of biological anomaly of man — something like the giraffe's neck, or the pelican's beak — that our vocal noises have so far outgrown in importance and frequency all our other methods of signaling to one another. Language is obviously essential for human beings, but it is not the whole story of human communication. Not by a long shot.

Consider the following familiar fact. When leaders in one of the less well developed countries decide that they are ready to introduce some technology that is already highly advanced in another country, they do not simply buy all the books that have been written about that technology and have their students read them. The books may exist and they may be very good, but just reading about the technology is not enough. The students must be sent to study in a country where the technology is already flourishing, where they can see it firsthand. Once they have been exposed to it in person and experienced it as part of their own lives, they are ready to understand and put to use the information that is in the books. But the verbal message, without the personal experience to back it up, is of little value.

Now what is it that the students learn by participating in a technology that they cannot learn by just reading about it? It seems obvious that they are learning something important, and that whatever it is they are learning is something that we don't know how to put into our verbal descriptions. There is a kind of nonverbal communication that occurs when students are personally involved in the technology and when they interact with people who are using and developing it.

Pictures are one kind of nonverbal communication, of course, and moving pictures can communicate some of the information that is difficult to capture in words. Pictures also have many of the properties that make language so useful — they can be taken in one situation at one time and viewed in an entirely different situation at any later time. Now that we have television satellites, pictures can be transmitted instantaneously all over the world, just as our words can be transmitted by radio. Perhaps the students who are trying to learn how to create a new technology in their own country could supplement their reading by watching moving pictures of people at work in the developed industry. Certainly the pictures would be a help, but they would be very expensive. And we don't really know whether words and pictures together would capture every thing the students would be able to learn by going to a more advanced country and participating directly in the technology.

Let me take another familiar example. There are many different cultures in the world, and in each of them the children must learn a great many things that are expected of everyone who participates effectively in that culture. These things are taken for granted by everyone who shares the culture. When I say they are taken for granted, I mean that nobody needs to describe them or write them down or try self-consciously to teach them to children. Indeed, the children begin to learn them before their linguistic skills are far enough developed to understand a verbal description of what they are learning. This kind of learning has sometimes been called "imitation," but that is much too simple an explanation for the complex processes that go on when a child learns what is normal and expected in his own community. Most of the norms are communicated to the child nonverbally, and he internalizes them as if no other possibilities existed. They are as much a part of him as his own body; he would no more question them than he would question the fact that he has two hands and two feet, but only one head.

These cultural norms can be described verbally, of course. Anthropologists who are interested in describing the differences among the many cultures of the world have developed a special sensitivity to cultural norms and have described them at length in their scholarly books. But if a child had to read those books in order to learn what was expected of him, he would never become an effective member of his own community.

What is an example of the sort of thing that children learn nonverbally? One of the simplest examples to observe and analyze and discuss is the way people use clothing and bodily ornamentation to communicate. At any particular time in any particular culture there is an accepted and normal way to dress and to arrange the hair and to paint the face and to wear one's jewelry. By adopting those conventions for dressing himself, a person communicates to the world that he wants to be treated according to the standards of the culture for which they are appropriate. When a black person in America rejects the normal American dress and puts on African clothing, he is communicating to the world that he wants to be treated as an Afro-American. When a white man lets his hair and beard grow, wears very informal clothing, and puts beads around his neck, he is communicating to the world that he rejects many of the traditional values of Western culture. On the surface, dressing up in unusual costumes would seem to be one of the more innocent forms of dissent that a person could express, but in fact it is deeply resented by many people who still feel bound by the traditional conventions of their culture and who become fearful or angry when those norms are violated. The nonverbal message that such a costume communicates is "I reject your culture and your values," and those who resent this message can be violent in their response.

The use of clothing as an avenue of communication is relatively obvious, of course. A somewhat subtler kind of communication occurs in the way people use their eyes. We are remarkably accurate in judging the direction of another person's gaze; psychologists have done experiments that have measured just how accurate such judgments are. From an observation of where a person is looking we can infer what he is looking at, and from knowing what he is looking at we can guess what he is interested in, and from what he is interested in and the general situation we can usually make a fairly good guess about what he is going to do. Thus eye movements can be a rich and important channel of nonverbal communication.

Most personal interaction is initiated by a short period during which two people look directly at one another. Direct eye contact is a signal that each has the other's attention, and that some further form of interaction can follow. In Western cultures, to look directly into another person's eyes is equivalent to saying, "I am open to you — let the action begin." Everyone knows how much lovers can communicate by their eyes, but aggressive eye contact can also be extremely informative.

In large cities, where people are crowded in together with others they neither know nor care about, many people develop a deliberate strategy of avoiding eye contacts. They want to mind their own business, they don't have time to interact with everyone they pass, and they communicate this fact by refusing to look at other people's faces. It is one of the things that make newcomers to the city feel that it is a hostile and unfriendly place.

Eye contact also has an important role in regulating conversational interactions. In America, a typical pattern is for the listener to signal that he is paying attention by looking at the talker's mouth or eyes. Since direct eye contact is often too intimate, the talker may let his eyes wander elsewhere. As the moment arrives for the talker to become a listener, and for his partner to begin talking, there will often be a preliminary eye signal. The talker will often look toward the listener, and the listener will signal that he is ready to talk by glancing away.

Such eye signals will vary, of course, depending on what the people are talking about and what the personal relation is between them. But whatever the pattern of eye signals that two people are using, they use them unconsciously. If you try to become aware of your own eye movements while you are talking to someone, you will find it extremely frustrating. As soon as you try to think self-consciously about your own eye movements, you do not know where you should be looking. If you want to study how the eyes communicate, therefore, you should do it by observing other people, not yourself. But if you watch other people too intently, of course, you may disturb them or make them angry. So be careful!

Even the pupils of your eyes communicate. When a person becomes excited or interested in something, the pupils of his eyes increase in size. In order to test whether we are sensitive to these changes in pupil size, a psychologist showed people two pictures of the face of a pretty girl. The two pictures were completely identical except that in one picture the girl's pupils were constricted, whereas in the other picture her pupils were dilated. The people were asked to say which picture they liked better, and they voted in favor of the picture with the large pupils. Many of the judges did not even realize consciously what the difference was, but apparently they were sensitive to the difference and preferred the eyes that communicated excitement and interest.

Eye communication seems to be particularly important for Americans. It is part of the American culture that people should be kept at a distance, and that contact with another person's body should be avoided in all but the most intimate situations. Because of this social convention of dealing with others at a distance, Americans have to place much reliance on their distance receptors, their eyes and ears, for personal communication. In other cultures, however, people normally come close together and bodily contact between conversational partners is as normal as eye contact is in America. In the Eastern Mediterranean cultures, for example, both the touch and the smell of the other person are expected.

The anthropologist Edward T. Hall has studied the spatial relations that seem appropriate to various kinds of interactions. They vary with intimacy, they depend on the possibility of eye contact, and they are different in different cultures. In America, for example, two strangers will converse impersonally at a distance of about four feet. If one moves closer, the other will back away. In a waiting room, strangers will keep apart, but friends will sit together, and members of a family may actually touch one another.

Other cultures have different spatial norms. In Latin America, for example, impersonal discussion normally occurs at a distance of two or three feet, which is the distance that is appropriate for personal discussion in North America. Consequently, it is impossible for a North and a South American both to be comfortable when they talk to one another unless one can adopt the zones that are normal for the other. If the South American advances to a distance that is comfortable for him, it will be too close for the North American, and he will withdraw, and one can chase the other all around the room unless something intervenes to end the conversation. The North American seems aloof and unfriendly to the South American. The South American seems hostile or oversexed to the North American. Hall mentions that North Americans sometimes cope with this difference by barricading themselves behind desks or tables, and that South Americans have been known literally to climb over these barriers in order to attain a comfortable distance at which to talk.

Within one's own culture these spatial signals are perfectly understood. If two North Americans are talking at a distance of one foot or less, you know that what they are saying is highly confidential. At a distance of two to three feet it will be some personal subject matter. At four or five feet it is impersonal, and if they are conversing at a distance of seven or eight feet, we know that they expect others to be listening to what they are saying. When talking to a group, a distance of ten to twenty feet is normal, and at greater distances only greetings are exchanged. These conventions are unconscious but highly reliable. For example, if you are having a personal conversation with a North American at a distance of two feet, you can shift it to an impersonal conversation by the simple procedure of moving back to a distance of four or five feet. If he can't follow you, he will find it quite impossible to maintain a personal discussion at that distance.

These examples should be enough to convince you — if you needed convincing — that we communicate a great deal of information that is not expressed in the words we utter. And I have not even mentioned yet the interesting kind of communication that occurs by means of gestures. A gesture is an expressive motion or action, usually made with the hands and arms, but also with the head or even the whole body. Gestures can occur with or without speech. As a part of the speech act, they usually emphasize what the person is saying, but they may occur without any speech at all. Some gestures are spontaneous, some are highly ritualized and have very specific meanings. And they differ enormously from one culture to another.

Misunderstanding of nonverbal communication is one of the most distressing and unnecessary sources of international friction. For example, few Americans understand how much the Chinese hate to be touched, or slapped on the back, or even to shake hands. How easy it would be for an American to avoid giving offense simply by avoiding these particular gestures that, to him, signify intimacy and friendliness. Or, to take another example, when Khrushchev placed his hands together over his head and shook them, most Americans interpreted it as an arrogant gesture of triumph, the sort of gesture a victorious prize fighter would make, even though Khrushchev seems to have intended it as a friendly gesture of international brotherhood. Sticking out the tongue and quickly drawing it back can be a gesture of self-castigation in one culture, an admission of a social mistake, but someone from another culture might interpret it as a gesture of ridicule or contempt, and in the Eskimo culture it would not be a gesture at all, but the conventional way of directing a current of air when blowing out a candle. Just a little better communication on the nonverbal level might go a long way toward improving international relations.

Ritualized gestures — the bow, the shrug, the smile, the wink, the military salute, the pointed finger, the thumbed nose, sticking out the tongue, and so on — are not really nonverbal communication, because such gestures are just a substitute for the verbal meanings that are associated with them. There are, however, many spontaneous gestures and actions that are unconscious, but communicate a great deal. If you take a moving picture of someone who is deeply engrossed in a conversation, and later show it to him, he will be quite surprised to see many of the gestures he used and the subtle effects they produced. Sometimes what a person is saying unconsciously by his actions may directly contradict what he is saying consciously with his words. Anthropologists have tried to develop a way to write down a description of these nonverbal actions, something like the notation that choreographers use to record the movements of a ballet dancer, but it is difficult to know exactly what the significance of these actions really is, or what the important features are that should be recorded. We can record them photographically, of course, but we still are not agreed on how the photographic record should be analyzed.

Finally, there is a whole spectrum of communication that is vocal, but not really verbal. The most obvious examples are spontaneous gasps of surprise or cries of pain. I suspect this kind of vocal communication is very similar for both man and animal. But our use of vocal signals goes far beyond such grunts and groans. It is a commonplace observation that the way you say something is as important as what you say, and often more important for telling the listener what your real intentions are. Exactly the same words may convey directly opposite messages according to the way they are said. For example, I can say, "Oh, isn't that *wonderful"* so that I sound enthusiastic, or I can say, "Oh, isn't *that* wonderful" in a sarcastic tone so that you know I don't think it is wonderful at all. Because the actual words uttered are often misleading, lawyers and judges in the courtroom have learned that it is sometimes important to have an actual recording and not just a written transcript of what a person is supposed to have said.

Rapid and highly inflected speech usually communicates excitement, extremely distinct speech usually communicates anger, very loud speech usually communicates pomposity, and a slow monotone usually communicates boredom. The emotional clues that are provided by the way a person talks are extremely subtle, and accomplished actors must practice for many years to bring them under conscious control.

A person's pronunciation also tells a great deal about him. If he has a foreign accent, a sensitive listener can generally tell where he was born. If he speaks with a local dialect, we can often guess what his social origins were and how much education he has had. Often a person will have several different styles of speaking, and will use them to communicate which social role he happens to be playing at the moment. This is such a rich source of social and psychological information, in fact, that a whole new field has recently developed to study it, a field called "sociology of language." . . .

One of the most significant signals that is vocal but nonverbal is the ungrammatical pause. . . . In careful speech most of our pauses are grammatical. That is to say, our pauses occur at the boundaries of grammatical segments, and serve as a kind of audible punctuation. By calling them "grammatical pauses" we imply that they are a normal part of the verbal message. An ungrammatical pause, however, is not a part of the verbal message. For example, when I . . . uh . . . pause within a . . . uh . . . grammatical unit, you cannot regard the pause as part of my verbal message. These ungrammatical pauses are better regarded as the places where the speaker is thinking, is searching for words, and is planning how to continue his utterance. For a linguist, of course, the grammatical pause is most interesting, since it reveals something about the structure of the verbal message. For a psychologist, however, the ungrammatical pause is more interesting, because it reveals something about the thought processes of the speaker.

When a skilled person reads a prepared text, there are few ungrammatical pauses. But spontaneous speech is a highly fragmented and discontinuous activity. Indeed, ungrammatical pausing is a reliable signal of spontaneity in speech. The pauses tend to occur at choice points in the message, and particularly before words that are rare or unusual and words that are chosen with particular care. An actor who wanted to make his rehearsed speech sound spontaneous would deliberately introduce ungrammatical pauses at these critical points.

Verbal communication uses only one of the many kinds of signals that people can exchange; for a balanced view of the communication process we should always keep in mind the great variety of other signals that can reinforce or contradict the verbal message. These subtleties are especially important in psychotherapy, where a patient tries to communicate his emotional troubles to a doctor, but may find it difficult or impossible to express in words the real source of his distress. Under such circumstances, a good therapist learns to listen for more than words, and to rely on nonverbal signals to help him interpret the verbal signals. For this reason, many psychologists have been persistently interested in nonverbal communication, and have perhaps been less likely than linguists to fall into the mistaken belief that language is the only way we can communicate.

The price of opening up one's attention to this wider range of events, however, is a certain vagueness about the kind of communication that is occurring—about what it means and how to study it. We have no dictionaries or grammars to help us analyze nonverbal communication, and there is much work that will have to be done in many cultures before we can formulate and test any interesting scientific theories about nonverbal communication. Nevertheless, the obvious fact that so much communication does occur nonverbally should persuade us not to give up, and not to be misled by our success in analyzing verbal messages.

Recognizing the great variety of communication channels that are available is probably only the first step toward a broader conception of communication as a psychological process. Not only must we study what a person says and how he says it, but we must try to understand why he says it. If we concentrate primarily on the words that people say, we are likely to think that the only purpose of language is to exchange information. That is one of its purposes, of course, but certainly not the only one. People exchange many things. Not only do they exchange information, but they also exchange money, goods, services, love, and status. In any particular interaction, a person may give one of these social commodities in exchange for another. He may give information in exchange for money, or give services in exchange for status or love. Perhaps we should first characterize communication acts in terms of what people are trying to give and gain in their social interactions. Then, within that broader frame of reference, we might see better that verbal messages are more appropriate for some exchanges and nonverbal messages for others, and that both have their natural and complementary roles to play in the vast tapestry we call human society.

≡

FOR DISCUSSION AND REVIEW

1. According to Miller, why is reading about some advanced technology developed in another country not enough? Why must students actually *go* to the country? In answering this question, try to use specific, original examples.

2. Miller asserts that along with their language, children also learn certain nonverbal "cultural norms" that "are communicated to the child nonverbally." Drawing from your own experience, describe three of the cultural norms that American children learn.

3. Keep track for a day of the way people you meet use their eyes to make or avoid eye contact. Write a brief description of the behavior you have observed. Do your findings agree with Miller's statements about the way Americans use their eyes? If not, what are the differences?

4. Miller uses two examples of the use of clothing to communicate. Based on your own experience, give two additional examples.

5. Spatial norms vary from culture to culture. Describe any differences between American norms and those of other countries that you have noticed while traveling abroad. If you haven't had such experiences, ask two or three of your friends about theirs.

42

Languages and Writing

John P. Hughes

Most Americans take mass literacy for granted; they find it difficult to imagine not being able to read and write, and they are surprised to learn that even today a significant proportion of the world's currently spoken three thousand to five thousand languages lack writing systems. In the following selection from his book The Science of Language, *Professor John P. Hughes suggests the limitations that the lack of a writing system can impose. He traces in detail the evolution of writing systems, sometimes logical and sometimes not, from the earliest Cro-Magnon cave drawings to present-day systems. Important to note is his explanation of the advantages of alphabetic systems and the unique nature of their origin.*

It has been said that the two oldest and greatest inventions of man were the wheel and the art of controlling fire. This is probable enough: and if one wished to make a group of three, surely the development of writing must claim the third place. Without a system of writing, no matter how wise or sublime the thought, once uttered it is gone forever (in its original form, at least) as soon as its echoes have died away.

Indeed, it would seem that without a means of preserving wisdom and culture, civilization, which depends on the passing on of a heritage from generation to generation, could not develop. The facts, however, are otherwise: noteworthy civilizations *have* arisen and flourished without possession of any form of writing, usually by forming a class of society whose duty and profession it was to keep in memory what we write down in books (and, too often, subsequently forget). Even the average citizen in such a society took as a matter of course demands upon his memory which we today would consider beyond human capacity.

All the same, one may question whether a really complex civilization — one capable of governing large areas, for instance — could be supported by such a system. If there ever was one, we may be sure it has been grossly slighted by history — which, after all, depends almost entirely on written records. Who, for example, has ever heard the Gaulish version of Caesar's campaigns?

IDEOGRAPHIC WRITING

There seems to be no reason to doubt that the many systems of writing which have been developed at different times by various peoples during mankind's long history all grew, by steps which we can and shall trace, out of man's ability to draw pictures.

Suppose you wish to preserve a record of your catching a twenty-pound trout, but happen to be illiterate. The obvious thing to do would be to draw and hang a picture of yourself catching the big fish. It was, apparently, an equally obvious thing to do some fifty thousand years ago, for the caves which yielded us the remains of the Cro-Magnon man first attracted attention because of their beautifully drawn pictures of a procession, perhaps a hunt, of animals. We shall never know whether this was a mere decoration or a record.

Given the ability to draw well enough so that your representations of persons and objects can be readily recognized, it is, of course, not difficult to tell a complete story in one panoramic picture, or in a series of uncaptioned sketches. The range of information that can be conveyed in this way can be greatly extended if a few simple conventions are agreed upon between the artist and his prospective audience: the use of a totem-sign for a certain tribe; considering a prone man to be sick or wounded if his eyes were open, dead if they are closed, and so on. Several tribes of North American Indians made use of this kind of communication (Figure 42.1).

In these circumstances, it will be noted, pictures act as a means for the communication of thought, and thus are somewhat like a language in themselves. Indeed, some authorities include this kind of communication

FIGURE 42.1. An Indian pictographic message. This message of friendship was sent from an American Indian chief to the president of the United States — the figure in the White House. The chief, identified by the lines rising from his head, who is sending the message, and the four warriors behind him, belong to the eagle totem; the fifth warrior is of the catfish totem. The figure at lower left is evidently also a powerful chief. The lines joining the eyes indicate harmony, and the three houses indicate the willingness of the Indians to adopt white men's customs. (From Henry R. Schoolcraft, *Historical and Statistical Information Respecting the Indian Tribes of America,* I, 418.)

among various forms of "language," but we have deliberately excluded it from our definition. It is common and conventional to call this kind of writing *ideographic writing,* and while the term is convenient, this is properly in no sense either language or writing, as we shall proceed to show.

Note, first, that the kind of communication achieved in Figure 42.1 is totally independent of the language or languages of the persons who make the drawing and of those who read it. The "text" may be correctly "read" in any language. It is not an effort to record the *language* in which the event is described, but, like language itself, to record the *original events:* we might even say it is a system alternative to language for symbolizing events. And therefore it is not strictly writing; for writing is always a *record or representation of language.*

Ideographic "writing" cannot be strictly language either, for it has two limitations which would make it unworkable as a system for expressing human thought. First, it is not within everyone's competence: some of us have no talent for drawing. This, however, could be offset by conventionalizing the characters to a few simple strokes, not immediately recognizable as the original picture except by previous knowledge of the convention (see Figure 42.2).

But then the second, more serious objection still remains: even with such conventionalization, the system cannot adequately express the whole range of human thought; and to do so even partially will require thousands of characters and a system of such complexity that exceedingly few in the society could master it.

The Chinese people have an ancient and beautiful script which was originally, and still is largely, ideographic. The characters have been conventionalized, but it is still quite easy to recognize their origin, as is shown in Figure 42.2. Although there are many mutually unintelligible dialects of Chinese, the same written text can be read by any native (each in his own dialect), and the gist can even be made out by one who knows the principles of the system, but little of the language. Chinese writing is thus one of the strongest forces toward Chinese cultural unity. . . . But

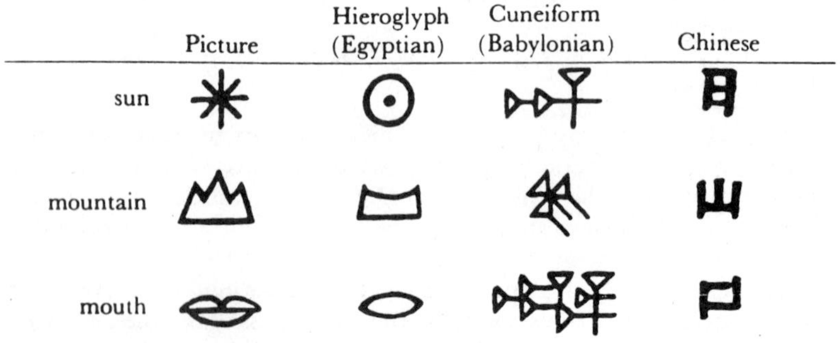

	Picture	Hieroglyph (Egyptian)	Cuneiform (Babylonian)	Chinese
sun				
mountain				
mouth				

FIGURE 42.2.   Conventionalized symbols.

it is estimated that 70,000 to 125,000 characters exist (not all, of course, used with equal frequency), and it is said that a scholar takes seven years to learn to read and write Chinese if he already speaks it, while over 80 percent of the native speakers of Chinese are illiterate in their own language.

Where there is considerable divergence between a language and its written representation, as in the case of Chinese or Italian, where many different dialects are written with the same spelling, or in French or English, where the language has changed considerably since the stage for which the writing was devised, a tendency may arise to consider the written language the "correct" language, of which the spoken language is a deformation which should be "corrected" to agree with the writing. This is particularly true when the writing either records, or once recorded, or is believed to record, the speech of a class of society which enjoys prestige, to which many native speakers would like to assimilate themselves.

This, however, always obscures things and puts the cart before the horse. Actually, the prestige class of any society probably least conforms its speech consciously to writing: sure of their status, its members do not worry about betraying an inferior origin in speech or behavior. It is said that if a man's table manners are absolutely disgusting, he is either a peasant or a duke. Writing is, in its essence, nothing but a means of recording language with some degree of efficiency. Whether one form or another of the language is "good" or "correct" is an entirely different question; a system of writing is good or bad according to how it records, accurately or otherwise, whatever form of the language it is aiming to record.

However, because of the prestige of letters in largely illiterate populations (which is so great that *gramarye* has even been thought to have magic power), the opposite tendency to "correct" language according to written forms has been so strong as to lead to such things as the creation of a word like "misle" from a misreading of the word "misled."[1] Many similar examples could be given.

PICTOGRAPHIC WRITING

Any nation which finds occasion to use a form of ideographic writing with any regularity, even if all the writing is the job of one relatively small social group, will probably sooner or later take the simple and logical step

---

[1] This is an extreme case of what is called "spelling pronunciation." More typical examples are the pronunciation, by Americans in England, of words like *twopence* and *halfpenny* as written.

to *pictographic writing*. In this case, the written sign, which in ideo-graphic writing is the symbol for an *idea*, becomes the symbol of a *word*. For example, a device like

which represents the floor-plan of a house, now becomes a sign for *per*, the Egyptian word for "house," or of *beyt'*, the Hebrew word for "house." Another example: the picture

conventionalized to

$\forall\!\!\!/$

which of course represented the snout of an ox, now becomes a sign for *alep*, the ancient Hebrew word for "ox."

The advantages of this step for the improvement of communication are evident. The written sign now symbolizes, not an idea, but a word, and a word is a far more precise symbol of a mental concept than any other which can be devised. With a sufficient stock of symbols of this new type, the writer can distinguish among a house, a stable, a barn, a shed, and a palace; whereas with ideographic writing he is pretty well limited to "house" vs. "big house" or "small house" (as there is no sepa-rate symbol for the adjective, the bigness or smallness cannot be specified and can range from "largish" to "enormous"). Much ambiguity is avoided: if you have tried to convey messages ideographically . . . you know how easy it is for an intended message "the king is angry" to be interpreted "the old man is sick."

Pictographic writing is, moreover, true writing, since it is a means of recording language, not just an alternative way of expressing the concepts which language expresses.

All pictographic writing systems that we know have developed from ideographic systems, and show clear traces of this, notably in their ten-dency to preserve ideographic symbols among the pictographic. Thus, the ancient Egyptians had an ideograph for water, a representation of waves or ripples:

〰〰〰

Eventually they derived from this a sign

〰〰〰
〰〰〰
〰〰〰

standing for the *mu*, which meant "water." But they often wrote the word *mu* as follows:

〰〰〰   〰〰〰
9   〰〰〰
        〰〰〰

And in writing of a river, the word for which was *atur,*

they also added the water sign: *atur* was written

The purpose of these ideographic "determinants" was probably to help the reader who did not know the particular word or sign by giving an indication of its general connotation. Nouns denoting persons were usually given the "determinant" of a little man —

or a little woman —

For, despite the noteworthy increases in efficiency which pictographic writing represents, thousands of characters are still necessary; and one advantage of the ideographic system has been lost — the characters are no longer self-explanatory. (This is only a theoretical advantage on behalf of ideographic script, since, while the ideographic character for a bird should presumably be readily recognized as a bird, in practice the characters have to be conventionalized for the sake of those who do not draw well.)

A considerable number of pictographic writing systems have been developed at different times in different parts of the world, but, Sunday-supplement science to the contrary notwithstanding, quite independently of one another, so that we have no ground for talking about the "evolution" by man of the art of writing. There is no evidence whatever for a First Cave Man who sat with hammer and chisel and stone and figured out how to chisel the first message, after which man made improvement after improvement, until the peak (represented, of course, by English orthography of the present day) was reached. Actually, nations once literate have been known to lapse into illiteracy as a result of ruinous wars and social disorganization.

SYLLABIC WRITING,
UNLIMITED AND LIMITED

The step from pictographic to syllabic writing is an easy, logical and, it might very well seem, self-evident one; yet there have been several nations which developed the first without ever proceeding to the second. It would probably be safe to say, however, that a majority of those who came as far as pictographic writing took the step to syllabic script.

In pictographic writing it is, of course, as easy to develop a stock of thousands of characters as in ideographic; yet, strange as it might seem, there is still always a shortage. This shortage arises because it is extremely difficult or impossible to represent some words in pictures. Take "velocity," for example. Is there any picture you could draw to express this that might not be read as, say, "the man is running"? Or, if you think you could picture "velocity," how would you handle "acceleration"? If you still think you could manage this one, what sort of picture, pray, would you draw for the word "the"?

The first step toward syllabic writing is taken when you permit yourself to cheat a little and take advantage of homophones. There is, let us say, a good pictograph for "the sea"; you use it to express the Holy "See," or "I see" (writing, perhaps, the characters for *eye* and *sea*).

When you have expressed the word "icy" by the characters for *eye* and *sea*, or *belief* by the characters for *bee* and *leaf*, you have turned the corner to syllabic writing. Any relationship whatever between the character and the *meaning* of the syllable it stands for is henceforth entirely irrelevant. The character expresses nothing but a sequence of sounds — the sounds making up one of the syllables of the language.

The first result of this is a gain of efficiency: a decrease in the number of possible characters (since more than one word or syllable can be written with the same syllabic character — in fact a great number can be written with varying sequences and combinations of a rather small number of characters). This gain is largely theoretical, however, for there will still be several thousand characters. The superiority of syllabic writing over pictographic from the point of view of efficiency will largely depend on the structure of syllables in the language using it. If syllables are generally or always simple in structure, a syllabic system of writing may work extremely well.

In every type of language, however, ambiguity and duplication are likely to be discovered in this kind of *unlimited syllabic* writing. It is often uncertain which of various homonymous readings is intended (e.g., does a character for "deep" joined to one for "end" mean "deep end" or "depend"?). And conversely, there are almost always two or more ways to say the same thing.

If the users of a syllabic system have a sense of logic, they will soon tend to adopt the practice of always writing the same syllable with the same character. The immediate result of this is for the first time to reduce the number of signs to manageable proportions: the sequence *baba* will always be expressed by signs expressing BA BA — never by signs for syllables such as BAB HA, BA ABA, 'B AB HA. Hence the number of signs is not so great as not to be within the capacity of the more or less average memory.

Since many languages have only one syllable-type — CV (i.e., consonant followed by vowel) — application of the principle above to the syllabic writing of such a language results in a very simple, logical and efficient system, next to alphabetic writing the most efficient writing possible.

The simplicity and efficiency are likely to prove elusive, however, when applied to languages of more complex syllabic structure. Even so, one almost inevitably arrives at the idea of having a series of signs representing syllables in which each consonant of the language is paired with each vowel: BA, BE, BI, BO, BU; DA, DE, DI, DO, DU; FA, FE, FI, FO, FU; and so on. A list of such signs is called a *syllabary*.

Some time after this stage of *limited syllabic writing* has been reached, the thought may occur that the inventory of signs can be further reduced by taking one form, without any specification, as the form for, say, BA; and then simply using diacritic marks to indicate the other possible syllable structures: something like the following:

| $\triangle$ BA | λ BI | $\triangle$- BU |
| φ BE | -$\triangle$ BO | |

This brings us very close to alphabetic writing. The last step in syllabic writing and the first in alphabetic writing might come about by accident; suppose a class of words ends in a syllable *-ba*, and in the course of time the vowel ceases to be pronounced. Now the syllabic sign $\triangle$ stands for B alone, not BA; and some sign (in Sanskrit *virāma*, in Arabic *sukūn*) is invented to express this situation: e.g., $\triangle$ will express BA, and $\triangle$ will express B. By use of this sign the vowel of any syllabic sign can be suppressed, and any sign in the syllabary can be made alphabetic.

A situation like that just described is seen in the Semitic writing systems (Arabic, Hebrew), of which it is often said that they "write only the consonants." Actually, all the Arabic and Hebrew letters were originally syllabic signs, representing the consonant *and* a vowel (see Figure 42.3).

ALPHABETIC WRITING

As will be clear by now, true alphabetic writing consists in having a sign for each *sound* (technically each phoneme) of the language, rather than one for each *word* or one for each *syllable*. This is the most efficient writing system possible, since a language will be found to have some thousands of words and at least a couple of hundred different syllables, but the words and syllables are made up of individual speech sounds which seldom exceed sixty to seventy in number, and sometimes number as few as a dozen. Hence an alphabetic writing system can, with the fewest possible units (a number easily within anyone's ability to master), record every possible utterance in the language.

It would seem that the different stages we have traced, from drawing pictures to ideographs, to pictographic and syllabic writing, so logically

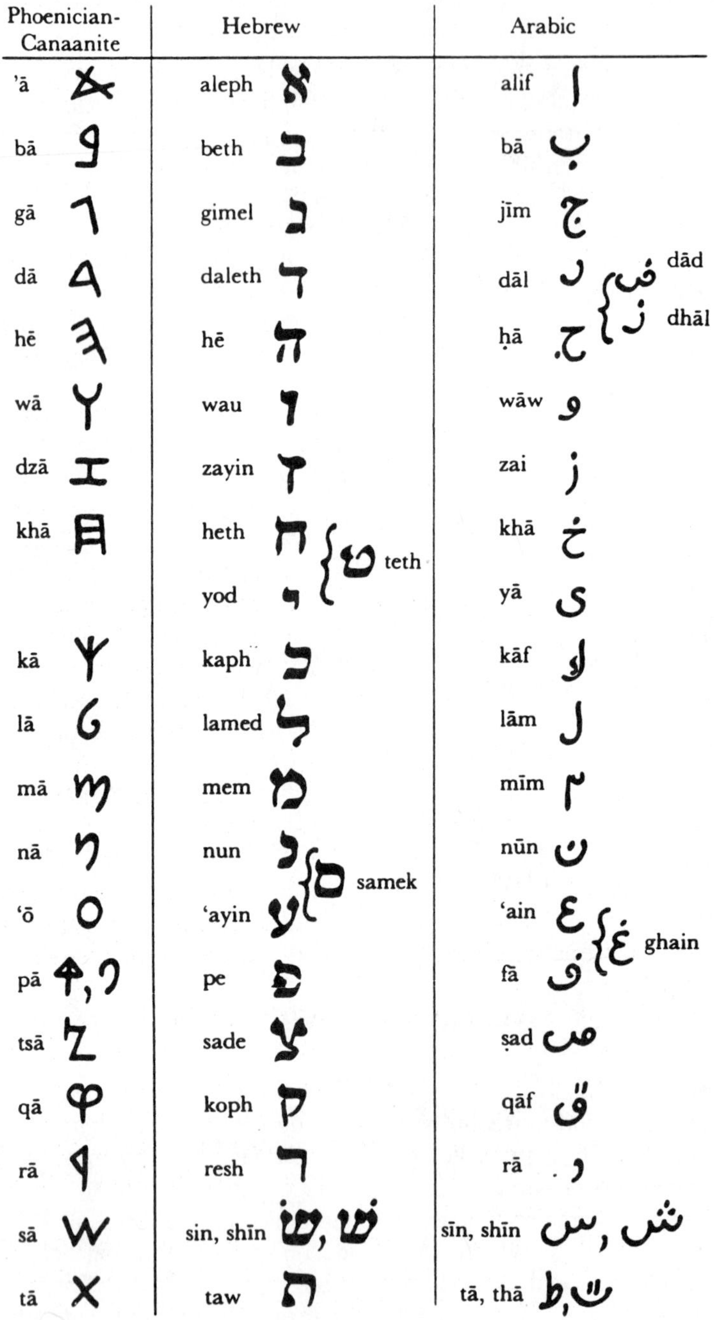

Phoenician-Canaanite		Hebrew		Arabic	
'ā	𐤀	aleph	א	alif	ا
bā	𐤁	beth	ב	bā	ب
gā	𐤂	gimel	ג	jīm	ج
dā	𐤃	daleth	ד	dāl / dād / dhāl	د ض ذ
hē	𐤄	hē	ה	ḥā	ح
wā	𐤅	wau	ו	wāw	و
dzā	𐤆	zayin	ז	zai	ز
khā	𐤇	heth / teth	ח ט	khā	خ
		yod	י	yā	ى
kā	𐤊	kaph	כ	kāf	ك
lā	𐤋	lamed	ל	lām	ل
mā	𐤌	mem	מ	mīm	م
nā	𐤍	nun / samek	נ ס	nūn	ن
'ō	𐤏	'ayin	ע	'ain / ghain	ع غ
pā	𐤐	pe	פ	fā	ف
tsā	𐤑	sade	צ	ṣad	ص
qā	𐤒	koph	ק	qāf	ق
rā	𐤓	resh	ר	rā	ر
sā	𐤔	sin, shīn	ש	sīn, shīn	س ش
tā	𐤕	taw	ת	tā, thā	ت ث

FIGURE 42.3. Semitic alphabets. The names of the letters of the Phoenician-Canaanite (Old Semitic) alphabet are surmises. Letters in one alphabet which do not have correlatives in the others are set off to the side. The traditional order of the Arabic letters has been modified slightly to stress parallels.

follow each other as inevitably to lead a nation or tribe from one to the next until ultimately an alphabetic writing would be achieved. But such is simply not the case. Many great nations, for example the Japanese, have come as far as syllabic writing, and never seemed to feel a need to go beyond it. Indeed, in all the history of mankind, alphabetic writing has been invented only once, and all the alphabets in the world that are truly so called are derived from that single original alphabet. It seems likely that but for a certain lucky linguistic accident, man would never have discovered the alphabetic principle of writing. Had that been the case, the history of mankind would certainly have been very, very different.

There is a strong probability that it was the ancient Egyptians who first hit on the alphabetic principle; but we cannot prove it, for we cannot show that all or even a majority of the characters which ultimately became the alphabet we know were used in Egyptian texts of any period (though an apparently sound pedigree can be made for a few of them).

Of course, the hieroglyphic writing had a stock of thousands of characters, and might well have included the ones we are looking for in texts which have disappeared or not yet been discovered. What is harder to explain, however, is that when the Egyptians wrote alphabetically, they gave alphabetic values to an entirely different set of characters (Figure 42.4). Yet the Egyptians had been using a writing system for literally thousands of years, and had gone through all the stages. It does not seem likely that some other nation came along just as the Egyptians were on the point of discovering the alphabetic principle, snatched the discovery from under the Pharaohs' noses — and then taught *them* how to write alphabetically! There is certainly a mystery here which is still to be solved, and much fame (in learned circles) awaits him who solves it. If the Egyptians did indeed fail, after three thousand years, to discover the principle of alphabetic writing, it is striking evidence that man might never have had this art except for the lucky accident which we shall now proceed to describe.

Not being able to prove a connection between the alphabet and Egyptian writing, for the present we have to say that the oldest known genuine alphabet was the Old Semitic, ultimate ancestor of the scripts used today to write Arabic and Hebrew. This alphabet had, of course, been a syllabic script. How had it turned that all-important corner into alphabetic writing? It seems probable that it was prompted in this direction by the structure of the Semitic languages.

To us, the "root" of our verb *ask* is the syllable *ask*, to which various other syllables are prefixed or suffixed to make the various verbal forms, for example the past tense *(ask-ed)*, the progressive present tense *(is asking)*, the third person singular present *(ask-s)*, and so on.

With verbs like *drive* or *sing*, however, we might say that the root is a syllable *dr-ve* or *s-ng*, where the dash indicates some vowel, but not always the same vowel, since we have *drive, drove, driven, sing, sang,*

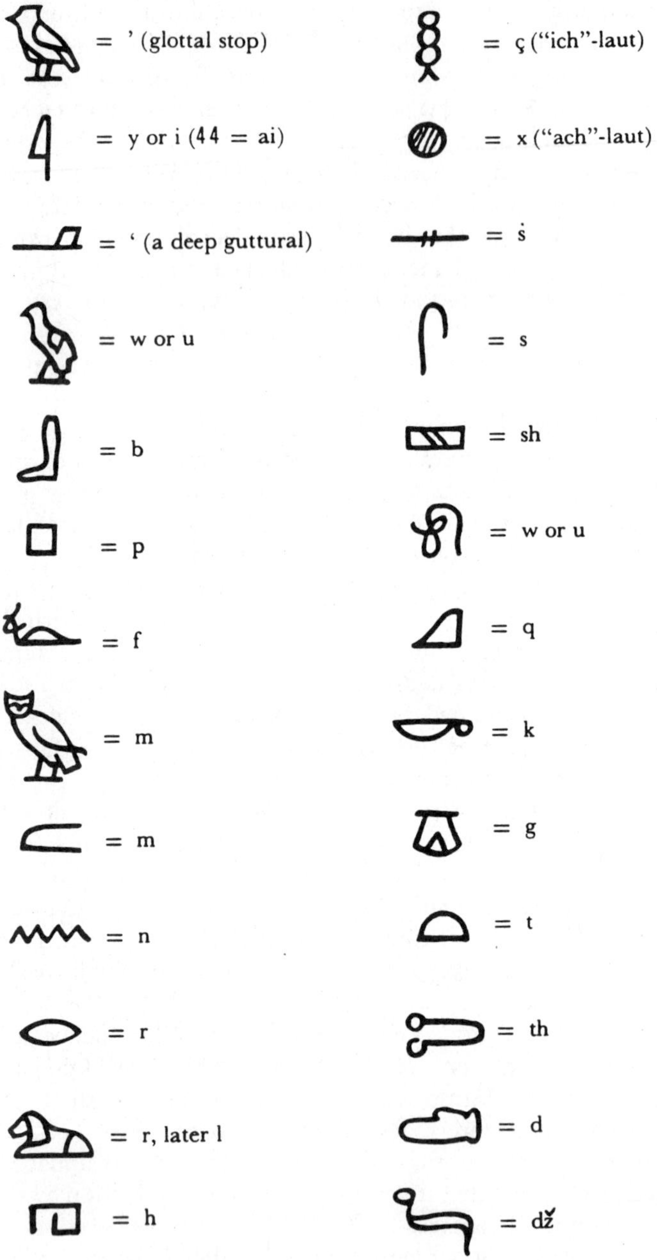

🦅	= ' (glottal stop)	𐃏	= ç ("ich"-laut)
𓇌	= y or i (𓇌𓇌 = ai)	⬤	= x ("ach"-laut)
▱	= ' (a deep guttural)	⚊	= ṡ
🐦	= w or u	∩	= s
𓃀	= b	▱	= sh
□	= p	𓎛	= w or u
🐍	= f	◿	= q
🦉	= m	⌣	= k
⊂	= m	🔺	= g
⋀⋀⋀	= n	⌒	= t
⬯	= r	⚶	= th
🦁	= r, later l	🖐	= d
🔲	= h	🐍	= dž

FIGURE 42.4. Egyptian alphabetic characters.

sung. Something is expressed by the alternation of these vowels, to be sure . . . , but the root of the verb is still a *syllable,* even with a variable vowel.

It was probably some kind of [alternating vowel] system like this which led to the situation now characteristic of Semitic languages (which is really just a further step in this direction), whereby the meaning of "driving" would inhere in the consonants D-R-V, that of "asking" in '-S-K. In Semitic languages the "root" of a word is really a *sequence of consonants* (usually three), modifications of the root being effected by kaleidoscopic rearrangements of the vowels intervening.

Thus, anything to do with writing shows the consonants *K-T-B,* but "he wrote" = *KaTaBa,* "it is written" = *meKTūB,* "he got it written" = *KaTtaBa,* "scribes" = *KuTtaBūn,* and so on. Words which seem to us quite unrelated turn out to be, in this system, derived from each other, like *SaLāM,* "peace," *iSLām,* "the Mohammedan religion," *muSLiM,* "a Mohammedan." (From *salām* we get *'aslāma,* "he pacified, subjugated"; *islām* is "subjugation, submission" to God, and *muslim* is "one who has submitted.")

Obviously, no other type of language is better adapted to suggest to its speakers that there is a unit of word structure below the syllable; that BA is in turn composed of B- and -A. This is precisely what other nations might never have guessed. In Semitic, where BA alternates constantly with BI and BU, and sometimes with B- (the vowel being silenced), it is almost inevitable that every user of the language should develop a concept of the phoneme — a notion which is fundamental to the development of true alphabetic writing.

The structural nature of the Semitic languages is, therefore, in all probability the happy accident which became the key that unlocked for mankind, for the first and only time, the mystery of how to record speech by the method of maximum efficiency — one which does not have so many characters as to make learning it a complex art demanding years of training nor require a skill in drawing which few possess, nor consume large volumes of material for a relatively small amount of recorded message.

The consequences of this lucky accident are truly tremendous. If we did not have the alphabet, it would be impossible to hope for universal literacy, and therefore (if Thomas Jefferson's view was correct) for truly representative government. Writing could have been kept a secret art known only to a privileged few or to a particular social class which would thus have an undue advantage over the others. Information could not nearly so easily be conveyed from nation to nation, and the levels of civilization achieved by the Romans and ourselves might still be only goals to strive for. Truly, Prometheus did not do more for human progress than the unnamed scribe who first drew an alphabetic sign.

THE WANDERINGS OF THE ALPHABET

Let us here stress again that as far as can be ascertained from the available records, the principle of alphabetic writing has only been discovered once — hence, in the whole world *there is only one alphabet.* It follows that any people which writes in alphabetic signs has learned and adapted the use of the alphabet from another people who, in turn, had done the same. When the wanderings of this most potent cultural innovation are plotted, it makes an impressive odyssey. But the same would no doubt be true of every other discovery which has figured in an advance of civilization, if the same means existed for following its trail.

The earliest preserved inscriptions in alphabetic script date to about 1725 B.C. and were found in and around Byblos, in the country then known as Phoenicia (now Lebanon). It would seem that an alphabetic script which we might call Old Semitic was fairly familiar in that region at that time, though, as we have said, we cannot establish precisely where this script was invented, or by which Semitic tribe. It has been suggested that several Semitic peoples might have hit on the alphabetic principle at around the same time; but, if so, they seem to have soon adopted a common set of symbols.

This Old Semitic alphabet is of course the ancestor of the Hebrew, Phoenician, and Aramaic systems of writing. From these northern Semites, the knowledge of the alphabet appears to have passed, on the one hand, to the Greeks of Asia Minor, and on the other, to the Brahmans of ancient India, who developed from it their *devanagari,* the sacred script in which the religious rituals and hymns of the ancient Hindus were recorded.

With this exception, it seems that the genealogy of every other alphabetic system of writing goes through the Greeks. And it was because of the structure of *their* language that the Greeks were responsible for the greatest single improvement in the system: the origination of signs for the vowels.

The Semitic dialects had certain sounds which did not exist in Greek. The symbols for some of these, such as *qoph* (Q), the sign for the velar guttural which had existed in Indo-European but had everywhere been replaced by *p* in Attic Greek, were simply discarded by the Greeks (except in their use as numbers, but that is a different story). In other cases, however, the Greeks kept and used the symbol for a syllable beginning with a non-Greek sound, but pronounced it *without the foreign consonant* — so that the symbol became a sign for the syllable's vowel.

Thus, the first sign in the alphabet originally stood for the syllable *'A,* where the sign *'* represents the "glottal stop," a contraction and release of the vocal cords — not a phoneme in English, but used often enough as a separator between vowels (e.g., oh-'oh), and you have heard it in Scottish dialect as a substitute for T: *bo'le* for *bottle, li'le* for *little.* Some dialects of Greek had this sound, and others did not. Those which did ultimately lost it, so that the sign Ɐ (by now written in a different direction, A) everywhere became the sign, not for 'A, but for the vowel A.

Other Semitic gutturals had had the tendency to influence adjacent vowels in the direction of O or U, and they accordingly, by the process just described, became the signs for those vowels.

A rather good illustration of what was going on is found in the sign H, standing for the syllable HE. In Ionic Greek, where the sound h was eventually eliminated, H became the sign for the vowel e. In Sicilian Greek, however, where syllables beginning with h still remained, the same H became the sign for h — which is our usage also, because we got the alphabet from the Romans, who got it from the Greeks, who followed the Sicilian tradition.

This fact explains deviations in *our* values for the alphabetic signs as compared with those of the standard (Attic) Greek alphabet (see Figure 42.5). Since the alphabet had not been invented as a tool for writing Greek, each Greek dialect which adopted it had to modify it a little — to assign different values to some of the signs, and discard the excess signs or use them in new ways, according to the phonology of their own speech.

While practically all modern nations which have alphabetic writing got it directly or indirectly from the Romans, there are a few to whom the tradition passes directly from the Greeks, in some cases concomitantly with direct northern Semitic influence. Between the third and fifth centuries A.D., the spread of Christianity occasioned the devising of the ornamental and highly efficient Armenian, and the intriguing, delicate Georgian alphabets. And when the feared Goths were marauding throughout Latin Christendom, Ulfilas, child of a Gothic father and a Greek mother, became the St. Patrick of the Goths, Christianizing them and translating the Bible into their language, writing it with an alphabet which, according to repute, he invented, basing it on Greek. Ulfilas' lucky bilingualism not only gave us our oldest extensive records of any Germanic language, but also, it is believed, served as the basis of the Scandinavian "runic" writing, although some think it was the other way around.

Later, in the ninth century, when Christianity reached the Slavic peoples, two principal alphabets, the "glagolitic" and the "Cyrillic" (the latter named in honor of one of its reputed inventors, St. Cyril, who died 869 A.D.; the other inventor was his brother, St. Methodius, d. 855 A.D.), were devised to represent the then most generally used Slavic dialect. From these developed in the course of time the national alphabets of those Slavic peoples who were evangelized from Byzantium — the Russians, the Ukrainians, the Bulgarians, and the Serbs (Figure 42.6). (In contemporary Russia the Cyrillic alphabet has in turn been adapted for writing many non-Indo-European languages of the Soviet Union.)

Slavs who got their religion from Rome had to struggle to put their complex Slavic phonology into the Latin alphabet, with what often seem (to English speakers) jaw-breaking results, as seen in names like Przmysl,

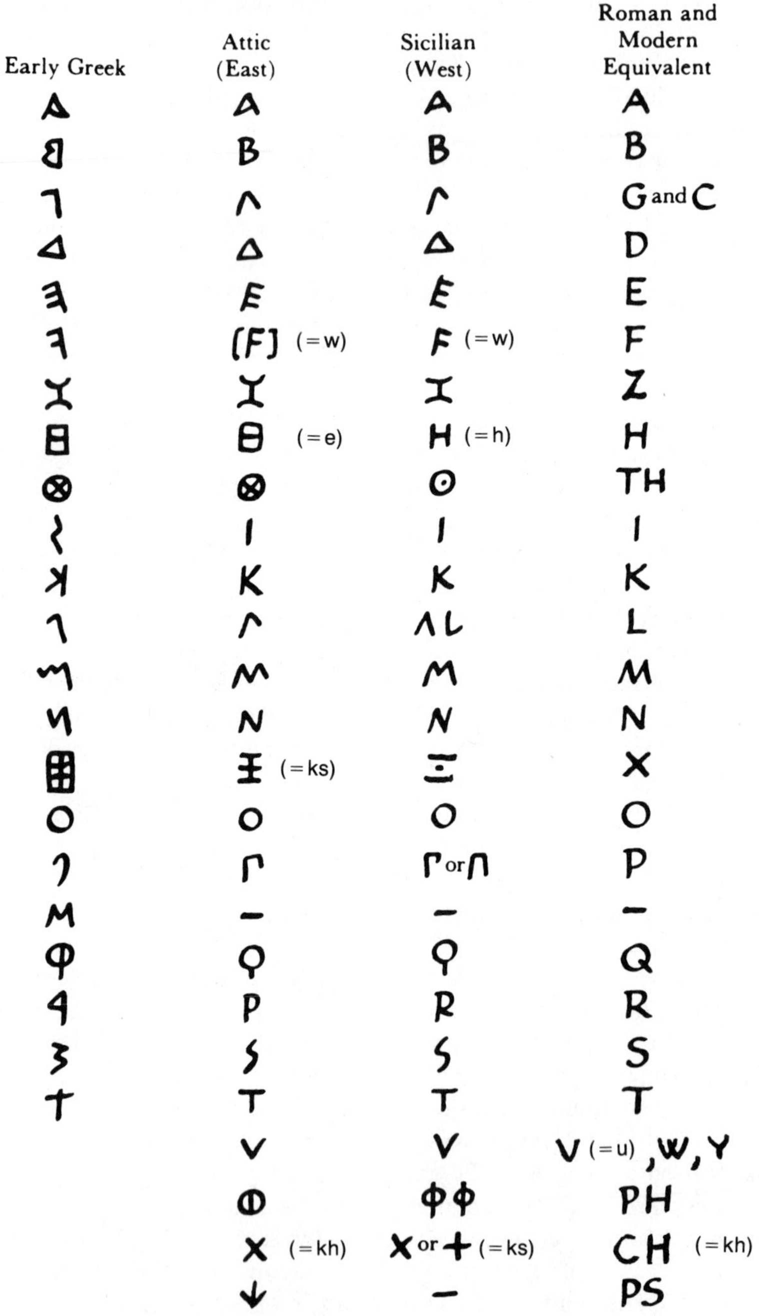

Early Greek	Attic (East)	Sicilian (West)	Roman and Modern Equivalent
A	A	A	A
ꓭ	B	B	B
ꓴ	∧	ℾ	G and C
◁	△	△	D
ꓱ	E	E	E
ꓱ	(F) (=w)	F (=w)	F
I	I	I	Z
日	日 (=e)	H (=h)	H
⊗	⊗	O	TH
⟨	I	I	I
K	K	K	K
⌐	∧	∧ L	L
᲌	M	M	M
Ꞑ	N	N	N
⊞	Ξ (=ks)	Ξ	X
O	O	O	O
ꓸ	⌐	⌐ or ∏	P
M	–	–	–
Φ	φ	φ	Q
ꓼ	P	R	R
Ƨ	ꓢ	ꓢ	S
†	T	T	T
	V	V	V (=u), W, Y
	Φ	φφ	PH
	X (=kh)	X or ✛ (=ks)	CH (=kh)
	ψ	–	PS

FIGURE 42.5. Greek alphabets. Note changes in direction of writing and variation of values between Attica and Sicily (after E. M. Thompson).

Cyrillic	Russian	Equivalent	Cyrillic	Russian	Equivalent
ⱄ	а	a			
Б	б	b	Ȣ	у	u
В	в	v	Ф	ф	f
Г	г	g	Ѳ	ѳ*	f (originally th)
Д	д	d	Х	х	kh
Є	е	ye	Ѡ		ō
Ж	ж	zh	Ш	ш	sh
Ѕ		dz	Ѱ	щ	shch
Ꙁ	з	z	Ч	ц	ts
Н	и	i	Ѵ	ч	ch
І	і*	i	Ъ	ъ*	"hard sign"
Ћ		d', t'	Ꙑ	ы	ӱ
К	к	k	Ь	ь	"soft sign"
Ⰾ	л	l	Ѣ	я	ya
М	м	m	Ю	ю	yu
N	н	n	Ѥ	ѣ*	ye
О	о	o	Ѧ, Ꙗ		ę, yę
П	п	p	Ѫ, Ѭ		ǫ, yǫ
Р	р	r	Ѯ		ks
С	с	s	Ѱ		ps
Т	т	t	Ѵ		ü

*These letters were abolished in 1918.

FIGURE 42.6. Slavic alphabets. Some of the Modern Russian letters are given out of standard order for purpose of matching.

Szczepiński and Wojcechowic. The name Vishinsky, as a rough transcription from the Cyrillic, is identical with the Polish name Wyszinski.

From the great Roman empire the art of alphabetic writing passed, by inheritance or adoption, to virtually all the peoples who know it today. They were responsible for many interesting and important innovations in the basic system which there is not space to detail here, but which may be found in any thorough and complete history of the alphabet. We shall just point out a few of the most significant ones.

The Romance-speaking peoples simply inherited their alphabet; in many cases, they did not realize that they were not still speaking, as well as writing, genuine but perhaps rather careless Latin. When they made an effort to write Latin more correctly, only then did they realize that theirs was actually a different language.

It was during the time when Latin was still spoken, however, that the first modifications had to be made in the alphabet — leading to the first diacritic signs. The sound *h* became silent in colloquial Latin in the first century B.C. and in standard Latin by the second century A.D. Thereafter the letter was a zero, expressing nothing, and hence could be used with other letters to express variations: TH for something like T that was not quite a T; GH for something like G that was not a G, and so on.

Another early diacritic, perhaps the earliest, was the letter G. Words like *signum* had shifted in pronunciation at a very early period from SIG-NUM to SING-NUM to, probably, [seɲo] (where the sign ɲ stands for what is technically a "palatized n," as *gn* in French *mignon* or *ñ* in Spanish *cañón*). This made the G, in this particular position, another zero: and the idea logically arose that any sound could be distinguished from a palatalized correlative by prefixing G to the latter: N/GN; L/GL. Hence Romance languages blossomed with forms like *egli, Bologna, segno, Cagliari*. But Portuguese used the faithful H to express these sounds *(filho, senhor)*, and Spanish, which had divested itself of doubled consonants, used a doubled letter *(castillo, suenno)*, and later used an abbreviation for a doubled *n (sueño)* — for the Spanish *tilde* is nothing other than the well-known medieval Latin MS. abbreviation for an M or N *(tā, dõinū, ītētiõẽ)*. Thus, the American who reads the Italian name *Castiglione* as *Cas-tig-li-o-ni* is murdering the harmonious genuine sound, since the spelling stands for *Ca-sti-lyo-ne*.

When the practice ceased of using as names of the letters the names of the objects they had pictured (or some meaningless derivative thereof, like *alpha, beta*), there arose the custom of naming a letter by giving (in the case of a vowel) its *sound*, or (in the case of a consonant), its sound *preceded or followed by [e]*. (In English this latter sound has uniformly shifted to [i], so we say the letters of the alphabet [e], [bi], [si], but Frenchmen say [a], [be], [se].) In some exceptional cases, however, phonetic shift has eliminated the letter's sound from its name. Our name for R is [ar] (from earlier [er] by the same change which gives us *heart, hearth, ser-*

geant). In English pronunciation, however, R is silent after a vowel, so the name of the letter R is *ah* — with no R in it.

Again, our name for *h* is *aitch*, a meaningless word in English but a preservation of French *la hache* "the hatchet" — suggested by the letter's appearance, to be sure

— but originally containing its sound; no [h] has been pronounced in French, however, for over a century, so the name of this letter, too, fails to contain its sound . . .

Our present letters J and W are known to have been invented in the sixteenth century. In Latin, since all W's had become V's by the second century A.D., the letter U, however written (V, U), expressed that sound — the choice between the rounded and the angular form being purely a matter of calligraphy. The English language, however, had both the V sounds and the W sounds; so, to express the latter, English printers of the sixteenth century "doubled" the former, writing *vv* (or *uu*).

Latin also lacked any sound like English J; but this sound appeared in Old French in words where Latin had had *i*, either as *ee* or as *y* (*Fanuarius* > *janvier*; *iuvenis* > *jeune*), and printers traditionally used *i* for it. Medieval scribes often extended this letter downwards in an ornamental flourish at the end of a number (thus: xiiij), and no doubt it was this which suggested the adoption in English printing of this alternative form of *i* for the *j*-sound. For quite a while, however, many printers continued to regard i/j and u/w/v as interchangeable and to print *Iohn, starres aboue, A VVinter's Tale, Fnterlude*, and so on.

We have been able to mention here only a few of the vicissitudes undergone by the alphabet — *the* alphabet, only one, always the same — in its long journey through space and time from the eastern shores of the Mediterranean to the far islands of the Pacific.

FOR DISCUSSION AND REVIEW

1. According to Hughes, "ideographic writing" is "properly in no sense either language or writing." How does he support this statement? Do you agree or disagree? Defend your answer.

2. The characters of written Chinese each represent, in general, one morpheme or one word. Explain the advantages of such a system, which does not involve any linking of sound to the written characters, to the Chinese as a nation. What are the disadvantages of such a system?

3. Justify Hughes's statement that "Pictographic writing . . . is true writing."

4. Describe the development of syllabic writing systems from picto-

graphic systems. What are the advantages of the former? How might a limited syllabic system develop into an alphabetic system? Is such a logical progression more or less inevitable? Why or why not?

5. Why is alphabetic writing "the most efficient writing system possible"?

6. Explain how the structure of the Semitic languages and the development of the concept of the phoneme led to the development of the alphabet.

7. Summarize chronologically what Hughes calls "the wanderings of the alphabet." In doing so, be sure to explain the important contribution made by the Greeks and how the structure of their language made this improvement possible.

8. What is a diacritic sign? Give three examples (draw them from at least two languages). Describe the development of diacritic signs as part of alphabetic writing.

9. Hughes describes the development of an alphabetic writing system as a "lucky accident" and as "truly tremendous." Describe the kind(s) of cultures that might have developed had an alphabetic writing system not evolved. (Consider, for example, Ray Bradbury's *Fahrenheit 451* or George Orwell's *1984*.)

43

Dictionaries, Change, and Computers

James Larkin

James Larkin is a professor of education at the University of Pennsylvania. In this article, Larkin examines dictionaries and the ways they record language, and how they reflect, legitimate, and even cause linguistic change. From the earliest modern English dictionary to the most recent publications, dictionaries have been used to define our language and, if possible, to facilitate the accessibility of information. While the use of dictionaries today is as prevalent as in the past, Larkin describes the new and growing role computers play in the creation of dictionaries and how they may permanently change the future of dictionaries. He stresses the importance of modern dictionaries as sociological, historical, and cultural documents. As computers continue to change the ways in which dictionaries are produced as well as the speed at which language change is recorded, their importance cannot be overlooked.

Is English a living language? Here's a test.

As the scholar, a renowned compiler of ancient languages, spread the scroll across the table in her favorite diner, she marveled at her own command of the subject: bits of information seemed to queue up in her memory, and then come crashing out in her controversial academic papers. She felt smart. Ambition, drive, and access to a good collection of historical dictionaries had gotten her out of a dumb, dead-end job sweeping up the airport B terminal. As she picked up a menu, a mouse scuttled across the floor in front of her. . . .

The challenge: at least 16 words in the previous passage (extracted from what someday could be a bestselling novel) mean something they didn't 25 years ago, according to their dictionary definitions. What's more, the new meanings of these 16 words have something in common with one another.

Words change; language changes; social organizations change. Dictionaries reflect change, legitimate it, and cause it. The faster we change, the more important it is to keep in touch with our words, language, and society. Dictionaries help us do that.

Although books of knowledge have been around for thousands of years, dictionaries are a relatively recent kind of knowledge book descended directly from encyclopedias. English dictionaries have been around in their modern form for a little over 200 years; earlier "dictionaries," dating to the 13th century, were primarily language-translation books (mostly from Latin to English or other languages) or encyclopedic references in which entries were organized by topic. Of course, translation references have been around much longer, dating at least to post-Sumerian translation guides inscribed on clay tablets, starting about 2300 B.C.

The earliest modern English dictionaries, starting in the early 17th century, were "hard word" books, intended in part for those who lacked formal education, including women. The first was Robert Cawdrey's *A table Alphabetical, conteyning and teaching the true writing, and understanding of hard usuall English wordes,* published in 1604. Over the next 75 years, dictionaries that included specialized words from the arts and sciences, divinity, and law appeared, and offered etymologies as well.

During the 18th century, the audience for dictionaries became more general, and dictionary writers produced more ambitious works: 1735, for example, saw the publication of B. N. Defoe's *A Compleat English Dictionary. Containing the True Meaning of all Words in the English Language: Also The Proper Names of all the Kingdoms, Towns, and Cities in the World: . . . Design'd for the Use of Gentlemen, Ladies, Foreigners, Artificers, Tradesmen; and All who desire to Speak or Write English in its Present Purity and Perfection.*

Works of this time were a kind of lexicographic last gasp for the age of rationalism, reflecting the sense that obtaining perfect knowledge of the world was a large but finite task, within human capabilities. A dictionary was where one documented "the True Meaning of all Words in the English Language," and an individual lexicographer could influence the language in ways that are incomprehensible today.

Prescriptive dictionaries — meant to specify and mold the language — became obsolete, however, with the publication of Samuel Johnson's *Dictionary of the English Language* in 1755. Although Johnson had set out to write a definitive, prescriptive national dictionary on the model of the Académie Française's *Dictionaire de la langue française* (1694), he realized with some regret that standing athwart a language and yelling "Stop!" would not somehow freeze the language in its ideal form. At best, he thought his dictionaries might slow the process of degradation. To this end, he assembled citations from "the best writers" to support and illustrate definitions. This was an important contrast to other dictionaries of the time, which relied heavily on etymologies to define words, taking rather less notice of changing and additional meanings used in everyday writing and, especially, speaking.

Here in the United States, nearly a hundred years passed before Noah Webster published the first of his two dictionaries, which owe a conceptual debt to Johnson's work. Other word books and dictionaries had been published in the States, but Webster set out to describe *American* English. This meant that he added new words, including many adopted from Native American languages, such as *skunk* (Massachusett) and *squash* (Narragansett). He also regularized spellings to bring them more in line with American pronunciation: *labour* became *labor*, *specialise* became *specialize*, for example.

It was Samuel Johnson, though, with his assembling of citations, who provided our model of modern dictionaries (and reference books in general). Johnson's methods presaged what has become the crown jewel of dictionary publishing today: the relational database. By drawing on a body of information to support word definitions, Johnson moved dictionaries a step towards value-neutrality, although he did omit words deemed impolite by his sensibilities. (You know which words — the ones we always look up first in a new dictionary. He also excised a few that you might not suspect — *leg*, for example, he thought a bit racy, and so he substituted *limb*.)

One convention that predates Johnson also contributes to the notion of a dictionary as an archetypal database product: the alphabetic organization of entries, which dissociated words with similar or related meanings. As in a modern database, the location of an entry is irrelevant to understanding its meaning. Instead, the relationships between entries are the currency of understanding. These relationships are made explicit by definitions, cross-references, pronunciation guides, usage notes, and so forth.

The dictionary always has been a database in a way, says David Jost, chief lexicographer at Houghton-Mifflin. Now on-line dictionaries, such as traditional dictionaries on CD-ROM or electronic spelling dictionaries and thesauruses, break down this overt organization even further. "If I have access to a dictionary on line, maybe I have stopped thinking of it as an alphabetic organization," he says. "Now the organization is almost unseen." In both literal and figurative ways, electronic dictionaries may help redefine the word *dictionary*, which most dictionaries currently define as an alphabetic reference.

There are other ways to organize a dictionary besides alphabetically. One dictionary, the *Longman Lexicon of Contemporary English*, organizes information by topic. An entry for *horse*, for example, might contain a drawing of a horse, with its parts labeled, a table explaining related terms (for example *filly, colt, stallion*), and a description of the major uses of horses. (Does this sound anything like hypertext-on-a-page?) Each main and subsidiary entry is listed in an index, so the user can still look up a word alphabetically. This type of dictionary is intended primarily for people learning English.

The idea of alphabetizing reference books took hold gradually over 300 to 400 years during the Middle Ages, in part because nontopical organization violated Scholastic taxonomies; instead of organizing similar topics together, it scattered them across hundreds of pages. The organization of information in physical space became less important because alphabetical organization emphasized navigating the links between entries. Some scholars argue that movable type was the essential technology that encouraged this "nonthematic," modular ordering, since entries could literally be moved around in pieces — and alphabetizing also reflected the way compositors organized metal type in their trays.

DICTIONARY AS DATABASE

Underlying every dictionary is one or more databases. A dictionary database is the soul of the publisher's efforts; the printed dictionary has become a kind of by-product of the primary editorial work of a dictionary publisher, which is to feed and update the database. These databases are of two types: the sources on which a dictionary relies for its authority, commonly called citations; and the entry database, which contains words and definitions, and from which printed and electronic dictionaries are drawn.

Dictionary publishers have a foot in the past and a toe in the future. Many large citation databases are still on index cards, although some are being converted to digital format. Some publishers use a combination of paper and on-line citations, and see no compelling reason to put their older citations on line. At the same time, most entry databases are electronic, and can be linked to a computerized page-layout system.

These technological changes, as well as those in the world at large — for instance, worldwide communications technology — mean both that the language is changing faster, and that dictionaries can respond to and document those changes more rapidly. As a result, modern dictionaries are sociological documents as well as historical and cultural ones. This is a fundamental expansion in the role of dictionaries, closely tied to their shift from a prescriptive to a descriptive mission.

Entries and citations are drawn from a much broader reservoir than ever before, notes Jack Horner, associate publisher of the Random House *Webster's College Dictionary*. "You need a dictionary that reflects the society as it happens to be today," he says. "Our aim is to publish an elegant communications tool that responds to the needs of the public." In a political season, these needs can include definitions to entries like *smoke and mirrors* and *spin control*; in the social realm, to *hit on* now means to engage a person in conversation intended to seduce him or her, in addition to its sense in the phrase "to hit on a good idea." The presence or absence of entries like these can help you judge how frequently and thoroughly a publisher updates a dictionary.

In addition to the information you see on the page of a printed dictionary, a publisher's on-line entry database contains a combination of formatting instructions and vitally important links to other words, such as cross-references. These links help keep a dictionary up-to-date and accurate. For example, when East and West Germany reunited in 1990, Random House was able to update over 300 entries within a few weeks, a month before going to press — not only references to the countries, but, for example, locations of geographical features such as rivers. In the past, the necessity of painstakingly completing and then "locking" (disallowing further entries or changes) each section of a dictionary well before publication made such changes difficult, and most were deferred to a subsequent edition. Database publishing systems also make it easier for publishers to add new words and meanings between major editions. Houghton-Mifflin added *AIDS*, for example, when reprinting an edition.

Going electronic not only keeps publishers competitive, but allows them to expand their product offerings. Random House, for example, promotes their College Edition dictionary as being drawn directly from the unabridged Third Edition. Merriam-Webster draws on its conventional and electronic database for its other products, which include nearly 50 reference books (such as a thesaurus and legal and medical dictionaries), the electronic spelling dictionary that comes with PageMaker, and electronic spellers manufactured by Franklin Electronics.

PUBLISHING A DICTIONARY

A dictionary publisher creates a new edition about every ten years, and may add from several dozen to several hundred new words a year between new editions. (A typical new college edition has 10,000 or more new words.) Creating a dictionary is a collaborative, iterative process, involving a professional staff and outside advisors, in total, several hundred experts in various aspects of the language.

1. *Construction of citation database.* The citation database is the foundation of the modern dictionary, which, like case law, is based on the evidence of precedent — the scientific method applied to language. Citations can come from any published source. In the past, this meant primarily literary sources, but now commonly include citations from advertisements, and from television and radio.

Creating a citation database is a monumental task. The original citation work for the *Oxford English Dictionary* is the most striking example: although the entire dictionary project was initially allotted 10 years, compiling the initial citation database alone occupied the first 22 years of what became a 71-year project, from 1857 to final publication in 1928. (And at that, lexicographer and author Tom McArthur notes, the dictionary was not completed when the whole work was finally published; rather "a truce was established with the language," and supplements were immediately planned.) By the time of publication, the *OED* database consisted of 5 million citations, Merriam-Webster's citation database, now over 100 years old, contains nearly 15 million entries.

New citations come from staff readers and consultants. An editorial staff member may spend several hours a day reading books, magazines, newspapers, watching television, or listening to the radio. One editor watched the Clarence Thomas confirmation hearings with paper and pad at the ready.

Publishers also collect citations from their readers. Some now encourage readers to call in words; Houghton-Mifflin has a toll-free telephone number for readers to call in their own cite sightings. But although many may call (or write), not all are chosen. Some readers contribute words that they make up, including "one person who wanted a word formed on his girlfriend's name," Houghton-Mifflin's Jost recalls. "We sent him a nice letter." (That's not the way to get your made-up word in the dictionary, anyway. You have to prove that other people use the word.)

Although an electronic database seems ideal for dealing with millions of citations and their cross-references, many if not most citation systems are still on millions of index cards. Some publishers are moving towards getting their citations into an electronic format, but the job is a huge one and, ultimately, less important than getting the other part of the process into an electronic format: the writing and editing.

2. *Writing and editing.* Most often the task for writers and editors is to revise a previous edition of an existing dictionary. They may propose to add new words if there is sufficient evidence in the form of citations (it takes more than a few). For example, *DOS* is so widely used in daily language that it is considered by at least one dictionary as a noun, and not just as an acronym for *Disk Operating System.*

Editors may revisit a word to determine whether additional definitions are needed because new senses have entered the language (*mouse* as a computer pointing device is a good example). For the preparation of the third edition of the *American Heritage Dictionary,* Houghton-Mifflin relied on its own citation database for this information, and used NEXIS, an on-line text-retrieval service, to validate its judgments. (For example, an on-line search gathered 5,000 citations that demonstrated that writers use *sneaked* much more often than the formerly nonstandard *snuck,* but that they do use both.)

In some cases, the most common use has changed, requiring reordering of definitions. This depends on the dictionary; not all dictionaries arrange definitions with the most-often-used definitions first. Some are listed etymologically, with new uses of words listed last — a problem for nonnative speakers of English, since they can end up using the archaic forms. (Example: Suppose you're learning English and you encounter a word that you don't know: *satisfaction,* in the sentence *I receive satisfaction from my relationship with my spouse.* The first definition in the *Random House Dictionary of the English Language* is "an act of satisfying; fulfillment; gratification." However, a dictionary that listed definitions in chronological order would tell you first that it was "an act of doing penance or making reparation for venial sin." In this example, perhaps either definition would fit, but the first would likely be more common than the second.)

The role of consultants and usage panels has grown with the quickly changing nature of the language. Both consultants and usage panels, like on-line text services, short-cut and support the citation process. They may include professional specialists across disciplines, who serve to check and correct definitions. They also vote on the appropriateness of parts of speech (for example, the abominable use of *hopefully* to mean "one hopes that"). Many of these specialists are prominent in their fields — writers and other communicators, scientists, linguists — and dictionaries customarily publish the list of panel members, a sort of endorsement by association.

3. *Construction of an entry database.* This is the newest part of publishing a dictionary, and it's not so much a step as a process that affects the writing, editing, and publishing, as well as the business orientation of the publisher. For some publishers, the writing system is some form of a relational database paired with an editing system and a page-composition system. Writers and editors work on line, and are actually modifying a database as they do. The database contains relational features, such as cross-references and the ability to search and extract entries based on user-specified criteria. These links between cross-referenced words are essential for the publisher to respond to changing definitions (for example, Germany is now one country, and the U.S.S.R. no longer exists).

The database can also include codes that the publisher's composition system uses to format text and create publishable pages. The net effect is a much shorter time between writing and publication, and the ability to make more substantial additions and revisions for each new printing of an edition. (The dictionary business is competitive and risky; publishers we talked with preferred not to reveal details about their proprietary publication systems.)

Finally, the database forms the foundation for related products the publisher markets — thesauruses, college and pocket dictionaries, specialized legal and other professional dictionaries, pronouncing and spelling dictionaries, biographical dictionaries, etymological dictionaries, even crossword puzzle dictionaries. The database serves as a basis for electronic products as well, such as on-line versions of printed dictionaries, on-line spelling dictionaries and thesauruses, or hand-held spellers or foreign-language translators. The publisher may also do custom jobs for corporate or government clients.

4. *Production and printing.* Because most publishing systems are integrated with the writing process, updates and corrections to dictionaries can appear much more frequently than in the past. Whereas in the past a publisher might have added a few words, perhaps several dozen,

between printings, electronic page composition means that publishers can now add and correct entries more easily. Some add more than a hundred words a year, and major dictionaries may go to press several times a year, each time with a few changes.

A NEW MATURITY

The dictionary, our most authoritative secular book, is entering a new maturity in which its rapid change both contributes to and feeds on changes in technology and communications. Words come into general currency incredibly quickly; where the *OED* may trace the development of a definition over centuries, a new definition for the word *Patriot*—as an anti-missile missile—appeared in an American dictionary a month after that sense of the word came into general use during the 1991 Gulf War.

Dictionaries still tie us to our histories and our cultures by helping us share rather than balkanize our language. The faster our language and our culture change, the more we need to know what stays the same.

═══

FOR DISCUSSION AND REVIEW

1. How do dictionaries reflect, legitimate, and cause change?
2. What were the purposes of the earliest modern English dictionaries? Do these uses differ from the uses of dictionaries today?
3. What are "prescriptive dictionaries"? How did Samuel Johnson's *Dictionary of the English Language* differ from this prescriptive format? What did Johnson hope to achieve with his dictionary?
4. What do modern dictionaries owe to Johnson's dictionary?
5. What does Larkin cite as the convention of modern dictionaries that predates even Johnson? In what ways is this helpful for word organization?
6. What are some nontraditional ways in which dictionaries can be organized? Include in your answer the ways in which computers are challenging the definition of *dictionary*.
7. What are the "databases" that underlie every dictionary?
8. How are computers changing dictionary databases? What do the changes suggest about our language?
9. In what ways are modern dictionaries sociological, historical, and important cultural documents?
10. How have database publishing systems made dictionaries more efficient?

11. In the process of creating a dictionary, what difficulties arise in the construction of a citation database? An entry database?

12. What is the job of a dictionary's editor? What problems does this person face?

13. How are dictionary entries ordered? Why is this important for a user to know?

14. Larkin says that "Dictionaries still tie us to our histories and our cultures by helping us share rather than balkanize our language." What does he mean? With respect to the rate of language change, how can dictionaries ever be seen as truly valid?

44

Speaking with a
Single Tongue

Jared Diamond

As the industrial nations of the world grow and technology expands, many animal species dramatically decrease in number. Some species weaken and eventually become extinct, gone forever from the earth. This pattern, unfortunately, is also recognizable among the cultures of the world. As we rush to create a global community we run the risk of over-looking and losing some of the world's most precious cultures. Jared Diamond is a contributing editor of Discover *magazine, a professor of physiology at the UCLA School of Medicine, and a research associate at the American Museum of Natural History. He is author of* The Third Chimpanzee: The Evolution and Future of the Human Animal. *In this selection Diamond discusses the inseparability of language and culture: one cannot exist without the other. Diamond warns us that as languages around the world are threatened with extinction, so too is the survival of several indigenous cultures. As a form of communication, identity, and individuality, all language must be regarded as invaluable. With improvements in our international communication systems over the past few decades, and increasing exposure to the more commonly used languages of the world, more and more languages have become extinct. Diamond stresses the urgency and necessity of recording every nearly extinct language for no other reason than to maintain a valuable piece of the history of human culture and evolution.*

"*Kópipi! Kópipi!*" In the jungle on the Pacific Island of Bougainville, a man from the village of Rotokas was excitedly pointing out the most beautiful birdsong I had ever heard. It consisted of silver-clear whistled tones and trills, grouped in slowly rising phrases of two or three notes, each phrase different from the next. The effect was like one of Schubert's deceptively simple songs. I never succeeded in glimpsing the singer, nor have any of the other ornithologists who have subsequently visited Bougainville and listened spellbound to its song. All we know of the kópipi bird is that name for it in the Rotokas language and descriptions of it by Rotokas villagers.

As I talked with my guide, I gradually realized that the extraordinary music of Bougainville's mountains included not only the kópipi's song but also the sounds of the Rotokas language. My guide named one bird after another: *kópipi, kurupi, vokupi, kopikau, kororo, keravo, kurue, vikuroi*. . . . The only consonant sounds in those names are *k*, *p*, *r*, and *v*. Later I learned that the Rotokas language has only six consonant sounds, the fewest of any known language in the world. English, by comparison, has 24, while other languages have 80 or more. Somehow the people of Rotokas, living in a tropical rain forest on one of the highest mountains of the southwest Pacific, have managed to build a rich vocabulary and communicate clearly while relying on fewer basic sounds than any other people.

But the music of their language is now disappearing from Bougainville's mountains, and from the world. The Rotokas language is just one of 18 languages spoken on an island roughly three-quarters the size of Connecticut. At last count it was spoken by only 4,320 people, and the number is declining. With its vanishing, a 30,000-year history of human communication and cultural development is coming to an end.

That vanishing exemplifies a little-noticed tragedy looming over us: the possible loss of 90 percent of our creative heritage, linked with the loss of 90 percent of our languages. We hear much anguished discussion about the accelerating disappearance of indigenous cultures as our Coca-Cola civilization spreads over the world. Much less attention has been paid to the disappearance of languages themselves and to their essential role in the survival of those indigenous cultures. Each language is the vehicle for a unique way of thinking, a unique literature, and a unique view of the world. Only now are linguists starting seriously to estimate the world's rate of language loss and to debate what to do about it.

If the present rate of disappearance continues, our 6,000 modern languages could be reduced within a century or two to just a few hundred. Time is running out even to study the others. Hence linguists face a race against time similar to that faced by biologists, now aware that many of the world's plant and animal species are in danger of extinction.

To begin to understand the problem, we should take a look at how the world's languages are divvied up. If the global population of about 5.5 billion humans were equally distributed among its 6,000 tongues, then each language would have roughly 900,000 speakers—enough to give each language a fair chance of survival. Of course, the vast majority of people use only one of a few "big" languages, such as Mandarin Chinese, English, or Spanish, each with hundreds of millions of native speakers. The vast majority of languages are "little" ones, with a median number of perhaps only 5,000 speakers.

Our 6,000 languages are also unevenly distributed over the globe. Western Europe is especially poorly endowed, with about 45 native languages. In 1788, when European settlement of Australia began, aboriginal Australia was considerably richer: it had 250 languages, despite having far fewer people than Western Europe. The Americas at the time of Columbus's arrival were richer yet: more than 1,000 languages. But the richest region of the globe, then and now, is New Guinea and other Pacific islands, with only 8 million people, or less than .2 percent of the world's population, but about 1,400 languages, or almost 25 percent of the world's total! While New Guinea itself stands out with about 1,000 of those languages, other neighboring archipelagoes are also well endowed—Vanuatu, for example, with about 105, and the Philippines with 160.

Many New Guinea languages are so distinctive that they have no proven relationship with any other language in the world, not even with any other New Guinea language. As I travel across New Guinea, every 10 or 20 miles I pass between tribes with languages as different as English is from Chinese. And most of those languages are "tiny" ones, with fewer than 1,000 speakers.

How did these enormous geographic differences in linguistic diversity arise? Partly, of course, from differences in topography and human population density. But there's another reason as well: the original linguistic diversity of many areas has been homogenized by expansions of political states in the last several thousand years, and by expansions of farmers in the last 10,000 years. New Guinea, Vanuatu, the Philippines, and aboriginal Australia were exceptional in never having been unified by a native empire. To us, the British and Spanish empires may be the most familiar examples of centralized states that imposed their state language on conquered peoples. However, the Inca and Aztec empires similarly imposed Quechua and Nahuatl on their Indian subjects before A.D. 1500. Long before the rise of political states, expansions of farmers must have wiped out thousands of hunter-gatherer languages. For instance, the expansion of Indo-European farmers and herders that began around 4000 B.C. eradicated all preexisting Western European languages except Basque.

I'd guess that before expansions of farmers began in earnest around 6000 B.C. the world harbored tens of thousands of languages. If so, then we may *already* have lost much of the world's linguistic diversity. Of those vanished languages, a few—such as Etruscan, Hittite, and Sumerian—lingered long enough to be written down and preserved for us. Far more languages, though, have vanished without a trace. Who knows what the speech of the Huns and the Picts, and of uncounted nameless peoples, sounded like?

As linguists have begun surveying the status of our surviving languages, it has become clear that prognoses for future survival vary enormously. Here are some calculations made by linguist Michael Krauss of the University of Alaska at Fairbanks. Presumably among the languages with the most secure futures are the official national languages of the world's sovereign states, which now number 170 or so. However, most states have officially adopted English, French, Spanish, Arabic, or Portuguese, leaving only about 70 states to opt for other languages. Even if one counts regional languages, such as the 15 specified in India's constitution, that yields at best a few hundred languages officially protected anywhere in the world. Alternatively, one might consider languages with over a million speakers as secure, regardless of their official status, but that definition also yields only 200 or so secure languages, many of which duplicate the list of official languages. What's happening to the other 5,800 of the world's 6,000?

As an illustration of their fates, consider Alaska's 20 native Eskimo and Indian languages. The Eyak language, formerly spoken by a few hundred Indians on Alaska's south coast, had declined by 1982 to two native speakers, Marie Smith (age 72) and her sister Sophie Borodkin. Their children speak only English. With Sophie Borodkin's death last year at the age of 80, the language world of the Eyak people reached its final silence — except when Marie Smith speaks Eyak with Michael Krauss. Seventeen other native Alaskan languages are moribund, in that not a single child is learning them. Although they are still being spoken by older people, they too will meet the fate of Eyak when the last of those speakers dies; in addition, almost all of them have fewer than 1,000 speakers each. That leaves only two native Alaskan languages still being learned by children and thus not yet doomed: Siberian Yupik, with 1,000 speakers, and Central Yupik, with a grand total of 10,000 speakers.

The situation is similar for the 187 Indian languages surviving in North America outside Alaska, such as Chickasaw, Navajo, and Nootka. Krauss estimates that 149 of these are already moribund. Even Navajo, the language with by far the largest number of speakers (around 100,000), has a doubtful future, as many or most Navajo children now speak only English. Language extinction is even further advanced in aboriginal Australia, where only 100 of the original 250 languages are still spoken or even remembered, and only 7 have more than 1,000 speakers. At best, only 2 or 3 of those aboriginal languages will retain their vitality throughout our lifetime.

In monographs summarizing the current status of languages, one encounters the same types of phrase monotonously repeated. "Ubykh [a language of the northwest Caucasus] . . . one speaker definitely still alive, perhaps two or three more." "Vilela [sole surviving language of a group of Indian languages in Argentina] . . . spoken by only two individuals." "The last speaker of Cupeño [an Indian language of southern California], Roscinda Nolasquez of Pala, California, died in 1987 at the age of 94." Putting these status reports together, it appears that up to half of the world's surviving languages are no longer being learned by children. By some time in the coming century, Krauss estimates, all but perhaps a few hundred languages could be dead or moribund.

Why is the rate of language disappearance accelerating so steeply now, when so many languages used to be able to persist with only a few hundred speakers in places like traditional New Guinea? Why do declining languages include not only small ones but also ones with many speakers, including Breton (around 100,000) and even Quechua (8.5 million)? Just as there are different ways of killing people — by a quick blow to the head, slow strangulation, or prolonged neglect — so too are there different ways of eradicating a language.

The most direct way, of course, is to kill almost all its speakers. This was how white Californians eliminated the Yahi Indian language between 1853 and 1870, and how British colonists eliminated all the native languages of Tasmania between 1803 and 1835. Another direct way is for governments to forbid and punish use of minority languages. If you wondered why 149 out of 187 North American Indian languages are now moribund, just consider the policy practiced until recently by the U.S. government regarding those languages. For several centuries we insisted that Indians could be "civilized" and taught English only by removing children from the "barbarous" atmosphere of their parents' homes to English-language-only boarding schools, where use of Indian languages was absolutely forbidden and punished with physical abuse and humiliation.

But in most cases language loss proceeds by the more insidious process now underway at Rotokas. With political unification of an area formerly occupied by sedentary warring tribes comes peace, mobility, intermarriage, and schools. Mixed couples may have no common language except the majority language (for example, English or Pidgin English in Papua New Guinea, the nation to which Bougainville belongs). Young people in search of economic opportunity abandon their native-speaking villages and move to mixed urban centers, where again they have no option except to speak the majority language. Their children's schools speak the majority language. Even their parents remaining in the village learn the majority language for its access to prestige, trade, and power. Newspapers, radio, and TV overwhelmingly use majority languages understood by most consumers, advertisers, and subscribers. (In the United States, the only native languages regularly broadcast are Navajo and Yupik.)

The usual result is that minority young adults tend to become bilingual, then their children become monolingual in the majority language. Eventually the minority language is spoken only by older people, until the last of them dies. Long before that end is reached, the minority language has degenerated through loss of its grammatical complexities, loss of forgotten native words, and incorporation of foreign vocabulary and grammatical features.

Those are the overwhelming facts of worldwide language extinction. But now let's play devil's advocate and ask, So what? Are we really so sure this loss is a terrible thing? Isn't the existence of thousands of languages positively harmful, first because they impede communication, and second because they promote strife? Perhaps we should actually *encourage* language loss.

The devil's first objection is that we need a common language to understand each other, to conduct commerce, and to get along in peace. Perhaps it's no accident that the countries most advanced technologically are ones with few languages. Multiple languages are just an impediment to communication and progress—at least that's how the devil would argue.

To which I answer: Of course different people need some common language to understand each other! But that doesn't require eliminating minority languages; it only requires bilingualism. We Americans forget how exceptional our monolingualism is by world standards. People elsewhere routinely learn two or more languages as children, with little effort. For example, Denmark is one of the wealthiest and most contented nations in the world. Danes have no problem doing business profitably with other countries, even though practically no one except the 5 million Danes speaks Danish. That's because almost all Danes also speak English, and many speak other foreign languages as well. Still, Danes have no thought of abandoning their tongue. The Danish language, combined with polylingualism, remains indispensable to Danes being happily Danish.

Perhaps you're thinking now, All right, so communication doesn't absolutely require us all to have a single language. Still, though, bilingualism is a pain in the neck that you yourself would rather be spared.

But remember that bilingualism is practiced especially by minority language speakers, who learn majority languages. If they choose to do that extra work, that's their business; monolingual speakers of majority languages have no right or need to prevent them. Minorities struggling to preserve their language ask only for the freedom to decide for themselves—without being excluded, humiliated, punished, or killed for exercising that freedom. Inuits (Eskimos) aren't asking U.S. whites to learn Inuit; they're just asking that Inuit schoolchildren be permitted to learn Inuit along with English.

The devil's second objection is that multiple languages promote strife by encouraging people to view other peoples as different. The civil wars tearing apart so many countries today are determined by linguistic lines. Whatever the value of multiple languages, getting rid of them may be the price we have to pay if we're to halt the killing around the globe. Wouldn't the world be a much more peaceful place if the Kurds would just agree to speak Arabic or Turkish, if Sri Lanka's Tamils would consent to speak Sinhalese, and if the Armenians would switch to Azerbaijani (or vice versa)?

That seems like a very strong argument. But pause and consider: language differences aren't the sole cause, or even the most important cause, of strife. Prejudiced people will seize on any difference to dislike others, including differences of religion, politics, ethnicity, and dress. One of the world's most vicious civil wars today, that in the land that once was Yugoslavia, pits peoples unified by language but divided by religion and ethnicity: Orthodox Serbs against Catholic Croats and Muslim Bosnians, all speaking Serbo-Croatian. The bloodiest genocide of history was that carried out under Stalin, when Russians killed mostly other Russians over supposed political differences. In the world's bloodiest genocide since World War II, Khmer-speaking Cambodians under Pol Pot killed millions of other Khmer-speaking Cambodians.

If you believe that minorities should give up their languages in order to promote peace, ask yourself whether you believe that minorities should also promote peace by giving up their religions, their ethnicities, their political views. If you believe that freedom of religion but not of language is an inalienable human right, how would you explain your inconsistency to a Kurd or an Inuit? Innumerable examples besides those of Stalin and Pol Pot warn us that monolingualism is no safeguard of peace. Even if the suppression of differences of language, religion, and ethnicity did promote peace (which I doubt), it would exact a huge price in human suffering.

Given that people do differ in language, religion, and ethnicity, the only alternative to tyranny or genocide is for people to learn to live together in mutual respect and tolerance. That's not at all an idle hope. Despite all the past wars over religion, people of different religions do coexist peacefully in the United States, Indonesia, and many other countries. Similarly, many countries that practice linguistic tolerance find that they can accommodate people of different languages in harmony: for example, three languages in Finland (Finnish, Swedish, and Lapp), four in Switzerland (German, French, Italian, and Romansh), and nearly a thousand in Papua New Guinea.

All right, so there's nothing inevitably harmful about minority languages, except the nuisance of bilingualism for the minority speakers. What are the positive advantages of linguistic diversity, to justify that minor nuisance?

One answer is that languages are the most complex products of the human mind, each differing enormously in its sounds, structures, and pattern of thought. But a language itself isn't the only thing lost when a language goes extinct. Each language is indissolubly tied up with a unique culture, literature (whether written or not), and worldview, all of which also represent the end point of thousands of years of human inventiveness. Lose the language and you lose much of that as well. Thus the eradication of most of the world's accumulation of languages would be an overwhelming tragedy, just as would be the destruction of most of the world's accumulated art or literature. We English speakers would regard the loss of Shakespeare's language and culture as a loss to humanity; Rotokas villagers feel a similar bond to their own language and culture. We are putting millions of dollars into the effort to save one of the world's 8,600 bird species, the California condor. Why do we care so little about most of the world's 6,000 languages, or even desire their disappearance? What makes condors more wonderful than the Eyak language?

A second answer addresses two often-expressed attitudes: "One language is really as good as another," or conversely, "English is much better than any of those fiendishly complicated Indian languages." In reality, languages aren't equivalent or interchangeable, and there's no all-purpose "best language." Instead, as everyone fluent in more than one language knows, different languages have different advantages, such that it's easier to discuss or think about certain things, or to think and feel in certain ways, in one language than another. Language loss doesn't only curtail the freedom of minorities, it also curtails the options of majorities.

Now perhaps you're thinking, enough of all this vague talk about linguistic freedom, unique cultural inheritance, and different options for thinking and expressing. Those are luxuries that rate low priority amid the crises of the modern world. Until we solve the world's desperate socioeconomic problems, we can't waste our time on bagatelles like obscure Indian languages.

But think again about the socioeconomic problems of the people speaking all those obscure Indian languages (and thousands of other obscure languages around the world). Their problems aren't just narrow ones of jobs and job skills, but broad ones of cultural disintegration. They've been told for so long that their language and everything else about their culture are worthless that they believe it. The costs to our government, in the form of welfare benefits and health care, are enormous. At the same time, other impoverished groups with strong intact cultures — like some recent groups of immigrants — are already managing to contribute to society rather than take from it.

Programs to reverse Indian cultural disintegration would be far better than welfare programs, for Indian minorities and for majority taxpayers alike. Similarly, those foreign countries now wracked by civil wars along linguistic lines would have found it cheaper to emulate countries based on partnerships between proud intact groups than to seek to crush minority languages and cultures.

Those seem to me compelling cultural and practical benefits of sustaining our inherited linguistic diversity. But if you're still unconvinced, let me instead try to persuade you of another proposition: that we should at least record as much information as possible about each endangered language, lest all knowledge of it be lost. For hundreds, perhaps thousands, of the world's 6,000 languages, we have either no written information at all, or just brief word lists. If many of those languages do indeed vanish, at least we'd have preserved as much knowledge as possible from irreversible loss.

What is the value of such knowledge? As one example, consider that relationships of the languages that survive today serve to trace the history of human development and migrations, just as relationships of existing animal and plant species trace the history of biological evolution. All linguists agree, for instance, that we can trace existing Indo-European languages back to an ancestral Proto-Indo-European language spoken somewhere in Europe or western Asia around 6,000 years ago. Now some linguists are trying to trace languages and peoples back much further in time, possibly even back to the origin of all human language. Many tiny modern languages, the ones now most at risk of vanishing unrecorded, have proved disproportionately important in answering that question that never fails to interest each of us: Where did I come from?

Lithuanian, for example, is an Indo-European language with only 3 million speakers, and until recently it struggled against Russian for survival. It's dwarfed by the combined total of 2 billion speakers of the approximately 140 other Indo-European languages. Yet Lithuanian has proved especially important in understanding Indo-European language origins because in some respects it has changed the least and preserved many archaic features over the past several thousand years.

Of course, dictionaries and grammars of Lithuanian are readily available. If the Lithuanian language were to go extinct, at least we'd already know enough about it to use it in reconstructing Indo-European language origins. But other equally important languages are at risk of vanishing with much less information about them recorded. Why should anyone care whether four tiny languages, Kanakanabu, Saaroa, Rukai, and Tsou, spoken by 11,000 aborigines in the mountains of Taiwan, survive? Other Asians may eventually come to care a lot, because these languages may constitute one of the four main branches of the giant Austronesian language family. That family, consisting of some 1,000 languages with a total of 200 million speakers, includes Indonesian and Tagalog, two of Asia's most important languages today. Lose those four tiny aboriginal languages and these numerous Asian peoples may lose one-quarter of the linguistic data base for reconstructing their own history.

If you now at last agree that linguistic diversity isn't evil, and might even be interesting and good, what can you do about the present situation? Are we helpless in the face of the seemingly overwhelming forces tending to eradicate all but a few big languages from the modern world?

No, we're not helpless. First, professional linguists themselves could do a lot more than most of them are now doing. Most place little value on the study of vanishing languages. Only recently have a few linguists, such as Michael Krauss, called our attention to our impending loss. At minimum, society needs to train more linguists and offer incentives to those studying the languages most at risk of disappearing.

As for the rest of us, we can do something individually, by fostering sympathetic awareness of the problem and by helping our children become bilingual in any second language that we choose. Through government, we can also support the use of native languages. The 1990 Native American Languages Act actually *encourages* the use of those languages. And at least as a start, Senate Bill 2044, signed by former President Bush last October, allocates a small amount of money — $2 million a year — for Native American language studies. There's also a lot that minority speakers themselves can do to promote their languages, as the Welsh, New Zealand Maori, and other groups have been doing with some success.

But these minority efforts will be in vain if strongly opposed by the majority, as has happened all too often. Should some of us English speakers not choose actively to promote Native American languages, we can at least remain neutral and avoid crushing them. Our grounds for doing so are ultimately selfish: to pass on a rich, rather than a drastically impoverished, world to our children.

═══

FOR DISCUSSION AND REVIEW

1. How are languages linked to the survival of indigenous cultures?

2. How does Diamond divide the world's languages? In what ways do these divisions emphasize the gradual extinction of various languages?

3. Describe geographic differences with respect to linguistic diversity. How did these enormous geographic differences arise?

4. What does Diamond mean when he says that the "prognoses for future survival vary enormously"?

5. What does *moribund* mean? What does this have to do with language extinction?

6. Why has the rate of language disappearance been accelerating so quickly in recent years? What are the different ways of "eradicating" a language that Diamond describes?

7. What are the more "insidious processes" of the loss of language Diamond describes?

8. How has the media fostered the process of language decay?

9. "Multiple languages are just an impediment to communication and progress." Do you agree or disagree with this statement? Why?

10. How do historical figures such as Pol Pot and Stalin warn us that monolingualism is no safeguard for peace?

11. Diamond states that "a language itself isn't the only thing lost when a language goes extinct." What does he mean by this statement?

12. Why must we preserve as much information about endangered and minority languages as possible? What purposes would this information serve?

13. Diamond asserts that we are not helpless to prevent the process of language extinction. In what ways can we help to slow this process? Can you make any other suggestions?

Projects for "Broader Perspectives"

1. Obtain the book *Gender Advertisements* by Erving Goffman (New York: Harper Colophon Books, 1979). Read the excellent introduction by Vivian Gornick, and then examine at least one section of text and illustrative advertisements. Prepare a report of your findings, indicating to what extent the way you look at advertisements in the future will be affected by what you have learned.

2. Most of our feelings of territoriality are unconscious unless and until "our territory" is violated. Prepare a report in which you describe the reactions of another person when you do some or all of the following: (a) after a class has been meeting for at least three weeks, deliberately sit in a seat that you know has regularly been occupied by someone else; (b) in your library or snack bar, move someone else's books or food and sit down while the person is temporarily away; (c) in an uncrowded library or classroom, deliberately sit right next to another individual; (d) in your dorm room or at home, deliberately sit (in a chair, at a desk, etc.) where you know someone else "belongs."

3. Individually or in small groups, prepare answers to the following questions for a class discussion: (a) What are your three most common gestures? What are your instructor's three most common gestures? What conclusions (about personality, setting, etc.) can you draw from these? (b) In a conversation, how do you know when someone is losing interest? Is not losing interest? (c) What aspects of a person's appearance cause you to feel (at least initially) friendly? Hostile? (d) In what ways do you act differently at home from the way you do at a friend's? Why?

4. Study the above illustration of a typical buyer-seller relationship; the buyer is on the left and the seller on the right. Discuss the interaction

between the buyer and the seller in terms of their gestures, their personal appearances, and their proxemic arrangement. What general statements can you make about the buyer? About the seller?

5. Using the following diagrams of common classroom seating arrangements, devise an experiment that will test the effects on behavior of various arrangements. You may wish to poll the feelings of members of a number of classes and elicit reasons for their feelings. Which arrangement was judged most comfortable? Least comfortable? Why? Is there any relationship between seating arrangements and class size? Between seating arrangements and class or grade level? Between seating arrangements and types of classroom activities or subject matter? Explain.

"row-by-row"　　　　　　　"horseshoe"　　　　　　　"circle"

OOOOOOOOOOOOOOO

O = student
X = teacher

6. Study a short movie while the sound is turned off. Make notes on your observations of proxemics and body language and what you learn from these aspects of behavior. Turn on the sound and make notes on your findings once again. Write a paper that discusses the quantitative and qualitative differences in what you learned from both viewings. Ideally, you should try to determine the relative importance of body language, verbal communication, and proxemics.

7. If you know Russian, prepare a comparison of the Cyrillic and Roman alphabets. Which alphabet is a better fit for Russian? For English? Why?

8. A number of "expert systems" are currently available and being used in a variety of situations. Prepare a report describing one of the following systems: DENDRAL, MYCIN, PROSPECTOR, KAS, TEIRESIAS, MOLGEN, GUIDON, TATR, CATS-1, PUFF, ONCOCIN.

9. A good deal of interesting work has been done with the systems of communication of animals other than chimpanzees. Using items included in the bibliography for this section, write a paper in which you review the research that has been done with bees, birds, or dolphins. You should supplement your research materials by looking in the *Reader's Guide to Periodical Literature* and the *Social Sciences and Humanities Index*.

10. Prepare a report describing the research with one or more chim-

panzees involved in communication experiments. A good starting place is Eugene Linden's book *Apes, Men, and Language* (Pelican Books, 1976) and its bibliography, but be sure to go beyond this single source. An interesting variation would be to have the class divide into groups, with each group responsible for preparing an oral or written report on a particular experiment.

11. George Yule's essay "Sign Language" introduces us to alternative methods of communication, languages used by people who lack vocal-auditory capabilities. In class, play a game of charades. Watch your classmates closely to see what signs, gestures, and facial expressions are used to convey their messages to the class.

Next, you may wish to create a list of words that you have to draw in order to convey meaning to the class, similar to the popular game "Pictionary." Make notes of the most obvious gestures your pictures attempt to create. When you complete these games, discuss the statement: "We aren't as distant from signed languages as we might sometimes think." How have these exercises influenced your impressions of Signed English and ASL?

12. In his essay, James Larkin explores the new role that computers are playing in the study of the English language. Go to your school library and collect information on natural language processing by computers. Several studies are currently under way that attempt to program computers to process and respond to verbal commands as well as make judgments on what they have heard. Consult the bibliography that follows for sources that might contain useful information. From what you discover through your research, do you believe it will be possible to teach computers to learn language? What implications for the future do you foresee if scientists succeed in teaching computers how to process languages?

Selected Bibliography

Nonverbal Communication

Ardrey, Robert. *The Territorial Imperative.* New York: Atheneum, 1966. [An examination of the concept of territoriality, the relationship of men and animals to space.]

Ashcraft, Norman, and Albert E. Scheflen. *People Space: The Making and Breaking of Human Boundaries.* Garden City, NY: Anchor Books, 1976. [Two distinguished scholars, an anthropologist and a psychiatrist, examine the hidden rules that govern our use of space.]

Birdwhistell, Ray L. *Introduction to Kinesics.* Louisville: University of Louisville Press, 1952. [Introduction to the field of kinesics, with kinegraphs and what they symbolize.]

———. "Kinesics." *International Encyclopaedia of Social Sciences.* Ed. David L. Sills. New York: Macmillan and The Free Press, 1968. [A brief but technical introduction.]

———. *Kinesics and Context: Essays on Body Motion Communication.* Philadelphia: University of Pennsylvania Press, 1970. [An interesting collection of Birdwhistell's essays on nonverbal human communication; excellent bibliography.]

Davis, Flora. *Inside Intuition: What We Know About Nonverbal Communication.* New York: New American Library (Signet), 1975. [Despite its popular title, a good summary of recent research; complete bibliography; readable.]

Goffman, Erving. *Gender Advertisements.* New York: Harper Colophon Books, 1979. [Goffman is a widely recognized social scientist; here he investigates advertisements and the way in which they do and do not reflect reality; highly recommended.]

———. *Behavior in Public Places.* New York: The Free Press of Glencoe, 1963. [A psychiatrist's analysis of public behavior.]

———. *The Presentation of Self in Everyday Life.* Edinburgh: University of Edinburgh, Social Sciences Research Center, 1956. [An analysis of an individual's impressions of himself when appearing before others.]

Hall, Edward T. *Beyond Culture.* Garden City, NY: Doubleday, 1976. [A study of how some of the basic cultural systems such as time and space are used to organize human behavior.]

———. "Proxemics." *Current Anthropology,* 9 (April–June 1968), 83–104. [A good introduction to proxemics with charts, comments by authorities, and bibliography.]

———. *The Hidden Dimension.* Garden City, NY: Doubleday, 1966. [A fascinating discussion of human and animal use of space.]

———. *The Silent Language.* Garden City, NY: Doubleday, 1959. [A pioneer work on space and language.]

Harris, Christie, and Moira Johnston. *Figleafing Through History: The Dynamics of Dress.* New York: Atheneum, 1971. [An entertaining historical discussion of clothes and how they affect the self-conceptions of individuals in different societies.]

Henley, Nancy M. *Body Politics: Power, Sex, and Nonverbal Communication.*

Englewood Cliffs, NJ: Prentice-Hall, 1977. [A very important book; crucial to an understanding of the full impact of nonverbal communication.]

Hewes, Gordon W. "World Distribution of Certain Postural Habits." *American Anthropologist*, 57 (April 1955), 231–244. [Distribution and significance of certain standing and sitting positions.]

Hinde, Robert A., ed. *Non-Verbal Communication*. Cambridge, Engl.: Cambridge University Press, 1972. [An informative collection of fifteen essays on the nature of communication, communication in animals, and nonverbal communication in man.]

Knapp, Mark L. *Nonverbal Communication in Human Interaction*. 2nd ed. New York: Holt, Rinehart and Winston, 1978. [A very thorough survey of research; excellent notes and comprehensive bibliography.]

Michael, G. and F. N. Willis, Jr. "The Development of Gestures as a Function of Social Class, Education, and Sex." *Psychological Record*, 18 (October 1968), 515–519. [A study of eight groups of children differing in social class, education, and sex.]

Morris, Desmond. *The Human Zoo*. New York: McGraw-Hill, 1969. [A zoologist's analysis of sociological implications of population clusters.]

Pittenger, Robert E., Charles F. Hackett, and John J. Danehy. *The First Five Minutes: A Sample of Microscopic Interview Analysis*. Ithaca, NY: Paul Martineau, 1960. [An in-depth analysis with emphasis on paralinguistic features of a five-minute interview between a psychiatrist and a young female patient.]

Poyatos, Fernando. *Cross-Cultural Perspectives in Nonverbal Communication*. Lewiston, NY: C. J. Hogrefe Inc., 1988. [Gestures, painting, photography, clothing, and architecture are included as forms of nonverbal communication in this interesting study.]

Scheflen, Albert E. *How Behavior Means*. Garden City, NY: Anchor Press/Doubleday, 1974. [A pioneer in kinesics examines nonverbal communication, territoriality, the environment, and cultural context; highly recommended.]

———. *Body Language and the Social Order: Communication as Behavior Control*. Englewood Cliffs, NJ: Prentice-Hall, 1972. [A discussion of the uses of body language for purposes of social control.]

———. "The Significance of Posture in Communications Systems" *Psychiatry*, 27 (November 1964), 316–331. [A psychiatrist's analysis of the significance of postural activities and markers in interview and group situations; illustrated.]

Wolkomir, Richard. "American Sigh-n Language: 'It's not mouth stuff — it's brain stuff,'" *Smithsonian*. July 1992, pp. 30–41. [A captivating study of how deaf people communicate in our spoken world.]

Artificial Intelligence

Note: Much of the literature in this field is highly technical. The books listed below represent a small selection from the available material.

Barr, Avron and Edward A. Feigenbaum, eds. *The Handbook of Artificial Intelligence*. Volumes I, II, and III. Los Altos, CA: William Kaufman, 1982.

Bobrow, D. G. and Allan Collins, eds. *Representation and Understanding: Studies in Cognitive Science*. New York: Academic Press, 1975.

Boden, Margaret. *Artificial Intelligence and Natural Man.* New York: Basic Books, 1977.

Campbell, Jeremy. *Grammatical Man: Information, Entropy, Language, and Life.* New York: Simon & Schuster, 1982.

Feigenbaum, Edward A. and Pamela McCorduck. *The Fifth Generation.* Reading, MA: Addison-Wesley, 1983.

Hanson, Dirk. *The New Alchemists.* New York: Avon, 1982.

Hofstadter, Douglas. *Godel, Escher, Bach: An Eternal Golden Braid.* New York: Basic Books, 1979.

McCorduck, Pamela. *Machines Who Think.* New York: W. H. Freeman and Company, 1979.

Moll, Robert N., M. A. Arbib, A. J. Kfoury. *An Introduction to Formal Language Theory.* New York: Springer-Verlag Inc., 1988. [Explores issues in computational linguistics with the comparison of human language analysis to artificial intelligence.]

Powers, David M. W. and C. C. R. Turk. *Machine Learning of Natural Language.* London: Springer-Verlag London Limited, 1989. [Focuses on the methods children employ to learn language in an attempt to create packages for machines to do the same.]

Schank, Roger C., ed. *Conceptual Information Processing.* New York: American Elsevier, 1975.

Shwartz, Steven P. *Applied Natural Language Processing.* Princeton, NJ: Petrocelli Books, Inc., 1987. [An informative examination of the field of artificial intelligence and its correlation to the theories of human language processing.]

Simon, Herbert A. *The Sciences of the Artificial.* 2nd ed. Cambridge, MA: MIT Press, 1981.

Winograd, Terry. *Understanding Natural Language.* New York: Academic Press, 1972.

Winston, Patrick. *Artificial Intelligence.* Reading, MA: Addison-Wesley, 1977.

Animal Communication

Fleming, Joyce D. "Field Report: The State of the Apes." *Psychology Today,* 7 (January 1974), 31–38, 43–44, 46, 49–50. [A summary of research with Washoe, Lucy, Sarah, and other chimps.]

Ford, Barbara. "How They Taught a Chimp to Talk." *Science Digest,* 67 (May 1970), 10–17. [A discussion of the chimpanzee Washoe's sign language, with illustrations.]

Gardner, Beatrice T. and R. Allen Gardner. "Teaching Sign Language to a Chimpanzee." *Science,* 165 (August 15, 1969), 664–672. [Teaching the infant chimpanzee Washoe the gestural language of the deaf.]

———. "Teaching Sign Language to a Chimpanzee. VII: Use of Order in Sign Combinations." *Bulletin of the Psychonomic Society,* 4 (1974), 264. [More technical; Washoe at a later stage.]

———. "Early Signs of Language in Child and Chimpanzee." *Science,* 187 (1975), 752–753. [A comparison of Washoe's acquisition of signs with child language acquisition.]

Hayes, Catherine. *The Ape in Our House.* New York: Harper & Brothers, 1951. [The story of the Hayes family's experiences with the chimpanzee Viki.]

Krough, August. "The Language of the Bees." *Scientific American Reader.* New

York: Simon & Schuster, 1953. [A summary of Karl von Frisch's classic study of communication among bees.]

Lilly, John C. *Man and Dolphin*. New York: Pyramid Publications, 1969. [The story of one man's attempt to communicate with another species.]

———. *The Mind of the Dolphin: A Nonhuman Intelligence*. New York: Avon Books, 1969. [An introduction to the controversial world of communication among dolphins.]

Linden, Eugene. *Apes, Men, and Language*. New York: Pelican Books, 1976. [A chatty survey of most of the research then being done in this country with chimpanzees.]

Patterson, Francine. "Conversations With a Gorilla." *National Geographic* (October 1978), 438–465. [Excellent photographs.]

Premack, David, "The Education of Sarah: A Chimp Learns the Language." *Psychology Today*, 4 (September 1970), 54–58. [Describes the process of teaching a chimpanzee a nonvocal language.]

Riopelle, A. J., ed. *Animal Problem Solving*. Baltimore: Penguin Books, 1967. [A collection of reports on problem-solving experiments with animals.]

Sebeok, Thomas A., and Jean Umiker-Sebeok, eds. *Speaking of Apes: A Critical Anthology of Two-Way Communication With Man*. New York: Plenum Press, 1980. [Indispensable and totally comprehensive. Very complete bibliography.]

Terrace, Herbert S. *Nim: A Chimpanzee Who Learned Sign Language*. New York: Alfred A. Knopf, 1979. [A book-length study detailing Terrace's four-year work with Nim.]

Terrace, H. S., L. A. Petitto, R. J. Sanders, and T. G. Bever. "Can an Ape Create a Sentence?" *Science*, 206 (November 1979), 891–902. [A more technical and complete account than that which appeared in *Psychology Today*; extensive bibliography.]

Wilson, Edward O. "Animal Communication." *Scientific American*, 227 (1972), 52–60. [From insects to mammals, animals communicate — but man's language is unique.]

Writing

Barfield, Owen. *History in English Words*. 1953; Great Barrington: Lindisfarne Press, 1988. [An exploration of how our knowledge has been shaped by words and language and how language has evolved and changed through writing.]

Cleary, Linda Miller. *From the Other Side of the Desk: Students Speak Out About Writing*. Portsmouth, NH: Boynton/Cook Publishers, Inc., 1991. [An invaluable glimpse into the frustrating process of learning writing from the point of view of high-school students.]

Diringer, D. *The Alphabet*. New York: Philosophical Library, 1948. [A detailed history.]

Gelb, I. J. *A Study of Writing*. Rev. ed. Chicago: University of Chicago Press, 1963. [A highly recommended study of the origin and evolution of writing systems.]

Pyles, Thomas and John Algeo. *The Origins and Development of the English Language*. 3rd ed. New York: Harcourt Brace Jovanovich, 1982. [See Chapter 3, "Letters and Sounds: A Brief History of Writing," which traces the origin and development of English writing.]

Glossary

acoustic phonetics. The study of the properties of human speech sounds as they are transmitted through the air as sound waves.

affix. In English, a prefix or suffix (both are bound morphemes) attached to a base (either bound or free) and modifying its meaning.

affricate. A complex sound made by rapidly articulating first a stop and then a fricative. Affricates appear initially in the English words *chin* and *gin.*

allophone. A nonsignificant variant of a phoneme.

alveolar. A sound made by placing the tip or blade of the tongue on the bony ridge behind the upper teeth (e.g., the initial sounds of the English words *tin, sin, din, zap, nap,* and *lap*); also, a point of articulation.

alveolar ridge. The bony ridge just behind the upper front teeth.

ambiguity. Having more than one meaning; ambiguity may be semantic or syntactic.

American Sign Language (ASL, Ameslan). A system of communication used by deaf people in the United States, consisting of hand symbols that vary in the shape of the hands, the direction of their movement, and their position in relation to the body. It is different from finger spelling, in which words are spelled out letter by letter, and Signed English, in which English words are signed in the order in which they are uttered, thus preserving English morphology and syntax.

aphasia. The impairment of language abilities as a result of brain damage (usually from a stroke or trauma).

articulatory phonetics. The study of the production of human speech sounds by the speech organs.

aspiration. An aspirated sound is followed by a puff of air; the English voiceless-stop consonants /p, t, k/ are aspirated in word-initial position (e.g., *pot, top, kit*).

assimilation. A change that a sound undergoes to become more like another, often adjacent, sound.

back formation. A process of word formation that uses analogy as a basis for removing part of a word; *edit* was formed by back formation from *editor.*

base. In English, a free or bound morpheme to which affixes are added to form new words; *cat* is a free base, *-ceive* is a bound base.

bilabial. A sound made by constriction between the lips (e.g., the first sound in *pet, bet,* and *met*).

Black English. A vernacular variety of English used by some black people; more precisely divided into Standard Black English and Black English Vernacular.

blending. A process of word formation, combining clipping and compounding, that makes new words by combining parts of existing words that are not morphemes (e.g., *chortle* and *galumphing*).

borrowing. A process in which words, and sometimes other characteristics, are incorporated into one language from another.

bound morpheme. A morpheme that cannot appear alone. In English, prefixes and suffixes are bound morphemes, as are some bases.

Broca's area. One of the language centers in the left hemisphere of the brain.

caretaker speech. Used by parents in talking to children who are beginning to speak, it is characterized by simplified vocabulary, systematic phonological simplification of some words, higher pitch, exaggerated intonation, and short, simple sentences.

central. A sound, usually a vowel, made with the tongue body neither front nor back.

clipping. A process of word formation, common in informal language, in which a word is shortened without regard to derivational analogy (e.g., *dorm* from *dormitory*, *bus* from *omnibus*).

coinage. A rare process of word formation in which words are created from unrelated, meaningless elements.

comparative linguistics. The study of similarities and differences among related languages.

complementary distribution. A situation in which two allophones of a phoneme each occurs in a position or positions in which the other does not. See also *free variation*.

compounding. A process of word formation in which two or more words or bound bases are combined to form a new word.

consonant. A kind of speech sound produced with significant constriction at some point in the vocal tract.

conversational principles. What an auditor can expect from a speaker: that the speaker is sincere, is telling the truth, is being relevant, and will contribute an appropriate amount of information.

creole. A language that developed from a pidgin and that has a complex structure and native speakers.

derivation. A process of word formation in which one or more affixes are added to an existing word or bound base.

diachronic linguistics. Historical linguistics; the study of changes in languages over long periods.

dialect. A variety of a language, usually regional or social, set off from other varieties of the same language by differences in pronunciation, vocabulary, and grammar.

dichotic listening. A research technique in which two different sounds are presented simultaneously, through earphones, to an individual's left and right ears.

diphthong. Complex vowel sounds having one beginning point and a different ending point. The English words *hoist* and *cow* contain diphthongs.

dissimilation. A change in one or more adjacent sounds that serves to make a string of similar sounds less similar.

downgrading. A historical process in which the value of a word declines. Also known as *pejoration*, *devaluation*, and *depreciation*.

Early Modern English. The English spoken in England from about A.D. 1450 to 1700.

ethnocentricity. The belief that one's culture (including language) is at the center of things, and that other cultures (and languages) are inferior.

free variation. A situation in which two or more allophones of a phoneme can occur in a particular position. See also *complementary distribution*.

fricative. A sound produced by bringing one of the articulators close enough to one of the points of articulation to create a narrow opening; a manner of articulation.

front. A sound, usually a vowel, articulated with the body of the tongue set relatively forward.

function words. Function words (e.g., articles, prepositions, conjunctions), having little reference to things outside of language, indicate some grammatical relationship; the function-word class is small and closed.

functional shift. A process of word formation in English (made possible by the gradual loss of most inflectional affixes) in which a word is shifted from one part of speech to another without changing its form.

glide. Sounds that provide transitions to or from other sounds; they are vowel-like sounds, but sometimes act more like consonants. The English words *yet* and *wet* begin with a glide; the English words *my* and *cow* end with a glide.

glottal. A sound made by constriction of the vocal cords (e.g., English *uh-uh* has a glottal stop in the middle).

glottis. The space, within the larynx, between the two vocal cords.

Great Vowel Shift. A set of sound changes that affected the long vowels of English during the fifteenth century A.D., and that resulted in many discrepancies between the spelling and pronunciation of modern English words.

Grimm's law. A statement of the regular sound changes that took place in Proto-Germanic but not in other Indo-European languages.

high. A sound, usually a vowel, that is articulated with the body of the tongue set relatively high (i.e., close to the roof of the mouth).

historical linguistics. The study of change in languages over time.

holophrastic speech. The stage of language acquisition in which children use one-word utterances.

ideograph. A character in a writing system that stands for an idea and is, or was, pictorial.

ideolect. The variety of language spoken by one person. See also *dialect.*

illocutionary force. The intentions of a speaker, as far as those listening can discern from the context. *Implicit* illocutionary force is unstated; *explicit* illocutionary force is stated.

Indo-European. A group of languages descended from a common ancestor and now widely spoken in Europe, North and South America, Australia, New Zealand, and parts of India.

interdental. A sound made by placing the tongue tip between the teeth (e.g., the initial sounds of the English words *thin* and *then*).

International Phonetic Alphabet (IPA). A set of symbols and diacritical marks that permits the unambiguous recording of any perceivable differences in speech sounds; an alphabet with a different symbol for every different sound in the world's languages.

labial. A manner-of-articulation term under which are included the bilabials and the labiodentals.

labiodental. A sound made by bringing the lower lip into contact with the upper teeth (e.g., the first sound of the English words *fat* and *vat*).

larynx. The structure that contains the vocal cords.

liquid.   A sound in which the vocal tract is not closed off, nor is there sufficient constriction to produce friction; in English, the liquids are [1] and [r], both consonant sounds.

low.   A sound, usually a vowel, articulated with the body of the tongue set relatively low, away from the roof of the mouth.

manner of articulation.   The way in which the flow of air from the lungs is modified, usually in the mouth, to produce a speech sound. See also *place of articulation.*

mean length of utterance (MLU).   A measure of morphemes in the speech of young children; often used to determine the progress of language acquisition.

mid.   A sound, usually a vowel, articulated with the body of the tongue set midway between the roof of the mouth and the bottom of the mouth.

Middle English.   The English spoken in England from approximately A.D. 1100 to 1450.

minimal pair.   Two words with different meanings that are distinguished only by having a different phoneme in the same position in both words; e.g., in English, *bat* and *pat* are a minimal pair.

morpheme.   A morpheme is the smallest unit in a language that carries meaning; it may be a word or part of a word.

morphology.   The study of the composition or structure of words.

nasal.   A sound made with the velum lowered so that air resonates in the nasal as well as in the oral cavity and the airstream flows out of the vocal tract through the nose. A manner of articulation.

native speaker.   One who has learned a language as a child and therefore speaks it fluently.

Old English.   The ancestor of Modern English, Old English was the language spoken in England from about A.D. 450 to 1100.

orthography.   Any writing system that is widely used in a society.

palatal.   A sound made by bringing the tongue into contact with the front part of the roof of the mouth (e.g., the initial sounds of the English words *church, ship, judge, rim,* and *yet,* and the medial sound of *measure*).

palate.   The hard front part of the roof of the mouth.

perceptual phonetics.   The study of the perception and identification of speech sounds by a listener.

phoneme.   A speech sound that is a single mental unit but that usually has one or more physical representations (i.e., allophones).

phonetics.   The study of speech sounds.

phrase-structure rule.   A rule that expands a single symbol into two or more symbols (e.g., S → NP VP).

pictograph.   A character in a writing system that stands for a word. See also *ideograph.*

pidgin.   A rudimentary language with a simplified grammar and limited lexicon, typically used for trading by individuals who do not speak the same language. Pidgins are auxiliary languages; people do not learn them as native speakers.

place of articulation.   The place in the vocal tract where the airflow is modified, usually by constriction, in the production of speech sounds; also called *point of articulation.* See also *manner of articulation.*

pragmatics. The study of speech acts or of how language is used in various social contexts.

presuppositions. Those things that the speaker and the listener in a conversation can suppose each other to know; meanings that are presupposed but not overtly stated.

semantics. The analysis of the meaning of individual words and of such larger units as phrases and sentences.

sociolinguistics. The study of social dialects; the identification and analysis of dialect features that are significant indicators of social class.

spectrogram. A visual representation of speech made by a *sound spectrograph,* indicating the frequency, duration, and intensity of speech sounds.

speech community. A group of people who regularly communicate with one another and who share certain speech characteristics.

stop. A sound produced by completely blocking the airstream; a manner of articulation.

syntax. The study of the structure of sentences and of the interrelationships of their parts.

telegraphic speech. Speech that follows the two-word stage in language acquisition. It lacks function words and morphemes and is characterized by short, simple sentences made up primarily of content words.

trachea. The tubal area extending from the larynx through the back of the mouth as far as the rear opening of the nasal cavity.

velar. A sound made by bringing the tongue into contact with the velum (e.g., the final sounds of the English words *sick, rig,* and *sing*). See also *velum.*

velum. The soft, back part of the roof of the mouth.

vocal cords. Muscular, elastic bands within the larynx that, in speech, are either relaxed and spread apart (for voiceless sounds) or tensed and drawn together so that there is only a narrow opening between them (for voiced sounds).

vocal tract. The vocal tract includes the pharynx, the nasal cavity, and the mouth cavity. It is located above the vocal cords and used for the production of speech sounds.

voice-onset-time (VOT). The time between moving the lips and vibrating the vocal cords. In English, /b/ has a VOT of 0 milliseconds; /p/ has a VOT of +40 milliseconds.

voiced sound. A sound made with the vocal cords tensed and vibrating.

voiceless sound. A sound made with the vocal cords relaxed, spread apart, and relatively still.

vowel. A speech sound produced with a relatively free flow of air; vowel sounds are "open" sounds made by varying the shape of the vocal tract.

Wernicke's area. One of the language centers in the left hemisphere of the human brain.

Acknowledgments

"Language: An Introduction" by W. F. Bolton. Condensed by permission of Random House, Inc. from *A Living Language: The History and Structure of English*, by W. F. Bolton. Copyright 1982 by McGraw-Hill, Inc. Used with permission.

"Nine Ideas about Language" by Harvey A. Daniels. From chapter 4 from *Famous Last Words: The American Language Crisis Reconsidered.* Copyright © 1983 by the Board of Trustees, Southern Illinois University. Reprinted by permission of the publisher.

"Song of the Canary" by Lewis Thomas. Reprinted by permission.

"To Be Human: A History of the Study of Language" by Julia S. Falk. Copyright 1993 by Julia S. Falk.

"The Acquisition of Language" by Breyne Arlene Moskowitz. First appeared in *Scientific American* magazine, November 1978. Reprinted with permission. Copyright © 1978 by Scientific American, Inc. All rights reserved.

"Developmental Milestones in Motor and Language Development" by Eric H. Lenneberg. From *Biological Foundations of Language* by Eric H. Lenneberg. Copyright 1967 by John Wiley & Sons. Reprinted by permission of John Wiley & Sons, Inc.

"Predestinate Grooves: Is There a Preordained Language 'Program'?" by Jean Aitchison. Reprinted by permission.

"How Children Learn Words" by George A. Miller and Patricia M. Gildea. First appeared in *Scientific American* magazine, September 1987. Reprinted with permission. Copyright © 1987 by Scientific American, Inc. All rights reserved.

"Preschool Language Development: Brown's Stages of Development" by Robert E. Owens, Jr. Reprinted with the permission of Macmillan Publishing Company from *Language Development: An Introduction, 3/e* by Robert E. Owens, Jr. Copyright © 1992 by Macmillan Publishing Company.

"Learning and Using a Second Language" by Jeannine Heny. Copyright 1993 by Jeannine Heny.

"Brain and Language" by Jeannine Heny. Copyright 1985 by Jeannine Heny. Figures 11.1 and 11.3 from *Language and Speech* by George Miller. W. H. Freeman and Company. Copyright © 1981. Figure 11.2 from *Brain and the Conscious Experience*, edited by John C. Eccles. Springer-Verlag, 1966. Figure 11.4 from "The Great Cerebral Commissure" in *Left Brain, Right Brain*, Springer and Deutsch, W. H. Freeman, 1981. Copyright © 1981.

"The Loss of Language" by Howard Gardner from *Human Nature Magazine*, March 1978 issue, copyright © 1978 by Human Nature, Inc. Reprinted by permission of the publisher.

"Crazy Talk" by Elaine Chaika. Reprinted with permission from *Psychology Today* magazine. Copyright © 1985 (Sussex Publishers, Inc.).

"From Speaking Act to Natural Word: Animals, Communication, and Language" by William Kemp and Roy Smith. Copyright 1985 by William Kemp and Roy Smith.

"The Continuity Paradox" by Derek Bickerton. From *Language and Species* by Derek Bickerton. Copyright © 1990 by The University of Chicago Press. Reprinted by permission of The University of Chicago Press.

"Phonetics" by Edward Callary. Copyright 1981 by R. E. Callary. Revised 1984 by R. E. Callary.

"The Rules of Language" by Morris Halle. Reprinted with permission from *Technology Review*, copyright 1980.

"Morphology: The Minimal Units of Meaning and the Hierarchical Structure of Words." Reprinted from *Language Files: Material for an Introduction to Language, Fifth Edition*, copyright 1991 by the Ohio State University Press.

"The Identification of Morphemes" by H. A. Gleason. From *An Introduction to Descriptive Linguistics*, revised edition by Henry A. Gleason, copyright © 1961 by Holt,

Rinehart and Winston, Inc. and renewed 1989 by H. A. Gleason, Jr. Reprinted by permission of the publisher.

"Morphology: Three Exercises" by H. A. Gleason. From *Descriptive Linguistics Workbook* by Henry A. Gleason, Jr., copyright © 1955 by Holt, Rinehart and Winston, Inc. Reprinted by permission of the publisher.

"Word-Making: Some Sources of New Words" by W. Nelson Francis. Selection is reprinted from *The English Language, An Introduction,* by W. Nelson Francis, with permission of W. W. Norton & Company, Inc. Copyright renewed 1991.

"What Do Native Speakers Know about Their Language?" by Roderick A. Jacobs and Peter S. Rosenbaum. Reprinted with permission of the authors.

"Syntax: The Structure of Sentences" by Frank Heny. Copyright 1985 by Frank Heny.

"The Meaning of a Word" by George L. Dillon. From *Introduction to Contemporary Linguistic Semantics* by George L. Dillon. Copyright © 1977, pp. 1–25, 137–146. Reprinted by permission of Prentice-Hall, Englewood Cliffs, NJ.

"Bad Birds and Better Birds: Prototype Theories" by Jean Aitchison. From *Words in the Mind: An Introduction to the Mental Lexicon* by Jean Aitchison. Copyright © 1987 by Basil Blackwell Publishers. Reprinted by permission of Basil Blackwell Publishers.

"Pragmatics" by Madelon E. Heatherington. From *How Language Works* by Madelon E. Heatherington. Copyright 1980 by Little, Brown and Company.

"Discourse Routines" by Elaine Chaika. From *Language: The Social Mirror* by Elaine Chaika. © 1982 Newbury House/Heinle & Heinle Publishers.

"Girl Talk—Boy Talk" by John Pfeiffer. Reprinted by permission.

"Speech Communities" by Paul Roberts. From *Understanding English* by Paul Roberts. Copyright 1958 by Paul Roberts. Reprinted by permission of HarperCollins Publishers, Inc.

"Social and Regional Variation" by Albert H. Marckwardt and J. L. Dillard. From *American English, Second Edition,* by Albert H. Marckwardt, revised by J. L. Dillard. Copyright © 1980 by Oxford University Press, Inc. Reprinted by permission. Map, "Speech Areas, Eastern United States" from *Social Stratification of English in New York City* by William Labov. Washington: Center for Applied Linguistics, 1982. Reprinted by permission of the Center for Applied Linguistics. Chart, "Detailed Style Stratification" from *Word Geography of the Eastern United States* by Hans Kurath. Ann Arbor: University of Michigan Press, 1949. Copyright by the University of Michigan; renewed 1976.

"Dialects: How They Differ" by Roger W. Shuy. From *Discovering American Dialects* by Roger W. Shuy. Copyright 1967 by the National Council of Teachers of English. Reprinted with permission.

"The Study of Nonstandard English" by William Labov. From *The Study of Nonstandard English* by William Labov. Copyright 1970 by the National Council of Teachers of English. Reprinted with permission.

"Pidgins and Creoles" by David Crystal. From *The Cambridge Encyclopedia of Language,* edited by David Crystal. New York: Cambridge University Press, 1987. Reprinted with permission of Cambridge University Press and the author.

"Language among Black Americans" by Elizabeth Whatley. From *Language in the U.S.A.,* edited by Charles A. Ferguson and Shirley B. Heath. New York: Cambridge University Press, 1987. Reprinted with permission.

"Comparative and Historical Linguistics" by Jeanne H. Herndon. From *A Survey of Modern Grammars,* second edition by Jeanne H. Herndon. Orlando, FL: Harcourt Brace, 1976. Reprinted with permission.

"The Indo-European Language" by Paul Thieme. First appeared in *Scientific American* magazine, October 1958. Reprinted with permission. Copyright © 1958 by Scientific American, Inc. All rights reserved.

"Relationships of Some Indo-European Languages with Detail of English Dialects" by

Jeanne H. Herndon. From *A Survey of Modern Grammars*, second edition by Jeanne H. Herndon. Orlando, FL: Harcourt Brace, 1976. Reprinted with permission.

"A Brief History of English" by Paul Roberts. From *Understanding English* by Paul Roberts. Copyright 1958 by Paul Roberts. Reprinted by permission of HarperCollins Publishers, Inc.

"Language Change" by Jean Aitchison. Copyright 1976, 1983 by Jean Aitchison. Reprinted by permission of Universe Books, New York, and Hutchinson Publishing Group, Ltd., London.

"Sign Language" by George Yule. From *The Study of Language* by George Yule. New York: Cambridge University Press, 1987. Reprinted with permission of Cambridge University Press and the author.

"Nonverbal Communication" by George A. Miller, from *Communication, Language, and Meaning: Psychological Perspectives*, edited by George A. Miller. Copyright © 1973 by Basic Books, Inc. Reprinted by permission of Basic Books, Inc., a division of HarperCollins Publishers, Inc.

"Languages and Writing" by John P. Hughes. Reprinted with permission from Megadot, Upper Montclair: NJ, from *The Science of Language: An Introduction to Linguistics* (New York: Random House, 1962).

"Speaking with a Single Tongue" by Jared Diamond, from *Discover* magazine, February 1993, pp. 78, 81–82, and 84–85. Jared Diamond/© 1993 *Discover* magazine. Reprinted by permission.

Index